THE SECOND
GREAT WAR

Photo, British Official

BRITAIN'S MINISTER OF DEFENCE AND HIS CHIEFS OF STAFF

Responsibility for Britain's defence was largely the task of these four British leaders, seen in the garden of No. 10, Downing Street. They are (left to right) Air Chief Marshal Sir Charles F. A. Portal, G.C.B., D.S.O., M.C., Chief of Air Staff from October 5, 1940, and formerly A.O.C.-in-C., Bomber Command; General Sir Alan F. Brooke, K.C.B., D.S.O., appointed Chief of the Imperial General Staff on November 18, 1941 ; Mr. Winston S. Churchill, Britain's Prime Minister and Minister of Defence from May 11, 1940 ; Admiral Sir Andrew Cunningham, G.C.B., D.S.O., First Sea Lord and Chief of Naval Staff from October 4, 1943, previously Naval C.-in-C., Allied Expeditionary Force, North Africa and C.-in-C., Allied Naval Forces, Mediterranean.

THE SECOND GREAT WAR

A Standard History

Edited by

SIR JOHN HAMMERTON

Editor of The Great War, World War 1914–18, Europe's Fight for Freedom, etc.

Military Editor

Maj.-Gen. SIR CHARLES GWYNN, K.C.B., C.M.G., D.S.O.

Volume Eight
Pages 3085—3576

Published by

THE WAVERLEY BOOK COMPANY LTD.

in association with

THE AMALGAMATED PRESS LTD.
Farringdon Street, London, E.C.4

MADE AND PRINTED IN GREAT BRITAIN BY PURNELL AND SONS, LTD.
PAULTON (SOMERSET) AND LONDON

CONTENTS OF VOLUME EIGHT

LIST OF CHAPTERS

LIST OF CHAPTERS (Contd.)

HISTORIC DOCUMENTS

(The number of the page on which each document appears is given in brackets)

DIARY OF THE WAR, 1944—1945

MAPS AND PLANS

SPECIAL PLATES IN COLOUR

CHAPTERS CLASSIFIED ACCORDING TO SUBJECT—Vols. 1 to 8

CHAPTERS CLASSIFIED ACCORDING TO SUBJECT—Vols. 1 to 8 (Contd.)

ALLIED BOMBS ON JAPANESE-OCCUPIED HOLLANDIA
In the heaviest air assault made to that date under General MacArthur's command, 300 Liberators, Mitchells, Bostons and Lightnings, attacking in waves, dropped 400 tons of bombs on the Japanese base of Hollandia in Netherlands New Guinea on April 3, 1944. Landing strips and runways were blasted, 288 Japanese grounded planes destroyed or put out of action, and 26 interceptors shot down for the loss of one Allied machine. Other heavy raids preceded Allied landings on April 22. Here bombs are bursting on the village and anchorage. *Photo, U.S. Official*

AWAITING THE ORDER TO STORM THE 'ATLANTIC WALL'

A street in a southern English country town crammed with men and vehicles of the Allied invasion forces waiting ready for the Supreme Commander's final order to move to the assault. This photograph was taken on June 5, 1944, the day originally fixed (though this was not known at the time) for the onset; owing to bad weather the operation was postponed for 24 hours when, though still poor, conditions were slightly better. Below, landing craft massed in Southampton Docks, also ready for the word to move forward.

Photos, British Official; Planet News

Chapter 306

ALLIED AIR POWER REACHES OUT TO JAPAN

Air forces, land-based and carrier-borne, continued to aid the Allied advance in the Pacific during 1944. Capt. Norman Macmillan records that as one island after another was taken, enemy airfields were occupied and new ones constructed. Land-based bombing attacks on Japan itself began in June ; and Allied air strength contributed to the recapture of the Philippines.
For air operations in the Pacific in 1943, see Chapter 268

AIR CHIEF MARSHAL Sir Trafford Leigh-Mallory, appointed Air Commander-in-Chief, South East Asia, left the United Kingdom with his wife on November 14, 1944, flying in his personal transport to take up his appointment. The aircraft crashed in the Alps thirty miles east of Grenoble, and all its occupants were killed ; but the mystery of its disappearance remained unsolved until the wreckage was found by a farmer on June 4, 1945. Air Marshal Sir Guy Garrod, as Deputy Air C.-in-C., took over the post already vacated by Air Chief Marshal Sir Richard Peirse until the arrival in the early spring of 1945 of the new C.-in-C., Air Marshal Sir Keith R. Park, who had commanded the famous No. 11 Group of Fighter Command in the Battle of Britain, and, later, the R.A.F. in Malta.

In a radio broadcast in India, after handing over, Garrod said : "This is a theatre where . . . lack of land communications compels the Army to depend upon air supply. As a result the Army is developing new standards of mobility and flexibility. . . . The air forces engaged in the battle over Burma have been formed into the Eastern Air Command [December 1943] under . . . Major-General George E. Stratemeyer [U.S. A.A.F.]. At his command and at the H.Q. of the Allied Air Command, South East Asia, American and British officers work as members of a united inter-Allied staff."

The air force used in the Burma operations was a mixture of British, American and Indian Air Forces. But the aircraft losses reported by the South East Asia Command during 1944 showed how small was the Burma air war in comparison with the enormous scale

reached in Western Europe. In the twelve months 248 aircraft were reported lost and 317 enemy aircraft destroyed. Indian Observer Corps posts provided warning of Japanese air raids.

Lack of suitable airfield sites, especially in the forward areas, had hampered the Allied air force, at first handicapped,

COMMANDER-IN-CHIEF

Air Marshal Sir Keith R. Park

AIR COMMAND SOUTH EAST ASIA

EASTERN AIR COMMAND

Maj.-Gen. G. E. Stratemeyer

U.S.A. 10th A.F.

3rd TACTICAL AIR FORCE

STRATEGIC AIR FORCE

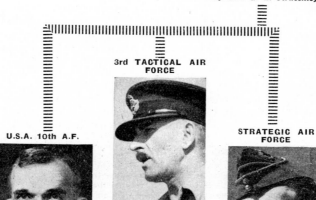

Air Marshal W. A. Coryton

Maj.-Gen. H. Davidson U.S.A.A.F.

Air Commodore E. W. Mellersh

TROOP CARRIER COMMAND

Brig.-Gen. W. D. Old U.S.A.A.F.

too, by the greater action radius possessed by Japanese fighters. This made it the more remarkable to fly the "Wingate Force" (3rd Indian Division) into the interior of occupied Burma by parachute and glider, and, when the first elements had constructed strip runways, to maintain and reinforce it by air transports, which on their return flights brought out the sick and wounded (*see* Chapter 299). In Burma the technique was first developed of bringing out wounded in gliders picked up by tugs that did not alight.

Mosquitoes, Spitfires, Thunderbolts, and Beaufighters (called by the Japanese "The Whispering Death") operated in Burma during 1944, and Allied Air supremacy was fully established. Probably the most difficult task was the interdiction of sampan traffic on the rivers at night. The Japs tried to bring down the low flying Beaufighters with trip wires strung across the rivers. A small force of Japanese bombers raided Eastern Bengal in the night of Christmas Eve ; two were shot down and two damaged.

R.A.F. and U.S. strategic bombers raided enemy base areas throughout the year ; among their targets were Rangoon, Singapore, Bangkok, and the Siam–Burma railway which ran through Moulmein ; these attacks were made first by Wellingtons and Liberators and later by Super-Fortress bombers of the U.S.A. 20th A.F.

Enemy rear areas were harried also by carrier-borne aircraft. Escorted by a strong force of Allied warships, these aircraft attacked Japanese airfields at Sabang and Lho-Nga in North Sumatra on April 19, damaging installations and shipping and destroying many aircraft. Another Allied carrier force, striking with naval escort in a combined South East Asia, Central and South West Pacific Commands operations, completely surprised the enemy at Surabaya in Java on May 17 : much damage was done to enemy shipping and shore installations, and 21 Japanese aircraft were destroyed for the loss of three. A night attack by U.S. Australian-based heavy bombers followed immediately. On June 21 an Allied naval and air attack was made on Port Blair, Andaman Islands, and R.A.F. heavy bombers, following up with a night attack against an enemy airfield there, covered the retirement of the force.

Sumatra received a succession of further naval and air attacks. The naval base at Sabang was bombarded by an

Attacks on Sumatra

Allied fleet assisted by carrier aircraft on July 25 ; in the night of August 24–25 a carrier-borne air force with naval support attacked industrial targets near Padang and its port, Emmahaven ; on September 18 Barracudas with Corsair and Hellcat fighters from aircraft carriers escorted by ships of the British Eastern Fleet attacked Sigli railway shops ; and on December 20 British naval aircraft from carriers attacked the harbour of Belawan-Deli, and oil storage tanks near by, and airfields in the Sabang area.

Air sweeps against enemy shipping were continuous. On May 2 R.A.F. bombers on reconnaissance sank an enemy submarine south-west of Socotra ; on August 19 a U.S. Liberator sank a 14,000-ton Japanese cruiser 100 miles east of Hongkong ; and on September 9 and 10 the R.A.F. attacked and hit 14 Japanese merchant ships, two sloops and a gunboat, leaving many of them ablaze or beached in the Andaman Islands area.

AIR MARSHAL GARROD
Sir A. Guy R. Garrod, K.C.B., O.B.E., M.C., D.F.C., was Deputy Allied Air Officer Commanding India and South-East Asia from April 1943 until February 1945, when he became C.-in-C. of the R.A.F. in the Mediterranean and Middle East and Deputy Allied Air C.-in-C. to Lieut.-General Eaker.
Photo, British Official

Owing to their increasing losses on sea lanes and the vulnerability of their harbours, the Japanese began in April to push overland into south-east China, eventually linking up with their forces in French Indo-China and Siam, and so obtaining a continuous overland route from Manchuria to Burma and Malaya. In November they drove northwards towards Kweiyang in Kweichow Province. In the process of these operations the tactical aircraft of the U.S.A. 14th Air Force commanded by Major-General Claire Chennault (*see* illus., pp. 2697 and 2709) had to withdraw from its bases in Kwangsi into Yun-nan, while

the strategic aircraft of the U.S.A. 20th A.F., formed on June 15, was temporarily withdrawn to India.

In the two years from its formation in March 1943 the 14th A.F. destroyed about 2,000 Japanese aircraft for the loss of 121, sank one-and-three-quarter million tons of shipping and 32 naval vessels, and destroyed about 400 locomotives, 200 trucks, 3,000 lorries, and 120 bridges. The loss of this air aid would have been a serious blow to Chiang Kai-shek's forces, and made an additional reason for the strenuous Chinese campaign to check and push back the advancing Japanese forces. Meanwhile supplies continued to be flown into China, and on October 5 President Roosevelt said that 20,000 tons of military materials were being transported every month over the southern slopes of the Himalaya Mountains in aircraft carrying their loads to 20,000 feet. In January 1945 this monthly lift over the " hump " (as it was called) rose to 44,000 tons. The greatest month's supply by trucks running on the Burma Road had been 18,000 tons. Part of the increase in air lift was due to the capture on May 17 of the two good-weather airfields near Myitkinya (*see* p. 3015) which provided an important staging post.

Exploits of 14th Air Force

It is doubtful if the many striking reverses to Japanese forces recorded in Chapter 299 could have been accomplished without air power. Air superiority harried the Japanese lines of communication and kept enemy air forces in check, thus enabling Allied transport aircraft to place troops and supplies where they were most needed. Mitchell bombers broke bridges in enemy-occupied Burma and cut railway tracks with 10-inch spike bombs. Without air supply it would have been difficult, perhaps impossible, to defend the Imphal plain ; without Wingate's airborne columns landed behind the Japanese lines to scourge their flanks and communications, Stilwell's advance would have been much less rapid.

AIR TRANSPORT OF SICK AND WOUNDED

Evacuation by air of sick and wounded was one of the things which gave the Allied forces superiority in the Burma fighting. East African drivers and stretcher-bearers took casualties from the front line to aircraft waiting on forward airstrips cut in the Burma jungle, whence they were carried to clearing stations. Left, an aircraft waiting to take off with wounded from an airstrip in a paddyfield. Right, an East African casualty being lifted out at a clearing station. (See also illus. in page 3005.)
Photos, British Official

The advance on the swampy Arakan peninsula depended entirely on air supply, yet by the end of 1944 Akyab had almost been reached.

After Wingate's death General Lentaigne commanded his force. The operations of this force combined with the defence of Imphal placed a tremendous strain on the supply aircraft of Transport Command and the Combat Cargo Group; but their response made it possible to defeat the Japanese in Northern Burma and the Manipur State.

Possession of the Philippine Islands was the strategic key to success in the South West Pacific, and General MacArthur's first main object was **Advance towards the Philippines** their seizure. To achieve this it was necessary to secure suitable bases for land-based aircraft farther and farther forward, which in turn would give carrier-borne aircraft greater freedom of movement, and enable them to make surprise attacks over an ever-widening area. Australian and U.S. troops completed the clearing of the Huon Peninsula (New Guinea) by February 11. On February 14 New Zealand and U.S. forces occupied the Green Islands off Buka, at the northern end of the Solomons, thus cutting enemy communications between that group and Rabaul (New Britain) (*see* map, p. 2858). On January 31 American amphibious forces began to land on the Marshall Islands away to the north-east, preceded and accompanied by softening-up bombardments from carrier-based aircraft and warships and land-based aircraft operating from the Gilberts; Jaluit, Japanese administrative centre in the Marshalls, and Wake Island, away to the north, were also bombed, and on February 18 the Americans captured Engebi, chief island of the Eniwetok atoll (Marshalls), and within land-based bombing range of Ponape (425 miles) and Truk (750 miles), the enemy's two chief bases in the Carolines. On half the Marshall Islands there is rainfall, and these were occupied; the rainless islands were bypassed.

WING COMMANDER CAREY

Wing Cmdr. F. R. Carey, D.F.C. and two bars, D.F.M., fought in the Battle of Britain, went to the Middle East, and then in 1944 to Burma. Early in 1945 he was credited in the Service with some eighty aircraft destroyed in three theatres of war—a record for both the First and Second Great Wars.

Photos, British Official ; Planet News

In the air, the year opened in the South West Pacific with Allied aircraft making powerful attacks on Rabaul, still the principal advanced Japanese naval and air base and G.H.Q. During January the air forces under MacArthur destroyed 546 Japanese aircraft, a record to that date for any one month in the Pacific. On February 3, 93 more were destroyed in two heavy attacks on Wewak airfield (New Guinea). On February 15, Kavieng airfield and harbour (New Ireland) were attacked and much damage was inflicted on the enemy; eight Allied planes were shot down by A.A. fire, but fifteen men were saved by a U.S. Catalina which, in face

of heavy fire, alighted four times on the blazing sea. The same day a Japanese convoy heading for the Bismarck archipelago was sighted about a hundred miles north-west of Kavieng by a U.S. Liberator, which bombed and damaged a 1,500-ton vessel and a destroyer. After midnight, U.S. Catalinas attacked and hit an 8,000-ton tanker, and at dawn Mitchells made a mass attack on the convoy, destroying a corvette and a freighter and leaving another freighter ablaze. The U.S.A. 5th A.F. (based in Australia) continued to attack, and on the 20th, General MacArthur's G.H.Q. announced that the convoy had been virtually wiped out, the Allies sinking two tankers of 8,000 and 7,500 tons, eight cargo ships of 1,500–2,000 tons, one 6,000-ton transport, one 500-ton freighter, one destroyer and two corvettes. All Japanese personnel were believed drowned.

Ponape was bombed on February 14. Powerful U.S. Navy task forces, aided by hundreds of aircraft, made a first attack on Truk at dawn on February 16, and a second next day; 201 Japanese planes were destroyed, **Air Bases in Admiralties Seized** and great damage inflicted both on the fleet and on shore installations. The Americans lost 17 aircraft. On February 29, MacArthur's forces landed in the Admiralty Islands, capturing Momote airfield the same day; an attempt by enemy " suicide squads " to recapture it on March 3 was defeated with heavy loss. On March 19, the enemy base at Lorengau, Manus Island (Admiralties) was also captured. This victory gave the Allies a strong air base astride the sea lanes to enemy bases in both New Britain and New Ireland.

The Japanese lost 26 (out of 40) fighters while trying to beat off an

ALLIED RAIDS ON THE NETHERLANDS INDIES

Left, fires left behind by a Barracuda at Sabang, off the north of Sumatra, after a seaborne air attack on April 19, 1944, when much damage was done to docks and installations, two Japanese destroyer escorts were left ablaze, two merchantmen hit, and 22 grounded aircraft destroyed. Right, Surabaya, Java, bombed by nearly a hundred Allied aircraft on May 17, 1944 ; ten ships were hit, believed sunk, shore installations damaged, 21 enemy aircraft destroyed.

HURRICANES AND MOSQUITOS IN BURMA

British, American and Indian Air Forces co-operated in operations against the Japanese in Burma. Here a R.A.F. Hurricane and a U.S.A.A.F. Thunderbolt are preparing to take off from a Burmese airstrip. Right, maintenance work on a R.A.F. Mosquito at Arakan. The British 14th Army's 1944 campaign in Arakan and the value of the air support it received are described in Chapter 299.

Photo, British Official

attack on Wewak on March 11, in which parked aircraft were destroyed, gun positions silenced, and fuel dumps fired. Eight days later Allied aircraft sank two Japanese troopships and three escort vessels taking reinforcements to Wewak. During an air attack on March 31 (one of a number) on Truk, 60 Japanese planes were destroyed, 49 of them on the ground. Air attacks against the enemy base at Hollandia (Dutch New Guinea) on March 30 and 31 destroyed 189 of 240 grounded enemy aircraft, and fourteen out of 30 interceptors ; and on April 3 the heaviest bombing attack of the Pacific war to date destroyed every one of 288 grounded enemy planes on the three airfields of Hollandia, while 26 interceptors were shot down, all for the loss of one Allied plane.

On April 1 MacArthur's forces occupied Ndrilo and Koruniat islands in the Admiralty Group, and on April 22 the largest assembly of Allied air, sea and land forces yet seen in the South West Pacific effected successful landings at Aitape (New Guinea) and at Hollandia and Tanahmerah Bay (Dutch New Guinea) (*see* Chapter 309). A week later a powerful naval and carrier-borne air attack on Truk did much ground damage and destroyed 60 enemy aircraft in the air and as many again on the ground. On May 17 MacArthur's forces landed

R.A.A.F. ENGINEERS AT AITAPE, NEW GUINEA

Tadji airfield, 2,000 yards inland, was captured on April 22, 1944, the day on which the Allies landed at Aitape. Allied planes were using it within 42 hours, thanks to the work of the Royal Australian Air Force Engineering unit landed with the ground forces. Within an hour of the landing, the R.A.A.F. unit got ashore a thousand tons of equipment including bulldozers, caterpillar tractors, mechanical shovels, and portable bridges. Here a Bristol Beaufort is being overhauled on the newly won airfield.

Photo, British Official

on Wakde Island off the coast of Dutch New Guinea 125 miles west of Hollandia, and on the following day occupied the airfield.

The Japanese, despite the attacks on their bases, tried to fight back in New Guinea, and on June 8 Allied aircraft attacked a Japanese cruiser and six destroyers off the Dutch New Guinea coast, and sank four of the destroyers, probably sank a fifth, damaged the cruiser, and shot down five enemy aircraft.

Japanese Warships Sunk

June 15 was a black day for Japan. On that day B-29 Super-Fortress bombers of the U.S. Army 20th Air Force, flying from bases in China, bombed the steel works at Yawata, the Japanese " Essen " : it was the first attack on Japan by land-based aircraft. The existence of the Boeing 29, officially named the Super-Fortress, had been revealed earlier in the year, but this was its first mention on a mission. After the Yawata raid, General Marshal,

PACIFIC AIR BASES

1. Middelburg Island, off Netherlands New Guinea, captured by the Allies without opposition, July 30, 1944, cleared of tropical growth and converted into an airfield. 2. U.S. parachute troops coming to earth on Kamiri airstrip on Numfor Island, off Netherlands New Guinea, captured. July 1. 3. Inflating barrage balloons to hover over L.S.T.s unloading on Green Island (off Buka) two days after its capture on February 14. 4. An Allied bomber, one of over a hundred which attacked Wewak, New Guinea, on March 19, gains altitude after bombing a Japanese troopship at mast height.

Photos, Associated Press; Popper

JAPAN HAMMERED BY SUPER-FORTRESSES

1. Brig.-Gen. Emmett O'Donnell; Lt.-Gen. Millard Harman, Deputy Commander, U.S.A. 20th A.F.; and Brig.-Gen. H. S. Hansell, Jr., head of 21st A.F. 2. A Super-Fortress takes off from Saipan. 3. Bombs from a China-based Super-Fortress falling on Showa Steelworks, Anshan, Manchuria, July 29, 1944. 4. 27-foot high tail fin of a Super-Fortress towers over a Keydet training plane. 5. Bombing-up 'Dauntless Dottie,' in which O'Donnell led the first Super-Fortress raid from Saipan on Japan, November 24.

Photos, U.S. Official; Associated Press; Keystone

U.S. Chief of Staff, stated that the Super-Fortress had introduced a new type of offensive against the enemy and had "created a new problem in the application of military force"; that because of its enormous range and heavy bomb-load it could "strike from many and remote bases at a single objective"; that its power was so great that it had been decided that it would be uneconomical to confine the Super-Fortress organization to a single theatre of war, and that a new air command, the U.S.A. 20th A.F., with centralized control had accordingly been created under General Henry H. Arnold, Chief of U.S. Air Forces, who would direct the bombing operations throughout the world.

The 53-ton Super-Fortress, designed to carry 1,000- and 2,000-lb. bombs, could carry an equal weight of small bombs—an unusual feature in bombers. Standard armament was ten half-inch machine-guns mounted in five electrically remote-controlled gun turrets, two upper, two lower and one tail. Electric synchronizing and computer sighting gear enabled one gunner to control two, or in one station three turrets simultaneously, bringing all guns in the turrets controlled to bear upon an enemy aircraft.

Also on June 15 U.S. assault forces landed on Saipan, largest of the Mariana Islands. This landing was followed by a strong Japanese air attack on the

Air-Sea Action off the Marianas American fleet at Saipan (June 18), in which 353 enemy machines were shot down for the loss of 21 American planes, one American battleship and two cruisers being superficially damaged. Next day U.S. carrier-borne aircraft surprised the Japanese fleet between Luzon and the Marianas. For the loss of 49 U.S. planes (many members of the crews were rescued), the following results were achieved: three hits with 1,000-lb. bombs on a 20,000-ton aircraft-carrier; a cruiser sunk and another left burning fiercely; at least one bomb-hit on a light carrier; a 30,000-ton battleship and another cruiser damaged; three destroyers damaged (one believed sunk); three tankers sunk and two left ablaze; and 15–20 aircraft destroyed. The Japanese fleet fled at nightfall towards the Formosa-Luzon channel.

MacArthur's forces continued to occupy new bases (see Chapter 309), until by September they were at Morotai in the Moluccas, only some 350 miles from Mindanao, southernmost of the Philippines. Throughout all the moves forward across the Pacific, Douglas air transports maintained a

continuous chain of air communication. The Japanese possessed no such force.

Meanwhile, Admiral Nimitz was also busy. On July 3, a carrier-borne air force sank five Japanese ships, damaged others, and destroyed 25 enemy aircraft in a bombing and shelling attack on Iwo Jima in the Volcano group and Haha in the Bonin Islands, for the loss of six U.S. aircraft. Air bombardment on Japanese positions on Guam (Marianas) began on the same day, and continued, with the aid later of shelling from naval guns, until U.S. Marines and infantry landed on July 20. Guam, captured by the Japanese two days after Pearl Harbor, was in American hands again by August 10. Tinian (Marianas) was invaded on July 23—still another base for U.S. aircraft.

Japanese positions on Mindanao were bombed for three successive nights from August 6 to 8. On August 16, General Stilwell's Chungking H.Q. announced that Liberators of the U.S.A. 14th A.F. had bombed Takao docks in Formosa. On September 1, U.S. Liberators, in the first major bombing attack on the Philippines since the Japanese occupation, dropped over a hundred tons of bombs on three airfields at Davao (Mindanao) and destroyed some 40 Japanese fighters and bombers on the ground as well as other fighters in the air. On September 11, carrier-borne aircraft destroyed more than 200 enemy aircraft on and over island airfields in the central Philippines. Three days later a successful landing was made on

Peleliu in the Palau group, due east of Mindanao. All the island except one pocket of resistance was in American hands by the end of the month, and in its airfield the Allies had secured the finest one in the area. On September 28, Australian-based U.S. Liberators made a 2,600 miles round flight to bomb oil installations at Balikpapan (Dutch Borneo), which was raided again on September 30, October 10 and 15. In these four attacks, 390 tons of bombs were dropped, and 146 enemy planes were destroyed for the loss of 19 U.S. bombers and six U.S. fighters.

By this time, concentrated air attacks were being made on targets in Mindanao, Luzon, Formosa and the Ryukyu Islands. Manila district was bombed by carrier aircraft on September 18 and again on the 19th. In these two attacks **Concentrated Bombing of Philippines** 357 enemy aircraft were destroyed, 40 ships and six small craft sunk, 11 ships probably sunk, 35 ships, 11 small craft, and two floating dry docks damaged, American losses being only 11 aircraft. Carrier-borne aircraft attacked targets in the Philippines on October 13, 14, 15, and 16, including northern Luzon and Manila Bay airfields; over a hundred Japanese planes were destroyed. Fighters making a first independent attack on the Philippines on October 15 destroyed most of a large motor convoy north of Valencia (Mindanao), and afterwards attacked horse troops.

PHOSPHORUS BOMBS AIMED AT LIBERATORS

Liberators of the U.S.A. 7th A.F. bombed an airstrip, dumps and gun positions on Iwo Jima (Volcano Islands), only 650 miles from Tokyo, on October 14, 1944, without loss, though eight enemy fighters attacked them. Here two phosphorus bombs dropped by Zeke fighters have burst in the path of the Liberators homeward bound after their successful attack.

Photo, New York Times Photos

SPECIAL PURPOSE BOMBS
A number of special types of bomb were developed in the course of the Second Great War. Here white phosphorus incendiary bombs dropped by a U.S. plane are bursting over the Japanese-held Lakunai airfield at Rabaul, New Britain. Left, 'Parafrag' bombs dropped by a raiding plane of the U.S.A. 5th A.F. about to hit a grounded Japanese plane on the nose during a raid on Oldnamlea airport, Buru Island, in the Moluccas. (See also illus. in page 2765.)
Photos, Planet News

Powerful blows by a carrier task force against Formosa began at dawn on October 11 and continued on the 12th and 13th. Japanese losses were at least 397 planes destroyed and 27 ships sunk; 62 ships were damaged, and a further 13 aircraft were shot down when the Japanese attacked the carrier fleet during the night of October 12–13. Sixty-six U.S. aircraft were lost. Following these carrier-borne attacks, China-based Super-Fortresses dropped hundreds of tons on Formosa on October 14 and 15. During October 13, 14 and 15, one U.S. task group off Formosa was attacked day and night; 95 enemy aircraft were shot down and five carrier-based U.S. aircraft were lost. On October 15, 50 out of 60 Japanese planes which attempted to attack damaged U.S. ships were shot down, and another 15 were destroyed by U.S.

Carrier Force Blows Against Formosa

patrols. The first American attack on the Ryukyu Islands, which extend south-westwards from Kyushu (Japan) to a point 73 miles from Formosa, occurred on October 9. Complete surprise was achieved and much damage done. Total Japanese aircraft losses in these Ryukyu-Formosa-Luzon attacks was given on October 17 as 915. On October 16, bombers of the U.S.A. 14th A.F. sank eight Japanese ships totalling over 40,000 tons, and damaged at least seven others in a raid on the anchorage at Hongkong, where ships had sought refuge from U.S. carrier-borne air attacks. A single Liberator, attacking two cruisers and four destroyers in the China Sea approaches to Formosa, blew up a 5,170-ton cruiser by direct hits on its magazine and sank a destroyer. China-based Super-Fortresses made their third attack on Formosa on the same day.

The pre-invasion air assault on the Philippines was switched to Leyte only in the final 48 hours before a powerful force landed there on October 20. This action produced a great sea-air battle which continued day and night from October 23–25.

The Japanese lost 66 transports and escort vessels and some 30,000 men out of nine convoys carrying reinforcements to Leyte up to December 12. A powerful carrier task force under Vice-Admiral McCain attacked Japanese airfields and installations in Luzon on December 12, 13 and 14. Next day 400 carrier planes swept over Luzon again, 100 attacking Clark Field aerodrome near

Manila, as American forces invaded Mindoro Island, to capture an airfield five miles inland. Between December 13 and 15, Pacific Fleet carrier planes sank 41 enemy ships and small craft and damaged 61 others off Luzon for the loss of 27 machines. U.S. Liberators bombed Clark Field on December 24, 25 and 26, destroying 144 Japanese aircraft in combat and on the ground; and on the 31st, targets on Luzon were again attacked. On the previous day, land-based U.S. aircraft sank, or probably sank, three enemy transports, two cargo ships, two destroyers and an escort vessel in the Lingayan Gulf.

The Super-Fortresses of U.S.A. 20th A.F. continued to attack Japan from China airfields. On July 7 they bombed Sasebo naval base, Yawata steel works, and the industrial centre of Omura, all on Kyushu. On July 29 they bombed Anshan steel works, twenty miles south-west of Mukden (Manchuria). On August 10 they bombed Nagasaki (and Palembang, Sumatra). On August 20 they attacked Yawata by day and night, losing four bombers and destroying 15 Japanese fighters. On October 25 they attacked targets on Kyushu, and on November 11 and 21, Omura aircraft works (Kyushu), Nanking and Shanghai. They then had to withdraw from China to India because of the Japanese threat to their airfields.

Super-Fortresses Raid Japan

But already a new task force, the United States Army 21st Air Force, under Brigadier-General Heywood S. Hansell, had been set up at the captured airfields on Saipan in the Marianas, and on November 24 Super-Fortresses of this force gave Tokyo its first air attack since the Mitchell raid from the carrier "Hornet" (April, 1942). On November 27 and 29 (at night) and December 3 they again attacked Tokyo, and although the distance from Tokyo to the centre of Saipan was some 1,500 miles, each bomber carried six tons of bombs. On December 6, Japanese aircraft attacked the airfields in Saipan, and on the following day U.S. air and sea forces counter-attacked the Japanese air base on Iwo Jima, between Saipan and Japan.

On December 7 industrial objectives in Manchuria and in Tokyo were bombed; on the 13th Nagoya was the target; on the 17th Nagoya and Hankow; on the 19th Omura, Shanghai and Nanking; on the 20th Tokyo was bombed before dawn; on the 21st, aircraft industrial plants at Mukden; on the 22nd Nagoya; and on the 27th Tokyo again. The bombing plan against Japan was beginning to unfold.

Chapter 307

THE 'MILITARY IDIOTS' PLAN INVASION

Operation 'Overlord'—the invasion of Normandy—was the biggest and most complex venture of its kind in the history of war. Its preparation and detailed planning by the men Hitler had called 'military idiots' were so brilliant that the Germans' much-vaunted Atlantic Wall was breached in a day and the first round in the battle for the liberation of Europe won. Here is some account of how Operation 'Overlord' was prepared

BEHIND the 4 000 ships, the thousands of assault craft and the gliders which took the invaders across the Channel under the protection of a giant air umbrella were more than three years of military planning, training and building-up of equipment. Everything that science and forethought could devise was at the disposal of the men who carried out the job. They were backed, too, by the all-out effort of the ordinary people of Britain who, since the time of Dunkirk, had worked and sacrificed to re-establish our armies on the mainland of Europe.

In planning, preparation and execution the invasion of Normandy was an Allied undertaking. Allied navies escorted the heavily laden ships across the submarine-infested waters of the North Atlantic to Britain, the great base from which the operation was mounted. The workers of Britain built immense camps and airfields to accommodate the flood of American men and equipment; railways were mobilized for their transportation. The free governments of the overrun European nations trained their forces and fostered the spirit of resistance in occupied Europe. Slowly, painstakingly, in the face of enemy air bombardment and determined attempts to cut the vital supply lines, the tempo of preparation increased, culminating in the avalanche of men and metal that fell upon the surprised Wehrmacht in Normandy on June 6, 1944.

As far back as the summer of 1940 when the fleet of little ships brought the battered B.E.F. home from Dunkirk, **Invasion the Ultimate Goal Even in 1940** it was appreciated that a direct offensive from Britain must be the ultimate goal of those who planned the course of military operations against Germany. The German invasion of Russia, which drew off a major part of the German Army from the West, and the entry of the United States into the war in 1941, enabled the military experts to view the problem in a new light, and early in the following year a three-Services planning staff was busily engaged in exploratory work, designed to lead eventually to the reopening of a

Western Front. Lieut.-General B. C. T. P a g e t (Commander-in-Chief, H o m e Forces) headed this staff with Vice-Admiral Lord Louis Mountbatten (Chief of Combined Operations) and Air Chief Marshal Sir Sholto Douglas (A.O.C.-in-C., R.A.F. Fighter Command). Admiral Sir Bertram Ramsay (Admiral Commanding Dover) was later appointed as chief naval representative.

LT.-GEN. F. E. MORGAN
Following the Quebec Conference of August, 1943, General Morgan was instructed to proceed with active preparations for the reopening of a western front. Making his headquarters in London, he started the production of new weapons, arranged training courses, and laid the foundations of the organization completed under the supreme command of General Eisenhower.
Photo, U.S. Official

The operations at St. Nazaire in March 1942 (*see* Chap. 226), the Dieppe raid in August of the same year (*see* Chap. 243), and other smaller raids on the enemy-held coast of France provided invaluable lessons in tactics and inter-Service co-operation. Furthermore, a mass of information was gathered about the German defences and a close study made of the topography and lines of communication farther inland.

With every operation and every reconnaissance, it became increasingly clear that to seize and supply a firm

bridge-head in Europe an immense number of special landing craft and other weapons and equipment, including a great force of troop-carrying aircraft, would be required. It was evident, too, that the substantial assault forces needed must be organized and trained to a degree to which no army had ever been trained before.

It was with these conclusions before them—coupled with the threat to Egypt by Rommel's counter-offensive in the Western Desert—that Mr. Churchill and President Roosevelt, meeting in **Decisions on Priority of Operations** Washington with their Chiefs of Staff in midsummer, 1942, decided that it would be sounder strategy to give priority to operations in the Mediterranean.

With a second decision—at Casablanca—in January of the following year, to concentrate on knocking Italy out of the war, it was clear that the reopening of the Western Front would have to be deferred until 1944. Preparations were, however, ordered to be made immediately, and in March 1943 a new Anglo-American staff was appointed in London to proceed with the planning with all vigour.

At the head of the new team of planners, consisting of high-ranking British and American officers of land, sea and air forces, was Lieut.-General F. E. Morgan, of the British General Staff. Designated Chief of Staff to the Supreme Allied Commander (not yet appointed), his job was to co-ordinate the plans of all Services for the great operation. Admiral Ramsay was charged with the responsibility of all naval operations and Air Marshal Sir Trafford Leigh-Mallory, A.O.C.-in-C. of R.A.F. Fighter Command, planned for the combined air arm.

The first task was to decide on what stretch of the enemy's long coastline the assault should be made. A correct balance of advantage had to be achieved from the standpoint of naval and air protection and of the capacity of the available beaches.

No decision was more important or more difficult to make. The success of the operation depended on the choice, and every possible consideration was

NEW WEAPONS FOR THE INVASION FORCES

Two aspects of the Armoured Vehicle (Royal Engineers), unofficially called the Petard, a tank made to carry a mortar and fascines. The fascines (see also illus. in p. 2634) were flexible tracks which could be laid to form a causeway across marshy ground or ditches. Below, a Cromwell tank mounting a 95-mm. howitzer which fired both high explosive and smoke shells, and could be trained on targets obscured from the view of the gunner. *Photos, Associated Press ; British Official*

weighed. Finally, the stretch of French coast between Caen and the eastern beaches of the Cotentin Peninsula was chosen. This area was well within the effective range of fighter aircraft ; the flat, sandy beaches would assist rapid disembarkation ; and it was comparatively lightly defended. If the landings went according to plan, it was hoped to expand the beach-head and capture either Cherbourg or Le Havre to assist the build-up. Again, the choice was influenced by the knowledge that the enemy had concentrated his defences in port areas on the assumption that the Allies would be unable to carry out such an operation without the capture of a first-class port—an assumption that greatly increased the possibility of achieving tactical surprise.

Following the approval of these basic plans at the Quebec Conference in August 1943, Lieut.-General Morgan was instructed to proceed with active preparations pending the appointment of the Supreme Commander. He made his head-quarters at Norfolk House, St. James's Square, London. His staff was rapidly converted into a fully integrated operational and administrative headquarters ; rigorous training schemes for all forces were begun and the amphibious craft and other specialized weapons required such as Churchill and Cromwell tanks mounting 95-mm. howitzers ; Crocodile, Wasp and Lifebuoy flame-throwers (*see* colour plate following p. 3102) ; " Armoured Vehicles (Royal Engineers) " (A.V.R.E.: new tanks carrying mortars and fascines) were put into production.

Preparations Begin, August 1943

Floating bombardment towers, mounting a battery of howitzers and a rocket-firing gun, were designed to be towed to positions off the French coast to support the landings. But not enough were ready in time and capital ships were used instead.

When, in January 1944, General Dwight D. Eisenhower arrived in Britain to take supreme command, bringing with him his own staff of officers and technicians, planning was already far advanced. He set up his headquarters at Bushey Park, Middlesex. The Supreme Commander ordered a further examination to check and revise the original estimate of forces required and the area of assault, and the final intricate co-ordination of action by all Services was completed down to the last detail.

As already emphasized, the Allied troops who were to carry out the assault on the European Fortress had to undergo very special training. Altogether

LANDING CRAFT UNDER CONSTRUCTION

Besides orthodox ships of all types and sizes, thousands of small craft of many descriptions were needed for the invasion of Normandy, and dozens of British firms—among them many that had never before contemplated building anything to float—were marshalled for their production. Here an assault landing craft is being built in an inland factory.

Photo, Fox Photos

there were nine training centres available in Britain for British and United States troops. Their provision had involved clearing many square miles of populated countryside so that live ammunition could be used and exercises carried out under realistic conditions.

At the same time, the specialists were rehearsing their tasks. Engineers were given replicas of all known defensive devices used by the Germans, and practised their destruction. Tank crews and lorry drivers were receiving instruction in the waterproofing of their vehicles to enable them to get through the shallow water separating the landing craft from the shore. The technique of waterproofing had been evolved by the Directorate of Mechanical Engineering, and involved the complete sealing of engines from the inrush of salt water with its corrosive effect. The work was to be done in the concentration areas immediately before the assault. Drivers were also trained in loading their vehicles on to landing craft and driving them through the water as they approached the beach. Through the same schools passed the Naval and Royal Marine crews of the small landing craft to see at first hand how their work fitted in with that of their Army colleagues. Even the Beach Groups, whose job it was to control the landings and beach defences (*see* Chap. 311), were mixed teams of soldiers, sailors and airmen.

Behind the training for the initial assault was the gigantic organization of

Schools for Specialists

supply. This was the responsibility of the Movements and Operations Branches of the Quartermaster-General's Staff. The complicated order of loading men and stores and their discharge in the right order of priority on the beaches had to be worked out by trial and error and in the light of lessons learned in the Mediterranean and other theatres. There was not a single one of the many supply services that had not to modify its normal methods to meet the situation.

The conclusion was soon reached that for the assault stage of the invasion it would be necessary to rely pre-

dominantly on coastal shipping—vessels whose draught would enable them to get as close inshore as possible and whose smallness would reduce their vulnerability to attack. Fortunately, many of these ships were already at hand, it having been appreciated as early as 1942 that, however great the building programme for special landing craft, ships of the Merchant Navy would take a major share in Operation "Overlord." Many of the smaller passenger vessels had been fitted out as landing ships and many coasters equipped with heavier derricks to enable them to carry vehicles.

Elaborate calculations were necessary to arrive at an approximate figure of the number of men and tonnage of stores which could be brought to the beach-head on the heels of the assault. Shipping routes all over the world were affected by the plans, for even at the peak of the invasion general war imports had to be maintained to sustain the base.

Inland Firms Build Sea-going Craft

To produce the thousands of assault craft required, British firms that had never dreamed of building anything to float—engineering firms, automobile firms, furniture factories, carpenters' shops, garages, every manner of industrial concern capable of working in metal and wood—were called on to contribute. Great constructional engineering firms got down to the job; some of them ran up shipyards of their own, for immediately after Dunkirk much larger landing craft than the original L.C.A.s (Landing Craft, Assault), which had run their first trials in 1939, were put in hand—big, ocean-going tank

WATERPROOFING THEIR TANKS

Some contact with seawater was unavoidable in getting vehicles ashore from the landing craft which took them in as close as possible, but not on, to the beaches. Tank crews and lorry drivers received careful instruction in waterproofing their vehicles to enable them to get safely ashore. Engines were completely sealed from the inrush of salt water with its corrosive effect.

OPERATION 'PLUTO'

Operation 'Pluto' (Pipe-Line Under The Ocean), described in page 3103, carried millions of gallons of petrol from England under the waters of the Channel to the Allied forces in France. 1. Three-quarter mile lengths of 3 in. diameter steel pipe, called 'Hamel' pipe, ready for winding on to the 'Conun.' 2. 'Conun' (short for 'H.M.S. Conundrum') being moved into position so that 'Hamel' pipe could be wound on to it. 3. A 'Conun' being towed across the sea paying out the first continuous length of pipe, 67 miles long. 4. Control room of Operation 'Pluto' in a seaside bungalow. 5. Pumping station hidden among the shingle of a south coast beach.

Photos, British Official; Sport and General

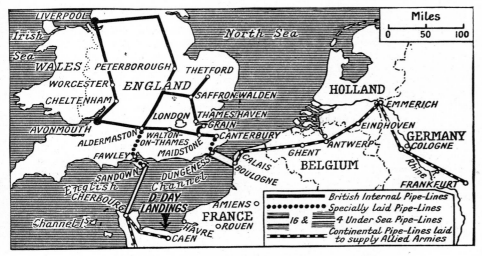

CROSS-CHANNEL PETROLEUM SUPPLIES

This map shows the position of the oil 'grid' constructed in England during the war (see page 3024), of the pipe-lines laid on the bed of the Channel (Operation 'Pluto'), and their continuation in the wake of the advancing Allied forces to feed vehicles and aircraft with the petrol essential to their progress.

By courtesy of the 'Sphere'

landing craft, for instance, which could be assembled only where they could be conveniently launched. Of the special types of vehicle designed for the operation, pride of place had been given to the D.U.K.W. (see illus., pp. 2869, 3048), the amphibious lorry which had already been used in operations against Sicily and the Italian mainland as a rehearsal for the much bigger assault on Western Europe, and also by Allied Forces in the Pacific.

The actual transportation across the Channel of all troops and their supplies (with the exception of the airborne forces) and their surface protection **Admiral Ramsay Naval C.-in-C.** against submarine and E-boat attack was the charge of Admiral Ramsay, who had been associated with the first planning team in 1942 and was now Naval Commander-in-Chief of the Allied Expeditionary Force. He was directly responsible to the Supreme Commander for the planning and execution of all naval operations off Normandy and the building up and continued supply of the Allied forces on the Continent. Under his command was massed a force which exceeded the total strength of the Royal Navy at the outbreak of war. The Channel had to be scoured for U-boats, the waters swept clear of mines, and each man-of-war allotted its specific task, whether it were to escort the convoys or to pour shells into the coastal batteries guarding the approaches to the beaches.

Complex though the problems of assembling the great armada had been, they were dwarfed by those of disembarkation on the enemy's side of the Channel. In previous opposed landings, the Allies had thought in terms of open beaches with the quick seizure and clearance of adjacent harbours. But for the invasion of Normandy, plans had to be made on the assumption that the ports would be heavily defended (as proved to be the case) and that the liberating armies would have to establish a foothold without the help of a harbour on a coast bristling with fortifications.

The problem was solved by prefabricating in Britain an immense system of breakwaters, piers and landing stages, to be towed across the Channel and assembled on the Normandy coast to form two complete ports. This undertaking, one of the most imaginative pieces of war engineering ever attempted, was worked out under the code name of Operation "Mulberry," and was one of the best-kept secrets of the invasion.

The decision that these artificial harbours would be essential to the operation had been made in 1943 and had been submitted as part of the general invasion plan to the Combined Chiefs of Staff at the Quebec Conference. On the approval of the plan, technical experts of the Admiralty and War Office were sent for and flew to join their United States counterparts to work out the details. It was realized that time was short and that the undertaking would be risky as it was very unlikely that all the necessary equipment could be produced in time to permit exhaustive tests or to make modifications. But the risks had to be accepted, and it was agreed that experiment and construction should proceed concurrently and that all the work should be done in the United Kingdom to save time—though labour and materials were much more plentiful in the United States.

The plan originally accepted was for two artificial ports, one in the British sector (Mulberry B), the other in the American (Mulberry A), each consisting of a breakwater formed of concrete caissons. The War Office, which had already been considering the project, undertook to produce the caisson designs. In spite of the great quantity of work to be done, and such essential experiments as the effect of wave action on the design, all details were complete by the end of November 1943.

To accommodate the necessary shipping and port equipment the size of each harbour had to be roughly the same as that at Dover; this entailed the construction of 150 caissons. For technical reasons, **Details of Operation 'Mulberry'** these could not be placed in water deeper than five and a half fathoms (33 feet), which meant that only a limited number of ships could use the harbour. It was therefore decided that the Admiralty should make an outer floating breakwater as well as that formed by the caissons. To provide immediate shelter for small craft, five short breakwaters (code name "Gooseberry") were to be formed by blockships along the invasion coast, and 60 vessels, including some old warships, were earmarked for this purpose. In

LAYING THE OIL 'GRID'

The pipe-line system a thousand miles long constructed in England to connect the ports with secret underground storage tanks and centres of consumption (see map) was linked with the Continent after the invasion of Normandy. Here is a section of pipe-line for the oil 'grid' being laid through the English countryside. *Photo, British Official*

the final lay-out of the breakwaters there were, therefore, three elements—the concrete caissons, the floating breakwaters, and the blockships, all of which had to be made ready in a very short time. The Admiralty was made entirely responsible for the floating breakwaters and blockships, and for the general lay-out of the artificial harbours. Many apparently insuperable difficulties were overcome, one of the greatest being to provide a pier which would ride up and down with the tide. The Prime Minister himself had given orders for such plans to be prepared as long ago as 1942. He wrote: "Piers for use on flat beaches. They must float up and down with the tide. They must ride out a gale. The anchor problem must be solved . . . Let me have the best solution worked out. Don't argue the matter. The difficulties will argue for themselves." The result emerged early in 1943. Prototypes of pier and pierhead were constructed which stood up well to severe sea tests, and were finally put into production. The total requirements

were several miles of pier and numerous pierheads with all the necessary adjuncts and appurtenances.

Some idea of the immense demands made on British building and engineering labour can be gauged by the fact that 20,000 workers had to be mobilized for the construction of the concrete caissons alone, and many more thousands were engaged on the other structures. Construction sites were mainly in the Thames (the port of London alone produced two-thirds of the caissons), Southampton and Portsmouth areas, but ports as far apart as Leith, Glasgow, Birkenhead and Hartlepool were also used.

The transportation of the blockships, the huge caissons, the floating breakwaters and the intricate pier equipment presented a tremendous task. A tug fleet of 85 ships was assembled, varying from very large American tugs of over 1,500 h.p. to small vessels of 600 h.p. not generally used in the open sea. Experts attached to the Naval Meteorological Service had been able to predict to the nearest foot the average height

of the breakers along the Normandy coast, and how the height would fluctuate with changes of the wind. This information, the result of months of skilled research, was of great value, and was, indeed, partly responsible for the Normandy coast being chosen for the assault. Despite the worst June gale for 40 years, "Mulberry B" was to enable the British armies, with all their vital supplies, to be put ashore in the most rapid military build-up in history. Parts of "Mulberry A" were lost in the stormy crossing of the Channel, and it was never completed. But the early capture of Cherbourg by the Americans minimized the importance of its loss.

The question of supplying the maximum air support for the invading armies during the assault and throughout the ensuing campaign on the Continent had been intensely studied since 1942. There was to be no repetition of Dunkirk, of Greece, or Crete where a powerful Luftwaffe had been able to work its will on thinly protected ground forces.

Providing Maximum Air Support

PRE-INVASION AIR ASSAULT

Left, rocket projectiles leaving a R.A.F. plane during an attack on enemy radio installations in northern France. Below, road bridge across the Seine at Rouen wrecked by U.S. bombers on May 27 and 28, 1944. The bridge on the left, put out of use by the R.A.F., had been partly repaired. Paralysis of the enemy's communications' system was the aim of 'Transportation Plan.'
Photos, British & U.S. Official

READY FOR THE ONSET

1. D.U.K.W.s parked on the sands at a south of England resort awaiting embarkation orders. 2. The interior of a loaded Hamilcar glider : it had a specially designed door in the nose through which vehicles could be driven into action in a matter of seconds after the landing of the aircraft. The tank shown is an American 'Locust.' 3. 'Priest' S.P guns, which did good service in North Africa and Italy (see illus., pp. 2555 and 2869) drawn up along a country road in southern England awaiting the order to embark. 4. L.S.T.s ready to leave a London dock.

Photos, British & U.S. Official ; Port of London Authority ; P.N.A.

HOW THE 'PHOENIXES' WERE BUILT

Here is one of the 150 concrete caissons for the prefabricated port (see page 3099) built at Arromanches in the first stage of construction in a riverside 'basin.' Below are caissons nearing completion afloat in a Port of London dock, and a finished caisson being towed down the Thames. Something of the inestimable value to the invading armies of this 'artificial' port is explained in Chapter 314. *By courtesy of Port of London Authority*

As a member of the 1942 Planning Staff, Air Chief Marshal Sir Sholto Douglas, A.O.C.-in-C., R.A.F. Fighter Command, was responsible for drawing up the early air plans. Twenty-two advance aerodromes for the use of fast fighters and fighter-bombers were to be constructed in Kent and other parts of southern England. For the protection of the armies after they had landed, a flexible force unrestricted by a static ground organization at elaborately constructed bases was brought into being. The various airfield services were made mobile—the intricate apparatus for controlling fighters in the air, workshops, signals and administration were put on wheels; barrack blocks gave place to tents and caravans. Special Airfield Construction Units, equipped with bulldozers, graders and excavators, were formed to work with the Royal Engineers. Moving with the forward elements of the Army, they were to choose sites for landing strips, clear and surface them with steel mesh netting, and get them ready for operations within a few hours. Mushroom airfields, complete with servicing facilities, portable hangars, supplies and defences, were to spring up in the wake of the advancing armies. Each squadron was organized to be able to pack up overnight and move on to the next landing strip, keeping up its support operations.

These general plans were already well advanced when Air Marshal Sir Trafford Leigh-Mallory took over R.A.F. Fighter Command, and the air planning for the invasion, in November 1942. Twelve months later the Allied Expeditionary Air Force, the largest single air component in history, came into being under the command of Leigh-Mallory (now Air Chief Marshal). The A.E.A.F. was an air team, with the newly-formed R.A.F. Second Tactical Air Force under Air Marshal J. H. D'Albiac and the U.S.A. 9th Air Force under Major-General Lewis H. Brereton as the offensive forward line, and the Air Defence of Great Britain, commanded by Air Marshal Sir Roderic Hill, responsible for the defence. (The Air Ministry announced the revival of the name "Fighter Command" for the air forces allocated to the defence of Great Britain on October 23, 1944.) The strategic air forces based in Britain—the R.A.F. Bomber Command and the U.S.A. 8th Air Force — remained outside the A.E.A.F., but their forces were on call for invasion purposes.

Modelled on the lines of the Desert Air Force, the Second T.A.F.—later commanded by Air Marshal Sir Arthur

A.E.A.F. Comes into Being

BRITISH PARACHUTE TROOPERS

Here are British parachute troopers in training. All volunteers, the men of this force were trained to the highest point of physical fitness, muscular co-ordination, and mental alertness by R.A.F. instructors of Army Co-operation Command. Parachute and other airborne troops, carried by an aerial armada extending for 200 miles, landed in Normandy on June 6, 1944, some little time before the onset of the seaborne forces, and by seizing key points behind the enemy's coastal defences helped materially towards the success of the main landings. Right, two parachute troopers, having made a training drop, and with their practice parachutes draped round them, watch others descending. Below, a mass descent of parachutists in training. Photographs showing American Marine parachutists in training were published in a plate following page 2874

Photos, British Official ; Crown Copyright

Colour photographs specially taken for The Second Great War

ALLIES BURN THEIR WAY TO GERMANY WITH LIQUID FIRE

Experiments with liquid fire for use against possible German invaders were made in June 1940. From them developed the three types of flame-thrower shown here. The Churchill 'Crocodile' (below and top left) went into action a few minutes after the landing in Normandy in June 1944. It threw a mass of flaming fuel over 150 yards, either in a rapid succession of 50-yard-long 'gouts' or in a continuous stream. Above, 'Wasp' flame-throwers, which had a range equal to that of the 'Crocodile,' but were fitted to Universal Carriers. Below, left, man-carried 'Lifebuoy' flame-throwers, used for smaller-scale operations. Large ring-shaped tubes (carried on the back) contained the fuel; the flame was projected from a gun fired in the manner of a rifle.

SUPREME COMMANDER, ALLIED EXPEDITIONARY FORCE, AND HIS STAFF

Towards the end of December 1943, and during January 1944, the names of the men who were to lead the Allied forces in reopening a Western Front were announced. This photograph, taken in January 1944, shows : seated, left to right, Air Chief Marshal Sir Arthur Tedder, Deputy Supreme Commander ; General Dwight David Eisenhower, Supreme Commander, Allied Expeditionary Force ; General Sir Bernard Law Montgomery, Commander-in-Chief, British Group of Armies ; standing, left to right, Lieut.-General Omar N. Bradley, Commander-in-Chief, American Group of Armies ; Admiral Sir Bertram Ramsay, Allied Naval Commander-in-Chief ; Air Chief Marshal Sir Trafford Leigh-Mallory, Allied Air Commander-in-Chief ; Lieut.-General Walter Bedell Smith, U.S. Army, Chief of Staff to General Eisenhower

Coningham—had its mobile squadrons formed into wings, under composite groups, consisting of fighter, fighter-bomber, light and medium bomber, reconnaissance and artillery spotting squadrons. The 9th Air Force was also a tactical force, with a strong medium bomber component and its own transport command. Both forces had their own forward repair and salvage units, airfield defence and signals units.

To provide the immense quantities of petrol that would be needed to keep forward aircraft in the air, and army vehicles moving, Operation "Pluto" (Pipe-Line Under The Ocean) was evolved. Comparable in its audacity of intention and achievement with the "Mulberry" ports, it envisaged the linking of the thousand-mile pipe-line network laid in England after the outbreak of the war (*see* page 3024) with the Continent by pipe-lines laid across the bed of the Channel, to be carried forward behind the armies and the airfields as they advanced. This "impossible" operation, suggested by Lord Louis Mountbatten, was made possible by the production and use of two types of pipeline—one somewhat like a submarine electric power cable without the cores and insulation, three inches in diameter and strengthened to withstand working pressures exceeding 1,200 lb. a square inch, the other a three-inch diameter steel pipe welded into continuous lengths of 30 miles or more. High-pressure stations on the English coast were camouflaged in an old fort, an amusement park, and a row of seaside bungalows, and a few weeks after the invasion began, petrol was being pumped across to Normandy with little or no danger of enemy air interception.

Absolute air superiority and the disruption of the enemy's communications and lines of supply were the two chief aims of the A.E.A.F. First, it had to be ensured that the Luftwaffe would be unable to make any serious challenge to the assault. For three years R.A.F. fighter pilots had been carrying out

'Operation Pluto' (marginal heading)

OPERATING A MECHANICAL SMOKE GENERATOR
Smoke screens were used on an increasing scale to protect special land targets, and as the time for the invasion of France approached they were used to shield from enemy reconnaissance planes the great masses of men and shipping assembling in and around the ports. The vital construction of 'Mulberry B' went on under a smoke screen. Here men are receiving instruction in the working of a mechanical smoke generator. *Photo, Daily Express*

offensive operations over France and the Low Countries, while German airfields and aircraft factories deep inside the Reich had been pounded by the four-engined bombers of the U.S.A. 8th Air Force and R.A.F. Bomber Command (*see* Chapter 296). The Germans saw the red light of impending invasion in 1943 and took strict measures to conserve their fighter aircraft. They switched almost entirely from bomber to fighter production and evaded combat whenever possible. But their wastage in men and machines mounted steadily, and in the two months before June 6, 1944, they lost more than 2,500 planes in air combat alone.

Behind their Army in France, the Germans possessed a magnificent system of rail and road communications whereby they could rush reinforcements to any threatened area. To deprive them of this advantage, a special section of the air staff drew up what was called the "Transportation Plan." A railway research worker and a university professor were called in to help with the choice of objectives and computation of bomb tonnages required for each target. The plan covered Northern and Central France and Belgium. It had a preparatory and tactical phase. The pre-

paratory phase, aimed at smashing rail centres on the Continent (chiefly executed by R.A.F. Bomber Command), was launched on March 6, 1944. By June 6, out of 80 centres scheduled for attack, 51 were completely out of action and 25 severely damaged. Bombing was widely dispersed so as to give the enemy no clue to the actual invasion area. Altogether, more than 66,000 tons of bombs were dropped in these operations.

The tactical phase, which began a few weeks after the opening of the assaults on stations and junctions, included attacks on running trains, open lines, roads, canals and bridges. The bridge programme was carried out chiefly by the U.S.A. 9th Air Force with such accuracy that only three bridges remained intact across the River Seine below Paris on the eve of the invasion. The bridges over the Loire, Somme, Marne and Oise were also listed for destruction. Meanwhile "choke-points" on roads and canals, which the enemy would be driven to use, were created and the transport attacked by R.A.F. rocket-firing Typhoons. The cumulative effect was such that when the battle began the enemy had to

'Transportation Plan' Air Attacks (marginal heading)

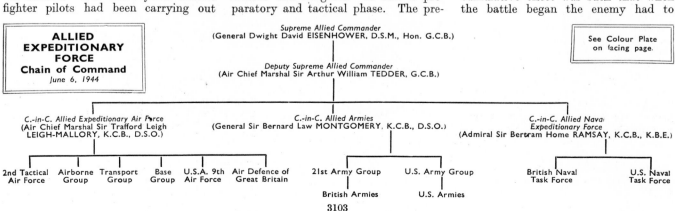

ALLIED EXPEDITIONARY FORCE Chain of Command June 6, 1944	Supreme Allied Commander (General Dwight David EISENHOWER, D.S.M., Hon. G.C.B.)	See Colour Plate on facing page.

Deputy Supreme Allied Commander
(Air Chief Marshal Sir Arthur William TEDDER, G.C.B.)

C.-in-C. Allied Expeditionary Air Force (Air Chief Marshal Sir Trafford Leigh LEIGH-MALLORY, K.C.B., D.S.O.)	C.-in-C. Allied Armies (General Sir Bernard Law MONTGOMERY, K.C.B., D.S.O.)	C.-in-C. Allied Naval Expeditionary Force (Admiral Sir Bertram Home RAMSAY, K.C.B., K.B.E.)

2nd Tactical Air Force	Airborne Group	Transport Group	Base Group	U.S.A. 9th Air Force	Air Defence of Great Britain	21st Army Group	U.S. Army Group	British Naval Task Force	U.S. Naval Task Force
						British Armies	U.S. Armies		

GENERAL MONTGOMERY EXPLAINS TO THE WORKERS

The men engaged in building the concrete caissons and other secret components required for the port of Arromanches, imagining they had been taken off war work for post-war reconstruction work, became restless. General Montgomery made a tour of factories and yards, and convinced the men that the work they were doing was vital to the campaign being planned. Here he is addressing a crowd of London's dock workers. *Photo, Planet News*

detrain far from the combat area, expend his precious petrol, shorten the life of his tanks and throw his divisions piecemeal into action. On one critical day he tried to move a whole division to the front on bicycles, and on another occasion German troops had to march 400 miles to reach the battle.

All the time the active preparations for the fighting were being made, the Luftwaffe was denied reconnaissance by a protective screen of fighters of

German Radar Reduced to Chaos

A.D.G.B. which Air Marshal Sir Roderic Hill threw round the south and south-east coasts. To increase the enemy's dilemma, the air planners sent fighter-bombers to attack his radar stations along the French coast. So thoroughly did they smash these small but vital targets that the German radar system was reduced to chaos, and the Allied armada sailed almost unmolested by the Luftwaffe. R.A.F. Coastal Command, meanwhile, was launching a vigorous offensive against U-boats in the Channel.

While the German commanders had to prepare for the coming battle little better than blindfold, Allied reconnaissance squadrons ranged far and wide. In the eight weeks before June 6 they flew 5,000 sorties. Each army unit knew exactly what beach obstacles barred its way; every coastal battery was pin-pointed and scheduled for "treatment"; and the air planners could see with what success this bombing programme was being carried out.

In addition to the frontal assault on Hitler's fortress, a leap over the Atlantic Wall by airborne troops had to be planned by the Allied invasion chiefs. In Britain, preparations for the formation of an airborne force had been made in the autumn of 1940. There had been little to work on apart from General Wavell's deductions from his visit to the Red Army demonstrations in 1936 and the great use that had been made of parachute troops by the Germans in their invasion of the Netherlands. Despite many difficulties, a strong force slowly came into being. The training of glider pilots and of troops in parachute jumping was undertaken by the R.A.F., who were also responsible for getting the force to the target area. (*See* colour plate facing page 3102.) The actual battle training was the job of the Army, under whose control the airborne men came immediately on reaching the ground.

By the end of 1943 there was, under A.E.A.F., a British Airborne Group commanded by Air Vice Marshal L. N. Hollinghurst and an American 9th Air Force Troop Carrier Command, commanded by Brig.-General B. F. Giles (later succeeded by Brig.-General P. L. Williams).

Airborne Invasion Forces

The two forces were organized to work with their respective divisions in the field. The invasion day plan of the British airborne forces was to seize bridges over the River Orne, knock out German batteries and create as much confusion as possible behind the enemy's lines. The Americans, meanwhile, were to assist the U.S. seaborne landing on the Cotentin beaches. The main airborne force was scheduled to leave on the eve of the seaborne invasion and drop about four hours before the beach landings. More

TRANSFORMING ENGLAND'S WINDING LANES

To make possible and easy the rapid passage of the immense quantities of men and material that had to be assembled by road at the points of embarkation for the invasion of the Continent, many of England's characteristic winding lanes were changed out of recognition. Civilians and service personnel worked on widening and straightening roads, strengthening bridges in the final stages of preparation. Here is one such road under reconstruction. *Photo, British Official*

U.S.-BUILT LOCOMOTIVES STAND BY FOR THE WESTERN FRONT
Some two thousand 'invasion specials' were run over the railway lines of Britain during the months of April and May 1944. Extra sidings and special loop lines had to be built to deal with the mass of invasion traffic carried. Here is a long chain, stretching out of sight, of American locomotives parked on a side line somewhere in England, waiting to be shipped across to the Continent. (See illus. p. 2367.) *Photo, Daily Mirror*

than 1,000 aircraft and 200 gliders were to be used, and three divisions of troops were to be dropped.

Final rehearsals were held under the eyes of General Eisenhower and his
Final Rehearsals Chiefs of Staff in the spring of 1944. Loading and unloading arrangements were thoroughly tested and assaults carried out along stretches of beaches similar to those to be stormed in Normandy. During these pre-invasion exercises, U.S. landing craft laden with troops were torpedoed off Weymouth by U-boats, and hundreds of the men became casualties and had to be treated in hospital. Staging and marshalling points in the Weymouth-Portland area were also subject to frequent air attack by the enemy. There were four major raids on embarkation ports, but by the time the attackers were overhead protective smoke-screens, operated by the Smoke Companies of the Pioneer Corps, were fully developed.

The immense task of moving all troops and their equipment from the great concentration areas to their marshalling camps in Southern England was then begun. Bridges had to be strengthened and roads widened to

carry the weight of traffic involved. Although British and American depots had been sited to lessen the burden on the railways, extra loops, additional sidings and yards had to be built to cope with the abnormal volume of freight, and no less than 2,000 "invasion specials" were run in April and May.

Despite the concentrated enemy air attacks of 1940 and 1941 and the subsequent intermittent aerial bombardments, it was from the Port of London that the bulk of the Allied armada of ships was loaded. The success of this operation was the result of the closest collaboration of the Admiralty, the War Office and the Air Ministry with the Port of London Authority. Special "hards" for L.S.T.s had to be constructed and marshalling areas prepared in the docks, as well as special access to some of the docks. The variety of vessels involved, and tidal conditions in the Port, made necessary extremely fine calculations by the Dock Masters and their staffs.

Towards the end of May, the most important D Day—invasion day—of the European War was fixed—for June 5. At the last moment the operation had to be postponed owing to unfavourable weather. Thousands of

Allied officers had to be re-briefed; but the basic plan was unchanged. The next day, though the weather was still far from favourable, General Eisenhower gave the word "Go" from a small headquarters in the village of Droxford, Hampshire, and the whole intricate machinery which had been built up in three years of preparation was set in motion. The armada sailed. The planners' job was over.

INVASION HEADQUARTERS
The village of Droxford, in Hampshire, was chosen as the site of the headquarters from which General Eisenhower directed the Normandy landing operations on June 6, 1944. Among those with him were Air Chief Marshal Tedder, General Montgomery, Field-Marshal Smuts, General de Gaulle, and Mr. Churchill. They lived and worked in a train on this stretch of permanent way.
Photo, New York Times Photos

AFRICAN TROOPS ON SERVICE IN BURMA

Tanganyika Infantry of the 11th East African Division on the road to Kalewa, which they secured without opposition on December 2, 1944, following a brilliant advance in most difficult conditions and against powerful enemy resistance in the Myittha gorge. Below, West African troops of the 81st Division in Arakan: they man-handled supplies through country where even mules could not be used, and drove the Japanese from Mowdok, a village in the Sangu Valley and not far from this spot, on October 8, 1944.   *Photos, British Official*

Chapter 308

COLONIAL AID IN MEN AND MATERIALS

Reviewing the year 1944 in the British Colonial Empire, Sir John Shuckburgh adjudges it one of continued and largely successful effort to cope with the still increasing demands made by the Allies, and particularly the Mother Country, on the Colonies' economic resources. While war had receded from the African Colonies (whose native peoples however gave a good account of themselves in overseas theatres of war), those of the Pacific still suffered its direct effects. The history of the Colonies in 1943 is recorded in Chapter 281

BY 1944, the African territories were no longer in the immediate war zone : the need for providing alternative military routes to the Middle East and India had largely disappeared. But if some tasks had been accomplished, there remained others still to be carried on ; and if the tide of war had ebbed from the coasts of Africa, it had acquired increased intensity in the Far East and the Pacific. African troops, who had rendered such a good account of themselves on their own continent against Germans and Italians, assisted in ever increasing numbers in the expulsion of the Japanese from Burma. Islanders in the Western Pacific still had the war on their doorstep and were still called upon for a maximum effort against the foreign invader.

A general review of the Colonial war effort was given by Colonel Oliver Stanley in the House of Commons on

Commons Review of Colonial Effort

June 6, 1944. He could not quote details of the size and strength of Colonial military contingents. That would have been inadmissible for obvious military reasons. But he was able to indicate in general terms how widespread was Colonial participation in the war. He reminded the House that East African troops were serving in Ceylon, troops from West Africa in Burma, Mauritians and Seychellois in the Middle East and Cypriots in Italy. Large numbers of men from different Colonies were employed as air crews or as ground staff in the Royal Air Force. In many territories naval units had been formed, some of which had been incorporated in the R.N.V.R.

Colonel Stanley went on to show that, remarkable as had been the contribution of the Colonies in the matter of manpower, the contribution in production had been equally outstanding. They had made strenuous efforts to render themselves self-supporting in the matter of food. The loss of Malaya and the Netherlands Indies had made it necessary to find substitutes for certain essential raw materials. Rubber (of which Malaya had been our

chief source of supply) was a conspicuous example, and immense efforts were made to increase rubber production in alternative areas—by speeding up production in Ceylon and by bringing back to life old plantations in other Colonies—in East and West Africa—which had been allowed to go out of production. Other products to which Colonel Stanley made special reference were tin, pyrethrum (an important insecticide), sisal (a fibre used for rope-making), sugar, foodstuffs and oil products, all of which in their several ways were vital to the Allied war effort. He revealed the interesting fact that the oil products of West Africa (palm kernels and ground nuts) were providing over 40 per cent of the fat ration allowed to people in the United Kingdom. "The impact on Colonial economies of this greatly increased and varied demand" had meant "a tremendous call for organization."

In the sphere of active military service, Colonial efforts were centred in two main theatres of operations : Burma, where in the course of the year the Japanese invaders were first checked and then steadily driven back from one point to another ; and the South Pacific, where there was a very similar story to tell and where the Allied Forces (predominately American in composition) were slowly asserting their superiority over the enemy. Among other successes, the year saw the expulsion of the Japanese from the British Solomon Islands Protectorate.

On the Burma front, West African troops went into action in 1943. In November 1944 it was announced that the 11th East African Division had arrived some months previously and had played a valu-

African Troops in Burma

able part in successful operations against the enemy. This Division, which had served with much credit in the East African campaigns of 1940 and 1941, contained men from Kenya, Uganda, Tanganyika, Nyasaland, Zanzibar and Somaliland. Their

SIGNALS TRAINING CENTRE ON THE GOLD COAST

Men of the West Africa Corps of Signals were trained at this centre at Accra, many of them serving afterwards in Burma where they helped to maintain communications, laying over a thousand miles of telephone wire through jungle, over hills and across rivers. Here they are receiving practical instruction in the maintenance and charging of batteries.

Photo, British Official

CHIEFS' VISIT TO R.W.A.F.F.
Early in 1944 eight chiefs of the Northern Territories of the Gold Coast visited the training centre of the Royal West African Frontier Forces. Here Lieut.-General Sir Francis Nosworthy, K.C.B., D.S.O., M.C., C.-in-C. West Africa, is talking with them. Lord Swinton, Minister Resident in West Africa, is on the left. *Photo, British Official*

merits obtained early recognition in their new surroundings. A Military Cross and two Military Medals were conferred upon men of a Kenya Battalion in the King's African Rifles after the first important engagement in which the Division took part. The awards were made for gallant conduct during an attack on a position on the Arakan front known as " Jumbo Hill " from which the Japanese were thrown back. As regards the two Military Medals, the official citation ended : " The initiative and prompt action of Corporal Malakwen and Private Kasulu in silencing the enemy's fire undoubtedly saved many casualties being suffered by two advancing platoons, and their actions are worthy of the highest praise."

During November the East African Division fought a series of successful actions in the Kalemyo district of the Chindwin front. In the course of the same month, two more East African Brigades were moved from Ceylon to take part in the Burma campaign. Both East and West African troops took part in the substantial advances made in Burma during December.

The West Africans continued to serve with distinction in this theatre of war. Early in the year a message was received in the Gambia from General Sir George Giffard, formerly G.O.C. West Africa. These were his words : " You will be pleased, I know, to hear that the West African troops are earning golden opinions both as tough fighters against the Japanese and as good soldiers in A.A., Signals and Engineers. Your Gambians have already been engaged, as have the Sierra Leonians, and have done well." The splendid fitness of the West African troops won high commendation later in the year from an officer who had arrived from India on special inspection duty. He said that " no other troops could possibly have undergone the same

West Africans Win Fame in India

LOADING GROUND NUTS
Forty per cent of the fat ration of the people of the United Kingdom was produced from West African ground nuts and palm kernels. Here 96 lb. sacks are being filled with ground nuts from two great mounds collected near Kuntaur village, Gambia, for transport by man-power to a steamer (left) lying 150 miles up the Gambia River.

physical exertions as the West Africans and come out of the Kaladan still smiling." He spoke highly of their prowess (which he declared had become renowned throughout India) in building jeep tracks and in constructing landing grounds for aircraft. It is clear that the West Africans stood up excellently to the hardships of jungle warfare. Their sickness rate was considerably lower than that of British and Indian troops in the same theatre. Moreover, they took kindly to a novel type of military activity : it was announced from Headquarters on July 4 that West African

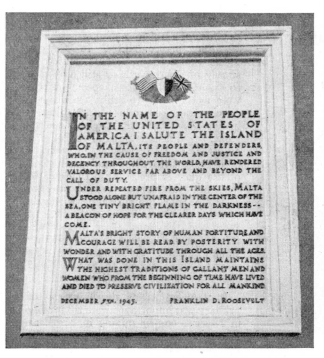

U.S.A. SALUTES MALTA
Following the Teheran Conference, President Roosevelt visited Malta on December 8, 1943. He was received by the Governor, Field-Marshal Lord Gort, V.C., and the Executive Council at Luqa airfield, where he read a citation to the people of Malta signed by himself. With his permission, his words were recorded on a bronze tablet (shown here), which was placed on the wall of the Palace at Valetta.
Photo, Sport and General

troops had operated with Wingate's "Chindit" columns. When the Chindits were placed under the command of General Stilwell, West Africans remained part of the force.

From the Pacific theatre there were many stories of the gallantry of the Fijians and other islanders. For some months of the year, two battalions **Fijians** of the Fiji Infantry **Serve** Regiment were engaged **Overseas** against the Japanese in the Northern Solomons. One of the two battalions returned home in August after fourteen months' service abroad, having accounted for many Japanese, itself suffering only slight casualties ; the other battalion remained behind and was employed in carrying out sea-borne raids in June and July. On July 13, it was reported that in one week they made three landings in enemy territory, captured nine field and anti-tank guns and blew up large dumps of ammunition. They constituted the fourth contingent to leave Fiji for service overseas. Two Fijian Commandos saw service in Guadalcanal, New Georgia and Vella Lavella (*see* illus., p. 2814).

The Fijian troops received a special mark of honour when the Victoria Cross was conferred posthumously upon Corporal Sukanaivalu for an act of

outstanding gallantry on Bougainville in the Solomon Islands on June 23. His platoon was ambushed, and the Corporal crawled forward to rescue men who had been wounded. After rescuing two men he was seriously wounded himself ; and his platoon, in trying to save him from falling into the hands of the enemy, suffered further casualties. Realizing that his men would not withdraw while they could see that he was still alive, the corporal raised himself up in front of a Japanese machine-gun and deliberately sacrificed his own life, knowing that it was the only way in which the remainder of his platoon could be induced to retire from a situation in which, if they had stayed on, they must have been annihilated. This was the first V.C. to be awarded during the war to a native member of the Colonial forces.

Another outstanding feat of arms was reported in 1944 : in a jungle skirmish in the Northern Solomons five Fijians accounted for fifty Japanese. The Fijians (all of whom were trained by New Zealand officers) were sent with two bren guns to hold a jungle trail junction. The enemy attacked, but one bren gunner held his fire until the Japanese were only a few yards away and then put them all out of action. After another twenty had been killed, the Fijians had to withdraw over the top of a ridge ; but from their new position they accounted for twenty more Japanese as they came over the skyline. By this time the party was almost surrounded, so they "went to bush" ; after a long night during which they were constantly on the move and several times narrowly evaded capture, they managed to rejoin the main Fijian force on the following morning.

There was much recruitment in the West Indies, both for the fighting services and for other purposes directly connected with the war. **Recruitment In West Indies** In March some 2,000 West Indians were brought to England for ground staff duties in the R.A.F. The majority of the party were Jamaicans, but recruits from all West Indian Colonies, including British Guiana and British Honduras, were among them. A further contingent, 1,935 in number, arrived in December, all Jamaicans ; 600 were recommended for trade training, the remainder for general duties as aircraft hands. West Indians were also accepted for air crew duty.

CHINESE MILITARY MISSION INSPECTS GIBRALTAR
A Chinese Military Mission headed by General Yang Chieh, former Ambassador to the U.S.S.R. and founder of the Chinese Staff College, arrived in London on January 29, 1944, having visited the Middle East, Malta, and Gibraltar on the way. Here the Mission, escorted by Brigadier Nugee, is seen against the rock of Gibraltar. General Yang Chieh is next to Brigadier Nugee.
Photo, British Official

WEST INDIANS WITH THE ROYAL AIR FORCE

Here is the gunnery crew of a launch undergoing training at a R.A.F. Marinecraft Training School in the United Kingdom. Below, Acting Flight-Lieut. Phillip Louis Ulric Cross, born in Trinidad in 1917, enlisted in 1941, commissioned 1942, awarded the D.F.C. June 1944 and the D.S.O. January 1, 1945. The citation announcing the D.S.O. award said, ' He has put in a very large number of sorties . . . against heavily defended targets. . . . His service has been of immense value.'

Photos. British Official ; Sport & General

They rendered conspicuous service : one of their number, Flight-Lieut. Ulric Cross of Trinidad, was awarded the D.S.O. and D.F.C. for exceptional navigational exploits, which also earned him the Pathfinder badge. A party of Bermudans of European descent (four officers and 106 other ranks) came to Europe to serve with the Lincolnshire Regiment, with which a number of their countrymen fought in the last war.

A contingent of the Caribbean Regiment (raised in the West Indies) proceeded first to the Mediterranean area and subsequently to the Middle East. An interesting ceremony took place prior to their departure from their training camp in the United States. They were reviewed on the King's birthday by the head of the British Army Staff in Washington, who addressed the Regiment and read messages to them from the Secretary of State for War and the Secretary of State for the Colonies. The ceremony was of some historical significance as the troops were probably the first British military force to be trained on U.S. soil since the American War of Independence. Military service did not exhaust the uses to which West Indian personnel was put. Arrangements were made in July for the recruitment of about 20,000 workers from the Caribbean area for employment in the U.S. under the War Manpower Commission.

British Troops Trained in U.S.A.

Among other Colonial units, the Cypriot Mule Companies deserve a special word of mention for their work in Italy, where they rendered outstanding service, especially with the Polish Corps at Cassino. The name of Malta was happily associated with the invasion of Europe in June 1944 : the 231st Malta Brigade—a British unit which earned its designation by services during the investment of Malta—was among the first British formations to land on the coast of Normandy.

The economic activities of the Colonial Empire followed much the same lines as in the previous year. The pro-

duction of rubber remained an outstanding preoccupation. In Ceylon, much the most important source of supply of natural rubber still available to the United Nations, special efforts were again made to stimulate output. A scheme was introduced in February, in agreement with the Ceylon Government, by which the price of rubber was adjusted each successive quarter in accordance with the actual production of the quarter preceding. In order to maintain the labour supply at the requisite level, application was made in June to the military authorities in India and the South East Asia Command for the importation of further Indian pioneer battalions ; by this means it was hoped to release local labour for rubber cultivation.

In Tropical Africa the industries of primary war importance were tin mining in Nigeria, copper mining in Northern Rhodesia, the cultivation of sisal and pyrethrum in Kenya and Tanganyika, and the production of foodstuffs and vegetable oils in almost every territory. It was in connexion with these industries that the conscription of labour had been introduced in four of the African territories earlier in the war. The step was taken with reluctance and was never regarded as more than a temporary expedient imposed by overriding military necessities. It could find its justification only in results achieved in the actual increase of production ; and, judged by this standard, it is fair to claim that it did in fact in great measure achieve its object. In Nigeria the additional output of tin, due directly to conscript labour, was estimated at over 3,000 tons for the year 1943. That was a notable advance ; but the system had its drawbacks : in particular, the demands of the mines tended to conflict with those of agriculture, which also urgently required labour for essential war purposes. It was decided, on a balance of considerations and in the interests of the war effort as a whole, to discontinue conscription for the tin mines at the end of April 1944. In Kenya, Tanganyika and Northern Rhodesia, the three other territories in which conscription of labour had been adopted, the system remained in force throughout the year. It was subject, in all cases, to special arrangements in regard to rates of pay, rations and working hours ; and the period of compulsory service was everywhere strictly limited, while every care was taken to minimize any hardship that might be imposed upon the labourers.

Industries of Tropical Africa

In general, Colonial commodities of many descriptions remained in immense demand throughout the year. There could be no prospect of a diminution in

Allied Nations' War Needs

the demand for tin and rubber so long as the Japanese remained in occupation of Malaya and the Netherlands Indies. Sisal was urgently required to replace lost supplies of Manila hemp. In the case of other commodities the considerations involved were, for the most part, of a more general character. Foodstuffs, sugar, pyrethrum, vegetable oils, cocoa, bauxite (for aluminium) and iron ore—to mention only a few items out of a long list—were still required in large quantities to satisfy the war needs of the Allied Nations.

In spite of the improved maritime situation, the pressure upon shipping space remained heavy and the obligation upon every Colonial territory to make itself as far as possible self-supporting in the matter of food and

FIJI ISLANDERS FIGHT OVERSEAS

Two battalions of the Fiji Infantry Regiment served in the Solomons during 1944, one battalion returning home in August after fourteen months' overseas service. Fiji Commando troops served in Guadalcanal, New Georgia, and Vella Lavella. Two men of the First Battalion of Fijian Infantry here stand guard over a Japanese Zero shot down over Kolombangara Island ; New Zealand officers are examining the wreckage. *Photo, U.S. Official*

CORPORAL SUKANAIVALU, V.C.

On June 23, 1944, during a withdrawal by sea from an advanced position at Mawaraka, Bougainville (Solomons), Corporal Sefanaia Sukanaivalu crawled forward and rescued two men who had been wounded when the platoon was ambushed. On his way to a third he himself was wounded and was unable to move. Realizing that his men would not leave him alive, he raised himself and was riddled with bullets. The first V.C. awarded to a Fijian went to him posthumously for his self-sacrifice.

Photo, British Official

other necessaries continued. Steady progress was made along approved lines —there were no striking new departures in fresh or unforeseen directions.

One or two points may be noticed. One important Colonial industry, towards the close of the year, outgrew the demands for its products. British Guiana had for some time past been the chief source of supply of bauxite for the aluminium factories of Canada. Production in the Colony increased from 476,000 tons in 1939 to 1,988,000 tons in 1943. Subsequently, owing to the decision of the Ministry of Aircraft Production to discontinue the purchase of aluminium from Canada, the figures began to decline. Efforts were made to stabilize the rate of production at between 400,000 and 500,000 tons per annum. There were indications that a similar situation might arise in connexion with Northern Rhodesian copper. The Ministry of Supply announced at one stage that they did not intend to renew their contracts with the copper producers after the end of January 1945 ; but the force of circumstances ruled otherwise, and in the event further purchases of copper had to be made on behalf of the United Nations.

So far as food production was concerned, a notable advance was made in connexion with the cultivation of rice in West Africa. Sierra Leone in particular raised its output considerably over the pre-war level, the object of the local authorities being not only to maintain and improve the food position

of the Colony itself but also to produce a substantial surplus for export. For this purpose an ambitious scheme of drainage and irrigation was undertaken which aimed at the reclamation of some 65,000 acres of swamp land on the coast and in the interior. Satisfactory progress was made with the project.

One episode of interest concerns Ceylon. The efforts of the school children to assist in local food production were recorded in a broadcast message. published in India in November 1944. The first paragraph ran : "When

Cingalese School Children Help

the full story of Ceylon's battle on her food front is told, perhaps its most dramatic chapter will be of the miraculous help her school children gave their country in her hour of dire need. It is a heartening story beginning with the slough of despond into which the country was pushed in 1942 with all its supplies of Burma rice cut off, and moving to a triumph of organization under which children cultivated school gardens and idle plots of land to help their country to surmount a great disaster." In the course of a single year the children ploughed and brought under cultivation no less than 20,000 acres of land ; they made a really effective contribution to the solution of the food problems of the Ceylon Government by extensive cultivation of school gardens and Crown lands allotted to them, by improving acreage of home gardens and by cultivating plots of

land belonging to private individuals in the neighbourhood of schools. A pleasant feature of the campaign was the zest with which girls threw themselves into the food production effort, producing large quantities of onions and raising extensive crops of leafy vegetables. In addition, the children took out War Savings Certificates and made deposits in the Post Office Savings Bank to the total value of over 700,000 rupees.

In August it was announced that the Royal Canadian Navy had established a training base in the island of Bermuda, where the U.S. Government had already, earlier in the war, acquired a base on a 99-year lease. Great Britain had maintained a naval establishment in Bermuda since the early years of the nineteenth century. Thus a situation was created in which three of the United Nations, two of them members of the British Commonwealth, were all in occupation of naval bases within the confines of a single British Colony.

Canadian Base in Bermuda

In Zanzibar on November 20, the 200th anniversary of the dynasty of the reigning Sultan was celebrated with appropriate ceremony. Cordial greetings were sent to the Sultan on the occasion both by His Majesty the King and by the Secretary of State for the Colonies, to which the Sultan replied in terms of equal cordiality.

Financial contributions received from the Colonial Empire during the year were not, and could not be expected to be, on the grand scale that marked the earlier stages of the war when princely donations were made by Malay Sultans and other wealthy individuals or communities to assist in meeting the expenses of military operations. Nevertheless, a steady flow of contributions was maintained throughout 1944 and a number of deserving funds benefited by Colonial generosity. The Red Cross funds, as was natural and right, were the main beneficiaries. The total Colonial subscription to these funds amounted in March to nearly £11,000 and in July the figure rose to £33,000. Tanganyika contributed a further £18,000 in September ; British Guiana £2,000 in October ; British Honduras £4,000 in November ; while

in the last month of the year a special Red Cross drive in British Honduras produced nearly £3,000 more. A flag day in the Bahamas resulted in the collection of over £4,000.

Aircraft production, in its various branches, was another object for which considerable sums were collected. By the beginning of July the Gold Coast Spitfire Fund had reached a total of £142,000. In July Aden made a gift of £2,175 for the purchase of aircraft. In September readers of the " Times of Ceylon " contributed £7,500 for a similar object (this brought the total contribution sponsored by this newspaper to war funds to the imposing figure of £369,000). In December the small Falkland Island community subscribed over £450 for a similar purpose.

King George's Fund for Sailors received donations from all parts of the

Colonial Empire. As the figures stood in June, Northern Rhodesia, though situated many miles from the sea in the centre of Africa, occupied third place in the list of Colonial contributors towards the fund. Ceylon was first with £32,900, Nigeria second with £13,000 and Northern Rhodesia third with £11,000. Other funds to which Colonial contributions were made included the Russian Relief Fund, the China Relief Fund, the Lord Mayor's Empire Distress Fund, the Shipwrecked Mariners' Society and the R.A.F. Benevolent Fund.

Chapter 309

ALLIES AT JAPAN'S INNER DEFENCES

With the fall of the Japanese base at Finsch Hafen in New Guinea on October 3, 1943 (see Chapter 276), the Allies gained control of Vitiaz Strait, which extends obliquely for a hundred miles between Long Island and the coasts of New Guinea and New Britain. The enemy's supply route from bases farther north was severed. Operations during the months which followed, described by Miss L. E. Cheesman in this Chapter, gave the Allies control over both shores of Vitiaz Strait and the north coast of New Guinea

THE 9th Australian Infantry Division (commanded by Major-General George F. Wootten) advanced north from Finsch Hafen, freeing villages along the coast. At the same time, inland operations were carried out independently by the 7th Australian Infantry Division (commanded by Major-General G. A. Vasey) on the wide plain of Ramu River. In this area airborne troops which had been landed on Kaiapit airstrip on Markham River made a forty-mile trek over the Markham Divide and took the village of Kaigulin on Ramu River on October 5. Next day they made a further advance and captured the civil aerodrome of Tumpu. From Tumpu is a motor road to Madang, fifty miles to the north.

Vigorous Japanese counter-attacks failed to dislodge the Australians from this important position, which, besides threatening enemy positions in the **Capture of Sattelberg** Finisterre Range and coastal regions, isolated a force between Tumpu and Finsch Hafen—remnants of the Finsch Hafen garrison which had escaped inland to the 4,827-foot Sattelberg, where they had been joined by belated reinforcements intended to relieve Finsch Hafen. This isolated Japanese force, advancing eastward, on October 21 retook Katika, two miles north of Finsch Hafen, and reached the coast a mile farther on at the mouth of Song River. Though these Japanese were not attempting to retake Finsch Hafen, but hoped to be rescued by sea, their infiltration in the rear of the Australian lines was a threat not to be ignored. Severe fighting on Song River, with persistent bombing from the air, forced the enemy to withdraw once more to Sattelberg. On November 17 Australian forces began a three-pronged drive against the mountain, making unremitting ground and air attacks. The greater part of the fighting was by infantry, supported by British Matilda tanks (*see* illus., p. 2765), the first heavy tanks used in New Guinea, against machine-gun posts hidden in *kunai* grass and on foxholes on razorback mountain ridges.

The Japanese proved to be short of ammunition for their mortars, on which they mainly relied for defence, and their supply trails were very vulnerable to air attack. But they held out tenaciously, and only bitter hand-to-hand fighting dislodged them. The Australians captured Sattelberg on

November 26. The remnant of the enemy force withdrew to Wareo, a few miles north, leaving 800 dead.

Off the coast north of Finsch Hafen, patrols of American M.T.B.s and the R.A.A.F. attacked the barge traffic on which alone the enemy coastal positions depended for supplies after Allied naval forces gained control of Huon Gulf. As the 9th Division advanced, it seized Japanese barge harbours and supply bases, taking Bonga on November 29, on which day also Allied light naval forces bombarded Sio, an enemy supply base farther along the coast. The Australians captured Bluecher Point on Dec. 28, and reached Fortification Point (Kitumala Point) two days later.

Troops of the U.S. 6th Army landed at Saidor on January 2, 1944, securing that harbour and airfield, and cutting off the Japanese forces between Saidor and the advancing Australians, who captured Sio on January 16. By February 11 the Australians had cleared the Huon Peninsula, and on the same day they linked up with the Americans at Vagomai, 14 miles south-east of Saidor. The Australians had covered 90 miles in 13½ days, forded 70 swollen rivers, and crossed difficult swamps. A Papuan infantry battalion had fought with them from Sio, showing

AUSTRALIA'S FLAG OVER SATTELBERG

Sergt. (afterwards Lieut.) Thomas Currie Derrick, D.C.M., a thirty years old Australian, won the V.C. for gallantry on November 24, 1943. His company after a gruelling day was ordered to retire ; he went forward alone, wiped out ten Japanese machine-gun posts unaided, and enabled the Australians to take the precipitous cliff face which made the capture of Sattelberg on the 26th possible. Here he is attaching the Australian flag to a tree at the summit of the mountain. He was killed at Tarakan off Borneo in May 1945.

Photos, Australian Official

great bravery and killing over 500 Japanese.

Allied patrolling by sea, land and air was so efficient that scarcely an enemy barge got through, and no larger surface vessels attempted to do so. As a result, it was found during clearing up operations that many Japanese in isolated posts had starved to death, for the forest of New Guinea is markedly poor in indigenous vegetation suitable for the support of human life. Such crops as the Papuans cultivate are not native, except the sago; and the Japanese by their callous and often cruel behaviour had alienated the Papuans, who deserted their villages rather than help the invader.

On the other hand, the co-operation of the native Papuans was a factor very valuable to the Allies. When they first learnt that Britain had declared war on Germany, the native constabulary sent deputies to the governor, Mr.

Isolated Japanese Starve

ADVANCE ALONG THE RAMU VALLEY
Japanese defence was only one of the difficulties the Australians had to overcome in their advance along the Ramu Valley towards " Shaggy Ridge " and the coast beyond. The country itself was extremely rugged and wild, full of rocky streams which were turned into swift torrents by violent rains. Here a line of Papuan porters is carrying supplies to a forward post across a rushing river which they had to cross some thirty times on their journey. *Photo, Paul Popper*

AUSTRALIAN ATTACK ON SATTELBERG
Australian infantrymen, going in behind Matilda tanks—the first heavy tanks used in the New Guinea fighting—, succeeded in capturing Sattelberg on November 26, 1943, after nine days of bitter hand-to-hand fighting against Japanese troops in machine-gun posts hidden in the kunai grass, or in foxholes dug into the mountain side. *Photo, Australian Official*

Hubert Murray, to request permission to join the British Army. They were sad when told that they could not survive an English winter. But it was definitely promised that if war came to their own country they should join the defence forces. This promise was fulfilled and not only the police but all sections of Papuan society served the Allies. Except for the temporary defection of one tribe, the Papuans in the British Territories remained loyal.

Excellent patrol work was carried out by the police units of the Papuan Infantry Battalion, commanded by Major William Watson. Corporal Sala won the M.M. for conspicuous bravery. Three other Papuans were decorated during the visit of Lord Gowrie to New Guinea in February 1944. Convoys of Papuan *kulis* were continually on the trails, taking supplies to the forward lines, locating supplies dropped by parachute, building huts, making clearings for airfields, cutting roads, acting as stretcher bearers, etc. The women and children brought food from village gardens.

Papuans Aid Australians

The Papuans refused Japanese paper currency as useless. Yet wounded survivors of an Australian unit who wandered for weeks during the Kokoda trail fighting in 1942 (*see* Chapter 249) before they found their way back to Port Moresby, obtained food and guides from the villages by presenting promissory notes. It was a great tribute to Australian administration that the Papuans had complete confidence these scraps of paper would be honoured. (*See* also illustration, p. 2759.)

to the ruggedness of the northern coast and the greater part of the interior, there have never been settlements in those areas. The Japanese had established themselves in coastal settlements, particularly those with airstrips, and had improved and fortified them. Rabaul, in the north-east of the island, was still a very strong base, in spite of unremitting Allied air attacks, and it was held by a large Japanese force.

The first point of attack was Arawe, 60 miles west of the Japanese secondary base at Gasmata (*see* map in page 3124). Following extremely heavy air attacks on Arawe and Gasmata in the preceding

During October 1943 the 7th Division, advancing inland, drove the Japanese from Ramu valley into the Finisterre Range where, six miles north of Tumpu, the enemy fortified a steep spur, "Shaggy Ridge," which terminates in a conical peak, "The Pimple." This ridge is 5,600 feet high and "The Pimple" is 100 feet higher; they dominated the Australian forward positions and were used by the Japanese as observation posts. They were also a defence for the motor-road which the Japanese had made to Madang from Yokopi. The enemy was in great strength in the area, especially on the crests. It was a naturally formidable position, and the Japanese had dug deeply among the rocks and constructed a network of intercommunication trenches. In places the crest was so narrow that there was not even space for two men to stand side by side.

Australians Storm 'The Pimple'

ALLIES MEET IN NEW GUINEA

On February 11, 1944, Australians advancing from Finsch Hafen met at Vagomai, 14 miles south-east of Saidor, Americans who had landed at Saidor. Here the Australian commander (centre left) shakes hands with a U.S. soldier at the linking up of the two forces, which marked the clearance of the enemy from the Huon Peninsula. Above, troops of the U.S. 6th Army land at Saidor, January 2, 1944. *Photos, Paul Popper; Associated Press*

The process of destroying the outposts went forward by air attacks, infantry charges with bayonets and hand grenades, and artillery and rocket gun bombardment. The Australians stormed "The Pimple" on December 27. For the final assault on the ridge a frontal attack was unavoidable, and the only approach was up a bare face of the mountain, denuded of forest by repeated air-raids and by artillery fire from 25-pounders mounted on the opposite slope. Torrential rain, thick mud, and the constant danger of landslides added to the attackers' difficulties. Several days' intensive dive-bombing by R.A.A.F. Boomerangs and U.S. Kittyhawks was succeeded by a heavy artillery barrage, under cover of which the Australian assault troops moved forward and climbed the exposed precipice. Thanks to the perfect co-ordination of the preliminary offen-

sive, the crest was almost reached before resistance was encountered. Then began savage hand-to-hand fighting for machine-gun nests, pillboxes and foxholes which had escaped destruction. To overcome some of these enemy pockets demanded much ingenuity and resource, and the difficulties of the terrain cannot be exaggerated; but on January 21, 1944, the enemy was driven from "Shaggy Ridge."

Advance towards the coast continued, though slowly, Japanese "suicide squads" putting up strong rearguard opposition. Bogadjim was taken on April 14, and Madang on April 24. Alexis Hafen fell two days later.

General MacArthur made his next "leapfrog" attack across the Vitiaz Strait to New Britain. This valuable island, which had been held by the Japanese since January 1942, had not been fully occupied by them. Owing

week, at 4 a.m. on December 15, light naval forces bombarded Arawe Peninsula for twenty minutes. A force which included a large number of Texans and was commanded by Lieut.-General Walter Kreuger, made a landing on Cape Merkus. U.S. Marines and Australian troops followed. The invasion barges reached shore unopposed and landed with tanks; but a diversionary U.S. commando force which attempted a landing on another part of the Peninsula before the bombardment was caught in enemy crossfire and half destroyed. Counter-attacks against the main landing point were too late, Zero fighters and bombers which attacked the beach-head being driven off by Australian fighters and by amphibious mounted guns. Sixteen Zeros were destroyed without Allied loss. By

Allies Attack New Britain

U.S. MARINES GO ASHORE AT CAPE GLOUCESTER, NEW BRITAIN

Following the first Allied landings in New Britain at Arawe on December 15, 1943, further landings were made on December 26 on both sides of Cape Gloucester. The troops, here seen leaving their landing craft and marching up the beach, came in convoy from New Guinea across the 54-mile-wide Vitiaz Strait. The landings, carried out under cover of smoke screens laid by Allied planes, met with no opposition, the enemy in the area having been blasted out of existence by preliminary naval and air bombardment, and not a man was lost. Below, U.S. Marines wading through the surf at another of the Cape Gloucester landing beaches. *Photos, U.S. Official ; New York Times Photos*

IN THE ADMIRALTIES

General Douglas MacArthur, C.-in-C., S.W. Pacific, his ears plugged with cottonwool to deaden the noise of the guns, watches the effects of the dawn bombardment of Los Negros on February 29, 1944, prior to the U.S. landings. Right, American 105 mm. howitzers landed on Manus Island trained on the Japanese-occupied base of Lorengau, captured March 18. Below, Australian Kittyhawk fighter-bombers on Momote air-field (Los Negros) six days after its recapture on February 29.
Photos, Associated Press; Key-stone; Paul Popper

the 18th the three-mile Arawe Peninsula was in Allied hands. Arawe airstrip was captured on the 19th.

During December U.S. forces advanced westwards, finding no Japanese in some bays, in others a strong force. On December 26 fresh landings were made at Silimati Point and elsewhere on Cape Gloucester. U.S. Marines got ashore unopposed without the loss of a single man, and neutralized the Japanese defences, which were facing another beach where Allied invasion

had been expected. Craft fitted with rocket-firing guns were used to cover these landings, and rocket guns played an important part in the subsequent land fighting. From "Target Hill," a 480-foot height to the west, Japanese batteries poured shells on the Allied troops, but could not stem their advance. Enemy dive-bombers were dispersed by air patrols, and numbers destroyed in every attack. "Target Hill" was captured on December 27, and U.S. Marines with tanks and artillery stormed one

Cape Gloucester airfield in the night of December 28–29, the other next day.

From Cape Gloucester beach-heads an offensive began against jungle pillbox defences in depth. Japanese counter-attacks were in strong force, but not co-ordinated; one enemy unit charging madly into machine-gun fire was annihilated. Fighting was severe; but on February 24, 1944, U.S. Marines pushing through from Sagsag and Cape Gloucester linked up with other units striking north-west from Arawe. A small scale landing against little opposition near Talasea (March 6), followed by a second landing in the same neighbourhood on March 9, led to the capture of the town and air base of Talasea on the 10th, and the isolation of a Japanese force on Willaumez Peninsula.

On April 11 General MacArthur announced that the major part of New Britain was under Allied control. The Japanese had abandoned Cape Hoskins and Gasmata and were preparing to stand at the neck of Gazelle Peninsula,

SHERMAN TANKS LANDED IN NEW BRITAIN

Towards the end of 1943, tanks began to be used in the South West Pacific. Matildas helped to capture Sattelberg in New Guinea (see page 3113), and troops of the U.S. 6th Army landing in New Britain at Arawe on December 15, and on Cape Gloucester on December 26, had tank support. Here a column of Shermans advances along the beach on Cape Gloucester.

Photo, U.S. Official

between Open Bay and Wide Bay, covering Rabaul. But Rabaul airfields and harbour had been damaged beyond repair by Allied air and naval attacks, and no shipping ventured in.

Emirau Island, 84 miles north-west of Kavieng, New Ireland, was occupied by U.S. Marines on March 19 without opposition.

Allied reoccupation of the Admiralty Islands, a group of about 160 volcanic and coral islands some 250 miles north of New Britain, began with a

Admiralties Reoccupied

landing on Los Negros Island on February 29 (*see* map in page 3124).

Following a naval bombardment at dawn, units of the U.S. 1st Cavalry Division (dismounted), commanded by Major-General Innis P. Swift, were put ashore under cover from air and naval forces. The slight enemy resistance was speedily overcome, and Momote airfield was captured almost undamaged. General MacArthur and Vice-Admiral Kinkaid, who directed the operations in person, went ashore within a short time of the

landings. Three days later, wave upon wave of Japanese troops attacked the Allied positions at dusk with desperate courage, but they were mown down by machine-gun fire and failed to dislodge the Allies. 3,000 of the enemy were killed or injured; American casualties were 61 killed, 244 wounded.

A landing was made on Manus Island on March 15. Very bitter fighting at close quarters followed: an elaborate system of bunkers (75 of which were destroyed) had to be overcome; but by the 18th Lorengau, the administrative centre (occupied by the Japanese April 8, 1942), was in Allied hands.

By April 2 only 400–450 of the original enemy garrison of 5,000 were still offering unorganized resistance in the Admiralties. The reoccupation of these islands provided the Allies with three valuable harbours and two airfields. It closed the Bismarck Sea to the enemy and removed the threat to Australia. Enemy supply lines were severed, and large numbers of Japanese were isolated in New Britain and New Ireland and on the New Guinea coast,

while Allied supply lines were safe from flanking attacks.

On April 22 the largest combined operation carried out to that date in the South West Pacific took place in the Hollandia district, which consists of the Cyclops Range, 24 miles in length from Humboldt Bay on the east to Tanah-merah Bay on the west, and Lake Sentani, south of the mountains. Humboldt Bay is 16½ miles wide at the mouth with two inner bays, Hollandia Bay and Jotefa Bay. The anchorages are good, except in the season of the north-west monsoon from November to March. Hollandia is a very small settlement in a trough-shaped valley with high slopes on three sides. A track follows the coast to Pim, thence passes north of the lake to Dempta in Tanahmerah Bay.

Humboldt Bay Landings

After the Japanese occupied Hollandia they made a large camp behind the range where they also constructed three airfields between the lower spurs of the mountains and the lake. They had converted sections of the track into good road. The position was excellently defended by the natural ramparts of the range. No attack was possible from the north owing to large scale land subsidence there; the highest peaks of

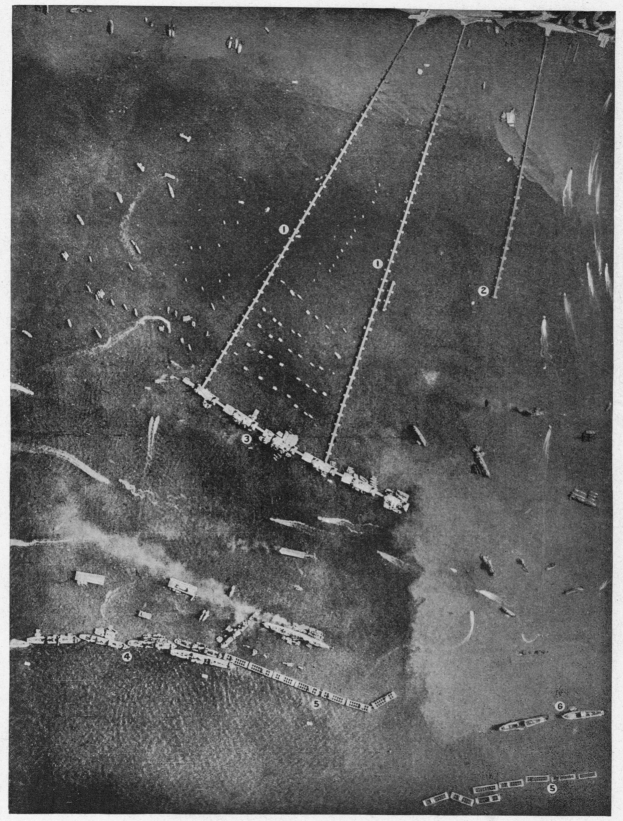

BRITISH BUILT PORT OF ARROMANCHES IN NORMANDY

Here, as seen from the air, are the main pierhead and pierways of 'Mulberry B'—the prefabricated improvised port built at Arromanches (see page 3099) following the first landings of the Allies in Normandy on June 6, 1944. (1) floating pierways nearly three-quarters of a mile long ; (2) pierhead for barges ; (3) main spud pierhead for coasters and medium-sized craft ; (4) line of blockships ('Gooseberry') ; (5) breakwater of concrete caissons ('Phoenixes') ; (6) moorings for Liberty ships. The comet-like streaks are 'ducks,' picket boats, and attendant craft.

AUSTRALIAN TROOPS DIG IN ON 'THE PIMPLE'

'The Pimple,' highest point of 'Shaggy Ridge' which dominated the Ramu Valley in New Guinea, was stormed by Australian infantry on December 27, 1943. Here it can be seen that some have dug themselves in to 'foxholes' on its precipitous sides. The razor-backed ridge, the crest of which was in places so narrow that there was not room for even two men to walk abreast, was cleared of the Japanese by January 21, 1944.   *Photo, Australian Official*

AMERICANS LAND ON THE ISLAND OF NEW BRITAIN

U.S. Marines under the command of Major-General William H. Rupertus (left) went ashore unopposed at Cape Gloucester, New Britain, on December 26, 1943, and captured one of the airfields in the vicinity during the night of December 28–29, the other next day. They linked up with Allied forces striking north from Arawe on February 24, 1944. The whole island (except Gazelle Peninsula, on which lies the once formidable Japanese base of Rabaul) was in Allied hands by April 11. *Photos, U.S. Official*

AUSTRALIANS CROSS THE FINISTERRE RANGE, NEW GUINEA

One of the fiercest battles of the New Guinea operations—that for "The Pimple" (captured December 27, 1943) in "Shaggy Ridge"—was fought in the rugged southern section of Finisterre Range. After clearing "Shaggy Ridge" on January 21, 1944, the Australians pushed on across Finisterre Range to the coast, to capture Bogadjim, abandoned by the enemy, on April 14, 1944. Here some of the men who fought through this exacting campaign pause for a rest on a deeply cleft spur of the range. (See map in page 3124.)

Photo, Australian Official

Lieut.-Gen. STURDEE   **Maj.-Gen. VASEY**   **Maj.-Gen. WOOTTEN**

The appointment of Lieut.-General V. A. H. Sturdee, C.B.E., D.S.O., to command the 1st Australian Army in succession to Lieut.-General Sir John Laverack (who succeeded General Sturdee as head of the Australian Military Mission in Washington) was announced on March 28, 1944. Major-General G. A. Vasey, C.B., C.B.E., D.S.O., who commanded the 6th and 7th Australian Infantry Divisions in New Guinea, was killed in an air accident off Queensland on March 6, 1945. Major-General George F. Wootten, C.B.E., D.S.O., commanded the 9th Australian Infantry Division in New Guinea.   *Photos, Australian Official*

the Cyclops form the coast; the foreshore has disappeared beneath the sea, and only one small landing beach, Torare Bay, exists.

In preparation for the Humboldt Bay landings, enemy airfields to the west were heavily bombed (*see* page 3090). The Japanese air force for almost the whole of New Guinea was paralysed, and not a single aircraft aided the defence of Hollandia.

Bombardment began at dawn. American, Australian and Dutch forces went ashore at three points, Cape Suaja, Cape Pie and Cape Cheweri, General MacArthur directing the attack from a destroyer. During the fighting he insisted on being landed to see the conditions, and narrowly escaped being sniped. Hollandia was captured next day, and Dr. Gerbrandy, the Netherlands Premier, sent a message to General MacArthur on the liberation of the first Dutch territory from the enemy. Dutch officials accompanied the Allied forces and

Capture of Hollandia

began immediately the restoration of Dutch civil administration at Hollandia, taking over further areas of Netherlands territory as they were liberated.

On April 25 U.S. infantry crossed the swampy Lake Sentani in "ducks," "buffaloes," "alligators" and other amphibious vehicles, and captured Sentani and Cyclops airfields. On the 27th, the Americans captured the main Hollandia airfield. Allied planes were able to use them immediately—and on July 11 it was announced that a daily courier-plane service was operating between Hollandia and Australia.

A large camp containing 720 prisoners was discovered on the shore of Lake Sentani. Prisoners from Malaya and the

Netherlands Indies, Indian troops, a few Europeans, Indonesian troops and civilians had been brought there to assist in making the camp and airfields. Women had been brought to wait on their captors, Indonesian and Eurasian missionaries, clerks, teachers, and some Dutch women. They were all suffering from malnutrition and neglect, and were without medical supplies and

many of the ordinary necessities of life, although the Japanese had large stores at Hollandia. No clothing had been issued, and the prisoners were wearing the rags of the clothing in which they had been captured two years before. Some of the women had obtained from the Sentani natives cloth made out of fibre. Fearing sabotage, their captors had forbidden the prisoners to approach the airfields, and not one had been injured by the bombing, while hundreds of Japanese were killed.

Further landings were made at Torare Bay and Dempta on May 5. From Torare Bay, a native trail, formerly used to fetch salt by inland tribes avoiding the hostile sea people of the coast, crosses the mountains to the beach. Thus the only escape routes of the enemy were cut. Fighting was severe during the next few days, but the enemy could not escape, and mopping-up operations of small pockets soon began. The Japanese combat troops fought to the end, but numbers of labourers surrendered without offering resistance. South of Lake Sentani are large areas of swamp inhabited by Papuan tribes, some of them still hostile to strangers since the time their territory was frequently entered by plumage hunters seeking birds of paradise. The

ALLIED CRAFT OFF TANAHMERAH BEACHES

Tanahmerah Bay lies some thirty miles west of Hollandia. Some of the forces taking part in the major Allied combined operation of April 22, 1944, which led to the capture of Hollandia on the 23rd, landed on these beaches, off which lie heavily laden landing ships (tanks). Smaller Allied craft are moving about the bay.   *Photo, Planet News*

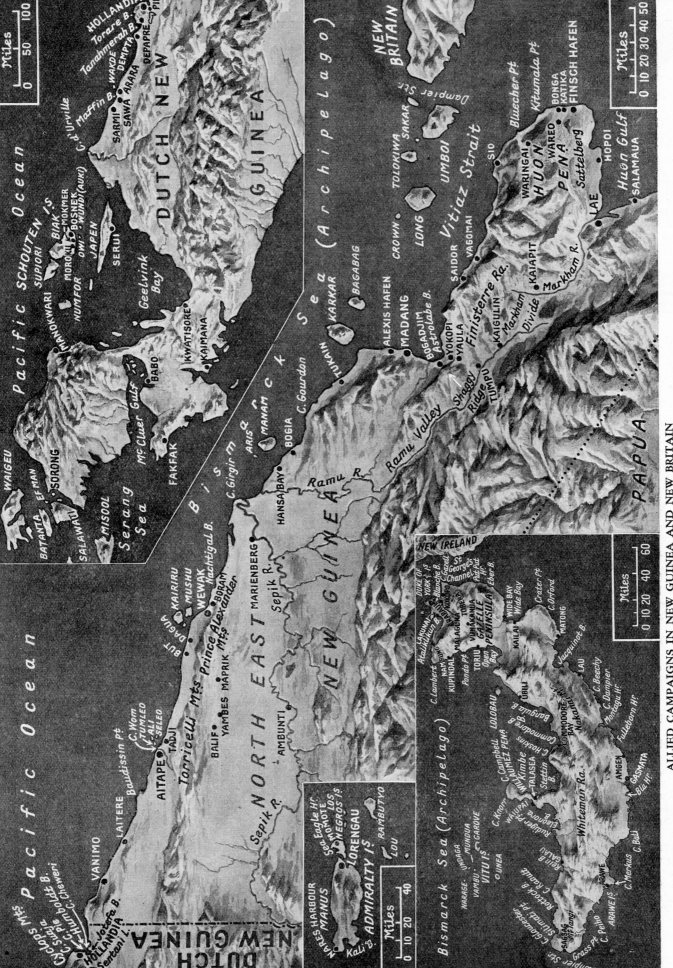

ALLIED CAMPAIGNS IN NEW GUINEA AND NEW BRITAIN

These four maps show, left corner, New Britain, where the Allies landed near Arawe on December 15, 1943. Above New Britain are the Admiralty Islands : the first Allied landing was made at Negros on February 29, 1944. The main map, of part of the north coast of New Guinea, includes the areas reoccupied by the Allies between October 3, 1943 and April 23, 1944. In the top right hand corner is Dutch New Guinea, first invaded by the Allies in the Hollandia area on April 22, 1944. For key showing relative positions of these areas, see opposite page.

Specially drawn for THE SECOND GREAT WAR *by Félix Gardon*

Japanese could not escape in that direction as they would not survive. Those who fled to the mountains were hunted out with zest by Sentani natives, who had suffered much at their hands. The Japanese casualties in this area were 1,422 killed and 410 captured.

The Allies had met no large-scale opposition at Madang and Alexis Hafen, which the enemy used mainly as bases for barges and as supply depots, and Australian patrols pushing west made no contact with enemy forces of any size, though they found that area more thoroughly mined than any hitherto recaptured. But on the coast beyond the mouth of Sepik River, which was reached on July 11, an organized system of defence had been built up in the area between Wewak and Aitape, which district was a pivot for enemy air operations in the South-West Pacific.

Australians Reach Sepik River

Wewak Harbour, which is deep and has good anchorages, had become an enemy naval base, with a seaplane base at Kairiru Island. The Japanese had

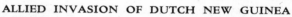

NEW GUINEA : KEY TO DETAILED MAPS OPPOSITE

On April 22, the same day as the combined assault on Hollandia, two other landings were made, at Aitape and at Tadji, where the airstrip was seized, and was made operational by Allied engineers in 42 hours—a record time, 24 hours ahead of schedule, on which they were personally congratulated by General MacArthur. The Japanese had three runways, the third incomplete. All had been constructed by manual labour, as was testified by shovels and wicker baskets for removing soil which were left where the labourers had been disturbed by the unexpected landing. All resistance in the Aitape area ceased by April 25 ; but on July 13 the Japanese launched a counter-attack in great strength. The Allies held their positions, and then started systematically to clear the area of the baulked enemy, small parties of whom took refuge in the Torricelli mountains whence they were hunted out with the help of the Papuans. A considerable force —estimated at 45,000 on July 20— remained some miles inland at Balif and Yambes between Wewak and Aitape.

The Japanese, planning a long-term occupation of New Guinea, were also developing the coastal area adjacent to Wakde Island (west of Hollandia), setting up an organized system of defences and intercommunication on similar lines to that of the Wewak–Aitape district but on a smaller scale. A triangle of air bases had been formed with airstrips on Wakde Island, Maffin Bay, and Sawa, south-east of Sarmi, which had been a Dutch Government station.

U.S. forces made a surprise attack on Wakde on May 17, catching the enemy unprepared and confused by preliminary concentrated bombing. By the 19th the small island was occupied, though organized resistance did not

ALLIED INVASION OF DUTCH NEW GUINEA

Following naval and air bombardment, Allied forces went ashore in strength at Hollandia in Dutch New Guinea on April 22, 1944. Left, all that remained of a street in Hollandia when American troops reached it. Below, Sherman tanks ready to pursue the enemy into the interior : the dense smoke rises from a blazing Japanese ammunition dump. *Photos, U.S. Signal Corps ; Paul Popper*

improved and enlarged five airstrips, at Boram, Wewak, Dagua, But and Tadji, and made the coastal track serviceable for heavy traffic. A very strong enemy force was established in the area, with large camps, and supply installations on Cape Wom, Wewak Peninsula, and Tumleo and Ali Islands. In 1943 the entire area had been subjected to continual Allied bombing (*see* pages 2672–74, 2765) ; but during the autumn extensive repairs were carried out by the Japanese, who restored the base to more than its previous air strength.

cease till the 21st. Allied casualties
were small; 833 enemy dead were
counted. The forces which landed at
Arara on the mainland opposite Wakde,
also on May 17, reached Maffin Bay on
the 24th; but the airfield was not taken
till July 1. Sawa airfield was secured
on July 14.

The capture of Wakde with its good
airstrip gave the Allies mastery over
Geelvink Bay and Manokwari, and it
formed a good forward base from which
to attack remaining Japanese bases in
Dutch New Guinea, Sorong on Doom
Island, and the rich oilfields at Babo.

Biak Island, largest of the Schouten
group, which lies some 200 miles west
of Wakde Island, had three airstrips.
Before dawn on May 27 Allied warships

LANDINGS AT AITAPE

1. American troops un-
loading stores during the
landings at Aitape on
April 22, 1944. 2. A
rapidly erected signals
post on Aitape beach:
the lamp on the tripod
was used to signal to
naval craft offshore. 3.
Lieut. Robert H. Pendle-
bury of Australia and
Major Joy R. Bogue of
Iowa examine some Jap-
anese prisoners.
*Photos, U.S. Signal
Corps and Coast Guard;
Tom Shafer*

approached its coast under cover
of Owi Island and heavily bombarded
enemy batteries. Units of the U.S.
41st Division, commanded by Major-
General Doe, and Australian troops
supported from air and sea made a
landing east of Bosnek, seven miles
from Mokmer airstrip. The Japanese
had withdrawn the bulk of their defensive forces from the Bosnek area to the
high ground between Bosnek and
Mokmer. Only light opposition was
met at first, the reef structure of the
coast presenting the chief difficulties
with which the Allied landing parties
had to contend.

The beach-head was held and troop-
carrying destroyers followed; tanks

were landed at jetties and shelving beaches. By 9.30 a.m. an important ridge overlooking Bosnek had been taken. Opposition stiffened in the afternoon, when enemy bombers appeared and attacked shipping and the beach-head; the only serious damage inflicted was by a Japanese bomber which crashed on a small naval boat. Bosnek was occupied within the next few days.

On June 2 landings were made without opposition on Owi and Wundi Islands by U.S. Marines and engineers; an airstrip constructed on Owi was in operation by the 20th.

Advance from Bosnek was difficult, owing to the nature of the high ground to the west. Enemy opposition increased and weather conditions hindered the Allied air offensive, and the Allies were halted two miles from Mokmer airfield. But by June 3 they had gained a ridge overlooking the little plain east of Mokmer, and brought the airfield defenders under fire. A tank battle on the plain—the first time tanks were used on both sides in the Pacific campaign—resulted in an enemy rout. Mokmer was surrounded on June 7 by the capture of another ridge to the south-west, and a few hours later the airfield had been won. The two remaining airfields, Moroku and Sorido, had been made useless by air attacks, but the enemy defended them fiercely until they were both captured on June 20, and Biak was freed except for a few pockets of resistance.

Tank Battle on Biak Island

Japanese casualties were probably over 2,000 killed—1,820 dead had been counted by June 18. Their air force, which had appeared in greater strength than for many months, suffered serious losses. During the operations the U.S.A. 5th Air Force used Japanese bombs found in ordnance dumps at Hollandia, re-rigged by the addition of new suspension bands.

The capture of Biak marked an important point in the South West Pacific campaign, for the distance between Darwin and Mokmer is 860 miles (less than that between Darwin and Port Moresby), Mindanao is less than 800 miles from Mokmer, Halmahera about 400 miles, and the Japanese naval base of Palau less than 600 miles to the north.

That both sides realized this importance is clear from the two following statements. In a communiqué issued on May 28, General MacArthur said of the Biak operations, " For strategic purposes, this marks the end of the campaign which has resulted in the reconquest or neutralization of the Solomons, the Bismarcks, the Admiralties, and New Guinea. From the most forward point reached by the Japanese, we have advanced our front 1,300 miles westward and 700 miles northward. These operations have effected the strategic penetration of the conquered empire which Japan was attempting to consolidate in the South West Pacific and have secured bases of departure for the advance to its vital areas in the Philippines and the Netherlands East Indies." The Japanese Imperial High Command spokesman on June 3 said, " By landing on Biak Island, the Americans have reached the inner line of Japan's defences. Biak Island is of paramount importance in the Pacific war, and Japanese operations around the Philippines would be much impeded if the Americans made Biak their base."

In September 1944 General Sir Thomas Blamey announced that 90,000 Japanese had been bypassed and had still to be dealt with. Ten divisions of Australians were being employed against them. In the Gazelle Peninsula of New Britain alone, between 6,000 and 7,000 Japanese soldiers were known to have settled in the fertile cultivated areas.

ALLIED COMMANDERS CONFER
Lieut.-General Walter C. Krueger (right), commander of the U.S. 6th Army, confers with Air Commodore Frederick R. Scherger, R.A.A.F. (back to camera), commander of the forces which re-established Tadji airfield after its capture by U.S. troops on April 22, 1944, and Wing Commander W. A. Dale, R.A.A.F. (facing camera) on further plans for the elimination of the Japanese from New Guinea.   *Photo, Keystone*

Gen. Blamey had no reason to think that Japan would readily surrender these conquests. Therefore tens of thousands of Australians must continue the fight, and Australia must maintain an even larger army to reinforce them.

The offensive measures necessary to deal with the remaining enemy forces in the Territories were by no means of the nature simply of mopping-up operations. The enemy was contained in definite areas, but although his communication lines had been cut and his forces were progressively disintegrating, yet parts of the country were held by well-equipped units which, though trapped, were well supplied. These outposts and isolated positions were being dealt with one by one in the remaining months of 1944 and through the turn of the year.

DRIVING THE JAPANESE FROM BIAK ISLAND

American and Australian troops which went ashore on Biak Island (Schouten group) in the early morning of May 27, 1944, cleared it by June 20. Both the Allies and the Japanese regarded possession of Biak as the key to the South West Pacific. Left, U.S. infantry attack a Japanese pillbox. Numerous strongpoints of this kind were stormed and destroyed by U.S. armour and infantry in a drive west of Mokmer airfield on June 11. Right, derelict enemy tanks on Biak beach : the first tank battle of the Pacific campaign was fought on this island.
Photos, Paul Popper ; Keystone

LENINGRAD LIBERATED

1. Only the shell remained of Pulkovo, most important meteorological observatory in Russia, after the Germans had been driven from the neighbourhood of Leningrad. Pulkovo lies ten miles south of the city. 2. The decorated locomotive of a relief train reaching Leningrad with arms, food, mail and troops. 3. Citizens undergoing military training pass St. Isaac's Cathedral. 4. Women begin repair work on a damaged building.

Photos, Pictorial Press ; Planet News

Chapter 310

LENINGRAD OFFENSIVE: CRIMEA RECOVERED

Leningrad, like Moscow and Stalingrad, proved a rock against which the German tide of invasion beat in vain. From the time it was invested, in November 1941 until January 1944, however, there was little movement on the Leningrad front. Then began the swift Russian advance towards Latvia, described by Major-General Sir Charles Gwynn in this Chapter, which also records the history of the reconquest of the Crimea. For the autumn and winter campaigns, 1943–44, in southern Russia, see Chapters 291 and 305

HAVING failed in 1941 to carry Leningrad by assault, when its defence depended on troops exhausted by a long and demoralizing retreat and citizens ill-armed and untrained (*see* Chapter 182), the Germans attempted to compel surrender by starvation and by air and artillery bombardment. In November 1941, by a bold thrust eastwards to Tikhvin, they cut the one remaining railway by which the trickle of supplies reaching the city across the ice of Lake Ladoga could be maintained. But their hold on Tikhvin lasted for ten days only, and the recapture of the town on December 8 by a vigorous Russian counter-attack was the first of the reverses the Germans suffered in the winter of 1941–42.

The Ladoga route was reopened; but it was totally inadequate to meet the needs of the city, and only a people of amazing spirit and powers of endurance could have accepted the sufferings of that terrible winter. The summer brought some relief, but although there was constant fighting the German ring of investment was not broken till January 1943, when Meretskov's army from outside joined hands with Govorov's army within the city (*see illus. in page 2679*), capturing Schluesselburg and establishing a narrow corridor through which one railway line ran.

Thereafter the city was never in immediate danger, though attempts to widen the corridor were fruitless and all railways giving direct communication with Moscow remained in German hands. The German lines of investment had by then been strongly fortified, both those facing the city and those facing eastwards. The latter ran from the strongly held town of Mga to Kirishi on the Volkov and thence along that river to Lake Ilmen, with Chudovo in the middle and Novgorod at its southern end forming hedgehog centres of resistance.

German Lines of Investment

Chudovo had special importance, as it not only stood on a railway which gave lateral communication along the front, but also blocked the main line to Moscow. Novgorod, in addition to its historic associations, also provided protection to the German lines of communication from attack from the east. The German investment line proper ran from Mga to the Gulf of Finland, passing north of the satellite towns of Pushkin and Krasnoye Selo to the Gulf of Finland east of Oranienbaum, where, however, the Russians held a detached enclave opposite Kronstadt. From their lines of investment German long-range guns could be trained on the important war industries of Leningrad, but never succeeded in putting them out of action, and the guns of the Baltic Fleet at Kronstadt frequently made effective reply to the German batteries. North of the city the Finnish position ran from the shores of Lake Ladoga about 80 miles north of Schluesselburg to the Gulf of Finland ten miles south-east of Terijoki, but this front remained comparatively quiet.

This broadly was the situation on the Leningrad front during the summer and autumn of 1943, and it was evident that the Germans had abandoned all idea

GENERAL LEONID GOVOROV
One of Russia's foremost artillery experts, Govorov commanded the troops which launched the attack on the Leningrad front on January 15, 1944. Govorov was promoted Marshal of the Soviet Union in June 1944.

of capturing the city. When, therefore, they were forced back to the Dnieper and presumably were anxious to shorten their front, there seemed to be a reasonable possibility that they might withdraw their northern armies, either to Riga and the line of the Dwina or at least to a line running from Narva to Pskov and thence to Vitebsk.

Yet in spite of the loss of the line of the middle and lower Dnieper and the increasingly serious situation in the Ukraine as the Russian winter offensive of 1943–44 developed, there were no definite signs of a **December Bombardment** withdrawal from the Leningrad front. Intensification of the bombardment of the city during December 1943 raised suspicions that the Germans were getting rid of reserves of heavy gun ammunition in view of a contemplated withdrawal, but the demonstration seems only to have been intended to increase the hardships suffered by the inhabitants.

There can be little doubt that the Germans, even if only as a routine staff precaution, had made plans for a withdrawal; but equally it is certain that they had not been put into operation, and the enemy was taken entirely by surprise when Govorov and Meretskov (*see illus. in page 1506*) took the offensive on a great scale, the former from Oranienbaum and southwards from Leningrad and the latter on the Volkov front as far south as Novgorod.

The Soviet offensive in the Leningrad area started on January 15, 1944, but it was not until the 18th that news of it was released. On the two following days Orders of the Day addressed to Govorov and Meretskov revealed more explicitly what had been achieved. Govorov after five days' stubborn fighting had broken through the strongly fortified German lines to a depth of $7\frac{1}{2}$ to $12\frac{1}{2}$ miles and to a width of 22 to 25 miles in both his sectors and had captured, among other places, Krasnoye Selo, Peterhof, Oranienbaum and Ropsha. Seven German infantry divisions had been defeated, 20,000 Germans killed, and among booty captured was a large group of heavy artillery which had

points and advanced depots in rear of their lines of investment, but these were captured in quick succession—among others Pushkin (Tsarkoye Selo) and Pavlovsk on January 24 and Gatchina (Krasnogvardeisk) two days later. The last is a particularly important railway junction standing on the Leningrad-Pskov line, and a lateral railway from Narva to Tosno, on the main Leningrad-Moscow railway, runs through it. These were achievements of Govorov's army. Meretskov, thrusting west from the Volkov, cleared the main Leningrad-Moscow railway by capturing the strongly defended railway towns of Tosno (27th), Lyuban (28th), and Chudovo (30th).

CZARS' PALACES DESTROYED

1. Cossacks of the Red Army advance guard reach the palace at Peterhof, about 15 miles from Leningrad on the Gulf of Finland, mid-January 1944.   Formerly a royal residence, it had been turned by the Soviet Government into a museum and cultural centre. 2. Men of the Red Army in white winter uniforms in front of the gutted palace (built by the Empress Catherine) at Pushkin (Tsarskoye Selo)—captured on January 24. 3. German mines extracted by Soviet sappers from the Oranienbaum-Peterhof road, and rendered harmless.
Photo, Planet News ; Pictorial Press

systematically shelled the city. Meretskov had forced the line of the Volkov and the northern end of Lake Ilmen and by a skilful outflanking manoeuvre had captured Novgorod. Other successes followed in rapid succession.

On January 21 Mga, the north-eastern keypoint of the German line, fell to a combined attack by troops under Govorov and Meretskov. Its capture marked the final liberation of Leningrad, for from it the railway running through the corridor opened the year before had been kept under fire. It had also blocked the railway running through Kirishi to central Russia. The Germans were still fighting desperately to hold towns which had formed strong-

The Germans were in full retreat— on Govorov's front, westwards towards Narva and southwards along the Pskov and Dno railways ; on Meretskov's front, south-westwards towards the Leningrad-Dno railway, the troops from Novgorod following the road and railway skirting the north-west of Lake Ilmen. The German losses before they could disengage were very heavy. The Russians claimed that they had routed ten divisions and had badly mauled two more ; great quantities of material had been captured. The nature of the fighting is indicated by the fact that between January 14 and 25 the Russians counted 40,000 dead to only 3,000 prisoners. The German troops, after many months of trench warfare, had deteriorated both physically and in tactical skill, and were in no condition to stand the surprise Russian onslaught. But by the end of January the efficiency of German staff work had begun to assert itself, and the retreat did not degenerate into a rout. The weather, which as elsewhere in Russia had been abnormally mild with frequent thaws, handicapped pursuit, tying the heavier weapons to roads in the marshy and forested terrain. Moreover, the Germans had the use of intact roads— probably developed both in number and quality by their engineers to facilitate the supply of the investing army—which they left ruined by demolition.

Germans in full Retreat

Rearguards under these conditions did not find much difficulty in checking direct pursuit, especially when the more thickly populated districts of the Leningrad region were left behind and outflanking movements in strength became difficult in forest country. Apart from harassing action by lightly armed ski troops and partisans, the chief dangers facing the Germans were (a) that the troops making a long retreat from the lower Volkov across the grain of the main road and railway

systems might be caught in a pocket, and (b) that the Dno and Pskov railways might be cut in the neighbourhood of Batetskaya and Luga by Meretskov striking west from Novgorod. Fortunately for the Germans, Govorov's pursuit southwards was easily checked south of Siversky, for at that point the road and railway entered dense forests and marsh land. The threat to Batetskaya was much more dangerous, for it involved the possibility of complete disaster. There was also the danger that Meretskov's columns skirting Lake Ilmen might cut the Dno railway farther south, although Shimsk near the south-west corner of the lake could be easily reinforced, and provided an obvious rallying point.

The Russians captured Siversky on January 31, but thereafter Govorov's advance southwards slowed down, and he did not begin to close in on Luga (captured February 12) till about February 9, by which time the Germans from the Volkov had in the main made good their escape, the Russians in direct pursuit of them having been greatly hampered by obstructions on the forest roads. Meanwhile Meretskov's thrust from Novgorod had met strong resistance as it approached Batetskaya, but that town also was captured on February 12, and Meretskov went on to enter the eastern suburbs of Luga as Govorov entered it from the north. The German stand in this area had, however, averted catastrophe, and Meretskov's left columns had been brought to a standstill at Shimsk.

While all this was happening, Govorov's right wing had pursued the Germans retreating towards Narva. Kingisepp, the chief stronghold covering the approaches to the Narva, was captured on February 1 after a hard fight, and the coast of the Gulf up to the mouth of the Narva was cleared. The lower stretches of the Luga river were also forced, opening the way to the north end of Lake Peipus. By February 6 the Russians reached the east bank of the Narva north and south of Narva town, but the river was a formidable obstacle in its incompletely frozen condition, and behind it the Germans were able to stabilize the front. The Russians did succeed in establishing a small bridge-head across the river, but the town of Narva was a strong centre served by good communications. Govorov's right wing now swung south along the east side of Lake Peipus in order to develop a second line of approach to Pskov. Gdov, from which a main road runs to Luga, was captured

Russians Reach Lake Peipus

ENEMY ON THE DEFENSIVE
1. German Grenadiers in a trench running through a 'ghost wood' south of Lake Ladoga await a Russian attack on a strongly defended sector of their line. 2. Field-Marshal Busch, commanding the Lake Ilmen front, with Lieut.-General Wegener (left). 3. One of a large number of heavy guns—used to bombard Leningrad —which were captured by the Russians in their drive of January 1944. Plenty of shells remained unused, in spite of the heavy bombardment to which the city was subjected during December 1943.
Photos, New York Times ; Keystone ; Planet

on February 13. Encountering little resistance, the Russians swept on, and for a time this force appeared to represent the most dangerous threat to Pskov.

The Germans had escaped the trap at Luga, but Govorov's main force was hard on their heels and Meretskov was free to drive down the Dno railway and thus co-operate directly with his force held up at Shimsk. This would soon imperil the communications of Staraya Russa on the south side of Lake Ilmen and of the whole German front which, to the south side of that place, ran along the Lovat River, through Kholm to the Dno-Vitebsk railway north of Novo Sokolniki. This front, from the marshy nature of the

RUSSIAN GUERILLA FORCES

Men—and women—who fought as guerillas behind the enemy lines during the years of occupation march towards Leningrad after its relief on January 27, 1944. Right, the northern front in Russia showing the country from which Generals Govorov and Meretskov drove the Germans during the early months of 1944.

terrain, did not favour a major Russian offensive, but it was already under considerable pressure by Popov's 2nd Baltic Army. On February 18 the Germans admitted that they were withdrawing from Staraya Russa, for which they had fought so hard a year before, and it soon became apparent that the whole of the Lovat front was in retreat to the Dno-Vitebsk railway. To cover this retreat, they made great efforts to hold Meretskov's drive, and Dno was actually captured on February 14 by Popov in co-operation with Govorov.

With Dno lost and with Novo Sokolniki in Russian hands since January 29, the Germans could make no lengthy stand on the railway between them. At Pskov, however, they had a strong pivot and south of it the Velikaya river provided a strong position, with the railways to Dvinsk and Polotsk giving good lateral and rearward communication. This front, moreover, included the defences of the old Stalin line. The German withdrawal therefore continued, and as Russian communications became longer and more difficult with the approach of spring, the momentum of pursuit diminished. Fighting, chiefly to secure some important centres, continued for a time, but broadly speaking the offensive died out and the northern front became stabilized on the general line, Narva, Pskov, Polotsk, by the middle of March.

The Russian offensive had on the whole achieved amazing success, especially as a large part of the armies employed had for many months previously been shut up in Leningrad under conditions which gave little scope for training in mobile operations. Not only had Leningrad and great tracts of

Soviet Pursuit Slows Down

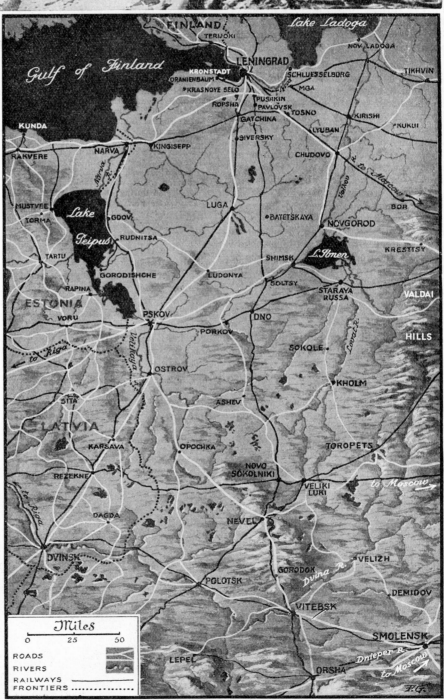

Specially drawn for THE SECOND GREAT WAR *by Félix Gardon*

GENERAL YEREMENKO

A portrait by the Russian artist Alexander Gerasimov of General Andrei Ivanovich Yeremenko, commander of the Independent Maritime Army which took Kerch on April 11, and advanced to capture Feodosia on the 13th and Yalta on the 16th. It later assisted in the investment of Sevastopol.

Photo, Pictorial Press

Russian territory been liberated, but a base for further operations served by immensely valuable railway and road communications had been secured. The Germans had been driven back into what might become a dangerous salient, but though they had suffered heavy defeats and immense losses, they had once again escaped disaster, owing to weather conditions (which restricted Russian capacity for winter manoeuvre) and also to their own executive skill.

Crimea Liberated

The Russian winter offensive of 1943–44 sweeping through the Ukraine and into Poland (*see* Chapter 305) had isolated the Crimea Peninsula. The Russians wisely refrained from diverting to what might prove a difficult and expensive operation forces which could be better employed in their main offensive. Yet if the spring thaw brought the main operations to a standstill, the chances of a Russian attack on the Crimea would increase.

There were three courses open to the Germans : (a) To evacuate the peninsula—a difficult operation and one involving loss of prestige, but probably easier to carry out while the Russians were fully engaged elsewhere than it might become later ; (b) To withdraw part of their force, leaving a garrison in the strong defences of Sevastopol in order to deny the port to the Russians ; (c) To hold on to the Crimea in the con-

fident hope that such a highly defensible stronghold could resist all attacks. The possession of the good airfields of the Crimea was also a matter of some importance for the protection of Rumania.

During the winter there were no signs of evacuation, but when by the end of March Nikolaiev had been captured and Odessa was closely threatened, evacuation from the Crimea had become much more difficult. At this late hour the first indications were given that tentative evacuation measures were in progress, though on no great scale. Probably they entailed the evacuation of convalescent establishments which the Germans were known to have established in the peninsula.

But while the Germans appeared to be debating what course to follow, the Russians struck. On April 10 a communiqué announced that some days previously Tolbukhin's 4th Ukrainian Army had gone over to the offensive against the Germans in the Perekop isthmus and on the southern shores of the Sivash (the Putrid Sea). It had broken through the Perekop defences and penetrated 12½ miles, had captured the town and railway station of Armyansk and reached the enemy's Ishun position covering the southern exit from the isthmus. Furthermore, it had forced a crossing of the Sivash east of Armyansk and captured the strongly held defile, by which the railway crosses the swamps, after two days' fighting. Orders of the Day of April 11 addressed to Generals

Tolbukhin (*see* illus. in page 2824) and Yeremenko respectively announced the capture by Tolbukhin of Zhankoi, the chief railway junction in the Crimea, and by Yeremenko's Independent Maritime Army of the Kerch fortress and an advance of 19 miles beyond it. With surprising speed the Russians had gained a foothold in the peninsula.

To appreciate fully the brilliance of this feat, it is necessary to recall the defensive potentialities of the Crimea. Its only connexions with the main land are by the Perekop isthmus, some three miles wide, **Natural Defences of the Crimea** and the narrow causeway along which the railway runs—both highly defensible defiles, especially at their southern exits where the defence could not only establish a ring of fire, but where the ground lent itself to armoured counter-attack. The German Ishun position had been established to exploit these advantages south of the Perekop defile, and the causeway was similarly protected on a smaller scale. Between the two defiles lies the Sivash, deemed to be an impassable barrier of swamps and lagoons. The remainder of the coast line, except at the Kerch Straits, gave few facilities for amphibious operations, especially in view of the fact that the enemy possessed numerous excellent airfields. The outer defences of the Crimea were therefore very strong; but the length of the perimeter required a considerable force to watch and hold it, although excellent internal com-

RUSSIAN ARTILLERY AGAINST SEVASTOPOL

The last battle for Sevastopol began on April 15, 1944, when long-range shelling from guns of this type played a decisive part in the Russian attack. The final assault by the Red Army started on May 8, and freed the city next day : it had been taken by the Germans in 1942 only after a nine months' siege. Front line dispatches announcing its liberation stated that 'under attacks by dive-bombers and a rain of high explosives, the German steel-and-concrete defence system was tossed into the air.'

Photo, Pictorial Press

RUMANIANS IN KERCH
Rumanian troops in considerable strength fought with the Germans in the Crimea, and took part in the defence of Sevastopol. Their casualties were heavy, the Rumanian 9th Cavalry Regiment, for instance, being wiped out in the retreat from Feodosia. Here two Rumanian soldiers are bringing up food for their comrades through Kerch's bombed streets. *Photo, New York Times*

munications favoured economical dispositions and facilitated prompt counter-attack.

The inner defences were equally formidable. The whole of the northern and western part of the peninsula is open country of a steppe character, very favourable for the use of armour, and behind this lies rugged country covering Sevastopol and a long stretch of the southern coast. Here the Germans had fortified three positions : an outer strong outpost position in country where tanks and wheeled vehicles were tied to the roads ; behind that, the main position, denying observation on Sevastopol, of very great strength, both

naturally and by reason of elaborate artificial defences of concrete and of caves hewn in rock ; and an inner position covering Sevastopol which, though equally strongly fortified with ample bomb-proof shelter, did not deny observation on the town and harbour nor keep modern artillery out of range. The names, British and Russian, of many of the works and tactical features dated from the war of 1854–56.

That was the nut the Russian commanders had to crack, and the sole advantages they held were that in the previous November Tolbukhin had carried his pursuit some distance into the Perekop isthmus. From the Kuban a lodgement had also been gained at Kerch, though without capturing the German fortifications.

There had, however, been plenty of time for preparation and Tolbukhin had made good use of it. At Perekop he had massed a great weight of artillery and the Germans had consequently reason to believe that was the danger point. But Russian plans were more subtle. It was known that the enemy on the south side of the Sivash had only small detachments of indifferent troops, and after thorough reconnaissance Tolbukhin was convinced he could cross the marshes by constructing causeways over the impassable places and utilizing the few comparatively dry ridges that existed. For this all necessary material was collected, and it was here his main blow came. The Russians, by refusing to be deterred by the apparently impossible, had again achieved surprise. It was an amazing venture, but skill and determination brought complete success. Too late, when the alarm was given, the Germans tried with aircraft to break up the causeways, but, attacked simultaneously at Ishun, they still underrated the danger. Before it was fully realized, Russian tanks were across the marshes,

and making straight for Zhankoi. Wheeling to the right after its capture, Tolbukhin's armour made for Eupatoria on the south-west coast, passing in rear of the Ishun defences which were already being heavily attacked in front.

With Yeremenko's important if less sensational success at Kerch, the German outer defences had been irretrievably broken, and retreat to the Sevastopol fortifications was inevitable. But the enemy had had disastrous losses and, with Russian armour in rear of their main force at Ishun, it was beyond even German competence to organize an orderly withdrawal before reaching the shelter of the southern hills. Retreat became a disorderly flight harried by Russian mobile troops.

On April 13 Marshal Stalin was able to announce the capture of Eupatoria (a possible evacuation port) and Simferopol, capital of the Crimea, by Tolbukhin, and of Feodosia by Yeremenko. By the 16th, Yeremenko had also captured Yalta, leaving Sevastopol as the only available port for a possible evacuation. South of Simferopol and west of Yalta the Russians, however, entered the hilly country in which the Germans, rallying in previously organized defences, were able to slow down pursuit.

THE CRIMEA
The swift Soviet campaign which liberated the Crimea between April 10 and May 9, 1944, is illustrated by this map. Figures after place names indicate the dates in April on which they were captured by the Russians.

3134

SHATTERED SEVASTOPOL IN RUSSIAN HANDS AGAIN

Red Navy signallers send out semaphore messages to Soviet ships in the Black Sea from the great naval base of Sevastopol, once more under Russian control from May 9, 1944. Below, Russian sailors enter the city during the last stages of the final Soviet assault, which began on May 7, and in which the Germans lost over 20,000 dead. *Photos, Pictorial Press ; Planet News*

Unable to use armour to advantage, the Russians nevertheless fought their way steadily forward with the aid of boldly used guns and mortars. By April 17 they had begun to make contact with the strongly held German main position, which could not be stormed without adequate preparation.

A period of bitter local engagements for the possession of tactical features then ensued, during which heavy guns and ammunition were brought up from Perekop. During that period the Germans made persistent, though not large scale, attempts to evacuate part of their troops—attempts rendered costly by the Red Air Force and the Black Sea Fleet. But Hitler seems to have issued orders that the fortress of Sevastopol was to be held at all costs.

Not till May 7, by which time Yeremenko had also closed in on the fortress, did Tolbukhin launch his full scale assault on the main German position. Under massed blows from the air, powerful artillery fire and determined infantry attack, the German line quickly crumbled ; but even then tactical surprise clinched the victory. The Germans had expected the main attack from the south. When it developed in the north, they tried to regroup, only to be caught in the consequent confusion by a decisive attack from the south.

Russians Recapture Sevastopol

The Germans fought hard, making numerous local counter-attacks, but by the third day their last defences had been overrun and Sevastopol had been taken by storm (May 9). The Germans made desperate last-moment attempts at evacuation, but from May 8 onward the harbour, under close artillery fire,

could not be used, and the remnants of the garrison retired to Khersonese Point in hopes of embarking there. A few parties may have escaped to sea in high-speed launches, but, by May 12, the Russians had closed in and surrender was inevitable.

In the final battle which began on May 7 over 20,000 Germans were killed and 24,361 were taken prisoner, including Lt.-Gen. Dehmut, Commanding the German 5th Army, while in the whole campaign their losses were over 111,000 including 61,587 prisoners, and enormous quantities of material.

The speed and sureness of touch with which Tolbukhin and Yeremenko carried out their task was all the more remarkable when compared with the 250 days it had taken the Germans to effect the capture of Sevastopol, at immensely greater cost (*see* Chapter 227). Tolbukhin especially had shown himself a commander of exceptional brilliance. The whole episode made a fitting end to the Russian winter campaign, and the fact that Rumanian troops in large numbers had been involved in the disaster seemed likely to affect the spirit with which Rumania would meet the danger which now clearly threatened her (*see* page 3082).

Diary of the War
MARCH and APRIL, 1944

March 1. Over 600 R.A.F. bombers attacked Germany at night; Stuttgart main target.

March 4. First daylight attack on Berlin by U.S.A. 8th A.F.

March 5. "Chindit" air invasion of Burma began.

March 6. Russians captured Volochisk. Major daylight assault by U.S. bombers on Berlin. U.S. Marines landed near Talasea (New Britain).

March 7. Loss of H.M.S. "Penelope" ("Pepperpot") off Anzio announced.

March 8. Major daylight blow at Berlin by 2,000 American aircraft.

March 9. Russians broke into Tarnopol. Strong U.S. bomber formations made day attack on Berlin.

March 10. Russian capture of Uman and Kristinovka announced. U.S. Marines captured town and air base of Talasea (New Britain).

March 11. Russians captured Berislavl.

March 12. 14th Army captured Buthidaung and Razabil (Burma).

March 13. Red Army captured Kherson. British and West African troops landed on Arakan coast 15 miles below Razabil; 17th Indian Division withdrew from Tiddim (Burma).

March 15. Russians crossed the Bug on 60-mile front. R.A.F. dropped over 3,000 tons on Germany; Stuttgart main target. M.A.A.F. dropped 1,400 tons on Cassino in 3½ hours; artillery, tank and infantry attack then secured two-thirds of town (Italy). M.A.A.F. bombed Sofia (Bulgaria). U.S. troops landed on Manus I. (Admiralties). Sharp attack by U.S. Liberators on Truk (Carolines).

March 16. Red Army captured Vapnyarka. Heavy night attack by R.A.F. on Sofia (Bulgaria). Wewak (New Guinea) and Kurile Is. bombed by Allied aircraft.

March 17. Red Army captured Dubno. U.S.A. 15th A.F. gave Vienna its first air raid. Americans captured Lorengau airfield (Manus, Admiralties). Wewak (New Guinea) and Kurile Is. bombed by Allies. Japanese launched attack on Assam.

March 18. Soviet forces captured Zhmerinka. 1,500–2,000 planes of U.S.A. 8th A.F. bombed Augsburg, Friedrichshafen and other targets in S. Germany; Frankfort-on-Main chief target for R.A.F. night attack. U.S. troops captured Lorengau (Manus, Admiralties).

March 19. Russians advanced to the Dniester. Germans crossed Hungarian frontier and started to occupy Hungary. Allied aircraft bombed Klagenfurt and Graz (Austria). U.S. Marines occupied Emirau I. Allied aircraft sank 2 Japanese troopships and 3 corvettes off New Guinea, and bombed Surabaya (Java).

March 20. Soviet forces captured Mogilev Podolski and Vinnitsa. Chinese under Gen. Stilwell cleared Japanese from Hukawng Valley (Burma).

March 22. Red Army captured Pervomaisk. Heavy day attack by U.S.A. 8th A.F. on Berlin; R.A.F. dropped more than 3,000 tons on Frankfort-on-Main.

March 23. 1,750 American planes attacked Hamm and other targets.

March 24. R.A.F. bombers dropped over 2,500 tons on Berlin. Chinese captured Shaduzup; Major-General O. C. Wingate killed in air accident (Burma).

March 25. Proskurov captured by Russians.

March 26. Red Army reached the Prut (Soviet frontier) on 55-mile front; captured Kamenetz Podolski. U.S. planes bombed military installations in Pas-de-Calais and Cherbourg areas; R.A.F. made night saturation attack on Essen. Fighting in Cassino, continuous since 15th, died down to artillery duel (Italy).

March 27. Russians forced the Upper Dniester. U.S.A. 8th A.F. bombed enemy aerodromes in France.

March 28. Red Army captured Nikolaiev. U.S. heavy bombers attacked enemy airfields in France.

March 29. Red Army captured Kolomyja. U.S. Fortresses bombed Brunswick. 14th Army captured western tunnel on Maungdaw-Buthidaung road (Burma). U.S. naval task force attacked Palau Is.; 23 enemy ships sunk, 6 probably sunk, 11 damaged.

March 30. Red Army captured Cernauti, capital of Bukovina. 1,000 R.A.F. bombers attacked Nuremberg at night. Heavy M.A.A.F. attack on Sofia (Bulgaria).

March 30 and 31. 203 Japanese aircraft destroyed in two air attacks on Hollandia (New Guinea).

March 31. Russians captured Ochakov. Americans heavily bombed Truk (Carolines).

April 1. Russians encircled 45,000 Germans at Skala. Entry into coastal areas of Great Britain prohibited. Truk and Ponape (Carolines) bombed by U.S.A. 7th A.F. Ndrilo and Koruniat (Admiralties) occupied by Americans.

April 2. Red Army crossed the Prut and advanced into Rumania. U.S.A. 15th A.F. bombed Steyr (Austria). Japanese crossed Imphal-Kohima road (Assam).

April 3. First major air attack of war on Budapest (Hungary) by U.S. bombers, followed by R.A.F. night attack. 300 Allied planes (1 lost) bombed Hollandia (New Guinea); 314 Japanese planes destroyed. 42 Barracudas of the Home Fleet bombed and damaged "Tirpitz" in Alten Fjord (Norway).

April 4. Bucharest (Rumania) heavily bombed by U.S.A. 15th A.F.

April 5. Red Army captured Razjelnaya. U.S.A. 15th A.F. bombed Ploesti (Rumania). Telephone service between Great Britain and Ireland suspended.

April 6. 14th Army captured eastern tunnel in Maungdaw-Buthidaung road.

April 8. Soviet forces reached Czechoslovak frontier. Brunswick and other places in Germany bombed by more than 1,000 U.S. planes. 152 tons dropped on Hollandia (New Guinea) by Allied aircraft.

April 9. Strong Soviet bomber force made night attack on Lwow. Focke-Wulf factories in Poland and E. Germany attacked by some 1,750 U.S. planes; heavy R.A.F. night attacks on French railway centres. Kohima (Assam) reported under Japanese pressure.

April 10. Red Army captured Odessa and Armyansk. R.A.F. dropped 3,600 tons on railway targets (France and Belgium).

April 11. Soviet forces captured Zhankoi and Kerch. Nearly 2,000 Allied planes attacked aircraft factories, railway centres, and airfields in Germany and enemy-occupied countries. All New Britain except Gazelle Peninsula in Allied hands.

April 12. Red Army captured Tiraspol. U.S.A. 15th A.F. bombed Wiener Neustadt (Austria). R.A.F. made heavy night attack on Budapest (Hungary). Over 200 Allied planes bombed Hollandia (New Guinea).

April 13. Red Army captured Feodosia, Eupatoria, and Simferopol. Nearly 2,000 U.S. planes attacked Augsburg, Schweinfurt and other targets in S. Germany.

April 14. Red Army captured Bakhchisarai and Alushta; death of Marshal Vatutin. Australians captured Bogadjim (New Guinea). Bombay Port (India) put out of action by explosion of ammunition ship.

April 15. Russians captured Tarnopol; cleared Skala "kettle." U.S. planes bombed Bucharest and Ploesti.

April 16. Russians captured Yalta. Imphal Plain (Assam) cleared of Japanese.

April 18. Russians captured Balaklava. Restrictions imposed on diplomatic representatives in United Kingdom. About 2,000 U.S. aircraft bombed Oranienberg, Rathenow and other places in N. Germany. 1,000 R.A.F. bombers attacked railway targets (France).

April 19. Allied aircraft struck heavily at Soe (Dutch Timor) and Sabang and Lho-Nga (Sumatra).

April 20. R.A.F. dropped 4,500 tons at night on railway centres in W. Europe.

April 22. Nearly 2,000 U.S. heavy bombers attacked Hamm; 1,000 R.A.F. bombers attacked Brunswick, Duesseldorf, and Laon. Strong Allied landings at Hollandia, Aitape, and Tanahmerah Bay (New Guinea). Japanese captured Chengchow (Honan, China).

April 23. S.E. Asia Command announced that Japanese offensive in Manipur had failed. Hollandia (New Guinea) captured by Allies.

April 24. British Home Office banned all overseas travel. U.S. heavy bombers attacked Munich area and Friedrichshafen; R.A.F. made heavy night attacks on Karlsruhe and Munich. Australians captured Madang (New Guinea).

April 25. U.S. infantry captured Sentani and Cyclops airfields (New Guinea).

April 26. R.A.F. delivered two major attacks, on Essen and Schweinfurt. Australians captured Alexis Hafen (New Guinea).

April 27. U.S. Strategic Air Force made major day attacks on Blainville and Chalons-sur-Marne marshalling yards, Toul and Nancy airfields. 1,000-bomber night raid by R.A.F. on Friedrichshafen. Sharp fighting continued at Kohima (Assam). Americans captured main Hollandia airfield (New Guinea).

April 29. American daylight assault on Berlin: 2,000 tons dropped.

April 29 and 30. Heavy air-sea attack by powerful U.S. task force on Truk (Carolines); 126 Japanese planes destroyed.

April 30. U.S.A. 8th A.F. bombed Clermont-Ferrand and Lyons airfields; attacked Pas-de-Calais targets.

Chapter 311

THE ALLIES REOPEN THE WESTERN FRONT

The Allies began to make plans for the invasion of Western Europe in 1942 ; but not till June 6, 1944, were their schemes brought to fruition. Something of the meticulous organization that preceded this most hazardous and most successful military operation in all history is described in Chapters 301 and 307. The story of the fighting begins in Chapter 314. Here Gordon Holman, who from the headquarters ship H.M.S. ' Hilary ' watched the troops go in to the attack, describes the actual assault on the Normandy beaches

In the month of May 1944, Rear-Admiral George Elvey Creasy, of the Royal Navy, Chief of Staff to Admiral Sir Bertram Ramsay, the brilliant Commander of the Allied Naval Expeditionary Force, concluded an address to Allied naval officers with these words : " Gentlemen, what Philip of Spain failed to do, what Napoleon tried and failed to do and what Hitler never had the courage to try, we are about to do, and with God's grace we shall."

For many days before those words were spoken an immense and intricate machine had been in motion (*see* Chapter 307). The assault forces gathered at innumerable points of embarkation along the southern shores of England—British and Canadians for the most part to the east, Americans to the west. Those who were to form the flood following in their wake assembled north, east and west on her long seaboard.

The final stages of this great initial movement saw an important link up between the disposition of ships and landing craft and the drafting of army units into the special marshalling areas near the coast.

To embark assault forces, a technique wholly different was required from that used for passing large bodies of troops to distant theatres of war. It was essential for the assault that, as far as possible, first wave troops should go in as self-supporting combat teams. It was also necessary that the support units should be well spread among the hundreds of ships so that any casualties inflicted by enemy air action would not unduly affect any particular angle of the assault.

Embarking Assault Forces

This important function of " breaking up " gave to the movement staffs in the marshalling areas the name " mincing machines." Each marshalling area was dependent, as to size, on the capacity of the embarkation area it served. As units passed from the marshalling camps they lost their identity and became serially numbered components of craft and ship loads. So, from the " hards " and quays, infantrymen, artillerymen, sappers and all the others who went to make up the 1944 army boarded the invasion ships and became part of a team that could fight its way up from the beaches.

The roads of southern England, hastily prepared less than four years earlier to meet the invader, were thronged with tanks, guns, bulldozers, lorries and " ducks." For miles inland, these assorted vehicles lined the way in almost unbroken chains, while fluffy vapour trails high in the heavens marked the path of the guardian fighter aircraft.

The R.A.F., with the U.S. air forces, had brought about a complete transformation since the dog-fighting days of the Battle of Britain. Both the armies and the mass of shipping that was to transport them could gather with little fear of major interference from the Luftwaffe. Indeed, as was to be proved in a few days, that vaunted service was not even capable of carrying out the thorough reconnaissance that would have given the Germans warning of the time and direction of our attack. The soldiers embarking in the ships were in great heart.

On June 4 everything was ready, and Admiral Ramsay (tragically killed in a flying accident on January 2, 1945) issued this memorable Order of the Day to the Allied Naval forces : " It is to be our privilege to take part in the greatest amphibious operation in history —a necessary preliminary to the opening of the Western Front in Europe which, in conjunction with the great **A Memorable** Russian **Order** advance, will **of the Day** crush the fighting power of Germany. This is the opportunity which we have long awaited and which must be seized and pursued with relentless determination ; the hopes and prayers of the free world and of the enslaved peoples of Europe will be with us, and we cannot fail them. Our task, in conjunction with the Merchant Navies of the United Nations and supported by the Allied Air Forces, is to carry the Allied Expeditionary Force to the Continent, to establish there a secure bridge-head, and to build it up and maintain it at a rate which will outmatch that of the enemy. Let no one underestimate the magnitude of this task. The Germans are desperate, and will resist fiercely until we out-manoeuvre and out-fight them, which we can and we will do. To every one of you will be given the opportunity to show by his determination and resource that dauntless spirit of resolution which individually strengthens and inspires and which collectively is irresistible. I count on every man to do his utmost to ensure the success of this great enterprise, which is the climax of the European war . Good luck to you all and Godspeed."

The secret of the point of assault was well kept. Many commanders

Rear-Admiral VIAN, R.N.   Rear-Admiral KIRK, U.S.N.

Admiral Sir Philip L. Vian, K.B.E., D.S.O., flying his flag in H.M.S. ' Scylla,' commanded the Eastern Force, Admiral Alan G. Kirk, in U.S.S. ' Augusta,' the Western Force of the Combined Fleet which escorted and assisted the Allied land forces in their invasion of Normandy. Admiral Kirk's appointment to the command of the U.S. Task Force operating as part of the Combined Naval Forces based on Britain was announced in February 1944. Both admirals received the K.C.B. for their part in the invasion— Admiral Kirk being the only American naval officer so honoured.

did not know where their men would go in until they had been embarked and "sealed" in landing craft. When the disclosure could be made, everybody wanted to study a map of the Bay of the Seine. The British, including the Canadians, were going in on the eastern beaches, with the Caen canal on their left flank and covered by airborne troops dropped a few hours earlier on the other side of the canal, while the Americans attacked to the west, where the broad bay sweeps round towards Cherbourg.

The Point of Assault

The vital sea lift was to be undertaken by two main forces—the Eastern Force under the command of Rear-Admiral Sir Philip Vian, of the Royal Navy, and the Western Force under the command of Rear-Admiral Alan G. Kirk, of the United States Navy. The Eastern Force consisted of three naval assault forces and one follow-up force,

and the Western of two naval assault forces and one follow-up force. The warships and larger vessels involved were 75 per cent British, but the over-all percentage, which took in many smaller craft, was 60 per cent British and 40 per cent American. The total number of vessels taking part in the assault—the figure was given to the writer personally by Admiral Ramsay—was 5,143.

On June 1, when the first meeting to discuss the weather forecast for D Day was held, the outlook was not good, and it deteriorated during the next three days. Throughout Sunday, June 4, the weather grew steadily worse. The sky was full of scudding clouds, and "white horses" crowned the waves even in the protected waters of the Solent. But this was the eve of the chosen day, and before noon the flat-bottomed landing craft, which had been assembled in a fleet stretching out

of sight along the Hampshire coast, were heading out towards the open sea. At the speeds they could make it was necessary that they should be well on the way by nightfall. (*See* illus., p. 3086.)

The wind continued to increase, and nobody was surprised when news came that a postponement of twenty-four hours had been decided upon. Tides on the other side of the Channel were all-important, however, and the expedition had to be undertaken on the 5th, 6th or 7th—or put off for a fortnight.

The wind was still blowing strongly next morning, June 5, but once again the little ships, recalled the previous night, began to leave the anchorage. And this time it was no false start. Up and down the coast, shipping was on the move,

Minesweepers in the Van

with the gallant minesweeping forces in the van—309 British, 22 American and 16 Canadian minesweepers. Having concluded preliminary sweeps, they had to open broad highways of more than thirty miles in length which ended only when they could get no closer to the Normandy beaches. They were followed by special vessels known as "danners," which laid danbuoys (to indicate dangerous areas) along the swept thoroughfares.

For the seaborne forces, H Hour in the eastern sector was fixed at 7.25 a.m. on June 6, the U.S. forces in the western sector going in fifty minutes earlier. Airborne landings were made several hours before that—in the vicinity of the east bank of the Caen canal, and astride the Cherbourg peninsula. Dropping by parachute or going in in

AIRBORNE TROOPS GO IN

1. A British Commando unit, landed by sea in support of glider-borne troops, digs in by a damaged glider. 2. General Sir Bernard Montgomery, C.-in-C. of all Allied ground forces during the opening phase of the invasion, in discussion with Air Chief Marshal Sir Trafford Leigh-Mallory, C.-in-C., Allied Expeditionary Air Forces. 3. American airborne infantry leap from their glider on arrival in Normandy.

Photos, British Official ; Associated Press

NORMANDY LANDINGS HELPED BY 'RHINO' FERRIES

The 'Rhino' Ferry, designed in the United States, was made of prefabricated hollow boxes of light steel and could be used as a pontoon bridge between landing ships and beaches, as a wharf or dry-dock, or as a self-propelled barge. Here it has been used as a barge to bring men and supplies ashore. In the background are landing ships (tanks).

Photo, Keystone

BRITISH LIBERATION

In his message to his Army Group just before the invasion
time has come to deal the enemy a terrific blow in western
which will live in history. . . . I have complete confide
photographs shown here were taken shortly after the first
craft going in to the beaches flying barrage balloons, and u
help in the unloading and disposal of guns, vehicle

Photos, British Officie

LANDS IN FRANCE

...andy on June 6, 1944, General Montgomery said : 'The
... To us is given the honour to strike a blow for freedom
... success of the operations about to begin. . .' The two
... That above, taken from H.M.S. 'Beagle,' shows landing
... of the Royal Navy. Below, men already ashore watch or
...es coming in a steady flow from 'Rhino' ferries.

...tish Newspaper Pool

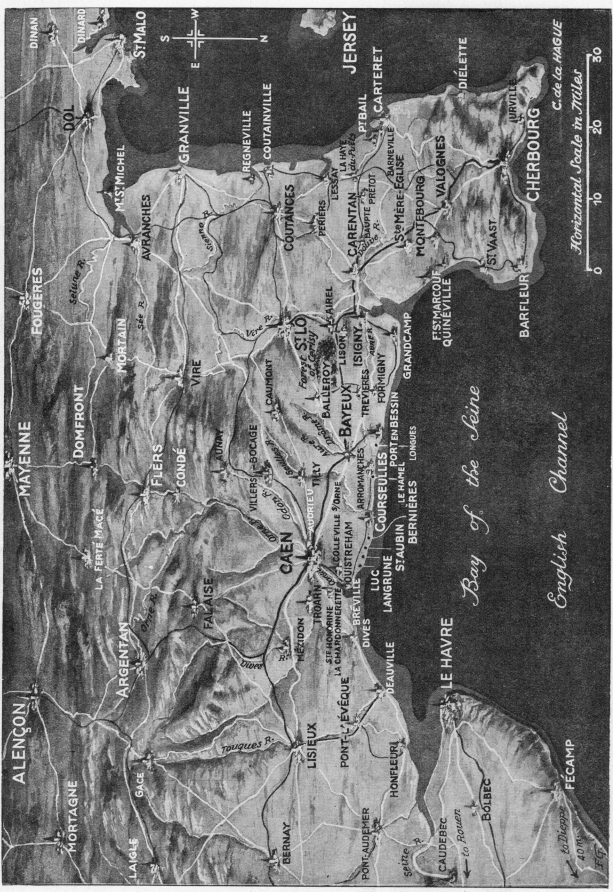

APPROACH TO THE NORMANDY BEACHES *Specially drawn for* THE SECOND GREAT WAR *by Félix Gardon*

This map shows the coastline of the Bay of the Seine as it lay before the approaching Allied armada on June 6, 1944. Seaborne landings beginning at 6.30 a.m. were made at points from the mouth of the Orne to the east coast of the Cotentin peninsula (on which Cherbourg stands). British and Canadians went in to the east, at Luc, Langrune, St. Aubin, Bernières, Courseulles and Longues—Americans to the west at 'Omaha Beach' (between Port en Bessin and the Vire) and 'Utah Beach' (between the Vire and the N.E. tip of the Cotentin peninsula). Airborne troops were dropped earlier east of the Caen canal and in the Cotentin peninsula.

3142

INVASION CHIEFS APPROACH ARROMANCHES
Rear-Admiral Sir Philip Vian, Air Chief Marshal Sir Arthur Tedder, General Bull, U.S.H.Q., Air Commodore Douglas Pennant (centre, facing camera) and Rear-Admiral J. W. Rivett-Carnac (extreme right), on board a L.C.P., pass a line of blockships (operation 'Gooseberry') making a break-water in the prefabricated British harbour at Arromanches in Normandy (see illus. in page 3119).
Photo, British Newspaper Pool

gliders (*see* illus., page 3084), these crack British and American troops secured important communication points and covered the flanks of the assault forces.

As darkness fell on June 5 over the heavy seas which tossed the flat-bottomed assault craft like so many corks, R.A.F. aircraft were preparing

R.A.F. Begins Battle of the Beaches to take off for the opening round of the battle of the beaches. In the early hours of the morning the drone of their engines could be heard above the whistle of the wind in the rigging of the ships. About 750 heavy bombers, guided by Pathfinders, carried out a concentrated bombing designed to soften up the German positions in the coastal area. They carried on until two hours before H hour, and then the " mediums " took over and pin-pointed the coast defence batteries.

As dawn broke on D Day, the fires started by the heavy bombers acted like beacons for the incoming ships. The coast of France was clearly visible when the heaviest air blow of all was struck immediately before H Hour. Fortresses and Liberators of the U.S.A. 8th and 9th Air Forces, covered by an umbrella of fighters, unloaded 2,400 tons of bombs on the British beaches and 1,900 tons on the American beaches. The complete absence of the Luftwaffe at this time must have been grimly suggestive to the stunned German defenders of things to come—if they were capable of appreciating the situation. All the same, until the Allies obtained their first landing strip in France, it was necessary to maintain ten fighter squadrons in the south of England in order that one should be continually over the beaches on the other side of the Channel.

The warships going in towards the coast seemed to be waiting for the guns of the Atlantic Wall to challenge them. Finally, as if they had despaired of the coming of the challenge, the bombarding ships opened up. Huge yellow flashes and big mushrooms of brownish cordite fumes split the horizon and, a few seconds later, the deep rumble that was to grow into a continuous roar came across the water to H.M.S "Hilary" (Commander [A] C. F. H. Churchill, R.N., commanding). With little more than forty minutes to go to H Hour, British " Hunt " class destroyers raced in boldly to engage in close duels with any surviving Nazi shore batteries. American destroyers, away to the west, were similarly at work, and the heavier guns of the battleships had taken up the onslaught and were hurling 14-inch, 15-inch and 16-inch shells across the beaches.

C-IN-C. VISITS THE 50th.
General Montgomery talking with Major-General D. A. H. Graham, C.B.E., D.S.O., M.C., who commanded the 50th (Northumbrian) Division when it took part in the opening attack in Normandy. General Graham went to France with the B.E.F. in 1939, and served in North Africa and Italy, where he was wounded, before being appointed in January 1944 to the command of the 50th. *Photo, British Official*

ALLIED TROOPS SEIZE A FOOTHOLD IN NORMANDY, JUNE 6, 1944

1. British infantry ride or carry their folding bicycles ashore to join men and vehicles already landed. 2. Landing craft moving towards the beaches from their parent ship and troops deploying on the shore—seen from the air. 3. On the American sector closely set beach obstacles faced units struggling to land under heavy machine-gun fire. 4. One of the massive wooden stakes topped with Teller mines which the Germans had set up along the invasion coast. At high tide the mines were just below the surface of the water—but first landings were made at low tide, and these obstacles were out of the water, as shown.

Photos, British and U.S. Official; Associated Press

WHERE THE ALLIES SET FOOT IN FRANCE AGAIN

Beaches in the British sector at Arromanches : here the great prefabricated harbour, 'Mulberry B' was assembled in the weeks that followed the initial landings. Right, 'Omaha Beach,' the stretch of coast from the estuary of the Vire river to Port en Bessin, looking from the American towards the British sector. The coast from the Vire to the north-east tip of the Cotentin Peninsula was called 'Utah Beach.' (Photographs taken in June 1945.)

Photos, Keystone ; News Chronicle

The final close-up punch before the assault troops poured ashore was delivered by rocket-firing craft (*see* page 3069 and illus., page 3071). The rockets cascaded on what remained of the German forward positions, and the vessels that fired them momentarily disappeared behind a sheet of flame from the rockets. Then, as H Hour arrived, there was a " silence " which, by comparison, was as impressive as the roar of the guns. In that lull the assault craft made the final run and bumped on to the beach. The tide was low, so that many of the enemy obstacles were exposed to view, but some of the assault craft were caught by angle irons and, with bottoms ripped open, were sinking as they made the French shore. Still the crews of the little craft had the grim satisfaction of knowing that they had

Attack by Rocket-Firing Craft

put their passengers ashore. Mines were touched off, but men thrown into the sea scrambled ashore and went forward with the rest. It is recorded that sailors from these gallant little vessels were so much with the troops that they left their craft and ran up the beaches in order to wish a final " Good Luck ! " to the soldiers.

Inevitably, some pockets of Germans escaped the amazing bombardment, because many of the concrete pill-boxes went deep underground. Even sentries were provided with concrete-

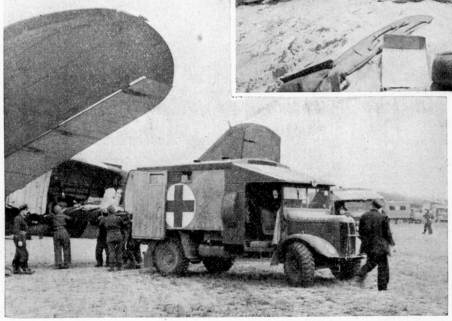

EVACUATION OF BRITISH AND AMERICAN WOUNDED
British casualties being transferred from a field ambulance to a transport plane on an airfield in Normandy which will take them to hospital in England. W.A.A.F. nursing orderlies tended the wounded on the French airfields and on the air journey. Above, American wounded at a beach dressing station waiting to be transported to England by sea.
Photos, British Official ; Associated Press

reinforced holes in the ground over which they could pull heavy concrete lids. At many points, therefore, the dash across the sands had to be made in the face of rifle and machine-gun fire.

The Canadian 3rd Infantry Division (commander, Major-General R. F. L. Keller, C.B.E.) and the Canadian 2nd Armoured Brigade (commander, Briga-dier R. A. Wynan) went in near Bernières and Courseulles. (The 1st Canadian Army did not leave England until towards the end of June, and though the 3rd Infantry Division and 2nd Armoured Brigade formed part of that army, commanded by Lieut.-General H. D. G. Crerar, they were for tactical purposes under the command of the British 2nd Army.) At Bernières, a single German gun held its fire until about a dozen craft were on the beach at

point blank range. Its courageous crew then opened fire and caused a number of casualties before they were wiped out by a rain of shells from the ships.

The hardest fighting on the whole length of the beaches came in an American sector not far beyond the British assault area. By one of the few strokes of misfortune that befell the Allies on that fateful day, the Ameri-cans found themselves confronted by strong and determined forces of the enemy. The explanation came later— the Germans had chosen the very time of the assault in that particular zone as the time for an anti-invasion exercise ! It was obvious to ships lying off-shore that some very hard fighting was going on, and that the Americans were finding it very difficult to get a foothold. Disregarding the risk they themselves

ran, the ships, including some Canadian minesweepers, got in as close as they possibly could and gave splendid gun support to the Americans.

The Canadian attack was on a 10,000-yard front in the region of Courseulles and Bernières. The sappers, working right in the front of the assault, as they did all along the line, cleared the dan-gerous obstructions, often with the aid of bulldozers, and the infantry went through four main gaps. Nor was the work of the Royal Engineers and American sappers finished when they had made the first safe paths through the extreme seaward defences. They continued to enlarge the openings, and days later were still making the beach areas safe for the great build-up.

Men of the Essex Scottish Regiment and the Fusiliers Mont Royal were among the first of the Canadians to storm across the beaches. A battalion of the Royal Berkshire Regiment went in with the Canadians, and many other English county regiments were strongly represented as the flood of our armies broke on to the Normandy shore. The Royal Warwickshires, the King's Own Yorkshire Light Infantry, the South Lancashires, the Durham Light In-fantry, the Cheshires are but a few of the regiments that added the assault on Normandy to their battle honours.

There was a place of honour in the forefront of the attack for the 3rd British Infantry Division—the division led by Major-General Montgomery, as he then was, in France in 1939–40, and at the landings on June 6, 1944, commanded by Major-General T. G. Rennie, and for the famous 50th (Northumbrian) Division (commander, Major-General D. A. H. Graham).

Maj.-Gen. RENNIE **Maj.-Gen. LYNE**

Major-General T. G. Rennie commanded the 3rd British Infantry Division (Montgomery's division in 1939–40) at the landings in Normandy on June 6, 1944. He was subsequently transferred to the command of the 51st (Highland) Division when it landed in France some little time later. Major-General L. O. Lyne commanded the 59th Infantry Division at the first landings.

Photos, British Official ; G.P.U.

The 50th was engaged in some hard fighting, but swept on to its objectives and well earned the praise of the Commander of the Corps to which it belonged : " Well done, indeed, 50th Division. Gradely lads. Champion !"

The 59th Infantry Division (commander, Major-General L. O. Lyne) was another British division early ashore.

Divisions Early Ashore

Famous cavalry regiments, fighting as armoured formations, were there. The 4th/7th Dragoon Guards were among the first armoured troops to land, and later led the advance towards Villers Bocage and assisted in the capture of Tilly. The 13th/18th Hussars, another armoured formation, landed at Colleville-sur-Orne.

A battalion of the King's Royal Rifle Corps was one of the first British units to land in France ; the Rifle Brigade and the Royal Ulster Rifles were there. The King's Own Scottish Borderers took part in the storming of the Atlantic Wall, but the full weight of those great fighters, the 51st (Highland) Division (commanded by Major-General T. G. Rennie, transferred from the 3rd Infantry Division), was felt by the Germans only in the days that followed, when the whole success of the campaign was ensured by the holding and smashing of the main German forces in the fierce battles that raged around Caen. The Black Watch, the Gordons and the Seaforths, the last particularly at Ste. Honorine la Chardonnerette, then proved again their superiority to the enemy.

Wales, the West Country, London— the 4th County of London Yeomanry (the Sharpshooters) went in as an armoured unit—were all fully represented on that great day, so that it

becomes almost invidious to mention a few names where so many should be recorded.

To return to events as they could be seen from the Bay of the Seine in the hours following H Hour : the lull in the bombardment that marked the actual time of landing was of very short duration. Even before the first reports came in from the forward observation posts the naval guns had found fresh targets and heavy shells were screaming inland.

Besides the battleships, 22 cruisers and many more destroyers joined in the bombardment, which was to continue as long as enemy forces remained within range. Among the famous ships (in addition to those mentioned in page 3074) that played a prominent part were the British cruisers " Apollo," " Argonaut," " Belfast," " Bellona," " Black Prince," " Ceres," " Danae," " Arethusa," " Diadem," " Enterprise,"

" Frobisher," " Glasgow," " Hawkins," " Mauritius," " Orion " and " Scylla," the American cruisers " Tuscaloosa," " Augusta " and " Quincy," and the Polish cruiser " Dragon." (*See* also illus., pages 3072 and 3084.) In the course of the bombardment, 56,769 shells of 4·7-inch or greater calibre were fired.

The naval guns not only offered continual support to the Allied troops but frequently intervened at specific points where their weight carried the day in the Allied favour.

Naval Gunners aid Land Forces

" Rodney " (nine 16-inch guns) and " Ramillies " (eight 15-inch guns), for instance, were called upon to put down a heavy fire on German forces attempting to split the British and Americans. The German effort failed, thanks largely to the work of the great naval guns. For a time the troops on the eastern end of the assault beaches were troubled by enemy artillery fire coming from the other side of the Caen canal. British cruisers attacked these batteries and their fire stopped.

Our air forces, too, continued to strike hard at the enemy. During the morning of D Day more than 1,300 Liberators and Fortresses, with an appropriate escort of fighters, bombed

CANADIAN TANKS IN A NORMAN VILLAGE

Canadian forces, comprising the 3rd Infantry Division, commanded by Major-General Keller, and the 2nd Armoured Brigade, commanded by Brigadier R. A. Wynan, went in to Normandy on D Day on a 10,000-yard front between Courseulles and Bernières, west of the estuary of the river Orne, and rapidly captured Bernières, Courseulles, St. Aubin, Ouistreham, and other villages. Here Canadian tanks are driving through in the Courseulles sector.

Photo, Canadian Official

mortar fire. They overcame this and quelled several machine-gun nests and then, despite the fact that every Marine carried a load of equipment, mortar ammunition, etc., amounting to nearly three-quarters of a hundredweight, decided to save time by pushing across country.

They arrived in sight of their objective, after covering ten miles, in time to see some of the preparatory work done by Army, Navy and Air Force. The Germans in the little port were bombed from the air, shelled from the shore and also from the sea. Still, the Germans had heavily concreted positions and the opposition was fierce when the Marines went into the assault. At one point the enemy twice counterattacked and won back the position, but

D DAY IN THE COTENTIN PENINSULA

A dressing station set up on a Cotentin beach. Above, German prisoners being shepherded to a farm cart and captivity by American airborne troops near Ste. Mère Eglise, in the heart of the peninsula, which they captured on June 6, 1944, the enemy garrison, taken completely by surprise, surrendering after a glider crashed on a roof and spilled its troops into the streets.

Photos, Associated Press ; Keystone

the Germans for two and a half hours, without a break. The Luftwaffe scarcely appeared. One of the most majestic attacks came at dusk a few evenings later. A fleet of bombers that filled the sky flew over the long anchorage and devastated E-boats and other German concentrations in Le Havre.

The enemy did attempt to attack the shipping in the anchorage by bombing on the night of D Day. The attack was not heavy and chiefly served to show the impressive number of anti-aircraft guns assembled in the ships and on the beaches. The whole anchorage seemed to be under a canopy of vivid tracer shells, while smoke made by the ships added to the confusion of the Nazi flyers.

During the morning of D Plus One (Wednesday, June 7) General Montgomery arrived from England in

Montgomery Goes Ashore

H.M.S. "Faulknor" (commander, Captain Sir James Paget, R.N.). He paid a flying visit to the headquarters ship "Hilary" before going ashore. In a final message to his troops he had wished them "Good hunting!" and, asked how the hunting was going, he replied, "Very well—everything is going excellently."

Anxiety about the success of the assault had, in fact, ended. In many sectors first, second and third objectives had been taken, and everything depended on the rapid build-up behind the front line which, in some cases, was already six to eight miles from the coastal strip.

British Commandos and American Rangers had pulled off spectacular feats, and one Royal Marine Commando was even at that time covering itself with glory. They went in to capture

Port en Bessin, a key point near the centre of the landings which was covered by three strong German defence positions. It was intended that the Marines should land at Le Hamel, but as their craft went in, they came under heavy fire from a German battery at Longues. They had to swing off a mile to the eastward and, as they attempted to land there, five of their fourteen L.C.A.s were mined and sank. The Marines from these swam ashore, salvaged what equipment they could and pushed inland with their comrades. They re-armed themselves with weapons captured from the enemy and went on through Les Roquettes to La Rosière, where they were met by heavy German

the Marines came a third time and the Germans had then had enough. When the Marine Commando made contact with the Americans they linked the whole Allied front in Normandy.

The most desperate German resistance at this time was in the direction of Caen, where later the great battle of "the hinge" was to develop. Heroic work was being done on the left flank by the British airborne troops, who had struck with such swiftness that bridges, locks and canal installations were in their hands before the enemy could press the plungers that would have blown these important military objectives sky-high.

At first the reception given to Allied troops by the French was cool. But

ALLIES ADVANCE INLAND

1. Vickers machine-gun section in action on the edge of a field of oats on the outskirts of Audrieu. 2. Tank crews of a British armoured unit snatch a rest while they can. 3. Taking cover from enemy snipers behind a M.10 tank destroyer. 4. Men of the British 6th Airborne Division, landed to the east of the river Orne, move a German anti-tank gun into position after capturing the village of Bréville, much damaged by their heavy mortar barrage.

(See map in page 3124.)

Photos, British Official

many people living in the coastal area of Normandy had had to face the shattering bombardment and bombing that destroyed so many German positions. They were dazed and shaken and, as a result, at first appeared apathetic. Already by D Plus Two a new and great hope was springing up in them. This was not a raid which would be followed by Nazi retribution, but Deliverance! With tears in their eyes they expressed their realization of this, and flags of France, with the double cross of Lorraine added to the centre panel, began to appear everywhere.

More troops and supplies were flowing over the beaches under the eyes of skilled naval Beachmasters who never for a moment allowed the flow to slacken. "Ducks" formed an endless belt, climbing up from the sea, going inland with their loads and passing back to the ships in the bay by another route.

The first of a number of old tankers and other ships had arrived, to be sunk close inshore to provide the beginnings of the "Gooseberry" shelters which protected the hundreds of small craft and probably saved the expedition from disaster when the big gale arose some days later (*see* illus. page 3119). A start had been made, too, on the construction of the "Mulberries," the prefabricated ports which had been planned to the last detail in England and towed to Normandy. Each concrete caisson displaced over 6,000 tons, and something like 150 of them had to be got into position. (*See* also page 3099.) As explained in Chapter 307, "Mulberry A," intended for the Americans, was never completed; but the British "Mulberry" at Arromanches at times handled as much as 9,000 tons of supplies in a day—three times as much as expected.

But it was several weeks before "Mulberry B" was working, and by then Navy and Army, with the ever

Beach Groups' Duties

watchful protection of the Air Forces, had accomplished wonders towards the build-up. During the first three days of the operation alone, thirty-eight convoys, comprising 743 ships and major landing craft, crossed the Channel with supplies and reinforcements (*see* illus., page 3010) which were landed on to

the beaches into the charge of Beach Groups. Each Beach Group included stevedore companies who unloaded the cargo, Field Dressing Stations and Beach Dressing Stations of the Royal Army Medical Corps, Pioneer Companies, R.A.O.C. and R.A.S.C. Beach Parties for running the stores dumps, Royal Corps of Signal sections, officers and men of the Army's Movement Control Branch; and each separate part of the Group had a small R.A.F. detachment working alongside it to

MR. CHURCHILL LANDS IN NORMANDY
On Monday, June 12, 1944, sixth day after the first landings, the Prime Minister, accompanied by Field-Marshal Smuts, Premier of South Africa, and Field-Marshal Sir Alan Brooke, visited General Montgomery's H.Q. in Normandy. He travelled in the destroyer H.M.S. 'Kelvin,' which went into action against German positions during the voyage, and he spent three hours ashore.
Photo, British Newspaper Pool

advise on the special R.A.F. problems. The Beach Group had to organize the beaches and the immediate hinterland in order to land, and then maintain, the assault, follow-up and build-up formations. Beach organization was the first step in the establishment and development of lines of communication and supply. The Beach Groups' responsibilities included the calling in of the craft to beach in the correct order; the bringing ashore of all supplies and stores, and all men and vehicles; the supervision of rearward movement and the embarkation of the wounded and of prisoners of war for evacuation to

Britain; the setting up and manning of anti-aircraft guns and searchlights to protect the beaches and the ships offshore. The Beach Groups landed in Normandy with some of their engineers even before the first assault troops, and supplies continued to go in over the beaches until the Channel ports had been captured.

At night the enemy came and dropped odd bombs in the anchorage, but did little damage. During the day planes appeared but were always driven off by our fighter patrols. In one conflict which might have been termed a battle, six F.W. 190s were shot down.

The Germans, in desperation, attempted to break into the anchorage with fairly powerful M.T.B.

Enemy M.T.B.s Forced to Withdraw

forces operating from Cherbourg and Le Havre. But this only gave an opportunity to the "little ships" of the Allies, and in the high speed actions which developed they took heavy toll of the enemy and eventually forced him to withdraw his boats from Cherbourg. As many as seven of these naval actions-in-miniature were fought in a single night. Losses among Allied ships remained extremely light (*see* page 3074).

Less than a week after D Day, on Monday, June 12, the Prime Minister set foot on the beaches and made an extensive tour with General Montgomery. He made the final lap, as so many others had done, in a "duck," and was smoking a large cigar when he climbed down from the big boat-cum-vehicle. With him were Field-Marshal Smuts and Field-Marshal Sir Alan Brooke, Chief of the Imperial General Staff. All were given a great welcome by the troops; Mr. Churchill's two fingers upraised in the Victory sign aroused the greatest enthusiasm.

The Luftwaffe made one of its few daylight attacks on the anchorage just before Mr. Churchill left to return to England, but their bombs fell harmlessly in the sea and then the Nazi planes were chased inland by Spitfires.

The Americans, by this time, had a strong grip on the Germans to the west and British battle plans were taking shape in front of Caen. Still, every man, gun, and tank was needed, and the Navy and Merchant Navies continued to labour without ceasing to get them ashore.

THE NAVY'S PART IN THE INVASION OF NORMANDY

On March 7, 1945, Mr. A. V. Alexander, First Lord of the Admiralty, in introducing the Naval estimates for the ensuing year, described the creation of the shipping required and the actual part played by the Royal Navy in what Admiral Sir Bertram Ramsay called "the greatest amphibious operation in history." Time may unfold a greater, but nothing like it had been seen up to June 6, 1944. Here are some vital extracts from the First Lord's speech

THE Naval forces required for the assault landing consisted of four main classes: minesweepers, to clear the way for all the ships and craft which would follow ; landing craft and ships of all kinds to carry the soldiers and the guns, tanks, transport and other equipment with which they would fight ; bombarding ships, whose task, with the Air Force, would be to destroy the enemy's opposition to the landing, and enable the Army to gain the lodgement which it requires before it can deploy its own weapons ; and finally escort and anti-submarine forces.

The minesweepers, bombarding ships and escort vessels already existed, though they were required in exceptionally large numbers. The landing ships and craft did not exist. They have all had to be developed and provided during the war from our own resources and those of our Allies. The process was started as soon as the armies of the United Nations were driven from the Continent, very many months before it became fashionable to chalk up on the walls demands for a " Second Front." . . .

While the Fleet with which we are familiar . . . was still being built and maintained . . . this strange new Fleet, containing ships of all sizes and odd shapes, each designed and developed for its special purpose, was brought into being. It included ships and craft for landing tanks and infantry, for giving close support fire, for landing guns and transport, for making smoke, and even floating kitchens and craft fitted with extending fire-escape ladders to put men up cliffs. In all, 4,066 landing ships and craft of over 60 different types took part in the operation. . . .

Shore works costing several million pounds had to be provided before the assault could be launched. . . . Another massive enterprise was the creation of the two artificial harbours, upon which the success of the whole operation depended. . . . Assault against an established enemy port was certain to meet the most powerful opposition. . . . An assault over open beaches, much less strongly defended, offered by far the best hope of getting a large force ashore quickly. But this was only half the problem. Once ashore, the Army had to be reinforced more rapidly than the enemy. To rely on the quick capture of an established port was to run great risk of disaster. The only answer was an assault over open beaches, accompanied by the creation of ports for rapid unloading and reinforcement.

The conception, like all great conceptions once made, seemed simple. Its fulfilment was an immense task. It required the preparation and sinking of 60 old ships, which provided breakwaters for both the British and American forces by the fourth day of the assault. In addition, two full scale ports, the " Mulberries," were constructed from 6,000-ton concrete caissons towed across the Channel. The British port alone used four-and-a-quarter miles of these caissons, weighing approximately 550,000 tons. On the twelfth day of the assault, 1,600 tons were discharged at this port, and by the thirty-fourth day an average of 6,000 tons a day was discharged.

One hundred and thirty-two tugs, including British, American, French and Dutch, were employed in towing the units of this harbour from sheltered anchorages in the United Kingdom to the Normandy coast. Nearly one thousand tows were made for this purpose in June and July. Tugs were mobilized from far and wide to accomplish this mighty task, made the more daunting by the rough and unseasonable weather in the Channel. . . .

No single topic was more anxiously debated in the planning of the operation than the date and hour at which it should take place. The appropriate choice depended on conditions of tide, conditions of light, the possibility of postponement for bad weather and other considerations, all of which were most carefully weighed. The date finally chosen was June 5, with the 6th and 7th as possible alternatives. . . . No one, however, expected the decision to be as difficult as it actually was. Even those of us who were in London remember the week-end before D Day, as we watched the low scudding clouds and heard the squalls of wind, as a time of almost unbearable anxiety. . . . The first meeting to discuss the weather forecast for D Day was held on June 1. The outlook was not very good, and it deteriorated during the next three days. On the evening of June 3, however, the Supreme Commander decided to allow the forces to move, despite the unfavourable outlook, in order to gain the many advantages of launching the operation on the first possible day. At 4.15 on the following morning it was clear that conditions the next day would not be acceptable, and a postponement of twenty-four hours was ordered. . . .

On the morning of June 5, the forecast stated that developments overnight showed slight improvement in the general situation, which appeared at that moment more favourable. On the strength of this forecast, the irrevocable decision to make the assault in the early hours of June 6 was taken. The decision was a terribly hard one. Events leave no doubt that it was right. Had the opportunity been missed, the operation could not have taken place for another fortnight, and by then the weather was even worse. In its combination of high winds and cloud, June 1944 was the worst June of the present century. Nevertheless, it seems likely that the wildness of the weather may have led the enemy to believe that we should not launch the assault, and it may therefore have contributed to his apparent unreadiness, and hence to the astonishing success of the assault. . . .

As our forces approached the French coast, without a murmur from the enemy, it was slowly realized that once again, almost complete tactical surprise had been achieved.

To the minesweepers fell the proud and dangerous honour of leading the assault forces to the beaches. The sweeping of ten approach channels was the largest single minesweeping operation ever undertaken in war. 309 British, 16 Canadian, and 22 U.S. minesweepers took part. . . . The minesweepers then had to widen all the approach channels and to sweep areas off the beaches for the reception of the vast numbers of ships needed to keep the Army supplied. . . . The operation was the greatest single achievement of a never-ending labour, in which over 15,000 mines have been swept since the beginning of the war. . . .

The next forces to go into action were the bombardment ships. . . . These forces took part in the drenching of the beach defences, immediately before the assault. . . . As one of the bombarding forces arrived in position at 5.15 a.m. four enemy E-boats and some armed trawlers from Le Havre made a half-hearted attack, and sank one Norwegian destroyer by torpedo. Our forces sank an enemy trawler, and damaged another, and the attack was not renewed. . . .

Then came the moment for which the whole world had waited : the moment when Allied Forces again set foot on the soil of France. . . . The outstanding fact of the day was that, despite the unfavourable weather, the Naval operations were carried out in every important respect as planned. Tactical surprise, which had not been expected, was achieved. Losses of ships and landing craft of all types were much lower than had been expected. . . .

During the first three days of the operation 38 convoys comprising 743 ships and major landing craft were sent across the Channel for the build up. This, of course, excludes the assault forces. . . . On June 19 a great gale blew up and at once stopped all unloading to the beaches. The sea did not finally go down until June 23 . . . but it may be said that the position of the Expeditionary Force was never in doubt after the third day of the assault. . . . By the tenth day half a million men and 77,000 vehicles had been landed. . . . By the end of July over 1,600,000 men, 340,000 vehicles, and 1,700,000 tons of stores had been landed. . . .

Chapter 312

NEUTRAL DIFFICULTIES AND FEARS DECREASE

As Axis power weakened and Allied strength grew, the difficulties and apprehensions of the neutral countries decreased, and Portugal, Spain, Sweden and Switzerland showed themselves more and more accommodating to the wishes and needs of the Allies. Eire, farther away from the actual combat zones, continued to maintain the strictest neutrality. Here the history of these five countries during 1943 and 1944 is recorded. Earlier developments will be found in Chapter 237

IN October 1943, Portugal granted Great Britain facilities in the Azores for the better protection of Atlantic shipping (*see* page 2658). The strategic importance of **PORTUGAL** these islands—they stand 900 miles out from Lisbon on the New York route (*see* map in page 2656)—was enhanced by the fact that when the agreement was made America was sending thousands of troops and vast quantities of stores to the United Kingdom in preparation for the invasion of Europe.

The facilities were granted under a treaty made in 1373 between King Edward III of England and King Ferdinand and Queen Eleanor of Portugal. Mr. Churchill, announcing the agreement to the House on October 12, said that it became effective at once. He emphasized that it was a temporary arrangement in no way affecting Portuguese sovereignty, and that all British forces would be withdrawn at the end of hostilities. In return, Britain would provide essential material and supplies to the Portuguese armed forces and assist the maintenance of Portuguese national economy. President Roosevelt, who had declared in 1941 that America would not permit an Axis occupation of the Azores, was kept fully informed of the negotiations.

When the agreement had been concluded, Dr. Salazar, the Portuguese Premier, informed the Spanish Government, in accordance with the terms of the Spanish-Portuguese treaty of friendship and non-aggression of July 30, 1940. Addressing the National Assembly in Lisbon on November 26, he said, " We were actuated by patriotism, not by bargaining. The British Government, despite their urgent need to defend their Merchant Navy in the Atlantic, abstained for years from raising this question. When they did raise it they limited their requests to the indispensable. War material which Britain was to send to Portugal under the terms of the agreement began to arrive in considerable quantities even before advantage was taken of facilities in the Azores."

The Germans protested vigorously on October 14 through their Minister in Lisbon, Baron Hoyningen Huene, declaring that the agreement was a serious breach of neutrality ; and on the 15th the Japanese Minister also protested. Possibly it was this protest that brought into prominence again the question of Portuguese Timor, occupied by the Japanese in February 1942 (*see* page 2348) and held by them since in spite of Portuguese representations. Some 500 Portuguese nationals had been evacuated by Allied warships from Timor to Australia in July 1943 ; and on November 26 Dr. Salazar said that there had been risings by the natives against the Japanese, who had murdered dozens of

people, and that some solution of the situation must be found. The Portuguese press took up the subject, and on March 8, 1944, it was announced that the Japanese would permit the holding of an inquiry into conditions in Timor.

Following several months of negotiation, Portugal agreed on June 5, 1944, to prohibit the export of wolfram " in order to shorten the war." "A decision," said Mr. Eden, British Foreign Secretary, in announcing the agreement, " comparable with the grant of facilities in the Azores." A decree issued on June 12, suspending indefinitely all mining and trading in wolfram, represented a serious sacrifice on Portugal's part. The wolfram mines were German-owned and the loss in taxes—£380 per ton when the price was controlled at £2,000—imposed a heavy burden on the Portuguese tax-payer, for Germany had been spending between four and five million pounds a year on Portuguese wolfram. Unemployment also resulted from the closing of the mines.

The food situation in Portugal was not easy—there were strikes in July 1943 owing to the scarcity of food, and bread rationing was introduced in Lisbon and other centres on April 20, 1944.

Count Jordana, Spanish Foreign Minister, declared on April 16, 1943, that Spain was ready to lend her good offices to achieve an immediate restoration of world **SPAIN** peace, a statement followed on May 9 by an appeal to the belligerents by General Franco to make peace. Later in May, the mounting power of the Allied air offensive (*see* Chapter 268) led to a campaign in the press against bombing—a campaign

R.A.F. TAKES OVER BASES IN THE AZORES

Following Mr. Churchill's announcement of October 12, 1943, that Portugal had accorded Great Britain the use of bases in the Azores for the greater protection of Allied shipping in the north Atlantic, the R.A.F. took over the areas assigned and turned them into airfields. Left, stores and equipment being unloaded at Angra. Right, local labourers moving metal strips for constructing runways. The use of the Azores bases reduced losses of Allied shipping and increased sinkings of U-boats. (See also illus. page 2656.) *Photos, British Official*

BOUND ON AN ERRAND OF MERCY

The full-masted Portuguese barque ' Foz do Douro ' sailed the Atlantic between an east coast port of the United States and Lisbon carrying food, clothing, and other comforts from the American Red Cross for transport by way of Geneva, headquarters in Switzerland of the International Red Cross Society, to American prisoners of war in German hands. She had her name, her country, and her flag painted on her hull to emphasize her neutrality. *Photo, Keystone*

without effect on Allied policy. A decree issued on May 26 ordered the construction of air-raid shelters in all cities of more than 22,000 inhabitants.

A conditional amnesty (estimated to affect 20,000 persons) granted on October 16, 1942, to all political prisoners serving sentences up to

Civil War Aftermath 14 years 8 months was extended on March 31, 1943, to those serving up to 20 years. Up to the end of July 75,000 prisoners had been conditionally released. A decree of June 3 allowed released prisoners to follow their former professions and occupations. On September 30 conditional liberty was granted to all prisoners over 70 ; and on December 28 it was announced that no further death sentences in connexion with the civil war would be carried out (a remission affecting 800 persons) ; over 200 others had been reprieved on December 24. On July 18, 1944, however, out of 271,139 people imprisoned during the civil war, 22,989 still remained in jail. The partly restored " University City " in Madrid, devastated during the civil war, was reopened by General Franco on October 12, 1943.

Obligatory National Health Insurance covering all workers in low-wage categories was introduced in February 1943.

The food situation in Spain was even more difficult than in Portugal. The bread ration in Madrid had been *increased* on September 1, 1942, to 150 grams (about 5¼ ozs.) daily for better-to-do persons, 200 grams for middle-class persons, and 250 grams for workers. During 1944, fresh milk, eggs, fish, poultry, vegetables, fruit, wine, cheese (since 1943) and toilet soap remained unrationed. An agreement signed on June 3, 1944, between Spain and

Argentina brought 1,000,000 tons of wheat, 500 tons of tobacco, and 10,000 tons of cotton to Spain in return for iron.

A complaint in the German paper " Das Reich " on July 11, 1943, alleged that 40,000 refugees from the labour call-up in France (*see* Chapter 289) had crossed the Pyrenees since the summer of 1940 and had been smuggled out of Spain to join the Fighting French forces.

Relations with the Allies continued strained. In August 1943 the British Ambassador, Sir Samuel Hoare, made it clear to General Franco **Strained** that as long as the **Relations** Spanish Blue Division **with Allies** (*see* page 2348) continued to fight against the Soviet Union, it was a serious obstacle to the development of cordial Anglo-Spanish relations. The British Government also took a grave view of the use made of the Tangier International Zone (seized by Franco in 1940) by the German consul-general and other Germans for activities against British interests.

British and American authorities were at last allowed to advertise their radio programmes in Spanish newspapers—but Spaniards continued to be punished for listening to B.B.C. broadcasts.

On the capitulation of Italy in September 1943, a number of Italian merchant ships lying in Spanish ports, and five warships which took refuge in the Balearic Islands, were seized by Franco, who refused to give them up despite strong Allied representations. The Germans pressed for Spanish

GENERAL FRANCO RECEIVES NEW GERMAN AMBASSADOR

Herr von Moltke, received very cordially by the Caudillo in January 1943 with praise of the German people's heroism, sacrifice and sufferings in their struggle against Bolshevism, died suddenly from appendicitis a few weeks after his appointment. He was succeeded by Dr. Dieckhoff, former Ambassador in Washington, who, accompanied by Count Jordana, the Spanish Foreign Minister (right), is here presenting his credentials to Franco.

recognition of Mussolini's Fascist Republic in Northern Italy.

On November 18 and 19, Spanish Falangists in uniform forced their way into the British Vice-Consulate at Saragossa. A similar incident took place at the American Consulate at Valencia on December 18. The Spanish Government expressed its regrets. In November the Spanish Government sent congratulations to José Laurel, the puppet president of the Philippines set up by the Japanese—and then explained to the United States that this was not recognition, except of the close racial, religious and cultural ties between Spain and the Philippines. In January and February 1944, bombs were found in ships carrying oranges from Spain to Britain. Following protests, Count Jordana declared that these acts of sabotage were regarded as detrimental to the state, and their originators were enemies of Spain.

Anti-Allied Demonstrations

On December 23, 1943, it was announced in Madrid that the Blue Division had arrived at San Sebastian the day before. In January, however, the Soviet Embassy in London stated that 12,000 Spaniards had been repatriated by the end of December, but that replacement battalions had been sent in September and October.

BOMB DAMAGED ORANGES

In January and February 1944, small time-bombs were found in several ships carrying cargoes of oranges between Spain and Britain. Count Jordana, the Foreign Minister, declared that such acts of sabotage were detrimental to the state. Here cases of oranges damaged by a bomb explosion are being examined.

SPANISH PRISONERS OF THE CIVIL WAR AT FORCED LABOUR

In July 1944, out of 271,139 people imprisoned during the Civil War (1936–39), 22,989 still remained prisoners. In September 1943, conditional liberty had been granted to all over 70, in December all those (some 800) still under sentence of death were reprieved. Here a group of prisoners who fought for the Republican Government are at work on the construction of the irrigation canal of Dos Hermanos i Guadalquivir. *Photo, March of Time*

Mr. Eden informed the Spanish Ambassador of the serious effect of Spain's continuing assistance to the enemies of the Allies, and again made strong representations on the detention of Italian ships. A little over a week later (January 28) the State Department of the United States announced that, in agreement with the British Government, and pending a reconsideration of trade and general relations between Spain and the U.S.A., all shipments of petroleum products to Spain had been suspended for the month of February.

Three of the fourteen Italian merchant ships held in Spanish ports were immediately released, and talks for the settlement of all points of difference were begun in Madrid. On May 2 it was announced by Britain and the United States that Spain had agreed to release all the Italian merchant ships except two whose ownership was in dispute; to have the disposal of the warships settled by arbitration (the release of the cruiser " Attilio Regolo " and four destroyers was announced on January 16, 1945); to close the German consulate at Tangier and expel certain German agents indicated by the Allies from the mainland, Tangier, and Spanish Morocco; and to cut exports of wolfram to Germany to approximately a third of those of the previous year. The Spanish Government gave an

assurance that all survivors of the Blue Division and the Blue Air Squadron had been withdrawn from Russia, apart from a few wounded and a small detachment supervising the withdrawal.

In April 1944 the government-inspired Spanish press appealed for a compromise peace. Then came the reopening of the western front (*see* Chapter 311). Count Jordana died on August 3; his successor, Señor José Felix Lequerica, **De Gaulle's Government Recognized** former ambassador to Vichy, received the delegate of the French Provisional Government for the first time on August 24. The French Provisional Government was recognized, and an ambassador in Paris appointed, on October 31.

On November 4, in a statement on Spanish policy made in an interview, General Franco said, " Those nations which have shown the desire for peace by remaining at peace must take part in the peace treaty." But this hint that Spain expected to be present at the peace negotiations was countered in the House of Commons on November 15 by Mr. Richard Law (Minister of State), who stated that H.M. Government saw no reason why any country which had not made a positive contribution to the Allies war effort should be represented at the peace conference.

Sweden went ahead with the five-year National Defence Plan introduced

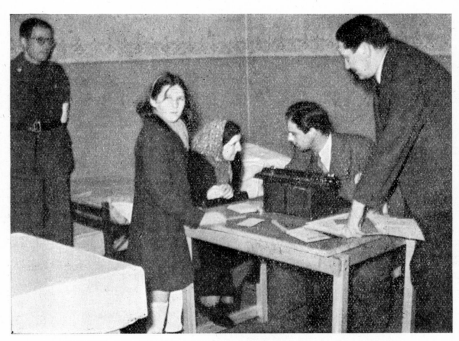

JEWISH REFUGEES FROM DENMARK REACH SWEDEN

In the evening on September 30, 1943, the Gestapo began a wholesale round-up of Jews in Denmark. Some 3,000, out of a total of 6,000 Danish Jews, reached Sweden in rowing boats and fishing smacks, thanks to Danish fishermen who risked German ' reprisals ' to carry them to safety. Here a Jewish mother and child are being received at a camp at Malmö. In April 1944 Sweden was sheltering 48,000 war refugees. All but a few hundreds had found work.

in January 1942, under which she planned to spend 3,778 million kronor (approximately £200 million at pre-war rates of exchange), in addition to an

SWEDEN annual expenditure of 1,200 million kronor on mobilization. By January 1943 she had an army of 600,000, into which the Home Guard, founded at the beginning of 1940, had been incorporated ; a developing air force of about 50 bomber, fighter and reconnaissance squadrons ; and a rapidly growing navy, the last addition to which in 1944 was a 7,000-ton cruiser, the " Tre Kronor " (Three Crowns), launched on December 16, when it was announced that a sister ship was under construction.

The increasingly outspoken stand of the Swedish press and public opinion against Quisling's regime in Norway led to open attacks on Sweden in the German press from the autumn of 1942 onwards. Sweden was accused of " indifference to the New Order " and " anti-German feeling " (a charge also levelled against Switzerland). Anti-Nazi feeling reached a new peak towards the end of 1943 following the mass arrests and deportation of students of Oslo University in November (see page 2720). On December 1 all Swedish universities and academic institutions flew flags at half-mast. An urgent request from the Swedish Government to Germany on behalf of the students brought the sharpest official rebuff so far administered by Germany, Sweden being asked to refrain from interfering in German-Norwegian questions.

Several incidents contributed to make Sweden uneasy as to Germany's intentions. The German carrier-plane which made a forced landing on February 24, 1943 (see page 2346), and was found to be carrying armed uniformed personnel and a dismantled machine-gun, was allowed to proceed after the arms had been removed ; but a second plane making a forced landing in July, and carrying six uniformed members of the German police force and a dismantled machine-gun, was seized and the crew interned. The German Government agreed to maintain strictly the non-warlike character of their planes, and their passage was continued until the end of May 1944, when the traffic was finally cancelled by Sweden.

Considerable alarm was caused when a German goods train at the Finno-Swedish frontier station of Haparanda was found on April 14, 1943, to contain a large number of detailed maps to a scale of 1 : 100,000 of Norway, Finland, and parts of the Swedish frontier zone. The maps concerning Sweden were confiscated. The following April, on the 15th, 23,000 freshly printed German ordnance maps of central Sweden were seized by the Swedish customs at Helsingborg after the arrival of the train ferry from Denmark. Documents with these maps showed that a consignment covering northern Sweden had already been sent to Oslo. A second consignment, of 3,000 road maps of the whole of Sweden, was seized on April 22, and a third covering the Swedish-Norwegian frontier on May 2. The German explanation of these " highly disquieting " discoveries was that the consignment of these maps was a " purely military routine measure," and it was " necessary for the German troops in Norway to possess maps of Sweden owing to circumstances which might arise independently of any steps taken by Germany." The Swedish reply, besides cancelling the carrier-plane service, was to cancel also the privilege accorded Germany of sending mail vans staffed by German postal officers through Sweden to Norway and Finland. All German mails thereafter were handled by Swedish staffs.

The Swedish submarine "Ulven" was missing on manoeuvres in April 1943. Another Swedish submarine " Draken," sent out to search for " Ulven," was fired on inside Swedish territorial waters by the German s.s. " Altkirch." After anchored mines had been found in Swedish waters and swept up by the Swedish Navy, Swedish warships were ordered to take action against any belligerent warships

BRITONS IN SWEDEN

After long negotiations, several thousand British and Allied prisoners of war in German hands were exchanged through Sweden in October 1943 and September 1944 for similar contingents of Germans in British hands. Here British soldiers are arriving at Roberts Hōld near Gothenburg for a 24 hours' break in their journey. They were received with great kindness by the Swedish Red Cross. (See also illus. in page 2590.)

Photos, Associated Press ; Keystone

SWEDISH SUBMARINE 'ULVEN' IN DRY DOCK

During naval manoeuvres in Swedish waters in April 1943, the Swedish submarine 'Ulven' disappeared. She was found on May 5 in the middle of a minefield laid by the Germans, and when raised on August 2 was found to have been sunk by striking a mine. Here the ill-fated vessel is being overhauled in dry dock after she was raised. Her sinking was one of a number of incidents that worsened German-Swedish relations. *Photo, New York Times Photos*

which contravened Swedish neutrality by minelaying or other offensive action inside Swedish waters. "Ulven" was found on May 5 in the middle of a German minefield, and when raised on August 2 was found to have been sunk through striking mines.

Difficulties with Britain also occurred. In February 1943 Britain protested at the building of 45 fishing vessels in

Difficulties with Britain

Swedish yards for the German firm of Hugo Stinnes, their design indicating that they were to be used as minesweepers. The Swedish Foreign Minister declared the allegation unfounded; but on June 21 it was announced in Stockholm that the Government had refused export licences for a number of such craft. On July 17 a Swedish note complained of the dropping of mines in Swedish waters by the R.A.F. on May 18 and June 10—a charge acknowledged by H.M. Government, which gave assurances against a recurrence.

Some 23 per cent of Sweden's total imports and 14 per cent of her exports in 1942 had been carried by five ships a month and one tanker a quarter to which the belligerents had agreed to give safe-conduct. In March 1943 Germany withdrew her safe-conduct (no ships had, in fact, passed since January). A new agreement was announced on May 7 by which Germany renewed her guarantees; but some six months later (October 28) Germany informed the Swedish Government that owing to

German military measures in the Skager Rak she could no longer give safe-conduct to Swedish vessels using the passage. It was about this time that a fleet of small, rapid, specially built British ships began to run the blockade to Sweden (*see* page 3036).

In May 1943 the Foreign Minister revealed that 500,000 tons of Swedish merchant shipping outside the blockade barrier of the Skager Rak (more than two-thirds of which had been lost) had been chartered to Britain, under an agreement made at the same time as the traffic transit agreement with Germany, and like it liable to be cancelled without notice.

Between August 1943 and April 1944, as part of their plan to prevent the manufacture of enemy aircraft, the Allies made twenty major air attacks on factories making ball-bearings at Schweinfurt, Steyr, Turin and elsewhere. As a result the ball-bearings Germany was receiving from Sweden became of increasing importance to her. On April 4, 1944, a joint Anglo-American note (of which the Russian Government later expressed support) was handed to the Swedish Government by the U.S. Minister in Stockholm requesting the cessation of the export of ball- and roller-bearing materials and machinery to Germany. Negotiations resulted in June in the announcement in Washington that a temporary understanding had been reached between the U.S.A., Great Britain and the Swedish ball-bearing concerns.

On September 9, all German non-military transit traffic through Sweden to and from Norway was suspended, except for the transfer of sick and wounded and of 500 nurses from Finland—the agreement for transit of troops had been cancelled a year earlier (*see* page 2731). Following Allied protests against Sweden's sending of supplies to Germany, the Swedish Government announced that from September 27 all Swedish Baltic ports would be closed to foreign shipping : which meant the virtual abolition of trade between Sweden and Germany.

An announcement published in Britain on April 30, 1945, revealed that an 8,000-lb. model of the V2 rocket bomb which had fallen almost intact near Kalmar in south-east Sweden during June 1944 had been released by the Swedish authorities following urgent diplomatic representations and flown to Britain in August in a Dakota transport plane : firm evidence for the Prime Minister's warning of August 2 to people who could do so to stay out of London (*see* page 3022).

With the elimination of the Axis from North Africa in May 1943 (*see* Chapter 277), Switzerland realized that an Allied attempt on the mainland of Europe, and probably on Italy, was a matter **SWITZER-LAND** of a very short time. In statements made towards the end of May, General Guinan, Commander-in-Chief, announced that Switzerland would defend the St. Gotthard, Loetschberg, and Simplon passes against any attacks ; and that she would regard as an enemy any armed force setting foot on her soil from whatever side it came. On the surrender of Italy (*see* Chapter 285), all frontier army units were mobilized (September 9), and the Alpine passes and their approaches were garrisoned. The suspension of traffic through the Simplon tunnel (September 20) was followed by the closing of the frontier between Switzerland and Italy to all passenger and rail traffic. In spite of German pressure, the Government stated on September 26 that Switzerland would refuse to allow the passage by land or air of foreign troops over her territory. A year later, when the fighting in France approached the Franco-Swiss border, there was a further mobilization of frontier defence units (September 5, 1944), and the Government ordered the deportation to Germany of all Gestapo and S.S. men coming from France to seek internment (September 19). The surrender of Italy led to a sudden increase in the number of refugees seeking safety in Switzerland : between September 9 and October 18, 1943, 24,000 crossed the Italian-Swiss border, bringing the total in the country to 61,500. The newly arriving refugees included some 1,000 prisoners of war, some of them British, from camps in Italy, and parties of Italian soldiers cut off in Savoy. Many Frenchmen also crossed the border to escape the Vichy Government's drastic labour call-up for work in Germany (*see* Chapter 289); and 800 young Alsatians crossed the frontier early in 1943 to escape conscription into the German army. By May 22, 1944, the number of refugees had risen to 74,662. Count Volpi, a former Fascist Finance Minister, was refused admission ; Mussolini's daughter, Countess Edda Ciano, who crossed the frontier secretly on January 9, 1944, and her three children, who had crossed the previous December 12, were interned. Some hundreds of prisoners of war who had escaped from Germany and Italy were allowed in September 1944 to leave for France.

While the ban on the Swiss Communist Party, imposed after the defeat of France, was raised on March 6, 1943, and the Federal Parliament decided on

Act to Deprive Swiss Citizens of Nationality December 28, 1944, to repeal the laws against Communism, a number of bodies of Fascist sympathy were suppressed. A departure from all Swiss precedent was made in the decree of May 18, 1943 (approved by the Swiss parliament on December 8 after long debates), which authorized the Government to deprive of their nationality Swiss citizens living abroad who had proved themselves unworthy of it by committing, at home or abroad, "serious crimes against the security and political independence of the country." This decree was the result of a number of cases in which Swiss citizens living in Germany, or who had fled there, were found guilty by Swiss courts of high treason and espionage.

Switzerland had occasion to complain on several occasions during 1943 and 1944 to the United States, British and German Governments of violation of the air space over her territory by their aircraft. The worst incident occurred on April 1, 1944, when a formation of U.S. Liberators bombed Schaffhausen : 37 were killed, 60 others injured, 300 made homeless. Bad weather was given as the explanation, and a first instalment of a million dollars (about £200,000) was handed to the Swiss Government on April 11 by the U.S. Minister at Berne by way of reparation. The blackout was completely lifted on

September 12 as a precaution against Allied bombing errors.

The professors and students of Zurich University and Technical College held a protest meeting on December 3, 1943, those of Basle on December 6, against the mass arrests by the Nazis of Norwegian students in Oslo (*see* pages 2720 and 3155).

On March 29, 1944, the National Council (lower house of parliament) adopted without opposition a motion to normalize relations with the Soviet Union. In accepting the motion on behalf of the Government, M. Marcel Pilet-Golaz, head of the Political Department (foreign affairs), explained that Soviet-Swiss relations had been on an informal basis preceding the assassination at the Lausanne conference in 1923 of the Soviet delegate, Mr. Vorovski, and the subsequent acquittal by a Swiss court of his assassin. Though the

Swiss Government had condemned the assassination, the Soviet Government prohibited all economic or other relations with Switzerland, which then placed a ban on the entry of Russian nationals. In 1937 both governments decided to lift their mutually prohibitive measures, and signed an agreement to that effect in Berlin. In February 1941 a trade agreement was signed in Moscow, but the outbreak of war between Germany and Russia prevented its taking effect. The Soviet reply (November 4, 1944) to the new overture, made on October 10 through the Minister in London, was an uncompromising refusal : Moscow alleged that the Swiss Government had for years been pursuing a hostile pro-Fascist policy towards the Soviet Union. M. Pilet-Golaz resigned on November 10.

Eire continued to maintain her neutrality, in spite of dangers, difficulties

TO COMMEMORATE SWISS MOBILIZATION

Following the surrender of Italy, all frontier army units in Switzerland were mobilized on September 9, 1943, and the Alpine passes and their approaches were garrisoned. A second mobilization took place a year later when the fighting in France approached the Franco-Swiss border. This monument, representing an eagle at rest, was erected on the Simplon Pass to commemorate the mobilization of Swiss forces during the Second Great War. *Photo, Keystone*

SWITZERLAND'S FLAG PAINTED ON SCHAFFHAUSEN STATION

The canton of Schaffhausen is an 'isthmus' of Swiss territory with a very irregular border jutting out by a narrow neck into Germany. On the neck stands the town and railway junction of Schaffhausen which, owing to its peculiar geographical situation, was several times bombed —the worst occurrence being on April 1, 1944, when 37 were killed. In an effort to obviate these tragic accidents, the Swiss flag, white cross on red ground, was painted on the station roof.

and hardships. That these were very real was illustrated by a statement made in September 1943 by Mr. de Valera, that Eire would have reason to

EIRE thank God very sincerely if she got through as she had done so far; and another by the Minister of Supply in the following month, that Eire's shipping capacity had been reduced by almost half through the loss of two of her best ships and other circumstances: "the main task now is to stay alive in a world where we have few friends." Eire's imports in 1943 were £26,102,904 (compared with £34,630,064 in 1942); her exports, £27,477,464 (compared with £32,666,343).

Great efforts were made by Eire to increase her own food production—the programme for 1943 provided for an increase in the acreage under the plough from 2,400,000 acres to 3,000,000. Restrictions on clothing styles and prohibition of the manufacture of some types of clothing were introduced on March 2, 1943. The tea ration was reduced to three-quarters of an ounce weekly on April 3. Since 1941, there had been no coal for private consumption in Eire, peat and wood being used instead.

The general election was duly held in June 1943, though a suggestion had been made in the Dail that it should be postponed, owing to the state of emergency. The results gave Mr. de Valera's party 67 seats against 71 among the opposition and independent parties (compared with 77 and 63 in the previous Dail). Mr. de Valera was again chosen Prime Minister, and his "no change" cabinet was approved.

The School Attendance Bill, introduced early in 1943, was held by the Supreme Court on April 15 to contravene the Constitution (section 42, which defines the rights of parents), and the President refused to sign it, thus setting a precedent in Eire for the overriding of Dail legislation by the written Constitution. A Children's Allowance Bill, passed just before Christmas, came into operation on April 1, 1944. It made an allowance of 2s. 6d. a week for each child after the second, payable half yearly till the child reached 16. An amendment to make the money payable to the mother was rejected. On May 9, 1944, the Government resigned after a defeat by one vote on the second reading of a Transport Bill designed to reorganize and transform Eire's railway and transport into one unified and well-planned whole. The election held on May 31 gave Fianna Fail 76 seats (other parties, 62); by 81 to 37, the new Dail re-elected Mr. de Valera Prime Minister.

The Government decided on January 4, 1944, to intern 162 German naval officers and men picked up and brought into Cobh Harbour (Queenstown) after the Bay of Biscay action of December 27–28, 1943 (*see* page 2751 and illus. in page 2752): a German request that they should be repatriated as ship-wrecked mariners was rejected. Eire also rejected the American request, published on March 10, that she should remove Axis consular and diplomatic representatives (*see* page 3019). The Government expressed surprise that so grave a note should have been addressed to it, nor could it entertain the pro-

posal " without complete betrayal of its democratic trust." For some months the German Legation had been prevented from using its radio transmitter; five German parachutists had been apprehended. As for the statement that Britain welcomed the American initiative, " it is not perhaps known to the American Government that the feelings of the Irish people towards Britain have during the war undergone a considerable change precisely because Britain has not attempted to violate our neutrality."

Many thousands of Irishmen had, indeed, enrolled in the armed forces of Britain, and a number had won battle honours. One of the German parachutists mentioned had, the Minister of Justice revealed in the Dail on July 9, 1943, been kept in hiding by the I.R.A. for eighteen months before his capture, and his paraphernalia included plans for the invasion and occupation of Eire.

With the resignation of Mr. William T. Cosgrave from the leadership of Fine Gael on January 18, 1944, on account of ill-health, a notable figure disappeared from Irish public life. Mr. Cosgrave was the first President of the Irish Free State, from 1922 to 1932, when he became leader of the opposition in the Dail. In spite of the armed resistance of Sinn Fein, led by Mr. de Valera, he secured the Dail's approval of the Free State constitution on Dec. 6, 1922, and restored order and normality to his country.

The United Nations addressed several warnings to the neutral states concerning the possibility that Axis war criminals might seek refuge with them from the consequences of their crimes. On September 5, 1944, **Neutrals, Attitude to War Criminals** the Swedish Minister of Social Welfare said in Stockholm, " It can be taken for granted that Sweden will close her frontiers " to those who " by their actions have defied the conscience of the civilized world." During October 1944 Mr. Eden was able to inform the House of Commons that Spain and Portugal had given assurances that they would not grant asylum to war criminals. The Swiss Government, in a statement on November 14, declared that their country would deny asylum to those who had violated the laws of war or whose conduct had been " irreconcilable with the traditions of right and humanity." On November 14 also, Eire stated that since the war began she had denied admission to all aliens whose presence would be inconsistent with the desire of the Irish people to avoid injury to the interests of friendly states, and it was not intended to alter this practice.

WITH THE CANADIAN THIRD INFANTRY DIVISION

Commanded by Major-General R. F. L. Keller, C.B.E. (top centre), this division was among the first units to go ashore in Normandy on June 6, 1944. Below, at an advanced Regimental Aid Post near Courseulles, a doctor renders first aid to a wounded man, who will later travel to the rear in the jeep standing by. Canadian chaplains worked closely with Regimental Aid Post personnel during the opening battles in Normandy.

Photos, Canadian Official

GERMAN PRISONERS CROSS THE NORMANDY BEACHES

On July 1, 1944, it was officially announced that the Allies had taken more than 40,000 prisoners in France since the landings in Normandy on June 6   Here is part of a long line of prisoners walking across the sands in the American sector soon after D Day for embarkation and transport overseas to internment.   In the foreground is a jeep bringing American wounded to the L.S.T. (landing ship tanks) from which the photograph was taken, for transport to England. American casualties up to June 20 were 3,082 killed, 13,121 wounded, 7,959 missing.   *Photo, U.S. Official*

Photo, Bri[...]

PORT EN BESSIN IN ALLIED HANDS

A Royal Marine Commando was instructed to capture the little port of Port en Bessin on June 6, 1944 (D Day). The men should have gone ashore at Le Hamel (see map in page 3142), but this proving impossible, they landed a mile to the eastward and working round inland took the port from the rear after its German defenders had been bombarded from the air and from the sea. The Marines then made contact with the Americans, and so linked the whole Allied front in Normandy. Here two British soldiers are looking at a German flak ship sunk in the harbour.

PORT OPERATING GROUP HEADQUARTERS STAFF LANDS IN NORMANDY

Port Operating Groups of the Corps of Royal Engineers were responsible for discharging supplies from ship to shore during Allied invasion operations. A number accompanied the invasion fleets making for France on June 6, 1944, and were fully employed discharging ships within forty-eight hours of the first landings. Tens of thousands of vehicles, from staff cars to 10-ton lorries, thousands of tons of ammunition, equipment, stores and food were successfully slung overside from ships into landing craft in spite of rough weather. Here craft manned by the Royal Canadian Navy are putting ashore the Port Operating Group Headquarters Staff. The house on the sky-line became the Beach Sub-Area Command Post.

Chapter 313

NAZI REGIME ESCAPES INTERNAL ATTACK

*The year 1944 was among the most fateful in the whole history of Germany.
It did not decide the outcome of the war in Europe—that was settled when the
tide of battle turned in 1942. Neither did it see the end of war on European
soil. But the fact that the events of 1944 enabled the Nazi regime to prolong
the struggle well into 1945 had a catastrophic effect on the German people.
Dr. F. Heymann, who in Chapter 278 set down the history of Germany from
July 1942—December 1943, here continues the record through 1944*

HITLER'S criminal resolve to fight on "until five minutes past twelve" not only caused the German people incomparably more death and destruction than they need have suffered : it also cost the Allies tens of thousands of lives. When the year 1944 started, there was still a chance that that utter lunacy might be avoided. There were still strong forces in existence which considered it possible to prevent the Hitler Gang from pursuing its policy to the bitter end.

By far the most important centre of this potential resistance was to be found in the German Army. The relations between the German Army, or rather the old German officers' caste, and the Nazi Party were matter for political speculation from the beginning of the Hitler regime. There was (contrary to the expectations of some people) no wide rift between the two before 1939, and so long thereafter as the war went well.

When Germany was no longer victorious, however, things began to change. Hitler came to distrust the generals and started to force upon them a strategy the folly of which became apparent at Stalingrad and Tunis. The generals resented this, and they realized that, from a military point of view, the war was already as good as lost.

They did not all react in the same way. Some, in particular the younger ones, had accepted the Nazi doctrine whole. But others clearly saw what was happening, and during the winter of 1943–44 most of the scores of German generals who were prisoners in Russia joined the Kremlin-sponsored German Officers' Union (*see* p. 2935) and started to exhort the German people, over the Moscow radio, to throw over Hitler and end the war.

**Paulus Speaks
Against
Hitler**

At least some of the senior officers of the Army in Germany (who did not feel themselves bound by the ban on listening to enemy broadcasts) were impressed by the voices of Field-Marshal von Paulus, Generals von Seydlitz, Daniels and others. Most of them had no need to be told by their comrades in Russian prison camps how

things stood. Yet the advice to overthrow Hitler was easier to give than to follow. To carry it out needed the most careful political and military preparation. And the organization of any such conspiracy suffered from the very beginning from the weaknesses of the main participators and of their position.

One of these weaknesses was lack of clarity of both motive and purpose. These men were more or less united in the knowledge that Hitler was fast destroying not only German material resources but the German people as well ; but they had no clear vision (except possibly a very reactionary one) of what should be done after successful revolt. Their fundamental motives moreover were dubious. Comparatively few of them despised Hitler and the Nazi regime as such. Some may have been actuated by sincere concern as to the fate of their people, but others simply thought in terms of 1918. The war had been lost—well, that was unfortunate, but what mattered most was to save, as had been done

26 years before, the German military tradition, the General Staff and with it the nucleus of a new German Army, and the possibility of trying again.

No such long term view was taken by the Nazi leaders. They knew and said openly that they were not likely to have another chance. For them defeat meant the end — for themselves personally and, probably, for their movement also, and their idea of a German world conquest. They did not want to acknowledge defeat so long as a " miracle," such as a split between the Allies, did not seem utterly impossible. The Nazi leaders knew that the chances of bringing about such a " miracle " by propaganda alone were slender. But a number of new weapons had been for some time in preparation, ranging from long-range missiles to be launched against southern England, through jet planes and a number of " One-Man-Weapons " to new types of U-boats, and these might tire out Britain to

**Nazi Hopes
of a
Miracle**

'HITLER YOUTH' BUILDS EAST PRUSSIA DEFENCES

In August 1944 there was a total mobilization of East Prussian men and women, Germans and Poles, from 15 to 65 for the building of fortifications on the frontier. The ' Hitler Youth,' boys and girls, was completely mobilized throughout Germany. The Nazi Party took control of the digging operations, which were in full swing by August 5, 10,000 Party leaders being active in the campaign. Workers and farmers, artists and professors worked without shelter, sleeping on the ground, labouring more than 12 hours a day. *Photo, Associated Press*

FIELD-MARSHAL ROMMEL'S BIER

Rommel's death was not announced by the Germans until October 15, 1944, and the facts about his end remained doubtful; but it seems likely that he died of injuries received when a staff car in which he was travelling near Dozulé, a village east of Caen in Normandy, on July 17, was 'strafed' and left burning by Typhoons of a Brazilian squadron of the 2nd Tactical Air Force. Right, Rommel boarding a patrol boat during an inspection of coastal defences at the mouth of the Scheldt.

raise his voice) intervened for him. He was given the choice of being either shot or degraded to the rank of private. He chose the latter, saying that Germany now needed efficient people in every rank more than ever.

Two symptoms indicated that the rank and file of the Army were growing more and more tired of the war. First, considerably more men in relation to the number of killed and wounded were being taken prisoner by the Russians. Secondly, a growing number of

War Weary Rank and File

such an extent that she might be prepared to conclude a compromise peace. Finally, the Nazi politicians thought that, even should defeat prove unavoidable, the war should be drawn out as long as possible, since the destruction thus wrought all over Europe would lead to a chaos in which they would have much more chance to continue a sort of guerilla war and so keep Nazism alive as an underground movement. For all these reasons the ruling gang, inside which Himmler had become by far the most powerful figure, were resolved to crush any move towards giving in. Against this background events developed in 1944.

A government order, announced on January 4, empowered the Reich Youth Leader Axmann to "accelerate the employment of German youth for auxiliary war tasks" (such as the servicing of anti-aircraft batteries) and to "regulate and direct the employment of German youth for war purposes," these decisions affecting all boys and girls over ten years of age. Classes of schoolboys were sent, under the leadership of young and reliable Nazi teachers, to do war work. Teaching (long considered quite unimportant) was left for occasional spare hours. (Compare with developments in Japan; see page 2897.) One of the main purposes of this and other measures was to break up the unity of families: Nazi rule had always tended towards "atomization" of the people, since this made organized resistance much more difficult.

German Youth on War Work

In January also all senior generals of the German Army were ordered to Berlin to listen to Goebbels, who gave them a lecture on the situation. That a "pep talk" of this sort was considered necessary by Goebbels and approved by Himmler (whom Goebbels had learned to fear and obey) showed that the Party suspected the loyalty of the Army.

The Russian spring campaign swept on. One German army was surrounded and annihilated near Korsun (see page 3076 and illus. in page 3077). A fraction of the doomed army was evacuated by air; but while none of the units of the regular German Army was thus saved most of the S.S. Viking Division was extricated. This was only one—perhaps the most spectacular—of many incidents, showing that the Fuehrer's headquarters regarded units of the S.S., the militant Nazi Army, as far more valuable and reliable than most units of the regular Army—and this was realized and commented on in the Army, from privates up to senior officers.

In March three Luftwaffe generals were sentenced to death by court martial, allegedly because out of cowardice they had disobeyed orders during the campaign in the Ukraine. Two were shot at once. The third, a close friend of Goering's, and a man popular with most of the high officers of southern Germany, was saved, when Goering (though he now seldom dared to

men—not considerable in total, but notable as a symptom—deserted while on leave and hid under false names. Their best chance of doing this happened if the city in which they spent their leave was subjected to Allied air attack. They could then disappear, "victims" of the air raid. It was not too difficult for them to go into hiding, or to assume another name, as many of the civil registers were destroyed by Allied bombs, and there was a regular black market in false identity papers.

The Nazis could not hope to "re-educate" the average German senior officer to the point of putting the Party above the Army. But they strengthened

UNDERGROUND FACTORIES

Allied bombing even of carefully dispersed surface industry drove the Nazis to construct immense underground factories, many of which were found intact when the Allies overran Germany. Most of those who laboured in these caverns were enslaved workers from the occupied countries. 1. The assembly line in a subterranean factory at Tarthun, near Magdeburg, where Junkers 162 jetplanes were under construction. 2. Entrance to a Daimler-Benz aero-engine factory built into a hill, and (3) machine-tools in one of the workshops inside. 4. A V2 rocket in course of production in an underground assembly plant at Nordhausen.

Photos, U.S. Official ; Associated Press

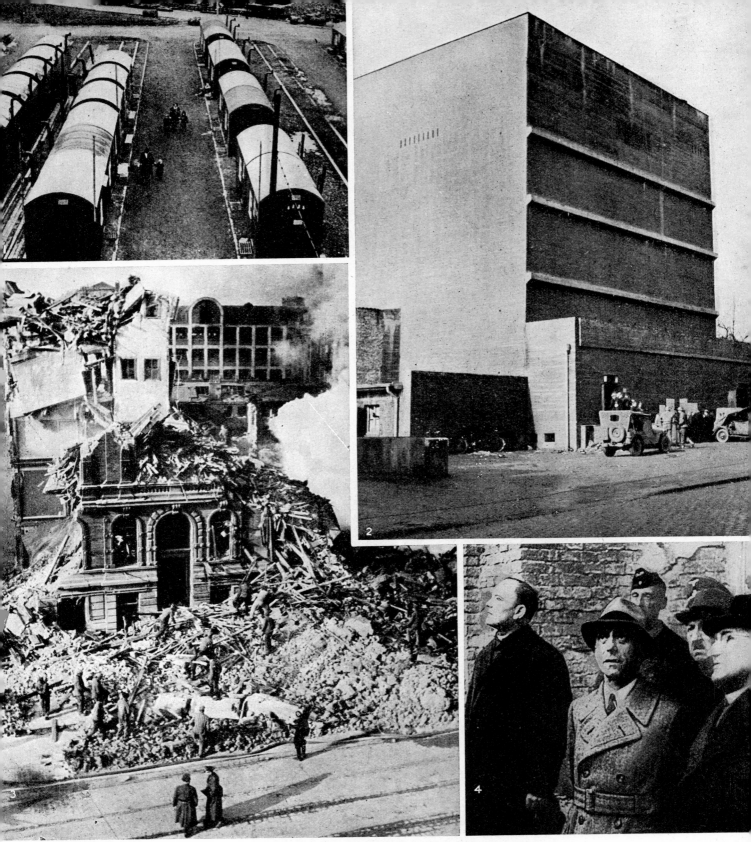

LIFE IN GERMANY UNDER ALLIED BOMBING

1. Rows of prefabricated huts put up to house bombed-out Germans. 2. Huge concrete air-raid shelter at Bonn : many of the people of all the heavily bombed towns of the Reich lived for months in similar erections, some never leaving them. 3. Apartment houses in Eppendorferbaum following an Allied air attack on April 7, 1944. 4. Dr. Josef Goebbels, Reichs Propaganda Minister, watches Allied aircraft over Berlin. From June 1943 official German propaganda for home consumption was more and more dominated by the severity of Allied air attacks on the Reich, neutral observers reporting that the people were becoming ' obsessed ' by bombing which had a greater adverse effect on morale than the reverses suffered by German arms in the Mediterranean and in Russia.

Photos, P.N.A.; Planet News; Associated Press

those whom they considered reliable, and promoted to important positions younger officers who had not been soaked, like their seniors, in the Army tradition, but whose whole thinking had been imbued by Nazi ideologies. In March 1944, a " general inspectorate to supervise the education of new leaders at the High Command of the Army " (Generalinspekteur fuer den Fuehrernachwuchs beim Oberkommando des Heeres) was created.

A more important step, announced on May 20, was the institution of " Nationalsozialistische Fuehrungsoffiziere " (National Socialist leadership officers).

Political Officers in the Army These were an exact imitation of the " Political Commissars " who had previously existed within the Red Army, been reintroduced after the outbreak of war, and then, when the Russian High Command realized that it could rely on the loyalty of the Army, converted into regularly commissioned officers. But German propaganda had always insisted that without the terrorist rule of the Political Commissars the Red Army would never have fought. Now they had to explain the necessity of establishing a similar institution in the German Army.

To counteract civilian anxiety about the growing danger of invasion from the West, German propaganda lauded the " impenetrable Atlantic Wall " (see illus. in page 2905) which, it was said, would make a successful Allied landing impossible. It was, in fact, highly desirable that the Allies should make the attempt, as its certain defeat might hasten the end of the war. Later, it was sometimes conceded that the Allies might manage to gain a small foothold somewhere, but that this would give the German Army all the more opportunity of destroying the expeditionary force of the Allies.

Field-Marshal Rommel, who, despite his defeats in Africa, was still the most

be wholly destroyed were intermixed with warnings about the material superiority of the Allies whose forces Eisenhower allegedly threw into the battle " without any regard for the frightful sacrifice in human lives." After the fall of Cherbourg and the conquest of the whole Cotentin Peninsula, even German propaganda could not pretend that the Allies would be thrown back into the sea.

And while a western front was thus firmly re-established, the eastern front was moving again. The Russians smashed the long established " Fatherland Line " along the upper Dnieper, then engulfed its northern and southern flanks, **Hitler's Strategy Again** moved deep into central Poland and caused the German Army losses of more than half a million men within a month. Again Hitler's personal strategy prevailed over the advice of his generals : the Baltic countries were not evacuated and an army of more than thirty divisions was thus cut off.

There was only one thing about which German propaganda could boast : the launching of hundreds of flying-bombs from the Pas de Calais against Britain (see Chapter 337). The destruc-

SECRET WEAPONS FOR THE DEFENCE OF THE REICH
1. The ' Tank Terror,' anti-tank gun similar in appearance to the Allied bazooka. According to German reports, many Allied tanks both east and west were destroyed by this weapon. 2. Radio-controlled midget tank, nicknamed ' Goliath,' being prepared for use on the Russian front : it was about six feet long, and could carry 1,000 lb of explosives. It had proved a failure in Italy. 3. One-man charge boat used for blowing up ships, bridges and other targets : the pilot could escape just before the explosion. *Photo, G.P.U. ; Associated Press ; Keystone*

popular German general, was appointed to supervise the defence of the coastlines of France and the Low Countries.

The successes the Allies won on and after June 6 threw the Goebbels machine into some confusion. Prophecies that the Anglo-American army would soon

tion wrought in London and southern England was painted in garish colours. By fantastic inventions and exaggerations as to the damage done and the " desperation of the English," Nazi propaganda succeeded for a short time in making at least some part of the

German people believe that "German science and new German weapons" could still compensate for Allied superiority in men and material. But those with more insight into the real state of affairs knew better. The commanders of the German Army saw clearly that the much-advertised Vergeltungswaffen (reprisal weapons) campaign was a military failure. Its start had been delayed by months; it had been hoped that the Allies would feel themselves forced to attack the V-weapon coast (that is to say, the Pas de Calais) where very strong German forces were waiting behind particularly formidable coastal defences.

But the Allies did not fall into this trap. The German generals had to fight a war on three European fronts, and a "Fourth Front"—the air front—against which the Luftwaffe, weakened by the concentration of effort upon the development of V-weapons, proved powerless, was steadily obliterating German production and communication centres. The army commanders saw clearly that it was only a question of a short time before Eisenhower's army broke out of Normandy.

Germans Fight on Four Fronts

Under the stress of this situation, those army circles which had, for many months, been secretly planning the overthrow of the Hitler regime, felt themselves compelled to act. The full story is not yet known—the Nazis naturally deliberately distorted it. But a plot had been worked out, in complete secrecy, by a limited number of high army officers. The general plan was to get rid of Hitler (thus freeing the Army from its military oath), to seize all the commanding centres in Berlin and the main cities of the Reich, to arrest the most important Nazi officials, and to disarm the S.S. The moment for the revolt, several times postponed, had been fixed for October, by which time it was expected that the climax of the war would have been reached and all preparations would have been completed. But the date was advanced by about three months, so that the venture was at least in part improvised, and this contributed to its failure.

The inner circle of the conspirators consisted almost exclusively of officers who belonged, or had previously belonged, to the German General Staff. Highest in rank was Field-Marshal von Witzleben. Beside him stood several Colonel-Generals (a rank between full general and field-marshal), among them two who had previously held the office of Chief of the General Staff: Beck, a man of the highest ability, who had retired after the invasion of Austria, and his successor Halder. The Chief of Staff at the time, General Zeitzler, seems also to have directly participated.

Three men had a particularly important role to play: General Olbrecht, Quartermaster-General of the Army, Colonel-General Fromm, C.-in-C. of the Home Army (Heimatheer) and therefore of almost all troops in Inner Germany, and Colonel-General Hoeppner. Olbrecht was, with Beck, the main driving force of the revolt, and his A.D.C., Colonel von Stauffenberg, was chosen to start the whole movement by eliminating Hitler. On July 19, Stauffenberg went to the Fuehrer's headquarters and deposited a small time-bomb (which he had carried in a big diplomatic case) in the room where a conference was to be held in Hitler's presence next morning. This—it had been expected by the conspirators—would be an underground room with concrete walls which would withstand and throw back the blast, thereby killing whoever was standing or sitting anywhere near the exploding bomb. Actually the conference took place in a

Attempted Assassination of Hitler

DICTATORS IN DECLINE

Official Italian circles in Venice believed that the attempt of July 20 on Hitler's life was meant to kill Mussolini as well—claiming that the same German military clique which engineered the plot had persuaded Mussolini to go to Germany earlier than he had planned. Here are the dictators shortly after the attempt on Hitler. Left to right, Grand Admiral Doenitz, Von Ribbentrop, the Fuehrer, Reichs Leader Bormann. Mussolini is talking to Reichs Marshal Goering.

wooden hut the walls of which collapsed easily. Hitler, at the moment of the explosion, had just left his chair under which the bomb had been deposited. Thus he was not killed but suffered only slight bruises.

Stauffenberg, however, who had managed to leave the hut a few minutes before the explosion was due, saw, or at least heard, the explosion. He at once boarded a plane for Berlin, certain that Hitler was dead. Everything now de-

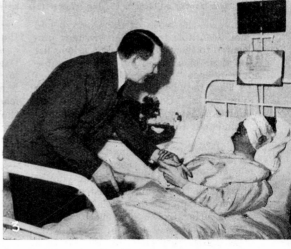

AFTER THE BOMB EXPLODED

1. According to the Germans, Hitler was standing on the spot indicated by a black arrow at the moment the time-bomb went off on July 20, 1944. 2. Field-Marshal Erwin von Witzleben, highest in military rank among the conspirators before the 'People's Court,' which condemned him to hang, together with seven other high ranking officers. 3. Hitler visits Lieut.-General Schmidt, wounded by the explosion.

pended on the speed and resolution of the main actors in Berlin. It was only by perfect co-ordination and quick action that there could be any hope of forestalling the countermoves which were certain to come from the Party. The key to all further moves was in the hands of the C.-in-C. of the Home Army, General Fromm.

The conspirators were masters of the War Ministry at the Bendlerstrasse, the centre and brain of the German military machine. All outgoing orders as well as incoming inquiries had to go through the teleprinting office there. When Stauffenberg arrived with the news that Hitler was killed the conspirators asked Fromm to give the orders necessary to secure Berlin and the main centres outside the capital. Some of these orders were given, but then Fromm suddenly lost his nerve and collapsed. Stauffenberg tried to take over, but being only a colonel met resistance

Conspirators Masters of War Office

from many officers in the War Ministry who might have obeyed Fromm. Colonel-General Beck, who tried to strengthen Stauffenberg's hand, had not sufficient authority, having been long in retirement. An open struggle ensued, and Beck and Stauffenberg fell in a fight with revolvers.

Although people in Berlin perceived little of what was happening, it was not until the evening that the Nazis were again in full control of the military machine, and that communication with Hitler was restored. In Hamburg, Munich and Vienna, the three most important places outside Berlin, the commanding officers received the first orders given by Fromm and acted accordingly. They told their officers that Hitler was dead, and that they were no longer bound by the oath on his name. State and Party buildings were occupied, and in some places fierce fighting started between Army and S.S.

units. These movements collapsed only after it was generally realized that Hitler was alive, and that the capital was under Party control.

In Vienna, the revolt continued throughout most of July 21. High Party and Gestapo officials were arrested. Army units participated, and the Austrian underground movement, led in Vienna by Socialist and Communist workers, came into the open. Workers with armlets of the People's Guards protected some of the main buildings as well as foreign consulates.

To the Nazis all this was a godsend. They had had many suspicions. But

PANIC-STRICKEN GERMANS SEEK SANCTUARY

The French 2nd Armoured Division, led by General Leclerc, formed the spearhead of the U.S. 7th Army's drive through the Vosges. On November 22 it liberated Saverne and advanced to within 20 miles of Strasbourg and the Rhine. On the same day the French 1st Army liberated Mulhouse. Numbers of fully-armed German troops, retreating before the French, crossed the Swiss frontier on bicycles seeking safety. (See also page 3156.) *Photo, Planet News*

what all the work of the Gestapo had not been able to provide was now presented to them gratuitously : a long list of their enemies—from left to right—throughout " Greater Germany."

They took frightful vengeance. They put up a " Court of Honour of the German Army," asking Field-Marshal Rundstedt to preside over it. There is

Army "Court of Honour"

nothing to show that Rundstedt was one of the conspirators, but there is little doubt that, had they won, Rundstedt would have been prepared to collaborate with them. He was the most successful, the most experienced and in many ways the most respected of all German Army commanders. Had he refused to preside over that court he would have shown that he approved of what the conspirators had done and would have been executed himself. But by making him the instrument of their vengeance, and the hangman of his comrades, the Nazis insured that the Army could never trust him as a possible leader against the Party.

After the " Court of Honour " had delivered all the accused officers, with Field-Marshal von Witzleben at the top, to the People's Court—because " by their deeds they had put themselves outside the ranks of the German

Army "—that Court, presided over by the notorious criminal Roland Freissler, quickly sentenced them all to death. Gallows were erected on big motor lorries, and after the accused had been hanged, the lorries with their horrible load went in slow procession through the streets of Berlin so as to show everyone that even a German Field-Marshal—a man considered a demi-god in old Prussia or the Kaiser's Germany—had to die this shameful death if he dared to conspire against the holy person of the Fuehrer. The relatives of the executed were forced to follow the gallows, and most of them were killed immediately afterwards. Whole families were thus murdered, in some cases down to children of four and five years old.

The mass killing continued throughout the year. As a matter of course, not only every officer and soldier, but anybody else, who could be suspected of having had anything to do with the attempted plot was put to death, and most of the victims were kept imprisoned and were tortured by the Gestapo in order to make them reveal their connexions and accomplices. (Fifteen hundred officers were arrested during the first few days after the revolt.)

Nor was that enough. This time the Nazi leaders were resolved to get rid

not only of those who had had anything to do with the events of July 20, but also of all potential enemies of the regime capable of exerting any influence. It was no

Well-Known Politicians Destroyed

chance that the second group of people condemned to death by the People's Court were not tried in public, as Witzleben and his comrades had been. This second group consisted almost entirely of well-known politicians of the Weimar Republic, drawn from all parties, from the Social Democrats (such as the former Hessian Minister Leuschner) to the German Nationalists (such as the former Mayor of Leipzig Goerdeler). There were also some professional diplomats, among them the former ambassador in Rome, Herr von Hassell. Without having been let into the secret of the time and place of the planned attempt on Hitler's life, some of these civilians had nevertheless been in contact with the conspirators—a connexion confirmed when, in July, 1945, the Bishop of Chichester, the Rt. Rev. G. K. A. Bell, made public information he had received for transmission to the British Government while he was in Sweden in May 1942. At that time, more than two years before the attempt, a German pastor, Dietrich Bonhoeffer, told him of the plot, and the names of the people involved in it. A few of these civilians had probably been selected as possible members of the—mainly military—government which it had been intended to set up. Others, however, were considered by the Nazis to be potential enemies of the regime, who might have been prepared to join any successful rising, and the Nazis put them all to death.

On the other hand, the Nazis were most anxious to prove to the German people that, as Hitler put it in a **Mystery of Rommel's End** hurried speech, " only a very small clique " of generals had taken part in the plot. They maintained that no one in a really responsible position had had anything to do with it, and they therefore had to suppress a number of the most important names. They did not mention Fromm, nor Zeitzler, whose name was not heard again after the announcement that as Zeitzler was " suffering from an infectious disease and could not carry out his duties for some weeks," Guderian had taken over the office of Chief of Staff. It is almost certain that the circumstantial reports given out of Field-Marshal Rommel's having suffered head injuries owing to a car accident due to an air attack, and having died in consequence, were lies. Rommel's end was announced on October 15, but rumours that he was dead had swept through the German army many weeks before that date. He had certainly at least given his blessing to the revolt, and all the tales about his wounds seem to have been designed to cover up the fact that Germany's most popular commander and Hitler's special favourite had made common cause with his enemies and shared their fate. (Allied correspondents reported that Rommel was injured on July 17 when his car was wrecked by British fighters in Normandy, and had died next day in Bemay hospital near Lisieux.)

The exact number of people murdered by the Gestapo during the months following July 20 is not yet known, but they amounted to tens of thousands. They ranged from hundreds of members of old, influential " society " families in Berlin and elsewhere (always including women, often children), to thousands of political prisoners in concentration camps, thousands of workers in Berlin, Munich, Vienna, Hamburg and western Germany (including a high percentage of the old leaders and officials of trade unions, whether Socialist or Roman Catholic). It was a mortal blow struck at every group which might have leanings in opposition to the regime and might supply the basis of a resistance movement before the final military collapse of Germany.

The destruction of all potential resistance was, however, only one of the benefits the Nazi regime derived from the events of July 20. There was also the legend of Hitler's miraculous escape : the Fuehrer, destined to " save Germany," clearly had " a charmed life." Hardly less important in Nazi eyes was the fact that a new " stab-in-the-back " legend had been secured. In 1918 it was alleged that the German Army, " undefeated in the field," had been stabbed in the back by " Marxist defeatists and traitors." This time the Party charged the " traitors in the Army " with having stabbed the fighting German people in the back. It was said that the treacherous generals had held back reserve troops, and so caused the breakdown of the Eastern front.

On July 24 it was announced from Hitler's headquarters that, at the request of all parts of the armed forces, the Hitler salute with the greeting " Heil **Hitler Salute in the Army** Hitler " would be substituted for the military salute. Much more important was an order by which professional soldiers, including the whole officers' corps, were allowed to join the Nazi Party, whereas previously any association with political bodies had been prohibited. Adherence to the Party now became an essential condition for personal success. There was a tendency also to replace the higher field commanders by S.S. generals,

HIMMLER ANNOUNCES THE ' VOLKSSTURM '

Hitler proclaimed the formation of the German People's Storm Army in a broadcast on October 18, 1944. A sort of Home Guard, it was modelled closely on Nazi Party lines, all commanders being trusted Party men. Heinrich Himmler, head of the Home Army since the failure of the July plot, was also head of the ' Volkssturm.' Here, also on October 18, in a town of East Prussia, he is personally announcing its formation. On his left is Field-Marshal Keitel, on his right Dr. Hans Heinrich Lammers, head of the Reich Chancellery. *Photo, Associated Press*

but the government soon realized that this would not work; highly efficient in suppressing and tormenting the foreign peoples from whose soil the German armies had been, or were just being, ejected, these S.S. commanders lacked the training and experience necessary for high commanders in the field. However much they suspected their loyalty, the Nazis had to leave the control of all military operations to the old Army commanders. Should they do anything that could be regarded as treasonable, their families would immediately be seized and punished.

In August, when the Allies had destroyed or routed the major part of the German armies in Normandy and freed almost the whole of France and Belgium, panic seized considerable parts of the remaining German troops in the West. Some streamed back in disorder towards and over the frontiers of the Reich, spreading fear also among the civilian population of western Germany. The Party tried to stop the rot by threatening all deserters or fleeing men with severe punishment. Special centres were set up where Nazi officers collected the remnants of routed troops and re-formed them into new "fighting groups" (Kampfgruppen), a rather vague expression which now frequently superseded the orthodox names of companies, battalions, and regiments.

Routed Troops Re-formed

Resolved to wage war, even at the risk of Germany's complete destruction, until "five minutes past twelve," the Nazis used the chance given to them by the shock of their new terror wave to arrange a new "total mobilization," more successful than previous attempts of a similar sort (*see page 2783*) mainly because it was pressed through much more ruthlessly. Sauckel, General Commissioner for the Employment of Labour, issued a decree on July 30 raising the age limit of women for compulsory registration for war work from 45 to 50. Goebbels, already Reichsminister for Propaganda and People's Enlightenment and "Gauleiter" and "Stadtpraesident" of Berlin, was made "Reich Trustee for Total War Mobilization" (Reichsbevollmaechtigter fuer den totalen Kriegseinsatz). His first step was to issue orders covering the following measures:

1. New limit of the right to employ domestic servants, all those released being sent to munitions work. All foreign domestic servants (among them many Polish and Russian girls) were sent into industry.

2. Closing of all theatres, concerts, cabarets and amusement centres with the sole exception of cinemas; further limitation of university study to work of immediate importance for the war effort; closing down of more newspapers and periodicals, many so-called "cultural workers" being taken over by the war industries.

3. New comb-out of the retail trade and all consumer goods industries to the very limit of possibilities.

4. Reduction by a fixed quota of employees of public services like railways, post office, municipal and provincial authorities and even the police (but not the Gestapo). Thus 10 per cent of the employees of city administrative bodies and 20 per cent of postal workers were to be released.

The industries hit by this cutting down of their manpower were ordered to make up for it by working harder, prolonging working hours to a minimum of sixty a week, and by cancelling all leave arrangements. Particular stress was laid, by a special decree, on ending all sham employment (*e.g.* girls being registered as employed by relatives, but not doing any real work). Heavy penalties were threatened for continuing such "employment" after a certain date.

Though the new, inexperienced, and untrained men and women in munitions did not equal the performance of highly skilled workmen, the war workers drafted into the army produced those new divisions required to build up a fresh western front from the mouth of the Maas river along the Siegfried Line to the Swiss frontier, and to mount the vigorous Ardennes offensive in December.

The Nazis kept the build-up of the new Home Army entirely to themselves. Its C.-in-C., successor to Colonel-General Fromm, was none other than Himmler.

Formation of the 'Volkssturm' The Party also sponsored the new force which was to be the last emergency levy: the "Volkssturm," organized on somewhat similar lines to the British Home Guard. Every man from 16 to 60 who was not in the army had to register for it. The original idea was to form it into two main cadres, the more able-bodied forming fighting groups who could be sent to the front even at some considerable distance from their homes, the others defending the towns or villages where they lived.

From the beginning the Volkssturm suffered from lack of equipment. In many districts firearms were even scarcer than they had been in Britain in 1940; and nowhere were there enough uniforms, though all possible apparel, from tram conductors' suits to the uniforms of fire brigades, were distributed together with Volkssturm armlets. The members of the Volkssturm were most unwilling to serve without uniform as they feared that the Allies might regard them as franc-tireurs. On the other hand, some to whom the brown uniforms of the S.A. were handed out tried by every means to get rid of them as they did not like the idea of being made prisoner in a dress which suggested that they were militant Party members.

For the German people in that small area of western Germany which was under Allied control towards the end of 1944, the war had, in the main, become a thing of the past. Elsewhere conditions grew worse, owing to the ever stronger impact of Allied air raids. Many of the larger German cities were reduced to heaps of rubble. Their millions of inhabitants had become cave dwellers. They lived and, to no small extent, worked underground—some of the most important munition factories having been made subter-

ranean. People lived in their own cellars or in public shelters, some of which were deep shelters, others giant concrete blocks of three or four storeys, without windows and with walls so strong that nothing except a direct hit by a "block buster" would have destroyed them. There old people, women and children lived dreary lives in hopeless apathy, sometimes not leaving their crowded mass quarters for days on end. Not only property but life itself lost all value, and juvenile criminality, even according to official German sources, mounted

steadily. Yet not all youths persecuted by the State were criminals. There was an opposition youth movement, called the "Edelweiss-Jugend" or "Edelweiss - Piraten." Though far from having any clear political ideology, these young people were united in their antagonism to the official "Hitler Youth" (in which they built up opposition "cells"), and their activities, which sometimes amounted to effective sabotage, led to strong measures of suppression by the Gestapo. This juvenile opposition must not be overrated, but it was one more sign that the Nazi regime was losing its attraction. After the Party victory of July 20, however, only the Allied Armies could bring about its downfall.

IN MUCH BOMBED COLOGNE

Berlin admitted 'a state of chaos' in Cologne already in July 1943, but workers were exhorted to attend work punctually (left), and shops were transferred to the basements, as is indicated by the arrowed signs in the photograph below, taken towards the end of 1944. When the 'bomb-shattered and battle-torn' city was taken by the U.S. 1st Army on March 6, 1945, about 150,000 civilians (peacetime population, 768,000) were still living in it.

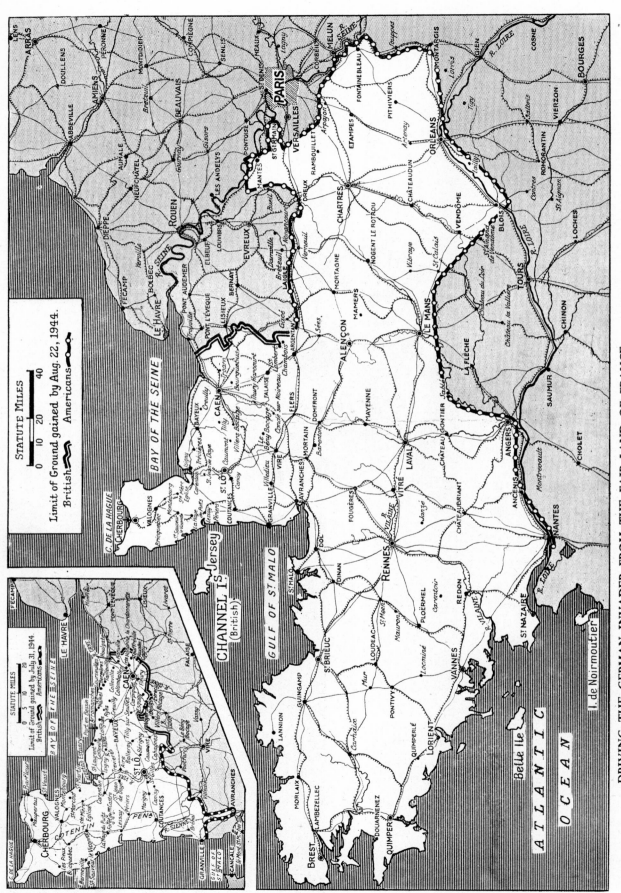

DRIVING THE GERMAN INVADER FROM THE FAIR LAND OF FRANCE

By August 22, 1944, eleven weeks after the first Allied landings in Normandy, the Americans had swept west to clear Brittany (except Brest, taken September 19, Lorient and St. Nazaire, which surrendered only on May 9, 1945, after the end of fighting in Europe), then east, and, with the French 2nd Armoured Division as their spearhead, were within a few miles of Paris. To the north-west of Paris, the Americans were already across the Seine, in the neighbourhood of Mantes. The British and Canadians, who had held down round Caen the bulk of the enemy's armour advancing from the east, were beginning also to advance eastward. Top left-hand corner: area of France liberated eight weeks after the landings.

Chapter 314

NORMANDY AND BRITTANY LIBERATED

In Chapter 311, Gordon Holman describes the onset of the Allied invasion forces on the coast of Normandy on June 6, 1944. Here Squadron Leader Derek Adkins describes the tough fighting which followed in the British and Canadian sector, and the initial difficulties and spectacular breakout of the American forces, culminating in the terrific battle of the Falaise Gap. The history of the second campaign in Western Europe is continued in Chapter 320

WHEN the Allied seaborne landings began at 6.30 a.m. on June 6, 1944, on the coast of Normandy, most of the shore batteries had been either subdued or put out of action by the preliminary air bombardment, and consequently opposition was less than expected. The seaborne landing on the east side of the Cotentin peninsula achieved almost complete surprise, but heavy seas and beach obstacles held up the initial landings on the beaches east of the Carentan estuary in the St. Laurent district. Farther to the east and as far as the river Orne, the opposition to the initial assaults was patchy, but heavy inland fighting developed here as elsewhere and enemy resistance stiffened as reserves came into action. On one of the American beaches the opposition was provided by a German division which happened to have been brought to the coastal sector for an exercise.

By the evening of the 6th, advance elements of the assault divisions were some few miles inland on the beaches to the east and west of Port en Bessin, the

First Allied Successes following places having been captured: St. Martin, St. Laurent, Colleville, Arromanches, Ryes, Creully, Tailleville and Ranville. Ste. Mère Eglise was captured by U.S. airborne troops. A bridge-head approximately 25 miles wide was established, which was quickly joined with the lodgement to the west to form one continuous front, with American forces in the Cotentin peninsula and just east of the Vire, Canadian and British troops on the left flank.

The bridge-head was steadily extended, and after Bayeux had been captured in the British sector on the 7th an armoured thrust in the direction of Villers Bocage secured a deep salient extending just south of Tilly sur Seulles (8 miles southeast of Bayeux). To the east British troops advanced to within three miles of Caen, while to the west U.S. forces penetrated to a depth of five miles south of Colleville and crossed the river Aure to the east of Trevières. Isigny (six miles east of Carentan) was captured on the 9th together with the high ground to the west, thus completing the contact with the lodgement in the Cotentin

peninsula. On the morning of the 12th, Carentan fell to U.S. troops who entered Montebourg on the following day, but were forced to give ground, the town, devastated in the fighting, being finally captured on the 19th.

Violent fighting, in which strong armoured forces were engaged by both sides, continued on all fronts, and many important positions changed hands several times. In the Caen area especially, enemy resistance stiffened, but no co-ordinated counter attack developed. This was partly due to the fact that the infantry component of the panzer divisions had had to be committed immediately on arrival in the battle area, while Allied air action against communications and activity by the French Forces of the Interior had considerably slowed down the rate of enemy reinforcement. In fact, the enemy's rate of build-up fell short of original estimates,

and in particular he lacked sufficient infantry to hold ground.

As a result of a powerful thrust, British tanks and infantry captured Villers Bocage on the 13th, but the Germans reacted strongly, and the British withdrew to the high ground east of Caumont, where the Americans, who were **Americans Make Slow Progress** in touch with the British forces, had expanded their difficult St. Laurent bridge-head to a depth of some twenty miles. The Americans' primary object, however, was to seal off the Cotentin peninsula, at the same time strengthening the southern flank of the salient to prevent the enemy relieving his formations cut off in the north. The Americans made slow progress until the 15th, when leading U.S. troops entered St. Sauveur Le Vicomte (captured next day). Thereafter opposition slackened and they

BAYEUX—FIRST TOWN OF WESTERN EUROPE TO BE LIBERATED
Bayeux, ancient city of Normandy, was taken undamaged on June 7, 1944. The liberating Allied troops received a frantic reception from the people who, with tears streaming down their cheeks, crowded the streets shouting, ' Vive la France! Vive l'Angleterre! Vive l'Amérique!' French, British and American flags, hidden during the four years of German occupation, fluttered from every house. Here a French war correspondent is addressing a Bayeux crowd.

CHERBOURG FALLS TO AMERICAN ARMS

1. Major-General Joseph Lawton Collins, commanding the U.S. 7th Corps, and his staff officers look across liberated Cherbourg towards the burning harbour area from one of the captured forts. 2. Germans, hands up, emerge from an underground fortress, to become prisoners. 3. Lieut.-General Carl Wilhelm von Schlieben Commander of the German forces in Cherbourg, and Rear-Admiral Hennecke, Sea Defence Commandant for Normandy, arrive at General Collins's H.Q. to surrender. The last strongpoint in Cherbourg fell on June 27, 1944. 4. Southern Railway Channel ferry, 'Twickenham Ferry,' lands the first cargo at Cherbourg, a 65-ton U.S. locomotive and train of wagons.

Photos, U.S. Official; British Newspaper Pool; Planet News

BRITISH TROOPS IN BOOBY-TRAPPED TILLY

Tilly sur Seulles, much disputed village in the British sector, was finally in Allied hands on June 19, 1944. British infantry, fighting their way in drenching rain through mines and booby-traps, cleared the enemy from house after house. British tanks engaged enemy 'Tiger' tanks, crushed machine-gun nests, and wiped out groups holding out in Tilly's shattered houses.

reached the west coast of the peninsula on the 18th at Barreville-sur-Mer. With Montebourg and Bricquebec firmly secured by the 19th, the Americans found themselves within ten miles of Cherbourg, and faced by elements of three German infantry divisions. They reached the main defences on the 21st, encountering fierce resistance from prepared positions. Intensive aerial bombardment and artillery fire on the 25th assisted the U.S. 7th Corps (Major-General Joseph Lawton Collins) to extend its initial penetration of the outskirts of the town ; while on the same day other American troops reached the coast at St. Vaast and Barfleur and made further advances on the opposite flank. By the 26th fierce street fighting was in progress in Cherbourg, during which Lieut.-General Carl Wilhelm von Schlieben, Commander of the German forces in Cherbourg, and Rear-Admiral Hennecke, Sea Defence Commandant for Normandy were captured. On the 27th the last strongpoint in the naval arsenal surrendered and resistance in the town ended. But enemy troops defending the Maupertus aerodrome, seven miles east of the town, and small pockets in the Cap de la Hague still held out, and it was not until July 1 that the north of the peninsula was firmly in Allied hands.

The approaches to the port of Cherbourg and the harbour itself had been heavily mined and the quays and docks were found extensively damaged, but certain hards and beaches were quickly put to use for landing of troops and supplies pending the restoration of the more important harbour facilities. Apart from heavy losses in killed and wounded, the Germans lost in Cherbourg some 20,000 troops as prisoners of war. (The total of prisoners taken in France since June 6 was over 40,000.)

As soon as the Allied armies had gained a foothold in Normandy, work began on the construction of the Mulberry harbours (see page 3099). The blockships were sunk and in use by D+5. By D+12 more than half the caissons were in position. But on D+13 a gale blew up from the north-east and continued for three days. Mulberry A, intended for the Americans, was badly damaged, and was never completed—the capture of Cherbourg reduced its importance. The British Mulberry B at Arromanches, protected to some extent by the Calvados reef, suffered less damage, though the gale took a heavy toll. Still, during this critical period, when the storms made unloading on to open beaches impossible, a small but important trickle of stores was landed in the Arromanches harbour. Even on the worst day, 800 tons of petrol and ammunition as well as many troops got ashore over the piers. A long spell of rough weather followed the gale, and the harbour was not unloading to maximum capacity until July. Scheduled to handle 7,000 tons a day, it thereafter at times handled as much as 9,000 tons daily. It remained in operation until November, when the great port of Antwerp came into use (see Chapter 325).

In the British sector intensive fighting continued, but the general line

Mulberry B at Arromanches

FIGHTING FRENCH LEADER LANDS IN FRANCE

In the darkest days of 1940, General Charles de Gaulle never despaired, and gradually he rallied to the cause of Free France thousands of his fellow countrymen and women. On June 14, 1944, he landed in France for the first time for four years from the French destroyer 'La Combattante.' He met General Eisenhower, and was welcomed tumultuously in Bayeux and other places. Here he is speaking to a crowd which gathered at Isigny. *Photo, Keystone*

WAR-DAMAGED NORMAN VILLAGES

A street in Carentan, at the base of the Cotentin Peninsula, after its capture by Americans on June 12, 1944, following heavy bombardment throughout the night of June 11-12 ; the Americans had fought bitterly all night, often waist-deep in water, in the marshes on the outskirts of the town. Right, the remains of the tower of the 600-year old church of Saint Jacques at Montebourg, entered by the Americans on June 13 after heavy fighting. *Photos, Keystone*

remained unaltered. On June 16 H.M.S. "Ramillies" (Capt. G. B. Middleton C.B.E., R.N.) bombarded enemy armour north-east of Caen while three U.S. battleships gave fire support to American troops near Isigny and Carentan. More enemy armour was shelled on the 18th by H.M.S. "Diadem," (Captain E. G. A. Clifford, R.N.) on which date S.H.A.E.F. announced that the enemy battery at Houlgate (east of Ouistreham) had been silent for 36 hours after bombardment by "Ramillies." Shelling of enemy targets by Allied warships continued.

A local advance resulted in the capture of Chardonnerette, three miles north-east of Caen, on the 23rd, and **British Reach the Odon** during the next two days further advances were made south of Tilly sur Seulles after hard fighting. By the 27th the British troops, including powerful armoured forces, had cut the Caen–Villers Bocage road and railway, and reached the river Odon at a point some two miles north of Evrecy. A firm bridge-head was established and included the important high ground to the north of Esquay. German reaction to this thrust was, as expected, violent. In addition to the strong armoured forces already in the area, panzer formations which the enemy had intended

to form into a reserve were used for immediate counter-attacks, and by July 1 the greater part of eight panzer and S.S. panzer divisions had been drawn into battle. The attack of the British 2nd Army (commanded by Lieut-General Sir Miles Christopher Dempsey, whose appointment was announced on June 28) was a fine piece of military strategy, for Rommel had hoped to be able to wait until these panzer divisions were fully ready and then launch them in a concentrated attack of his own choosing.

Armoured and infantry fighting of the most bitter nature developed. The close country prevented large armoured formations being employed at single points, but the Germans put in counter-attacks of company strength, supported by tanks, at numerous points in an attempt to infiltrate into the British lines. All failed. The bridge-head remained firm and was, in fact, enlarged.

While bad weather continued to delay the planned build-up of the Allied forces, the German rate of reinforcement was affected by the activities of the French Forces of the Interior which kept considerable German forces, including panzer divisions, tied down in the south of France, and by the effects of the "Transportation Plan" air attacks (*see* page 3103) : the 9th S.S.

panzer division, which had crossed Germany from the eastern front in seven days, took fourteen to travel from the Franco-German frontier to the Normandy battlefield.

The U.S. 1st Army (Lieut-General Courtney H. Hodges), having cleared the north-west tip of the Cotentin peninsula, was regrouped for a new drive southwards. The **U.S. 1st Army Drives South** attack opened in a blinding rainstorm at 5.30 a.m. on July 3, on a wide front south of St. Sauveur Le Vicomte. By the following day the Americans had captured the tactically important high ground to the north of La Haye du Puits, but enemy resistance in the town ceased only on the 9th after it had been outflanked on the east and the west. Simultaneously other American troops were fighting their way up the steep wooded slopes of the Forêt de Mont Castre in conditions that were described as jungle warfare, but by the 11th they reached the southern edge of the forest. The Americans also started to advance down the Carentan-Périers road, at the same time forcing a passage across the river Vire in the direction of St. Jean de Daye, which fell on the 8th. By the 11th advanced elements, pressing on through waterlogged country, were

IN FALAISE AFTER THE BATTLE OF 'THE GAP'

The ancient town of Falaise, capital of William the Conqueror's Norman dukedom, was captured by Canadians on
August 17, 1944, during the last stages of the battle of the 'Falaise Gap' in which British, Canadian, American,
Dutch, Belgian, and Polish Allied troops accounted for about 100,000 men of the German 7th Army. Killed exceeded
captured in number in what was one of the bloodiest battles of the western front in the Second Great War.

PREMIER VISITS

Mr. Churchill spent Aug.
14–20, 1944, on the Ital
front, addressing Briti
Canadian, Indian and N
Zealand troops of the
Army and U.S. and Bra
lian troops of the 5th.
personally fired a shell i
the German gun positio
on August 19. Here he
with Lieut.-General
Oliver Leese, command
the 8th Army, and Gene
Sir Harold Alexand
C.-in-C., Italy (whose p
motion to Field-Marsh
dating from June 4, v
not announced until N
ember 26). Left,
wreckage of the Ponte
Grazie, Florence, used
cross the Arno—at

Photos, British Official

—EIGHTH ARMY

lowest summer ebb—by Florentines returning to their homes after the Germans had evacuated the city on August 11. Right, train wrecked by Allied bombing on the line between Arezzo and Cortona. Italian roads, railways, bridges, marshalling yards received constant attention from Allied bombers before and after the Allies landed on the peninsula. Attacks on communications in the battle area were of almost daily occurrence during July 1944, when this photograph was taken. Below, checking over a Churchill tank in a back area in Italy.

Crown Copyright

RUINS OF HOTLY-CONTESTED CAEN

Round Caen, most important road junction in Normandy, and eastern bastion of the German defence positions, raged some of the fiercest fighting of the early days of the Allied invasion of France in 1944. It was captured on July 9, by which time artillery and air bombardment had reduced it to ruins. Here is the shell of the church of S. Pierre. Below is the wreckage of a once prosperous street, with the remains of the tower of S. Pierre in the background.

'CHURCHILL' TANKS IN THE ADVANCE ON CAEN

A massed attack in the direction of Caen began in the area east of Tilly sur Seulles at dawn on June 25, 1944. Strong resistance was encountered, and fierce tank battles were fought between 'Churchills' and German 'Panthers'; but by nightfall on the 28th, the British were threatening to outflank Caen to the south-west. Here British tanks and infantry are advancing across a cornfield; below, creeping forward under cover of a damaged wall at St. Maugieu.

within three miles of the important communications centre of St. Lô.

The British 2nd Army bridge-head across the river Orne held firm against repeated enemy counter-attacks, and on July 4 Canadian and British forces themselves attacked eastwards towards Caen. Intensive enemy artillery fire forced the British troops to withdraw slightly, but the Canadians, after capturing Carpiquet and part of the airfield south of the village, continued to defeat every attempt by the enemy to drive them out of their new positions, although bitter and inconclusive close quarter fighting continued for four days. Early on the 8th, however, after a highly concentrated bombardment from heavy and medium bombers, the British and Canadian divisions, contained for so long by the enemy north of Caen, launched an attack which carried them to the outskirts of the town the same night. The attack was well supported by fire from massed artillery and H.M. ships. By nightfall the following day the whole town except for suburbs south of the river Orne had been taken and small pockets in the rear were being rapidly eliminated, while the Canadians completed their capture of Carpiquet aerodrome.

By the 15th, the U.S. 1st Army was within sight of Lessay, Périers, and St. Lô. At the same time the American advance down the Carentan–Périers road and the widening of the bridge-head made earlier across the river Vire resulted in a straightening of the general line and the elimination of resistance in the flooded areas south of Carentan. To the east of St. Lô further steady gains were made between the 11th and 13th, including the cutting of the St. Lô–Berigny road. The town of St. Lô fell on July 18 after eight days' fierce fighting.

Fall of St. Lô

Following the capture of the northern part of Caen and the expansion eastwards of the Odon bridge-head, the British 2nd Army paused for regrouping before launching an attack at dusk on July 15 on the line Noyers–Bougy–Esquay. Good progress was made against stiff resistance, but the main achievement of the attack was that it held a considerable part of the enemy armour west of the Orne, where it became heavily involved with consequent losses. Then at 8.45 a.m., on the 18th, General Montgomery attacked again with powerful forces of infantry and armour south-east of Caen. The assault was preceded by the heaviest and most concentrated bombing undertaken to that date in support of military operations. Over 2,000 British and American heavy and medium bombers (only nine were lost) dropped 7,000–8,000 tons of bombs in an area of little more than 70 square miles, blasting a 7,000-yard-wide passage between the suburb of Vaucelles and the woods of Touffreville and Cagny. Armoured formations then crossed the river Orne

CARPIQUET AIRFIELD IN CANADIAN HANDS

After fierce hand-to-hand fighting, the Canadians captured Carpiquet, reduced to rubble but full of enemy strongpoints, on July 4, 1944, and went on to attack Carpiquet airfield, 300 yards to the south. Though not used by the Luftwaffe for some time, it had been converted into a formidable centre of resistance, and did not fall till July 10. Here Canadians examine a German 20-mm. A.A. gun on the captured airfield.

Photo, Associated Press

by specially constructed bridges and, through the gap made by the bombers, drove strong wedges in the direction of Cagny and Bourguébus.

Despite the initial success of the thrust by British armour to the east of Caen, the enemy defensive positions, and in particular the very heavy anti-tank screens to the south

Canadians Capture Fleury

and east of Bourguébus, halted the advance. By the afternoon of the day of the assault the momentum of the drive was slowing down in the face of this powerful opposition, and a pause was made to allow the infantry to come up. On the next day violent rainstorms so softened the ground that no movement was possible off metalled roads. Meanwhile Canadian troops had successfully cleared the southern and south-eastern suburbs of Caen, and British infantry had thrust out towards Troarn, clearing several fortified villages. A further Canadian attack across the Orne, west of Caen, resulted in the capture of Fleury and the clearing of the east bank of the river for some three miles due south.

A week after the British 2nd Army's offensive began the U.S. 1st Army achieved a spectacular breakthrough. The attack, which began west of St. Lô on July 25, made rapid progress, Marigny and St. Gilles, lying seven and four miles west of St. Lô respectively, being captured on the following morning. The attacking force, which included a large proportion of armour,

then fanned out into three columns, directed west, south and south-west. The first was within five miles of Coutances by the 27th, while another, after capturing Canisy (27th), swung west and reached a point ten miles north-east of Granville on the 29th. By the same date the third column was within seven miles of Villedieu. On the extreme right

flank Lessay and Périers fell on the 27th. An armoured column thrusting down the Périers–Coutances road occupied Coutances on July 28, there joining American forces advancing from the east.

Next day the sea was reached south of the Sienne estuary, and during that afternoon the tempo of the advance increased. By nightfall of the 30th American armour swept through Bréhal, and on the 31st reached and captured Avranches and Granville. Farther east United States forces captured Berigny on July 27 and straightened out the enemy salient south of the town on the 28th.

Two important attacks in the British sector (in which were the enemy's best armour and fighting troops) contributed to the success of the American operations farther west.
The first was launched on July 25 by the Canadians down the Caen–Falaise road.

British Attacks Help Americans

Although almost no ground was won owing to repeated and furious counter-attacks, the attack succeeded in containing the great bulk of the enemy armour at the vital moment of the American breakthrough. The centre of activity of the second was the area of Caumont, where British troops had secretly taken over from the Americans. A British armoured and infantry force made a major attack on the 30th, after a heavy preliminary air bombardment, and by August 1 had secured Cahagnes and Le Bény Bocage. The next two days

RUINS OF A DISPUTED MARKET TOWN

Villers Bocage, after its final capture by British troops on August 5, 1944; it had been first taken on June 13, and lost again. It lies 14 miles south-east of Bayeux and twenty miles inland. The Germans had made it a strongpoint in their defence system for the area, and the R.A.F. had been called on to help overcome resistance. Here a wrecked enemy tank lies across the roadway in a bomb- and shell-blasted street.

Photo, British Official

BATTERED CAEN AND ITS PEOPLE

1. A British sniper watching for stray Germans in the ruins of Caen after its capture on July 9, 1944: in the background the damaged tower of the church of S. Pierre. 2. The interior of the church of S. Etienne, where 1,500 people who had lost their homes in the bombardment found refuge. 3. Air view of Caen after its liberation. Though the people who remained in the capital of Calvados throughout the fighting spoke in horror of the concentrated Allied bombing, they gave the British and Canadians an enthusiastic welcome.

CAEN OFFENSIVE BEGINS

On July 18, 1944, the British 2nd Army started an offensive from Caen which carried it across the Orne into the flat plains to the south and south-east. 1. British tanks move into position in the early morning. 2. A flail-tank goes ahead. First used in the great break-through at El Alamein, described in Chapter 255, flail-tanks had in front a steel cylinder to which lengths of chain were attached and which rotated rapidly as the tank moved forward, the free ends of the chains beating the ground continuously and clearing a passage by setting off buried anti-personnel and anti-tank mines. 3. Lieut.-General Crocker, commander of the 1st Corps, watches the fighting. 4. British infantry in slit trenches on 'Hill 113,' in the Tilly-Evrecy sector, secured on the morning of July 16 after a night attack.

saw a further expansion of the initial assault towards Vire, Aunay sur Odon and Villers Bocage, and by the 4th the outskirts of all three villages had been reached. The much disputed villages of Evrecy and Esquay, south-west of Caen, were captured on August 4, ruined Villers Bocage on the 5th.

On June 25, S.H.A.E.F. announced that General Joseph Koenig, C.-in-C. of the French forces in Britain, had been vested by the French National Committee with the command of the French Forces of the Interior, acting under the direction of the Supreme Commander. In Brittany, the F.F.I. now seized high ground in advance of the thrusts by American armour and also engaged in guerilla warfare, to harass the Germans and to protect Allied lines of communication. Elsewhere in France they blew up bridges, put locomotives out of action, derailed trains, and cut the underground long-distance cable between Paris and Berlin.

F.F.I. Aid Allies

During the first days of August, the speed of the American advance into the Brittany peninsula resulted in a fluid front. One armoured column pushing southwards and westwards reached the area of Dinan on the 3rd, turned south and then altered direction towards Brest, liberating several Breton towns en route. Another column liberated Rennes, capital of Brittany, virtually intact, on the 4th and, advancing southwest, reached the river Vilaine on the 6th, thus sealing off the Brittany

ENEMY-HELD STRONGHOLD AT ST. MALO

The Fort National off St. Malo under attack from American artillery from the mainland. When the American 1st Army, with help from the F.F.I., liberated Brittany, the enemy-occupied coastal ports were left isolated. Brest held out till September 19, 1944, Lorient and St. Nazaire until the war in Europe had ended. At St. Malo, however, Colonel von Auloch surrendered on August 17. Below, Germans who surrendered at St. Malo march into captivity. *Photos, U.S. Official*

peninsula. An American column liberated Vannes (6th), and began to close in on Lorient on the 8th. Meanwhile U.S. infantry had attacked St Malo, the citadel of which did not surrender till the 17th. Other forces moved south, reaching Nantes and Angers on the 9th. Patrols crossed the Loire on the 11th.

At the eastern end of the United States sector a large area of country was cleared between Villedieu and Vire, and, while fighting was still proceeding in Mortain, advanced elements pushed on beyond Barenton. On the night of August 6–7, however, the Germans made a powerful counter-attack westward from the Mortain area, near the junction of the American and British fronts, and aimed at splitting the Allies by cutting through the bottleneck at Avranches. With the support of tank-buster aircraft, the Americans met, checked and held this attack, which was carried out by elements of four panzer divisions. Counter-attacking, they

German Counter-Attack

COMMANDER OF THE TWELFTH ARMY GROUP

Lieut.-General Omar Bradley, Commanding General of the 12th Army Group, which consisted of the U.S. 1st and 3rd Armies, with (left) Lieut.-General Courtney H. Hodges, commanding the U.S. 1st Army, and (right) Lieut.-General George S. Patton, commanding the U.S. 3rd Army. This photograph was taken in August 1944 at General Bradley's headquarters, following a conference in which General Montgomery took part. *Photo, Associated Press*

PREFABRICATED PORT OF ARROMANCHES SEEN FROM THE SHORE

Work on the prefabricated harbours designed to assist the Allied build-up in Normandy began immediately a foothold had been secured. Owing to the damage done by the mid-June gales, construction of Mulberry A was abandoned, but Mulberry B at Arromanches—"compared to which Dover seems small," said Mr. Churchill—was completed and in full use by July, 1944. A view of the harbour from the air is in page 3119.   *Photo, British Official*

prevented the enemy from disengaging while the jaws of a trap were closing between Argentan and Falaise.

The British and Canadians continued to pound steadily against the strongest defences yet encountered in northern

Strong Defences Delay British

France, and no dramatic results were achieved, but their contribution to the outcome of the first phase of the Battle of France should not be underestimated. On the night of August 6, the British left flank crossed the river Orne some 2½ miles north of Thury Harcourt. This bridge-head, which was the scene of hard fighting to retain a footing, was steadily expanded. An enemy salient between the British and Canadian forces was eliminated on the 12th. Canadian and British troops of the 1st Canadian Army (Lieut-General H. D. G. Crerar) had meanwhile attacked southwards at 11.30 p.m. on the 7th from their Caen positions. The Canadians, pushing steadily on were

within a mile of Falaise by the 15th. Progress was also made due east of Caen, in the direction of Lisieux. Other British troops fighting their way south through close and difficult country reached Flers and Condé sur Noireau.

With British and Canadians (including the 1st Polish Armoured Division: Major-General Maczek) steadily advancing from the north and Americans (including the French 2nd Armoured Division: General Jacques Phillipe Leclerc) closing in from the west and south, a large part of the German 7th Army was almost surrounded. It only remained to close the narrow Falaise–Argentan gap to cut the enemy's last escape route. This move was achieved by the Americans who, advancing from Le Mans with great weight

behind them, reached the Argentan area on August 12. It was the French armoured division, under the command of the Americans, which actually sealed the pocket when they met the Canadians at Chambois, south of Falaise, on the 19th. The enemy had been making frantic attempts to extricate his trapped forces through the narrowing gap, and the Allied air forces had taken full advantage of such a magnificent target.

Intensive fighting continued inside the pocket, and on the 20th, by sustained counter-attacks, the enemy succeeded in forcing a small break in the Allied line through which a portion of his armour escaped. But the gap was resealed. Terrible slaughter was inflicted on the enemy in and around the village of St. Lambert where, said war

Sergt.-Major HOLLIS

Company Sergeant-Major Stanley Elton Hollis, the Green Howards, awarded the V.C. for conspicuous gallantry in Normandy on June 6, 1944, when, charging a pillbox at Fleury single-handed under heavy machine-gun fire, he saved his company from heavy fire in the rear.

Captain JAMIESON

Captain David Jamieson, the Royal Norfolk Regiment, was in command of a company which established a bridge-head over the River Orne. On August 7-8, 1944, despite severe wounds, he with his company held the bridge-head against seven counter-attacks. He was awarded the V.C.

Corporal BATES

Corporal Sydney Bates of the Royal Norfolk Regiment, was awarded the V.C. posthumously for conduct at Sourdeval on August 6, 1944, when, single-handed and armed only with a light machine-gun, he checked a formation of the S.S. 10th Panzer Division. He died of his wounds.

Major CURRIE

Major David Vivian Currie, Canadian Armoured Corps, commanding a small force of Canadian tanks and infantry, captured the village of St. Lambert-sur-Dives on August 18, 1944, without artillery support and held it for three days against large-scale counter-attacks. He was awarded the V.C.

Lieut. WATKINS

Lieut. Tasker Watkins, the Welch Regiment, after all his superior officers had been killed, crossed open country under heavy fire at Bafour on August 16, 1944, wiped out two German posts with a sten gun and then led a successful bayonet charge. He received the V.C.

Photos, Canadian Official ; Fox Photos ; Lenare ; G.P.U.

correspondents, "German life had ceased with tragic and terrible suddenness." Dead choked the village street and surrounding meadows. By August 22 the disorganized remnants of Von Kluge's 7th Army had been taken prisoner and the pocket eliminated.

On August 15, it was announced that General Eisenhower had taken over

SECOND ARMY COMMANDER

Lieut.-General Sir Miles Dempsey, commander of the British 2nd Army in France, with Lieut.-General Richard Nugent O'Connor (left), commanding British tank formations in Normandy. General O'Connor, who was captured in Libya near Benghazi in April 1941, had made his escape in January 1944. *Photo, British Official*

personal command of the Allied Expeditionary Force; that General Montgomery was at the head of the 21st Army Group, consisting of the British 2nd Army (General Dempsey) and the 1st Canadian Army (General Crerar); and that Lieut.-General Omar Bradley was at the head of the 12th Army group, composed of the U.S. 1st (General Hodges) and 3rd (General Patton) Armies. General Montgomery issued his last order as C.-in-C., Allied Land Forces on August 20.

The opening battles of the new campaign in the west may be summarized thus:

First, there was the fight to protect the beach-head from fire and immediate counter-attack.

Second, the fight for the bridge-head —a long-drawn-out process of local operations to gain room for deployment and the build-up for the decisive attack and exploitation—day-to-day expenditure, of course, slowed down the build-up of reserves. This phase included the capture of the port of Cherbourg, and the securing of a starting line for the decisive attack, and it also helped to wear down enemy reserves.

Third, the opening of the main offensive to make way for a breakthrough. This began with the attack at Caen which the enemy evidently took to indicate the intention to break through there. The assault was taken up all along the line with varying weight and resulted, as had been hoped, in the Americans making an opening for an armoured break-out.

Fourth came the armoured break-out through the Avranches bottle-neck while the enemy was pinned down on the British front.

Fifth, there was the enemy's counter-attack to cut through the Avranches bottle-neck, made in inadequate strength because many of his reserves had been exhausted, could not arrive in time, or were committed to the British front.

Sixth, the enemy was deprived of the use of Brest, and the Allied right flank was protected, by the American break-out. When the Avranches counter-attack developed, the Americans swung north to trap the counter-attacking force while the British drive on the Caen front closed the trap on the other side. The enemy persisted in his counter-attack too long, and the trap closed on him.

BRITISH AND AMERICANS MEET AT ARGENTAN

Troops of the American 3rd Army, advancing from Le Mans, reached the Argentan area in great strength on August 12, 1944, but it was not till some days later that they made contact with British and Canadian troops closing in from the north on the Germans trapped in the 'Falaise Gap.' The bulk of the German 7th Army, commanded by Field-Marshal von Kluge, was destroyed in this battle. *Photo, British Newspaper Pool*

ALLIES REACH THE RIGHT SIDE OF THE CHANNEL

"The event of the year so far as the British Army is concerned is the re-entry into Europe from the West," said Sir James Grigg, Secretary of State for War, in introducing the Army estimates on March 13, 1945. The following extracts from his speech give important details concerning the build-up of the British Armies which help to explain the success of that great venture of war

FEW campaigns can ever have gone more " according to plan " than that of June, July and August, 1944. I remember being present, a month or six weeks before D Day, at a conference where the Land, Sea and Air Commanders expounded their plans, and gave out their provisional orders. . . . At the end of his exposition Field-Marshal (then General) Montgomery put on the wall a large map showing where he expected the Anglo-Canadian-American forces to be at D + 90. Somewhere about D + 80 I was visiting the General at his field H.Q. . . . The dispositions of the Allied Forces were almost exactly as they had appeared on the map I saw at the preview, but the position of the Germans was quite different. They had stood and fought on the wrong side of the Seine, a great part of them had been destroyed in consequence, and the way was open for a rapid advance beyond the Seine to the very German border. . . .

Normally it is not good policy to put a formation into the field unless there is a clear prospect of being able to provide enough reinforcements to keep it up to strength for as long as the operations are likely to last. But the campaign which was to start in the summer of 1944 held the chance of complete and final victory. . . . We therefore decided to throw everything we could into the battle. . . .

During this period of preparation we mounted and sustained offensives in North Africa and, after the destruction of the enemy there, we invaded Sicily in July of 1943 and Italy two months later. These operations provided many lessons for the new venture and many new devices were specially produced for it. And, of course, a great many old devices were developed and perfected. . . . I must mention the Bailey Bridge; the Flail tanks; the engineer assault tanks; the flame-throwing tanks which Field-Marshal Montgomery picks out as a particular success; self-propelled anti-tank guns and the special forms of anti-tank ammunition. Of the entirely new devices the most notable, perhaps, was the prefabricated harbour—the " Mulberry." . . A set of spare lock gates for the Caen canal were constructed and made ready to be floated over complete in case the Germans destroyed the existing gates. And again spare parts and assemblies for the repair of vehicles damaged in the early days were packed in special cases such that the required part could be found in the dark and issued without delay. . . . Two million 24-hour rations, specially packed in waterproof covers, were issued in the period immediately after landing, together with three million self-heating tins of soup and cocoa. Three and a half million cases of compo rations, sixty million gallons of tinned petrol and sixteen thousand tons of coal packed in five hundred thousand special rot-proof bags were got ready for early shipment. Twenty thousand feet of railway bridging and twenty-five thousand tons of steel trestling were prepared to reconstruct our supply lines as we advanced. . . . In the last 14 days alone Ordnance Depots issued one hundred and fifty thousand miles of telephone cable and eleven million yards of minefield tracing-tape. . . .

THEN began the movement to marshalling areas. The marshalling camps, which had been constructed near to all the ports of embarkation, were designed for two main purposes. First, they enabled the Movements staffs to sort out each unit into appropriate craft loads, and secondly, they served as hotels where troops arriving and departing at all hours of the day and night could be fed, bathed, accommodated and supplied with all their last-minute needs. It was in these camps, too, that the final stages of the waterproofing of vehicles were carried out. In all one hundred and fifty thousand were waterproofed, and despite the fact that many of them went ashore through five feet of water in heavy seas, less than two in every thousand were drowned off the beaches. . . .

By D–8 the loading of stores into coasters had been completed and the berths were clear for the loading of the assault

vessels. The road convoys moved down the last few miles from marshalling areas to ports, and the craft were loaded in the order planned long beforehand to ensure that what was first needed on the other side would be first off. . . .

The Supreme Commander, General Eisenhower, directed that the assault should begin on June 6. . . . He vested the command of all the ground forces engaged, of whatever nationality, in General Montgomery. This was to continue until the number of U.S. troops engaged warranted their separate control by a U.S. Army Group Commander. The assault began, therefore, under General Montgomery's direction in the early hours of June 6. . . . By June 10 the Allied Armies had won a continuous front along a narrow strip of the Normandy coast. . . . Generals Dempsey and Montgomery had already set up their Advanced H.Qs. ashore.

DURING this critical phase when we had no ports, our chief concern was to win what the Americans call the logistic battle. . . . The enemy's build-up was reduced because he couldn't make up his mind what was coming next and also because of the success of the R.A.F. policy of interdiction. Our own build-up was successful because of our months and years of careful preparation. . . . In the first fourteen days three hundred and ninety thousand men, seventy thousand vehicles and two hundred and thirty thousand tons of stores were landed for the British and Canadian forces alone, and the figures for the U.S. forces were of the same order. The gales which raged round about June 18 delayed the build-up and damaged the two Mulberries, one of them so badly that it was abandoned ; but though it delayed it never interrupted and in the end the logistic battle was won. . . .

Argentan was captured on August 13, the Canadians took Falaise on the 17th and to all intents and purposes the German 7th Army was hopelessly trapped. The time had now come for the U.S. troops to pass from General Montgomery's command, and he issued his last directive as Commander of all the Allied land forces on August 20. . . .

[Sir James Grigg then described the campaign which in eight months took the Allies " from the wrong side of the Channel to the Rhine and beyond."]

Let me say a little about tanks. . . . First as regards guns. The Royal Tiger, alone of the enemy's tanks, mounts a gun —a hotted up 88-mm., firing a 22½-lb. shot, with a muzzle velocity of 3,340 feet per second—which has a penetrative performance superior to that of our 17-pounder firing conventional shot. The standard 88-mm. mounted in the ordinary Tiger and the 75-mm. mounted in the Panther are both inferior weapons. But the 17-pounder firing the latest type of ammunition surpasses the performance of any German gun yet encountered or, so far as I know, in contemplation. Moreover, we have in action at least five tanks mounting a 17-pounder for every Royal Tiger the Germans have on the Western Front.

Then as to armour—it is true that the frontal thickness of the Tigers and indeed of the Panther makes them all three formidable defensive weapons. But we aren't any longer fighting a defensive war. . . . Field-Marshal Montgomery himself . . . thinks that British armour has come through the campaign in Western Europe with flying colours, and has proved itself superior in battle to German armour. He holds that if Rundstedt had been equipped with British armour when he attacked in the Ardennes on December 16, he would have reached the Meuse in 36 hours, which would have placed the Allies in a very awkward situation. And further that if the 21st Army Group had been equipped with German armour it could not have crossed the Seine on August 28, and reached Brussels on September 3 and Antwerp on September 4, thus cutting off the whole Pas de Calais area in eight days : which the Field-Marshal holds to be a very remarkable achievement with far-reaching results. . . .

'THIS SWELLING CRESCENDO OF DESTRUCTION'

"The story of the air war in the past year is largely the story of the Royal Air Force and the United States Army Air Force working in the closest partnership and harmony for the destruction of the common enemy," began Sir Archibald Sinclair, Secretary of State for Air, in introducing the Air estimates on March 6, 1945. Outstanding points in the story as he told it are recorded below

DDAY for the British and American armies of liberation was June 6 last year, but for the Royal Air Force the campaign had started long before. The weight of our invasion of Northern Europe would have been much reduced if the U-boats had been sinking even a fraction of the number of Allied ships which they were sinking in every month of the year 1943. Gradually, however, the squadrons of Coastal Command, . . . working in closest co-operation with the escort groups of the Royal Navy, had obtained an increasing mastery of the German submarines. Bomber Command, too, had contributed largely to this result by bombing the U-boats in their assembly yards and in their pens, and by their arduous, difficult and extremely successful mining operations.

The Germans had boasted that, thanks to the U-boat, no Allied soldier would set foot on the Continent of Europe. Coastal Command and the Royal Navy answered this boast with deeds. Together they swept the seas and kept open those channel lanes on which depended the security of our convoys and the nourishment of our armies.

In the opening stages of this great battle the burden of the fighting lay principally on Coastal Command. In the three weeks before D Day Admiral Doenitz was endeavouring to move up his reserves of U-boats from their bases in Norway to the threatened area of the Channel Coast. From Norway these U-boats began to slink out on their long trek through Northern and Atlantic waters to the Channel. The Commander-in-Chief, Coastal Command—Sir Sholto Douglas—had anticipated every move they made. Knowing what they had to expect the German Command had given their crews a concentrated course of training against air attack. In particular they were equipped with a new 37-mm. anti-aircraft gun. Their foresight was wise but unavailing, for these reinforcements were attacked and mauled by aircraft of Coastal Command. In the continuous daylight of the Northern summer, the battle was joined off the coasts of Norway, the Shetlands and the Faroes and even in the Arctic when the U-boats sought to escape the range of our aircraft. Many were sunk and damaged.

This was the opening bout. The main campaign, fought in the English Channel and its Western approaches, began on D Day. Previous to that date, single U-boats had penetrated into coastal waters with the aid of Schnorkels. When the invasion came, the Biscay U-boat fleet made their way to the Western approaches of the Channel on the surface. They were instantly engaged by Coastal Command, and U-boat prisoners have frankly admitted that entering the Channel was a nightmare. During the first four critical days from D Day, the Command made 38 sightings, which resulted in several destructive attacks. . . .

THESE successes of Coastal Command, won in unison with the Royal Navy, were decisive ; a blow was inflicted on the enemy from which he never recovered. . . .

The work of Bomber Command under Sir Arthur Harris and of the United States Strategic air forces under General Spaatz, in preparation for the launching of our armies, had been continuous over a period of years. All through 1943 and 1944 the great battles of the Ruhr, of Hamburg and Berlin, were steadily undermining the war power of Germany.

We had become aware that the Germans were making a tremendous effort to build up the biggest fighter force that the world had ever seen. . . . The British and American bomber forces, therefore, in the winter of 1943 and spring of last year turned their main effort against the German fighter factories and ancillary production. . . .

General Arnold, Commanding General of the United States Army Air Force, in his annual report to Congress says : " The week of February 20–26, 1944, may well be classed by future historians as marking a decisive battle in history— one as decisive and of greater world importance than Gettysburg." That great series of attacks against the German

aircraft production laid the foundation of the air mastery which the Allies enjoyed on D Day and now enjoy over Germany and the battlefields of Europe.

In the late spring, the destruction of German communications behind the intended invasion front took first place among our bombing objectives. . . . It was not a task upon which the Allied Air Forces entered lightheartedly, for it involved the destruction of railway facilities, some of which were in thickly populated areas of France. . . . Marshalling yards and railway repair facilities were destroyed on a great scale. 24 road and railway bridges over the Seine were selected for bombing ; by D Day all 24 had been either demolished or severely damaged. The result was to destroy one of the main assumptions on which the enemy's plan of defence was based. He had naturally assumed that he could reinforce his defensive front by road and rail more quickly than we could reinforce by sea. As things turned out, the weather favoured this calculation and for three critical days it was impossible to land troops or supplies over the beaches. Nevertheless, so thoroughly had the Allied Air Forces done their work and so complete was the mastery of the British and American Tactical Air Forces over the French roads and railways by day, that the Allied armies were able to reinforce much more rapidly than the Germans. . . .

TWO activities of Bomber Command call, I think the House will agree, for special attention on this occasion. The " Tirpitz " . . . was sunk by two squadrons of Bomber Command under Wing Commander Tait. They flew 1,200 miles to bomb from some 15,000 feet and scored 3 direct hits and two near misses. . . . I think Hon. Members will be gratified to reflect that this brilliant feat of arms was accomplished by British crews aiming, with a British bombsight of extraordinary complexity, ingenuity and accuracy a 12,000-lb. bomb of British design and manufacture from a British Lancaster—the only aircraft in the world to-day which could carry that bomb. . . .

When the peoples of Europe awoke from the nightmare of 1940, they found themselves powerless against the mechanized might of Nazi Germany. To the Royal Air Force fell the task of supplying arms to the resurgent peoples of Europe. . . . The task was exacting. Every crew was a pathfinder. They were searching, not for towns or marshalling yards, but for fields and points in the open country—often miles from roads and other landmarks. This entailed extremely low flying, with the aircraft—especially if it was a light night— an easy target for even the lightest flak. In difficult country the navigation risks were almost as formidable as the risks from the enemy. Frequently pilots had to land their aircraft in occupied territory to bring out leading members of the Underground movement. . . . Aircraft operating from this country dropped more than 160,000 parachute containers of arms and explosives, and 37,000 packages of specialized equipment. At least 15,000 tons of supplies were dropped from Great Britain alone. . . .

For four years the Allied Air Force was the only force from the West carrying the war to Germany. From Dunkirk to D Day they harried and pounded German war industry and transport. Had not the Luftwaffe been out-fought in the air, hammered on its airfields and smashed in its factories, there could have been no invasion of Normandy. . . .

Allied air bombing is on such a colossal scale that Dr. Goebbels has had to admit that " it can now hardly be borne." In the week ending February 12, 16,000 tons of bombs were dropped by the Allied Air Forces. This rose to 23,000 tons the next week, to 41,000 the week after that and in the following week 32,000 tons with some returns outstanding. This swelling crescendo of destruction is engulfing oil plants, tank factories and the communications of the German armies on every front, as from West, East and South the Allied Armies surge forward into Germany.

Chapter 315

AIR WAR IN THE WEST DURING 1944

Something of the work of the Allied Air Forces in connexion with the re-opening of the Western Front in Europe is told in Chapter 307. Here Captain Norman Macmillan, M.C., A.F.C., gives an account of other air activities of the Allies in Western Europe, the Mediterranean, and the Atlantic during 1944. He described the mounting air assault on German industry in Chapter 296

THE air war in 1944 is cleft by the date line June 6, the day of the invasion of Normandy. Preparation for that event brought changes in air appointments at the beginning of the year. On December 29, 1943, Air Chief Marshal Sir Trafford Leigh-Mallory, A.O.C.-in-C. Fighter Command, became Allied Air C.-in-C. under General Eisenhower. The R.A.F. created a 2nd Tactical Air Force to operate with the invasion forces, and the appointment of Air Marshal Sir Arthur Coningham to command it was announced on January 25, 1944. The arrival in England of Air Chief Marshal Sir Arthur Tedder from the Mediterranean to assume his duties as Deputy Supreme Commander to General Eisenhower was announced on January 16 (*see* plate facing page 3103).

Fighter Command was the pool which had to meet the demands of the new

Air Defence of Great Britain

organization, and at the beginning of March Fighter Command was replaced by a new Command called Air Defence of Great Britain (*see* page 3102), a name which

existed in the organization of the R.A.F. prior to June 1936.

Month after month Bomber Command broke its own records. In March 1944 its strategic night bombers delivered

R.A.F. BOMB TONNAGE ON GERMANY				
1944	Total Tonnage Dropped	Tonnage on Germany	Ratio of Tonnage Dropped by	
			Night	Day
July.. ..	57,500	13,000	5	1
August ..	65,000	14,000	5	8
September ..	52,400	21,000	2	5
October ..	60,000	50,000	10	7
November ..	53,160	53,000	2	1
December ..	48,600	48,600	5	2

the record tonnage of 20,000 tons on Germany and 8,000 tons elsewhere. On March 15 the night force sent out included more than 1,000 heavy four-engined bombers for the first time, and 3,000 tons were dropped on Stuttgart and subsidiary targets. In April—a month notable for strategic attacks against communications in Western Europe—Bomber Command dropped 33,000 tons, and the record for one night soared to over 4,500 tons. Among the month's targets were railways at Ville-

neuve St. Georges and Chambly (near Paris), Lille, Ghent, Tours, Tergnier, Aulnoye, Laon, Ottignies, Lens, La Chapelle, Vilvorde (near Brussels), Montzen, Achères and Somain; more than 1,000 bombers took part in many attacks. In May the Command dropped 37,000 tons and again railway targets in France, Belgium and Germany were the principal objectives. In June the bomb tonnage rose to 56,000.

The changed situation following the Allied invasion of France made it possible for Bomber Command formations, if necessary, to be escorted by fighters when they intervened by day in the battle areas in Europe. In the autumn of 1944 this great strategic night force was to a very considerable extent being used for day bombing in support of the Army of Liberation. This change in the Command's work, and, as the Army advanced, the rise in the tonnage it dropped on targets within Germany, are shown in the accompanying table.

Flight-Lieutenant HORNELL

Squadron-Leader BAZALGETTE

Squadron-Leader PALMER

Flying-Officer CRUICKSHANK

Flight-Lieutenant David Ernest Hornell, Royal Canadian Air Force, was awarded the V.C. for his action while pilot and captain of a Catalina on anti-U-boat patrol in Northern waters. His aircraft badly damaged and ablaze, he pressed home the attack and sank the U-boat. His crew were picked up 21 hours later from their dinghy ; two were already dead of exhaustion ; Flight-Lieut. Hornell himself died soon after.

Acting Squadron-Leader Ian Willoughby Bazalgette, D.F.C., R.A.F.V.R., master bomber of a Pathfinder squadron, carried out his mission in France on August 4, 1944, although his Lancaster was ablaze. He brought his aircraft down, thus saving two wounded members of the crew who could not use their parachutes. Killed when the machine later exploded, he was awarded the V.C.

Squadron-Leader Robert Anthony Maurice Palmer, D.F.C. and Bar, R.A.F., was awarded the V.C. for conspicious gallantry in an attack on Cologne on December 23, 1944 when, with his aircraft on fire and in imminent danger of blowing up with its bomb load, he pressed home the attack, dropping his bombs on the marshalling yards with devastating effect. His bomber was last seen going down in flames.

Flying-Officer John Alexander Cruickshank, R.A.F.V.R., received the V.C. for gallantry while on anti-U-boat patrol as captain and pilot of a Catalina in Northern waters. Sighting a surfaced U-boat, he attacked. The depth-charges failed to drop. His navigator-bomber was killed, two others of the crew were wounded, and he himself was wounded 72 times, but he attacked again and sank the U-boat.

Photos, British Official ; Elliott & Fry ; Keystone

R.A.F. GLIDERS LINE UP TO TAKE OFF FOR FRANCE

Part of the immense armada of aircraft which crossed to France in the hours preceding the land-fall of the invading armies on June 6, 1944. Below, camouflaged airborne troops aboard one of the gliders of an aerial train extending for 200 miles which dropped glider-borne and parachute troops to key points behind the enemy's coastal positions. *Photo, British Official*

As the ring tightened about Central Europe, the weight that fell upon German soil rose until it reached a hundred per cent of Bomber Command's tonnage. Duisburg got more than 10,000 tons in less than 18 hours on October 14 and 15. The Command's total tonnage for the year was 525,518 tons (plus 13,170 tons of sea-mines), more than twice the weight dropped from September 1939 to December 1943.

During 1944 the activities of the U.S.A. 8th, 9th, 12th and 15th Air Forces steadily increased, the 8th and 9th operating from the United Kingdom until the latter, a tactical force (like the 12th in Italy), moved to the Continent,

MAJOR-GENERAL R. N. GALE

Maj.-Gen. Richard Nelson Gale commanded the British 6th Airborne Division on June 6, 1944. In January 1945 he became Deputy Commander to Lieut.-General Lewis H. Brereton, commanding the Allied 1st Airborne Army set up in August 1944.

where each of the U.S. armies had its own Tactical Air Force in support of operations. The bombing distribution for the 400,000 (long) tons of bombs dropped by the 8th Air Force in 1944 was : Allied Army support, 32 per cent ; German aircraft industry, 29 per cent ; German oil industry, 13 per cent ; flying-bomb launching-sites and depots, 7 per cent ; tanks, ordnance and motor vehicle plants, 5 per cent ; shipyards and port installations, 1 per cent ; other miscellaneous targets, 13 per cent. The 8th Air Force had both bombers and fighters, and 6,129 German aircraft were

shot down and 1,044 more destroyed on the ground by the guns of its fighters and bombers ; the force lost 2,632 bombers and 1,446 fighters ; it destroyed 6,675 railway wagons 4,014 motor transport vehicles, 128 armoured vehicles, 41 tanks and 67 ammunition and fuel dumps, disabled 3,300 locomotives, and damaged many more. Both Bomber Command and the 8th Air Force dropped thousands of tons of weapons and supplies to the French Maquis and the Polish patriots in Warsaw.

The pounding of the aircraft factories in France, Germany, Czechoslovakia

ALLIED FIGHTERS OPERATE FROM AIRSTRIPS IN FRANCE

Airfield construction units and Servicing Commandos accompanied the assault troops on June 6, 1944, and moved inland with bulldozers to sites previously selected by photography.   By June 10, Spitfires were taking off and Dakota transports of the U.S.A. 9th A.F. were evacuating casualties from portable airstrips, the first Allied fighters to operate from French bases since 1940 being a Spitfire wing led by Wing-Commander Johnson, a Battle of Britain veteran. Here U.S. Thunderbolts are being serviced at one of these improvised airstrips.   *Photo, Keystone*

and Austria ; and of the oil installations in Germany, Austria, Hungary and Rumania by the three great Bomber Forces of Britain and America operating from Great Britain and Italy broke the power of the Luftwaffe to put aircraft into the air and find fuel for those that were left to fly ; and with the smashing of the rail communications, held up the precious oil that the Wehrmacht needed for its surface vehicles and tanks. (For the work and effects of the "Transportation Plan" air attacks, *see* page 3103.)

German radar stations along the French coast were smashed from the air (*see* page 3104) to prevent detection of the assault forces ; and from 11 p.m. on June 5 until sunrise on June 6, Bomber Command made ten attacks each with 100 or more heavy bombers against 40 German coastal heavy guns, bombing from 20,000 feet through tentenths cloud by Pathfinder radar control from home ground stations with the "Oboe" type radar instrument in the aircraft.   These bombers dropped over

5,000 tons and so damaged the guns and emplacements, or threw up such large mounds of earth in front of them as to render them useless for action against the great convoys that soon swarmed the seas off the coast of Normandy, and not a shot was fired by them on D day.

Over the invasion force more than 11,000 Allied aircraft operated under Leigh-Mallory. Before dawn the British 6th Airborne Division (commanded by Major-General R. N. Gale, D.S.O., O.B.E., M.C.), and the U.S. 82nd and 101st Airborne Divisions, the largest airborne force ever employed in war until that date, were placed behind the German coastal defences by parachute and glider (*see* Chapter 311). The Hamilcar glider, able to carry a light tank of about eight tons, or any other equivalent load, went into action for the first time (*see* illus., page 3101). The other firstline gliders were the Horsa, a three-ton transport, and the American Waco (CG4A), a two-tonner.

Once the invasion had begun the

Loire bridges were quickly bombed down to isolate the battlefield, and heavy bombers were used in close support of operations.

In the afternoon of June 30, 250 Lancasters with fighter escort went to the support of the British 2nd Army whose bridge-head across the river Odon was being **Bomber** fiercely counter- **Support for** attacked (*see* Chapter **Ground Forces** 314), and in fifteen minutes dropped more than 1,000 tons of bombs on Villers Bocage and a small wood sheltering enemy tanks. Preceding British ground attacks, on July 7 at dusk, 450 Lancasters and Halifaxes poured 2,300 tons of bombs on German troops, tanks, guns, defence posts, obliterating strong-points in the north-west outskirts of Caen where resistance had been powerful ; on July 18, Allied bombers flying east of Caen dropped between 7,000 and 8,000 tons of bombs in an area of little more than 70 square miles ; and of over 2,000 bombers engaged only nine were lost ; on July 30 another concentrated load fell on the triangle Villers Bocage—Caumont—Jurques.

Meanwhile, the Mediterranean Allied Air Force directed a great strategic air assault against key points in southern

France and the Rhône valley. Then, throughout the night of August 14–15, a concentrated air barrage descended on the German-defended Riviera coast —gun positions, troops, strong points, supply dumps, beach obstacles, inland airfields and communications. Some 200 naval aircraft from an Escort Carrier Support Force gave close support to the Allied landings (*see* Chapter 320), operating continuously for ten days with surprisingly few accidents from deck landings. The Riviera invasion began with the descent of waves of parachute troops (with sometimes more than 1,000 in the air simultaneously), followed by glider-borne troops with jeeps and 75-millimetre howitzers, and then the main seaborne assault force. Air mastery was quickly secured over an area stretching from the beach-head to 50 miles inland.

The tactical aircraft of the Allied Expeditionary Air Force drove the Luftwaffe steadily back from its forward airfields by constant attacks with rocket projectiles, bombs, cannon and machine-guns. Enemy ground forces

were battered northwards out of France through Belgium until the British 2nd Army stood on the line of the Albert and Scheldt canals. There the nature of the countryside, with its innumerable waterways, delayed the advance, and a great airborne operation was planned to force a corridor northwards along the route Eindhoven — Veghel — Grave — Nijmegen—Arnhem and seize the strategic bridges—the Grave bridge over the Maas, the Maas-Wahl Canal bridge, the Waal bridge at Nijmegen, and the Arnhem bridge over the Lower Rhine (Lek).

After enemy airfields had been cratered by bombs, the first landings were made on the afternoon of September 17. Over 1,000 troop-carrying or glider-towing aircraft—twin-engined Dakotas and four-engined Stirlings—took part. The U.S. 101st Airborne Division landed from Eindhoven northwards almost to

Grave ; the U.S. 82nd Airborne Division near Nijmegen ; and the British 1st Airborne Division at Arnhem. The operation was commanded by Lieut.-General F. A. M. Browning, Deputy Commander of the Allied 1st Airborne Army, and his Corps H.Q. landed with the 82nd Division in the Nijmegen area.

The second lifts of all divisions landed late on the second day, on account of bad weather in England, and troop-carrier aircraft flew through heavy flak, but at Nijmegen the second lift of 400 gliders landed within a few hundred yards of the ground fighting.

The 101st Division completed its task in two days, and the Guards Armoured Division linked up with the 82nd Airborne. On the third day, no lift could fly in, but a few supplies were dropped. Bad weather in the west next day again prevented Allied air operations, but the

CONCENTRATED R.A.F. ATTACK ON ENEMY ARMOUR

On June 30, 1944, 250 Lancasters of R.A.F. Bomber Command, supporting the 2nd Army, attacked the 2nd and 9th S.S. Panzer Divisions as they moved up through the village of Villers Bocage (14 miles south-east of Caen) to the fighting zone farther north. They dropped over 1,000 tons in fifteen minutes ; only two houses in the village remained standing. Here a few of the Lancasters are passing over the target area, which is invisible through the smoke of concentrated bomb bursts.
Photo, British Official

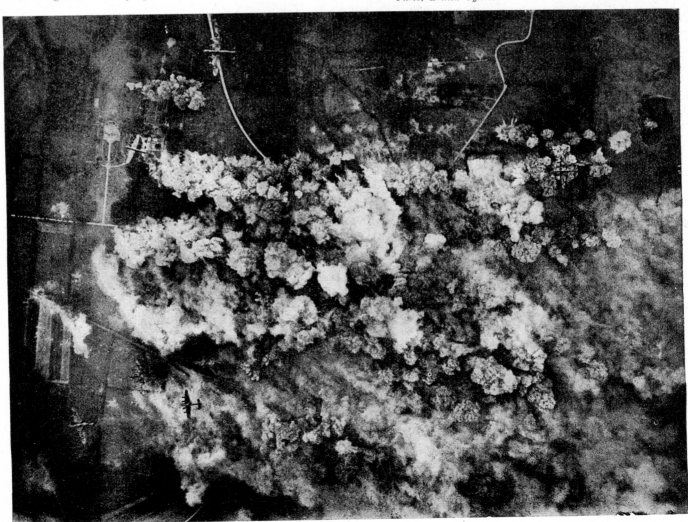

Luftwaffe appeared in strength for the first time for several months. On the fifth day part of the Polish Parachute Brigade flew through the bad weather and dropped to join the forces that had pushed through the corridor to the south bank of the Lower Rhine. On the sixth day weather caused failure in the air supply to the 1st Airborne Division, now within a constricted perimeter, and no reinforcements reached the 1st and 82nd Divisions, the latter also isolated through the cutting of the corridor farther south by the enemy.

On the seventh day no airborne operations save a partial re-supply of the 1st Division were possible. In the succeeding night part of the Polish Brigade got across the river and next day joined the 1st Division. Heavy fighting continued in the Arnhem and Nijmegen areas, and early on the ninth day it was decided to withdraw the 1st Division. After fighting their way to the river, the survivors withdrew that night in boats ferried across by the 43rd (surface) Division.

This airborne operation advanced the ground forces nearly 60 miles through most difficult country, and placed British and Canadian forces in positions whence, in February 1945, they initiated the western sector of the Battle of Germany. General Dempsey, commanding the forces fighting in the Nijmegen salient, said that the action of the 1st Airborne Army saved him at least 25,000 casualties.

Antwerp, captured intact on September 4, and much needed as a port for Allied supplies, was covered by the German-held Dutch islands of the Scheldt estuary. Bomber Command was again called in to aid the surface forces. In a daylight attack on October 3 the sea dyke, Westkapelle, Walcheren, was burst by 12,000-lb. bombs at high tide, and in succeeding attacks the German gun positions covering the estuary were smashed and flooded, although the final capture of Walcheren involved Canadians and British in heavy fighting.

On November 16, Bomber Command gave its first support to American ground forces, 1,150 R.A.F. bombers dropping more than 5,600 tons in an obliteration attack on Dueren, Juelich and Heinsberg—fully effective to the writer's knowledge at least so far as Heinsberg was concerned. On the same day, 1,200 U.S.A. 8th A.F. bombers dropped some 4,000 tons north of Eschweiler.

U.S. heavy bombers did not carry a heavier bomb than 2,000-lb. Bomber Command's 12,000-lb. one-piece, streamlined, 22-foot long bomb, nicknamed the "Tallboy," was a terrible weapon (*see* illus. page 2969):

Bomber Command's 'Tallboy'

when Brest was captured (September 19), the German-vaunted bomb-proof U-boat pens were found cracked or burst wide open by these missiles dropped on them on August 12. They broke the Kembs dam, 10 miles south-east of Mulhouse, on October 7, though the Sorpe dam in the Ruhr, attacked on October 15, resisted them as it had resisted the attack of May 17, 1943 (*see* page 2660). With them 29 Lancasters sank the battleship "Tirpitz" in Tromsö Fjord on November 12 (*see* page 2969 and illus., page 3070).

Both Bomber Command and the Tactical Air Force made spectacular pin-point attacks, apart from their continuous routine strategic and tactical work. On February 18, R.A.F. Mosquitoes under the command of Group Captain P. C. Pickard, D.S.O., D.F.C., attacked Amiens prison, where 100 French prisoners lay under sentence of death for aiding the Allies. The first wave of six planes breached the 20-foot high,

EFFECT OF A R.A.F. 'TALLBOY' ON A U-BOAT PEN AT BREST
Built of thick concrete reinforced with steel girders, the U-boat pens at Brest were considered bomb-proof until on August 12, 1944, escorted R.A.F. Lancasters dropped 12,000-lb. 'Tallboy' bombs on them in a daylight attack. After the fall of Brest on September 19, it was found that the roofs of three of the pens had been penetrated. Damage done to one of them is shown here.
Photo, British Official

ALLIED AIR FORCES IN THE INVASION OF THE SOUTH OF FRANCE

R.A.F. mechanics servicing a Spitfire at a landing strip newly constructed in the south of France following the Allied invasion between Nice and Marseilles on August 15, 1944. Below, part of Operation 'Uppercut'—the landing of parachute troops in southern France on August 15 by the U.S.A 12th A.F. Troop Carrier Air Division. Large numbers of British and U.S. parachute and glider-borne men were dropped behind the landing beaches.

ALLIED AIRBORNE TROOPS IN HOLLAND

Photographers of the Army Film and Photographic Unit accompanied the men of the Allied 1st Airborne Army who were dropped in the Nijmegen-Eindhoven-Arnhem area on September 17, 1944. Here airborne troops are unpacking supplies which have been dropped to them by parachute. Left, Lieut.-General Frederick Browning, Deputy Commander of the 1st Airborne Army, who was made K.C.B. in December 1944 for the part he took in these operations.

recht and caused the German Army's biggest funeral—one Field Marshal, two full Generals, 47 Staff Officers and 172 Other Ranks. Roermond bridge was one of many successfully attacked.

On December 16, when Von Rundstedt launched his counter-offensive in the Ardennes, over 500 Luftwaffe aircraft were sighted during the day. Next day 1,000 enemy aircraft were estimated to be covering the Aachen area. 2nd T.A.F. and the U.S. 9th T.A.F. (under Major-General Elwood R. Quesada, supporting the U.S. 1st Army) laid strips of anti-personnel fragmentation bombs among enemy troops. From the U.K., Bomber Command and the 8th A.F. attacked railways and communications, isolating the German battle area from its supply zones. On December 24 and 25 Allied sorties exceeded 10,000 against the enemy's 1,000. When captured in May 1945, Rundstedt said the cutting of his communications from the air made his offensive unworkable, and proved the major factor in his failure to achieve his object of placing the German defence line back on the river Meuse to protect the Ruhr industries. But even a defence

Allied Air Forces Against Rundstedt

3-foot thick wall, the second destroyed both ends of the gaol and the German guards' quarters. The crew of one Mosquito, filming the action, saw the prisoners running out into the surrounding fields. Group Captain Pickard was killed in the attack. On April 4, Mosquitoes of No. 2 Group led by Wing Commander R. N. Bateson, D.S.O., D.F.C., made an attack at 50 feet on a single five-storey house in The Hague, completely destroying the building, which contained lists of the Dutch population, without touching the houses on either side except for slight roof damage. A third pin-point attack of a similar kind occurred on October 31, when 24 Mosquitoes in four waves wrecked two buildings of the University of Aarhus used as Gestapo H.Q. in Denmark, and containing thousands of documents relating to the Danish population and resistance. Stockholm reported that about 100 Germans, including the Gestapo Chief for Jutland, were killed.

When 60 Mitchell and Boston bombers of No. 2 Group attacked motor transport waiting to cross the Seine at Rouen by ferry in the last days of August, 1,800 vehicles were destroyed and 6,000 Germans were later buried:

the bombers were in the air and but two minutes from a previously allotted target when they were diverted to the quayside at Rouen. On October 15 six squadrons of No. 84 Group attacked the German 15th Army H.Q. at Dord-

FRENCH PATRIOTS FREED FROM AMIENS PRISON

On February 18, 1944, a Mosquito wing of the 2nd Tactical Air Force carried out an attack on Amiens Prison, France, which enabled some hundred French patriots, imprisoned for helping Allied airmen and others, to escape. The attack was made from little more than roof-top level. The plane carrying Group Captain P. C. Pickard, D.S.O., D.F.C. (right), leader of the attack, and his navigator Flight-Lieutenant S. A. Broadley, D.S.O., was shot down.

PIONEERS CLEARING CAEN PAUSE FOR REFRESHMENT

The destruction wrought in Caen by war and by deliberate German savagery was immense—the whole centre of the town, with shops and industrial buildings, was demolished (see illus. page 3181) ; the churches of S. Pierre, S. Jean and S. Sauveur, the university and part of the castle built on the hill by William the Conqueror perished ; and for nearly five weeks before liberation on July 9, 1944, Caen had been without electricity, gas and water except that drawn from a few wells.   Here men of the Pioneer Corps are having a brief respite while engaged on repair work.

'MULBERRY' PORTS OFF THE FRENCH COAST: FAILURE AND SUCCESS

Two prefabricated ports were planned and prepared in Britain and towed in sections across the Channel as part of the operations immediately following the invasion of June 6, 1944. Parts of 'Mulberry A,' intended for the American sector, were lost at sea, and, as can be seen here, the floating pierways jutting into the Channel from 'Omaha Beach' (see illus. in page 3145) were damaged and twisted beyond repair by the great storm of June 19—the worst the Channel had known in June for forty years. Below, loading and unloading proceeding smoothly at 'Mulberry B' off Arromanches in the British sector ; it successfully rode out the storm that wrecked 'Mulberry A.'

Photos, British Official : U.S. Signal Corps

FALAISE—'HINGE' OF GERMAN DEFENCE IN NORMANDY—AFTER ITS CAPTURE

With the taking of the ancient town of Falaise on August 17, 1944, the Canadians smashed the German 'hinge' position in the first great battle of the new western front. In an order of the day for August 18, Lieut.-General H. D. G. Crerar said, 'The capture of Falaise marks a great historic step forward to final victory.' The town was in ruins, but immediately it was cleared of the enemy the inhabitants began to return (above). The beautiful 11th-century church of St. Gervais had been reduced to a shattered skeleton (below). *Photos, British Newspaper Pool*

Photo, U.S. Signal Corps

AMERICANS ADVANCE NEAR ARGENTAN

Heavy fighting in Argentan was already in progress by August 15, 1944, the Americans holding part of the town and the Germans struggling desperately to prevent their advance to link with the Canadians near Falaise. It finally fell to British troops on August 20. The battle for Argentan was one of the great deeds 'well and truly done by the whole Allied team,' to quote General Montgomery's special message of August 21, in the decisive ten-day battle of the Falaise Gap. Here American infantry patrols are advancing cautiously in the neighbourhood of Argentan.

R.A.F. ATTACK ON GERMAN TRANSPORT AT ROUEN

Rouen was liberated by the 1st Canadian Army on August 30, 1944. Some 35,000 Germans in what Lieut.-General H. D. G. Crerar described as 'frantic' retreat attempted to cross the river Seine in and near the city under incessant air and artillery bombardment. Here are the tangled remains of some of the 1,800 vehicles destroyed in the last days of August by 60 Mitchell and Boston bombers in one raid alone

line on the Meuse would scarcely have protected the Ruhr when Allied aircraft were battering it to pieces and the Germans had scarcely any defence against the overhead attack.

On January 8, 1944, Air Marshal Sir John Slessor was appointed Deputy to Lieutenant-General Ira C. Eaker, C.-in-C. Mediterranean **Mediterranean** Allied Air Force, and **Appointments** commander of all R.A.F. units in the Mediterranean. On January 12, Air Marshal Sir Keith Park succeeded Air Chief Marshal Sir Sholto Douglas as A.O.C.-in-C. Middle East when the latter took over Coastal Command.

More than 5,000 tons of bombs were dropped on airfields near Rome in the week before the Allied landings at Anzio on January 22 (*see* page 3047). Severe air action over the beach-head, and numerous air battles waged above the surface forces, followed.

Italian railway communications, strategically vulnerable to air attack, were constantly cut and disorganized; docks and railway yards of value to enemy communications were bombed in Italy, France and the Balkans. Islands held by the enemy, factories and oil plants,

airfields, gun positions, and troops were attacked. Monte Cassino monastery and the town of Cassino were violently bombed (*see* Chapter 302).

Throughout the year air attacks were made from Italy and the Middle East against targets in France, Czechoslovakia, Poland, Germany, Austria, Hungary, Yugoslavia, Rumania, Bulgaria and Greece; some were co-ordinated with operations of the 8th A.F. Athens (airfields), Avignon, Brno, Budapest, Chambéry, Friedrichshafen, Genoa, Grenoble, Innsbruck, Lyons, Marseilles, Munich, Nice, Nîmes, Nish, Ploesti, Regensburg (Ratisbon), Rome (railyards and airfields), Steyr, Toulon, Trieste, Ulm, Vienna, Wiener Neustadt, Zagreb and many other places came to know the bombers of the Mediterranean air forces. The U.S.A. 15th A.F. played a major part in the destruction of German oil reserves and in smashing her aircraft industry. Backed by the Allied air forces the Allied armies under General Sir Harold Alexander entered

Rome on June 4. By the end of the year they were far to the north of Rome, with their tactical aircraft smashing at the railway lines emerging from Alpine tunnels through which Kesselring's supplies had then to pass.

On October 13 British airborne troops landed in gliders on Mogara airfield 28 miles west of Athens, cleared landmines, and made landing strips for transport and combat aircraft. In a politically troubled Greece, the R.A.F. on December 10 bombed an E.L.A.S. column approaching Athens.

Three main organizations in the U.K. were concerned in the 1944 Atlantic air operations: Coastal Command, the Fleet Air Arm, and Transport Command. From bases in England, Scotland, Wales, Northern Ireland, the Orkney and Shetland Islands, the Azores, and (after the invasion of France) from the French coast, flying boats and landplanes of Coastal Command patrolled the ocean seaways, while Mosquitoes fought German aircraft over the Bay of Biscay and Spitfires gave ships protection in coastal waters. From Iceland, Newfoundland, Labrador, and the U.S.A. coast R.C.A.F. and U.S.N.A.C. patrols maintained watch over the western area of the North Atlantic. From the West Indies, British and U.S.; from the coast of Brazil, Brazilian; from the West Coast of Africa, Coastal Command; and from South Africa, S.A.A.F. aircraft maintained constant vigil to defeat the U-boat threat to Allied seaborne communication lines, radar detection equipment playing a great and growing part in their success.

Fleet Aircraft Carriers and Escort Carriers accompanied convoys crossing the ocean to the Mediterranean, Britain, Russia, Africa and India. Merchant Aircraft Carriers escorted convoys only to British ports, themselves laden with oil or grain. Some M.A.C.s ferried aircraft on their decks, mostly fighters for the U.S. air commands in Britain. (*See* illus., page 3043.)

In Air Sea Rescue the year's greatest development was the improvement of the airborne lifeboat—first carried by Hudsons and later by Warwicks—a life-saving development which began in Britain.

Up to November 1944 25,000 aircraft had flown the Atlantic, and half that number had been so sent to the battle fronts within the previous year. November 10, 1940 was the date of the first ferry flight, when seven Hudsons were the first war aircraft to make the journey. Later, Dakota, Liberator, Fortress,

TRANSPORTING FIGHTERS BY AIRCRAFT-CARRIER

To save time when a theatre of war urgently needed reinforcements of fighters and other short-range aircraft, these were frequently ferried across the Atlantic by the lighter classes of aircraft-carrier. Aircraft so conveyed reached port ready for flight, whereas machines carried in the ordinary way in crates had to be assembled on arrival. Both hangar and flight-deck of the carrier were filled with planes. Here is H.M.S. 'Smiter' packed with Corsairs in transit.

Mitchell, Lancaster, Mosquito, Boston, Marauder, Lodestar, Ventura landplanes and Catalina, Coronado and Mariner flying boats were the principal types to cross by air. The British, American, and Canadian Air Forces were all concerned in transatlantic traffic, together with British Overseas Airways Corporation, Pan-American Airways, Export Airlines and Trans-Canada Airlines. There were two classes of traffic : (1) delivery aircraft flown by ferry crews and (2) reinforcement aircraft flown by the operational aircrews who would fly them in operations against the enemy. Delivery aircrews were mostly returned by air to the Western Hemisphere, and mails and priority passengers flew to all parts of the world via the trans-

atlantic terminal. War-superannuated aircraft, such as Hampdens, were flown from Britain to Canada to serve as trainers ; only one Hampden failed to get across.

New airfields and settlements were created to meet the needs of the Atlantic Ferry. Dorval airport, Montreal, was the western terminus ; Prestwick airport, Scotland, the eastern. The northern run lay via Gandar airport, Newfoundland; or along an alternative **Airports for Atlantic Ferry** two-stage route via Goose Bay airport, Labrador, and Reykjavik airport, Iceland. The southern (flying boat) route ran from Bermuda, with feeder lines from Dorval, Elizabeth City, and Nassau. From Nassau the South Atlantic route lay via Para, Belem and Natal in Brazil to Ascension Island (*see* illus. in page 2812), thence to Takoradi and Accra on the African Gold Coast, Lagos, Kano, Fort Lamy, and so to Cairo.

Civilian aircrews wore dark blue uniform (pilots wore small metal wings) with braid to distinguish Captain, First and Second Officers. Military crews wore Service uniforms. Their work reduced delivery from three months to three weeks or less, and saved shipping space and risk of aircraft losses through submarine sinkings. Crews have breakfasted four mornings running on Ascension Island in mid-South Atlantic, who had been either in Africa or South America in the intervals between each breakfast. Men in a London club in the late evening might that morning have breakfasted in Newfoundland, and next day be far on their way to Australia. The Atlantic, graveyard of so many pioneer flights, in war was spanned by an aerial bridge built by courage of aircrews, skill of aircraft engineers, and devotion to duty of ground controllers.

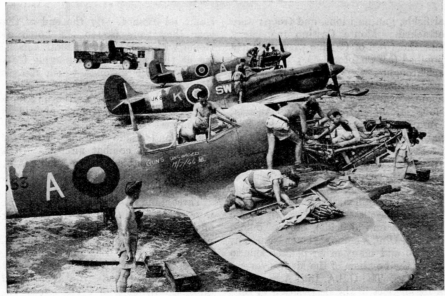

TRAINING YUGOSLAV PARTISANS IN ITALY

Specially selected members of Marshal Tito's Partisans went to Italy during 1944 for training in the servicing and operation of aircraft under the instruction of N.C.O.s of the Royal Air Force. Here Yugoslav Partisans and men of the R.A.F. are working together on Spitfires on an Allied airfield in Italy. *Photos, British Official*

Chapter 316

FOUR OCCUPIED LANDS GREET LIBERATORS

During 1944, the Allied armies of liberation reached and crossed the frontiers of Norway, the Netherlands, Poland, and Czechoslovakia. Their ordeal was not over—the Netherlands in particular had still grievous suffering to bear—but freedom was very near. Denmark alone of the five countries whose history is related in this chapter remained entirely under enemy domination. For internal events in these countries during 1943, see Chapter 273

IN Denmark, though the Germans paid and protected the Schalburg Corps (Danish Nazis—the dregs of the population—estimated at about 2,000 in Copenhagen and 6,000 elsewhere in Denmark), encouraging **DENMARK** them to murder prominent personalities and to assault defenceless women and children, they could not stem the tide of growing resistance, which manifested itself in sabotage against factories working for the Germans and vital German communications.

One notably daring attack was made on June 22, on the Riffel Syndikatet in Copenhagen, which, after Krupps and the Skoda Works, was the largest factory in Europe specializing in the manufacture of automatic weapons. It was making arms for the Germans to the value of £100,000 per month. The saboteurs drove off without one casualty, while the Germans called on Danish firefighting crews who, however, operated their engines · in such a way that the factory was completely destroyed. In retaliation the head of the Gestapo in Denmark, General Pancke, executed eight patriots in Jutland at the far side of the country—though he did not use the word reprisal.

There ensued from June 30 a general strike in Copenhagen, which the German authorities attempted to quell by cutting off supplies of water, gas and electricity; but Danish morale remained firm, and the Germans were compelled to make concessions: the Schalburg Corps was withdrawn from the streets on July 4, and the curfew was lifted on the 9th.

In September, the Gestapo made many new arrests and deported 190 hostages to Germany, while German soldiers opened fire on civilians in Copenhagen. Following a two-day strike, the Germans proclaimed a "state of emergency" and withdrew all power from the Danish police (1,680 of whom were sent to Germany), replacing them by members of the Schalburg (renamed Hilfspolizei) Corps. In October 400 persons arrested in Copenhagen were deported to Germany; the German police were reinforced; and arrested saboteurs were compelled to travel on German troop trains. But sabotage and wreck-

ing, in particular against enemy communications, continued.

Inside Norway the Gestapo and its agents continued their political offensive

against Norwegian patriots with increasing intensity. The Nazis still hoped, by a brutal suppression of the leading elements of resistance, to force some sections of the population to assist in the German war effort not only as slave labourers, but even as conscript soldiers. The attempt to realize this aim called forth the maximum resistance.

Early in the year it was discovered that Quisling, at a meeting with Hitler in January, had promised to mobilize three divisions of young Norwegians for military service with the **NORWAY** Wehrmacht on the Eastern front. The premature disclosure of this undertaking compelled the Nazis to postpone for several months any attempt to put it into practice, and enabled the patriots to make every possible preparation for effective resistance when the decisive trial came.

In May the Nazis called up three age groups of young men for so-called National Labour Service. Immediately the Home Front leadership instructed young Norwegians to ignore the calling-

'STATE OF EMERGENCY' IN DENMARK

On September 19, 1944, the Germans suppressed the Danish police force. The same day, in protest, a general strike broke out in Copenhagen, accompanied by street fighting, particularly in front of the royal palace, where several Germans and Danes were killed and wounded. Here members of the Danish police are on the defensive in the palace grounds. Above, police and civilians build barricades before the palace.   *Photos, Keystone*

'ALTMARK' COMMEMORATED

Near Joessing Fjord, where H.M.S. 'Cossack' released 299 British prisoners held on board the German ship 'Altmark' in the then neutral waters of Norway (see Chapter 63), the Germans erected this sign : 'Here on February 16, 1940, the Altmark was surprised by British pirates.' In 1945 the Norwegians presented this board to Admiral Sir Philip Vian—Captain of 'Cossack' in February 1940.

Photo, Associated Press.

up notices and to go into hiding in the forests and country districts. Gestapo search parties had little success.

The struggle against mobilization received much assistance from saboteurs who burned down registration offices, destroyed card indexes and so forth. Other sabotage was directed against German fuel supplies, one petrol tank after another being emptied, blown up or set on fire. Then came attacks on factories, such as the Kongsberg Ammunition Factory, the Holmestrand Aluminium Factory, the Lysaker Chemical Works, a large omnibus garage in Oslo containing 100 German aeroplane engines, and the Skefco Warehouse in Oslo.

One of the most important sabotage attacks culminated on February 20, 1944, in the blowing-up of the ferry-steamer "Hydro," on **Destruction of** Lake Tinnsjoe, with a **Norwegian** cargo of "heavy **'Heavy Water'** water" en route for Hamburg. The only considerable source in Europe of heavy water (deuterium oxide), used by the Germans in atomic energy experiments, was the Norsk Hydro Hydrogen Electrolysis plant at

Vemork in the Rjukan Valley, in the province of Telemark.

As far back as 1942, Allied plans had been made to sabotage this plant (and thus lessen the possibility of Germany's perfecting an atomic bomb) by landing airborne troops. The first attempts ended in failure, but on February 16, 1943, a Norwegian party was successfully parachuted into the district. Divided into a demolition group and a covering group, the attackers reached their objective on the night of February 27–28. Whilst the covering party surrounded the German guard-house, the demolition group entered a room adjacent to the target, found the door into the high concentration room open, and took the guard by surprise. The

saboteurs had practised in England on duplicate models built under the supervision of Major Leif Tronstad, formerly Professor of Industrial Chemistry at the University of Trondhjem. Now the demolition charges were slipped into position in the machinery, and the men were 20 yards outside the factory when they heard the explosion. It was calculated that 3,000 lb. of heavy water were destroyed, together with the most important parts of the high concentration plant.

From the members of the party who remained in Norway to report results, it was learned that General von Falkenhorst visited Vemork immediately after the disaster. He described the operation as " the best *coup* I have ever seen."

NORWEGIAN VICTIMS OF THE NAZIS

The bodies of 35 of the 45 Norwegian prisoners who lost their lives when the German prison ship 'Westfalen' sank in the Skagger Rak were recovered and buried in Gothenburg Cathedral, Sweden, with full military honours on September 14, 1944. Here are some of the coffins, covered with Norwegian flags, lying in the Cathedral before the service. *Photo, Norwegian Official*

ONCE A FISHING VILLAGE IN FINNMARK

The site of the fishing village of Berlevaag in the Arctic province of Finnmark after the Germans had razed every building in it—a part of the destruction they wrought in the province following the Russian advance into Norway in October 1944. Out of a population of 1,600, only 70 remained, living in cellars on the fish they were able to catch and use when the Germans had gone.
Photo, Norwegian Official

The German guards were removed and punished and German mountain troops patrolled the district, some of them firing nervously on one another. Reconnaissance aircraft hovered in the neighbourhood. The Gestapo combed the area and arrested many innocent Norwegians; mountain huts were broken into and burnt.

Following an attack by the U.S.A. 8th A.F. in November 1943, the Germans had decided to dismantle the Vemork installations and send the machinery to Germany. As soon as this information reached London, in February 1944, approval was obtained from the Norwegian Defence Minister to attack the stocks en route, despite risk of reprisals on the local inhabitants.

The Germans had drafted special S.S. troops into the Rjukan Valley, aircraft patrolled the mountains each day, and new guards were stationed on the railway line from Vemork to the ferry quay on Lake Tinnsjoe; but by some freak of folly not a single German guard had been posted on the ferry-boat "Hydro." At 1 a.m. on February 20, three Norwegians boarded her, and laid in the bows time-bombs constructed from alarm-clocks. At 11 a.m. the "Hydro" sank, after a "mysterious explosion," and with her 3,600 gallons of heavy water. So it was that the manufacture of heavy water ceased in Norway and all stocks available to German scientists from that source were lost.

By the end of the year more than 8,000 Norwegians were confined in prisons and concentration camps in Germany. Prison ships sailed from Oslo across the heavily mined Skager Rak to Denmark. One, the "Westfalen," sank on September 10 with some 50 Norwegians—of whom only five escaped—locked in the hold. The tragedy aroused such indignation in Sweden that the Swedish Government decided to refuse further transit visas to German civilians, who had been allowed to return from Norway on the "safe" route provided by the Swedish railways.

Following the signing of the Russo-Finnish armistice on September 19, the Russians advanced through Finland, to cross the Norwegian frontier on October 25. A week earlier, a representative of Terboven, Reich Commissioner for Norway, declared that Russian troops entering Norway would find every "military and civilian installation" destroyed, no single fireplace intact, and that the entire civilian population would be forcibly evacuated from the war zone, those who stayed behind being left to suffer the "white death" (*i.e.* die of cold). The Germans kept their word: as the Russians approached, they retreated southwards, driving the people out of their homes, burning towns, villages, isolated houses and farm buildings. Approximately 250,000 people were affected. Some escaped to Sweden or the mountains or the rocky inhospitable islands off the coast. Many died of cold, hunger and exposure. Some were shot while escaping. The Arctic province of Finnmark, where at the best of times life is very hard, was reduced to a dead country.

The Russian armies of the Ukraine (*see* Chapter 305) crossed the pre-war Russo-Polish frontier on January 4, 1944. On February 8, "Wolna Polska," organ of the Union of Polish Patriots in Moscow (*see* page 2940), announced the creation in Occupied Poland of a National Council which, in July, set up a Polish Committee of National Liberation (Polski Komitet Wyzwolenia Narodowego) that met at Chelm in liberated territory on July 22. What Moscow radio described as a "Polish Popular Assembly" met at Lublin on the 25th, invested the Committee with provisional powers until November 1, 1944, and declared Lub'in the temporary capital.

POLAND

During September, Mr. Osobka-Morawski, President of the Committee, and the Governments of the Soviet Republics of the Ukraine, White Russia and Lithuania signed agreements for the removal from the area east of the "Curzon Line" (claimed by Russia—*see* page 3212) of some 4,000,000 Poles. On December 31 the Committee

IN MAIDANEK EXTERMINATION CAMP, LUBLIN

When the Russians captured Lublin on July 24, 1944, they overran Maidanek camp, where they found prisoners of war from the Polish armies of 1939, Soviet prisoners, citizens of Poland, France, Belgium, Italy, Holland, Czechoslovakia, Greece, Yugoslavia, Denmark, Norway and other countries. A commission of inquiry they set up established that 1,380,000 corpses of people killed in the camp by shooting, gas, starvation and torture had been burned in the cremation furnaces and on bonfires. Lublin residents are seen inspecting the camp. *Photo, Planet News*

declared itself "the first Provisional Government of Liberated Democratic Poland," with Mr. Morawski as Premier.

The activities of the underground movement in Poland kept half a million Germans occupied. Its members carried out death sentences passed by the underground on German officials. One of its most vital tasks was the destruction of German communication lines and military transport.

Owing to the constant derailment of trains round Lublin, the governor of the area asked the German authorities to reinforce the military police on the railways with 3,000 men. On March 16 several battalions of S.S. men and military police were sent from Cracow. Half way between Cracow and Warsaw, 7½ miles from Kielce, the troop train carrying them was derailed by iron obstacles placed in its path. The Germans were then attacked by a detachment of the underground army waiting in ambush. The skirmish lasted one and a half hours; many Germans were killed and 250 were made prisoners. On April 5 a train of 30 wagons of anti-tank guns and ammunition passing through the coal basin of Dabrowa was suddenly attacked at a station near Katowice. The fight with the German guards lasted barely half an hour. Then some of the ammunition and 200 German soldiers were trans-

Attacks on German Troop Trains

ported on waiting lorries to the nearest base of the underground army. The rest was set on fire.

As a result of these and other exploits, a proclamation issued in June 1944 by the German management of the "Eastern Railways" named "fourteen dangerous sectors" and "eight dangerous centres" on the Polish railway network, where "communications have to be carried on with the utmost care owing to the activities of the underground army." So nervous were the Germans that on June 30 the military authorities issued an order that "anyone coming within 550 yards of the rails will be shot."

On June 11, 1944, Pinczow, a town in central Poland, was entered by the patriots and remained in their hands for several hours. Their task was to liberate from prison 400 eminent political prisoners who had been condemned to death. The whole German garrison and the police were disarmed and taken prisoner. Some of the Gestapo officers previously condemned to death by the underground were executed. On March 11 two attacks were carried out by men of the Polish underground army in Berlin, chiefly as a propaganda measure. Leaflets were scattered round the two Berlin railway stations, 15 Germans were killed and 26 wounded. Expeditions were also sent to Silesia, Slovakia and East Prussia.

Polish Underground in Berlin

Units of the Secret Home Army, attacking the Germans in the rear, helped the Red Army to capture Vilna (July 13), Lwow (July 27) and other places. But their greatest effort was the rising in Warsaw in which some 80,000 Polish troops fought. By July 31, a Russian mobile column had advanced as far as the outskirts of Praga, an outer suburb of Warsaw on the east bank of the Vistula. General Tadeusz

UNDERGROUND ARMY UNIT RECEIVES ITS STANDARD

The Polish Telegraphic Agency in London announced on July 18, 1944, that units of the secret Underground Army, to the strength of a division, had co-operated with the Soviet General Chernyakhovsky's forces in the assault on Vilna, captured on July 13. Here the 23rd Brigade, serving in south-east Poland, receives its standard after it has been blessed, July 1944. *Photo, Keystone*

BATTLE OF WARSAW

1. German anti-tank gun in Theatre Square, Warsaw, firing at the ruins of the Town Hall, one of the last centres of resistance by the Polish Home Army in the heroic battle of August 1-October 3, 1944. 2. General Thadeusz Komorowski (known as General Bor), commander of the Home Army in Warsaw, in civilian clothes after his surrender. 3. Countess Tarnowska, President of the Polish Red Cross, and Dr. Bartoszewski, delegates for the surrender, arrive in the enemy lines. 4. Citizens who survived the terrible battle.

ROCKET SHELLS ON DEVASTATED WARSAW

Following their defeat of the Russians at Praga, the suburb of Warsaw on the east bank of the Vistula, the Germans turned the full force of their armour and their bombers against the Polish patriots who had risen in considerable force in the city itself, under the command of General ' Bor ' (Thadeusz Komorowski). This remarkable photograph shows a rocket shell discharged into a devastated area where the Home Army was still holding out. *Photo, Planet News*

Komorowski (known as General Bor), commander of the Polish Home Army in Warsaw, had been authorized by the Polish Government in London to use his own judgement about the time for a general uprising in the city, and the nearness of the Russians decided him to strike at 5 p.m. on August 1. A heroic struggle followed. But strong reinforcements of picked S.S. troops rushed to Praga defeated the Russians and stopped their advance.

General Bor's forces achieved great initial success, but both his intelligence staff work and his liaison with the Russians seem to have been at fault, and he was unable to co-ordinate his movements with the Soviet command. The Germans, having halted the Russians, turned the full force of their bombers and their armour against the Poles in Warsaw who, however, short as they were of weapons and ammunition, held out until October 3. Some outside help came to them from the R.A.F., which dropped weapons and supplies (up to September 12, 250 Allied airmen, including 98 Poles, were lost on these missions), and after September 14 from the Red Air Force, while on September 16 the largest force of shuttle bombers of the U.S. Strategic Air Force ever to leave Britain dropped arms, ammunition, food and medical aid over Warsaw and flew on to Russia.

Civilian sufferings in the city were indescribable—the Germans carried out incessant air bombings at roof-top height, and artillery bombardment was almost continuous. After September 8 both electric light and the water supply failed. The Warsaw rising was the greatest single defeat suffered by the Poles during the war. Their losses were high—only 15,000 men surrendered—and their capital was almost totally destroyed. The Germans completed its destruction after driving the 400,000 inhabitants to a huge concentration camp at Pruszkow, many thousands being sent for forced labour in Germany.

During the operations which led to the liberation of Lublin (July 24), the Red Army overran the Maidanek " extermination camp." The findings of a subsequent joint Russo-Polish commission fully substantiated the unbelievable reports of the destruction there of Polish and other Jews, political victims of many countries, and Polish and Soviet prisoners of war. Of Poland's pre-war Jewish population of 3,325,000, only some 250,000 hunted creatures living in the woods remained. Many thousands of victims from Austria, Germany, France, Hungary, and other countries had also vanished.

The Germans had already inundated a considerable area of the Netherlands— according to estimates made by the Government in London, 25 per cent of the arable land of the country—by the end of 1941. In the early months of 1944 they flooded new areas, in Zeeland and the provinces of North and South Holland, forcibly evacuating the inhabitants. There was also great activity in the building of fortifications, with increasing pressure upon Dutch labour. Exerted through the rationing system, the withdrawal of unemployment pay and, wherever possible, through direct compulsion, it resulted in the transportation of some quarter of a million Dutch workers to Germany, while another 40,000 were sent to Belgium or France.

THE NETHERLANDS

Underground resistance was bold and continuous. One raid had for its object the appropriation of radio sets for the use of the underground. A number of confiscated sets were stored in the municipal offices at Groothuizen under the day and night guard of two men.

The guards were overpowered, and 76 wireless receivers were removed. The Germans considered the lower ranks of the police so unreliable that they disarmed them. Their revolvers were stored in a barracks at s'Hertogenbosch. Next morning the room was found to have been burgled, and the revolvers had disappeared. The pin-point raid by the R.A.F. in May on a single building at The Hague (described in page 3194) was the result of co-operation between the Dutch underground and the R.A.F.

RESISTANCE CAPTIVE

Allied troops crossed the Dutch-Belgian border on September 11, 1944, and everywhere received assistance from Dutch resistance elements. Here two members of the Netherlands Underground movement are questioning a prisoner rounded up at Valkenswaard, just inside the border.

Photo, British Newspaper Pool

As the British and Canadian armies advanced, hope ran high that the liberation of the Netherlands would be accomplished as swiftly as had been that of France and Belgium. On September 4, Seyss-Inquart, Reich Commissioner for Occupied Holland, proclaimed a "state of emergency." German troops were ordered to open fire on all demonstrations of over five people; a curfew from 8 p.m. to 4 a.m. was imposed. Troops of the British 2nd Army crossed the Dutch-Belgian border near De Groote on September 11, and six days later came the airborne landings in the Arnhem-Nijmegen-Eindhoven area (*see* Chapter 325). The same day General Eisenhower broadcast a message to the people of the Netherlands, telling those in the area south of the River Lek (Lower Rhine)

British Troops Cross the Dutch Border

that "the hour for which you have been waiting so long has struck" and that "your qualities of courage and discipline . . . are now called on for one last supreme effort." The population of the still unliberated areas were advised not to rise, but to give help, shelter and information to the Netherlands Forces of Resistance. At the same time, the Netherlands Government in London called on all Dutch railway workers to strike in order to impede enemy transport and troop movements.

Dutch resistance elements were at the various landing and dropping zones during the airborne invasion, and guided the airborne forces to their targets; Dutch women in the villages provided hot meals for them. Ground forces coming up in support liberated Eindhoven on September 19, Nijmegen on the 20th; but what was left of the British 1st Airborne Division had to be withdrawn from Arnhem on the 27th. The Netherlands south-west of the river Maas was cleared by the end of the year; but the rest of the country, in which lay the great centres of population, was still in enemy occupation, and demolition charges in position there threatened another million acres of arable and pasture land (17 per cent of the national total) with inundation by salt water if touched off.

The Germans used the continuing railway strike not only as an excuse for bringing no food into the country, but also as a pretext for confiscating the small reserves of foodstuffs built up by the Dutch Food Ad-

FLOODS IN HOLLAND

Flooding of certain strategic areas was a recognized method of defence in the Netherlands; and to the floods they let loose the Germans added, as can be seen in this photograph, obstacles of various kinds to impede airborne landings and amphibious operations. The Dutch Government in London estimated that twenty-five per cent of the arable land of the Netherlands had been inundated by the end of 1941, and further flooding took place in 1944 as the Allies approached the Netherlands frontier.

Photo, Associated Press

ministration, and all available transport A population of 7,000,000 was faced with imminent starvation; the daily ration in the province of South Holland fell in October to 780 calories a day, in December to 460 (compared with the 3,000 required by the normal human being for health). There was no fuel in the towns either. Yet in that densely populated, unforested, meticulously cultivated land, hundreds of thousands still eluded the intensive German labour call-up.

German oppression in Czechoslovakia continued in 1944; but the whole atmosphere in the country changed with the approach of the Red Army, which reached the Soviet-Czechoslovak frontier on April 8. Acting under directions from the exiled Government in London, partisans increased both passive resistance and sabotage. National councils were set up in Bohemia, Moravia, Slovakia and Ruthenia, as well as a number of district committees. The task of the organizations was, as areas were liberated, to safeguard order, remove collaborators from public office, see that the people were fed, and carry on interim administration pending the election of a free Parliament.

CZECHO-SLOVAKIA

Dr. Tiso, President of Slovakia, and his Foreign Minister, Dr. Tuka, were received by Hitler at his H.Q. on May

IN LIBERATED HOLLAND

1. Prince Bernhard of the Netherlands, husband of Princess Juliana, the Heir Apparent to the throne, being cheered when he paid a visit to Nijmegen after its liberation on September 20, 1944. 2. The people of Tilburg, freed by British armour on October 27, nail a portrait of Princess Juliana to a boarded-up shop front. 3. Refugees from Nijmegen find rest and care in a stocking factory turned into an emergency hospital. 4. In November, Prof. Pieter S. Gerbrandy, Dutch Premier, visited the Netherlands. He is seen here in Breskens.

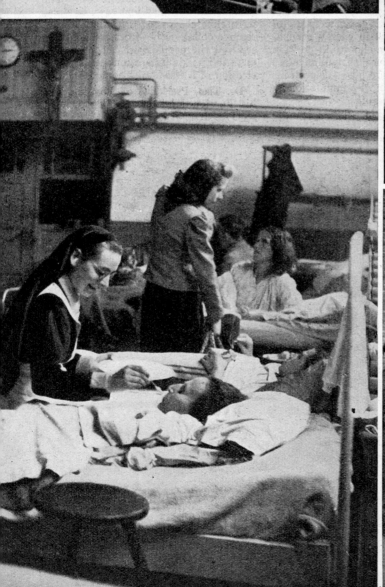

13 for discussions on the relations between Germany and Slovakia at which Field-Marshal Keitel, Ribbentrop, General Catlos (Slovak War Minister) and Tido Gaspar (Slovak Propaganda Minister) were also present.

Following the entry of four German divisions from Moravia into Slovakia on August 29, the Czech Forces of the Interior came into the open, and, with Slovak partisans, captured Csacza, a junction on the railway from Bratislava to Cracow and Berlin. Fighting also broke out in the areas of Zilina, most important railway junction in central Czechoslovakia, and of Trencin, which dominates the Vlara Pass in the White Carpathians. These operations were carried out under the orders of the Slovak National Council, representing all democratic parties and acting on general instructions from London.

The rising was followed by the dismissal on September 2 of General

CZECHS RETURNING TO THEIR VILLAGES

Villagers driven from their homes in the Carpathians as the fighting advanced took refuge in the mountains. Here is a group returning after their district has been cleared of the enemy. The Red Army, and with it the Czechoslovak Brigade formed in Russia in 1941 (see page 2579), reached the frontier of Czechoslovakia on April 8, 1944, but progress through the difficult border country was slow, despite substantial internal help.
Photo, Pictorial Press

Catlos from his positions as Slovak War Minister and C.-in-C., on the grounds that he had introduced " Bolshevist and pro-Allied " officers into the Slovak Army, had prepared the rising of the Slovak partisans (which, the Slovak radio declared, was started by Slovak Army officers), and had attempted to make contact with the Czech Government in London. President Tiso continued to express his confidence in the Reich as " protector of Slovak independence."

The incorporation of all patriot forces fighting in Slovakia into the Czechoslovak 1st Army, under the command of General Rudolf Viest (who resigned his appointment as Under-Secretary of War in the London Government to take up his new post) took place in mid-September. The first Czechoslovak community to be liberated was Vyssi Kormarnik in Slovakia, reached on October 6 by the Czechoslovak 1st Army after it had forced the Dukla Pass in the Carpathians in a bitter struggle which cost it very heavy losses.

Red Army Enters Slovakia

As in Poland, however, the Russian forces did not advance so rapidly as had been hoped, and S.S. troops occupied Banska Bystrica on October 28, taking prisoner over 12,000 Czechs, including General Viest himself, and capturing 284 guns, 65 aircraft, 62 tanks, and 98 heavy weapons which had been concentrated in the area by General Catlos, after consultation with the Soviet Command. The end of the year found the Red Army advancing slowly but steadily into Slovakia through very difficult mountainous country.

NETHERLANDS AIRMEN HOME AGAIN

The Burgomaster of the town of Helmond, in the province of North Brabant, presents shields of his town and province to men of the Royal Dutch Naval Air Service on their return to the Netherlands with the first three of their Mitchell bombers. This squadron had flown with the Royal Air Force for four-and-a-half years (see illus. in page 2733).
Photo, British Newspaper Pool

NORWEGIAN ARMY IN NORWAY AGAIN

1. Norwegian troops trained in Britain on board a British cruiser on their way to Norway to co-operate with the Russians on the Arctic front in the liberation of their country. 2. Units bearing their national flag march into the port of Kirkenes, freed by the Russians on October 25, 1944. 3. The 'Vestmannrod,' one of a number of Norwegian merchant vessels included in the great international armada that carried the Allies to France on June 6, 1944, unloading supplies on to the Normandy beaches. 4. Members of the small Norwegian garrison guarding the metereological station on arctic Jan Mayen Island bring home supplies.

Chapter 317

EXILED GOVERNMENTS PREPARE FOR HOME

The thoughts of the exiled governments of Norway, the Netherlands, Poland and Czechoslovakia turned during 1944 towards preparations for their return home. None of them saw their native land that year, however ; and the Polish Government, failing to adjust its differences with Russia, steadily lost weight in international affairs. The internal happenings in these countries and in Denmark for the year are described in Chapter 316. For the earlier history of the exiled governments, see Chapter 274

"I MUST congratulate all of the Danes in this country," said Mr. Eden in January 1944, "and Danish seamen who sail the seas in the Allied cause on the way in which you have upheld the name and fame of Denmark. . . . Danish ships and Danish seamen have shared with the Merchant Navies of the Allies **DENMARK** all the perils of the war at sea, and so it is fitting that Danish ships in our service should be flying the Dannebrog, which now rightly takes its place alongside the flags of the United Nations." More than 800,000 tons of Danish shipping with some 5,000 men were enlisted for the cause of the free nations. Many of these ships and crews volunteered to take part in the invasion of France.

Early in 1944, Danish seamen serving with the Royal Navy took over two recently commissioned motor minesweepers, which flew both the Danish and White Ensigns. A number of Danes volunteered for service in the "Buffs," of which regiment King Christian is honorary colonel ; Danes served in the Royal Norwegian Air Force, and in the Royal Norwegian Navy.

Iceland on June 17, 1944, proclaimed itself a republic, severing the union with Denmark as it had the right to do after twenty-five years under the Act of Union of December 1, 1918.

Three weeks before the Allied onset in Normandy, the Norwegian Government in London signed identical agreements with Britain, the United States and Russia providing for **NORWAY** the administration of Norway as she was liberated. Russian forces reached Norway first, on October 25. Next day King Haakon broadcast a welcome to them, and on the 28th Mr. Trygve Lie, the Premier, and Mr. Terje Wold, the Minister of Justice, went first to Stockholm, where they arranged for a credit from Sweden of 100,000,000 kroner (about £6,000,000) to cover the support of 15,000 Norwegian refugees in Sweden, the training in Sweden (already carried out) of 10,000 Norwegian police, and the supply of certain goods. They then went on to Moscow, where they reached agreement on the use in liberated Norway of their Swedish-trained police force. On November 15 Mr. Wold paid a flying visit from Moscow to Kirkenes—the first Norwegian minister to set foot in free Norwegian territory since the German occupation of 1940. He found only 28 houses standing, food supplies limited and the health position serious. (*See* page 3203.)

A Norwegian Military Mission, sent from Britain and under the control of Major-General W. Steffens, the Norwegian Military Attaché in Moscow, was attached to the Russian Command on the Arctic front, on which Norwegian troops specially trained in Britain co-operated. Other Norwegian forces served with the Allies on the western front : a Norwegian Commando took part in the capture of Walcheren in November 1944.

In September it was announced that, of the 1,022 ships totalling about 4,000,000 tons placed by Norway at the disposal of the Allies following the German invasion in 1940, 475, of nearly 2,000,000 tons, had been lost in Allied service up to September 1, 1944. Ships of the Norwegian merchant navy were among those that took the Allies to Normandy, and a Norwegian ship was the first to sail into Antwerp after the Scheldt had been cleared in November.

The crossing of the pre-war Polish frontier by the Red Army on January 4, 1944, brought a new element into the relations between Poland and the Soviet Union. **POLAND** The London Government issued a statement on January 5 affirming its reliance on the principles of the Atlantic Charter, and stating that though no agreement had been reached between it and Russia, it had instructed the Polish underground forces to "intensify their resistance to the German invaders, to avoid all conflict with the Soviet armies entering Poland in their battle against the Germans, and to enter into co-operation with the Soviet

DANES TAKE OVER MINESWEEPERS
Vice-Admiral E. L. S. King, C.B., M.V.O., Principal Liaison Officer to the Allied Navies, addresses Danish seamen serving with the Royal Navy at the ceremony at a Scottish port when two of H.M. motor minesweepers were handed over to Danish crews. On Admiral King's left are Count Reventlow, the Danish Minister, and Captain A. M. Bingeman of H.M.S. 'Lochinvar.'
Photo, British Official

POLISH FORCES ON WESTERN AND SOUTHERN FRONTS

Tanks of the 1st Polish Armoured Division rolling past a windmill near Hooge-Zwaluwe in the Netherlands. Above, General Maczek, commander of this Division, in conversation with General Montgomery, C.-in-C., 21st (British) Army Group, of which the Polish troops in the west formed part. Below, General Kasimierz Sosnkowski, Polish C.-in-C., inspecting Polish troops of the 8th Army in snow uniform during his visit to the Italian front in April 1944.

Photos, British Official ; Keystone

commanders in the event of the resumption of Polish-Soviet relations."

In a statement published on January 11, Russia insisted on the rectification of the Polish-Russian frontier, but intimated that she would support an extension of Poland westwards. Later developments made it clear that she wanted the so-called " Curzon Line " (proposed as the boundary by the Supreme Council on December 8, 1919) to be recognized as the basis for discussions of Poland's eastern frontier. The Polish Government, however, had no intention of yielding up the territories overrun at Russia's expense during the period of her weakness following the war of 1914–18, and countered with the suggestion that the settlement of both east and west frontiers should be left until after the war when a Polish parliament would be able to ratify any changes.

There was no resumption of relations between the London Government and the Soviet Union, and the likelihood of agreement decreased when in July Russia allowed the Lublin Committee (*see* page 3203) to administer liberated Polish territory. During a visit paid to Moscow in October by Mr. Churchill and Mr. Eden, consultations were held at which both the Lublin Committee and the London Government were represented—the latter by Mr. Mikolajczk, the Premier, who returned to London to consult with his Cabinet. He could not persuade its members to agree to the proposals he brought, and he resigned, to be succeeded by Mr. Arciszewski, who formed a government on November 29 which included no representatives of Mr. Mikolajczk's (the Peasant) Party.

Russo-Polish Difficulties Continue

General Kasimierz Sosnkowski, Polish C.-in-C., said in April 1944 that more than 100,000 Poles were fighting in the reconstituted Polish army, navy and air force, apart from the guerilla army in Poland itself (*see* page 3204). Polish Commando troops appeared on the Sangro and Garigliano (Italy) in January 1944, and in February it was announced that the 2nd Polish Corps, commanded by General Wladyslaw Anders, and comprising the "Carpathian" and " Kresowa " Divisions, was in action in Italy after intensive training in the Middle East. (The part this well-equipped, well-trained corps of brave men played in the Italian campaign is mentioned in Chapters 302 and 338.) Polish forces also fought with distinction in western Europe, the 1st Armoured Division, commanded by General Maczek, achieving great things in the

'PRINCESS IRENE BRIGADE' APPROACHES HOLLAND

An official statement published in August 1944 announced that the Princess Irene Brigade of the Netherlands Army (formed in 1942 and named after Princess Juliana's second daughter, born a month before the outbreak of war) was fighting with the 1st Canadian Army in France. Here transport of the brigade is moving through a Belgian village only 25 miles from the Dutch frontier, which was crossed by the Allies on September 11. *Photo, Pictorial Press*

battle of the Falaise Gap (*see page 3184*). Infantry and airborne units fought with the British and Canadians through France and the Low Countries. Sir Bernard Montgomery (promoted Field-Marshal on September 1) was awarded the highest Polish military honour, Virtuti Militari, on November 25, while fourteen Poles, including General Maczek, were awarded the D.S.O. and other British decorations.

By an Anglo-Polish agreement of April 6, 1944, the Polish Air Force—third largest in Britain—received an autonomous status, Air Vice-Marshal Mateusz Izycki, its Inspector-General, being appointed A.O.C.-in-C. At that time, the force consisted of thirteen squadrons—seven Fighter, three Bomber, one Night-Fighter, one Coastal Command, one Army Co-operation Command—with over 12,000 personnel. It continued to co-operate in all the activities of the R.A.F. Britain received advance information about flying-bombs smuggled out by Poles employed in France and Germany in their manufacture, which they actively sabotaged; while Polish fighter pilots had by September 7 destroyed 223 of these missiles sent against England.

Polish Air Force Becomes Autonomous

Polish losses during the war were given by Polish sources in London as : Killed and wounded, Polish campaign (September 1939), 220,000 ; Narvik (April-May 1940), 300 ; France (May-June 1940), 6,500 ; Libya (1941), 900 ; France, Belgium, the Netherlands, Italy (1944), 10,600 ; Polish Air Force and Navy (1940–44), 10,600 ; Polish Home Army (until March 1944), 25,000. With war prisoners in Germany (420,000) and internees in other countries, total losses of the Polish armed forces abroad to the end of 1944 and at home to March 1944 amounted to about 886,700.

A statement made by the secretary of Dr. Gerbrandy, the Dutch Premier, on April 4 outlined the arrangements made by the exiled government in anticipation of an early return to the Netherlands. Each part of territory as it was liberated would automatically come under a State of Siege. As soon as the Queen returned to her country, the Government would resign. The Collaborators would be dismissed from their posts, suspected collaborators would be suspended. Action would be taken against traitors under a new "special penal law" administered by special courts. Relief measures would be put in hand ; and the judicial position created by the German occupation would be carefully overhauled. Steps would be taken immediately to build up the Netherlands armed forces, to provide security in Holland and in the Netherlands Indies, to create an occupation force, and to fight alongside the other Allies against Japan. A Royal decree issued on July 31 implemented these arrangements.

THE NETHERLANDS

Separate but identical agreements signed on May 16 at the Foreign Office in London with the British and United States Governments provided for military control of the Netherlands during operations and the handing over of authority to the Netherlands Government as soon as the military situation allowed.

A Customs Union between Belgium and Luxemburg (already bound by an economic union since 1921) and the Netherlands, to come into force provisionally immediately the contracting governments were re-established in their own countries, was entered into on September 5. It followed a monetary agreement made on October 21, 1943,

QUEEN WILHELMINA INSPECTS DUTCH WARSHIPS

In March 1944 Queen Wilhelmina of the Netherlands, accompanied by Prince Bernhard, paid a visit to Portsmouth where, after visiting Admiral Sir Charles Little, C.-in-C. Portsmouth, she went on board the Dutch gunboats 'Flores' and 'Soemba,' inspected the ships' companies, and presented medals. She is seen here with the officer commanding 'Flores.' *Photo, British Official*

LIBERATED CZECHOSLOVAKIA

The Czechoslovak 1st Army Corps, operating with the Red Army, forced its way through the Dukla Pass in the Carpathians, and on October 6, 1944, liberated Vyssi Kormarnik; 1½ miles to the south, first Czech community to be freed. Here men of the Czechoslovak 1st Army dressed in Russian uniforms are erecting a new frontier post near the Dukla Pass.

and though temporary in character, was intended to facilitate a later permanent Customs Union.

Queen Wilhelmina became the first reigning foreign queen to be admitted to the Order of the Garter since its institution in 1348, when King George VI invested her with it on September 24.

The Princess Irene Brigade of the Netherlands Army, raised in 1942 and named in honour of Princess Juliana's second daughter, fought through France as part of the 1st Canadian Army. The Supreme Commander's appointment, with the approval of the Netherlands Government, of Prince Bernhard of the Netherlands as Commander of the Dutch Forces of the Interior was announced on September 3.

Towards the end of November, Dr. Gerbrandy and several other members of the London Government visited the parts of Holland already liberated. They were warmly welcomed (*see* illus. in page 3208). But at Eindhoven the Premier reiterated that his government intended to resign as soon as the whole country was liberated.

"We announce news of historic importance," began a statement issued by the Czechoslovak Government in
London. "Today, Easter **CZECHO-SLOVAKIA** Sunday, April 8, 1944, the Red Army and with it the Independent Czechoslovak Brigade in the Soviet Union, have reached the frontier of Czechoslovakia. The Czech flag has been hoisted on the top of the Carpathians." (For formation of Czechoslovak Brigade, *see* page 2579.) But, as in the case of the Netherlands, the liberation of Czechoslovakia did not go forward so rapidly as had been hoped. (*See* Chapter 316.)

An agreement announced on April 30 between the Soviet and Czechoslovak Governments placed supreme power and responsibility for military operations in the hands of the Soviet C.-in-C. and arranged that as liberated territory ceased to be in the operational zone full powers of administration were to pass to the Czechoslovak Government. It was approved by the British and United States Governments before its publication. Dr. Frantisec Nemec, the Minister for Reconstruction, Industry and Commerce, and General Rudolf Viest, Under-Secretary for War, were appointed by the London Government as delegates to take over the administration of Czechoslovakia as it was liberated (July 2); and on July 23 President Benes signed a decree restoring the Czechoslovak constitution within the limits of pre-Munich Czechoslovakia: it nullified all German and Hungarian legislation automatically except for such measures (which were in no case to be retained for longer than one month) as must be temporarily retained to avoid administrative chaos.

On August 22 the Czechoslovak Government signed an agreement in London with the French Provisional Government (recognized on June 13) declaring the treaties of Munich and their consequences null and void, and re-establishing the former relations between Czechoslovakia and France.

Czechoslovak troops fought in Normandy and contained the German garrison in by-passed Dunkirk.

DUNKIRK CONTAINED BY CZECHOSLOVAK TROOPS

When the 1st Canadian Army by-passed the Channel ports (see chapter 320), Czech troops serving with it were given the task of containing Dunkirk, and it was to these units that the German garrison surrendered on May 11, 1945, following the unconditional surrender of Germany. Here Czech sappers, patrolling a flooded area near Dunkirk in a motor-boat, land on ground occupied by the enemy. *Photos, British Official ; Keystone*

BLANKET BOMBING OF ENEMY AIRFIELDS

On August 15, 1944, over 1,100 Lancasters and Halifaxes of R.A.F. Bomber Command dropped more than 5,000 tons of bombs on nine airfields in the Netherlands and four in Belgium, all bases for German night-fighters. Visibility was excellent, there was little opposition, and only two bombers were lost. Here are the cratered landing ground and runways of Le Culot airfield (Belgium) after this attack.

Photo, British Official

FIRST LARGE DUTCH TOWN LIBERATED

Units of the Allied 1st Airborne Army landed in the Netherlands on September 17, 1944, and the following day in the triangle, Eindhoven, Nijmegen, Arnhem. The U.S. 101st Airborne Division landed at Eindhoven. On the 18th, forces of the British 2nd Army, pushing forward from Valkenswaard, overcame stiff resistance by German Panther tanks and entered the town at 6.30 p.m. The British troops received a great welcome from the inhabitants, whose reaction to their liberation was described by correspondents as 'a moving mixture of thanksgiving and jubilation.' Here British armour is driving through an Eindhoven street hung with Dutch flags brought out of hiding to celebrate freedom.

Photo, British Official

EINDHOVEN WELCOMES BRITISH ARMOUR

The town of Eindhoven, seat of one of the largest radio works in Europe, and with a population of 110,000, was liberated on September 18, 1944, without much fighting and was found to be little damaged, though earlier R.A.F. raids had destroyed much of the works (see illustration in page 2180). Professor Gerbrandy, Premier of the exiled Netherlands Government, during his visit to liberated Holland towards the end of 1944, announced at a press conference he held at Eindhoven on December 4 that as soon as the whole country was freed, he and his government would resign so that a fresh government could be formed in tune with the new temper he discovered among the people.

COSSACKS ASSEMBLED IN A WHITE RUSSIAN WOOD

Horse-mounted Cossack regiments fought with success in the Soviet armies that defeated and drove back the German invaders from the Caucasus to Germany. Cossack cavalry formed part of Marshal Rokossovsky's 1st White Russian Army during the summer campaign of 1944, aiding Marshal Rotmistrov's armour in its rapid and successful attack on Minsk (July 3) and taking a notable part in the capture of Baranowicze (July 8). Here a detachment, ready mounted, is waiting orders in a wood in Polyesye. (See also illus. in pages 2682 and 2712.)

Photo, Pictorial Press

Diary of the War
MAY and JUNE 1944

May 1, 1944. Over 3,000 Allied planes (1 lost) kept up offensive in western Europe from dawn to dusk; at night R.A.F. Bomber Command sent out 1,000 planes (10 lost) against seven important targets. Ponape (Carolines) bombarded by U.S. battleships.

May 2. Chinese evacuated Hulao Pass (Honan, China).

May 3. M.A.A.F. attacked Bucharest.

May 4. M.A.A.F. attacked Budapest.

May 5. Allied landings at Torare Bay and Depapre (New Guinea).

May 6. Heavy night attack by R.A.F. on Mantes-Gassicourt. M.A.A.F. flew 2,000 sorties, mostly over Rumania.

May 7. Nearly 1,000 U.S. bombers attacked Berlin. 14th Army evacuated Buthidaung (Burma). Guam (Marianas) bombed by U.S. Liberators.

May 8. 2,000 American bombers and fighters attacked Berlin and Brunswick. Guam (Marianas) again bombed. U.S. Senate extended lend-lease to June 1945, with amendment forbidding President to make any post-war commitment in connexion with lend-lease.

May 9. Russians took Sevastopol by storm. Heavy day raids by U.S.A. 8th A.F. on marshalling yards and airfields in France and Belgium; day and night attacks on Channel coast batteries and other targets in France. Japanese captured Lushan, capital of Honan (China).

May 11. Soviet bombers made heavy night attack on Lublin (Poland). Allied assault on Gustav line (Italy).

May 12. U.S.A. 8th A.F. attacked synthetic oil plants at Brux (Czechoslovakia), Leuna and other German centres. Americans captured Ventosa (Italy). Russians cleared Crimea.

May 13. U.S.A. 8th A.F. bombers attacked Tutow, Osnabrueck, and Stettin. Chinese recaptured Suiping (Honan).

May 14. M.A.A.F. flew 2,500 sorties against targets in occupied Italy. Kohima cleared of Japanese (Assam).

May 16. Indians captured Pignatoro (Italy). Chinese recaptured Chumatien, Honan, and passed through Mamien Pass after crossing Salween river, Yunnan.

May 17. Myitkyina airfield captured by " Merrill's Marauders " (Burma). Allied landings on Wakde I. (New Guinea).

May 18. Allies captured Cassino and Monte Cassino (Italy).

May 19. U.S. heavy bombers attacked Berlin and Brunswick; cross-Channel air offensive continued. M.A.A.F. bombed Genoa, Spezia, Leghorn.

May 20. Nearly 5,000 Allied aircraft attacked targets in France and Belgium. General Eisenhower's first orders to Europe's " underground army " broadcast. Americans captured Itri, Fondi, and Gaeta (Italy).

May 21. Extensive day air attacks in France and Germany; 700 R.A.F. bombers attacked Duisburg (night).

May 22. Night attack by 1,000 planes of Bomber Command on Dortmund and Brunswick. M.A.A.F. heavily attacked enemy road communications between Rome and front. New Allied offensives on Anzio and Hitler line fronts (Italy).

May 23. Chinese cut Burma Road at Chefang, 24 miles from Burma border.

May 24. Dawn to dusk Allied air offensive against targets in Western Europe; night attack on Aachen. Americans captured Terracina; Canadians smashed through Hitler defences; M.A.A.F. flew nearly 3,000 sorties against communications between Rome and the front (Italy).

May 25. Heavy air attacks on enemy-held railways in France and Belgium. Anzio patrols linked with main 5th Army (Italy). M.A.A.F. flew over 3,000 sorties.

May 27. Full-scale day and night air offensive in west. M.A.A.F. flew 3,000 sorties over Italy, Yugoslavia and France. U.S. forces landed on Biak I. (New Guinea).

May 28. 4,000 sorties flown in Allied western dawn-to-dusk air offensive; heavy night attack by R.A.F. Lancasters on Angers (France). New Japanese offensive in Hunan (China).

May 29. Soviet aircraft in great force attacked Rumanian airfields. Targets in Germany bombed by U.S.A. 8th A.F.; cross-Channel air offensive maintained. M.A.A.F. flew about 3,000 sorties over Italy and Austria.

May 30. Powerful German attack against Russians in Rumania. Allied air offensive in west continued. M.A.A.F. flew 2,400 sorties over Italy, Austria and Yugoslavia.

May 31. Allies bombed objectives in Germany and France by day and night. Australians captured Bunabun (New Guinea).

June 2. U.S. bombers from Italy made first landing in Russia in " shuttle service " after attacking Rumanian objectives in support of Red Army. Heavy air attacks on Pas de Calais targets. Americans captured Velletri and Valmontane (Italy). M.A.A.F. flew 2,700 sorties over Italy, Hungary, Rumania. British attacked from Kohima (Assam).

June 3. Cross-Channel air offensive continued.

June 4. Rome liberated by Allies. Russians repulsed Germans in Rumania.

June 5. Western air offensive maintained. Strong Allied air attack on Bangkok (Siam).

June 6. Allies landed in Normandy.

June 7. British captured Bayeux (France). Allies captured Civita Vecchia (Italy).

June 8. Powerful Allied air formations bombed Rennes, Le Mans, and Laval; also communications (France).

June 9. Americans captured Isigny (France). Allies took Viterbo, Orsogna, and other towns (Italy).

June 10. Announced that General Montgomery had set up his Advanced Headquarters in France, and that R.A.F. was operating from French bases. M.A.A.F. flew 2,400 sorties in Italy and the Balkans. Red Army offensive opened in Karelian Isthmus.

June 10-13. Powerful U.S. naval and carrier forces struck at Saipan, Tinian, Guam (Marianas)

June 12. Carentan taken by Americans; Mr. Churchill visited Normandy front (France). 14th Army reoccupied Naga Village (Assam).

June 13. First flying-bomb reached S.E. England; attacks continued

throughout June. Heavy day and night attacks by M.A.A.F. on Munich area.

June 14. General de Gaulle visited Normandy. 1,500 U.S. Bombers attacked targets in France, Belgium, Holland and Germany; 300 R.A.F. Lancasters dropped 1,200 tons on E-boat pens at Le Havre. 8th Army occupied Orvieto (Italy). Budapest (Hungary), Zagreb (Croatia), and Nish (Yugoslavia) attacked by M.A.A.F. U.S. task force attacked Japanese bases in Bonin and Volcano Is.

June 15. Allied air forces in west flew over 3,000 day sorties; R.A.F. Bomber Command attacked enemy shipping at Boulogne. Allies captured Terni, Todi and other places (Italy). Super-Fortresses of the U.S.A. 20th A.F. bombed Yawata (Japan). U.S. landings on Saipan (Marianas).

June 16. Americans captured St. Sauveur-le-Vicomte; King George VI visited Normandy (France). Allies captured Spoleto, Trevi, and other towns (Italy). Kamaing (Burma) captured by Gen. Stilwell's 22nd Chinese Division.

June 17. French landed on Elba.

June 18. Americans captured Barneville-sur-Mer (France). 1,300 U.S. bombers attacked Hamburg and other targets in N.W. Germany. Red Army smashed Mannerheim line (Finland). 8th Army took Assisi (Italy). Japanese air attack on American fleet at Saipan (Marianas): 353 enemy planes shot down; 21 American planes lost, 3 ships slightly damaged. Japanese captured Changsha, capital of Hunan (China).

June 19. Americans captured Bricquebec and Montebourg; British, Tilly sur Seulles (France). 8th Army reached Lake Trasimene; captured Perugia (Italy). Organized resistance on Elba ceased. Surprise attack by U.S. carrier-borne aircraft on Japanese fleet between Luzon and Marianas: 14 ships sunk or damaged.

June 20. Allied air forces in west flew some 6,000 sorties against targets in Germany and France. Red Army captured Viborg (Finland).

June 21. 1,000 U.S. bombers dropped 1,300 tons on Berlin.

June 22. Japanese cleared from Kohima-Imphal road (Assam).

June 23. New Russian offensive began in White Russia. Ploesti and Giurgiu oil installations attacked by U.S. bombers (Rumania). U.S. carrier-borne aircraft attacked Iwo (Volcano Is.).

June 25. Massed attack by British east of Tilly. 500 U.S. heavy bombers of M.A.A.F. attacked targets in S. France.

June 26. Russians captured Vitebsk and Zhlobin. 8th Army took Chiusi (Italy). M.A.A.F. attacked Vienna area. Mogaung fell to Allies (Burma).

June 27. Americans captured Cherbourg. Russians captured Orsha.

June 28. Russians captured Mogilev.

June 29. Leipzig and other targets in Germany heavily attacked by U.S. heavy bombers. Russians took Bobruisk; cleared Leningrad-Murmansk railway.

June 30. R.A.F. Lancasters dropped 1,000 tons on Villers Bocage (France). M.A.A.F. flew 2,600 sorties over Italy, Yugoslavia, Hungary. U.S. severed diplomatic relations with Finland.

THREE YEARS AFTER GERMANY'S ATTACK ON SOVIET RUSSIA

This map shows the vast area of the Soviet Union over which the Germans advanced and retreated during the three years following Germany's assault on June 22, 1941. Leningrad, though virtually surrounded, did not fall; nor did Moscow. Stalingrad, on the Volga, which Hitler had vowed to capture, also held the enemy and proved the turning point of the war in Russia. In the eighteen months between December 16, 1942, and June 22, 1944, Soviet troops forced the enemy back to the line on the left of the shaded portion. *By courtesy of The Soviet War News Weekly*

MIDSUMMER OFFENSIVE IN WHITE RUSSIA

Major-General Sir Charles Gwynn, the Military Editor, described the Russian reconquest of the Crimea and the relief of Leningrad in Chapter 310—prelude to the tremendous leap forward of the Red Armies in White Russia during the high summer of 1944, the history of which he records here. The simultaneous operations in the Baltic Republics and Finland are dealt with in Chapter 329; those in Rumania, Czechoslovakia and Hungary in Chapter 340

BY the beginning of May 1944 nearly the whole Russian front had become stabilized after the winter offensive, the recapture of Sevastopol on May 9 being the last important event of that great series of campaigns.

In the far north six or seven German divisions stood between Murmansk and Petsamo. Farther south the Finns were entrenched south of the River Svir between Lakes Onega and Ladoga, thus blocking the Murmansk-Leningrad railway in its southern stretches, while on the Karelian Isthmus their lines were within artillery range of Leningrad with the heavily fortified Mannerheim line behind their forward positions.

The German main armies were disposed in four groups, Lindemann's group in the Baltic States holding a front from Narva on the Gulf of Finland to the Dvina east of Polotsk. Lake Peipus covered a long stretch of this front, and south of it Pskov was a strong hedgehog bastion at the northern end of the entrenched "Panther" line running through marshy country to the Dvina. The Germans clung to territory north of the Dvina, which clearly might become a dangerous salient, in order to maintain communications with Finland and to shut in the Russian Baltic Fleet. Actually the front to be held was not longer than an east to west front from Polotsk to Riga would have been, but its communications were much longer and more exposed. Furthermore the Russians by capturing the main railways leading south from Leningrad had secured excellent lateral communications, providing a base for offensive operations.

Between the Dvina and Pripet marshes, Von Busch commanded the German group holding the very strongly fortified positions covering the main avenue from Moscow to Warsaw. Its northern flank was protected by the marshy region of the Dvina and its southern by the Pripet marshes, while the upper Dnieper added to the strength of the greater part of the front. Vitebsk and Orsha, formidable hedgehog centres, flanked the dry corridor between the Dvina and Dnieper. The Germans were very confident in the strength of

this sector, but it had elements of weakness. Vitebsk was already outflanked to the north-west, and on the southern flank Rokossovsky had secured a crossing over the Dnieper by capturing Rogachev (February 24, 1944), and also held the railway across the Pripet at Mozyr. He was in a position to turn the line of the Beresina and to threaten the hedgehog centres of Zhlobin and Bobruisk which guarded the German right flank. Moreover railway communication had been restored to Veliki Luki, Smolensk and Gomel, which provided valuable advanced bases for a Russian offensive.

RUSSIANS REJOICE AT ADVANCE ON VITEBSK

The capture by storm of Vitebsk on June 26, 1944, was the climax to a concerted movement of envelopment carried out by the 3rd White Russian Army under General Chernyakhovsky and the 1st Baltic Army under General Bagramyan. Here a group of Soviet soldiers fire their tommy-guns into the air to celebrate the capture of a bridge across the Dvina leading to Vitebsk. Top right, a monument at Vitebsk commemorating the retreat of Napoleon in 1812, mined by the Germans but saved by Russian sappers. *Photos, Pictorial Press*

Between the Pripet marshes and the Carpathians, Model's Army Group had halted Zhukov's winter drive short of Lwow, but it was in this sector that the Germans expected a renewal of the Russian offensive, though probably not until there had been sufficient time to improve communications.

Model's group was widely separated from Kleist's, which covered the approaches to Rumania between the **Situation on the Eastern Front** Dniester and the Seret, but the Carpathians provided an easily held barrier in the interval through which no large scale Russian drive could penetrate. Kleist was holding a strong position, and so long as his Rumanian contingent remained reliable appeared to be in no great danger.

Such was the general situation on the Eastern front when, on June 10, four days after the Allies had landed in Normandy, the Russian offensive opened unexpectedly with an attack on Finland under the well-tried partnership of Govorov and Meretskov. This time the Mannerheim line, although it had been further strengthened, failed completely to hold up the Russian attacks, and on June 20 Viipuri (Viborg) was captured by Govorov (promoted Marshal of the Soviet Union on June 18). Attacking between Lakes Onega and Ladoga on June 21, General Meretskov forced a crossing of the Svir, and by the 24th was across it along its whole length. By June 29 this thrust had cleared the Leningrad-Murmansk railway. Thereafter the Russians drove the Finns out of the whole area between the lakes. Having removed all dangers on the Finnish front, however, the Russians showed no intention of carrying out an aggressive campaign and offered very reasonable terms to Finland (*see* Chapter 327). Except in so far as it continued to affect German strategy, the curtain raiser in Finland had thenceforward little military significance.

The great Russian summer offensive started on June 23, not as the Germans had expected on Model's front, but on Von Busch's. A tremendous artillery bombardment was closely followed by an infantry attack, which in its power and speed clearly achieved an element of surprise. The first objective was the encirclement of Vitebsk, by General Bagramyan's 1st Baltic Army striking from the northeast across the upper Dvina and by General Chernyakhovsky's 3rd White Russian (Byelorussian) Army from the south-east. On June 24, one Order of the Day announced that Bagramyan had broken through the Vitebsk defence on a 20-mile front, widening it on the second day to 50 miles with penetrations of from 12 to 50 miles, and reaching the Dvina on a 23-mile front. Another Order of the Day of the same date announced that Chernyakhovsky had broken through south of Vitebsk on a front of 18 miles, widening it to 50 miles with penetrations of 18 miles. Furthermore that his southern wing had simultaneously broken through on a front of 12 miles and had advanced 10 miles towards Orsha by the right bank of the Dnieper, which here flows from east to west before turning south at Orsha.

On June 25 the encirclement of Vitebsk was completed when Bagramyan, having crossed the Dvina, joined hands with Chernyakhovsky on the Vitebsk-Lepel high-**Vitebsk Taken by Storm** way, the last remaining escape route for the garrison. The ring was tightly held and this great centre, which had long resisted Russian attacks, was taken by storm on June 26, with the destruction of the five divisions allotted to its defence. Thereafter Bagramyan's army was set free to carry out the drive towards the Baltic described in Chapter 329.

The capture of Vitebsk opened the way for Chernyakhovsky's further operations against Von Busch's group. The left prong of his two-pronged attack had aimed at the encirclement of Orsha. He had taken full advantage of the marsh-free gap between Vitebsk and the Dnieper to use strong armoured forces with paralysing effect. By June 25 they had cut the Orsha-Vitebsk railway and, reaching the Orsha-Lepel railway the following day, turned southwards to establish themselves on the Orsha-Minsk road and railway. Attacking from the east and northwest, Chernyakhovsky captured Orsha on June 27. The northern half of Von Busch's front was broken, and

General ZAKHAROV
Colonel-General Georgi Zakharov commanded the 2nd White Russian Army which in the summer campaign of 1944 fought through difficult country between that covered by the 1st and 3rd White Russian Armies, south and north respectively, to capture Mogilev on June 28 and Byelostok on July 27. He had previously been Chief of Staff to Malinovsky.

General CHERNYAKHOVSKY
Army-General Ivan Danilovich Chernyakhovsky commanded the 3rd White Russian Army which swept from the vicinity of Vitebsk (captured June 26, 1944) into East Prussia, where Chernyakhovsky was killed, aged 36, on February 18, 1945. A Jew, he was the youngest of the Red Army commanders, and an outstanding strategist.

STATE THEATRE AT MINSK AFTER GERMAN OCCUPATION

Minsk, capital of White Russia, was recaptured by assault in a combined outflanking movement by the 1st and 3rd White Russian Armies, under Marshal Rokossovsky and General Chernyakhovsky, on July 3, 1944. The first important Soviet city to fall to the Germans in 1941, it had been in their hands for three years and six days. About fifteen miles from the pre-war Polish frontier, it lay less than 140 miles from East Prussia.   *Photos, Pictorial Press*

RUSSIAN ARMOUR IN MOGILEV

Troops of the 2nd White Russian Army, commanded by Colonel-General Zakharov, forced the Upper Dnieper and captured the town and regional centre of Mogilev by assault on June 28, 1944. During the fighting, the German 12th Infantry Division was wiped out, its commander Lieut.-General Bauer and his staff and the commander of the Mogilev garrison, Major-General Ellendorff, being taken prisoner.   *Photo, Pictorial Press*

simultaneously the southern half was receiving equally devastating blows.

Starting on June 25, General Rokossovsky's 1st White Russian Army exploited the position he had secured during the winter across the Dnieper and on both sides of the Beresina to drive north-west towards Bobruisk. Zhlobin he surrounded and captured on June 26 but, more important, by the 28th his left wing had completely encircled Bobruisk on the west, while his right against stiff opposition had closed in on it from the east. On the following day the five divisions holding this vital strongpoint surrendered with a loss of 16,000 killed and 18,000 prisoners.

Meanwhile, between Chernyakhovsky's and Rokossovsky's Armies, Colonel-General Zakharov's 2nd White Russian Army was fighting its **Russians** way over difficult **Take** marshy country **Mogilev** towards Mogilev, another hedgehog town on the Dnieper. Its starting line was farther east than that of the other armies and it had the Pronya River as well as the Dnieper to cross. Nevertheless, it broke through on a 25-mile front on June 25, and two days later had crossed the Dnieper on each side of Mogilev, which it took on June 28. Most of the garrison

appears temporarily to have made good its escape, for owing to the marshy nature of the terrain Zakharov's army was composed of infantry and had no armoured pursuit force.

Thus all the hedgehog strongholds on Von Busch's supposedly impregnable front had fallen in five days, and the shattered remnants of his front line formations were in disorderly flight. But even worse was to come. Chernyakhovsky, after capturing Orsha, called to his support armour under Marshal Rotmistrov (*see* illus. in page 3077). It reached the upper Beresina by June 29, and fanning out, not only closed all the roads leading west from Vitebsk and Orsha, but, striking to the north-west at great speed, reached the roads and railway leading north-west from Minsk to Vilna by July 2. Meanwhile Rokossovsky's armour and Cossack Cavalry, after the capture of Bobruisk, struck west and north-west to reach the Minsk-Baranowicze railway on the same date. Zakharov in the centre was still far behind—he did not reach the Beresina till July 1, where he met with stiff resistance, for in the Minsk area

Von Busch had a reserve Corps and this he had attempted to use to defend the city from the east, only to be caught in a double pincer trap. The long-range mobile tentacles of the two flanking armies closed in on Minsk, capital of White Russia, which they captured on July 3, while their main bodies wheeled in on the flanks of the Germans opposing Zakharov.

Within ten days, the amazing manoeuvres which culminated in the capture of Minsk and the trapping of almost the whole of Von Busch's Army Group had made an immense gap at the most vital sector of the German front. It remained to Rokossovsky (promoted Marshal of the Soviet Union on June 29) and Chernyakhovsky to exploit the gap, Zakharov being left to complete the work of annihilation. Seldom can a victory have been more complete, and it clearly was the result of perfect co-ordination between the four armies employed—including that of Bagramyan to the north. Strategically it was a masterpiece, but it also involved the skilful tactical use of all the resources available, both mobile troops and slower-

FERRYING TANKS ACROSS THE DVINA RIVER

The Dvina was one of the natural obstacles which General Bagramyan had to overcome when he opened the midsummer offensive on his sector in 1944. His forces reached the river on a 23-mile front on June 24, crossed it the next day, and completed the encirclement of Vitebsk by joining hands with General Chernyakhovsky's army advancing from the south-east.

Photo, Planet News

moving masses. As usual the Russian artillery and the work of the engineers contributed immensely to the initial breakthrough, although it was the bold and swift use of mobile columns that produced decisive results.

It was an amazing feat for such comparatively lightly armed forces to have captured Minsk, which as a great road and railway centre was Von Busch's advanced base and a strategical key centre of vital importance, not only for the German defensive position but for the further development of the Russian offensive. From it road and railway communications ran north-west to Vilna and Kovno, Chernyakhovsky's next objectives, while to the south-west the main Moscow-Warsaw communications, running through Baranowicze and Brest-Litovsk, indicated the direction of Rokossovsky's further advance. Between these armies Zakharov's provided a connecting link, with Grodno and Byelostok as his objectives. But Chernyakhovsky's right flank needed protection from counter-strokes by Colonel-General Lindemann's armies. Bagramyan, therefore, after the fall of Vitebsk, was directed first towards Polotsk, which he captured July 4, and thereafter advanced south of the Dvina towards Dvinsk, having the co-operation of Yeremenko's 2nd Baltic Army, which

Steady Soviet Advance Westward

took the offensive on July 10 from the Sokolniki region north of the Dvina. It was also clear that Rokossovsky, in his advance towards Brest-Litovsk, required more direct lines of communication on his left. On July 5, therefore, he opened operations west of Mozyr, advancing along the Gomel-Pinsk railway north of the Pripet, and on July 6 he attacked north-east of Kowel, a town

on the Kiev-Brest-Litovsk railway south of the Pripet marshes, whose loss to the Russians, admitted by the Germans, was confirmed by Marshal Stalin on the same day.

The immediate task after the capture of Minsk was, however, to exploit the gap left by the destruction of Von Busch's group—a gap that the Germans were already attempting to close by rushing up reserves. Chernyakhovsky's advance was swift. On July 5 he took Molodechno where the Polotsk-Warsaw railway crosses the Minsk-Vilna line, by July 9 he had captured Lida, 100 miles to the south-west on the former railway, and on July 13 by an encircling attack secured Vilna. By that time Zakharov, having liquidated Von Busch's armies, had resumed his advance and was west of Minsk, clearing the area south of the upper Niemen, while to the north Bagramyan had cut the Dvinsk-Kovno highway. But Chernyakhovsky, although by July 15 he secured bridge-heads over the Niemen south-east of Grodno, then met stiff opposition. In co-operation with Zakharov he captured Grodno on the 16th, and thus greatly facilitated Zakharov's operations toward Byelostok (captured July 27).

STREET-FIGHTING IN LEPEL

The Red Army, piercing the enemy's fortifications south of Polotsk, took Lepel and 100 other places in the region on June 28, 1944. Great columns of Russian reinforcements and supplies pushed on westwards through wide gaps in the former German defences as fast as the heavy ground permitted, such German forces as had extricated themselves falling back in disorder.

Photo, Planet News

Meanwhile, between Minsk and the Pripet region, Rokossovsky's right wing advanced rapidly towards Baranowicze, which he took on July 8, overthrowing German reserve formations rushed up to attempt to check his progress by counterattacks. By July 10, farther to the southwest he had forced the line of the Shara, a tributary of the Pripet, and with his force advancing from the Mozyr region was threatening Pinsk. The Germans made a great effort to hold this important centre, but it fell on July 14. They had fought stubbornly against the Russian advance up the Pripet, for they had been using the river as an important supply line to their White Russian front. In the marshy country it was difficult to dislodge them by land operations, but Rokossovsky, fertile in expedients, employed vessels of the Dnieper River Flotilla to co-operate with his land troops, and was thus frequently able to by-pass and encircle the enemy's centres of resistance.

Having reached and passed Vilna, Grodno and Pinsk, the White Russian offensive had come up in line with the front established south of the Pripet by Zhukov's 1st Ukrainian Army during the

SOVIET TRAFFIC REGULATOR IN LIBERATED POLOTSK

Polotsk, powerful enemy strongpoint covering the road to Dvinsk, was taken by assault by General Bagramyan's 1st Baltic Army on July 4, 1944. An important communications centre with lines running to Pskov, Nevel, Vitebsk, Molodechno and to Latvia and Lithuania via Dvinsk, its capture was accomplished only after very bitter fighting through three powerful lines of fortifications and large minefields. *Photo, Pictorial Press*

winter, and on July 18 an Order of the Day announced that an offensive had started on that front, now under the command of Koniev, previously in command of the 2nd Ukrainian Army, on the Bessarabian front.

Koniev's offensive resulted in an immediate penetration of 30 miles on a front of 125 miles. It was in contact with Rokossovsky's left wing which twelve days earlier had taken the offensive about Kowel, though only apparently to break the crust of the German resistance in that marshy area. With Koniev on the move he was able to strike deeper, and on July 20 it was announced that he had broken through the German front and had reached the Western Bug. The whole eastern front from Lake Peipus in the north to the foothills of the Carpathians was now ablaze, for on July 19 an Order of the Day announced that the 3rd Baltic Army, commanded by Colonel-General Maslennikov, had taken the offensive and had broken through the Panther line south of Ostrov. (See Chapter 329.)

In a month the three White Russian Armies and Bagramyan's 1st Baltic Army had not only broken through but had completely destroyed the defensive position **Achievements of Four Russian Armies** which the Germans, taking every advantage of marshy country and river lines, had fortified in depth and manned so strongly that they had deemed it impregnable. Having broken through by skilful tactical manoeuvre and admirable co-operative employment of all available weapons, the Russians exploited their success at amazing speed and with the utmost boldness, direct pursuit being supplemented by wide

RUSSIAN ATTACK ON ENEMY KEYPOINT

The Germans called on every available man—sappers, mechanics, cooks—to aid in their defence of Polotsk, captured by the Russians on July 4, 1944. The main Soviet thrust was made by tanks pushing north from Lepel. Guards infantry followed, and cleared the town street by street. Bridges thrown by the attackers across the Ulla River were repeatedly destroyed, and heavy air fighting marked the later stages of the battle. *Photo, Planet News*

WHITE RUSSIAN SUMMER OFFENSIVE, 1944

Following successful offensives in the Ukraine and on the Leningrad front, the Red Army in White Russia, after a lull of several months in that area, went over to the offensive on June 23, 1944. The shaded part of this map shows the country recovered up to July 20 in the campaign described in this chapter, which took the Russians well into Poland and Lithuania.

By courtesy of The Times

tion of the struggle before the war "sweeps into and destroys the whole of Germany," was no doubt based on a professional appreciation of the military situation and was not dictated by political views or personal resentment.

It seems probable that many of the generals and highly placed officers caught in Zakharov's round-up shared the views expressed in the appeal, for it is difficult to believe that a considerable number could not have escaped if they had made a determined effort. It is normally the duty of regimental officers to remain with their men, and even higher officers should do so so long as they can exercise any control of the situation; but once control is hopelessly lost their obvious duty is to escape to a position where a directing influence can be re-established. The number of occasions on which German generals and Staff officers have been flown out of traps is a proof that to attempt to escape in such circumstances in no way violates German conceptions of military honour.

Zakharov's Round-up of Enemy Officers

The Germans claim that this great disaster was due to overwhelming numerical strength; but even after the end of hostilities it was not possible to ascertain even approximately the strength of the forces engaged on either side. That the Russians had greatly superior numerical strength may, however, be taken for granted, for it is the inherent advantage of offensive strategy that a superior concentration of force can always be ensured at the points selected for attack: a superiority likely

armoured thrusts which enveloped the enemy's reserves and his potential rallying pivots at fortified centres in the rear. The whole was a strategic masterpiece, but the co-ordination of action in its execution depended greatly on the initiative, drive, and brilliant grasp of the situation by individual commanders.

The front of these four armies north of the Pripet had been advanced over 300 miles on a width of approximately 300 miles, and the momentum of the advance was far from exhausted. But more important than the territorial gains were the immense losses in men, material and prestige inflicted on the enemy. Here are some of the items of the bag. In killed and prisoners, Bagramyan's army had accounted for over 64,500, Chernyakhovsky's for over 161,280, Zakharov's for over 131,500 and Rokossovsky's for over 182,200. In all, 381,000 officers and men were killed and about 158,500 taken prisoner, including the remarkable figure of 22 generals. Material captured or des-

troyed included in round numbers 630 planes, 2,700 tanks and self-propelled guns, 8,700 guns of various calibres, 5,700 mortars, 23,000 machine guns and 57,000 lorries.

It is not surprising that while this catastrophe was occurring the Germans should have directed all their reserves to make good the gap in the Eastern front and have perforce trusted to Rommel to seal off the Allies in the Cherbourg peninsula, since he could not be given reinforcements sufficient to mount a major counter-offensive against them. Nor is it surprising that Field-Marshal von Paulus and his fellow captive generals in Moscow should have at this stage "seen the writing on the wall" which the successive disasters in the east and south and the reopening of the western front meant, and have made their appeal to their brother officers in the German armed forces. That appeal, calling for a resolute break with Hitler and his associates with a refusal to obey his orders and a cessa-

IN THE WAKE OF THE GERMAN RETREAT TO THE WEST

From June 23–27, 1944, on the 3rd White Russian front alone 32,000 Germans were killed, 20,000 captured. Here is part of one German burial ground left behind in White Russia by the retreating Wehrmacht. Below, Vilna after its capture on July 13 by General Chernyakhovsky. Seized by the Poles from Lithuania in 1920, it was included in Poland at the outbreak of war in 1939. After Poland's collapse, the Russians transferred it to Lithuania again, and at its liberation Marshal Stalin's Order of the Day described it as the capital of the Lithuanian Soviet Republic.

Photos, Pictorial Press

RUSSIANS ADVANCE THROUGH MARSHLANDS

In the area north of the Pripet, the Red Army overwhelmed strong German defences by bold and skilful advance through marshy country deemed by the enemy to be impassable. Here Soviet sappers are building corduroy roads to ensure communications in the area. Below, Russian infantry wade through mud and water in the wooded marshlands of Polyesye.

Photo, Pictorial Press

to be all the greater when the defender has, as in this case, failed to foresee correctly where the blow will fall. The battle was in fact a triumph for offensive as opposed to over rigid defensive strategy, and although no doubt air power played its part in securing success it certainly did not make a decisive contribution to victory. We need look no further for the reason for the Russians' success than brilliant leadership and the admirable qualities their troops displayed.

Great variety of method was employed in the strategical and tactical handling of their forces, and the troops responded to every demand made on them. The speed **Admirable** with which every phase **Qualities of** of the operations was **Russian Troops** carried through did much to disorganize the enemy's attempts to use his reserves in counter-attacks, and the timing of the rapid succession of attacks did much to ensure that reserves were seldom available where most needed. The maintenance of the speed and striking power of the encircling thrusts over great distances gave proof of the efficiency of the administrative organization and the flexibility of the transport services, and it is amazing that after a rapid advance of 300 miles the momentum of the offensive had not been lost, except where stiffening resistance was encountered in highly defensible areas.

Chapter 319

ITALY STRUGGLES TO ACHIEVE DEMOCRACY

Chapter 285 describes the Italian revolution against Fascism, a movement simultaneous and closely connected with the victorious march of the Allied armies, though not entirely dependent on strictly military events. The story of liberated Italy from the armistice of September 1943 to the end of 1944, told here by Ruggero Orlando, is full of hope : it shows that such ideas as liberty and democracy can survive despite long and dire oppression, and take concrete shape again, even amongst ruins, death and misery

MUSSOLINI and his regime fell on July 25, 1943. The armistice between Italy and the Allies was signed on September 3 at Cassibile, near Syracuse, in Sicily (*see* illus. in page 2865). Until the evening of September 7, the Italians had no idea that its announcement was imminent. They learned of it only through the arrival in Rome of two high American officers, Brig.-General Maxwell D. Taylor and Colonel William T. Gardiner. They had not expected the announcement to be made until, at the earliest, September 12.

On learning that General Eisenhower intended to make public the conclusion of the armistice within the next 24 hours, Marshal Badoglio wired to Allied headquarters asking for a postponement : the Italian forces were not sufficiently prepared to meet a likely German onslaught. In fact, it was either too early or too late for the announcement, and, in view of subsequent events, it was more probably too late.

Mussolini's fall had left King, High Command and Government unprepared to answer the question : " Can a country that proclaims itself no longer Fascist, carry on a Fascist war ? " Marshal Badoglio had postponed the issue by declaring, in his proclamation of July 25, " the war goes on," very much to the consternation of people, soldiers, and the lower ranks of the officers. The motives for this decision were varied, but probably the most decisive one was fear, coupled with the vain hope that Hitler would withdraw his troops and leave Italy, geographically a blind alley for any invader coming from the south, to her fate. The best Italian divisions had been shattered in North Africa. On July 25, the majority of the remaining divisions were scattered over the Balkans. The Air Force was almost non-existent, and the position with regard to petrol, equipment and other supplies was disastrous. Only a whole-heartedly anti-German, anti-Fascist leadership would have declared immediate war on the Germans.

When the Italian High Command on August 12 finally decided to send their

Badoglio Proclaims 'War goes on'

delegate, General Castellano, to Lisbon to ask from the Allies military collaboration against the Germans, the Nazis were already pouring troops into the country. One hour after Mussolini's fall two Schutzstaffel divisions stationed in Belgium and the Adolf Hitler division in Russia had received orders to move to Italy. From then onwards German divisions flowed continuously into Italy. (At the last Hitler-Mussolini meeting at Feltre, one week before the fall of Fascism, Hitler had replied to the Duce's urgent appeal for help that he could not spare any troops.)

In the first days of September, the Germans in Italy had swollen to twenty divisions, in great part shock troops and highly motorized. In the Rome area alone, there was a parachute division, containing, instead of the usual four thousand, fourteen thousand men. And the German Grenadier division was composed of 20,000 to

25,000 men, instead of 8,000 to 10,000.

The counter-preparations on the Italian side, on the other hand, were held up, partly by the half-heartedness of political and military leaders : many officers had hoped for the fall of Fascism only in order to invigorate and make more efficient their war effort on the German side ; partly by the need for the purge of pro-German elements from the Army ; and above all by the exaggerated secrecy with which all anti-German preparations were carried out. Though the Germans showed clearly that they knew and were preparing for an Italo-Allied armistice, Marshal Badoglio said nothing to most of his ministers, even after the armistice had been signed. The Minister for the Navy was informed of it only on September 6, and complained bitterly that, had he known of it earlier, he would have prevented the concentration of so many warships in northern ports.

ALLIED C.-IN-C., MEDITERRANEAN, RECEIVES MARSHAL BADOGLIO
On September 29, 1943, Marshal Badoglio, accompanied by members of his military, naval and air staffs, had a conference with General Eisenhower, Allied C.-in-C., at Malta on board H.M.S. 'Nelson.' Here are Field-Marshal Lord Gort (Governor and C.-in-C. Malta), Air Marshal Sir Arthur Tedder (Allied C.-in-C. Air), Marshal Badoglio, Lieut.-General F. N. Mason Macfarlane (Governor and C.-in-C. Gibraltar), General Eisenhower, and General Sir Harold Alexander (Deputy Allied C.-in-C.) at the meeting. *Photo, British Official*

ROME UNDER NAZI CONTROL

1. Parachute trooper on guard outside the Ministry of the Interior. 2. Italian volunteers (left) in front of the German Embassy, which they helped German troops to defend against supporters of Badoglio until German parachute troops (right) came to their aid. 3. Parachute troops patrolling in St. Peter's Square, outside the white line which marked the border between Rome and the Vatican City.

Photos, Keystone; Associated Press; G.P.U.

Thus, when on September 7, they learned of the imminent armistice announcement, Marshal Badoglio and the General Staff almost gave way to panic. The Allies took no heed of Badoglio's telegram asking for postponement: they felt it fully within their rights to decide the date and manner of announcement, the Italians having signed unconditional surrender.

Another telegram left Rome that night for Allied headquarters. It was signed by General Taylor and cancelled the Allied plan to land an American parachute division near the five airports in and near Rome. The two American officers had been sent to Rome precisely to arrange with the Italians for that action and to place themselves at the disposal of the officers commanding the defence of Rome. The division was to start descending in the night of September 8–9, while the Italian Armoured Corps of Rome, consisting of four divisions, was to hold the airports against German attacks for four consecutive nights—the time necessary to land the whole division.

General Carboni, Commander of the Armoured Corps, dissuaded the Americans from the project, because the airports were "virtually in German hands."

Parachute Landing Cancelled

"Moreover"—and these are the words he wrote in his report to the Commission inquiring into the breakdown of the defence of Rome—"any attempt to seize the airports on our part would have been a signal for Marshal Kesselring's forces to attack us." His arguments were later confirmed to the two Americans by Marshal Badoglio himself, and consequently the whole scheme was cancelled.

Preoccupation with a desire to give the Germans no pretext for attack, and the stupid hope that they might withdraw after the announcement of the armistice, were dominant not only in Carboni's mind, but also in the minds of those from whom he took his orders. Even during the night of September 8–9, while German troops were already marching towards Rome, the Chief of the General Staff issued the following order: "Let the Germans pass through the lines held by the Armoured Corps, if they present themselves without shooting."

However, before this order, which would have given the Germans possession of the capital without firing a shot, reached the Commands, Italian and German troops had already become involved in fighting. The Italians held their own, but how long could they do so? The air support, which the Italian Government had asked from the Allies

in a memorandum dated September 6, was not forthcoming. Apparently this important document never reached the Allies. General Castellano, who had, without consulting anybody, evolved the parachute plan, was accused during subsequent inquiries of having prevented the officer carrying the memorandum from seeing any responsible person at Allied headquarters.

No German troops had yet penetrated into Rome when suddenly at dawn on September 9, the King, the Service

King Victor Emmanuel Leaves Rome

Ministers, except the War Minister, and the High Command decided to leave the capital and seek refuge with the Allies. Next morning the telephones rang in the Service ministries, and in the High Command offices. Dispatch riders came in. So did telegrams from all over Italy, from the islands, from the Balkans. There was nobody to give orders, nobody to give news. Rumours went about, "an armistice has been signed with the Germans," "the King has been taken prisoner"; secret papers were lying about abandoned, even on Marshal Badoglio's desk. Nobody had been informed of the flight. Only General Sorice, Minister of War, had been ordered by Marshal Badoglio to ring up Ricci, Minister of Interior, and ask him to take over the administration of the capital. Ricci declined. Nobody had been appointed to take control in the absence of General Ambrosio, the head of the armed forces, who was in Southern Italy.

Shortly before leaving, General Roatta, Assistant Chief of the General Staff, called General Carboni and ordered him to transfer his command and two

of his four divisions, which were already engaged in heavy fighting, to Tivoli. Only the Grenadiers division was left behind. The "Centauro" black-shirt division no longer counted. When General Carboni showed himself puzzled by the order, Roatta told him : "In Tivoli or farther on on the road to Avezzano you will find me and Ambrosio or further orders." Carboni obeyed. Neither in Tivoli, nor on the road to Avezzano did he find Ambrosio or Roatta, by now safely embarked at Pescara ; nor any further orders.

On the following day, Carboni, acting on his own initiative, went back to Rome and decided to call back the two divisions uselessly moved to Tivoli. But it was too late. The Grenadiers had fought heroically, supported by the civilian population—supplied with weapons, some secretly stored in the preceding weeks by the democratic parties, mainly the Communists and the Action Party, some taken from deserting Italian and German soldiers in the muddle. For it must not be forgotten that, immediately after

the announcement of the armistice, a great part of the German troops was seized by utter confusion and defeatism. Many sold their arms for civilian clothes, many threw them away.

Meanwhile, Marshal Caviglia, some ninety years of age and the highest ranking officer in the area, assumed command. He was assisted by Marshal de Bono, a man who during the First Great War had been dismissed from his post because of inefficiency and who, nevertheless, had reached again high military commands during the Fascist period (although causing an Italian defeat during the Abyssinian war), because he had been one of the "quadrumviri" of the March on Rome. On the instigation of General Calvi di Bergolo, Commander of the "Centauro" black-shirt division and son-in-law of the King, they entered into negotiations with Kesselring.

In a desperate effort to save the situation, General Carboni through the rest of the night distributed arms to the civilian population ;

Germans Threaten to Bomb Rome

he also tried in vain to contact the Allies through the British Embassy at the Vatican. He then asked the Committee of National Liberation to order a popular insurrection. The request was not accepted by the anti-Fascist parties, but nevertheless thousands of civilians fought on even after an armistice with the Germans was signed on September 10, at four o'clock in the afternoon. Its conditions were accepted in face of a German threat of an all-out bombing attack on Rome.

General Calvi di Bergolo was appointed commander of the "open city"

ALLIED MILITARY GOVERNMENT IN ITALY

1. Main entrance to the headquarters of Allied Military Government of Occupied Territory in Palermo, Sicily.
2. Civilians unloading salt brought into Florence by A.M.G., officials of which entered the northern half of the city on August 13, 1944, following the German withdrawal on the 11th. 3. Regulations governing civilian life posted up in Naples by A.M.G. 4. Salvaging a tapestry, one of many art treasures found in a castle at Mignano (south-east of Cassino), where every building was mined and destroyed by the Germans. 5. Italian policemen (Carabinieri) continue their duties under A.M.G.O.T. authorization.

Photos, British Official; Pictorial Press

of Rome. He was on excellent terms with the Germans ; yet, as he was the King's son-in-law, it was thought that the people would trust his loyalty to the legitimate Italian Government appointed by the King.

From the military point of view, Rome cannot be defended without sufficient forces to prevent enemy concentrations in the Tuscan maremma to the north. The Allies are said to have made verbal promises to General Castellano at Cassibile that they would land with fifteen divisions. But only four divisions were landed at Salerno. The Italians, it seems, had reason also to expect that heavy artillery would be landed at the mouth of the Tiber. But the expectation was not fulfilled. That there was truth in these reports was later confirmed by an American eyewitness of the parleys, the war correspondent David Brown who wrote : "The Allies launched a gigantic bluff. . . . The Italians never knew how imminent the landing was, nor how meagre the forces dedicated to it."

It is in any case certain that the subsequent divisions in Italian politics were due far more to the events which immediately followed the Allied-Italian armistice of September 8, 1943, than to recriminations over the Fascist past or ideological differences between parties. To the dramatic events connected with the German occupation of the country, and not to memories of Fascist times (about which there was not much controversy) was due the impossibility of retaining Badoglio as Prime Minister after the liberation of Rome ; the widespread and acrimonious discussions over the Monarchy, the military caste and the higher ranks of the bureaucracy ; and the fact that the Italian resistance movement was not simply anti-Fascist, but also Republican, although it was made up of men of both right-wing and left-wing views.

Much discussion turned on whether the Germans occupied Italy, and in particular Rome (thus adding at least **Panic Spreads from Italian H.Q.** a year to the duration of the Italian campaign) through criminal acts committed by the Monarchy and Marshal Badoglio. If there was an "Allied bluff," that would have been an extenuation of their conduct. But whether their acts were criminal or not, they gave way to panic, showing themselves absolutely unfit for political and military leadership. The panic at headquarters in Rome spread to responsible leaders throughout the country. Almost everywhere civilians seized arms and fought, together with disbanded

soldiers, while regular formations melted away. The Turin workers, having received petrol and weapons from the disbanded army stores, distinguished themselves in severe and lengthy street fighting. When led by decided commanders, regular soldiers fought to the end, as at Spezia, Treviso and Trieste ; confronted by a firm Italian garrison, the Germans had to evacuate Sardinia (announced September 19). The "Turin" division fought for the whole month of September near Gorizia.

Leadership did not fail in the Navy, the least "fascistized" of all Italian armed forces. An example unique in history, the Italian Navy, ordered at very short notice to sail towards Allied ports, despite ferocious attacks by the German air force, obeyed immediately (*see* page 2848). They had but their A.A. guns to defend themselves against the Luftwaffe. "The Italian Fleet did not surrender ; they fought their way out," Lord Cranborne stated later in the House of Lords on behalf of the British Government.

Once the Army was disbanded, the cadres broken up and the individual soldier thrown on his own resources, the traditional hatred for barbarity of the Italian people came again to the fore. Hundreds of thousands of young men preferred to go to German prisons and concentration camps rather than adhere to the German puppets, the new Fascists.

On September 12, Nazi parachutists released Mussolini from a winter-sport hotel on the top of the Gran Sasso, the highest mountain of the Appenines. He was taken to Germany, thanked Hitler (*see* illus. in page 2789), recovered from the shock, but **Rescue of Mussolini** did not dare to return to Rome. Instead he went to live near Salò, on the shores of Lake Garda, and set up the "Italian Social Republic," a definitely quisling regime, held in contempt even by its Nazi masters. The members of the Fascist Grand Council, who, on July 25, 1943, voted Mussolini out of power, were tried at Verona for treason—all except six *in absentia*. Cianetti, former Minister of Corporations, was sentenced to 30 years' penal servitude. Count Galeazzo Ciano (Mussolini's son-in-law), Marshal de Bono, and three others were shot on January 11, 1944.

The Germans, as they retired northward, left behind them the greatest possible misery and confusion, thus increasing popular resentment against Badoglio's government. President Roosevelt and Winston Churchill, on the signature of the armistice, broadcast a message to the Italians : "Strike hard, strike home ; all will be well in the end," they said. But the anti-Fascist parties felt that every Italian was prepared to follow this encouraging advice, except the Government. On

WATCHING THE ADVANCE OF THE EIGHTH ARMY
People of Canosa, which lies just south of the river Ofanto, stand on their hillside to watch the 8th Army moving across the Apulian plain in the direction of the great air base at Foggia, occupied on September 27, 1943. In this area of Italy the enemy offered little resistance, and the advance of the 8th Army was very rapid with comparatively little damage to the countryside.
Photo, British Official

ITALY'S SECOND POST-FASCIST PREMIER

When the Allies entered Rome, Badoglio resigned. He was succeeded by 71-year-old Signor Ivanoe Bonomi, Prime Minister of the last pre-Fascist government of Italy. Here Signor Bonomi early in 1945 is signing an agreement by which Italy doubled the 50 million dollars (about £11,000,000) contributed by U.N.R.R.A. (see illus. in page 2949) to the relief of Italy. With him is Mr. Spurgeon M. Keeny, chief of the U.N.R.R.A. Italian Mission.   *Photo, P.N.A.*

September 29, 1943, Marshal Badoglio met General Eisenhower, Commander-in-Chief of the Allied Mediterranean Forces, and General Alexander, Deputy Allied Commander-in-Chief, on the British battleship "Nelson" at Malta. He signed the 44 clauses which elaborated the temporary armistice signed on September 3. It was agreed that they should remain secret.

On October 1 Naples was liberated (*see* Chapter 286). On October 13 Italy declared war on Germany. The King opposed this step, and even Marshal Badoglio "was no longer on speaking terms" with him. The Italian Government instanced the atrocities the Germans were committing in the provinces they occupied as justification for the step. A tripartite announcement published in London, Washington and Moscow recognized Italy as a "co-belligerent." The Conference of Foreign Secretaries at Moscow, October 19–30, issued a declaration reaffirming the attitude of their governments in favour of the restoration of democracy in Italy, and agreed to set up an Advisory Council for Italy.

Italy a 'Co-Belligerent'

Meanwhile A.M.G.O.T. (Allied Military Government of Occupied Territory) or A.M.G., followed the armed forces to organize territory as the Germans were expelled from it. Italian territory occupied by the Allies and behind the combat zones was governed by the Allied Control Commission (A.C.C.) instituted on November 10, and working

in concert with the Italian government.

Badoglio approached politicians of the various Italian parties, which, thanks to the liberty of the press and of organization granted by the Allies, were no longer "underground," with a view to forming a representative government; but his efforts encountered growing hostility from the Committee of National Liberation set up in Naples, and representing all Italian anti-Fascist parties—Liberals, Christian-Democrats, Labour Democrats, Action Party, Socialists, and Communists—which declared itself against collaboration with the King.

Count Sforza, once Foreign Secretary in pre-Fascist times, and one of the most prominent anti-Fascist exiles, returned to Italy from America, via London. He met President Roosevelt and Mr. Churchill; he agreed with them to overlook the constitutional question,

which turned on the responsibility of the monarchy for the misdeeds of the Fascist regime, and to help Marshal Badoglio in constituting a representative government. But he conditioned his support of Marshal Badoglio and the monarchist government by their efficiency in furthering the common war effort.

As soon as Count Sforza reached Italy, he decided that Badoglio's government was too closely linked with the Fascist past to stir enthusiasm amongst Italians for the anti-German war, and he declared himself unable to support the Marshal.

Marshal Badoglio then formed (November 16) a cabinet of "experts," made up of military chiefs and technicians with a very few political figures, none representing currents of opinion inside the Committee of National Liberation. This Government took steps to reorganize the Army so as to take an active part in the war (the first Italian unit went into action on the side of the Allies in December 1943) and to reform the administrative structure, freeing it from Fascist elements.

The six parties of C.N.L. conducted a violent campaign against the King, accusing him of direct responsibility for Italy's past and recent ruin, and against the monarchy itself. Their activity culminated in the Congress at

ITALIANS WOUNDED FIGHTING WITH ALLIES NEAR MIGNANO

Badoglio's government reorganized the army so that it could take an active part in the war on the Allied side, and on December 16, 1943, Italian troops, including Bersaglieri, won their first victory of the campaign when, in action with the 5th Army, they gained all their objectives in an attack on the crest of a steep hill blocking the southern entrance to the Liri valley during operations against the Gustav line (see Chapter 302).   *Photo, Keystone*

GERMANS SHOW THE WHITE FLAG AT VILNA

On July 8, 1944, strong tank and infantry forces of the 3rd White Russian Army broke into Vilna, which was completely surrounded by July 10. The enemy garrison barricaded itself in the centre of the city and offered violent resistance to the Red Army. It was not finally overcome till July 13, after 8,000 of its number had been killed. Here are some of the 5,000 taken prisoner coming out to surrender. Below, Soviet machine-gunners in the street fighting that went on inside Vilna for five days.

Photos, Pictorial Press

ALLIED MILITARY GOVERNMENT BRINGS WATER TO NAPLES

The Allies entered Naples on October 1, 1943, to find that the Germans had destroyed port installations, many public buildings, all important hotels except two—and the water supply system. Col. Knox, U.S. Navy Secretary, said on October 8 that the population of Naples was starving and without drinking water. Here Neapolitans are drawing water from taps set up by A.M.G., which made the provision of water for civilians one of its first tasks.

Photo, Pictorial Press

CANADIANS ON PATROL IN CAPTURED CALAIS

By-passed in the rapid advance of the 21st Army Group during the end of August and beginning of September 1944, Calais was attacked by the Canadians on September 28, when, fighting through torrential rains across minefields and inundations, they drove into the town and stormed the citadel. A twenty-four-hour truce to allow of the evacuation of the citizens was followed at noon on September 30 by an all-out attack supported by artillery and aircraft. By 7.30 a.m. on October 1 the town had been cleared. *Photo, Associated Press*

TRIUMPHAL ENTRY INTO RHEIMS

In their drive towards Belgium after the retreating Germans, General Patton's U.S. 3rd Army liberated the ancient city of Rheims, Metropolitan See of France, on August 30, 1944, without the firing of a shot. The cathedral, here seen with its main entrance well protected against blast, was untouched, and the city had suffered little damage ; but the great airfield nearby was studded with bomb craters, its hangars and other buildings riddled with holes, from R.A.F. and U.S.A.A.F. raids. Seventy-five aircraft were found abandoned on it.

Photo, Keystone

Bari, held on January 28–29, 1944, in which participated, beside the representatives of the six parties of the southern C.N.L., political figures from parts of Italy occupied by the Germans and politicians returned from abroad. The result of this first democratic congress held in liberated Europe was the adoption of a motion creating a permanent executive committee, to which was given the task of taking the necessary steps to secure the King's abdication, as being "the undeniable pre-requisite for the moral and material reconstruction of Italy."

The executive committee did not achieve its purpose. Mr. Churchill, speaking in the House of Commons,

British Support Badoglio declared explicitly that he did not consider it possible to form any other Government in Italy capable of obtaining obedience from the Italian armed forces, and that the United Kingdom would give its support to the King and Marshal Badoglio, promising, at the same time, to examine the situation afresh after the liberation of Rome.

During the first phase of the political battle between the Monarchy and the Committee of National Liberation, three events caused resounding echoes both inside and outside the country. In mid-February 1944, the Italian Government left Brindisi for Salerno, and all the territory south of the northern boundaries of the provinces of Salerno,

PALMIRO TOGLIATTI

The Italian Communist leader, Togliatti, after spending most of the Fascist period in exile in Moscow, returned to Italy in the spring of 1944. At a party meeting in Naples on March 31–April 1, he made a speech of great moderation, insisting on the need for Italian unity. As a result, the party decided to reverse its policy, and to agree to the postponement of a settlement of the question of the Monarchy, and to participation in an all-party interim Government.

Photo, New York Times

BRITISH COAL FOR THE ALLIED FORCES IN ITALY

While the north of Italy remained under German control, the south was cut off both from the coal it had been accustomed to receive from Germany and Poland, and also from its sources of electric power; and the railways had to be kept going for the use of the Allied occupation and fighting forces on coal imported from Britain. Here a collier from Cardiff is discharging her 9,000-ton cargo at Taranto. *Photo, British Official*

Potenza and Bari was handed over by A.M.G. to Italian administration.

In the early part of March 1944, the Soviet Union recognized Badoglio's Government and decided to establish diplomatic relations with it.

The arrival in Italy from Moscow on March 28, 1944, of the Italian exile and leader of the Italian Communist Party, Palmiro Togliatti, a member of the executive of the defunct Comintern, marked the beginning of a new phase in the question of the Monarchy. Togliatti, unlike Count Sforza (who, though linked with the Action Party, was not formally a member of it), had behind him a strong, disciplined party and was able to achieve what Count Sforza had failed to do: he brought the C.N.L. inside the Badoglio Cabinet.

On August 12 the King, in a public declaration, announced his desire to withdraw into private life after the liberation of the capital, and to appoint as Lieutenant of the Realm his son Umberto, Prince of Piedmont. The attitude of the Communists, shared by the Socialist Party, and the decision taken by the King removed the obstacles to the collaboration of the six parties of the C.N.L. with the Government, and the King accepted the resignation of the cabinet on April 17. On the 27th, he charged Marshal Badoglio with the formation of a new Government, and after four days of consultations a Government was formed, composed of representatives of the parties of the Committee of Liberation, with a few

military men and technicians. The fact that a leader coming from Moscow had succeeded where Count Sforza, coming from Washington and London, had failed, strongly increased the already existing dislike for Sforza in British diplomatic circles. But the solution of the Italian crisis was warmly welcomed by Russia, Britain and the United States alike.

The new Government repudiated the whole foreign policy of the Fascist regime in a public declaration on May 23; in particular, it condemned the Fascist incursions into France, Greece, Yugoslavia, Russia and Albania.

On the liberation of Rome, June 4, 1944 (see Chapter 302), the King retired from public life, appointing Prince Umberto as Lieutenant of the Realm. The Government, resigning at Salerno in accordance with constitutional custom, was re-formed at Rome, the President of the Committee of National Liberation, Ivanoe Bonomi, taking the place of Marshal Badoglio as President of the Council. Bonomi's Government included many more representatives of the six anti-Fascist parties. It decided to take an oath of loyalty not to the Monarchy, but to the Nation, and its members pledged themselves not to take action which might compromise the party truce and the solution of the question of the Monarchy.

King Retires from Public Life

The dismissal of Marshal Badoglio took British circles by surprise. Only local information from Rome, where the memories of September 8, 1943, were still bitter, convinced the London Government that further support of the Marshal would lead to serious trouble ; and not until July 15 was the veteran anti-Fascist Ivanoe Bonomi able to preside over the first regular meeting of his cabinet in the capital. (For military operations following the capture of Rome, which had important effects on Italian political developments, *see* Chapter 338.)

On July 20 the provinces of Foggia, Campobasso, Benevento, Avellino and Naples were restored to **More Provinces** Italian administration ; **under Italian** on August 15 those of **Administration** Rome, Frosinone and Littoria. The city of Naples remained under Allied Military Government, in view of the capital importance of the port for Allied Military supplies.

During August, Mr. Churchill spent fifteen days in Italy (*see* plate following page 3178) and met the new Italian Government. Before leaving Italian territory, he sent a message to the Italians, stating how much he appreciated the co-operation afforded to Allied armed forces, and fixing the principles on which, in his opinion, a true democracy must be founded ; he finally wished to an Italy based on such principles the speediest return amongst the peace-loving peoples. On August 29 British and American trade union delegates arrived in Italy to get in touch with the Italian Confederation of Labour.

MR. CHURCHILL IN ROME

The Prime Minister, in Italy from August 11-28, 1944, visited the front, inspected Allied forces about to land in southern France, had an audience with the Pope, and met Prince Umberto, Lord Lieutenant of the Realm, and the Italian Government. He is seen here with Prince Umberto ; behind the Prince stands General Sir Henry Maitland Wilson, Allied Supreme Commander, Mediterranean.
Photo, British Official

This organization was founded on June 13, 1944 and, for the first time in the history of Italy and of many European countries, unions with Socialist and Communist leadership merged with Catholic organizations ; the progress made by the Italian Confederation, despite the difficulties of the organizers owing to bad economic conditions, unemployment and the lack of links between one province and another, was considered by many observers the first outstanding success in the democratic reconstruction and rehabilitation of Italy.

As new provinces were liberated, the popular feeling against Fascists and " collaborators " was violent ; the difficulties were immense of disciplining to acceptance of legal justice the masses, the partisans, and the many unruly elements who often appear when waters are troubled. The police, who under Fascism had been principally a body for political repression, were partially

DISORDER IN ROMAN COURT

A few minutes before Enrico Caruso, ex-Chief of the Rome Police and an active collaborator with the Germans against his fellow-citizens, was due to appear in the Supreme Court at Rome, a disorderly crowd burst into the courtroom, seized Donato Carretto, Fascist prison governor and a witness for the defence, and lynched him. Here an Allied officer spectator is appealing for order.
Photo, British Official

disbanded; those who remained were bewildered and powerless, often without transport or telephones, and ridiculously underpaid while prices were soaring. The authority of the Italian Government was seriously undermined by Allied control, and by the fact that some Allied authorities took time before trusting a totally anti-Fascist Government as much as they had trusted Badoglio (a great loss in this sense was the resignation in July 1944 for reasons of health, of the intelligent, popular and tactful General Sir F. Noel Mason Mac-Farlane, as head of the Allied Control Commission). But Bonomi, diplomatic yet upright, held together the most intransigent anti-Fascists, while dealing with Court circles and Monarchist bureaucracies; he speeded up anti-Fascist purges and trials of war criminals. Some unpleasant incidents, such as the lynching of a former vice-director of prisons (who was a witness in the trial of Enrico Caruso, the "butcher" of the Romans under Nazi occupation) received great publicity in Italy and throughout the world; nevertheless, cases like that were sporadic, and not more numerous than in other European countries following liberation.

The tribunals passed only one capital sentence, on Caruso. The Governor of the Bank of Italy, who allowed the Nazis to seize the Italian gold, and some generals who failed in their duty of resisting the Germans after the armistice, were condemned to imprisonment.

Foreign relations progressed step by step. On September 26, 1944, it was announced that, following the second Quebec Conference (*see* Chapter 339), President Roosevelt and Mr. Churchill had had further discussions, and a joint statement was issued modifying the terms of the Instrument of Surrender signed by Badoglio on September 29, 1943 (*see* page 3234 and Hist. Doct. CCLXXXI) and reducing the powers of the Allied Control Commission (whose name was changed to Allied Commission from October 21, 1944). The Italian Government was invited to appoint representatives to London and Washington; U.N.R.R.A. help was extended to Italy; and Anglo-American economic assistance towards Italian rehabilitation was promised. The Allied envoys in Rome (Mr. Alexander Kirk, United States; Sir Noel Charles, Great Britain; Mr. Krylenko, Soviet Union) were raised to Ambassadorial status, as were the Italian representatives in Washington, London, and Moscow. Count Nicolò Carandini was accepted as Italian Ambassador in London.

Italian Representatives Abroad

Signor Bonomi had to face serious opposition within his cabinet. In the absence of any assembly, the cabinet itself acted as a parliament, where different and often conflicting tendencies were represented. The most intransigent republicans, for instance, charged Bonomi with violation of the constitutional truce, because he had appointed the veteran politician Vittorio Emmanuele Orlando, President of the lower House, and Count della Torretta, President of the Senate. No lower House existed; the Senate was in process of purging. But the heads of the two Houses, according to the Italian constitution, were the highest counsellors of the King in case of a cabinet crisis. These appointments were therefore considered as an attempt by the Crown, with the connivance of Bonomi, to wrest power from the hands of the Committee of Liberation which claimed to represent the popular will.

After many attacks on this and other issues, Bonomi resigned on November 26. The crisis lasted two weeks; political polemics broke out into the open, made easier by the relative standstill of military operations in the winter season and made harsher by the British "veto" on the appointment of Count Sforza as Foreign Secretary; until, on December 10, Bonomi formed a new cabinet. The Socialist and Action Parties, although they remained in the Committee of Liberation, refused to participate in the new Government which was thus based on four parties, Liberal, Christian-Democrat, Labour-Democrat and Communist.

Meanwhile, in northern Italy the size and organization of the resistance movement had grown stronger and better; frequent contacts were established between north and south, and the voice of the northern partisans began to play a prominent part in Italian politics. On December 29, 1944, the Italian Government decided that as areas were liberated partisans could enter the Army

ITALIAN PARTISANS WITH THE ALLIES

On May 22, 1944, the first communiqué on the operations of Italian partisans behind the enemy lines was issued from General Alexander's headquarters. It stated that they were keeping six German divisions occupied, and detailed some of their activities. This photograph is of Luigi Piazza, parish priest of San Valentino, with the leader and other members of one Partisan band which, after five months' fighting in the mountains, passed through the British lines for rest and re-equipment.

with the same rank they had held in their partisan units, up to that of lieutenant-colonel; that partisans' families resident in liberated zones should receive the same treatment as soldiers' families, and that partisans were eligible to receive military awards reserved for the regular armed forces.

GERMAN ARMOUR IN MILAN

Resistance by the Italian civilian population in the part of Italy under German occupation followed the Italo-Allied armistice, and led to ruthless repression. A state of emergency was declared in Milan, where machine-guns were mounted and 1,750 hostages were seized. Continued trouble led to the use of armoured units against Italian patriots in Milan and Turin. Here is a S.S. tank before Milan Cathedral.

Photo, Associated Press

CROSSINGS OF THE RIVER SEINE

Such elements of the German 7th Army as escaped from the Falaise pocket (see page 3184) streamed eastward towards the Seine, relentlessly pursued by the British and Canadian armies. The first British crossing of the river was made at Vernon on August 25 by Wiltshires and Somersets of the 43rd Divn. who launched the assault within two hours of arrival there. 1. Enemy transport approaching the west bank of the river at Muids, between Vernon and Les Andelys, where it was loaded on to an improvised ferry. 2. British infantry cross by assault boat at Vernon. 3. Ferrying bren-carriers over at Elbeuf. 4. British troops and vehicles pouring across a pontoon bridge.

KEEP 20 YARDS
OVER BRIDGE

Chapter 320

ALLIED ARMIES ENTER PARIS AND BRUSSELS

In Chapter 314, Squadron Leader Derek Adkins described the fighting that followed the reopening of the Western Front in June 1944, up to the liquidation of the Falaise 'pocket,' and the destruction there of the greater part of the German 7th Army. Here he continues the history of the campaign to the relief of Brussels and Antwerp by Gen. Dempsey's British 2nd Army, early in September, describing also the new landings in the south of France on August 15 and the successful Allied sweep up the Rhône valley

FOLLOWING the elimination of the Falaise pocket, troops of the British 2nd and 1st Canadian Armies thrust hard towards the Seine, driving the battered remnants of Von Kluge's 7th Army before them. While the battle of the Falaise Gap was actually in progress, however, American armoured columns to the south, having liberated Le Mans (August 9, 1944), fanned out to reach Châteaudun and Orléans on August 16, Chartres and Dreux on the 17th and Mantes–Gassicourt, on the Seine itself, 31 miles west of Paris, by the 18th (*see* map in page 3174). At the same time advanced elements reached Arpajon, south of the city. U.S. infantry followed on the heels of this armour to mop up and consolidate the captured territory. This wide sweep by the Americans to the east and north-east caused the enemy great distress by forcing him to use the difficult river crossing of the Seine to bring up supplies and reinforcements.

Allies Cross the Seine — While Allied armour continued to push up the western bank of the Seine towards the estuary, the infantry succeeded in forming a bridge-head in the Mantes–Gassicourt area, and during the 19th and 20th two regiments were successfully put across. By the 22nd other American troops had penetrated to Sens, 60 miles S.E. of Paris, and Etampes, pushed through Melun and Fontainebleau, to liberate Troyes on the 25th. On the west bank of the Seine they were forty-five miles north-west of the capital by the 22nd. These forces, driving towards the mouth of the river and fanning out to include Evreux and Breteuil, made contact with British troops in the area of Laigle, captured by the British on the 22nd, during that day.

Other forces of the British 2nd and 1st Canadian Armies, with Polish, Dutch and Belgian contingents, also advanced eastward. They reached Lisieux on the 22nd (cleared 23rd), the Belgians took Deauville on the 22nd and the enemy salient, between the American armoured forces at Elbeuf and the British and Canadian troops, was eliminated on the 25th.

3243

~~~~~~~~~~~~~~~~~~~~~~~~~~~~~~~~~
THE TASKS OF
21st (BRITISH) ARMY GROUP

In a lecture given to the Royal United Services Institution in London on October 3, 1945, Field-Marshal Sir Bernard Montgomery said that after the defeat of the German armies in the Battle of Normandy the immediate tasks of 21st Army Group were .

1. The destruction of the enemy in N.E. France.
2. The clearance of the Pas de Calais with its V-bomb sites.
3. The capture of airfields in Belgium.
4. The capture of Antwerp.
~~~~~~~~~~~~~~~~~~~~~~~~~~~~~~~~~

Between August 25 and 30, new crossings were secured over the Seine. One, at Vernon, was established in brigade strength by British troops on the morning of the 26th, a bridge having been rapidly built for the purpose. At Pont de l'Arche, ten miles due south of Rouen, Canadian armour made another crossing in face of stiff opposition. In this sector a German ferry was captured intact. Both bridge-heads were steadily extended during the next few days, and a third was established at Elbeuf. By the 29th British armour was nearing Gournay, and any hope the Germans had had of holding the line of the Seine had gone. Nevertheless, fierce fighting continued near the mouth of the river as the enemy engaged in a last desperate rearguard action to allow as many of his troops as possible to escape. Some succeeded in doing so, at a cost of the bulk of their heavy equipment, but by

BURNT-OUT ENEMY EQUIPMENT IN A SEINE VILLAGE
The lower reaches of the river Seine were the scene during the last days of August 1944 of terrible destruction by the Allied air forces of German troops, transport and armour struggling to escape eastward after the defeat of the 7th Army in the Falaise pocket. Here is burnt-out and abandoned enemy transport in the devastated village of La Mailleraye-sur-Seine.

the 29th the last pockets holding out in the Forêt de Bretonne had been eliminated, and the main strength of the British and Canadian armies was pouring across the Seine.

The liberation of Paris was announced on August 23 by the French Forces of the Interior as having taken place the previous day; but in point of fact a certain amount of enemy resistance remained to be overcome. In the evening of the 24th tanks of the French 2nd Armoured Division (General J. P. Leclerc) entered the Port d'Orléans, and advanced to the Ile de la Cité to meet the leaders of the F.F.I. The main force of the division entered the city next morning and by nightfall all organized resistance had ceased. At this date, north of Troyes, only a small corner at Rouen remained in enemy hands west of the Seine. In this congested space, the

Liberation of Paris

FIGHTING IN PARIS STREETS

Right, General Jacques Phillippe Leclerc, Commander of the French 2nd Armoured Division, the first Allied force to enter Paris, reaches the Boulevard Montparnasse on August 25, 1944. Below, men of the 2nd Armoured Division near the Arc de Triomphe on guard against Nazi snipers and pro-Nazi French militia (see page 2902) who had fired on other members of the Division guarding German prisoners, some of whom were killed. Their guard escaped injury. *Photos, U.S. Official*

confused remnants of several German divisions endeavoured to make a stand, while some of their troops, at the cost of the greater part of their heavy equipment, made the perilous crossing of the river under Allied gunfire and constant attack by the Allied air forces.

On the night of August 14–15, the Allies opened one more front in Europe, in the south of France. This operation was under the direction of General Sir Henry Maitland Wilson, Allied Supreme Commander, Mediterranean, and was led by Lieut.-Gen. Alexander

M. Patch, commanding the American 7th Army. The initial attacks were made by a combined British and American airborne force, dropped behind the beaches between Hyères and Cannes to block the movement of enemy reserves (*see* illus. in page 3193); and by U.S. Rangers and French Commando units against the west flank of the assault area. The Commandos rapidly overran resistance on the islands of Levant and Port Cros, and at Cap Nègre.

On the morning of August 15 three infantry divisions—all seasoned in the hard school of Italy—were landed across the beaches between Agay and the Baie de Cavalaire. Opposition was neither extensive nor formidable and forces were rapidly pushed forward into the pine-clad Esterel and the Monts des Maures. Within forty-eight hours, the bridge-head had been extended as far as the valley of the Argens, through which run the main road and railway from Marseilles and Toulon to Cannes. Fréjus, St. Raphael, Draguignan, Le Luc and Carnoules were quickly captured, and near the coast Allied forces were soon closing in on Bormes. Advances to places as much as thirty-five miles inland had been made by the evening of the 18th, when American reconnaissance units in the northern sector entered Grasse and Castellane. To the west a task force reached the river Durance at Oraison and began to move northward on both sides of the river (*see* map in page 3249), while in the central sector Allied forces were on the outskirts of Aix en Provence by the 19th and entered the town next day, crossing the river Durance to the north in the direction of Pertuis. Meanwhile French armoured forces operating south of the main road leading through Aix en Provence pushed towards Aubagne and Marseilles, while in the extreme south other French forces succeeded in encircling Toulon and were soon on the outskirts of Hyères. To the west the coast road was cut by the capture of Bandol. In all these operations the French Forces of the Interior contributed materially to the rapid advance of the Allied forces, for the whole of

ALLIED TROOPS LAND ON THE RIVIERA

Still another front was opened in Europe when the American 7th Army, which included French and British units, landed at various points between Hyères and Cannes on August 15, 1944. Here men of the American Medical Corps and military police hug the beach just after coming ashore in the face of mortar fire. Below, troops moving inland from the assault beaches. Losses in these landings were unexpectedly light.　　*Photos, Keystone ; Planet News*

GENERAL DE TASSIGNY

Condemned to ten years' imprisonment by Vichy in 1943, General de Lattre de Tassigny escaped after eight months. He led the land forces which captured Elba (see illus. in page 3069), and was in command of the French forces forming part of the U.S. 7th Army　　*Photo, French Official*

France south of the Loire was virtually under their control, with the exception of the Bordeaux area, Marseilles and the Rhône valley.

The position was then exploited in three main thrusts. The first, towards Digne and Grenoble, threatened to break German communications. The second was beyond Aix en Provence towards the Rhône ; the third was towards Toulon and Marseilles.

It is worth comparing the progress of General Patch's columns northwards to Grenoble with the march of Napoleon and his 1,100 men, on the return from Elba in March 1815. Napoleon landed in the Golfe Jouan, nearer to Cannes than the beaches where the Allies landed in 1944 ; and his desire to be clear of the dangerous Royalist region of coastal Provence impelled him into Grasse on D+1. American reconnaissance elements did not reach the town until D+3, but as it lay to the flank and not on the main line of their advance this relative slowness was not entirely to their

CANADIANS PASS THROUGH LIBERATED ROUEN

Canadian Army, after several days' heavy fighting with enemy rearguards in the Elbeuf
ent patrols into Rouen on the evening of August 29, 1944, and liberated the city next day.
demolitions and Allied bombing, particularly of German transport trying to escape east-
ee illus. in page 3199), had severely damaged the beautiful old city. This glimpse of the
Canadians passing through Rouen is from a window in the ruined opera house.

disadvantage. The routes of the two
armies converged at Castellane on the
river Verdon. Napoleon passed through
here—travelling on foot and supporting
himself with a stick—on D+2; the
Allies on D+3. For the Emperor the
passage of the gorges at Sisteron was
vital, for it was there that he feared interception from the regulars summoned
from Marseilles, but by forced marches
he reached the Durance west of Digne
on the evening of D+3, and from here
he sped through Sisteron to Gap in one
day's march of forty miles. General
Patch's columns crossed the Durance
early in D+4 and took Gap, after stiff
fighting, early on August 21 (D+6).
The gates of Grenoble were laid at
Napoleon's feet on D+6, but after his
advance of 200 miles he rested there
for thirty-six hours, and it was D+8
before he was moving north of the river
Isère; the Allies entered the city on
D+7, and the following day were six
miles north.

The thrust towards the lower reaches
of the Rhône was carried out by two
American infantry divisions. Enemy
forces imposed some
initial delay around **Recovery of**
Brignoles, but, having **Provence**
overcome this resist-
ance, the Americans swept rapidly across
the Durance to Manosque and Pertuis,
and on north-westwards towards
Carpentras. (*See* map in page 3248.)

The enemy garrisons in Toulon and
Marseilles put up a resolute defence
against General de Lattre de Tassigny's
French forces. Having lost the actual
city of Toulon by August 26, the enemy
withdrew to fortified peninsulas across
the bay and did not surrender until
August 28, a week after their escape route
to the west had been severed. Equally
hard fighting took place in and around
Marseilles, which fell on August 23,
unorganized resistance continuing, however, until the 28th. Meanwhile French
armour, relieving the Americans west of
Aix en Provence, occupied Tarascon, the
ancient city of Arles, and Avignon, once
the seat of the Papacy, on the 25th.

In northern France, American forces
continued to make good progress on a
fifty-mile stretch of the Marne between
the capital and Château Thierry, while
other elements advanced across the
line of the river Aisne from Soissons
eastwards. Still other forces advancing
from positions in the Melun–Troyes area
liberated Vitry, Chalons, Rheims and
Verdun, which fell on September 1, and
by September 3 were approaching the
German border; while troops on the
left of this thrust were driving their way
against patchy opposition across the old
battlefields of the First Great War.

ROLLING ON TO BRUSSELS

1. Lieut.-General B. G. Horrocks (who fought in the Western Desert), commanding 30th Corps, watches British troops and transport passing through Amiens, freed by British tanks under Lieut.-General Sir Richard O'Connor (see illus. page 3185), another Western Desert veteran, on August 31, 1944. 2. German prisoners captured by the F.F.I. being driven through the streets of Arras after the British had passed on September 1. 3. British motor-cycle column rides by burning German transport on the outskirts of Brussels. 4. German prisoners watch British armour advancing along the main road to the Belgian capital, which fell on September 3. The British 2nd Army advanced 220 miles from the Seine to Antwerp in a week.

Photos, British Official .

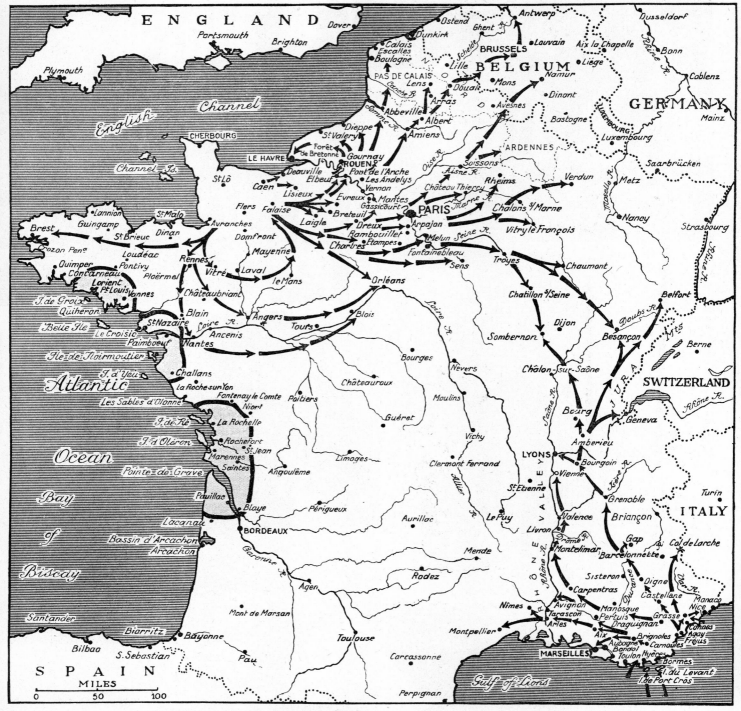

CLEARING FRANCE OF THE ENEMY

This map indicates the principal lines of Allied movement: in the north, from the clearance of the Falaise pocket on August 22, 1944, to the capture of Antwerp on September 4; in the south, from the landings on the Riviera on August 15 to the linking of the armies from the south and the north-west at Sombernon, near Dijon, on September 11. Shaded areas along the coast round Lorient, St. Nazaire, La Rochelle and Dunkirk remained in enemy hands

The British 2nd Army made an equally spectacular advance from their bridgeheads over the Seine. After a rapid night march, they entered Amiens on August 31 and by midday had crossed the Somme there. By September 2 Arras, Douai, Albert and Lens had all been liberated. On the same day, British forces crossed the frontier into Belgium beyond Douai, Americans crossed it south of Avesnes. On the 3rd British armour entered Brussels after an advance probably never equalled for speed. Even after the liberation of the capital the advance continued: next day the great port of Antwerp was seized almost intact. The British 2nd Army had accomplished the remarkable feat of advancing 220 miles from the Seine to Antwerp in one week. Escape was impossible for the large numbers of German troops, disordered remnants of many divisions completely demoralized and confused, which were cut off in the Pas de Calais, and enormous hauls of prisoners came in daily as a result of the lightning advance.

In the coastal sector British and Canadian troops of the 1st Canadian Army advanced in conformity with the British 2nd Army on their right. After freeing Rouen on August 30, they pushed on swiftly towards the Somme, while other forces turned into the Havre peninsula. The same Canadian regiments—the Essex-Scottish, Royal Hamilton Light Infantry, and Royal Regiment of Canada—that had raided

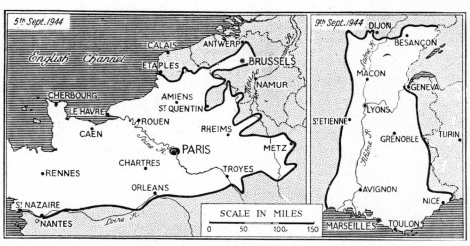

LIBERATION SPREADS THROUGH FRANCE

The unshaded parts of these maps indicate the areas in the north and south of France in which, by the dates shown, the only Germans left were prisoners. Liberating forces had already pushed on into Belgium, and stood on the Franco-Swiss frontier. To the left is a detail map of the Riviera beach-heads where Allied landings were made on August 15, 1944.

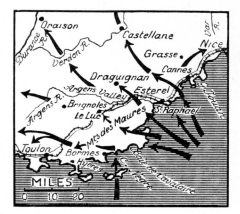

Dieppe in 1942 (*see* Chapter 243) liberated the town on September 1. St. Valery fell on September 2 to the 51st (Highland) Division, under Major-General T. G. Rennie, who was taken prisoner when two brigades of the same

AMERICAN PATROL IN THE FRENCH ALPS

On August 25, 1944, U.S. troops and the F.F.I. captured Briançon, a powerful Alpine fortress and garrison town on the Route des Alpes near the Franco-Italian frontier, and some fifty miles as the crow flies south-east of Grenoble. Here an American patrol moves cautiously through a small village in the neighbourhood.

Photo, Keystone

division had been compelled to surrender there in 1940 (*see* page 954) but had escaped ten days later. On the 2nd the Canadians, with the Polish Armoured Division, reached the Somme at Abbeville. All but one of the bridges had been destroyed. In addition, this was one of the few places where the Germans offered any resistance. This was overcome, however, and the Canadians moved up to the Canche, where more fighting was necessary before a crossing was secured. By September 6, against stubborn resistance, they reached the sea on either side of Calais, having by-passed Boulogne, which was firmly held by the enemy. In the Havre peninsula, the town alone remained in enemy hands.

In the south of France the Allied forces compelled the German 19th Army into a full retreat despite bitter resis-

tance by the 11th Panzer Division. On the Riviera or eastern flank, the river Var was forced. Nice was occupied on August 30, and patrols began to probe the densely mined hill country north of Monaco. Strong columns advancing

COMMANDER, U.S. 7th ARMY

Lieut.-General Alexander M. Patch (centre), who led the U.S. forces on Guadalcanal (see page 2488), was in command of all Allied ground forces constituting the U.S. 7th Army which landed in southern France on August 15, 1944. With him here are Lieut.-General Lucian K. Truscott, commanding the U.S. 6th Corps, and Lieut.-General Jacob Devers, commanding the 6th Army Group, of which the U.S. 7th Army was part. *Photo, Associated Press*

northwards reached the Col de Larche, east of Barcelonnette. West of the Durance, Carpentras fell on August 25, and powerful attacks were made up the Rhône towards Montelimar. The small plain about Montelimar was overrun on the 28th, and discomfited enemy

GERMANS LEAVE BRUSSELS AS ALLIES ENTER

Brussels was liberated on September 3, 1944, by the Guards Armoured Division, led by Major-General Allan H. S. Adair, C.B., D.S.O., M.C., followed closely by the 11th Armoured Division, both under the command of Lieut.-General B. G. Horrocks. The British were given a delirious welcome in Brussels, from which the enemy had pulled out in such haste that all bridges were left intact. Here German cyclist troops are making for the Porte de Namur as the British entered the city on the opposite side. Below, Allied forces passing the Royal palace.

forces were attacked at the crossings of the river Drome, south of Livron.

Valence was cleared on the 31st and the Americans swept on towards Vienne, occupied on September 2. Other troops meanwhile had forged **Lyons Occupied Without Attack** ahead from Grenoble to reach Bourgoin on August 28 and Amberieu on the 30th. Lyons was occupied on September 3, but it had already been outflanked to the north-east by American and French forces which had swept on to Bourg-en-Bresse. (The F.F.I. had also been so active in Lyons that no formal attack had been necessary.) Motorized Algerian infantry of the French forces introduced into the vanguard on the right flank, extended the line as far as the Swiss frontier west of Geneva—also on September 3—and in three days the French advanced through the foothills of the Jura to within twenty-five miles of the historic fortress of Belfort.

On the lower reaches of the Rhône armoured units fanned out northwards and westwards to occupy Nîmes on August 28, Montpellier on the 31st. The main thrust northwards then became very rapid. The key town of Besançon was captured on September 8 by American forces after they had forced the river Doubs and beaten back enemy resistance around the city, and Dijon

YPRES—BATTLEGROUND OF THE FIRST GREAT WAR—FREED AGAIN
On September 7, 1944, Polish troops of the 1st Canadian Army liberated the historic town of Ypres, almost obliterated in four great battles fought in the First Great War when the British held an all-out German drive for the Channel ports. Here Canadians examine the famous Cloth Hall and church of St. Martin, reconstructed between the wars. *Photo, Associated Press*

fell to French troops on September 11, on which date also the first waves of General Patch's 7th Army, having advanced 350 miles in 28 days, made contact with the forces of General Patton's U.S. 3rd Army (operating from the north-west) at Sombernon, 16 miles west of Dijon. The Allied front had now become continuous from the Swiss border—north to the Channel ports and south to the Riviera.

Meanwhile the enemy continued to hold the great ports of Brest, Lorient, and St. Nazaire in the Brittany peninsula; a hundred-mile stretch of coast round the estuary of the river Garonne; Le Havre, the second largest port in France, **Ports Still in Enemy Hands** whose garrison commander at the end of August rejected an ultimatum to surrender; and the smaller Channel ports of Boulogne, Calais and Dunkirk in the Pas de Calais.

The French Forces of the Interior not only gave direct support to the advancing Allied armies, but also, outside the zones of military operations, harassed the Germans by tying up large numbers of garrison troops, by delaying the movement of enemy reserves and by disorganizing communications. Orders issued by General Koenig (whose appointment as Military Governor of Paris was announced in Algiers on August 21) on September 4 to the F.F.I. in the Pas de Calais, Nord and the Ardennes are of particular interest as illustrating the tactics which contributed, among other things, to the eventual liberation of the Channel ports.

BRITISH TROOPS AMUSE ANTWERP CITIZENS
Smiling men and women and fascinated children watch the crew of a 17-pounder anti-tank gun demonstrate their weapon in an Antwerp street after its liberation on September 4, 1944. The Germans had pulled out so quickly and in such disorder that the city was left virtually undamaged, with most of the docks intact except for earlier damage by Allied bombing. *Photo, British Official*

ALLIED ASSAULT ON LE HAVRE

At 11.30 a.m. on September 12, 1944, thirty-six hours after British troops of the 1st Canadian Army had launched an all-out assault on the great French port of Le Havre, the German garrison surrendered. An unprecedented air and naval barrage preceded and supported the land assault, and most of the city was devastated. British losses were 400 killed and wounded ; 8,000 prisoners were taken. Here tanks and infantry are advancing to the attack.

An extract from these reads : " Our troops will do everything to impede the orderly withdrawal of the enemy. Those formations which already have fighting experience will form solidly led companies with part of their effectives. The remainder of the effectives will go to form very mobile guerilla groups which will maintain very close contact with the companies whose aid they will request when meeting a strong detachment from which they would not be able to disengage themselves. Every time liaison is possible, appeal should be made to armoured units when strong units are engaged in a locality or fortified centre. Tactics should be those of harassing German columns with a view to their disintegration. Battle will be accepted only when our unit is stronger than the enemy unit. It is not a matter of launching a company to attack a battalion, but to divide the battalion

Gen. Koenig's Orders to F.F.I.

until complete dispersion and the destruction of the small isolated formations. In every town and village, set up a patriotic militia which must include the whole able-bodied population with a view to crushing the Boches. Place watchers who will warn the F.F.I. of the approach of German columns. Block access to the locality by means of barricades, trees, etc."

When the German commander at Le Havre refused to surrender, British troops of the 1st Canadian Army attacked, and, after thirty-six hours' battering, took the port by assault on September 12. A week later in Brittany the long investment of Brest ended on the 19th, when all organized resistance ceased in the town and the enemy was

driven from the Crozon peninsula by American forces. Meanwhile Canadian troops of the British 2nd Army launched an all-out attack on Boulogne on September 19. Enemy positions at Calais and Dunkirk were gradually reduced by constant pressure on their perimeters. The concentrated attack on Boulogne carried the assaulting infantry into the central defences of the town, where heavy fighting continued in clearing strong points until the 22nd, when all resistance ceased. Three days later, on September 25, a similar strong attack preceded by a heavy air bombardment, was launched against Calais by troops advancing from the south and east. The fortress of Escalles, six miles west along the coast, and some important high ground to the west of the town were captured. The German commander of the port itself, Col. Schoerner, surrendered unconditionally at midnight on September 30–October 1, and by

SURRENDER OF BREST—ENEMY 'HEDGEHOG' IN BRITTANY

All organized resistance ceased in Brest on September 19, 1944, when American troops cleared the Crozon peninsula, to which the German commander, Major-General Ramcke (seen below with his walking-stick, dispatch case, and Irish setter after his surrender) had escaped. General Ramcke led the German airborne invasion of Crete (see Chapter 159). Left, British 'Crocodile' flame-throwers move up for the final assault on Brest.

Photos, British and U.S. Official

ENTRY INTO BOULOGNE

The last remaining stronghold of Boulogne, at Le Portel, fell to the Canadians at 4 p.m. on September 22, 1944. Prisoners taken numbered 7,500 and included Lieut.-General Ferdinand Heim, seen (left) discussing the surrender with Brigadier J. Rockingham, who led the final assault. The photograph above shows a French sailor, once a Boulogne taxi-driver, guiding a Churchill tank into the city. *Photos, British Newspaper Pool ; Associated Press*

7.30 a.m. Calais was completely liberated. The enemy was still entrenched in the fortress town of Dunkirk, the two ports of Lorient and St. Nazaire, and round the Garonne estuary ; but these isolated enemy bastions in no way affected the main front, where the Allies had their hands too full to spare the attention needed to reduce them.

To summarize the strategic results of these operations : Lieut.-General Omar Bradley's 12th Army Group, after having in co-operation **Strategic** with Field-Marshal **Results of** Montgomery virtually **Operations** annihilated the 7th German Army and liberated Paris, struck east with his right into Lorraine and with his left into eastern Belgium. Montgomery, after crossing the Seine, struck north, and with his left cleared the Channel ports from Le Havre to Calais inclusive which, as they were freed of mines and obstructions, became useful subsidiary bases. His right, breaking through scattered groups of the German 15th Army attempting to escape eastwards, entered western Belgium, liberating Brussels and, more important, capturing the port of Antwerp intact ; although before that great port, vital to further operations, could be developed as a base the Scheldt had to be cleared.

In the south General Patch's U.S. 7th Army had cut off and rendered innocuous the greater part of the German 19th Army, and his spearhead had entered the Belfort gap into southern Alsace on Omar Bradley's right.

Three German Armies had thus suffered disastrous defeat and almost the whole of France and Belgium had been liberated. But in front of Patch and Omar Bradley lay difficult mountainous and forest country backed by the Siegfried Line, and in front of Montgomery was the intact German garrison in Holland with the lower Rhine and innumerable canals on which to fight. With these obstacles in front and with immensely lengthened lines of communication, the momentum of the advance obviously could not be maintained and a pause was inevitable till new bases could be established and communications shortened and improved. By leaving garrisons in the Channel ports and by demolitions, the Germans had emphasized the inherent difficulty of maintaining a long advance from restricted bases.

The dispersion of the Allied advance over so wide a front evoked some criticism, but it must be realized that greater concentration of effort would only have increased congestion on roads, and railways were out of action. Also, if not engaged everywhere, the enemy might have organized a counter stroke.

GERMAN CROSS-CHANNEL BATTERY SILENCED

By September 30, 1944, all the long-range guns round Calais had been captured and the English towns of ' Hellfire Corner ' freed from four years of intermittent shelling. Here is one of the enemy's 406-mm. (16-inch) guns captured near Calais. Before the final assault on Calais itself (cleared on October 1), a twenty-four-hour truce was arranged for the evacuation of some 25,000 civilians, a group of whom are here being helped across an improvised bridge over a canal.

Chapter 321

AMERICA PREPARES FOR THE LAST LAP

As in the other Allied countries, the successful reopening of the Western Front in Europe had outstanding significance in the U.S.A. during the year 1944. Combined with the return of American armies to the Philippines in October, it called forth, as Mr. Selden Menefee here records, a realistic determination to end the war as quickly as possible and to prepare for the problems of peace. The Dumbarton Oaks Conference in the autumn was the first step towards setting-up an international organization to maintain peace and security. American affairs in 1943 are covered in Chapter 294

THE great day of 1944, for Americans as well as Britons, was June 6 —D Day in western Europe. This was what they had been working, building towards, for more than two years. All eyes were on the Normandy beaches and the roads to Paris and to Germany. This was the supreme test. Once the Allied forces started to roll forward, a great wave of optimism swept the United States. Betting pools were made up on the date of Berlin's fall, and few guesses were later than Christmas. But when Christmas came, and the Allies were holding back Rundstedt's counter-attack in the Ardennes, realism prevailed once more.

Invasion Optimism in U.S.A.

In the Pacific theatre, the outstanding event of the year was the invasion of the Philippines by General MacArthur's forces, in October. This meant the beginning of the end for the Japanese, for without the Philippines they could no longer control the sea lanes to the Netherlands East Indies. To most Americans it meant more than that : at last they were back in the islands where they had been so badly defeated in 1942, and Bataan and Corregidor were about to be avenged. But even this prospect was almost an anti-climax after the excitement of D Day in Normandy.

At home, also, a battle was fought— the bitter political tug-of-war which resulted in the re-election of Franklin D. Roosevelt for a fourth term as President and of Harry S. Truman as Vice-President. Once this was over, people settled down once more to the big job of supplying the men, machines and munitions that were needed to continue the great offensive overseas.

In the hot months of June and July, preliminary preparations for the presidential election began. The renomination of President Roosevelt was considered inevitable by Democrats and Republicans alike, and interest among the Democrats therefore centred on the fight for the vice-presidential nomination. Incumbent Henry Wallace, with a half-hearted endorsement from the President and the enthusiastic support of labour and the progressive wing of the Party, had the advantage. But he could not swing the necessary two-thirds majority of delegates to the Democratic nominating convention, because of opposition from the conservative Southern section of the Party and from Democratic politicians who feared that conservative Democrats would break with the party if Wallace won the nomination.

Wallace had become the leading liberal spokesman for the Administration, and by his ringing statements on the rights of labour, Negroes, small business men, and others, had made many enemies. Mr. Roosevelt, knowing that the election would be close, apparently felt that he could make a better race with a running mate not labelled as a " New Dealer."

Accordingly, Senator Harry S. Truman of Missouri became the compromise candidate. Mr. Truman had made an excellent reputation as chairman of a special Senate committee investigating war expenditure, which saved the treasury billions of dollars by keeping a close check on the money spent by war agencies. At the same time, his voting record showed that he was completely in accord with the Roosevelt programme of reform, although he was not by nature a crusader. He was therefore acceptable to labour and the conservative Southerners alike, although he was not widely known among the American people. On the very eve of election, a public opinion poll showed that only 55 per cent of the people could even name the vice-presidential candidate, so greatly did the actual presidential race dominate the scene.

Compromise Candidate for Vice-President

The Republican candidate for the presidency, Governor Thomas E. Dewey of New York, was a young man who had won fame as a fighting district attorney in the crusade against gangsterism in New York City. With the defeat of Wendell Willkie,

NEW SECRETARY FOR THE NAVY

Colonel Frank Knox, the Republican appointed Secretary of the Navy by President Roosevelt in 1940, died on April 28, 1944, and was succeeded by Mr. James V. Forrestal, Democrat, who had been Under-Secretary to Knox. Here (left) he is taking the oath on his appointment, administered by Rear-Admiral Thomas L. Gatch, Judge Advocate General of the Navy. In the background is Admiral Ernest J. King, Naval C.-in-C.   *Photo, Associated Press*

SUPREME COMMANDER, ALLIED EXPEDITIONARY FORCE

Major-General Dwight David Eisenhower's appointment as Commander of U.S. Forces in the European theatre of war was announced on June 25, 1942. On July 7 came his promotion to the rank of Lieutenant-General. He commanded the Allied forces which landed in North Africa on November 8, and became Allied C.-in-C. North Africa on February 6, 1943. General Eisenhower's appointment as Supreme Commander of the Allied Expeditionary Force organizing in the United Kingdom for the liberation of Europe was announced on December 24, 1943.

ITALY RE-ENTERS THE WAR AS CO-BELLIGERENT OF THE ALLIES

The Italian surrender to the Allies was signed on September 3, 1943 ; Italy declared war on Germany on October 13. Retrained and re-equipped Italian troops began serving with the Allies in the following December ; Italian partisans behind the enemy lines rendered the Allies invaluable aid. Here on a Sicilian airfield is an Italian pilot who volunteered for service with the U.S. Army Air Force. Below, Italian troops fighting on the Allies' side outside their headquarters at a town in Sicily.

Photos, Pictorial Press

ALLIES FIGHT THEIR WAY NORTH IN ITALY

The difficulty of reducing Cassino, reached on February 2, 1944, kept the 5th and 8th Armies virtually stationary before the Gustav line until May 18, when a combined assault by the two armies carried town and mountain after a week's hard fighting (see Chapter 302). Here a British soldier is sniping in the ruins of Cassino. Below, a man of the Royal Signals repairing a line on a recently shelled pontoon bridge across the Garigliano river, after the 5th Army's successful attack across it on the night of January 16–17, 1944.   *Photos, British Official : Crown Copyright*

PREMIER AND PRESIDENT WITH THEIR CHIEFS OF STAFF AT QUEBEC

Mr. Winston Churchill reached Quebec on September 10, 1944 for a conference with President Roosevelt. (See Chapter 339.) Here, on the terrace of the Citadel, are : Front row, left to right, General Marshall (U.S. Chief of Staff), Admiral Leahy (Chief of Staff to President Roosevelt), President Roosevelt, Mr. Churchill, Field Marshal Sir Alan Brooke (Chief of the Imperial General Staff), Field Marshal Sir John Dill (British Chief of Staff at Washington) ; back row, left to right, General Sir John Lavarak (Chief of Australian General Staff), Lieut.-General Sir Hastings Ismay (Chief of Staff to Mr. Churchill as Minister of Defence), Admiral King (C.-in-C., U.S. Navy), Marshal of the R.A.F. Sir Charles Portal (Chief of Air Staff) General Arnold (Chief of Staff, U.S. Army Air Forces), Admiral of the Fleet Sir Andrew Cunningham (First Sea Lord).

Republican candidate in 1940, in the 1944 Presidential primaries, his nomination was assured, for he had shown his ability to secure votes in the key state of New York when he ran for governor in 1942. Very little was known about his views on international affairs except that he favoured a military alliance between Britain and the United States. Soon after his nomination, however, he made a speech calling for full American participation in a world organization. He also supported the extension and improvement of the social security laws of the Roosevelt Administration, to the dismay of his predominantly conservative backers.

Mr. Roosevelt then pointed out that previous Republican administrations had not been notable for their success in averting depressions, and that the

Roosevelt's Criticism of Republicans

Republicans had been tardy in preparing for the war and for the peace to come. This spurred Mr. Dewey into an ill-considered series of attacks on the President, and the issue quickly became simply whether one was for or against Mr. Roosevelt. In the end, most of the people were for him, at least to the point of not wanting to experiment with untried leadership, especially in international affairs, until the war was over.

The Roosevelt campaign was a simple but masterful one. The President braved cold and rain in New York,

FORMULATING A DRAFT CHARTER FOR A WORLD LEAGUE

Representatives of Great Britain, the U.S.S.R., and the U.S.A. met at Dumbarton Oaks in Washington on August 21, 1944, and formulated a draft charter of world peace and security for later consideration by all the United Nations. Left to right, Sir Alexander Cadogan, Lord Halifax, Mr. Cordell Hull, Mr. Andrei Gromyko, and Mr. Edward R. Stettinius. The Russian delegation withdrew on September 29, and a Chinese delegation took its place in the deliberations.

Chicago and Philadelphia to prove that rumours concerning his health were baseless (he was in good condition at that time). He based his campaign on America's foreign policy, and was caustic about the records of Republican isolationists. Mr. Dewey, on the other hand, founded his plan of battle on criticism of Roosevelt's domestic policy. His supporters used every possible device, from referring to the " Roosevelt dynasty " to identifying the Administration with communism because the Communists were supporting it.

One major issue of the campaign was the Congress of Industrial Organizations' Political Action Committee, or P.A.C., as it was called. Having seen an anti-labour Congress elected in 1942 because the labour vote did not turn out that year, the C.I.O. was determined to prevent the same thing from happening in 1944. A year before the election a well-financed organization was set up, and preliminary campaigning set in motion. The P.A.C. used the same technique as the old-fashioned political machine—personal contacts and door-bell ringing to register the voters, and then intensive campaigning in the shops and neighbourhoods to win them over to the Democratic ticket. (Actually, however, the P.A.C. was non-partisan in its approach ; in several places it supported liberal Republican candidates.)

The Republicans soon turned the spotlight on Mr. Sidney Hillman, Russian-born chairman of P.A.C. and head of the Amalgamated Clothing Workers' Union. He was called a Communist, and the power behind the Democratic

Party. It was alleged that President Roosevelt had told Democratic leaders at the convention that the Democratic vice-presidential candidate must be satisfactory to Hillman. Whether or not this was true, " Clear everything with Sidney " became the unofficial campaign slogan of the Republicans. But in the final analysis, the P.A.C.'s ability to mobilize the labour vote far outweighed the effect of these propaganda attacks.

Public opinion polling also received a test in the election. The " Fortune " Survey predicted that Roosevelt would receive 53·5 per cent of the popular vote ; he actually received 53·7 per cent.

Election Result Forecasts

The Gallup Poll underestimated the Democratic vote by about 2 per cent. One of the most revealing polls taken, however, concerned the reasons Democratic voters gave for supporting Roosevelt. About 26 per cent simply liked the man or his personality. Another 24 per cent said " To win the war." Faith in Roosevelt's policy of international co-operation was cited by 22 per cent, and belief that a Democratic administration would mean more jobs and prosperity in the future by 19 per cent.

Again, the people showed that they did not take their opinions from newspaper editorials. More than 60 per cent of the daily newspapers in the country, with over two-thirds of the circulation, supported Dewey, while only 22 per cent of the dailies, with little more than a sixth of the circulation, supported Roosevelt, according to the magazine

CHAIRMAN OF P.A.C.

Mr. Sidney Hillman, head of the Amalgamated Clothing Workers' Union and chairman of the Political Action Committee of the Congress of Industrial Organizations, played an important part in securing a big labour vote for Franklin D. Roosevelt at his fourth presidential election.

Photos, P.N.A. ; Keystone

"Editor and Publisher." Other estimates put the Dewey figure at 80 per cent or more of the daily press, pointing out that in ten states not one daily supported the President. The conclusion to be drawn is that newspapers are big business, and this was a people's election. Forty-eight million people voted, and a decisive majority felt that their future would be safer in the hands of Roosevelt and Truman than in the hands of Dewey and Bricker, who were unknown quantities in international affairs. (The official figures were: Roosevelt, 25,602,505; Dewey, 22,006,278; a majority for the President of 3,596,227.)

Three international conferences met in the United States during 1944 to make recommendations for later development. The first, the United Nations Monetary and Financial Conference at Bretton Woods, New Hampshire, opened on July 1. It recognized that satisfactory international economic relations depended on stable currency exchange rates, and it recommended on July 22 the establishment of (1) an International Monetary Fund to control matters relating to international exchange; (2) an International Bank for Reconstruction and Development to assist in making post-war reconstruction as rapid as possible by providing capital for projects which would raise the productivity of the borrowing country.

Three International Conferences

The Moscow Declaration of November 1943 (*see page 2709*) was taken a step further when Mr. Edward R. Stettinius, U.S. Under-Secretary of State, Mr. Andrei Gromyko, Soviet Ambassador in Washington, and Sir Alexander Cadogan, Permanent Under-Secretary of the British Foreign Office, with experts, met at Dumbarton Oaks on August 21 to prepare the ground for a conference of all the States concerned which would draw up the Charter of the new international "League to Enforce Peace." On September 29 a joint announcement stated that "a large

measure of agreement" had been reached in the Anglo-American-Soviet talks. The Soviet representatives withdrew, and Dr. V. K. Wellington Koo, Chinese Ambassador in London, then joined Mr. Stettinius and Sir Alexander Cadogan. The conference ended on October 7, the Chinese delegation having approved the draft that had been worked out.

An Assembly and a Council with permanent and non-permanent members, an International Court of Justice and a Secretariat were proposed as the main organs of the organization envisaged in the Charter suggested at Dumbarton Oaks, as they had been of the old League of Nations. Under the Covenant, however, both the Assembly and the Council could take action. Under the Charter the Security Council alone could take action, and it would be armed with powers of enforcement (including military force) which had not been accorded to the League.

On November 1, a Civil Aviation Conference met in Chicago. Fifty-four nations, including all the United Nations except the U.S.S.R., were represented. It soon became clear that there

were marked divergences of view, particularly between the United States and the British Commonwealth. The U.S. accepted the need for an international air authority, but held that its powers should be limited to the regulation of technical matters and to consultation. British Commonwealth representatives favoured giving it a high degree of control over economic matters also. Discussion centred round the five so-called "freedoms of the air": (1) the right of air transit; (2) the right to land for servicing;

PRESIDENTIAL ELECTION

Mr. Thomas E. Dewey, Governor of New York, was selected as Republican candidate for President, Mr. Franklin D. Roosevelt as Democratic candidate in 1944. 1. Roosevelt acknowledges an ovation after delivering an address on his foreign policy at a Foreign Policy Association banquet. On his left are Mr. William W. Lancaster, Chairman, Foreign Policy Association ; Mr. Henry L. Stimson, Secretary of War ; Mr. James Forrestal, Secretary of the Navy ; and Mr. Herbert H. Lehman, Director General, U.N.R.R.A. 2. Governor Dewey addresses an enthusiastic audience at Oklahoma City. 3. Recording the soldiers' vote in the S. Pacific. 4. Crowds in Times Square, New York, watch election figures flashed on the bulletin board.

(3) the right to carry passengers, freight, and mails from the country of origin to any place in the world ; (4) the right to bring passengers, freight and mails back to the country of origin from any place ; (5) the right to pick up and set down passengers along an international air route. The fifth " freedom " also showed up much divergence of view.

The final act of the conference, which ended on December 5, advocated among other things—many technical —the recognition of the complete and exclusive sovereignty of each nation over its air space, and the establishment of an International Civil Aviation Organization whose functions were set out in detail. Mayor La Guardia's summing up of the conference was, " Everybody is against bad weather."

War production, which had risen rapidly in 1943, levelled off in 1944. But its momentum was sustained, and by the year's end, reckoning the dollar at 4 to the £1, £15,000 million worth of munitions had been produced, out of a total of some £50,000 million worth of goods and services. The Government was spending at the rate of about £62,500,000 a day. This fact alone spelled the doom of the Axis. East and West, the United Nations produced about £18,500 million worth of combat munitions, of which the U.S. share was nearly £11,000 million, compared with a *total* Axis production of around £6,750 million.

War Production Steady

Put in specific output, the record of U.S. war production in 1944 was even

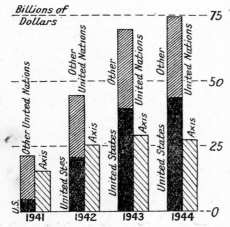

Billions of Dollars

RELATIVE WAR PRODUCTION
This diagram illustrates the relation between war production in the United States and in the other United Nations and the Axis countries for each year from 1941 to 1944. America was not a belligerent until after Pearl Harbor (December 7, 1941). (In America the term billion stands for a thousand million.)

more impressive : 96,359 planes, including 16,048 heavy bombers ; 30,889 ships ; 17,565 tanks ; 595,330 Army trucks ; 152,000 Army aircraft rocket launchers ; 215,177 bazookas ; 1,416,774 short tons of ground artillery ammunition, and much more besides. Aircraft production was about 15 times that of the period just preceding American entry into the war. Despite design changes, manpower shortages, and other difficulties, twelve times as many B-29 Super-Fortresses were turned out as in 1943. Production of B-24 Liberators, Mustangs, Wildcats, Hellcats, Corsairs, Commandos and Skymasters all doubled or tripled the 1943 output.

RATION TOKENS
These tokens made of plastic fibre came into use on February 27, 1944, in conjunction with the blue and red coupons (see illus. in page 2951) already distributed.

Production of merchant shipping dropped slightly, to 16·5 million tons. Guns and combat and motor vehicles also dropped, and war construction fell off sharply. But these trends represented the change in America's military position. War plants, trucks and guns were already in existence. And as the Allies had gone from the defensive to the offensive, the content of the U.S. munitions programme changed. Shipyards had to change to building combat landing ships, even at the expense of merchant ships. But thanks to the huge output of ships and trucks in 1943, most of which were still in use, this was possible without impairing the war effort.

The United States devoted almost one-fourth of its national production to the manufacture of combat armament in 1944—nearly as large a proportion as Great Britain, the Soviet Union, or Germany, though probably a somewhat smaller proportion than Japan. But this did not mean that Americans sacrificed as much as Britons and Russians, as the annual report of the War Production Board clearly pointed out. The United States escaped devastation and its attendant loss of civilian lives, and because of high total output, American civilians had higher living standards than during the depression period before the war.

The American consumer spent almost £1,750 million more on goods and services in 1944 than he did in 1943, but he

obtained very little more than in the previous year. He spent nearly £25,000 million on goods and services, but at the end of the year he had less household equipment than a year earlier, and fewer clothes in his wardrobe. His table was set more generously than civilian tables in any other country, but even so he and his wife had less meat, butter, fresh fruits, and certain other foods than they would have liked.

Ration point values of meats, dairy products and canned goods were increased. But the important fact was that while the American productive system was feeding munitions and supplies to the enemy's funeral pyre on all fronts, the American consumer still had more goods and services than in either 1942 or 1943.

The average family income in the United States was about £650 in 1944, compared with only £325 in the pre-war period 1936–39 ; and the factory workers' take-home pay averaged £11 10s. compared with £6 in 1939 and £6 15s. in the pre-depression year 1929. Similar prosperity was felt in other sections of the community. Such an increase in incomes would have meant inflation except for a strict and efficient price control system under the Office of Price Administration. From May 1943, when President Roosevelt issued an order to hold the price line at any cost, to the end of 1944, living costs rose only 1·5 per cent. Clothing prices went up 11·6 per cent and household furnishings 14 per cent, but food prices actually dropped by almost 4 per cent. Rents were held stationary by a system of controls affecting 80 per cent of all dwellings.

Average Incomes

This achievement was the more remarkable in that enforcement machinery was very sketchy. O.P.A. had only about 3,000 investigators—one for every 43,000 civilians. Much of O.P.A.'s work was done by volunteers, organized into local price panels. Here is a typical morning's work of one of them :

Complaint : a customer alleged she had been overcharged on lettuce and bananas. The dealer said he had been overcharged by the wholesaler. He was let off with a warning until the wholesaler's charge could be investigated. A dealer quoted 35 cents instead of the 33-cent ceiling price for loin of pork. Since this was his first offence, he was merely asked to sign a compliance statement. Another dealer had been systematically charging 2 cents too much for pork. He was required to pay $62.40 to the U.S. Treasury, representing his estimated illegal profits over a period of six months. An automobile was

CENTRES OF UNITED STATES AIRCRAFT PRODUCTION

Production of aircraft in the United States increased enormously in 1944. The size of the plants that were achieving records can be gauged from this photograph of the north wall and part of the staff parking ground of the Bell Bomber plant in Georgia. Below, the 17-ton centre section of the main wing of a Super-Fortress (B.-29) for the U.S.A. 20th A.F. (based in China—see page 3094) being lowered to join the fuselage at the Wichita (Kansas) plant of the Boeing Company.

sold at $50 over the ceiling price. The dealer was warned, and required to refund the $50 to his customer.

Despite the Government's efforts to control prices, black market activities became widespread in certain fields—petrol, meat ration points, and cigarettes and other scarce commodities were sold secretly at prices far higher than the ceiling. Such racketeering was estimated to have cost the consumer £500 million in 1944.

Income tax took a sharp rise in 1944, personal exemptions being cut to $500 (£125), so that the tax hit almost everyone. The tax was

Relation of Taxes to Expenditure

put on a pay-as-you-earn basis, and deducted from current pay cheques. These deductions, together with a voluntary 10 per cent deduction for war bond purchases which was almost universal, helped to control the tendency to inflation. But only a little more than 40 per cent of America's war expenses was being financed out of current taxes, compared with 50 per cent in Great Britain. Here, again, the American civilian came off relatively lightly.

Labour troubles flared up at times during 1944, but on the whole were less troublesome than in the previous year. In May some 290,000 workers

were involved in strikes, but this affected less than one-fifth of one per cent of the nation's working time.

June 6 had an electric effect on the workers. Three days after the landings in Normandy, the National War Labour **Invasion Aids Settlement of Disputes** Board reported that all strikes referred to it had been settled, for the first time in two and a half years. William Green, president of the conservative American Federation of Labour, cabled the news to General Eisenhower, adding. "We hope this information will encourage you and your brave men in the grave task ahead." Two unions of the Congress of Industrial Organizations, the liberal or left wing of labour, enforced the no-strike pledge in war industry to the point of fining members or sections indulging in strike action.

In the autumn strikes began again, but on a small scale, usually prompted by the desire to break through the wage ceiling, which limited hourly wage increases to about 15 per cent above the April 1942 level, while prices had increased almost twice as much. But the wage ceiling held.

Another cause of unrest was a wave of uneasiness about the temporary nature of war employment. Early in the year there were rumours of imminent reductions in ship production. So many workers left their jobs that Rear-Admiral Emory S. Land, chairman of the U.S. Maritime Commission, said shipyard production was being virtually sabotaged. Other war industries, already short of manpower, were also affected by the rush to find peace-time jobs. But June 6 put a stop to this, and by the end of the year speculation about reconversion had largely vanished. With the casualty list approaching the million mark, people were realizing the war more personally and taking it more seriously. (In December 1944, some 85,000 workers were involved in strikes, compared with 200,000 in December 1943.)

The civilian labour force declined slightly during 1944. With 11,900,000 men and women in the armed forces at the end of the year, the number of men in the labour force dropped by almost a million to 33,720,000, while the number of working women increased by about 400,000 to 17,530,000. Throughout the year there was discussion of the need for a national service act. The general public favoured it. But the labour unions and many conservative employers opposed it, and Congress turned it down.

A small minority of employers continued to oppose all government action, war or no war. One of these went so far as to refuse to recognize an order of the War Labour Board to settle a strike by negotiating with the union in his Chicago plant. As a result, the Army seized the plant and evicted the employer bodily from the premises. This became a *cause célèbre*, and was used by business men of Republican persuasion as a basis for charges of "dictatorship" against the Administration, especially after a U.S. court branded the seizure as an unwarranted invasion of property not primarily concerned with war production.

As for racial troubles, there was a great decline in tension compared with the previous year, when anti-Negro riots occurred in several cities. The only thing **Reduced Racial Tension** comparable was an unauthorized strike of transit workers in Philadelphia, directed against the advancement of Negro workers to skilled jobs. This deprived almost a million war workers of their transportation for several days, but was finally resolved by the Government and the C.I.O. union, which opposed racial discrimination in any form. The lessening of racial tension was probably due to the "shaking down" of personnel in war industries, and to organized community efforts to remove the causes of racial friction in hundreds of cities and towns following the riots of 1943.

GERMAN PRISONERS BOUND FOR THE LAND OF THE FREE

Between June 6 and October 31, 1944, the Allies in western Europe took a total of 637,544 German prisoners, of whom some 390,000 were captured by the four American armies operating in that area. Here are some hundreds of these prisoners on a troop transport crossing the Atlantic under guard by U.S. Coastguardsmen for internment in camps in the United States.

Photo. Keystone

PRESIDENT ROOSEVELT VISITS PEARL HARBOR

Between July 21 and August 18, 1944, President Roosevelt travelled by cruiser to United States bases in Hawaii and the Aleutians. He is seen here at Pearl Harbor, Hawaii, which he reached on July 26, with General Douglas MacArthur, C.-in-C. South-West Pacific on his right, Admiral William D. Leahy, his personal Chief of Staff, on his left, listening to Admiral Chester W. Nimitz, C.-in-C. Pacific, explain his strategy. *Photo, Keystone*

American interest in world affairs remained at a high level during 1944. All public opinion polls showed that

Majority Favours World Organization

seven Americans out of every ten favoured full participation in a world organization to preserve the peace—a complete reversal of pre-war isolationism. This was true even in the Middle West. A majority wanted to start building such an organization immediately, rather than wait until the war was over. Most Americans were even willing to sacrifice some " sovereignty " in order to help ensure peace. But they were not too well informed on these matters ; 72 million out of 90 million adults were willing to admit, for example, that they did not have a very clear idea of the Dumbarton Oaks proposals.

The people supported the Allied unconditional surrender policy for Germany by an eight to one majority. An even larger proportion believed that the peace treaty should be more severe than the treaties negotiated by the United States with Germany, Austria and Hungary in 1921. They believed that the Allies should occupy Germany for several years, and supervise the training of German youth to prevent a recurrence of the war. They thought the Germans should pay reparations, and a slight majority favoured the use of German workers to rebuild the homes and industries they had devastated in occupied territory. Similar views were held regarding Japan,

except that in the United States feeling was much higher against the Japanese than against the Germans.

As for the Allies, opinion towards Russia took a sharply favourable turn in 1944. A majority felt that the Soviet Union would enter the war against Japan, and that Russia could be trusted to co-operate with the United States when the war was over. Opinion towards Britain was still very favourable, but was somewhat disturbed at the end of the year by two things : the forthright criticism of American foreign policy in the London " Economist," which many Americans felt was unjustified and in bad taste ; and widespread criticism (in liberal circles) of British policy in southern Europe. There was a significant decline in opinion favourable to the British after the reports of fighting between British troops and Greeks in Athens.

A significant poll made near the end of the year showed that 48 per cent of the American public felt their country would get along better with Russia after the war than before the war, 22 per cent thought relations would be worse, and 20 per cent that they would be about the same. When the same question was asked about England, only 31 per cent thought relations would be better after the war than

before, 19 per cent thought they would be worse, and 43 per cent that they would be about the same.

On domestic questions, a large majority continued to support the social legislation of the Roosevelt administration. Only a minority was generally in favour of further reforms—although in some specified cases, such as the question of extending social security benefits to a larger proportion of the population, and adding health insurance to the government programme, a majority gave its approval.

In general, the politicians and the public opinion polls were in agreement on the basic aims of the American people. They were three in number :

(1) To win the war as quickly as possible.

(2) To ensure peace by a programme of international co-operation and collective security against future aggression.

(3) To provide jobs for all returning veterans and war workers.

As the end of the war came closer, more and more attention was concentrated on the third of these objectives. Americans everywhere were asking : If we can produce like this in wartime, why not in peacetime ? The future of America's democratic form of capitalism would depend on its ability to answer that question positively.

AMERICAN FORCES IN THE MARSHALLS

The atolls of the Marshall group were heavily bombed and shelled before ground forces landed on February 1, 1944. Roi was captured in less than an hour, Namur fell on the 2nd, Kwajalein on the 5th. Control of the Marshalls was completed by the occupation of Parry Island in Eniwetok atoll on February 22. 1. Two Japanese out of twenty emerge alive from a blockhouse on Kwajalein after it had blown up. 2. Marines killed in the attack on Parry Island are transferred to a landing craft for burial ashore. 3. Marines wounded on Eniwetok atoll receive treatment with blood plasma before being moved to waiting transports. *Photos, U. S. Coast Guard ; Planet News*

Chapter 322

AMERICANS REACH THE PHILIPPINES

The 'island-hopping' advance of American ground forces from the Gilbert Islands (described in Chapter 287) to the Philippine Islands forms the subject of this chapter by Lt. Bernard Brodie, U.S.N. Simultaneous land operations in New Guinea are recorded in Chapter 309. An account of air operations in the Pacific during 1944 is to be found in Chapter 306, of naval operations in the same area and period in Chapter 334. Consult also map in page 3274

THE strategy in the Pacific after the taking of Tarawa and Makin in the Gilberts (*see* page 2888) was to advance upon the core of Japanese strength from two directions. One was from the south-west, where the combined Allied army and naval forces under General MacArthur had already secured the Solomons, had landed on Bougainville, and were working their way along the northern coast of New Guinea. The other was from the Hawaiian Islands, whence, under Admiral Nimitz's direction, the most powerful naval and amphibious forces in history were to strike directly across the archipelagos of the central Pacific. The mobile power embodied in the major combatant ships of the Pacific Fleet was to cover operations along both routes of advance and at the same time contain the Japanese Navy.

By this time the disparity between Allied naval and air power and that of the enemy was such that it was not **Japanese Positions Isolated** necessary, in order to control the seas and to render secure a route from Hawaii westward, to occupy every atoll. It was sufficient to seize those islands essential for Allied use, by-passing others and thereby effectively isolating them. Such isolated positions were, if strongly held, subjected subsequently to neutralizing air raids and bombardments, and were in time rendered innocuous. Often the mere cutting of supplies was enough. The Japanese were to learn how unprofitable it was to establish outposts across seas over which they could not maintain command.

On January 29, 1944, after raids on twenty consecutive days, American forces began an attack on the Marshall Islands. The operations, the largest of the kind undertaken to that date, were supported by a great fleet of co-ordinated carrier task forces under Vice-Admiral R. A. Spruance. Attacks by carrier planes were delivered simultaneously on Kwajalein, Roi, Maloelap, Taroa, and Wotja. In addition, Taroa and Wotja were bombarded by cruisers, and shore-based aircraft bombed all four atolls together with Mille and Jaluit. Battleships entered the bombardment of Kwajalein and Roi on January 30, and the air attacks were extended to Eniwetok. Two squadrons of U.S. naval aircraft also made a heavy attack on Wake Island some 800 miles to the north.

The small and undefended atoll of Majuro was taken on January 31, and on the following day landings were made on Roi, Namur, and Kwajalein. Roi Island was captured in less than an hour; Namur was captured on the 2nd; the occupation of Kwajalein itself was completed on February 5, by which day the 19 most important islands of the 32 in the group had been secured. Engebe, chief island of the Eniwetok atoll, was seized in six hours on February 18, and by February 22 control of the entire Marshalls group (administered by Japan under mandate before the war) had passed to the United States; Japanese losses in the operations being nearly 12,000 killed. The atolls not invaded were engulfed within the Allied area of command, and the stranded Japanese garrisons effectively neutralized during succeeding months by air bombardments.

The pattern of attack at Kwajalein represented merely a development of the system adopted at Tarawa and Makin, and it was to prove also the pattern of innumerable other amphibious operations in the succeeding year and a **Attack on Kwajalein** half. The preparatory bombardment had reached a new crescendo of fury, no fewer than thirteen battleships, as well as cruisers and destroyers, participating in the direct bombardment of the one atoll. This greater volume of fire, together with improvement in the projectiles used and in methods of firing, no doubt accounted in large part for the relatively few casualties sustained by the Allied forces—in fortunate contrast to the bloody experience at Betio in Tarawa Atoll (*see* page 2889). At Kwajalein, too, preliminary footholds on lightly held islets were secured, and fire from mortars and field artillery could be used as well as

STARS-AND-STRIPES FLIES ON KWAJALEIN

Heavy air raids and bombardment from the sea on Kwajalein in the Marshalls were followed on February 1, 1944, by landings of the U.S. 7th Infantry Division under Major-General Charles H. Corlett. Supporting air attacks were made by carrier and shore-based aircraft—the latter from the Gilberts. Here, immediately the island was secured on February 5, technical units start putting up telephone wires.   *Photo, U.S. Navy*

AMERICAN MEMORIAL TO TWENTY-TWO BRITONS

The announcement in March 1945 that the George Medal had been awarded to Captain Holland, a New Zealander, and Lieut. Morgan, an Australian, was the first intimation published that these two men had for months after the Japanese invaded Tarawa in the Gilberts in December 1941 maintained contact with the outside world by means of a portable wireless transmitter concealed in a remote village. Lieut. Morgan was one of twenty-two unarmed British prisoners murdered by the Japanese on October 15, 1942.

Photos, Rob Wright, by courtesy of The London Missionary Society

In memory of twenty-
two British subjects mur-
dered by the Japanese at
Betio on the 15th of
October 1942.

Standing unarmed
to their posts, they
matched brutality with
gallantry and met death
with Fortitude.

R.G.MORGAN
B.CLEARY
J.R.HANDLEY
A.M.M°ARTHUR
A.L.SADD
A.C.HEENAN
J.J.M°CARTHY
H.R.C.HEARN
A.E.M°KENNA
A.L.TAYLOR
T.C.MURRAY
C.A.PEARSALL
L.B.SPEEDY
C.J.OWEN
D.H.HOWE
R.J.HITCHON
R.JONES
R.A.ELLIS
C.A.KILPIN
J.H.NICHOL
W.A.R.PARKER
R.M.McKENZIE

the heavy naval artillery in advancing upon the main objectives.

The bases secured in the Marshalls were developed for a new operation which in boldness and breadth of strategic conception easily surpassed the already impressive performance of the preceding months. Westward from the Marshalls lies the long chain of the Carolines, with Truk their centre and their strongest point. A continuation of the strategy already laid down seemed to dictate a penetration of that vast archipelago. But by now the American High Command was thinking in terms of by-passing not only individual islands and atolls but whole archipelagos.

Beyond the Carolines to the north-west lie the Marianas, which form the southern end of an almost continuous chain of islands extending 1,350 miles

Advance to the Marianas

south-eastward from Japan. Several islands of the Marianas group provided airfields and bases which the Japanese were using as stepping stones for air and sea communications between the home islands and Truk, and the eastern Carolines, the Marshalls, the western Carolines, the Philippines and other Japanese-held territories. The capture of the Marianas would cut one of the main arteries feeding the enemy's maritime fortresses and give the Allies bases from which they could control sea areas farther west in the Pacific and base aircraft to bomb the Japanese home islands. To the task of taking the Marianas was devoted a force comprising some 600 vessels, ranging from aircraft carriers and battleships to high-speed transports and tankers, more than 2,000 aircraft and some 300,000 Army, Navy, and Marine personnel.

Preliminary moves involved the neutralization of the enemy air bases on Marcus and Wake Islands to the north-east, the Palaus to the south-west (*see* Chapter 334). From June 10–12 carrier planes from a powerful task

force under Vice-Admiral Marc A. Mitscher struck heavily at the Marianas themselves, destroying 141 Japanese planes, sinking thirteen ships and damaging sixteen other ships for the loss of fifteen Hellcat fighters.

The first objective was Saipan, a rugged island of some 72 square miles in extent which was the key to the Japanese defences. In preparation for the assault, surface ships ranging from fast

PACIFIC COMMANDERS

Vice-Admiral Marc A. Mitscher (left) commanded the carrier task forces which supported the landings in the Marshalls (February 1944) and the Marianas (June 1944). Rear-Admiral R. K. Turner directed amphibious operations on both occasions.

Photos, Associated Press ; Central Press

U.S. MARINES GO IN TO LAND ON ENGEBE

A Pearl Harbor communiqué on February 20, 1944, announced that the U.S. 22nd Marine Corps had completely occupied Engebe, chief island of the Eniwetok atoll in the Marshalls, on the 18th, within six hours of landing. Here Marines are zig-zagging to the beach in assault boats. The island itself is shrouded in the smoke of the heavy preliminary naval and air bombardment which smashed the shore defences.
Photo, U.S. Navy

battleships to destroyers began to bombard the island on the morning of June 12. while fast minesweepers cleared the waters for the assault ships. On June 13 a contingent of older battleships arrived and together with the cruisers and destroyers took over the brunt of the bombardment. Finally, on the morning of June 15, an amphibious force of transports, cargo ships, and L.S.T.s under Vice-Admiral R. K. Turner came into position off the west coast and landings began. The 2nd and 4th Marine Divisions landed first and were followed by the 27th Army Division.

The landings on Saipan immediately provoked into action the long dormant Japanese Fleet (*see* page 3093). Because

Landings on Saipan

the Battle of the Philippine Sea was not the full fleet action which the American public had been led to expect, it was written off in the press as an abortive action, but it was in fact one of the three or four decisive naval battles of the Pacific War.

The Japanese could not think of meeting in a full-fledged naval action the whole bulk of the huge force under Admiral Spruance. But they knew that that force had the primary commitment of covering the amphibious operations for the taking of Saipan, which would necessarily impede and embarrass its movements. Admiral Spruance was in fact determined not to let his carriers and battleships be drawn so far away to westward that they could not protect the amphibious units from a possible " end run " by an undetected enemy force. The force whose approach was reported to him on the very day of the Saipan landings was, while strong, clearly not the whole of the Japanese Fleet. The Japanese hoped, moreover, to use the airfields still in their hands on Guam and Tinian as a refuelling base for their carrier aircraft, which would enable them to launch their attacks at about twice the normal range. They hoped, in other words, to strike a crushing blow at the Allied fleet while standing entirely outside the maximum striking range of Allied forces.

The plan, shrewdly devised, failed with losses that were disastrous to the already grossly inferior Japanese Fleet. The deterioration in its fighting strength was to tell markedly in the greater battle off the Philippines four months later (described in Chapter 334). The more immediate result was the collapse of any Japanese hopes for the relief or support of their beleaguered and desperately resisting garrison on Saipan. Once more a Japanese garrison was to fight to the end hopelessly isolated from outside aid.

Organized resistance on Saipan was finally quelled on July 9. The fighting was intense, and the American casualties were heavy: 2,359 killed, 11,481 wounded, 1,218 missing. Ninety-five per cent of the Japanese garrison,

AMERICANS RETURN TO THE ISLAND OF GUAM

Guam, southernmost of the Mariana Islands, belonging to America since 1899, was a U.S. naval base before war began in 1941, although the rest of the Marianas were mandated to Japan. Guam was captured by the Japanese on December 9, 1941. U.S. Marines and infantry, commanded by Major-General Roy S. Geiger, went ashore on the island on July 20, 1944, to meet stubborn opposition not overcome until August 10. Here are the skeletons of the Pacific Cable Company's offices at Sumay. Below, a warship of the U.S. 5th Fleet supports the landings with shellfire.

estimated at 19,000, perished. The land campaign was constantly supported by naval forces, both surface and air. Between June 13 and July 9, over 11,000 tons of shells were fired on the one island, as well as many aerial bombs. But the rugged terrain and numerous caves, of which the Japanese took full advantage, reduced the effectiveness of Allied fire.

The unexpectedly stiff resistance on Saipan and the sortie of the Japanese Fleet delayed Allied landings on Guam. This delay, however, permitted a period **Air and Sea Bombardment of Guam** of air and surface bombardment which in severity and duration exceeded anything previously experienced in the Pacific. Between July 8 and the landing on the 20th of amphibious forces under the command of Rear-Admiral Richard L. Connolly, Guam was bombarded by battleships, cruisers and destroyers, and bombed by carrier-borne aircraft. An official report indicated the extent of the devastation caused to Japanese gun emplacements : " coastal defence guns, heavy and light A.A. guns, dual-purpose guns and all types of defence installations were rendered impotent prior to the landing of troops. . . . It is believed that not one fixed gun was left in commission on the west coast that was of greater size than a machine gun." The fighting in Guam was less intense than on Saipan, but enemy opposition was stubborn, and it was not until August 10, 1944, that organized resistance on the

AMPHIBIOUS INVASION OF TINIAN ISLAND

U.S. Marines landed on Tinian in the Marianas on July 23, 1944, capturing the airfield on the 25th and gaining control of the island by August 1. Here a long line of amphibious tanks is streaming towards the shore of Tinian carrying troops and supplies to reinforce ground forces which have already carried the fighting inland. *Photo, Associated Press*

island (captured by the Japanese two days after Pearl Harbor) ceased; the elimination of isolated pockets of opposition went on until the middle of November.

The conquest of Tinian, 2½ miles south-west of Saipan, was assisted by artillery fire from that island. Resistance was much less stubborn than on the other islands. Troops were landed on July 23, by August 1 the island was declared secure, and the occupation phase was completed on August 7.

The occupation of Biak Island off N.W. New Guinea (*see* page 3126) was followed on July 1 by the seizure of Numfoor Island, between Biak and the mainland, and on July 30 by a landing on the Vogelkopf Peninsula at Cape Sansapor, near the western tip of New Guinea. Thus the southern flank of the Allied lines of communication across the Pacific was completely secured. In none of these operations were ships larger than heavy cruisers used.

To complete the isolation of the enemy-held central and eastern Carolines, including the base at Truk, and to prepare for the invasion of the Philippines, it was necessary to secure the Palaus. **Descent on the Palaus** These islands, lying to the west of the Carolines chain (though sometimes considered part of that archipelago), lay on the right flank of any approach to the Philippines from New Guinea, where the major part of the Allied forces were gathered.

In preparation for the landing on Peleliu Island in the Palaus, widespread air and surface attacks on targets ranging from the Volcano and Bonin Islands to the Philippines were made to neutralize or destroy Japanese forces which might have interfered. The attacks in the Philippines were especially heavy and profitable (*see* page 3093). Strong forces of carrier-based planes attacked the Palaus themselves on September 6, leaving seventeen small

JAPANESE SHIPS ABLAZE OFF SAIPAN

In the preliminary bombardment of Saipan, Tinian, and Guam in the Marianas, carried out by an American task force between June 10 and 12, 1944, thirteen enemy ships (including a destroyer and three corvettes trying to escape from Saipan) were sunk, and sixteen others were damaged. Here Japanese shipping in Tanapag Harbour, Saipan, is blazing after the American bombardment. *Photo, U.S. Navy*

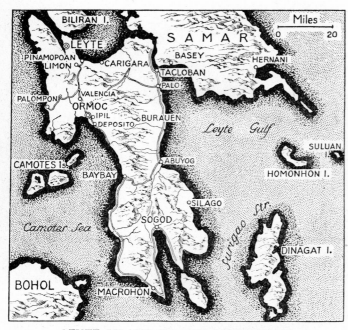

LEYTE ISLAND IN THE PHILIPPINES

Contrary to the expectations of the Japanese, the Americans on October 20, 1944 made their first landing in the Philippines in the centrally situated island of Leyte instead of the more southerly Mindanao (see map in page 3274). Some idea of the ruggedness of the country, and the consequent difficulties of the campaign, can be gained from this map.

enemy ground forces neutralized. The Japanese had meanwhile abandoned Ulithi Atoll (Western Carolines), and U.S. troops landed there on September 23.

On September 14, the day of the landing on Peleliu, an amphibious force under General MacArthur's personal command invaded Morotai in the Halmahera group of the Molucca Islands, securing it with little resistance. By this move the south as well as the north flank to the New Guinea–Philippines invasion route was covered.

In his report of March 27, 1945, to the Secretary of the Navy, Fleet Admiral E. J. King disclosed that the initial plans for the re-entry of the Philippines provided for a landing on Mindanao some time in November, but that the decision to accelerate the advance and to make the initial landings on Leyte in the central Philippines was reached in mid-September, when the Third Fleet air attacks revealed the weakness of the enemy's air opposition. A landing on Leyte would by-pass and isolate large Japanese forces on Mindanao. Moreover, Leyte had sufficient anchorage facilities and aerodrome sites, and provided good access to the remainder of the central Philippine islands.

Decision to Land on Leyte

Concentrated bombing of the Philippines followed this decision (see page 3093). Besides inflicting heavy damage on enemy ships and planes, complete photographic coverage of the area of Leyte and Samar, where the landings were to take place, was obtained.

Japanese political and military leaders had more than once publicly acknow-

ships ablaze, wrecking the grounded aircraft, and setting warehouses on fire.

A three-day intensive preparatory bombardment preceded the landing of units of the 1st Marine Division on Peleliu on September 14, the operation being made under the command of Vice-Admiral Wilkinson and Major-General Julian Smith. Three days later the 81st Infantry Division went ashore on Angaur Island, six miles to the south. A second landing on September 20 completed the subjugation of Angaur, and part of the 81st Division was then sent to Peleliu, where the fighting was much more severe and the Marines had suffered heavy casualties. By September 25 communication between the northern and southern Japanese pockets left on the island had been severed, and on October 1 the U.S. Navy Department announced that, with the exception of "Bloody Nose Ridge" (Mount Umurbrogal) on Peleliu, the islands of Peleliu, Ngesubus, Kongauro, and Angaur in the Palaus were in American hands. No landing was made on Babelthuap, the largest of the Palau group. Its rough terrain was heavily garrisoned, and since it had no favourable airfield sites or other advantages, there was no reason to incur the costly losses that its conquest would have involved. From Peleliu and Angaur, the rest of the Palaus could be dominated and the

Severe Fighting on Peleliu

BEACH ASSAULT IN THE PALAU ISLANDS

An American landing was made on Angaur Island, southernmost of the Palau group, on September 17, 1944 ; a second followed on the 20th, when all organized resistance ceased. Six hundred Japanese were killed in the fighting. Here U.S. infantrymen are going in to shore in landing vehicles tanks (armoured) : by virtue of their caterpillar treads, these vehicles could creep over hidden reefs that sometimes held up other types of landing craft. *Photo, Paul Popper*

U.S. FORCES CAPTURE PELELIU IN THE PALAUS

1. Major-General Roy S. Geiger, commanding the 3rd Amphibious Corps; Colonel Harold D. Harris; and Major-General William H. Rupertus, commanding the 1st Marine Division, plan the final stages of the conquest of Peleliu (where the 1st Marines landed on September 14, 1944) in a building abandoned by the Japanese. 2. Marines of the 1st Division enjoy a short rest in a captured searchlight position during severe fighting. 3. Rocket-firing L.C.I.s move in to the shore of Peleliu. 4. Marine veterans dig in after landing.

ledged that loss of the Philippines must inevitably mean loss of the war for Japan. For not only would the islands present the Allies with a great staging base for future operations, but the establishment of Allied naval and air forces there, coupled with Allied control of the Palaus and the Marianas, would make it possible to sever Japan's communications with all the lands between the Bay of Bengal and the Solomon Sea. And these lands contained, besides the vast wealth of strategic resources for which Japan had originally gone to war, the cream of the Japanese army. No nation could afford such a loss.

A more critical strategic situation could not arise, short of an invasion of Japan itself, and the landing on Leyte on October 20 was therefore the signal

Surprise Achieved in Philippines

for the Japanese Combined Fleet, which had avoided battle for almost two years, to move in for the show-down fight (*see* Chapter 334). The landing, which was preceded by devastating naval and air bombardment, was a complete surprise, for Leyte had been regarded by the Japanese as safe from attack, on account of its position in the centre of the occupied Philippine Islands. All their defensive preparations had been made on Mindanao. The main beach opposition came from 6-inch and 8-inch naval guns, which were knocked out by the 14-inch and 16-inch guns of the American fleet. Machine-gun nests were dealt with by 6-inch guns, and rocket-firing craft (*see* page 3069 and illus. in page 3071) covered the trenches. With the continued help of naval guns, beach-

heads were secured in the Tacloban area with small casualties. Two airfields, Tacloban and Dulag, were immediately overrun. U.S. troops, numbering over 100,000 and comprising elements of the 6th Army (under Lieut.-General Walter Krueger) with veterans from the New Guinea campaigns, began to advance. By October 22 they had established themselves on the north coast, thus gaining control of the San Juanico Strait separating Leyte from Samar, and had taken Palo on the east coast. San Pablo airfield was captured on the 24th. Landings were made on Samar on the 27th.

A typhoon interfered with operations, but by the 30th the 6th Army controlled the whole east coast of Leyte (212 miles) and all important road junctions and

communications, and were within ten miles of the west coast of the island; while nearly all Samar had been freed. Reinforcements reached the enemy from Mindanao, Cebu and others of the Philippine Islands, but the convoys bringing them were subjected to heavy American attacks, and many failed to get through (*see* Chapter 334).

After October 31, the chief centre of resistance was Ormoc, a west coast port with an airfield, where General Yamashita, who led the Japanese troops in Malaya in 1941 and captured Singapore, was in command. The U.S. 1st Cavalry Division was involved in heavy fighting which developed round Carigara; while to the south the U.S. 7th Division cut across the island to reach the west coast

OPERATIONS IN LEYTE
U.S. military supplies and equipment move through the streets of Tacloban, capital of Leyte, first of the Philippine Islands to be freed from the Japanese. Left, a church turned into a hospital by the U.S. 36th Evacuation Hospital Group. Tents have been pitched outside its walls for casualties who could not be accommodated inside the building.
Photos, Planet News; Associated Press

26 miles south of Ormoc on November 1. The U.S. 24th Division captured Pinamopoan on November 5. Japanese air activity over the island was greatly reduced by heavy U.S. bombing attacks on aerodromes in the other islands of the Visayan group.

Ormoc came under fire from American long-range artillery on November 8. The Japanese fought for the town with fanatic intensity, but U.S. infantry,

ATTACK ON JAPANESE CAVE POSITIONS IN PELELIU

In Peleliu, island of the Palau group (Western Carolines), U.S. Marines encountered the toughest terrain they had experienced in the Pacific. Landing there on September 14, 1944, they had occupied three-quarters of the island by the 22nd, but its complete subjugation was held up by Japanese occupying fortified cave positions on Mount Umurbrogal ('Bloody Nose Ridge'), a jagged limestone ridge a few hundred yards inland. Here a bulldozer-tank is attacking enemy cave positions.

Photo, U.S. Official

GENERAL MacARTHUR RETURNS TO THE PHILIPPINES

General Douglas MacArthur, Commander-in-Chief, South-west Pacific, watched the landings on Leyte in the Philippines on October 20, 1944, from the cruiser U.S.S. 'Nashville,' and afterwards went ashore himself, declaring that he had come ' to stay for the duration.' Here he is (left) wading ashore with Lieut.-General Richard Sutherland (centre), his Chief of Staff. Right, monument set up on ' Red ' Beach, near Tacloban, to commemorate the General's return to the Philippines.   *Photos, Keystone ; New York Times Photos*

BRINGERS OF FREEDOM TO THE FILIPINO PEOPLE

L.S.T.s, including number 18, veteran of amphibious invasions from the Solomons onwards, lie off the shore of Leyte Island in the Philippines on October 20, 1944, as men, armaments and supplies come ashore. U.S. Coast-guardsmen and troops are already busy filling sandbags for beach gun-emplacements. Below, Philippine civilians welcome American troops among the wreckage left near the shore by the bombardment which preceded the landings. An Australian Naval Squadron, under the command of Commodore John A. Collins, R.A.N., and three Australian passenger ships converted into landing ships took part in the invasion.

Photos, Paul Popper

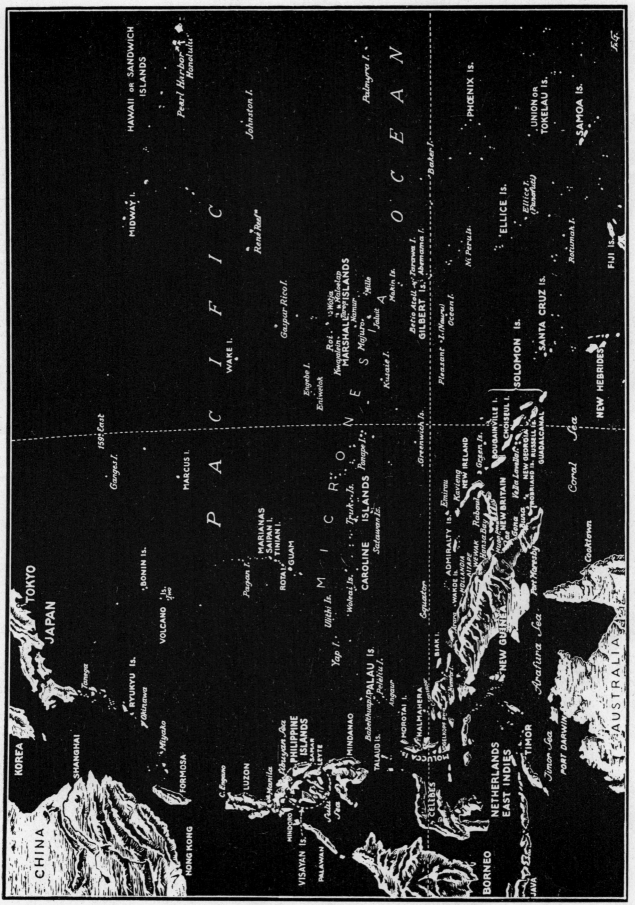

JAPAN'S SHORT-LIVED EMPIRE IN THE SOUTH-WEST PACIFIC

Japan began her campaign of conquest in the South-West Pacific on December 7, 1941, with an attack on Pearl Harbor in the Hawaii Islands, which neutralized the American Fleet lying there. Within a few months she had gained control of all the islands, large and small, between Japan and Australia except for a small area in south-east New Guinea. But this rapidly-won empire began to shrink when on August 8, 1942, American troops landed in Guadalcanal, and in October, Australian forces turned back the Japanese thirty-two miles from Port Moresby. Thereafter the Allied advance went on unchecked until by October 1944, U.S. forces were back in the Philippines and New Guinea was virtually clear of the enemy. *Specially drawn for* The Second Great War *by Félix Gardon*

LIBERATION OF THE PHILIPPINES PROCLAIMED

From the steps of the Government building in Tacloban, capital of Leyte Island, General MacArthur proclaims the liberation of the Philippines. Behind him (left to right) stand Lieut.-General George C. Kenney, Commander of the Far East Air Force ; Vice-Admiral Thomas C. Kinkaid, U.S.N., Commander of the Allied Naval Forces, S.W. Pacific ; Lieut.-General Walter Krueger, Commander of the U.S. 6th Army ; Lieut.-General Richard K. Sutherland, General MacArthur's Chief of Staff ; Lieut.-General Richard Egeberg, aide-de-camp ; and Sergio Osmena, President of the Philippines, who landed with General MacArthur. *Photo, Planet News*

linked up at the village of Deposito, and took Ormoc after fierce street fighting on December 10, wiping out the Japanese garrison. The town of Valencia, headquarters of the Japanese 35th Army, was captured on the 19th, and a special communiqué issued by General MacArthur on the 20th, the third anniversary of his retirement to the Bataan Peninsula (*see* page 2088), announced that the Leyte campaign had ended with the capture of Palompon. The Japanese had lost 113,221 men on Leyte. U.S. losses were 2,623 killed, 8,422 wounded and 172 missing.

Under strong air cover and with the support of cruisers, destroyers and rocket-firing craft, U.S. troops on December 15 made an almost unopposed landing on Mindoro at a point some 300 miles north-west of Leyte and only 75 miles south **U.S. Troops Land on Mindoro** of Manila—a move which virtually cut the Philippines in two. The invasion convoy had made a 600-mile voyage within enemy waters, taking the route from waters south of Leyte across the Mindanao Sea, and up the Sulu Sea to Mindoro Strait. The little enemy resistance encountered was quelled by December 30, and the turn of the year found the United States forces poised ready for descent on Luzon.

supported by Sherman tanks, heavy artillery, and dive-bombers, made slow progress, driving the enemy point by point from the series of ridges which were a natural protection to the port on the landward side, and had been used by General Yamashita as the basis of a strong line of defence. War correspondents described the fighting as the fiercest in the South-West Pacific since the Kokoda-Buna campaign in New Guinea (*see* Chapter 249). A strong Japanese counter-attack was repulsed on November 18. Then came torrential rains and a typhoon which washed away bridges, turned streams into torrents, and roads into rivers : conditions were as bad as the worst encountered in New Guinea. But operations went on.

The Americans crushed a Japanese outpost at Limon on November 23, crossed the Leyte river next day, and pressed on. Ormoc was bombarded by **Pressing on to Ormoc** naval units on the 28th. Torrential rains continued. The Japanese began a series of fierce but unsuccessful " suicide " charges on December 1. Six days later the U.S. 77th Infantry Division (Major-General Andrew Bruce) landed near Ipil, three miles south of Ormoc. The 7th and 77th Divisions, converging on the port from three sides,

ROCKET SHIPS ATTACK MINDORO

With strong air cover and supported by cruisers, destroyers and rocket-firing craft, U.S. troops made a landing almost unopposed on the south-west coast of Mindoro on December 15, 1944. This second landing divided the Philippines in two (see map opposite) and, said General MacArthur, "enables us to dominate sea and air routes which reach to the China Sea." *Photo, Associated Press*

Diary of the War
JULY and AUGUST 1944

July 1. 1944. Enemy resistance in Cotentin Peninsula ceased (France). U.S. infantry landed on Noemfoor Island (Netherlands New Guinea). Evacuation from Greater London reopened. International financial conference met at Bretton Woods, U.S.A. (to July 22).

July 3. Siena captured intact by French (Italy). Red Army liberated Minsk. 14th Army captured Ukhrul (Assam). Iwo Jima (Volcano Is.) and Haha (Bonin Is.) heavily attacked by U.S. task force.

July 4. Canadians captured Carpiquet (France). R.A.F. dropped 12,000-lb. bombs on caves of St. Leu d'Osserat, 30 miles N.W. of Paris, used as flying-bomb dump. Red Army liberated Polotsk.

July 5. Red Army captured Salmi (Finland), Molodechno, Smorgon.

July 6. Red Army captured Kowel.

July 7. Over 1,100 U.S.A. 8th A.F. Fortresses and Liberators bombed Leipzig area; massive night attack by R.A.F. Lancasters on caves of St. Leu d'Osserat; 2,300 tons dropped by R.A.F. on enemy defences N.W. of Caen (France). U.S.A. 20th A.F. bombed Sasebo, Yawata and Omura (Kyushu, Japan).

July 8. Red Army captured Baranowicze. M.A.A.F. bombed Vienna area.

July 9. British captured Caen; Americans, La Haye du Puits (France). 5th Army captured Volterra (Italy). Red Army captured Lida. U.S. bombers from Italy attacked Ploesti (Rumania). Resistance on Saipan (Marianas) ceased.

July 11. Over 1,100 bombers of U.S.A. 8th A.F. attacked Munich area. U.S. heavy bombers attacked Toulon.

July 12. Over 1,200 bombers of U.S.A. 8th A.F. (26 lost) attacked Munich area; over 1,300 aircraft of Bomber Command (12 lost) attacked railway centres, flying-bomb sites, etc., at night. Red Army captured Idritsa.

July 13. Red Army captured Vilna.

July 14. French troops seized San Gimignano and Poggibonsi (Italy). Red Army carried Pinsk by assault. U.S.A. 15th A.F. attacked Budapest.

July 16. Over 1,000 bombers of U.S.A. 8th A.F. attacked Munich area. 8th Army took Arezzo (Italy). Red Army captured Grodno.

July 18. Americans captured St. Lô (France). U.S.A. 8th A.F. attacked Peenemunde, Zinnowitz, and targets in the Kiel area. R.A.F. made heavy night attacks on Berlin and Cologne, and other targets. Some 300 lost and up to 1,000 injured in explosion of two ammunition ships at Port Chicago, Cal. (U.S.A.).

July 19. 5th Army captured Leghorn (Italy). U.S.A. 15th A.F. bombed Munich area.

July 20. Attempt to kill Hitler. U.S.A. 8th A.F. attacked central Germany. U.S. forces landed on Guam (Marianas).

July 21. About 1,100 U.S.A. 8th A.F. bombers attacked Regensburg, Schweinfurt, and other targets in south Germany.

July 23. Red Army took Pskov.

July 24. Red Army captured Lublin (Poland). R.A.F. Bomber Command attacked Stuttgart in force (night).

July 25. R.A.F. Lancasters dropped 12,000-lb. bombs at Watten, (France). Second heavy concentrated night attack by R.A.F. on Stuttgart. M.A.A.F. attacked Hermann Goering works at Linz (Austria). Heavy bombardment of Sabang (Sumatra) by Eastern Fleet. Polish National Committee set up at Lublin.

July 26. Red Army captured Narva (Estonia), Deblin (Poland). M.A.A.F. attacked Vienna area.

July 27. Red Army captured Byelostok, Stanislavov, Dvinsk, Rezekne, Lwow, Shavli.

July 28. 1,500 – 2,000 Fortresses attacked Leuna synthetic oil plant; 1,000 R.A.F. aircraft attacked Stuttgart and Hamburg (night). M.A.A.F. bombed Ploesti (Rumania). Red Army captured Brest Litovsk, Yaroslav, and Przemysl.

July 29. U.S.A. 8th A.F. bombed Leuna and other German targets. U.S.A. 20th A.F. bombed Mukden (Manchuria).

July 31. Americans captured Avranches (France). Over 1,200 U.S.A. 8th A.F. Fortresses and Liberators bombed Munich and Ludwigshafen and airfields in France. Red Army captured Siedlce, Jelgava.

August 1. British 2nd Army captured Le Beny Bocage. Red Army captured Kovno (Lithuania). Polish Underground Army rose in Warsaw.

August 4. Americans liberated Rennes (France). About 1,200 bombers, escorted by 1,000 fighters, of U.S.A. 8th A.F. bombed targets at Peenemunde, Hamburg, Bremen, Harburg, Anklam, Rostock and Wismar. Allies captured Myitkyina (Burma). Chinese recaptured Tengchueh (Yunnan).

August 5. British captured Villers Bocage (France). Over 1,100 U.S.A. 8th A.F. bombers attacked targets in Germany; in France 16 escorted R.A.F. Lancasters dropped 12,000-lb. bombs on U-boat pens at Brest. Red Army captured Stryj.

August 6. Americans sealed off Brittany peninsula (France). Over 1,000 U.S.A. 8th A.F. bombers attacked targets in Berlin, Brandenburg, Kiel and Hamburg areas. R.A.F. attacked flying-bomb depots near Paris and at Watten. U.S.A. 15th A.F. bombed Toulon and targets in Rhône valley.

August 7. Red Army captured Borislav.

August 9. French Forces of the Interior captured Quimper; Americans, Le Mans. R.A.F. laid mines in Dortmund-Ems canal.

August 10. Americans entered Nantes and Angers. Formation of Allied 1st Airborne Army announced. U.S.A. 20th A.F. bombed Nagasaki (Japan). Japanese captured Hengyang (Hunan, China). Resistance on Guam (Marianas) ceased.

August 12. Second R.A.F. attack with 12,000-lb. bombs on Brest U-boat pens. Germans withdrew from Florence.

August 12 and 13. U.S.A. 15th A.F. swept Riviera coast and attacked targets in Rhône valley.

August 14. 1st Canadian Army launched major attack near Falaise; U.S. heavy bombers pounded enemy installations on Riviera coast.

August 15. Allied invasion of south of France. 2,000 Allied bombers attacked airfields in Germany and the Low Countries.

August 16. M.A.A.F. flew about 1,800 sorties over southern France. Over 1,000 bombers of U.S.A. 8th A.F. escorted by 1,000 fighters attacked targets in central Germany; R.A.F. made major night attacks on Stettin and Kiel, laid mines in Stettin canal.

August 17. Liberation of Dreux, Chartres, Châteaudun, and Orléans announced; Canadians captured Falaise; final surrender of Germans in St. Malo.

August 18. Red Army captured Sandomierz.

August 19. Allied forces closed Falaise pocket; F.F.I. rising in Paris.

August 20. British captured Argentan; U.S. 7th Army reached Aix-en-Provence (France). U.S.A. 20th A.F. bombed Yawata (Japan).

August 21. U.S. troops across the Seine at Mantes-Gassicourt. Conference to draft world charter opened at Dumbarton Oaks, U.S.A. (to October 7).

August 22. Destruction of German 7th Army in Falaise pocket completed; U.S. 7th Army entered Grenoble; French liberated Hyères. Red Army captured Jassy (Rumania).

August 23. Rumania accepted Allied armistice conditions.

August 24. French 2nd Armoured Division entered Paris; Cannes, Antibes, Grasse liberated (France). Over 1,300 heavies of U.S.A. 8th A.F. escorted by about 1,000 fighters attacked targets in Germany and Czechoslovakia. Hostilities between U.S.S.R. and Rumania ceased.

August 24–25 (night). Heavy attack by Eastern Fleet on Padang and Emmahaven (Sumatra).

August 25. Paris liberated; General de Gaulle entered the city; French troops entered Avignon, Arles, and Tarascon; U.S. troops captured Carpentras and Briançon. Over 1,100 bombers of U.S.A. 8th A.F. attacked targets in Peenemunde, Luebeck, Wismar, Rostock, Stettin, and Luftwaffe air bases. R.A.F. sent out over 1,400 bombers (27 lost) in night operations. Red Army captured Tartu (Estonia). Rumania declared war on Germany. Japanese cleared from Assam.

August 26. Liberation of Vichy and Aix-les-Bains by F.F.I. announced; Germans bombed Paris at night; Toulon liberated. R.A.F. bombed Koenigsberg (E. Prussia) at night. Bucharest freed of enemy. Bulgaria announced her withdrawal from the war.

August 27. Red Army captured Galatz. F.F.I. liberated Nîmes, Montpellier, and Carcassonne.

August 28. U.S. tanks crossed the Marne, liberated Château Thierry; enemy resistance in Marseilles ceased.

August 29. U.S. 1st Army liberated Soissons and crossed the Aisne. Allies captured Urbino (Italy). Major R.A.F. blows at Stettin and Koenigsberg (night). Red Army captured Constanza (Rumania).

August 30. U.S. 3rd Army liberated Rheims; British, Beauvais and Gournay; Canadians, Rouen; F.F.I., Clermont Ferrand. Red Army captured Ploesti.

August 31. British liberated Amiens. Red Army entered Bucharest.

Chapter 323

CHINA MANAGES TO CONTINUE THE FIGHT

Save for their success in clearing the enemy from the China end of the Burma Road, the military forces of China, still receiving all too little direct Allied aid, suffered almost unrelieved reverses during 1944. The turn of the year found them holding yet another Japanese threat to Chiang Kai-shek's capital, Chungking. China's social and political history, however, showed increased awareness of the need for change and promise of improved conditions. The history of China for 1943 is told in Chapter 271

WITH the Allies during the year 1944 advancing steadily on many fronts towards final victory in both Europe and the Pacific, the situation in China presented the only major, and lengthening, shadow on a picture of general triumph. Throughout the year China was, in the main, still strategically isolated from her Allies, while with her own poor resources she had to meet the most sustained and dangerous Japanese offensive mounted against her since 1938. In the field she suffered serious, if temporary, setbacks, and these defeats combined with the economic and political stresses of long defensive warfare to create and intensify important internal dissensions.

The gloom of the military picture during the year was not, however, unrelieved. In May, in conformity with a plan made at the Quebec Conference of August 1943 (*see* pages 2701, 2799), China's first general offensive of the war was launched under Marshal Wei Li-huang across the gorges of the Salween River in west Yunnan along the route of the Chinese end of the Burma Road, with the object of linking with the Chinese Army under General Stilwell which was fighting its way through northern Burma from India over the ground on which the Ledo Road was being built (*see* page 3011). Strengthened by American arms, air support and technical direction, the Salween offensive made good progress, capturing Tengyueh at the beginning of August— a success which, combined with Stilwell's capture of Myitkyina on August 4 after a two-and-a-half months' siege, reduced the gap between the two forces to 50 miles as the crow flies. Marshal Wei captured Wanting on the Burma-China frontier on January 3, 1945, after months of fighting in most difficult country, and so cleared the Chinese section of the Burma Road from enemy control. By the 21st he had advanced to drive the enemy from the last stretch of the road, and a special Order of the Day issued from Kandy by Admiral Mountbatten, Supreme Allied Commander, S.E. Asia, on January 23

China's First General Offensive

announced that land communication to China was again open. But the Air Transport route over the Himalayan "hump," made much safer by the capture of Myitkyina airfields on May 17, 1944 (*see* page 3015), was maintained even after the reopening of the land route, which was used for the transport of artillery, lorries and other heavy equipment that could not be flown in.

During 1944 there was a great increase in the tonnage of supplies flown over the "hump," but even so they were described by President Roosevelt in August as "still only a relative trickle." He explained also that most of the supplies sent into China were destined not for the Chinese forces, but for the American Air Forces operating in China. Of such supplies as did go to the Chinese, the bulk went to the force attacking across the Salween. Problems of interior communication

(such as the absence of heavy lorries and railway equipment) meant that little help reached the hard-pressed east China front, about which a Chinese National Military Council spokesman said in October : " The actual tonnage of American supplies afforded to the Chinese Armies in east China from Pearl Harbor to the present would not be sufficient to sustain a single British or American Army division in combat for a week."

These armies of east China were in action, and in retreat, almost continuously from April to the end of the year. To secure land lines of communication between their inner defence sphere in the north and the rich territories of southeast Asia, Japanese armoured columns struck heavily in mid-April in the province of Honan (still affected by the previous year's grievous famine

The Armies of East China

COMMANDER OF AMERICAN FORCES IN CHINA
General Joseph Stilwell's recall to America was announced on October 28, 1944. Three days later Major-General Albert Coady Wedemeyer arrived in Chungking to take over the command of the United States forces in China. Here he is being greeted at a forward airstrip in Yunnan by Marshal Wei Li-huang, commander of the Chinese 2nd Army during the operations which freed the Chinese end of the Burma Road. *Photo, New York Times Photos*

CHINESE CAPTURE TENGYUEH

Marshal Wei Li-huang's American trained and equipped Chinese 2nd Army, fighting its way south-westward over the Salween River in Yunnan to meet General Stilwell's Chinese army in Burma, captured the Chinese city of Tengyueh near the Burma border on August 4, 1944. 1. Infantry move forward to scale the wall of Tengyueh. 2. Chinese wounded receive treatment at an improvised dressing station : casualties were heavy. 3. A Chinese soldier uses a portable flame-thrower (see plate following page 3102) against a Japanese strongpoint in the city. 4. War invades the peace of a temple.

Photos, Associated Press; Planet News

MARSHAL WEI LI-HUANG'S FORCES CROSS THE SALWEEN

Between May 10 and 13, 1944, a Chinese army of 20,000, commanded by Marshal Wei Li-huang, crossed the Salween River in Yunnan on a 130-mile front north and south of the Burma Road. After the crossing, which was made by boat and raft, the Chinese troops, equipped with material flown in 'over the hump,' began a drive towards Tengyueh. *Photo, U.S. Official*

—*see* illus. in page 2708), and in about a month drove the Chinese from their positions astride a 200-mile stretch of the north-south Peiping-Hankow railway. Thus securing for the first time in seven years a direct rail link between his north and central China garrisons, the enemy then proceeded to drive west along the south bank of the Yellow River (Hwang Ho) to capture the ancient Chinese capital of Loyang (now capital of Honan province) and to gain control of the east-west Lunghai railway along the greater part of its length.

Towards the end of May the Japanese developed their main offensive of the year in Hunan, southward from Hankow and north and west from Canton, to complete their land supply line on from central China to the Indo-China border, and at the same time to cut the American Air Forces off from the main east China bases from which they had been successfully harrying strategic targets in occupied China and shipping in the China Sea. For the fourth time, they attacked Changsha, capital of Hunan, previously the scene of successful Chinese defence (*see* page 2287), and this time overran it (June 18) in circum-

stances which caused the Chinese to court-martial and execute the garrison commander and members of his staff.

From Changsha the enemy armoured columns pushed rapidly south until they were checked by a patch of determined Chinese resistance in the rail junction town of Hengyang in southern Hunan. Hengyang was the hub of the supply network feeding both the Chinese armies and the American air bases in east China, and outside it was an important American air base. The air base was captured on June 26; but the walled town held out for forty-seven days, during which relieving Chinese columns made desperate efforts to reach the city from the south-west. Hengyang fell on August 10 when the relief columns were only a few miles away. The garrison of about 20,000 was killed almost to a man, and the Japanese tide moved forward towards another base and communications centre—Kweilin, capital of Kwangsi.

Other Japanese columns from Canton pushed north and west up the valley of the West River (Si Kiang), also in the general direction of Kweilin and of another American air base town, Liuchow, a hundred miles to the south-west. Another Japanese force farther south moved towards the town of Nanning and the Indo-China border. Caught between these mobile columns, and themselves lacking the mobility necessary to a modern army, the Chinese put up a patchy defence with periods of stout-hearted resistance and sudden local collapses. It was not good enough, and by the beginning of December the Japanese had occupied all these towns, forced the U.S.A. 14th A.F. to abandon its bases at Kweilin, Liuchow, and Nanning, driven a corridor clear through from Manchuria to their fief in Indo-China, and split free China in two. A new drive westward in Kweichow

U.S.A. 14th A.F. Driven from Bases

PILLBOXES IN CHANGSHA, CAPITAL OF HUNAN PROVINCE

In May 1944 the Japanese attacked Changsha, centre of the richest 'rice-bowl' area of China, for the fourth time, and, despite preparations such as these defensive pillboxes in the Nan Tsen Road, they succeeded in taking it after bitter street fighting and heavy bombing from the air. The garrison commander and members of his staff were subsequently court-martialled and executed.

Photo, Keystone

reached Tuhshan (70 miles south-east of Kweiyang) and threatened both Kunming in Yunnan, the main remaining U.S. air base in China, and Chungking, the capital; but this drive was checked and the Japanese were pushed back into Kwangsi before the end of the year.

During September, Japanese forces in the coastal area began a drive on the ports still in Chinese hands. Wenchow (in Chekiang), near which were situated Allied air bases, fell to them on September 11. A month later (October 8) they took Foochow (in Fukien), thus gaining control of all the important ports on the south coast of China.

In relation to these Chinese reverses (called by Mr. Churchill "most disappointing and vexatious"), one American observer with the Chinese armies commented, "Unfortunately one could not hope to trample the enemy to death." Other commentators were less charitable; and the announcement in Washington on October 28, at the very time of the battle for Kweilin, that General Joseph Stilwell had been relieved of his command in South-East Asia, and of the posts of Chief of Staff to Generalissimo Chiang Kai-shek and deputy to Admiral Mountbatten, Supreme Allied Commander, South-East Asia, and recalled to Washington, brought into the open growing Allied criticism of China as militarily, politically and economically inefficient and corrupt. Major-General Albert C. Wedemeyer, who arrived in Chungking on October 31, was appointed to command United States forces in

Stilwell Recalled to U.S.A.

China, and to be deputy Chief of Staff under Lord Louis. (Lieut.-General Daniel I. Sultan took command of American forces in the India-Burma theatre, formerly also under Stilwell.)

No satisfactory explanation was given for General Stilwell's recall, President Roosevelt stating that it had been done at the Generalissimo's request because of a "difference of personalities" between General and Generalissimo. Dr. T. V. Soong, China's Foreign Minister, said: "The recall of General Stilwell was entirely a question of personality and has nothing to do with any difference of policy between China and the United States."

Some Allied correspondents accused the Chungking Government of subordinating the requirements of the war against Japan to those of a feud with the Chinese Communist regime established by Mao Tse-tung at Yenan in Shensi province. Some declared that many reported battles and victories against the Japanese existed only in the imaginations of Chinese propaganda services, and complained that restrictions on their movements and political censorship had prevented them while in China from securing and transmitting a true picture of the situation.

Accusations Against Chungking

These charges reached a peak in the United States where they caused a violent reaction after the encomiums which

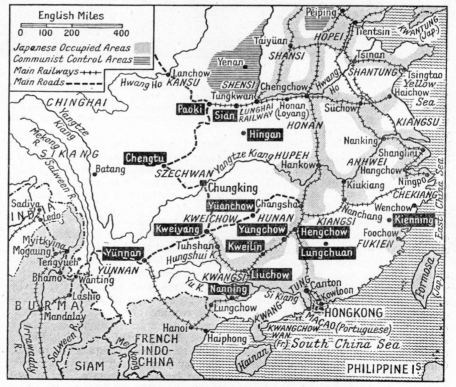

CHINA'S IMMENSE BATTLEGROUND, DECEMBER 1944

By the end of 1944 the Japanese had ousted the Chinese from control of all the main railway lines in the eastern half of the country, and, though it was continually attacked, had secured a corridor from Manchukuo (Manchuria) to French Indo-China, which was also in Japanese occupation. The shaded areas showing Japanese occupation and Communist control (see left-hand top corner of map for key) are approximate. Names in white on black are those of the principal U.S. air bases, several of which were lost during the year.

American, as well as Chinese, sources had hitherto showered on China almost without interruption. In Britain the reaction was less violent and more in line with the view of a great number of President Chiang's Chinese supporters. A reflection of this more moderate attitude was seen in November, when the Chungking Government underwent a reshuffle, in which some of the less popular Ministers were replaced. General Chen Cheng became War Minister in place of General Ho Ying-chin, who had been accused of interesting himself solely in operations against the Communists. Dr. H. H. Kung, whose simultaneous tenure of office as Minister

FIRST CONVOY OVER THE NEW LEDO-BURMA ROAD

A special Order of the Day issued from S.E.A.C. headquarters on January 23, 1945 announced that land communication with China, closed since April 1942, had been reopened. As a tribute to General Stilwell, the new 620-mile highway built behind his advancing army from Ledo in Assam to Mongyu on the old Burma Road was officially named the Stilwell Road. Left, signpost on the Ledo-Burma Road at the Burma-China frontier.

Photos, L.N.A.; News Chronicle

of Finance and President of two Government banks had been the subject of unfavourable criticism at the September meeting of the People's Political Council, left the Finance Ministry, where he was succeeded by Mr. O. K. Yui. Dr. Wang Shih-chieh (who headed the Chinese goodwill mission which came to Britain at the end of 1943 and on the way home visited Turkey and the Middle East, and who had an international reputation as a leader of the Liberal wing of the Kuomintang) returned to his old post as Minister of Information, and steps to ease the burden of censorship—under way since early in the year—were accelerated.

Chinese internal politics during the year were dominated by efforts to bridge the differences between the Central **Chungking-Communist Differences** Government at Chungking and the Communist regime at Yenan. In May, Dr. Wang with General Chang Chih-chung, on behalf of President Chiang, met representatives, headed by Mr. Lin Tsao-han, of the Yenan Government at Sian (Shensi).

He returned to Chungking accompanied by Mr. Lin Tsao-han, who had a conference with President Chiang

Kai-shek, and spent two months in the capital. Discussions continued intermittently for several months, but remained abortive, each side accusing the other of bad faith.

During the year Chungking enforced two important special measures, a *habeas corpus* act, of less significance and scope than those protecting the individual in Britain and America, but none the less imposing a sharp curb on the arbitrary powers of policemen and local political or military chiefs; and a measure restricting child labour—long a major blot on China's social life.

In the political field, China under the guidance of Chiang Kai-shek took new steps towards representative institutions. A law of September 9, 1939, had laid down that the *hsien* (county) was the essential unit of local self-government and that all Chinese over 20, both men and women, resident in a *hsien* for more than six months could exercise the franchise. On a pyramidal framework based on representation for each *pao* (group of approximately a hundred households) elective village, town, and *hsien* councils were set up over a growing area. By April 18, 1944, the *hsien* system was in effect in 1,103 counties spread over 21 provinces of free China; and the Central Government ordered that representative bodies in all *pao*, village, town and *hsien* units should be set up before the end of 1944.

The *hsien* system aimed at training the Chinese people to exercise political freedom locally before they began to participate in national affairs, and was part of a general five-year programme of popular education whose object was the **Reducing Illiteracy** eradication of illiteracy and the establishment of one "People's School" in each *pao*. At the beginning of 1944 it was estimated that there were still nearly 155 million illiterates in China. By September 1944 there were stated to be 203,785 People's Schools, with 35,949,198 child (70 per cent of the total children of school age), and 8,468,662 adult pupils.

In national affairs, the general trend of the year was towards a freer expression of views. The People's Political Council, consisting of 240 members, of whom 164 were elected by provincial or municipal councils, met for its third annual session on September 5. Non-Kuomintang parties were represented by only twenty members, among them six Communists (including Mr. Lin Tsao-han). The session was marked by lively discussion of the reports presented by various Ministers, and though the non-Kuomintang members were few, they were able to present their case.

The still-tight Chungking censorship prevented full distribution of the texts of speeches and criticisms, but in a final speech President Chiang said that he was very much pleased at the attitude

CHINESE INFANTRY MOVE IN TO BATTLE

Hengyang, old walled town in southern Hunan, was the centre of determined Chinese resistance in the summer of 1944. The American air base close by was captured by the Japanese on June 26, but the town did not fall until August 10, after the garrison of 20,000 had been almost completely wiped out. Here Chinese infantry is moving in to attack an enemy strongpoint in the vicinity of Hengyang. *Photo, Keystone*

and spirit of members who had criticized and at the same time supported the Government, and the spirit of frankness which permeated the session was a certain guarantee against further internal splits and would enhance confidence in the realization of democratic government in China.

In the same speech, President Chiang announced that the Government was considering bringing to an end earlier than previously expected (one year after the end of the war) the " political tutelage " stage of China's revolution in which the country was governed by one Party, the Kuomintang. " Our hope," he declared, " is to put our country on a firm foundation and to enable the people to exercise their political rights."

China's most important visitor during the year was U.S. Vice-President Wallace, who arrived in Chungking on June 20 on a mission from President Roosevelt. A joint statement issued at the end of five days of conferences said: " Mr. Wallace and Generalissimo Chiang Kai-shek discussed in an informal, frank and friendly atmosphere matters of

common interest and concern. They have exchanged views to their mutual advantage and found themselves in agreement on the basic principles of their objectives." After leaving Chungking Mr. Wallace visited the headquarters of the U.S.A. 14th and 20th Air Forces, and inspected Chinese industrial, agricultural and educational enterprises, arriving back in Washington on July 9.

On September 6, the arrival of Mr. Donald Nelson, Chairman of the U.S. War Production Board, and Major-General Patrick Hurley, President Roosevelt's personal envoy, was announced in Chungking, to discuss means of increasing China's industrial capacity for the furtherance of her war effort. The Americans' recommendations having been approved, Mr. Nelson returned to Washington for discussions with President Roosevelt. On November 16 he arrived back in Chungking, accompanied by experts with whose help a Chinese War Production Board, headed by Dr. Wong Wen-hao, Minister of Economic Affairs, was set up to direct, supervise and

co-ordinate Government and private production agencies. " My main job here," said Mr. Nelson, " is to help China get bigger production from her existing industrial facilities. . . . If all goes well, Chinese economy as it stands will soon produce considerably more of certain key industrial war material than it has been producing. I would expect, too, that as the Chinese people sense their growing industrial power their morale will likewise be strengthened for the hard fight

CHINESE COMMUNIST LEADER

Mao Tse-tung, leader of the Communists who controlled a large part of Shensi province, with Major-General Patrick J. Hurley, appointed United States Ambassador to China on November 27, 1944. *Photo, Associated Press*

SUPPLIES BY AIR FOR CHINA

1. Work began in October 1943 on an oil pipe-line to run from Calcutta through Assam and Burma, and terminate eventually in China. The line, rising in places to 10,000 feet above sea level, when completed was to be 1,800 miles long. Here lengths of piping for the line are being unloaded in Burma from a C-47 cargo aircraft. 2. American aircraft drop supplies by parachute to Chinese soldiers waiting to collect them. 3. Inspecting the cargo of a C-87 transport plane before it takes off 'over the hump.' 4. An aeroplane arrives back at base in India after a 'hump' trip. The 20,000th such trip was made in the summer of 1944.

Photos, U.S. Official ; Planet News ; Associated Press ; New York Times Photos

ahead. Conceivably China may be about to enter a new and decisive phase of her prolonged effort." General Hurley was appointed U.S. Ambassador to China on November 27, in succession to Mr. Clarence Gauss, whose resignation had coincided with the recall of General Stilwell.

Two agreements with Britain, signed on May 2, provided under a British offer of February 2, 1942, (1) for a British loan

Agreements with Britain

of up to £50,000,000 to finance goods and services for war purposes in the sterling area ; (2) to provide arms, munitions and military equipment on Lease-Lend terms. On July 7, eighth anniversary

of the Japanese attack on China, Mr. Churchill sent a message to President Chiang, regretting that the heavy calls on Britain's strength in Europe had prevented her from bringing " to our Chinese Ally the assistance we could wish." At the same time the Prime Minister declared : " When victory in the West is won, we shall fulfil our pledge to bring our whole weight to bear on Japan, an enemy whose odious and barbaric conduct has filled the hearts of my countrymen with implacable and remorseless detestation."

A treaty formally abolishing Canadian extraterritorial rights in China was signed at Ottawa on April 12 (*see* page 2697 for similar treaties with

CHINA'S FOREIGN MINISTER
Dr. T. V. Soong, China's Foreign Minister and former Ambassador to the U.S.A., represented China at the 1943 Quebec conference (see page 2799). On December 4, 1944, he was appointed deputy to Chiang Kai-shek in the Generalissimo's capacity as President of the Executive Yuan.
Photo, Karsh, Ottawa

REFUGEES FROM THE ADVANCING JAPANESE
The heavy fighting, and the advance of the Japanese, in Hunan and Kwangsi provinces during the summer of 1944 led to more mass migration of the Chinese peasantry. According to statistics issued by the police bureau, the population of Chungking in mid-October was 1,026,794—an increase of 24,214 since the beginning of the month—and the influx was continuing. This group of refugees has made a temporary ' home ' of a goods wagon in a railway siding.
Photo, Planet News

Britain and the U.S.A.) ; and in July Mr. Mackenzie King, Canadian Prime Minister, expressed the hope that a solution would be found to prevent the Chinese from feeling themselves discriminated against as a race by Canada (the only Chinese allowed to enter that country, under a law of 1923, were diplomats, experts and students). President Roosevelt welcomed the approval by the House Immigration Committee on October 7, 1943, of the adoption of amendments to the U.S. immigration laws which would allow Chinese nationals (excluded by acts dating from 1882) to enter the U.S. and acquire U.S. citizenship. But nothing was done during 1944 in either Canada or the U.S. to implement these expressions of goodwill. Ecuador announced on November 21 that she had repealed her Chinese Exclusion Law, and that President Velasco Ibarra had informed Chiang Kai-shek that " honest persons, regardless of race or religion," would be allowed to enter the country.

A Sino-Mexican treaty of amity, taking the place of a treaty concluded in Washington on December 14, 1899, which had expired in 1928, was signed on August 1. China was a participant in the Dumbarton Oaks conference and in the Chicago Aviation Conference (*see* page 3256).

Chapter 324
WAR TOUCHES THE JAPANESE HOMELAND

Assured at the beginning of the year 1944 that Great Britain and the United States were 'short of breath' although they had reached only the outer defence ring of 'Greater East Asia,' the Japanese people found that the passing months brought a breathless succession of Allied advances, resulting before the year was out in a crescendo of Allied air raids on the mainland.
For the history of Japan in 1943, see Chapter 288

THE peculiar sensitiveness of Japanese governments to reverses in the field was shown in February 1944 when the Allied invasion of the Marshall Islands (*see* page 3263) was followed by Cabinet changes, and the replacement of the Chiefs of Staff of the Army (Field-Marshal Sugiyama) and the Navy (Admiral of the Fleet Nagano) by, respectively, General Hideki Tojo himself (already Premier and Minister for War, Education and Munitions) and Admiral Shimada, the Navy Minister.

General Tojo speeded up shipbuilding, in order to try to replace losses (*see* Chapter 334). He also gave priority to aircraft production (a l r e a d y doubled during 1943) in an effort to counter growing American air superiority. Japan had so far experienced only one air raid, that led by Major-General Doolittle in April 1942 (*see* page 2125); but the possibility of air attacks was growing, and a great programme of evacuation and dispersal of population and industry was drawn up, and all citizens began training in fire-fighting. There were, however, few shelters except in war factories, and little fire-fighting equipment beyond buckets of water and sand. The Super-Fortress raid on Yawata of June 15 (*see* page 3090) found Japan little prepared to meet heavy attack from the air. Japan's successful drive in Hunan and Kwangsi (*see* page 3279) against the American air bases in southern China was largely designed to obviate attacks from these bases on the Japanese mainland, and

on shipping in the China seas. But the homeland was also menaced by Allied island bases creeping ever nearer Japan. The loss of Saipan in the Marianas (*see* page 3264) was too great a setback to be compensated by a mere Cabinet reshuffle, and on July 18 Tojo resigned, after an announcement earlier the same

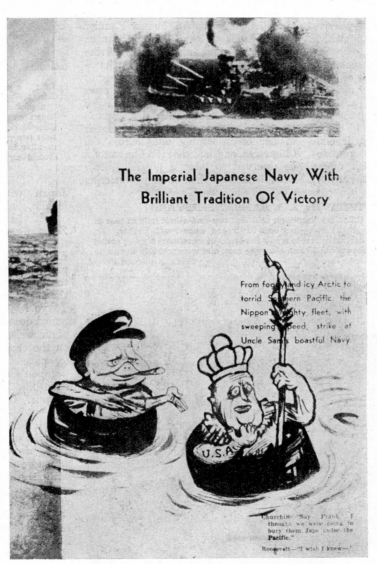

The Imperial Japanese Navy With
Brilliant Tradition Of Victory

From foggy and icy Arctic to torrid Southern Pacific, the Nippon's mighty fleet, with sweeping speed, strike at Uncle Sam's boastful Navy

Churchill "Say Frank, I thought we were going to bury them Japs under the **Pacific**."

Roosevelt—"I wish I knew—"

JAPAN TRIES TO WIN THE FILIPINOS
This was a page in one of the propaganda magazines issued by the Japanese in the Philippines, where they made great efforts to persuade the Filipinos that Japanese occupation was to their advantage, and to enlist their support for 'co-prosperity' and the consolidation of 'Greater East Asia.'
Photo, Central Press

day that he had been relieved as Chief of the Army General Staff and succeeded by General Yoshijiro Umezu, C.-in-C. of the Kwantung Army. The previous day, it had been announced that Admiral Naokuni Nomara had become Chief of the Naval Staff. Broadcasting (July 18) on the loss of Saipan, Tojo said, "I am moved by great trepidation at the thought of the deep anxiety caused to His Imperial Majesty... The situation now approaches when opportunities will occur to crack the enemy and to win victory. The real war is yet to be fought. Let us one and all renew our faith and our determination to the s u p r e m e sacrifice and thereby set the mind of his Imperial Majesty at rest."

A new Cabinet was formed on July 22 under the premiership of General Kuniaki Koiso (nicknamed " The Bull "), Governor - General of Korea, with Field-Marshal Sugiyama as War Minister and Admiral Mitsumasa Yonai as Navy Minister. The civilian element was somewhat stronger than in the previous government, Mamoru Shigemitsu being Foreign Minister and Minister for Greater East Asia ; Takakora Ogata, Minister of State and head of the Board of Information ; Ginojiro Fujiwara, a prominent industrialist, Minister of Munitions ; Sotaro Ishiwara, Finance Minister ; and Shigeo Odate, a former prefect of Tokyo, at the Home Office.

This radical change was w i d e l y interpreted by Allied observers as an indication both of internal quarrels among Japan's behind-the-scenes masters and of multiplying doubts among them about the progress of the war. Koiso himself was, like Tojo, an "expansionist." Some of his appointments—for instance, that of Field-Marshal Sugiyama—were a direct criticism of the outgoing Government. On the other hand, Mamoru Shigemitsu continued as Foreign Minister (*see* illus. in page 2895). Japan's last Ambassador in London, he was a man of considerable popularity among some sections of the Western peoples ; while for the first time in years two representatives of Japan's impotent political parties, *Seiyukai* and *Minseito*, were given posts as Ministers of State.

Japan was on the defensive, and the Koiso Cabinet had a threefold significance in its composition : first, it was **Japan on the Defensive** strongly representative of the basic aggressive militarist policies which were part of the national religion of Japan ; secondly, it included a sufficient element of long-muted public opinion to be able to present a bold face to the anti-war spirit which was increasing from day to day among the unvocal subjects of the divine Emperor ; thirdly, it contained pseudo-democratic and pseudo-internationalist elements which might suffice (if the worst came to the worst)

to bamboozle the Western Allies into making a compromise peace. Koiso could thus, in a Japanese metaphor, like a bamboo, bend with the storm without breaking. As China's War Minister, General Ho Ying-chin, remarked, "Tojo's exit should not be taken as a hint that Japan intends to sue for peace, but we should be on our guard against Japanese trickery."

Some ten days later, on August 2, 18 of Japan's 48 provincial governors were replaced in the biggest home-front reorganization since the war began. Soon afterwards the new Premier took the unusual step of bringing these new governors, and those who had retained their posts, to Tokyo to hear an exhortation, the text of which was not disclosed to the public, by the Emperor himself. On August 18 the new Premier admitted difficulties of "unprecedented seriousness," and said : "Until Divine help comes, we must endure every hardship and do everything in our power to overcome this trial," which might even end in invasion. On the same day a naval spokesman explained that Japan's greatest danger lay in the Allied threat to her ocean supply lines across the China seas, and said that the Fleet would be reserved to meet a possible direct naval attack on the sea-lane connecting

TOJO'S SUCCESSOR
General Kuniaki Koiso gave up the Governor-Generalship of Korea to become Premier of Japan on July 22, 1944. He succeeded General Hideki Tojo, Premier since October 1941 (see page 1965), who resigned on July 18 after the American conquest of Saipan evoked strong criticism of his leadership.
Photo, Associated Press

Japan with Shanghai, Hongkong, Manila, Saigon and Singapore.

A kind of Home Guard, based on the *Zaigo Gunjinkai* (Reservists' Association), was formed : in the words of Koiso, "the only way to overcome the present crisis is for the whole nation to unite in a determined effort to crush the enemy's counter-offensive" ; and in Tokyo itself ten thousand houses were pulled down to create fire-breaks in case of air raids. The anticipated air attacks on the capital began on November 24 (*see* page 3094).

Japan's anxieties were accentuated by the Allies' progress against Germany in Europe. Only two months before his fall (and less than a month before the Allied invasion of Normandy), Tojo assured the **Anxiety due to Events in Europe** Japanese people that "in conjunction with the Japanese drive in East Asia" Germany had prepared a counter-offensive which would alter the picture of the war.

Such a statement, at such a time, referred obliquely but primarily to the Soviet Union, still a neutral in the Far East war, but one at whom the Japanese were forced to give continual nervous glances over the shoulder. During March, Russia reached agreements favourable to herself in two matters which had been sources of Russo-Japanese diplomatic

WARTIME ACTIVITY IN A JAPANESE SHIPYARD
In September 1943 Colonel Knox, U.S. Navy Secretary, said that two-and-a-half million tons of shipping—one-third of Japan's merchant fleet—had been destroyed since Pearl Harbor. By intensive building, Japan made ineffectual efforts to repair her losses of merchant shipping and of war vessels—also enormous—which continued at an alarming rate, and were probably the prime cause of her defeat.
Photo, Associated Press

friction for years—a clear reflection of the success of the Red Army winter offensive in Europe. Under the first agreement, Russia recovered (subject to payment of compensation) the oil and coal concessions in Northern (Russian) Sakhalin, which she had been forced in 1925 to yield to the Japanese, who since 1905 had controlled the southern half of the island. The second agreement renewed the Soviet-Japanese Convention relating to fishing rights off the Siberian coast, but on terms much more favourable to Russia. Both Washington and London considered these agreements a triumph for Soviet diplomacy, and a measure of Japan's anxiety

to ensure the U.S.S.R.'s maintenance of neutrality in the Far East. Despite the big concessions made, Japanese propaganda indulged in a riot of praise of the harmonious relations existing with her great neighbour.

Less easy to gloss over was the shock administered in November when Stalin, in his annual speech commemorating the anniversary of the Revolution, bluntly branded Pearl Harbor as the work of an aggressor state on a par with the actions of Nazi Germany. This downright indication of Soviet sentiment towards Japan stirred *Domei*, the official Japanese news agency, to put the country on record as " surprised and

SUPER-FORTRESS SHADOW OVER JAPAN

B -29s (Super-Fortresses) of U.S.A. 20th A.F. based in Saipan (Marianas) made their first attack on the Japanese mainland on November 24, 1944, when they struck Tokyo at mid-day. Thereafter the strength and frequency of raids by Super-Fortresses increased steadily. Right, a B.-29 over the Tama river on its way to Tokyo. Below, smoke rising from more than forty hits on the Mitsubishi aircraft factory at Nagoya during a raid by Super-Fortresses on December 13, 1944.

JAPANESE ENCAMPED IN NORTH-EAST CHINA

The Japanese first entered north-east China in 1931, on the excuse that they must put down banditry. As the years went by, the number of armed Japanese immigrants and settlers grew. When Japan made a direct attack on China in 1937, she put an army, which became known as the Kwantung Army, into Manchuria, where it lived on the by no means highly productive country, reducing the inhabitants to extreme poverty. Here is an encampment of a ski detachment of the Kwantung Army taken during winter manoeuvres. *Photo, Associated Press*

offended " at Stalin's words, " because Japan is fighting for the liberation of Greater East Asia from the British and Americans." Press comment generally took a similar line, and four days after Stalin had spoken an official spokesman of the Japanese Government found it necessary to defend his country, insisting that Japan was not an aggressor nation.

Behind this self-exculpation lay strategic uneasiness. Hard-pressed as they were, the Japanese had earlier in the year (when they still be-
Uneasiness about the U.S.S.R. lieved in the possibility of a successful German counter-offensive on the Eastern Front) moved south several of their crack divisions from the Manchurian border to take part in their summer offensive in China (*see* page 3279) and were therefore probably less well prepared than at any previous time during the war to meet possible Russian intervention in the north.

The China offensive was, in fact, the one crumb of solid comfort Tokyo's propagandists could give to the Japanese people throughout the year. The long-promised land link joining all Japan's mainland conquests became at last an actuality, though it was of no great practical value in view of the precariousness of the Japanese hold on parts of it, developments on other fronts, and the ever-tightening aerial blockade of Japan.

But if the army could be presented as " invincible " at least against the almost unarmed, ill-organized Chinese, the navy, on which lay the prime responsibility for halting the Allies' island-hopping advances in the Pacific, was in very different case. Far from halting the Allied advance, it was in fact being steadily smashed as a fighting force (*see* Chapter 334), though the Japanese people were not told anything of this. What they could not help noticing, though, was that the Chief of Naval Staff was changed three times

in the year ; that Admiral Koga in May followed his predecessor as Commander-in-Chief of the Combined Japanese Fleet, Admiral Yamamoto, to a death in action, which is unusual among the highest officers of victorious navies ; that the Imperial Navy was talking in terms merely of the defence of home waters ; and, above all, that island after island—some recent Japanese conquests, some old mandates, many pronounced as vital to the defence of Japan—cropped up in the news as it was invaded by the Americans and then mysteriously disappeared from it as it was lost to Japan.

The year's great naval engagements came in October, when the Japanese Navy renounced its own announced principle of fighting in home waters only and steamed south to resist the American invasion of the Philippines. The Japanese naval staff organized a well-prepared encounter which gave them a good chance of success. Only the brilliance of the American commanders turned a potential defeat of the Allied invaders of Leyte into a Japanese rout.

But the Japanese propagandists did not await the result of the battles

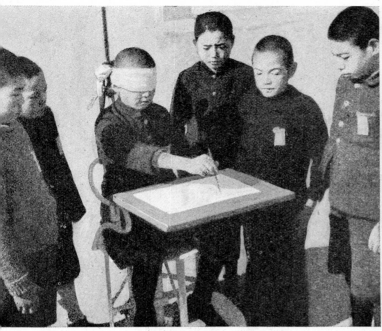

YOUNG JAPAN AS PART OF THE WAR MACHINE

Less and less normal schoolwork was done in the schools of Japan as the war went on (see page 2897). Here a group of young lads is being trained to fit them to become good airmen : after being spun round in a movable chair, the blind-folded boy has placed his pointer on a chart. The nearer he gets to a chosen point, the better his sense of balance and his powers of co-ordination and recovery. Right, pupils of a Japanese high school receive instruction in an armaments plant.

Photos, Keystone ; Associated Press

before communicating to the public their anticipated outcome. While the battles of the Philippine Sea were still in progress, the Japanese were told : " At the end of this battle Halsey's fleet will have ceased to exist, and the successes scored so far surpass in numbers and strategic importance the victories of Pearl Harbor and of Malaya." But the true story of this complex interlocking series of sea fights (told in Chapter 334) was very different, and by the end of the year

the Allies were in control of the Philippine islands of Leyte, Samar and Mindoro (*see* Chapter 322).

Nor could Japan's leaders wholly conceal from the people the Navy's failure in its other main task—the protection of merchant shipping. At the very beginning of the year Tojo

had admitted to the Diet that losses at sea " could be by no means minimized," and in March Tokyo radio confessed that communication with the south Pacific (from seizure of whose riches so much " co-prosperity " had been promised) could be carried on only by small wooden ships, hiding by day and dodging forward by night across " an ocean on which rains a torrent of bombs and shells."

Such gloomy revelations, which through the year became an ever more insistent accompaniment to the

ALLIED PRISONERS OF WAR IN JAPANESE HANDS

The Japanese used the labour of prisoners of war in a number of ways, from the building of railways to the rolling of cigarettes. The two photographs below, smuggled out of the Netherlands East Indies during the Japanese occupation, show, left, prisoners making uniforms, and, right, rolling cigarettes for their captors.

Photos, Paul Popper

hysterical claims of victories and destruction of Allied ships and aircraft, were generally coupled with increasingly urgent appeals to the people to increase production.

A serious problem for Japan's war economy was the production of food. It was theoretically possible for the Japanese to live at their accustomed subsistence level off the produce of their own soil, but the organization of the war machine had brought about over a period of years a pronounced drift from the farms to better-paid work in factories (*see* page 2897). Had it not been for the Allied blockade, this drift might have been offset by imports from the rich conquered areas, but just as increased sinkings called for more and more new ships, so they brought a new and conflicting demand for the maximum of workers on the farms. Tojo, in February, had declared that the country's food situation was secure, thanks to the soya and millet of Manchuria, which required only a short and comparatively safe sea haul; but by the end of the year his successor, Koiso, found it necessary to drive for complete self-sufficiency in food within the home islands. In this he was undoubtedly, though ironically, helped, at the cost of war production, when large-scale Super-Fortress attacks began on industrial areas. Brave as they

Japan's Manpower Difficulties

are as soldiers in attack or last-ditch defence, the Japanese do not take kindly to the nerve strain of bombing, and in Tokyo, at least before the actual attacks began, factory workers were reproached with having "lost their calmness" when a few Super-Fortresses flew over the city on reconnaissance. By the end of 1944 the great heavy industry factories, as well as the innumerable backyard machine shops on which Japan relied to so large an extent for her war production, were losing workers. The people, poor and hungry, were scattering back to their ancestral fields. An earthquake on December 7 indicated to the superstitious (and they were many in Japan) the true significance for them of that infamous anniversary, which the Government celebrated in far less lively fashion than in the two preceding years before the war, started so safely and so far away, had come home to the Japanese mainland.

JAPANESE PRISONERS OF WAR IN ALLIED HANDS

Casualties among the Japanese were high in the Pacific campaign, but they were mostly killed and included few prisoners. Here are four prisoners clad in new clothing supplied by their captors coming ashore at a U.S. base. Above, prisoners taken on Eniwetok atoll, where 3,000 Japanese were killed during the fighting in February 1944, have a meal under the eyes of U.S. Marines while waiting for shipment to a prison camp.

Photos, U.S. Official; Keystone

JAPANESE TORPEDO-BOMBER CRASHES OFF SAIPAN *Photo, U.S. Navy.*

A communiqué issued from Admiral Nimitz's headquarters at Pearl Harbor on June 13, 1944, stated that a powerful American task force had struck heavily at Saipan, Tinian and Guam in the Marianas from the 10th to the 12th. Thirteen enemy ships were sunk, sixteen damaged, and 141 planes were destroyed. In this photograph (selected as one of the hundred best pictures of the war taken by photographers of the U.S. Navy, Marine Corps and Coastguardsmen) a Japanese torpedo-bomber crashes off Saipan after a hit from a carrier's A.A. guns during this action.

LAND CONVOY
REACHES YÜNNAN

The British withdrawal from
Burma in April 1942 cut the
last link between the Allies
and China—by land over the
Burma Road, maintained after
the Japanese blockade of
China's coasts had put an end
to any contact from the sea.
The hazardous air route over
the Himalayas (nicknamed by
the airmen who flew it the
'Hump' route) was established
and accomplished wonders,
especially in the provision of
supplies and equipment for
the U.S. Air Forces operating
in China ; but many things
which China needed could be
taken in only by sea or land,
and it was to provide a surface link that Lieut.-General
Stilwell began his drive from
Ledo in Assam in March 1944
(see Chapter 299).   The route
was completed in January 1945,
and here is the crowd which
greeted the arrival in the city
of Yünnan of the first convoy
over it.

Photo, Associated Press

ALLIED FIRST AIRBORNE ARMY DESCENDS ON THE NETHERLANDS

Waves of parachutists of a U.S. Airborne Division drop from troop-carrying aircraft into the fields near Grave : cattle are grazing indifferently near gliders which have landed earlier. Below, more parachute troops float down to join comrades already landed by parachute and glider : a photograph taken by a R.A.F. Photographic Reconnaissance Spitfire during the gigantic airborne operation in the Netherlands of September 17, 1944.

Photos, British & U.S. Official

Chapter 325

BATTLE FOR THE ROAD BRIDGE AT ARNHEM

The capture of Brussels and Antwerp (see Chapter 320) was followed by the biggest airborne operation of the Second Great War, which is here described by Squadron Leader Derek Adkins. Though not completely successful, it achieved much ; and the stand of the British 1st Airborne Division at Arnhem is one of the heroic episodes of war that will live in history. The contemporaneous clearing of the Scheldt estuary is described in Chapter 332

THE speed of the Allied advance through the Pas de Calais and into Belgium suggested that if sufficient strength could be concentrated and maintained for the task, one powerful and full-blooded thrust deep into Germany would overwhelm the enemy and carry with it decisive results. The best axis along which such a thrust could be developed was the route north of the Ruhr leading to the plain of northern Germany. It was realized that the enemy was likely to concentrate strong forces to defend this vital axis and also the industrial area of the Ruhr. Speed was therefore essential if full advantage was to be taken of the disorganized state of the enemy's forces, for weather conditions would inevitably deteriorate from mid-September onwards and handicap the use of air power and airborne forces.

The Supreme Allied Commander decided, however, that the early opening up of a deep-water port and an improvement of maintenance facilities were prerequisites to the final assault on Germany itself. He therefore directed that the immediate aim should be the establishment of bridges over the Rhine throughout its entire length, and that until Antwerp or Rotterdam could be opened up operations would not be further developed. In view of the time factor, it was then agreed that the 21st Army Group under General Montgomery (promoted Field-Marshal on September 1) should launch its thrust to the Rhine before attempting the clearance of the Scheldt estuary.

It was at this juncture that the Allied armies in France were regrouped from north to south as follows : 21st Army Group (Field-Marshal Montgomery) comprising the 1st Canadian Army (General Crerar) and the British 2nd Army (General Dempsey) ; the 12th Army Group (General Bradley) consisting of the U.S. 1st Army (General

Hodges) and the U.S. 3rd Army (General Patton) (on September 13 it was announced that the U.S. 9th Army, under the command of Lieut.-General William H. Simpson, was also in the field as part of the 12th Army Group) ; the 6th Army Group (General Devers) formed by the U.S. 7th Army (General Patch) and the French 1st Army (General de Lattre de Tassigny).

The Germans had withdrawn from Antwerp without contesting it (*see* page 3248), but they made a determined attempt to stand on the Albert Canal. On September 6 British troops of the 2nd Army liberated the ancient city of

LINE OF THE GERMAN STAND IN BELGIUM
After the destruction of the German 7th Army in the Falaise pocket on August 22, 1944, the enemy's retreat was little better than a disorganized rout until, after the fall of Brussels (September 3) and Antwerp (September 4), the Germans made a determined attempt to stand on the line of the river Scheldt and the Albert Canal. The Belgian battle area is shown in this map.

Ghent. On the same day reconnaissance units reported that all the bridges over the Albert Canal had been destroyed ; but next day it was forced near Beeringen, and the bridge-head thus made was enlarged against bitter opposition. A second bridge-head near Gheel was won on September 9 and this too became the object of furious counter-attacks, all of which were held.

On the following day an armoured unit reached and forced the passage of the Meuse-Scheldt canal at a point 12 miles north-east of Beeringen, after a successful action with the enemy's batteries. West of Antwerp the general push north towards the Dutch border continued, and on the 11th armoured patrols crossed the frontier into the Netherlands near Groote.

The 1st Canadian Army, including elements of British, Polish and other Allied troops, was forced to move

more slowly in the coastal sector, since it had either to by-pass or overcome the German garrisons left in the Channel ports north of Le Havre, and had also to cross the rivers in its path at their broadest. It was therefore given the task of reducing the pocket of German troops in the north-west corner of Belgium and Zeeland-Flanders south of the Scheldt. It liberated Bruges and crossed the Zeebrugge-Bruges-Ghent canal on the 12th. Canadian armoured forces then wheeled eastwards and crossed the Leopold Canal on the 13th, but next day were forced to withdraw from the bridge-head they had formed. Polish armour joined British units in and around Ghent and they also drove eastward. They, too, were driven back. After more hard fighting, the Canadians recrossed the Leopold Canal at six different points on September 15. Next day the Poles crossed the Dutch frontier, and on the 17th cut the Hulst-Axel road and crossed the Hulst Canal, but were forced back. Recovering, they pushed rapidly into the Netherlands, liberating Terneuzen on the Scheldt on September 21.

Canadians Cross the Leopold Canal

The Germans were determined to hold the Scheldt pocket as long as possible, in order to deny the channel to Allied shipping ; while in the Meuse-Scheldt canal area, where a second bridge-head had been secured north of Moll (captured on the 15th) the enemy, beginning to recover his balance, was throwing in repeated and fierce counter-attacks : " so that," explained Field-Marshal Montgomery in a lecture he gave on October 3, 1945 to the Royal United Service Institution, " the urgency of launching the thrust to the Rhine was underlined," its purpose being to cross the Maas (as the Meuse becomes in the Netherlands) and the Rhine and thus place the British 2nd

Army in a suitable position for the subsequent development of operations towards the northern face of the Ruhr and the north German plain.

On Sunday, September 17, the battle of Arnhem began with the launching of the greatest single airborne operation of the war. The essential feature of the plan was to lay a carpet of airborne troops across the parallel west-east waterways of the Rhine delta lying north of the Meuse-Scheldt canal to the Lower Rhine (Neder Rijn or Lek), on the general axis of the road through Eindhoven to Uden, Grave, Nijmegen and Arnhem, so that bridge-heads could be seized over the successive river-lines of the Maas, the Waal (main stream of the Rhine), and the Lower Rhine. Along the corridor, or airborne carpet, 30th British Corps was to advance and establish itself north of the Lower Rhine with bridge-heads across the river Ijssel, facing east, over which the British 2nd Army might in due course pour to break down the last remaining barrier defending the Reich, thus gaining direct access to the Ruhr.

LIEUT.-GENERAL SIMPSON

On September 13, 1944, it was announced that a new formation, the U.S. 9th Army, was in the field in France under the command of Lieut.-General William H. Simpson. General Simpson had served with the American Expeditionary Force in France in 1918 as chief of staff of the 33rd Division.

Photo, U.S. Official

Operation " Market " was preceded by an intense air bombardment to neutralize the ground defences, which were formidable and increasing daily. Nevertheless, little opposition to the actual landings was encountered, in spite of the **Operation 'Market'** fact that the long columns of aircraft coming from Britain had to fly low over the Dutch islands on which the Germans had heavy concentrations of anti-aircraft batteries. On the night of September 16–17 R.A.F. Lancasters bombed enemy airfields, railway marshalling yards and other targets in Germany and Holland, and on the morning of the 17th over 750 Flying Fortresses of the U.S.A. 8th A.F. bombed German gun positions over a wide area in the Netherlands. Before the gliders and transport aircraft landed their troops, Mitchell and Boston medium bombers of the R.A.F., together with squadrons of Mosquitoes, Typhoons, Spitfires, Mustangs and Lightnings, bombed and strafed barracks and gun sites.

Altogether well over 5,000 aircraft took part in the airborne operations, undertaken by the Allied 1st Airborne Army (the formation of which had been announced by S.H.A.E.F. on August 10). It included British, American and Polish units. Lieut.-General Lewis H.

CANADIANS LIBERATE THE ANCIENT CITY OF BRUGES

On September 12, 1944, the 1st Canadian Army occupied Bruges, Belgian city of canals, without a struggle, and thrust on across the Zeebrugge-Bruges-Ghent Canal, in the direction of Terneuzen, to within five miles of the Netherlands border. (See map in page 3295.) Here citizens of Bruges cheer and wave to the incoming Canadians.

Photo, New York Times Photos

Brereton, formerly commanding the U.S.A. 9th A.F., was its commander, with Lieut.-General F. A. M. Browning (*see* illustration in page 3194) of the British Army as Deputy Commander.

The plan involved the landing of three separate forces. Its most striking feature was that the whole operation was to be carried out in daylight. The British 1st Airborne Division (*see* table in page 3301), under the command of Major-General R. E. Urquhart, C.B., D.S.O., with a Polish parachute brigade in support, was to be dropped at Arnhem, where one rail and two road bridges (one a pontoon bridge) spanned the Lower Rhine. Their principal task was to seize and hold the main road bridge. Elements of the U.S. 82nd Airborne Division were to establish the section from Grave to Nijmegen, where there were vital bridges over the Maas and the Waal respectively. They were also to capture the high ground south of Nijmegen overlooking the exits from the Reichswald. The third force was the U.S. 101st Airborne Division, which was to create that part of the corridor from the outskirts of Grave to Eindhoven, an important road junction some 37 miles south of Nijmegen. The U.S. 82nd and 101st Airborne Divisions were among the airborne troops who jumped the Atlantic Wall on June 6 (*see* page 3190). The British 1st Airborne Division had seen service in North Africa, Sicily and Italy (*see* Chapters 256, 283 and 286).

Disposition of Airborne Forces

As success at Arnhem depended on success also at Eindhoven and Nijmegen, and there were insufficient carrying planes and gliders to take all the divisions in in one lift, the Eindhoven and Nijmegen forces were given priority

CASUALTIES IN THE ADVANCE ON NIJMEGEN

Eindhoven, where the U.S. 101st Airborne Division had been dropped on September 17, 1944, was reached and liberated next day by troops of the British 2nd Army, who pushed on immediately towards Nijmegen. The Germans, using self-propelled guns, attacked the advancing column, but were driven off by British tanks and R.A.F. Typhoons. Here men wounded in this action find some slight cover in a ditch by the roadside.   *Photo, British Official*

in available aircraft, and it was decided to land the 8,969 officers and men to be dropped at Arnhem in two lifts—first the 1st Parachute Brigade, the 1st Air Landing Brigade and about half the available sappers and gunners and other divisional troops; then the 4th Parachute Brigade and the remaining divisional troops, with the Polish Parachute Brigade following later as reinforcements. The first lift was to seize the main road bridge and, if possible, the pontoon and railway bridges down stream. The second lift was to establish a perimeter outside and surrounding the town of Arnhem.

From the start of the operations, however, adverse weather conditions

ASSAULT ON THE BELGIAN WATERWAYS

The British 2nd Army met stubborn resistance to its passage of the Albert and Meuse-Scheldt Canals. British infantry, sappers and men of the Pioneer Corps carry an assault craft to the Meuse-Scheldt Canal, first crossed on September 10, 1944. Right, a 25-pounder of a British artillery field regiment defends the bridge-head seized over the Albert Canal at Beeringen on September 7, and held against repeated counter-attacks.   *Photos, British Official*

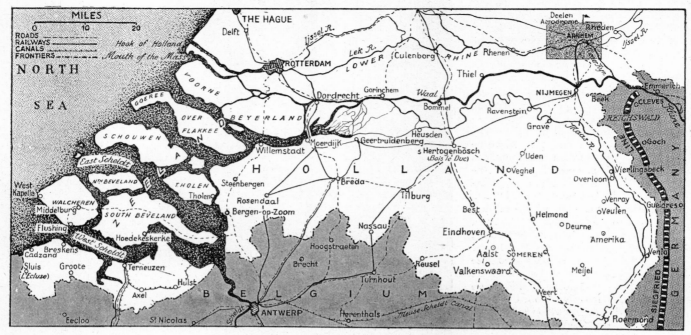

SCENE OF THE GREATEST AIRBORNE OPERATION OF THE WAR

After the remnants of the German 15th Army were forced back across the Seine, the enemy could make a stand before the German frontier was reached only along the line of the streams which debouch into the North Sea through the Rhine delta. It was to secure a foothold on the northern side of this triple water barrier that the great airborne operation of September 17, 1944 was planned and executed. (Shaded area round Arnhem is shown in large scale in page 3304.)

prevailed ; in fact during the eight days' battle that followed there were only two days on which the weather permitted even a reasonable scale of offensive air support and air transportation. As a result the airborne formations were never completed to strength (the U.S. 82nd Airborne Division, for example, was without a complete glider-borne combat team). Moreover,

it had been intended to fly in the 52nd Division, but this project had to be abandoned. In addition, resupply missions were repeatedly cancelled, and even when flown were often on a greatly

reduced scale. It was also unfortunate that the heavy commitments of the Allied air forces in respect of the 82nd and 101st Divisions necessitated the placing of the British 1st Airborne Division third on the priority list, for their task proved the most difficult of all and only narrowly fell short of success.

The 101st Airborne Division drop was completely successful. The British 2nd Army in a great thrust at dawn on September 18 from Valkenswaard near the Dutch-Belgian border overcame stiff resistance from German Panther tanks near

British 2nd Army Reaches Eindhoven

Aalst and advanced to link up with the airborne troops at Eindhoven, which they entered at 6.30 p.m. (see illus. in pages 3216 and 3217). Tanks of the Guards Armoured Division reached Nijmegen and the south end of the 600-yard-long bridge across the Waal on September 20. American parachutists, crossing the river in rubber boats under heavy shell and machine-gun fire, reached the north end of the bridge, which the two forces succeeded in capturing intact, forestalling enemy preparations for its demolition. The 2nd Army was ready to move on to Arnhem.

The country around Arnhem is well wooded, and the number of open areas suitable for landing is limited. Four were eventually chosen outside the range of the heavy flak concentrated at Arnhem and the guns defending the

BRITISH FORCES REACH HELMOND

Troops of General Dempsey's 2nd Army reached Eindhoven at 6.30 p.m. on September 18, 1944, built a bridge overnight to replace one which the airborne forces had not succeeded in saving from destruction by the enemy, and advanced next day to Grave on the Maas, liberating on the way a number of towns in the Dutch province of North Brabant—among them Helmond. Here British bren-gunners are covering the road into that town. (See also illus. in page 3209.)

CAPTURE OF THE GREAT BRIDGE AT NIJMEGEN

At Nijmegen on September 19-20, 1944, the U.S. 82nd Airborne Division, supported by the Guards Armoured Division, fought one of the fiercest actions of the war to secure the great road bridge over the river Waal. 1. A 17-pdr. anti-tank gun guards the approach to the bridge. 2. Royal Engineers dismantle explosive charges from the piers of the captured bridge. 3. The Waal at Nijmegen : the upper bridge in the photograph is the one round which the furious battle of September 19-20 was fought. 4. A priest tends German wounded at the approach to the bridge.   *Photos, British Official ; British Newspaper Pool*

followed almost at once by the billowing parachutes of the 1st Brigade under the command of Brigadier G. W. Lathbury, D.S.O., M.B.E. In the British Army magazine " Soldier," Captain J. W. Shaw describes how the parachutists went into battle : " From 1300 onwards they came in. Multi-coloured parachutes like bunches of giant flowers, red, blue, yellow and white, sailed down bringing men and stores. The Brigade battle-cry, ' Whoa, Mahomed !', picked up from Arabs in Tunisia hailing each other and their cattle, rang through the air. Gliders skimmed the tree-tops to make perfect landings. Casualties were negligible. The Red Devils were in Holland."

The three battalions of parachutists and a parachute squadron of Royal Engineers moved off at once. The 2nd Battalion, commanded by Lieut.-Colonel J. D. Frost, D.S.O., M.C. (*see* illustration in page 2253), advanced quickly through

the village of Heelsum, and moved along the southern road running close to the north bank of the Lower Rhine. The 3rd Battalion, under the command of Lieut.-Colonel J. A. C. Fitch, pushed up the Heelsum-Arnhem road, in order to approach the bridge from the north. The 1st Battalion, under Lieut.-Colonel D. T. Dobie, D.S.O., was held in reserve. The 1st Air Landing Reconnaissance Squadron, which should have attempted a *coup de main* against the bridge, was unable to do so as most of its transport failed to arrive.

The 2nd and 3rd Battalions met light opposition at first, but they soon ran into strong enemy positions and came under heavy fire from 88 mm. guns, machine guns and mortars. The railway bridge was **Parachutists Enter Arnhem** blown up while some men of the 2nd Battalion were actually on it, though no one was hurt. The rest of the

aerodrome at Deelen to the north. These are shown on the plan in page 3304 at " Y," " S," " L," and " X." A fifth, marked " V," was selected as the supply dropping point after the main landings had been effected.

After the 21st Independent Parachute Company, under the command of Major B. A. Wilson, had reached the dropping zones to act as a marker force, the gliders carrying the 1st Air Landing Brigade and Divisional Headquarters flew in,

ACCIDENTS OF LANDING

Inverted landing by one American parachutist on September 17, 1944, and (left) a crashed glider being examined by American airborne troops. The U.S. 101st Airborne Division went in near Eindhoven, the U.S. 82nd near Nijmegen. Both Divisions jumped the Atlantic Wall on June 6.
Photos, U.S. Official

battalion pressed forward, only to come under fire from the high wooded ground at Den Brink. One company then skirted the position to the south, entered Arnhem, reached the bridge and seized the buildings commanding its northern end. A second company, having captured Den Brink, set out to cross the 150-yard wide river in order to outflank the southern defences of the bridge, but no barges were available and the pontoon bridge had been destroyed. At dawn on the 18th, a mixed force of between 600 and 700 men still held the northern end of the main bridge, but all that day the enemy kept up continuous shell and mortar fire, and in the evening made a heavy attack supported by tanks and self-propelled guns, which was successfully driven back although four of the houses held by the parachutists were set on fire.

The 3rd Battalion suffered severe casualties and only a few men from one company reached the school close to the bridge to join the sappers fighting with the 2nd Battalion. The other companies, surrounded on the 18th near the railway station by an ever-increasing number of the enemy, were split into two groups and could make no progress until dawn the following day when all that were left seized the Pavilion by the

BRITISH 1st AIRBORNE DIVISION
Commanded by Maj.-Gen. R. E. URQUHART, C.B., D.S.O.

1st Parachute Brigade
1st, 2nd and 3rd Parachute Battalions
16th Parachute Field Ambulance

1st Air Landing Brigade
2nd Battalion South Staffordshire Regiment
7th Battalion King's Own Scottish Borderers
1st Battalion Border Regiment
181st Field Ambulance

1st and 2nd Anti-tank Batteries of the R.A.

4th Parachute Brigade
10th, 11th, and 156th Parachute Battalions
133rd Parachute Field Ambulance

21st Independent Parachute Company

1st Air Landing Reconnaissance Squadron

1st & 4th Parachute Squadrons

9th and 261st Field Companies of the R.E.

1st Air Landing Light Regiment

Detachments of the Royal Army Service Corps, the Royal Corps of Signals, the Royal Army Medical Corps and the Royal Electrical and Mechanical Engineers

reached the St. Elizabeth Hospital and was in touch with the 2nd Battalion, which had been urgently demanding reinforcements to maintain its hold on the bridge.

Meanwhile the 1st Battalion of the Border Regiment and the 7th Battalion of the King's Own Scottish Borderers, arriving on schedule by glider, held the landing grounds and dropping zones so that the second lift containing the

balance of the division, due to land before 10 a.m. on the 18th, might do so in safety. Cloud and foggy weather, however, held up its take-off until midday, and the landings were not made until the afternoon. The loss of so many vital hours in the arrival of these reinforcements complicated still further a situation that had already become extremely difficult.

The 2nd South Staffords and the 11th Parachute Battalion advanced as far as the St. Elizabeth Hospital by daybreak of the 19th, but increasing pressure from the enemy made further progress impossible. **Attempt to Establish Perimeter** While these efforts were made to reinforce the dwindling and hard pressed forces at the northern end of the bridge, the rest of the Air Landing Brigade and the 4th Parachute Brigade (under Brigadier J. W. Hackett, D.S.O., M.B.E., M.C.), which had come in with the second lift, sought to establish the planned perimeter around Arnhem. A confused and bitter struggle followed, in which the Glider Pilots —1,126 strong—fought alongside the Border Regiment, the King's Own Scottish Borderers, and the Independent Parachute Company. Casualties were

FIRST AIRBORNE DIVISION LANDS AT ARNHEM
Parachutists of the 1st Parachute Brigade land near Arnhem. The first two gliders of the 1st Air Landing Brigade to arrive (right), bringing Headquarters signallers, jammed wings. The landings near Arnhem were made with very little loss or damage, and all units were able at once to set about the tasks allotted to them. *Photos, British Official*

river. Covering fire from a Spandau, however, prevented any further advance.

The 1st Battalion followed the 2nd and 3rd down the railway. The Germans, having been reinforced, closed in behind them. Fierce fighting continued throughout the night of the 17th-18th and raged all the following day, but by 6.30 p.m. the battalion

CORPORAL HARPER
(York and Lancaster Regiment)
Corporal John William Harper, to whom the V.C. was post-humously awarded, commanded the leading section in an assault on September 29, 1944 on a strongly held natural defensive position. The personal gallantry of Cpl. Harper, who was killed, ensured the success of the operation.

CAPTAIN QUERIPEL
(Royal Sussex Regiment)
The V.C. was awarded to Capt. Lionel Ernest Queripel for courage, leadership and devotion to duty in the Arnhem operations. On Sept. 19, 1944, he commanded a parachute company which held up the enemy for 9 hours. Though badly wounded, he covered the withdrawal of his men.

LIEUT. GRAYBURN
(Parachute Regiment)
Lieut. John Hollington Grayburn commanded the platoon which attempted on Sept. 17, 1944, to seize the road bridge at Arnhem. Forced to withdraw from the bridge, his platoon held a house near it until the 20th. Killed while directing the withdrawal of his men, and posthumously awarded the V.C.

LCE-SERGT. BASKEYFIELD
(South Staffordshire Regiment)
At Oosterbeek by Arnhem on September 20, 1944, L.-Sergt. John Daniel Baskeyfield, himself severely wounded, continued single-handed to fire his six-pounder anti-tank gun. His own gun put out of action, he crawled to another and fired it until he was killed. Posthumously awarded the V.C.

MAJOR CAIN
(Royal Northumberland Fusiliers)
From Sept. 19–25, 1944, a company of the South Staffordshire Regiment, commanded by Major Robert Henry Cain, succeeded in holding a key position during the Battle of Arnhem. He personally knocked out several Tiger tanks with a 'Piat.' His coolness and courage won him the V.C.

FLT.-LIEUT. LORD
(Royal Air Force)
With his starboard engine burning furiously, Flt.-Lieut David Samuel Anthony Lord flew on on Sept. 19, 1944, to drop supplies to the airborne men at Arnhem. His mission completed, he ordered his crew to abandon the Dakota, himself remaining at the controls. Posthumously awarded the V.C.

positions were continually overrun, ammunition was running short, the key house had been burnt down and the wounded reached serious proportions.

By the 20th the remaining force, of some 110 men and five or six officers, was fighting in ruins close to and underneath the bridge. But with each hour the situation became more hopeless. The Official Account of the British Airborne Divisions describes the end simply in these words : " There was no more ammunition, there had been no food for a long time, and hardly a man but was wounded. The very ground on which the defenders stood or crouched was constantly seared by flames from the burning houses about it, and no man could remain there and live. So in the end the gallant remnant were dispersed or captured."

Fight for the Bridge Ends

By September 20 a perimeter of defence was established to the west of

MAJOR-GENERAL URQUHART
Major-General R. E. Urquhart, C.B., D.S.O., commanded the British 1st Airborne Division dropped near Arnhem on Sept. 17, 1944. He landed with his men and was with them when the 2,490 that remained of the original force of 10,095 were withdrawn across the river. He is seen here outside his Arnhem H.Q. *Photo, British Official*

high, and as the Germans had brought up further reinforcements and were pressing on all sides the whole Brigade was ordered in the afternoon of the 19th to move south of the railway and occupy the high ground between Oosterbeek and Arnhem. By the evening the strength of the Brigade had been reduced to about 250. It had almost no ammunition left, and the Germans were still attacking. The troops on the bridge could not be reinforced and the decision was therefore reluctantly taken to form a perimeter on the western edge of Oosterbeek bounded on the south by the Lower Rhine, and there to hold out until the long expected relief from the British 2nd Army arrived : a decision that resulted in all but a very small part of the supplies dropped from the air with indomitable courage and persistence falling into enemy hands, since the dropping ground " V " was not within the new perimeter, and wireless contact could not be established with headquarters.

On the bridge itself the valiant defenders prepared for a final stand. Their

BRITISH STAND AT ARNHEM

1. A parachutist in action in a ruined house at Oosterbeek, just west of Arnhem. 2. Two German prisoners captured by parachutists. 3. Manning a 75-mm. gun on the outskirts of Arnhem. 4. Major 'Jock' Neill (left), who fought on though wounded in both legs and arms, and Lieut. McCartney giving orders to machine-gun crews. Photographers of the Army Film and Photographic Unit landed with the Allied 1st Airborne Army in the Netherlands. One of those at Arnhem, writing on Sept. 20, 1944, said, 'This is the fourth day of fighting and camera work is almost out of the question. All day we are under shell, mortar and machine-gun fire.' But they succeeded in bringing out some remarkable photographs, as the illustrations to this chapter testify.

Photos, British Official

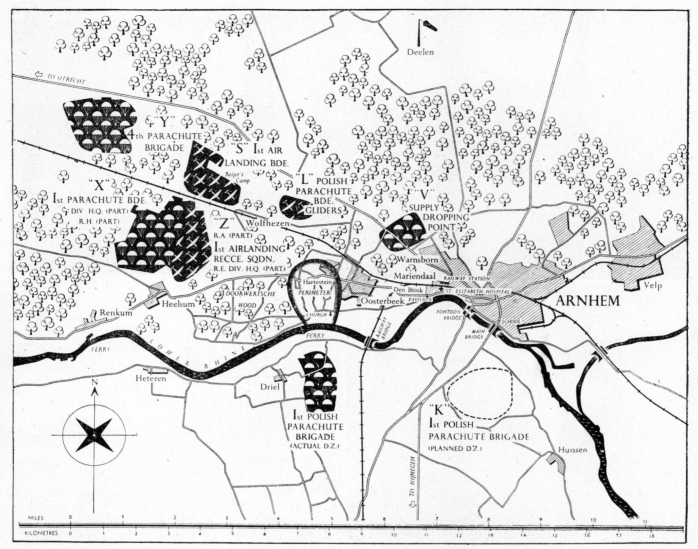

THE BATTLE OF ARNHEM

Along this stretch of the Lower Rhine running through and west of the pleasant garden city of Arnhem was fought one of the great battles of British arms. Here for ten days a force of ten thousand men, flown in to enemy-occupied territory, maintained a hold, reduced at the end to the area just across the river from Driel, waiting in vain for ground forces to come up to them.

Crown Copyright

Oosterbeek, the centre of which was Hartestein. Here for more than five days the remnants of the British 1st Airborne Division stood. Only 250 of the Polish Parachute Brigade, dropped south of the Lower Rhine near Driel on the 21st to reinforce them, succeeded in getting across the river, despite desperate efforts during four nights. The western half of the perimeter comprised a detachment of Glider Pilots, the remainder of three companies of the Border Regiment, the Poles and a number of Royal Engineers, all commanded by Brigadier P. H. W. Hicks, D.S.O., M.C. The other half consisted of three Glider Pilot detachments, the Borderers, the Reconnaissance Squadron, the 21st Independent Parachute Company, elements of the Royal Army Service Corps now

fighting as infantry, all that remained of the 156th and 10th Parachute Battalions, elements of the 1st, 3rd and 11th Parachute Battalions, and the 2nd South Staffords. This eastern half was under the command of Brigadier Hackett. Every officer and man fought during those last grim days with "a gallant tenacity, equalled perhaps, but never surpassed by any soldiers of the British Army either now or at any other time in its long and honourable history."

Throughout the fighting, courageous Dutch civilians cooked food, supplied water, acted as stretcher bearers, nursed the wounded, and maintained the civil telephone service, which was of inestimable value when wireless contacts failed.

If the British 2nd Army could have continued their thrust into the Nether-

lands up the one road that splits into two after leaving Nijmegen and joins together again near Arnhem, the 1st Airborne Division might well have been relieved. But no tank or armoured vehicle could leave that road without becoming **Why the 2nd Army did not Come Up** bogged, and large stretches of it were under enemy observation from higher ground and could be shelled at will. During those vital days, the road was never continuously under Allied control nor free from the enemy's fire. Sometimes it was cut for hours on end, and sometimes the point of the Allied spearhead was blunted by frontal counter-attacks. Two hundred and fifty men of the Dorsetshire Regiment succeeded in reaching the southern bank of the Lower Rhine west of Arnhem on September 22, where they made contact with the Polish Parachute Brigade and, like the Poles, tried desperately to get across.

On September 22, General Urquhart sent Lieut.-Colonels C. B. Mackenzie and E. C. Myers, C.B.E., D.S.O., to find General Browning and report. They returned with the order to evacuate. On the nights of September 25-26 and 26-27 the majority of those who remained of the heroic British 1st Airborne Division were withdrawn across the river in assault boats. The Division, which went in 10,095 strong (including the glider

THESE SUPPLIES ARRIVED
The Supply Dropping Point (see plan opposite) was outside the perimeter formed west of Arnhem, but owing to the breakdown of communications, supplies continued to be sent down, with severe losses of aircraft, in the appointed spot : only 7·4 per cent of tons dropped, including this parachute-load, was collected by the beleaguered division. *Photo, British Official*

pilots), had lost 7,605 officers and men in killed, wounded and missing. As Mr. Winston Churchill said in his war survey on September 28, the words " Not in Vain " might be the pride of those who survived, and the epitaph of those who fell, for " in attack most daring, in defence most cunning, in endurance most steadfast, they performed a feat of arms which will be remembered and recounted as long as the virtues of courage and

' THEY OFFERED US WATER AND APPLES—ALL THEY HAD '
Throughout the battle of Arnhem, Dutch civilians co-operated with the British, cooking food, supplying water, helping the wounded, keeping civilian telephone lines working. After the battle, the town was cleared of all its inhabitants. When they returned after the liberation of the Netherlands eight months later, those who were fortunate enough to find their homes standing found them empty—stripped bare by the ' Herrenvolk.' *Photo, British Official*

resolution have power to move the hearts of men."

The Battle of Arnhem had indeed not been in vain, for the Allies had secured all the bridges over two of the three great defences of the northern Netherlands and now possessed a firm base for further operations. Moreover, the enemy had been compelled to use and maintain on the Lower Rhine a large force that might otherwise have been thrown against the U.S. 82nd and 101st Divisions farther south. His losses, too, had not been light at a time when every man counted in the defence of the Rhine delta and of the Scheldt estuary.

Apart from the great qualities displayed by the troops, operation " Market " will always be a classical example of the strategic use of airborne forces. It revealed their potentialities and also their limitations which even further

GERMAN TANK IN THE STREETS OF ARNHEM
On September 19, lightly armed Airborne men, trying to get through to support comrades who had seized the north end of the road bridge on the 17th, were met by German tanks as they entered Arnhem, and were forced to withdraw from the position they had reached near the St. Elizabeth Hospital. *Photo, German Official*

SURVIVORS WHO REACHED NIJMEGEN

At noon on September 22, 1944, General Urquhart decided that he must send two officers to acquaint General Browning with the position at Arnhem. They got through and returned, and the plans they had made for evacuation were put into effect. By noon on the 27th, all who remained of the gallant band—less than a fourth of the original ten thousand—were back in Nijmegen. A few of them are seen here sorting arms they managed to bring out with them.

developments of air transport cannot eliminate. Their operations are particularly sensitive to weather conditions and the nature of the terrain can seldom be such as to present no difficulty in finding landing grounds for large numbers of aircraft. The chief limiting factor must however inevitably be the length of time during which the force landed can meet the enemy's reaction without the support of the main army. Reinforcement by air may prolong the period but not indefinitely. On the other hand, the time the supporting army will take to come up naturally depends not only on the distance it has to traverse but also on the enemy's opposition to its advance.

In the case of the Arnhem landing it must have been evident that limiting conditions would be so nearly reached that great risks would have to be taken. The distance, some sixty miles, that the supporting army would have to traverse, including the crossing of three large rivers, might well have been considered impossible. Nevertheless, the importance of the object to be gained and the need of speed fully justified the acceptance of risks. Weather, no doubt, was largely responsible for the failure to secure complete success ; but probably the inability to deploy sufficient force to protect, effectively, the sides of the corridor through which the supporting army advanced was the chief reason it was held up in the last ten-mile stretch beyond Nijmegen. Apparently congestion on the immensely long line of communication stretching back to Normandy limited the size of the force that could be kept in action.

On the whole, the degree of success achieved by the enterprise was more remarkable than its partial failure.

Objects Aimed at Justified Risks Taken

OOSTERBEEK BURNS AFTER THE BRITISH WITHDRAWAL

The last stand of the British airborne forces landed near Arnhem was made on the slightly higher ground to the west of the suburb of Oosterbeek. There, with dwindling ammunition, little food, and towards the end, no water—for the Germans cut off the town water supply— they held out from September 20, 1944, until their evacuation a week later in conditions that worsened from hour to hour.

Photo, Keystone

Chapter 326

BELGIUM & LUXEMBURG REGAIN THEIR LIBERTY

The greater part of Belgium, victim of the German onslaught of May 1940, was liberated with spectacular rapidity in a few days of September 1944. Her people's continued stubborn fight against Hitler's " new order " by sabotage and passive resistance is described here as well as the coming of their freedom. For her history in 1943, see Chapters 273 and 274. Something of the struggle of Luxemburg, incorporated into the Greater Reich in 1942, and freed in 1944, is also set down in the following pages

By 1944 approximately 97 per cent of the Belgian people were resisting the Germans in some way or another. A large number resisted actively, the remainder did all they could passively to make the Germans realize that they and their "New Order" were the hated enemy. Largely through the trade unions, officially suppressed but in fact still secretly active, resistance among workers became so widespread and highly organized that the indispensable supply of skilled Belgian labour fell far short of the Germans' objective. Moreover, an increasing number of deportees made their way back to Belgium from Germany and went into hiding. By the end of 1943 there were at least 300,000 of these *réfractaires*, and at the beginning of 1944 the Germans themselves acknowledged that the number of people in hiding threatened to exceed the number of German troops in Belgium.

One of the chief weapons used by the Germans to coerce Belgian workers was their control of the country's food. By keeping the average worker's ration just above starvation level they were able to blackmail hundreds of thousands into their service. From the beginning of 1943 the elaborately organized Food Office proved entirely inadequate to its tasks, for the black market had become so widespread that the Germans were forced to set up their own black market organization to maintain control of agricultural production.

Strength of the Resistance Movement

The Resistance Movement was staunchly supported by all classes of the community : the Church, the Universities, the Magistrature, the personnel of the Central and Communal administrations, the Police Force, and even the Labour Offices, defied the German authorities and allied themselves to the cause of freedom.

Various organizations were formed by the *réfractaires* with the immediate object of providing a livelihood for their members, and the ultimate aim of expelling the invader. Apart from numerous clandestine organizations, the two chief Resistance Movements were the Secret Army (Armée Blanche), which came into existence towards the end of 1942, and the " Front de l'Indépendance," founded in 1941. The latter, with strong left tendencies, was more feared by the Germans. One of its clandestine papers declared in January 1944 that it was the duty of all partisans to become the advance-guard of the Allied armies, and appealed to the Belgian Government in London to provide it with arms. The Secret Army consisted mainly of more traditionally-minded patriots and was organized on military lines. It followed Allied directives and went into action on June 6, the day of the Allied invasion of France. On September 3 General Eisenhower appointed Major-General Yvon Gérard, who fought in the Belgian campaign of 1940, as Commander of the Belgian Forces of the Interior. Their first communiqué revealed that during August the Forces of the Interior had carried out more than 415 operations on the Belgian railway network, effected 53 derailments and collisions, destroyed 18 bridges, and sunk two German torpedo boats in Antwerp harbour. Acts of sabotage committed by patriots in the first six months of 1944, far too numerous to record in detail, were mainly attacks on railways, canals and power cables.

German reprisals became increasingly severe. During the first four months of the year, the Germans published the names of 111 hostages whom they had put to death. According to a statement by Mr. Hubert Pierlot, Premier of the exiled Government (August 1944), no fewer than 7,500 Belgians were shot, 10,000 put into concentration camps, and 500,000 deported between May 1940 and August 1944. But repression did not curb the Belgian spirit of resistance.

German Reprisals

BELGIAN POLICE SEARCH CIVILIANS IN BRUSSELS

Resistance in Belgium was widespread and persistent, and the Germans resorted to the methods of repression common in their treatment of all the occupied countries. On January 18, 1944, the Belgian Government in London stated that they had a list of 1,200 Belgians executed since the beginning of the war, including 700 hostages shot without trial. Here, in blacked-out Brussels, Belgian police under Gestapo orders search passers-by for arms and resistance literature.

SUPPLIES FOR THE BELGIAN SECRET ARMY

The Secret Army, one of the two chief resistance movements in Belgium, came into existence towards the end of 1942. Arms and ammunition for its use were dropped by parachute into agreed fields by Allied airmen. Here a container, dropped in daylight after the invasion of Normandy, is being collected by a farm cart. Below, a nurse of the Secret Army gives first aid to a British soldier during the occupation of Antwerp (September 4, 1944).

Photos, British Official ; British Newspaper Pool

By May 23, 1944, as a result of the increased facilities for sabotage and banditry afforded by the severe Allied aerial bombardments, and the fact that many civil servants and railwaymen had taken the opportunity to disappear, General von Falkenhausen, the German Military Commander, issued a special order decreeing the punishment, by penal servitude, imprisonment or even death, of anyone leaving his place of work, or failing to resume work when this had been interrupted by force of circumstance. New methods of oppression included the establishment of a special summary court martial, an increase in the powers of the Gestapo and S.S., mass executions, the application of more than medieval tortures, and the ruthless extermination of Jews.

In the summer of 1944, moreover, important changes took place in the German administrative system. A decree issued by Hitler on July 13, 1944, replaced the previous military administration in Belgium and northern France by a civil administration under a Reich Commissioner. It was announced that in future the rights of military sovereignty exercised by the Military Commander would be vested in the Commander of the Armed Forces in Belgium and Northern France, serving under the Reich Commissioner. This post was given to Grohe, Gauleiter of Cologne-Aachen, while General of Infantry Grasse was appointed Military Commander. Gauleiter Grohe and General Grasse took over from General von Falkenhausen on July 18.

On August 9, however, it was announced that Jungclaus, General of the S.S. and Lt.-General of Police, had been appointed by Hitler as Chief of the S.S. and Police in Belgium and Northern France. This **Closer Control by S.S. in Belgium** was followed by the news on August 14 that Jungclaus had been appointed Commander-in-Chief of the Wehrmacht in Belgium—a move indicating close control by the S.S. of German troops in Belgium.

Late in 1943 there was a considerable drop in the number of supporters of the "New Order" in Belgium, and quisling organizations began to disintegrate as the certainty of German defeat grew daily more apparent. At the beginning of 1944 Belgian quislings could be roughly divided into two groups : those hoping to save themselves by leaving the sinking Nazi ship ; and those who fanatically continued to cling to the wreck. Belgicists and

LIEUT.-GENERAL TSCHOFFEN

General Paul Tschoffen, a barrister of Liége, escaped from occupied Belgium in 1942. Appointed head of the Civil Affairs Mission on July 8, 1944, he returned to his country immediately on the entry of the Allied troops, who first crossed the Belgian border on September 2.   *Photo, Pictorial Press*

some traitors belonging to the Flemish Nationalist Movement (Vlaamsch National Verbond, or V.N.V.) were in the first group; other V.N.V. adherents and members of the Walloon Nazi Movement, "Rex," and of the German Flemish Collaborationist Community, "Devlag," were in the second. The Germans entrusted these quisling organizations with no real power, though they used their militias in support of German army and police forces.

During 1944, "Rex" and "Devlag" came to the fore at the expense of the V.N.V. While the leader of "Devlag,"

Activities of Belgian Nazis
Van de Wiele, and the Rexist leader, Degrelle, toured Belgian workers' camps in Germany in July on a recruiting drive for the S.S. formations, the V.N.V. leader's tour of Flanders received no support from the Germans. The dismissal of Von Falkenhausen left greater power in the hands of the auxiliary police formations of "Rex" and "Devlag." Large-scale reprisals against patriots were subsequently carried out by these terrorist organizations.

In February 1944, the S.S. Walloon Brigade, fighting on the Russian front, was encircled by the Russians in the Cherkassy pocket and all but wiped out. Degrelle, who was fighting with the Brigade, succeeded to its command on the death of Lucien Lippert. A few days later, leaving the remnants of his troops still fighting, he escaped by plane with some of his officers to

Hitler's headquarters, where the Fuehrer decorated him with the insignia of the Knight's Cross of the Iron Cross " for his heroic deeds."

In August 1944 Degrelle again returned to the Russian front and the Walloon S.S. Brigade as well as the Flemish S.S. Brigade, Langemark, took part in the final battles in the Baltic area.

As in previous years, the Germans in 1944 were obliged to rely on the Belgian Secretaries-General of the various government departments to administer the country. Resistance among the rank and file of the administrative personnel was stimulated by the mili-

tary successes of the United Nations. The most treacherous among the Secretaries-General began to produce excuses, and even Romsée, Secretary-General for Home Affairs and one of the most notorious collaborators, showed a change of heart. The V.N.V. leader, Elias, repeatedly attacked the Secretaries-General for their " conservative policy." Van Coppenolle, the chief of the Gendarmerie, continued to collaborate wholeheartedly. Patriotic functionaries were still in the central and local administration, and resistance was evident even in the Food and Labour Offices. Dismissals of patriotic burgomasters during 1943 and 1944 became

PRINCE CHARLES ASSUMES THE REGENCY

King Leopold of the Belgians was removed from Belgium to Germany on June 7, 1944. When the Government returned to Brussels in September, Parliament was assembled and, in accordance with the constitution, on September 20 elected as Regent Prince Charles, Count of Flanders, brother of the King. After Leopold's removal, Prince Charles took to the maquis and remained with the resistance group in the Ardennes until September 11.   *Photo, Planet News*

frequent, and by the middle of 1944, out of nine provincial governors, four were former V.N.V. politicians and three former Rexists.

On January 1, 1944, Mr. Pierlot broadcast from London a message to the Belgian people in which he expressed his confidence that Belgium would be liberated during the year. In the following months the Belgian Government strengthened its armed forces and prepared by decree new laws (published in the official gazette, the "Moniteur Belge") to be applied after liberation.

Preparations for Liberation

Mr. Camille Gutt (Minister of Finance and Economic Affairs) announced the future application of monetary and financial measures, and sweeping decrees were issued which abolished all laws illegally introduced by the Germans during the occupation. Further measures provided for a quick purge of the collaborationist administration.

The Minister of Information and Justice, Mr. Antoine Delfosse, declared in a broadcast speech on January 22: "Faithful to the nation's mandate, the Belgian legitimate Government, reassembling all Belgian forces distributed across the world, has continued the war on land, at sea and in the air."

In the ensuing months the Govern-

BELGIAN PREMIER WITH A BELGIAN SPITFIRE SQUADRON
The Belgian Air Force, reformed in Britain after Belgium was overrun by the enemy, flew with the R.A.F. in the Battle of Britain. On January 15, 1944, it accounted for its hundredth enemy aircraft. Here Mr. Hubert Pierlot, Premier of the exiled Belgian Government, is speaking to the pilots and ground staff of a Belgian Spitfire Squadron stationed in England which he visited on the eve of Belgium's National Day (July 21). *Photo, British Official*

ment intensified preparations for a speedy return to a liberated Belgium. Meanwhile, plans were co-ordinated with the British Government, and on May 16 Belgium signed agreements with the United Kingdom and the United States relating to the administration of Belgian territory after liberation. Consequently, Mr. Pierlot and Mr. Paul-Henri Spaak (Minister of Foreign Affairs) were heavily attacked by the German-controlled press and radio in Belgium. The statement that Belgium would remain in Allied occupation as long as the war lasted was particularly resented by the Germans. On June 8 the British Foreign Secretary, Mr. Anthony Eden, reaffirmed that the Belgian Government in London was recognized by Britain as the legal and constitutional Government of Belgium.

The transfer of King Leopold from Belgium to Germany on June 7 came to the knowledge of the Belgian people through a broadcast on June 13 by the Belgian radio service in London, which, during the years of exile, broadcast regularly in French and Flemish. Several days before June 6 the Belgian people were warned to be on the alert against possible false orders and provocative statements emanating from the enemy, and Mr. Pierlot appealed to them to assist the forces of the Resistance with all possible means. Detailed advice on how to assist the Allies was given in radio broadcasts by a spokesman at Supreme Headquarters, Allied Expeditionary Force.

Warning Against False Orders

On July 8, Lieut.-General Paul Tschoffen was appointed as Chief of the Belgian Civil and Military Affairs Mission to Belgium. Belgian troops, trained in England, fought with the 1st Canadian Army across northern

REMOVING TRACES OF THE INVADER AT EUPEN
Eupen, one of the three towns ceded to Belgium by Germany after the war of 1914-18 and reincorporated in the Reich in 1940 (see page 2725), was captured in the night of September 11-12, 1944, by the U.S. 1st Army. The people, while not actively hostile, were silent and did not greet the Allied troops with the jubilation they met elsewhere in Belgium. Here Nazi insignia are being removed from Eupen police station. *Photo, Planet News*

GREAT BRIDGE AT NIJMEGEN IN ALLIED HANDS

The battle for the road bridge across the river Waal at Nijmegen in the Netherlands raged for twenty-four hours before American parachutists, who crossed the river in assault boats under withering fire to capture the north end, on September 20, 1944, joined tanks of the Guards Armoured Division roaring across after a fierce struggle for the south end. Here a British soldier stands guard at the entrance to the bridge after it was safely in Allied hands. Note the portrait of a smiling Hitler left by the former German guard. *Photo, British Newspaper Pool*

BRITISH AIRBORNE TROOPS AT OOSTERBEEK BY ARNHEM

Men of the British 1st Airborne Division, dropped near Arnhem in the Netherlands on September 17, 1944, reached and seized the northern end of the road bridge it was their object to capture intact; but relief by ground forces did not come, and they were driven back to the western suburb of Oosterbeek, where, under constant artillery and mortar fire, and hemmed in by superior forces, they held on grimly for a week until those who remained were evacuated.   Here a patrol of parachutists is searching the ruins of a house at Oosterbeek.   *Photo, British Official*

THE LAST POST SOUNDS AGAIN AT THE MENIN GATE

From July 1927 when Lord Plumer unveiled the Menin Gate memorial—erected at Ypres to the memory of the Allied soldiers who fell defending the salient in the First Great War—until May 10, 1940, when the Germans again invaded Belgium, the nightly ceremony of sounding the Last Post there was carried out by Belgians. With the liberation of Ypres on September 6, 1944, the ceremony recommenced. The two buglers here seen at the Gate are members of the Ypres Fire Brigade and assistants at the local police station. (See also illustration in page 884.) *Photo, British Official*

RED ARMY'S SELF-PROPELLED GUNS THRUST ON TO RIGA
Units of General Yeremenko's 2nd Baltic Army broke through German defences on the Latvian border in mid-July 1944 and captured Dvinsk. In the following month they encountered stiffer resistance on both sides of the Riga highway, where the many natural obstructions had been reinforced and strengthened by enemy artillery and mortars. But Yeremenko's mobile units pushed on to co-operate with Maslennikov's 3rd Baltic Army in the storming of Riga on October 13. Here self-propelled guns are crashing through forest land.   *Photo, Planet News*

France, and participated in the liberation of their own country.

On September 5 Mr. Pierlot in a farewell broadcast from London announced the beginning of the liberation of Belgium in the following words: "The Allied armies have entered Belgium. They advance with irresistible dash, and with every step they deliver a fraction of our territory."

Several days later the Pierlot Government returned to Brussels. Four years of German occupation had not broken the thread of legal continuity which linked the exiled Government to the people.

The liberation of Belgium was effected with exceptional speed by the Allies, assisted by the Belgian Resistance Movement. On September 2 British and American forces crossed the Franco-Belgian frontier. Next day British tanks entered Brussels, and Antwerp was liberated on the 4th, though some time elapsed before the freeing of the Scheldt estuary permitted the use of the port. (*See* Chapters 320, 325 and 332.) The liberators were received everywhere with great enthusiasm by the Belgians.

Enthusiastic Reception of Liberators

With the approach of the Allies, a mass flight of German and quisling

MAJOR-GENERAL GÉRARD

Both before and after the Allied breakthrough into Belgium, resistance groups, organized by the Belgians themselves, seriously disrupted German communications. Major-General Yvon Gérard's appointment as Commander of the Belgian Forces of the Interior by General Eisenhower—approved by the Belgian Government—was announced on September 3, 1944. He had served in the campaign of 1940.

LIFE IN BELGIUM BEGINS AGAIN

By mid-October 1944, transport, police and public services in Belgium were resumed in many districts, and shops reopened for business. Typical of the return to normal was Turnhout, 26 miles north-east of Antwerp; here at a street corner, a few weeks after liberation, a member of the Civil Police directs Allied dispatch-riders. Nearby is the penal colony of Merksplas: hence the inscription which runs, 'We want the Boches in quod.' *Photo, British Official*

officials with their families took place. One last act of the Germans before leaving Brussels was to set fire to the "Palais de Justice," which contained the records of the Gestapo.

After its return to Brussels on September 8, Mr. Pierlot's Government resumed its functions. Relations with S.H.A.E.F. followed the plans agreed upon. Lieut.-General Tschoffen announced on the 9th that all the Secretaries-General who had served under the occupation had been suspended. Vital ordinances were issued and parliamentary activity was resumed without delay. The Belgian Senate and the Chamber of Deputies reassembled in joint session on September 19—their first meeting since May 1940. On the following day Prince Charles, brother of King Leopold, was elected Regent for the King, who remained a prisoner in Germany. In accordance with the intention he expressed in July 1943, Mr. Pierlot and his Government resigned. Since, however, no general election could be held until the return of deported workers and prisoners of war, at the Regent's invitation Mr. Pierlot resumed the Premiership and formed a new interim Coalition Government whose composition was announced on September 26. Of its nineteen members, seven were Catholics, five Socialists, three Liberals, two Communists, one non-party, and one representative of the Resistance Move-

ment. Besides Mr. Pierlot, only three members of the London Government were included: Mr. Spaak (Foreign Affairs), Mr. Gutt (Finance), and Mr. de Vleeschauwer (Colonies). Mr. Victor de Laveleye (Liberal), originator of the "V" campaign (*see* pages 1790, 1796 and illus. in page 2017) became Minister of Education. Dr. Marteaux and Mr. F. Demany, founders of the "Front de l'Indépendance Belge," were Minister of Public Health and Minister without Portfolio respectively. The new Government was the first in which the Communists held office. A bill extending the "special powers" accorded to the Government in 1939 was passed by the Chamber on November 28, by the Senate on December 7.

Meanwhile, the leaders of the Resistance and of the extreme left claimed that the Government, though most of its members had been in Belgium during the occupation, was far from reflecting or understanding the Belgian people's post-liberation outlook. Differences of opinion on the measures to disarm the Resistance groups and their incorporation into the regular army led in November to the resignation of three Ministers, representing the extreme left and the Resistance.

Government Resignations

The Government was faced from the first moment with vast and complex political and economic problems. Chief

THE FREEING OF BRUSSELS

Men and women of the Belgian Resistance Movement—notably the Armée Blanche and the Front de l'Indépendance—did much to harass the German armies in retreat and prevent Nazi destruction as the British 2nd Army made its spectacular dash from the Seine. Though Brussels was soon taken by 'desert tactics,' to use the phrase of Lieut.-General B. G. Horrocks, of XXX Corps, a few enemy outposts were left as British forces hurried in. 1. Armed with pistols, patriots in street-fighting helped to speed the German withdrawal. 2. Field-Marshal Montgomery with the Burgomaster, Mr. van de Meulebroeck, outside the Hôtel de Ville, on September 7, 1944, after the civic reception held in his honour. 3. The Palais de Justice, containing Gestapo dossiers, was set ablaze by the retreating enemy.

Photos, British Official ; British Newspaper Pool

3

of them were the extreme shortage of transport, food and fuel, the currency situation, the need for a purge of collaborators from public life, and for the punishment of traitors. The purge of collaborators began immediately after the Government's return, but severe criticisms were levelled at the dilatoriness of legal procedure, and it was hinted that too many industrial collaborators were allowed to escape.

The immediate economic problems confronting the country in September 1944 were considerable as a result of the German occupation and the absence of normal sources of supply. Shortage of raw materials, coal, food and transport caused severe hardships. Theoretically rations at the beginning of October were : 9 ozs. bread daily ; 9 ozs. butter, 7 ozs. margarine, 4 lb. 7 ozs. sugar, 3½ ozs. cheese, 2 lb. 5 ozs. meat, 2 lb. preserves, 33 lb. potatoes monthly ; but it was rarely possible for the people to secure their full supplies. The food situation, however, began to improve towards the end of the year in spite of the V-weapon attacks on Antwerp (*see* Chapter 337) and the Rundstedt offensive in the Ardennes (*see* Chapter 336).

Drastic currency measures counteracted a serious threat of inflation, and coal production, which had fallen to 10,000 tons per day in September (pre-war figure, 30,000 tons), had risen to 40,000 tons daily by mid-November.

The Grand Duchy of Luxemburg was the one independent European state to be incorporated as a whole into the Greater German Reich.
Luxemburg Freed According to an official German definition, all Luxemburgers were " Volksdeutsche," *i.e.* Germans who did not possess German nationality as they resided outside the Fatherland ; but this view was unacceptable to all but a small minority of the population. In October 1941 the Germans held a census in which 98 per cent of the population indicated that they wished to retain Luxemburg nationality. This census, however, the Germans declared invalid and in August 1942 all Luxemburgers were made " subjects of the Reich," like the people of the annexed Belgian area Eupen-Malmédy-St. Vith (*see* page 2725).

The administration of the country was entirely in German hands. Workers were conscripted to work in German factories, and young men were called up for service with the armed forces or the S.S. By the end of 1943, approximately 10,000 Luxemburgers had been compelled to join the German army, and many died on the Russian front.

A decree introduced in August 1940

PUNISHMENT OF BELGIUM'S COLLABORATORS DEMANDED
Differences between the new Pierlot Coalition Government and Resistance and Communist groups followed the liberation of most of Belgium by the end of September 1944. Here, anti-Pierlot demonstrators, carrying banners in French and English, parade in Brussels—without incident—on November 19. Below, at Bruges High Court a Belgian schoolmaster charged with diverting tobacco to the Germans and with recruiting young Belgians to fight against the Russians.
Photos. British Newspaper Pool ; Associated Press

ordered the use of the German language only, and the German educational system was enforced throughout Luxemburg. In April 1944, to complete and unify intellectual Germanization, the whole complex of German cultural law was introduced into the country. But the Luxemburgers refused to regard themselves as Germans, and their stubbornness caused their overlords no little trouble.

After a general strike in September 1942 the death penalty for striking was enforced, and continued desertions from the Wehrmacht led to an official warning, published on January 31, 1944,

that desertion would be " most severely punished and that anyone who incites men to desert, or tries to depress their morale, is also liable to severe punishment."

On February 7 Gauleiter Simon, Chief of Civil Administration, announced that desertion would be punishable by death. In spite of all these warnings, however, resisters continued to desert, and 22 Luxemburgers were executed in March 1944 for helping men to desert.

Meanwhile, the Grand Duchess Charlotte, legal sovereign of Luxemburg, the Royal Family, and the Luxemburg

IN FREED LUXEMBURG

Following their liberation in September 1944, patriots and people of Luxemburg rounded up collaborators, some of whom are here paraded at Pétange before being handed to the Allied authorities. The portraits of enemy leaders had been removed from German installations. Left, Prince Felix, husband of the Grand Duchess Charlotte, 'chaired' by crowds on his arrival in the capital.

Photos, U.S. Official ; Keystone

Government in London made preparations to return to their country. A Grand-Ducal decree of July 13, 1944, provided for the abolition of all measures introduced by the enemy ; and a thorough purge of collaborators was planned to follow liberation.

On September 1 Gauleiter Simon fled as the Allies approached the frontier, but the German Military Commander forced him to return, and only on September 10, when the Allies ultimately crossed the frontier, did the Germans finally leave the country. The Allied liberators were given a tumultuous welcome. Radio Luxemburg, Europe's second most powerful radio station, was left almost intact by the retreating Germans and soon became an important propaganda weapon for the Allied cause.

Luxemburg proclaimed her perpetual neutrality and disarmament in 1868, but a decree of November 1944 introduced compulsory military service in the Grand Duchy, and on December 21 the Government announced that it was abandoning neutrality.

The German counter-attack in the Ardennes (*see* Chapter 336), during which part of Luxemburg became the scene of bitter fighting, delayed the return of the Grand Duchess and her family, who arrived in Luxemburg on April 14, 1945, in an aeroplane placed at their disposal by General Eisenhower.

Following the defeat of Rundstedt's offensive, immediate surveys were made of the devastated areas of Luxemburg. Within a short period it had changed from a rich to an impoverished country, with thousands of the population homeless. Nearly one-third of the country had been wrecked, with enormous destruction of villages, livestock and forests, and a shortage of manufactured goods, fuel and food.

GERMANY'S SATELLITES FALL AWAY

The doubts which were beginning to assail the Axis satellites in 1943 (see Chapter 279) became certainties during 1944. Finland, Rumania and Bulgaria in succession capitulated to the Allies and signed agreements which entailed the waging of war against their former ally. Hungary, two-thirds overrun and her capital besieged by Soviet troops by the end of the year, had ceased to be an effective support of Germany's rapidly deteriorating position

FINLAND's war weariness, already apparent through 1943, continued to grow, particularly after the Russian Leningrad offensive launched on January 15, 1944 (*see* page 3129) threatened the long quiescent Russo-Finnish front with renewed activity. But operations swept westward instead of north, and for the time being the front remained quiescent.

On January 31, however, the United States delivered to the Finnish Government a strong note, pointing out that there were two obstacles to an improvement in their mutual relations : (1) the collaboration between Finland and Germany ; (2) the state of war existing between Finland and the Soviet Union, ally of the U.S.A. The note caused a deep impression—it was the first blunt indication for many Finns that their country no longer enjoyed the undiluted admiration of America.

Twelve days later, Mr. Juho Paasikivi, a negotiator of peace in 1940 (*see* page 758) and long regarded as leader of the anti-war party, **FINLAND** arrived by air in Stockholm on what was ostensibly a private visit. There he was put in touch with the Soviet Minister, Madame Kollontai, and he returned to Finland carrying the terms for an armistice, the chief points of which were: that Finland should break with Germany immediately and intern all German troops and warships in Finland, a task in which the Soviet Union was prepared to assist her if it was beyond her power; the immediate repatriation of Soviet and Allied prisoners of war and civilians in concentration camps; the re-establishment of the treaty of 1940; other matters to be negotiated later.

They were considered by the Finnish Diet in secret session on February 29. Negotiations through Stockholm continued, and though in a second secret session the Diet rejected the terms, Mr. Paasikivi and Mr. Carl Enckell, a former Foreign Secretary and a friend of Field-Marshal Mannerheim, flew secretly to Moscow on March 29, bringing back with them important clarifications considered by the Diet, again in secret session, on April 12. Helsinki

issued no statement; but Mr. Vyshinsky, Deputy People's Commissar for Foreign Affairs, announced on the 22nd to the Soviet and foreign Press in Moscow that Finland had rejected the Soviet terms.

Taking into account the breaking by Finland of the 1940 treaty, the tremendous damage which Finnish participation in the war had done to the north-western frontier zone of the Soviet Union, and in particular to Leningrad, the terms offered could not be considered as other than moderate, and this was the view of Finland's friends in Sweden and the United States. The only comment describing them as "harsh" and "intended to destroy Finnish liberty and the whole Finnish nation" came from Germany. The Fuehrer himself, in the first interview with a foreign newspaper correspondent he had accorded for years, told Mr. Christer Jaederlund of "Stockholms Tidningen" that the object of the terms was "to place the noose round the victim's neck and tighten it in the ripeness of time."

On June 10, **four days after the** Allies landed in Normandy, the Russians attacked in the Karelian isthmus (*see* page 3222), to capture Viborg on the 20th. The U.S. State Department announced on **U.S. Severs Relations with Finland** June 16 that the Finnish Minister in Washington and three Councillors at the Legation had been handed their passports and asked to leave because of activities "inimical to the United States," though it also stated that this did not mean breaking off relations with Finland. Ribbentrop arrived in Helsinki on June 22. By promising effective aid, and at the same time threatening that the Finns would "fare just as ill as the Italians if they try to betray Germany," he extracted from President Risto Ryti and Mr. Ramsay, the Finnish Foreign Minister, an agreement by which Finland undertook not to attempt to make a separate peace or armistice. On the 28th, fresh German troops were reported to be in Helsinki; while additional German

RED AIR FORCE RENEWS ITS ATTACKS ON HELSINKI

By February 1944 Finland was weary of a profitless war and in a mood to consider a truce with the U.S.S.R. Negotiations were set on foot, but the armistice terms offered by Moscow, though moderate in the circumstances, were rejected in April. Meantime, the Finnish capital was subjected to Soviet air attack and here sleighs laden with household possessions of the bombed-out are leaving the city.
Photo, Keystone

FINLAND SURRENDERS TO ALLIES

Fighting between Finland and the Soviet Union ceased on September 5, 1944. The Finnish peace delegation, already on the way to Moscow, reaches the frontier (left) marked by white flags. Led by the Premier, Mr. Antti Hackzell (above right) and Gen. Walden (above left) the emissaries cross the demarcation line to enter the cars waiting to take them to the Soviet capital (below). *Photos, Pictorial Press*

warships had been lying off Turku for some days. The United States officially announced severance of relations with Finland, because of her new alliance with Germany, on June 30.

President Ryti had made this alliance without consulting the Diet, and the **Mannerheim** result was g r o w i n g **Chosen** unrest both among its **President** members and among citizens outside. On August 1 it was announced that the President had suddenly resigned, and that the Diet had met in camera to consider the situation. Three days later the Diet passed an emergency law by which a new President could be elected by itself instead of by the Electoral College provided for in the Constitution, and Field-Marshal Mannerheim was chosen President. He immediately made it clear to the Germans that he

did not consider himself bound by the unconstitutional Ryti agreement. At his invitation, Mr. Antti Hackzell, who had been Finnish Minister in Moscow from 1922–27 and spoke Russian fluently, formed a government in which Mr. Enckell became Foreign Minister.

Mr. Gripenberg, Finnish Minister to Sweden, arrived in Helsinki on August 11, and returned to Stockholm on the 14th to inform Madame Kollontai that Finland was prepared to discuss terms. An official request for the reopening of negotiations was handed to her on August 25. Four days later, in agreement with Great Britain and with the approval of the U.S.A., Russia agreed to begin talks provided Finland announced a break with Germany and demanded from her the withdrawal of German troops from Finnish soil within a fortnight after the signing of pre-

liminary conditions, and at latest by September 15.

From 8 a.m. on September 4, Finnish troops ceased operations. At 8 a.m. next day, the Red Army on the Finnish front sounded the " cease fire." Two days later (September 7) a Finnish peace delegation arrived in Moscow, and on September 19 negotiations were concluded between Finland on the one hand, the U.S.S.R. and Great Britain on the other. The principal terms are given in Historic Document 283, page 3328.

Large scale withdrawals of German troops from northern Finland were reported for several days before September 15, but a great part of the German 20th Army, under the command of General Lothar Rendulic, still remained on Finnish soil, and was not expelled from the country till the end of November, and that only after heavy fighting (described in Chapter 329). During this last phase in Finland, the Germans behaved as they did in other occupied countries, burning, looting and destroying whole villages, thus leaving the Finnish people in no doubt as to the character of their former friends. On the other hand, the Russians kept their promise not to interfere with the internal structure of Finland.

Conditions were difficult—war waged with only a short pause since 1939 had exhausted much of the country's manpower and economic resources, and the Finns now had to make good also some of the damage they had done to Russia. They could, however, look forward to the task of peaceful reconstruction with more confidence than many of the countries whose peoples had not fought on the wrong side, but which had been much more ravaged by war and the German occupation than had Finland.

The first active intimation that by breaking from the Axis Rumania might regain Transylvania came from a man who had been the in-

RUMANIA timate friend and collaborator of Rumania's greatest modern statesman Nicolas Titulescu : President Benes of Czechoslovakia. In January 1944, after his visit to Moscow during the previous month, Dr. Benes revealed in an interview that in Moscow the Vienna Award

GERMAN ARMY HOLDS ON IN FINLAND

General Lothar Rendulic's German 20th Army, remained in northern Finland when that country made peace with the Allies, and was finally driven out only after bitter fighting. Here one of its units, halted during a withdrawal on the Kandalaksha sector, watches a camouflaged field gun passing to the rear. *Photo, Associated Press*

(*see* page 1289) was not considered a just and durable solution of the frontier problem between Rumania and Hungary. His declaration made a strong impression on all those politicians inside Rumania who were opposed to the war, some of whom still had access to King Michael.

Russian troops crossed the river Prut, the pre-war state frontier between the U.S.S.R. and Rumania, on April 2 (*see* page 3080). The same day Mr. Molotov declared that the Soviet Union did not covet any part of Rumanian territory and did not intend to interfere with the social and political structure of the country, but that her army in Rumania had orders " to pursue the enemy until his final rout and capitulation."

A few days later it was learned that Prince Stirbey, an old man who had once played a considerable role in Rumanian politics, had arrived in Cairo in order to find out whether his country could come to terms with the Allies. He could not have made the journey without the knowledge of the " Conducator," Marshal Ion Antonescu, who must therefore have yielded to the pressure put on him by the anti-war groups and the King. Prince Stirbey approached the British, who referred the matter to the Moscow government as the power primarily concerned, and on April 12, after consultations between Moscow, London, and Washington, the Rumanian emissary was presented with conditions for an armistice, which were rejected by Marshal Antonescu, though Mr. Churchill described them in the House of Commons on August 2 as generous.

Seeking Peace with the Allies

PAYING THE PRICE OF ALLIANCE WITH GERMANY

At Helsinki, in December 1944, the War Damage Indemnity Agreement between the U.S.S.R. and Finland is signed by Colonel-General Shdalnov on behalf of Russia. Standing on the left is Mr. Juho Paasikivi, negotiator of his country's peace in 1940 and in 1944. Beside him is the chairman of the Soviet Military Commission. Making good some of the damage done to Russia was but a part of the heavy price Finland had to pay for supporting Germany. *Photo, Planet News*

RUMANIA'S CAPITAL WELCOMES THE RED ARMY

Although the Allies offered armistice terms to Rumania on April 12, 1944, these were not accepted until August 23 owing to German pressure and the intransigence of the dictator Antonescu, who on that date was summarily arrested by order of King Michael. Eight days later, troops of the 2nd Ukrainian Army entered Bucharest after a 35-mile advance from Ploesti in 24 hours.

Photo, Pictorial Press

The Russians launched a new offensive in Rumania on August 22, capturing Jassy, capital of the ancient province of Moldavia, and over two hundred other places in one day. On August 23 Antonescu, after an audience with the King in which he vainly tried to defend his policy of continuing the war, was arrested on the King's order, together with members of his government. The King, acting with great swiftness and determination, invited General Constantin Sanatescu, Marshal of the Royal Court, and his own aide-de-camp, to form a government, which he did the same evening, rallying to his support the four main democratic parties. Mr. Grigoire Niculescu-Buzesti, a friend and disciple of Titulescu, became Foreign Minister. Dr. Juliu Maniu (National Peasant Party), Mr. Constantin Bratianu (National Liberal Party), Mr. Constantin Petrescu (Social Democratic Party), and Mr. Lucretiu Patrascanu (Communist Party) became Ministers without portfolio. The new Government immediately accepted the Allied terms offered in April, and broke off relations with Germany and her remaining Allies.

Hostilities between Rumania and the Soviet Union ceased at 4 a.m. on August 24; but the Germans were not forced out of the country without considerable further heavy fighting (*see* Chapter 340). Fighting broke out

Rumania Accepts Allied Terms

between Germans and Rumanians, particularly in the neighbourhood of Bucharest, which was attacked by the Luftwaffe, and on August 25 Rumania declared war on Germany. The German Minister in Bucharest, a Nazi extremist, Baron Manfred von Killinger, committed suicide.

Prince Stirbey, Mr. Patrascanu and other Rumanian delegates arrived in Moscow on August 30. The terms of the armistice (*see* Historic Document 282, page 3328) were announced on September 13. While the terms resembled in many respects those accepted by Finland, they included the recognition by the Allies of Rumania's claim to northern Transylvania, which district was transferred to Rumanian administration in March of the following year after its liberation by the Russians. Bessarabia and the northern Bucovina went to the Soviet Union under the clause restoring the 1940 Soviet–Rumanian frontier.

By September 18 the Soviet High Command, " in view of the fact that Marshal Antonescu's group may prove to be suitable candidates for inclusion in the list of war criminals," had arrested the " Conducator " himself; Mihail Antonescu, former Foreign Minister; General Pantazzi, former War Minister; and others, including Dr. Karl Clodius, German economic envoy in Bucharest, negotiator of those trade agreements which had been a main

element in the strong political hold Germany had secured in the Balkans.

Owing to differences which arose among the four parties represented in the Cabinet, the Socialists and Communists, with an agrarian group (the " Ploughmen's Front ") and a new political group called the Union of Patriots, formed a National Democratic Front. At the beginning of November Lieut.-General Vinogradov, Vice-President of the Allied Control Commission, protested to Sanatescu at his Government's delay in carrying out the armistice conditions. A second Sanatescu Cabinet gave greater representation to the newly formed National Democratic Front. But on December 2 this Government also resigned and at the King's request General Radescu formed a new one which, while retaining a number of the members of Sanatescu's second Cabinet, included also Dr. Petre Grozea, Chairman of the Ploughmen's Front, as Vice-Premier, and Professor Vladescu-Racoasa, head of the Union of Patriots, as Minister for Minorities. The Communist Patrascanu became Minister of Justice. Maniu, Bratianu and Petrescu were dropped.

National Democratic Front Formed

A Royal decree of September 4 reestablished the liberal constitution abolished by King Carol in 1938. Decrees of November 12 provided for the arrest of all former Iron Guard members; the abrogation of all racial legislation; and the post-war expulsion from Rumania of over 300,000 Germans born in the country.

In Bulgaria the Bojiloff Government tried by brutal suppression to counter

GERMANS RESIST IN BUCHAREST

As in Finland, the Germans fought fiercely after their ally had surrendered, particularly against the Rumanians themselves in and around Bucharest. 1. The National Theatre burns after being hit in an attack by the Luftwaffe. 2. After a bitter struggle, the first German prisoners are taken. 3. Overjoyed citizens parade the streets of the capital to celebrate the signing of the armistice between Rumania and the Allies on September 12, 1944.

Photos, Associated Press

GREETINGS FOR THE RED ARMY IN SOFIA

Throughout the summer of 1944, Allied political pressure on Bulgaria increased, especially from Moscow ; and on September 8, Army General Tolbukhin's armies drove over the frontier, the Black Sea port of Varna being occupied on that date. The Russians reached the Bulgarian capital a week later, and an armistice was concluded towards the end of October. *Photo, Pictorial Press*

the unrest and dissatisfaction of the peasantry and much of the Army. But continuing arrests and executions of Communists and other " troublemakers "

BULGARIA led to increased unrest, and many people in opposition fled to the mountains. Disorganization of communications and administration resulted from the heavy Allied air raids on Sofia and Plovdiv, which went on with growing intensity from November 1943 to April 1944. Reports from Turkey put the number of people who had left Sofia at about two-thirds of the city's population of 450,000. On January 14, Sofia radio, after a twelve-hour silence, broadcast an order to all doctors, nurses, and chemists to return to the capital within twenty-four hours. A 6 p.m. to 6 a.m. curfew was imposed in Sofia on January 16, and extended to the whole country on February 9. All public and private employees who had left the capital were ordered to return to their duty by January 28 under threat of severe penalties : fourteen high officials who failed to return—among them the Under-Secretary of the Ministry of Communications and the Governor of Sofia—were deprived of their posts.

During February the Government decreed the " total mobilization " of intellectuals, who were forbidden to leave Sofia (all writers, journalists and scientists being ordered to produce at least two patriotic articles or stories a month), doctors, pharmacists, judges and law officers. Health resorts and hostels, convents and monasteries were opened to bombed-out evacuees. A decree of March 18 ordered the immediate evacuation of all women and children from Sofia, free transport on the state railways being provided. All

motor traffic was put under military control.

The Sobranje (Grand National Council) met on January 25 and 26, and though in the official report complete approval of the Government's policy was said to have been expressed, the opposition had tabled a motion demanding the withdrawal of Bulgarian troops from occupied areas to which no claim could be maintained ; further strengthening of relations with the Soviet Union (with which, it will be remembered, Bulgaria was not at war—*see* page 2797) and Turkey ; and the formation of a government of national unity.

A few days later, Bulgarian troops, far from being withdrawn from areas already occupied, took over from the Germans the occupation of Edessa, Florina and Kastoria, extending their hold on Greece to the Albanian frontier.

Mr. Lavritcheff, Soviet Minister to Bulgaria, left for Moscow on March 25, ostensibly on leave. May 20 brought a note from the Soviet Union which left no doubt that if Bulgaria did not cease aiding Germany, Russia would sever relations with her. Twenty-four hours later Bojiloff resigned. Professor Filoff, one of the Regents (*see* page 2798), visited Hitler at Berchtesgaden on May 29, and received an ultimatum that a friendly and more co-operative government must be formed. Mr. Ivan Bagrianoff, a former Minister of Agriculture, took the Premiership on June 1, and in company with Filoff went to Berchtesgaden on June 4.

No outward change occurred in Russo-Bulgarian relations. Yet German influence was in fact waning, and the Bagrianoff Government took a number of steps indicating an altered policy. For instance, during July two Sofia

dailies which were under Nazi domination, " Dnes " and " Vecher," were suppressed ; a number of senior Gestapo-trained police officers were removed ; Mr. Protich, an outspoken anti-Nazi, was appointed chief of the Department for Jewish Affairs, and a decree issued in August raised the ban on the residence of Jews in Sofia, from which they had been banished for nearly two years.

At an extraordinary meeting of the Sobranje on August 17, Bagrianoff declared that his Government was " determined to remove all obstacles which stand in the way of the Bulgarian people's love of peace." **U.S.S.R. Declares War on Bulgaria** The German Government was asked to withdraw its troops from Bulgarian territory on the 25th, and next day it was announced over the Sofia radio that Bulgaria was withdrawing from the war and would henceforth be neutral. With the Red Army close to the Bulgarian border— General Tolbukhin crossed the frontier on September 8 (*see* Chapter 340)—Mr. Stoicheff Mushanoff, a former Premier and President of the Sobranje, arrived in Cairo to open negotiations with Britain and the U.S.A. They had scarcely begun when the Bagrianoff Government fell (September 1) following a sharp note from Russia.

A new Government was formed (September 2) by Mr. Kosta Muravieff,

'ARROW CROSS' LEADER

On October 15, 1944, Budapest radio announced that Hungary had asked for an armistice. Twenty-four hours later, Ferencz Szalasy, chief of the Fascist organization 'Arrow Cross,' seized power and repudiated the broadcast. Szalasy is here seen during a visit to Hitler on December 4. *Photo, Associated Press*

a leader of the right wing of the Agrarian Party who had been in retirement for ten years. On September 5 he broadcast a statement of policy, dwelling on his Government's desire to restore " normal diplomatic relations with all freedom-loving peoples." On the evening of the same day the Soviet Union declared war on Bulgaria in a note pointing out the leniency of the Soviet attitude in view of Bulgaria's aid to Germany during the preceding three years, and her refusal, in spite of changed circumstances, to break with that country.

In the early hours of the following day the Bulgarian Minister in Ankara informed the Soviet Ambassador to **Bulgaria Asks for an Armistice** Turkey that his Government asked for an armistice with the Soviet Union, stating that Bulgaria had declared war on Germany — a declaration denied in Berlin. Not until formal declaration of war was made on September 8 did Russia change her attitude. Next day, Colonel Kimon Gheorghieff, leader of the opposition, formed a new Government; the Regents Prince Kyril and General Michoff were dismissed (Professor Filoff had disappeared), their places being taken by Professor Venelin Ganeff (Radical Democrat), Mr. Zoetko Bobeshevsky (Communist), and Mr.

Todor Pavloff (Communist); and Moscow announced that the state of war between the U.S.S.R. and Bulgaria had ceased, and armistice conditions were being worked out by the Allies.

During September a number of pro-Nazi politicians, including Bojiloff; the three former Regents; Beckerle, German Ambassador in Sofia, and members of the Embassy staff and of a mission from Mussolini's "government" were arrested and handed over to the Red Army. But Bulgarian troops still remained in Yugoslavia and Greece. On October 11 Moscow announced that the Soviet Union, Great Britain and the United States having stipulated that before negotiations could begin these forces must be withdrawn within fifteen days, Bulgaria had agreed to this condition. A Bulgarian delegation, headed by Professor Stainoff, the Foreign Minister, reached Moscow on October 15, and an armistice (the terms of which are given in Historic Document 284, page 3328) was signed there on October 28.

The Horthy regime in Hungary was, despite its semi-fascist harshness, regarded with deep suspicion by the Nazis. They knew that the Hungarian ruling class, glad though they were to receive an ample jackal's share of territory taken from Czechoslovakia, Yugoslavia and Rumania, would be

HARVEST GUARD

In an attempt to frustrate sabotage of standing crops, special volunteer country police units were raised in Hungary during the summer of 1944. One of these guards is seen here between soldiers of the German and Hungarian armies with whom they closely co-operated. *Photo, Associated Press*

prepared to change sides should this prove advantageous.

On March 16, 1944, Admiral Horthy was summoned to Berchtesgaden, where he saw Hitler on the 18th. Hitler was reported to have demanded that all able- **HUNGARY** bodied men of military age who had been exempted or released from the Army should be mobilized; that all units of the Army down to regimental formations (equivalent to British battalions) should be commanded by German officers; that the railways and the important Danube traffic should come under a mixed general staff; that the food reserves and production of the country should go into a common pool for equal distribution among all countries associated with Germany; that censorship and press control similar to that in Germany should be imposed.

Horthy refused to accept these demands. He returned to Budapest next day, to find German troops already in occupation. German parachute units seized the airfields, and all important railway centres and Danube ports were taken over by German garrisons. Some opposition was encountered but was quickly suppressed. The Prime Minister, Mr. Kallay, resigned and fled to the Turkish legation. On March 22 Mr. Sztojay, Hungarian Minister in Berlin,

GERMANY'S FOURTH ALLY GIVES IN

The Bulgarian armistice was delayed by the Allied insistence that her troops in Yugoslavia and Greece must be withdrawn before negotiations could begin. This was effected in the stipulated fifteen days and the agreement was concluded at Moscow on October 28, 1944. Marshal F. I. Tolbukhin, commander of the 3rd Ukrainian Army, here signs for the U.S.S.R.; on the left is Mr. Molotov.

Photo, Pictorial Press

HUNGARIAN C.-IN-C.
Following the Szalasy coup d'état in October 1944, the Hungarian Commander-in-Chief, General Bela Miklos, joined the advancing Russian forces, taking with him the Hungarian 1st Army. On the formation of a Provisional Government in December he was appointed Premier.

formed a new government, which the Hungarian ministers in Stockholm, Madrid, Berne, Lisbon, and Helsinki refused to recognize.

The Social Democratic, Smallholders and Liberal Parties were dissolved.

Important opposition newspapers were suspended. Trade union funds were confiscated. Persecution of the Jews, against whom (except in Ruthenia) only half measures, according to German standards, had been taken, was intensified : within three months a series of decrees drove them from professional and business life and forced them into newly created ghettoes. Reports published in July stated that tens of thousands of Jews had been deported to Polish death camps.

On July 4 the King of Sweden sent a personal telegram to Horthy urging him " in the name of humanity" to save Hungarian Jews from further persecution. On the 5th Mr. Eden made a protest in the House of Commons. On the 14th Mr. Cordell Hull voiced the horror and indignation of the American people. On the 19th the International Red Cross announced from Zürich that the Hungarian Government had agreed to suspend the deportation of Jews. An informal offer made to Britain by the Germans in May to forgo the extermination of Hungarian Jews in exchange for 10,000 lorries of food, medical and other supplies (which, it was stated, would not be used on the western or southern

fronts) was made public in the same month. This " barefaced attempt to blackmail the Allies " was rejected.

The Russians entered Hungarian-occupied Transylvania on August 29 (*see* Chapter 340), and on the same day Sztojay resigned, to be succeeded by General Latakos, a strong supporter of Horthy. The inclusion in the armistice terms with Rumania (*see* page 3328) of the return to her of Transylvania made the new Hungarian Government resolute in its determination to continue the war. Russian and Rumanian troops crossed the border into Hungary proper on October 6. A few days later Horthy asked for an armistice, but he was overthrown in a coup d'état by Szalasy, leader of the " Arrow Cross," who seized power. The Commander-in-Chief, General Bela Miklos, went over to the Russians, taking with him the Hungarian 1st Army. The Russian advance continued, and at the turn of the year the capital, Budapest, was under siege.

In liberated Hungary, elections for a Provisional National Assembly were held during December. Professor Bela Zsedenyi was elected President, and General Miklos was appointed Premier of a Provisional Government which declared war on Germany on December 29.

BUDAPEST TRAINS AUXILIARY FIRE-FIGHTERS

By December 26, 1944 the Russian 2nd and 3rd Ukrainian Armies had encircled the Hungarian capital where German resistance ended only on February 13, 1945. For months the city had been subjected to Allied air attack, and this fire-fighting unit was one of many enrolled to assist the municipal brigades. Note the out-of-date equipment in the background. *Photo, Associated Press*

SURRENDER TERMS SIGNED BY GERMANY'S EX-ALLIES

By the end of 1944, four of Germany's allies had abandoned her. Here are the principal additional terms signed by Italy on September 29, 1943 (for the terms signed on September 3, *see* page 2866), and the conditions imposed on Rumania, Finland, and Bulgaria

The following extracts from the 44 conditions, additional to those of September 3, 1943, signed by Italy on September 29, 1943, are taken from White Paper Cmd. 6693 issued by H.M. Stationery Office (4d.) in November 1945.

1. (*a*) The Italian Land, Sea and Air Forces wherever located hereby surrender unconditionally.

(*b*) Italian participation in the war in all Theatres will cease immediately. There will be no opposition to landings, movements or other operations of the Land, Sea and Air Forces of the United Nations.

2. The Italian Supreme Command will give full information concerning the disposition and condition of all Italian Land Sea and Air Forces.

3. The Italian Supreme Command will take the necessary measures to secure airfields, port facilities, and all other installations against seizure or attack by any of Italy's Allies

4. Italian Land, Sea and Air Forces will within the periods to be laid down by the United Nations withdraw from all areas outside Italian territory notified to the Italian Government by the United Nations and proceed to areas to be specified by the United Nations. . . . All Italian officials will similarly leave the areas notified except any who may be permitted to remain by the United Nations. Those permitted to remain will comply with the instructions of the Allied Commander-in-Chief.

5. No requisitioning, seizures or other coercive measures shall be effected by Italian Land, Sea and Air Forces or officials in regard to persons or property in the areas notified under Article 4.

7. Italian warships of all descriptions, auxiliaries and transports will be assembled as directed in ports to be specified by the Allied Commander-in-Chief and will be dealt with as prescribed by the Allied Commander-in-Chief.

8. Italian aircraft of all kinds will not leave the ground or water or ships, except as directed by the Allied Commander-in-Chief.

9. All merchant ships, fishing or other craft of whatever flag, all aircraft and inland transport of whatever nationality in Italian or Italian-occupied territory or waters will, pending verification of their identity and status, be prevented from leaving.

10. The Italian Supreme Command will make available all information about naval, military and air devices, installations and defences, about all transport and inter-communication systems established by Italy or her Allies on Italian territory or in the approaches thereto, about minefields or other obstacles to movement by land, sea or air and such other particulars as the United Nations may require. Italian forces and equipment will be made available as required by the United Nations for the removal of the above-mentioned obstacles.

13. The manufacture, production and construction of war material and its import, export and transit is prohibited, except as directed by the United Nations.

14. (*a*) All Italian merchant shipping and fishing and other craft, wherever they may be, and any constructed or completed during the period of the present instrument will be made available in good repair and in seaworthy condition by the competent Italian authorities at such places and for such purposes and periods as the United Nations may prescribe.

(*b*) All Italian inland transport and all port equipment will be held at the disposal of the United Nations for such purposes as they may direct.

15. United Nations merchant ships, fishing and other craft in Italian hands wherever they may be (including for this purpose those of any country which has broken off diplomatic relations with Italy), whether or not the title has been transferred as the result of prize court proceedings or otherwise, will be surrendered to the United Nations. . . . The Italian Government will take the necessary measures to insure that the vessels and their cargo are not damaged.

16. The Italian authorities will conform to such measures for control and censorship of press and other publications, of theatrical and cinematograph performances, of broadcasting, and also of all forms of inter-communication as the Allied Commander-in-Chief may direct.

17. The warships, auxiliaries, transports and merchant and other vessels and aircraft in the service of the United Nations will have the right freely to use the territorial waters around and the air over Italian territory.

18. The forces of the United Nations will require to occupy certain parts of Italian territory. The territories or areas concerned will from time to time be notified by the United Nations, and all Italian Land, Sea and Air Forces will thereupon withdraw from such territories or areas, in accordance with the instructions issued by the Allied Commander-in-Chief.

19. In the territories or areas referred to in article 18 all Naval, Military and Air installations, power stations, oil refineries, public utility services, all ports and harbours, all transport and all inter-communication installations, facilities and equipment and such other installations or facilities and all such stocks as may be required by the United Nations will be made available in good condition by the competent Italian authorities with the personnel required for working them. The Italian Government will make available such other local resources or services as the United Nations may require.

20. Without prejudice to the provisions of the present instrument, the United Nations will exercise all the rights of an occupying power throughout the territories or areas referred to in article 18.

25. (*a*) Relations with countries at war with any of the United Nations. or occupied by any such country will be broken off.

(*b*) The United Nations reserve the right to require the withdrawal of neutral diplomatic and consular officers from occupied Italian territory.

29. Benito Mussolini, his Chief Fascist associates and all persons suspected of having committed war crimes or analogous offences whose names appear on lists to be communicated by the United Nations will forthwith be apprehended and surrendered into the hands of the United Nations.

30. All Fascist organizations, including all branches of the Fascist Militia (M.V.S.N.), the Secret Police (O.V.R.A.), will in so far as this is not already accomplished be disbanded in accordance with the directions of the Allied Commander-in-Chief.

31. All Italian laws involving discrimination on grounds of race, colour, creed or political opinions will in so far as this is not already accomplished be rescinded, and persons detained on such grounds will, as directed by the United Nations, be released and relieved from all legal disabilities to which they have been subjected.

32. (*a*) Prisoners of war belonging to the forces of or specified by the United Nations, and any nationals of the United Nations, including Abyssinian subjects, confined, interned, or otherwise under restraint in Italian or Italian-occupied territory will not be removed and will forthwith be handed over to representatives of the United Nations or otherwise dealt with as the United Nations may direct.

(*b*) Persons of whatever nationality who have been placed under restriction, detention or sentence (including sentences *in absentia*) on account of their dealings or sympathies with the United Nations will be released under the direction of the United Nations and relieved from all legal disabilities to which they have been subjected.

33. The Italian Government will comply with such directions as the United Nations may prescribe regarding restitutions, deliveries, services or payments by way of reparation and payment of the costs of occupation during the period of the present instrument.

34. The Italian Government will carry out during the period of the present instrument such measures of disarmament

demobilization and demilitarization as may be prescribed by the Allied Commander-in-Chief.

35. The Italian Government will supply all information and provide all documents required by the United Nations. There shall be no destruction or concealment of archives records, plans or any other documents or information.

37. There will be appointed a Control Commission representative of the United Nations charged with regulating and executing this instrument under the orders and general directions of the Allied Commander-in-Chief.

The principal provisions of the armistice between Rumania and the United Nations, signed on September 12, 1944, were :

Rumania to declare war against Germany and Hungary, for which purpose she is to put into the field at least 12 infantry divisions with reinforcements. The Government and High Command undertake to disarm and intern all the armed forces of Germany and Hungary on Rumanian territory and intern their nationals.

The frontier between Rumania and Soviet Russia established by the agreement of June 28, 1940, to be restored (Article 4).

Rumania to surrender at once all Allied prisoners of war, and to look after them until repatriation ; also to release all persons imprisoned in connexion with activities in favour of the Allies or in view of their racial origin, and to rescind all discriminatory legislation (Article 6).

Rumania to hand over all United Nations' vessels in her ports. She will also provide regularly the funds in Rumanian currency required by the Allied (Soviet) High Command for the execution of its functions and place at its disposal industrial and transport undertakings, public utilities, power stations, food, fuel, etc. Rumanian merchant vessels to be subjected to operational control by the Allied High Command.

Rumania to pay reparations to make good the damage suffered by the Soviet Union ; but as she is waging war against Germany and Hungary she will pay only in part, the sum being $300 million (American) (£75,000,000) spread over 6 years. She will also pay for damages suffered by other Allied nations and their civilians in Rumania (Article 11).

The Rumanian Government to co-operate with the Allied (Soviet) High Command in the arrest of war criminals.

Rumania to disband at once all organizations of Fascists and others hostile to the United Nations (Article 15).

Local circumstances permitting, Rumanian civil administration to be re-established in all Rumanian territory lying not less than 32½ to 62½ miles from the line of the front.

An Allied Control Commission to be set up to control the execution of the agreements till the peace is signed.

The Allied Governments consider the decisions of the Vienna Award [see page 1288] as not valid, and agree that Transylvania, or the greater part of it, shall be returned to Rumania (Article 19).

The principal provisions of the armistice signed on September 19, 1944, between the U.S.S.R. and the United Kingdom, on the one hand, and Finland, on the other, were :

Finland to withdraw her troops behind the frontier line of 1940, and to disarm all German forces still in Finland after September 15 and hand over their personnel to the Allied (Soviet) High Command as prisoners of war ; and to intern German and Hungarian nationals (Articles 1 and 2).

Finland to make available to the Allies the airfields on her western and south-western coasts, with all equipment, during the period necessary for air operations against the Germans in Estonia and the German Navy in the northern part of the Baltic (Article 3).

Finland to place her Army on a peace footing within 2½ months from the signature of the armistice (Article 4).

The effect of the treaty with the Soviet Union of March 12, 1940 [see page 746] to be restored subject to the changes in the present agreement (Article 6).

Finland to return to the Soviet Union the Oblast of Petsamo (Article 7), and the Soviet Union to renounce its rights to the lease of Hangö peninsula. Finland, for her part, to lease to the Soviet Union territory and waters for the establishment of a naval base in the area of Porkala-Ud (Article 8).

The agreement of October 11, 1940, concerning the Aaland Islands to be restored (Article 9) [i.e. the Aalands to be demilitarized].

Finland to hand over at once all Allied war prisoners, and also Allied nationals who had been interned in or deported by force to Finland ; Finnish prisoners and interned persons in Allied territory to be transferred to Finland.

Finland to indemnify the Soviet Union for losses caused to the amount of $300 million (£75,000,000), over 6 years. Provision also to be made for the indemnification by Finland of losses caused to other Allied States (Article 11).

Finland to collaborate with the Allies in the apprehension and trial of war criminals ; also to transfer to the Allied (Soviet) High Command as booty all war material of Germany and her satellites, including ships (Articles 13 and 15).

Finland not to permit the export or expropriation of any property belonging to Germany or Hungary or to their nationals (Article 16).

Finnish merchant ships to be handed over for use in the general interests of the Allies ; also all ships in Finnish waters belonging to the United Nations (Articles 17 and 18).

Finland to remove all discriminatory legislation, and to dissolve all pro-Hitler organizations and all others conducting propaganda against the United Nations (Article 21).

An Allied control commission to be established to regulate and supervise the execution of the agreement, until the conclusion of peace.

The principal provisions of the armistice signed on October 28, 1944, between Bulgaria and all the nations at war with her, were :

Bulgaria to disarm the German armed forces and hand them over as prisoners of war ; to intern nationals of Germany and her satellites ; to maintain and make available such land, sea and air forces as may be specified for services under the Allied (Soviet) High Command. On the conclusion of hostilities the Bulgarian armed forces to be demobilized under the supervision of the Allied Control Commission (Article 1).

Bulgarian merchant vessels to be subject to the operational control of the Allied (Soviet) High Command.

Bulgarian armed forces and officials to be withdrawn from territories of Greece and Yugoslavia in accordance with the pre-conditions accepted by Bulgaria on October 11, and to evacuate from those territories all civilians who were citizens of Bulgaria on January 1, 1941 (Article 2).

Bulgaria to assure complete freedom of movement over her territory to Soviet and other Allied forces, put at their disposal industrial and transport enterprises, power stations, fuel and food, and make regular payments in Bulgarian currency to the Allied (Soviet) High Command.

Bulgaria to release immediately all Allied prisoners of war and internees and all persons detained because of Allied sympathies, or for racial or religious reasons, and to provide them with food, clothing, medical and sanitary requirements, and the means of transport to their own countries. Also to repeal all discriminatory legislation (Articles 4 and 5).

Bulgaria to co-operate in the apprehension and trial of war criminals and to dissolve all pro-Hitler or other organizations hostile to the United Nations (Articles 6 and 7).

Bulgaria to accept censorship of all literature, films and theatrical performances, and broadcasting, and of post, telegraph and telephone services by the Allied (Soviet) High Command.

Bulgaria to restore all property and the rights and interests of the United Nations and their nationals, including Greek and Yugoslav property ; to return all valuables and materials removed from United Nations' territory either by Germany or Bulgaria ; and to hand over all United Nations' vessels in Bulgarian ports for the use of the Allied (Soviet) High Command.

Bulgaria to hand over as booty to the Allied (Soviet) High Command all German and German satellite war material on Bulgarian territory, including vessels in Bulgarian waters, and to prohibit the removal of any form of property belonging to Germany or her satellites (Articles 12 and 13).

Bulgaria to pay reparations to the United Nations, the amount to be determined later (Article 9).

An Allied Control Commission to be set up to regulate and supervise the execution of the armistice terms.

Bulgaria to make foodstuffs immediately available for the relief of Greece and Yugoslavia.

Chapter 328

SOVIET FORCES CROSS INTO EAST PRUSSIA

In Chapter 318 the progress of the White Russian offensive for the month after its start on June 23 is described. Along the whole front, the pre-1939 Russian frontier was crossed and left far behind, while on the right Chernyakhovsky passed out of Poland into Lithuania with Bagramyan's 1st Baltic Army covering his northern flank. This chapter records the course of operations culminating in the invasion of East Prussia. The simultaneous campaigns in the Baltic and on the Danube are covered in Chapters 329 and 340

GENERAL CHERNYAKHOVSKY'S 3rd White Russian Army reached and crossed the middle Niemen south of Kovno (*see* page 3224), but it then encountered stiffening resistance to its attempts to encircle that city and to close on the East Prussian frontier some 50 miles ahead. A pause to gather strength was necessary, though not a relaxation of attempts to secure more extensive bridge-heads. On Chernyakhovsky's left Colonel-General Zakharov was advancing towards Byelostok, a strongly fortified town the scene of a Russian disaster in the early days of the war.

Marshal Rokossovsky's 1st White Russian Army north of the Pripet was, in spite of now very long lines of communication, advancing rapidly towards Brest Litovsk, outflanking it from the north, and cutting the railway thence to Byelostok. His army south of the Pripet, having broken through on the Kowel front, crossed the Western Bug River, and on July 24 his capture of Lublin was announced. This thrust outflanked Brest Litovsk from the south, and was also clearly designed to co-operate with the new offensive by Marshal Koniev's 1st Ukrainian Army on the Lwow front.

Interest centred on the race to the Vistula of the armies commanded by Rokossovsky and Koniev. Nevertheless, the operations of the armies under **Approach to East Prussia** Chernyakhovsky and Zakharov (2nd White Russian) continued greatly to influence the strategic situation, although their progress became less spectacular. Their approach to the frontiers of East Prussia and the pressure they maintained unquestionably induced the Germans to weaken their Vistula front by concentrating a disproportionate part of their available force in that province, to which for sentimental as well as strategic reasons they attached immense importance. It was the traditional homeland of the Junker officer class; and it provided a potential springboard for a counter-offensive against an army advancing towards the Vistula. It had also become the southern abutment of the

bridge by which communications with Colonel-General Lindemann's armies in the Baltic States could be maintained.

Thus Chernyakhovsky and Zakharov not only threatened East Prussia with invasion but, if that proved impracticable owing to the defensible character of the approaches, could still, by maintaining pressure, deprive the province of its strategical value to the enemy. The importance of their operations was greatly enhanced by the progress of the three Baltic Armies farther north, and by the evident determination of the Germans to cling to their dangerous position in the Baltic States in hopes of inducing Finland, already wavering, not to withdraw from the war. On July 26 Marshal Govorov, commanding on the Leningrad front, captured the ancient Estonian city of Narva, thereby opening a passage into Estonia north of Lake Peipus and thus further increasing the probability that Finland might shortly find herself isolated.

On the 1st Ukrainian Front, Tarnopol had been captured on April 15 (*see* page 3082), but Brody, some forty miles north-west of Tarnopol, though the scene of heavy fighting, remained in German hands and **On the Road to Lwow** marked presumably the outer ring of the deep defences covering Lwow. It is not surprising in view of the nature of the country south of Lwow, hilly and intersected by the Dniester tributaries, that Koniev, while striking directly westwards towards that city, made it his primary aim to develop an outflanking manoeuvre to the north of it. With Rokossovsky's army operating in the Kowel region, each army protected a flank of the other, even though they tended to diverge and were not aiming at pincer effects.

In his breakthrough (*see* page 3225), Koniev captured on July 18 Brody and Krasnoye on the direct road to Lwow, as well as Kamenka to the north of the

RUSSIAN ARMOUR ENTERS BYELOSTOK

On the lateral railway between Vilna and Brest Litovsk, the heavily defended town of Byelostok was the immediate objective of Colonel-General Zakharov's 2nd White Russian Army driving for the East Prussian frontier with the 3rd White Russian Army in July 1944. The fall of this town—announced on July 27—was part of the collapse of the whole German defence line from Narva to Stanislavov. (See map in page 3331.)   *Photo, Pictorial Press*

was deteriorating was proved by the long list of Russian successes announced on July 26, 27, 28. On the 26th Rokossovsky, driving on from Lublin, captured Deblin (Poland) on the east bank of the Vistula; on the Gulf of Finland Narva (Estonia) fell to Govorov. On the 27th, five Orders of the Day announced, from north to south, the capture of Dvinsk and Rezekne by General Yeremenko (2nd Baltic Army), and of Shavli (Lithuania) by General Bagramyan (1st Baltic Army); of Byelostok by Colonel - General Zak-

German Situation Deteriorates

city and more than fifty other places. Thereafter, while maintaining his direct pressure on Lwow, his right wing continued to advance in true blitzkrieg style. On July 20 he captured Rava-Russka and Vladimir-Volynski, the latter place bringing him in close contact with Rokossovsky, whose breakthrough on the Kowel front had that day carried him to the Western Bug (*see* page 3225). Brest Litovsk was thus left with only one railway, leading west, and was in danger of complete encirclement.

On July 24 Koniev's spearhead, on a sixty-mile front north of Yaroslav, reached and crossed the San River, the tributary which prolongs the north to south line of the middle Vistula. This thrust, though it threatened to turn the line of the Vistula, was no doubt aimed primarily at outflanking and encircling Yaroslav and Przemysl, both on the west bank of the San. With their capture, railway communications to Lwow from Cracow and Silesia would be cut. Like Lwow, Przemysl was a great fortress town in the frontier defences of the old Austrian Empire which had stood a notable siege in the First Great War.

It was by now clear that the Germans, in order to seal off the gap caused by the White Russian offensive, had gravely weakened their front in southern Poland. Presumably they hoped to retain Lwow as a pivot to strengthen their position in the Carpathian foothills. They certainly transferred thither some formations from the Bessarabian front, in the hope of remedying their weakness. Such attempts to be strong at all points in defence is, however, notoriously apt to result in weakness everywhere. The Germans, who appear always to have underestimated Russian strength, especially in armament, may have con-

Koniev Crosses the San River

LWOW FAILS TO STEM THE SOVIET ADVANCE

In a determined effort to hold the vitally important pivot-position of Lwow, the German High Command reinforced the garrison with troops withdrawn from Bessarabia. But by July 27, 1944 it was in Marshal Koniev's hands, and his victorious 1st Ukrainian Army was greeted by streamers of welcome put out by the populace (top). On the outskirts, the driver of a caterpillar motor-cycle is captured (above).

Photos, Pictorial Press; Planet News

sidered it improbable that Koniev had resources adequate to stage a dangerous offensive in view of the great concentration of Russian force in the north. To that extent, Koniev's offensive may have effected a strategic surprise. Although Koniev's most spectacular advance was north of Lwow, his direct drive towards the city paid good dividends: west of Brody five German divisions were surrounded and their final liquidation on July 23 yielded 17,175 prisoners, including Major-General Lindemann (commanding the 361st Infantry Division) and General Nedgig (commanding the 45th Security Division); while among the 30,000 dead was Major-General Beutler (commanding the 340th Infantry Division). A large quantity of booty was also captured. Other offensive operations were in progress southward towards Stanislavov.

How rapidly the German situation

harov, and of Lwow and Stanislavov by Marshal Koniev. Apart from these six towns mentioned in Orders of the Day, the Red Army liberated on July 27 nearly 2,000 other localities in the long front from south-west of Pskov to Galicia. On the 28th, Brest Litovsk fell to Rokossovsky's northern wing and Yaroslav and Przemysl to Koniev's spearheads. These were all devastating blows, the loss of Lwow and Brest Litovsk in particular, proving how completely the German front had been broken and of how little worth were their strongest hedgehog centres. The capture of Deblin and Przemysl by spearhead troops furthermore indicated that the momentum of the offensive had not been checked, and that the whole line of the Vistula was in danger. Nearly all these successes appear to have been won in a very similar way: bold encircling movements by mobile troops

DEPUTY SUPREME COMMANDER, ALLIED EXPEDITIONARY FORCE

Air Chief Marshal Sir Arthur W. Tedder, G.C.B., was appointed deputy to General Eisenhower (see plate facing page 3254) on December 27, 1943. As A.O.C.-in-C., R.A.F., Middle East (1941-43), he had helped to perfect air-land co-operation ; in General Montgomery's Desert advance (October 23, 1942-January 23, 1943 : see Chapters 255 and 257) the R.A.F. brilliantly employed 'Tedder's Carpet'—a path cleared through enemy defences by pattern bombing. From February to December 1943 he was in command of the Mediterranean Allied Air Forces. On September 11, 1945 he was promoted Marshal of the R.A.F., and on January 1, 1946 became Chief of Air Staff and was created a Baron.

THE BOARD OF ADMIRALTY MEETS IN LONDON

IN its historic board-room in Whitehall the Board of Admiralty meets to plan the Royal Navy's part in the Second Great War. The Board includes a First Lord (a member of the Cabinet) ; the Civil Lord and the Parliamentary Secretary (also drawn from the Houses of Parliament) and five Sea Lords. The last-named, professional seamen, consist of the Chief of Naval Staff, the Chief of Naval Personnel, the Controller, the Chief of Supplies and Transport, and the Chief of Naval Air Equipment. Other members are the Deputy Chief and the Assistant Chiefs of the Naval Staff and the Permanent Secretary (a Civil Servant).

In this photograph reading from Lord Bruntisfield, M.C., Parliamentary Secretary (with arm on desk at near end), in anti-clockwise direction are : Sir James Lithgow, M.C., T.D., Controller of Merchant Shipbuilding and Repairs ; the Rt. Hon. G. H. Hall, M.P., Financial Secretary ; Rear-Admiral D. W. Boyd, C.B.E., D.S.C., Fifth Sea Lord and Chief of Naval Air Equipment ; Vice-Admiral F. H. Pegram, C.B., D.S.O., Fourth Sea Lord and Chief of Supplies and Transport ; Vice-Admiral Sir W. Frederic Wake-Walker, K.C.B., C.B.E., Third Sea Lord and Controller of the Navy ; Vice-Admiral Sir William J. Whitworth, K.C.B., D.S.O., Second Sea Lord and Chief of Naval Personnel ; Sir H. V. Markham, K.C.B., M.C., Permanent Secretary ; the Rt. Hon. A. V. Alexander, C.H., M.P., First Lord of the Admiralty ; Sir J. Sidney Barnes, K.B.E., C.B., Deputy Secretary ; Admiral of the Fleet Sir A. Dudley Pound, G.C.B., G.C.V.O., First Sea Lord and Chief of Naval Staff ; Admiral Sir Charles E. Kennedy-Purvis, K.C.B., Deputy First Sea Lord ; Vice-Admiral Sir E. Neville Syfret, K.C.B., Vice-Chief of Naval Staff ; Rear-Admiral J. H. Edelsten, C.B.E., Assistant Chief of Naval Staff ; Rear-Admiral W. R. Patterson, C.B., C.V.O., Assistant Chief of Naval Staff ; and Captain R. A. Pilkington, M.C., M.P., Civil Lord.

Photo, Topical Press

FIRST LORD OF THE ADMIRALTY

The Rt. Hon. Albert Victor Alexander, C.H., M.P., appointed to the Admiralty in 1940, held the same post in the second Labour Government from 1929-31. He was Secretary of the Parliamentary Committee of the Co-operative Congress. His was the responsibility to Parliament for the Royal Navy's part in the Normandy invasion of June 6, 1944, described by Admiral Sir Bertram Ramsay as 'the greatest amphibious operation in history' (see page 3151) in which 4,066 landing ships and craft of over sixty different types took part.

SECRETARY OF STATE FOR AIR

The Rt. Hon. Sir Archibald Sinclair, Bt., K.T., C.M.G., M.P., who succeeded Sir Kingsley Wood at the Air Ministry in 1940, was Liberal M.P. for Caithness and Sutherland from 1922 and was elected Leader of the Liberal Parliamentary Party in 1935. On March 6, 1945, he declared in the Commons (see page 3187) that R.A.F. Coastal Command's blows against the U-boats during the invasion of Western Europe —delivered in unison with the Royal Navy — were 'decisive.'

Direct colour photographs by Fox Photos

COMMANDER-IN-CHIEF, FIRST CANADIAN ARMY

The appointment of Lieut.-General Henry Duncan Graham Crerar, C.B., D.S.O., to command the 1st Canadian Army was announced from Ottawa on March 20, 1944. Four months later—on July 18—he set up his all-Canadian H.Q. in France. It was the first time in the history of the Dominion that an independent Canadian army had taken the field. He had commanded the 1st Canadian Corps in Britain, and later in Italy, from December 1941 to March 1944. He was Chief of General Staff, Canada, 1940-41 ; and G.O.C. the 2nd Canadian Division Overseas in 1941. His promotion to full general was announced on November 21, 1944, and in July 1945 he was appointed a Companion of Honour.

Direct colour photograph by Illustrated

were quickly followed by determined frontal attacks, which generally completed the capture of the strongholds in a few days' hard fighting.

The city of Lwow itself was the centre of an elaborate system of strongly fortified towns and villages, each of which was carried by the same process on a small scale of encirclement and direct assault. The defence was thus broken before the city itself was entered, and in consequence it escaped serious damage, although the Germans had been determined to hold it at all costs.

Amazing as had been the success of the Russian offensive, the resulting exhaustion and lengthening lines of communication would seem to have given the Germans prospects of at least partially retrieving the situation before the Red Army was in a condition to exercise again its full power. In the Baltic States they still had thirty divisions of Lindemann's group which, though under pressure, had not yet been heavily defeated and had still a line of retreat open by which they could join the strong group in East Prussia. Whether they withdrew or held their ground, they necessitated the diversion of strong Russian forces. Similarly, in East Prussia there was a strong group in a highly defensible area which might become a menace on the flank of the Russian drive towards the Vistula. In the south lay the easily defended region of the Carpathians where, moreover, Hungarian troops might be trusted to fight in defence of their own frontiers, unwilling though they would probably be to take part in counter-offensive operations outside them ; no large German forces were, therefore, required in this area except so far as they might be reinforced to threaten Koniev's lines of communication as he advanced westwards. On the Rumanian frontiers, although Von Kleist was threatened by the 2nd and 3rd Ukrainian Armies, he similarly was in a good defensive position and had the support of Rumanian troops.

On the whole, therefore, the pressing German problem was to find sufficient troops to hold the line of the Vistula uncovered by the defeats they had suffered.

It is impossible to say exactly what reserves the Germans still had available for the purpose, but the landing in Normandy (*see* Chapter 311) had made it out of the question to withdraw any formations from the western front, nor could any be withdrawn from Italy, where Kesselring was reorganizing his

Possibilities of German Defence

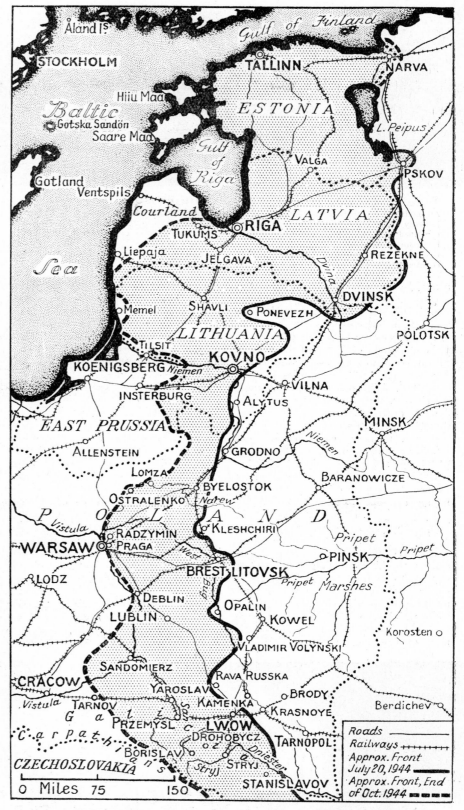

THE SOVIET ARMIES ROLL FARTHER WESTWARD

The Russian summer campaign in Poland and Lithuania which began on June 23, 1944, slowed down by the beginning of August though fighting went on until late October. German losses were immense, and while the enemy made a partial recovery the beginning of the end was clearly in sight. The shaded area in this map indicates the ground recovered by the Baltic and White Russian armies of the Soviet Union between July and October 1944. Concurrent operations in Latvia and Estonia are described in Chapter 329 ; those in Bessarabia and Rumania, in Chapter 340.

KOVNO IS RESTORED TO THE LITHUANIANS

Advancing from his hard-won bridge-heads over the river Niemen to the South, Gen. Chernya-khovsky's 3rd White Russian Army, adopting the familiar Russian tactics of a frontal attack combined with encircling movements, entered the Lithuanian capital on August 1, 1944. The battle for Kovno opened on July 25, with Russian armour and infantry attacking from several directions ; but the Germans fought bitterly to hold this strongly fortified bastion, mounting counter-attacks until almost the last moment. *Photo, Pictorial Press*

army after his retreat from Rome. It is probable, however, that when the Allied summer offensives opened there was still a substantial central reserve located in western Poland and Germany, although parts of it would have been in no condition for immediate front-line service. Probably there were some good S.S. Divisions and old regular divisions withdrawn for re-equipment and reconstitution after the winter disasters, as well as a number of new divisions, in many cases bearing old numbers, formed to replace those completely lost.

Of the divisions in reserve in western Poland, some were certainly rushed up in an attempt to check the White Russian breakthrough. Although unsuccessful in that, these and some troops of the front-line armies would have made good their retreat to the Vistula. Throughout Germany there were training establishments and depots of convalescent units, from which the ranks of incomplete formations could be quickly filled with trained personnel. Over a month had

German Strength in Men

passed since the scale of the disaster in White Russia must have been recognized, and strenuous measures must have been taken to bring reserve divisions up to war establishment and to dispatch them to the front. With excellent rail communications available the process could have gone on rapidly.

When the Russians reached the Vistula, they found the position strongly held. At Deblin, Rokossovsky did not make a determined effort to secure a crossing. Instead, he wheeled northwards, clearing the east bank. An element of caution may have been introduced into Russian strategy owing to the difficulty of maintaining supplies for strong forces at the end of long lines of communication and the possibility of a counter-offensive.

From the beginning of August, although the Russian offensive continued, progress became much less rapid ; determined resistance was being encountered.

In the north Bagramyan, thrusting north from Shavli (where he had cut the last railway leading from Latvia to East Prussia), on July 31 captured

Jelgava, on the approaches to Riga. The following day he reached Tukums on the southern shore of the Gulf of Riga, cutting the last road and thus completing the isolation of Lindemann's armies. General Chernyakhovsky, after bitter fighting in the bridge-heads he had established across the Niemen south of Kovno, on August 1 captured that city.

This was a notable achievement, for Kovno was not only an important railway centre, essential as an advanced base for the development of an attack on **Importance** East Prussia, but it **of Kovno** had been fortified as a strong bastion on the line of the Niemen, where the Germans made great efforts to stem the Russian advance towards the East Prussian frontier forty miles away. Moreover, Kovno was naturally highly defensible, skirted as it was by the 250-yards-wide Niemen on the south and with a considerable tributary giving protection on the north. As usual, the Russian success was due to a skilful combination of encirclement and direct attack. The Germans had, however, succeeded in gaining time to reinforce their defences, and there could be no immediate question of Chernyakhovsky undertaking an invasion of East Prussia. Nevertheless his hard fighting had drawn and pinned large German forces to the defence of the frontier.

Somewhat similarly Zakharov by his capture of Byelostok on July 27 had gained an important communication centre and had forced the Germans to strengthen the southern approaches to East Prussia, although for the time being an attempt at invasion was impossible. His role for some time to come was in fact mainly to provide, and extend as necessary, a defensive flank to Rokossovsky's operations.

Rokossovsky after the capture of Brest Litovsk by his right wing certainly appears to have aimed at the capture of Warsaw before the Germans had time to consolidate their position on the Vistula.

Resistance Grows Near Praga

His advance at first made rapid progress, in spite of the determined resistance of isolated German detachments. In the first instance these were generally by-passed, but when stronger and better organized resistance was encountered on the approaches to Praga, the suburb of Warsaw on the east bank of the Vistula, they constituted serious blocks on Russian lines of communication and troops were necessarily diverted to their liquidation. The situation at this period is somewhat obscure, but it is evident that the Germans had concentrated a strong force for the defence of Praga with the object of holding it as a bastion bridge-head on their Vistula defence line, and it was too strong to be rushed by Rokossovsky's advanced troops with long and weak communications behind them. Instead, on reaching the outskirts of Praga Rokossovsky extended his front northwards, capturing Radzymin (July 31) on the south side of the Bug, but thereafter encountered stiff resistance in the strongly fortified area at the confluence of the Bug and Vistula. By the end of the first week of August Rokossovsky was definitely held and, though the mopping up of pockets of resistance in his rear proceeded, a threatening German salient existed between Byelostok and Praga on both sides of the Bug. Zakharov's pressure on the north-eastern side of this salient, however, prevented its becoming a serious danger to Rokossovsky.

The wave of optimism caused by the unbroken success of the Red Army led to an under-estimation of German powers of recovery, and at the end of July, although Rokossovsky had to fight harder and

German Power Under-estimated

harder as he approached Praga, it was generally assumed that he would capture that area without much difficulty and probably also Warsaw itself. General Komorowski (known as General Bor), leader of the Polish underground army, given authority to exercise his own judgement by the Polish Government in London started a general rising. The course of the heroic and tragic struggle is described in page 3206. Praga, strongly fortified bridge-head suburb on the east bank of the Vistula was, as it has always been, the

RED ARMY REACHES PRAGA—SUBURB OF WARSAW

Self-propelled gun of Marshal Rokossovsky's 1st White Russian Army in action in the streets of Praga (1), eastern suburb of the Polish capital whence across the Vistula Warsaw itself can be seen (3). Although the Soviet forces had approached the outskirts of Praga by late July 1944, so tough was the German defence of this key-position that it took Rokossovsky until September 14 to reduce it   Troops of the Polish 1st Army shared in the street fighting (2)

GERMANY COMPELLED TO FIGHT ON HER OWN SOIL AT LAST

In a Russian Order of the Day dated October 23, 1944, the historic announcement was made that General Chernya-khovsky's 3rd White Russian Army, taking the offensive on a large scale, had crossed the frontier into East Prussia, penetrating to a depth of 18 miles on an 85-mile front. 1. Soviet heavy artillery moving up through Schirwindt, one of a number of German towns taken after savage fighting. 2. Powerful steel and concrete field fortifications demolished by Russian shell fire   3. Ilyushin-2 bombers of the Red Air Force support the advance into Germany.

Photos, U.S.S.R. Official ; Planet News

CHERNYAKHOVSKY'S GUNS ON THE BANKS OF THE NIEMEN
Again and again during their retreat to the west in the summer and autumn of 1944, the German armies sought to make a stand on the succeeding river lines. The Russian bridge-heads over the Niemen, from which the 3rd White Russian Army broke out to capture Kovno (Kaunas), on August 1, were particularly fiercely contested. Here Soviet artillery is about to cross the river after the fighting had moved north-westwards. *Photo, Pictorial Press*

key to Warsaw in an attack from the east, and the Germans fought hard for it. They launched counter-attacks of great violence with a considerable measure of success, and Rokossovsky did not take it until September 14, when he had cleared pockets in his rear and closed up his army.

By that time, bridges had been blown up, the Germans had consolidated their defences on the west bank and the Poles in Warsaw were in a desperate con- **Germans Consolidate on the Vistula** dition. But Rokossovsky considered it impracticable to attempt to force the river to their assistance in face of the formidable defences. Instead, he directed his operations northwards towards the Narew, on which river Zakharov had extended his front westward by capturing Ostralenko (September 6) and Lomza (September 13).

After his capture of Yaroslav, Przemysl and Lwow at the end of July, Koniev swung his spearhead north to clear the line of the San up to its confluence with the Vistula, and to join hands with Rokossovsky's left on the east bank of the latter river. This operation was completed by July 31,

and by August 3 considerable progress had also been made along the Yaroslav-Cracow railway towards Tarnov. On that date a more important success was gained, a bridge-head being secured across the Vistula. In a few days it was considerably expanded in spite of violent and persistent counter-attacks, although Sandomierz, an important stronghold on the left bank, was not taken until August 18. At this stage Koniev may have intended to thrust north-west in order to assist Rokossovsky in forcing a passage of the Vistula farther north; but the intention, if formed, was abandoned in view of the growing strength of the German opposition. In fact he maintained his bridge-head with difficulty, in face of increasing attempts by the Germans to eliminate it.

Koniev's progress eastwards was also halted short of Tarnov by the middle of August; but south-westwards of Lwow he had by then made considerable progress in the upper Dniester valley and

in the Carpathian foothills. On August 5 Koniev was credited with forcing the Stryj River, a tributary of the Dniester, and capturing Stryj.

An important regrouping of Russian forces in that region was revealed when an Order of the Day for August 6 announced that the 4th Ukrainian Army had captured Drohobycz. **Thrust to the Carpathian Passes** This army, which included troops accustomed to mountain warfare in the Caucasus, had last been heard of in the Crimea under Tolbukhin's command, but now General Petrov was its commander. This reinforcement relieved Koniev of anxiety on his left flank and enabled him to concentrate for operations westwards. But Petrov's immediate objective was the important oilfield centred on Borislav, which he captured on August 7. In some quarters it was suggested that Petrov had been given the task of forcing the Carpathian passes and carrying the war into the Hungarian

ALLIED EQUIPMENT AIDS THE RED ARMY'S OFFENSIVE

The weapons of war speedily sent by Britain and America to aid their Russian ally soon found their way to those sectors of the vast battle front best suited to their specialized use. Here, in the open country of the Ukrainian front, British Valentine Mark 9 tanks move forward with the Red Army advance in August, 1944. Trucks from the U.S.A. were used by this same Russian unit.
Photo, Pictorial Press

plains, but at the time it seemed improbable that he would do more than attempt to seize the passes as a defensive measure, and possibly with a view to an ultimate offensive.

By the middle of August, the Soviet offensive in Lithuania and Poland had exhausted its momentum.

Chernyakhovsky after his capture of Kovno (August 1), continued to meet stubborn resistance as he worked his

Chernya-khovsky in East Prussia

way nearer the East Prussian frontier in a series of local engagements. It was however, not until October 23 that an Order of the Day announced that he had taken the offensive on a large scale and had broken into German territory to a depth of 18 miles on an 85-mile front, capturing a number of frontier

towns and Goering's hunting lodge. Nothing could have done more to stimulate morale on both sides than the fact that the German frontier had been crossed, and fighting was savage, the Germans counter-attacking violently though without recovering much lost ground. They, however, held an immensely strong and heavily fortified defensive zone of great depth and, after the first break in, the front was soon stabilized except for fierce local attacks and counter-attacks. Chernyakhovsky can have had little expectation of breaking through the notoriously strong Insterburg gap towards Koenigsberg. The

object of his offensive was probably to draw still more troops to East Prussia, thus reducing the possibility that they might be used in a counter-offensive against Rokossovsky. His offensive and the further localized operations Chernyakhovsky conducted in the late autumn also gave Bagramyan greater freedom for his operations in Latvia.

The Russian summer campaign in Poland and Lithuania had thus run its course, and the Germans had succeeded in staging a partial recovery which enabled them again to present a stabilized front. Nevertheless the Soviet forces had brilliant achievements to their credit in this campaign, and the enemy's losses had been immense and irreplaceable. Moreover, in Latvia and Estonia (*see* Chapter 329), in Rumania and Bessarabia (*see* Chapter 340), they had suffered further disasters.

HOW RUSSIAN ARMOUR CROSSED THE VISTULA

Successful forcing of river barriers, frequently considered impassable by the German defenders, was largely the result of the unorthodox tactics adopted by the Russian engineers. Pneumatic floats for infantry, rubber assault boats, rafts of all kinds and massive ferries, towed by motor-boats like that here seen conveying tanks and their crews across the broad Vistula, were among the methods employed. (See also illus. in pages 3224 and 3340.) *Photo, Planet News*

Chapter 329

FREEING OF BALTIC REPUBLICS AND FINLAND

*The Military Editor, Major-General Sir Charles Gwynn, here continues the
history of the successful campaigns fought by Soviet Armies during the summer
and autumn of 1944 in Finland (which in September changed sides) and in the
Baltic Republics. Except for the Courland promontory, where remnants of
a German army were penned, Estonia, Latvia, Lithuania and Finland were
cleared of the enemy by the end of the year. For other Soviet operations in
1944, see Chapters 305, 310, 318, 328, and 340*

AFTER co-operating with Chernyakhovsky's 3rd White Russian Army
in the capture of Vitebsk (June 26),
Bagramyan's 1st Baltic Army struck
north-west along both banks of the
Dvina, which he had crossed from the
north in effecting the encirclement of
Vitebsk. His first objective was the
great railway junction of Polotsk which
had resisted Russian attacks successfully in the spring. After it had been
outflanked to the south-west, Polotsk
was captured by storm on July 4, the
day after Chernyakhovsky and Rokossovsky captured Minsk. Thereafter
Bagramyan's right pushed on along the
Polotsk-Dvinsk railway on the north
bank of the Dvina for about thirty
miles to Trudi, but the weight of his
army advanced south of the river. His
object was to strike at the communications of Colonel-General Lindemann's
Group in the great salient it occupied in
Latvia and Estonia, while at the same
time covering the right of Chernyakhovsky's thrust into Lithuania from a
possible counter-attack. Thus by July 10,
while his right remained poised about
Trudi, Bagramyan's left had outflanked Dvinsk and was fighting " south
and south-west of the city " cutting the
railway and highway leading to Kovno.

The Russians had, however, no intention of giving Lindemann liberty to
concentrate for a counter-stroke, and
on July 12 it was an-
nounced that the 2nd
Baltic Army under
General Andrei Yere-
menko (last heard of in the Crimea—
see illus. in page 3133) had taken the
offensive on the Novo Sokolniki front,
west of Veliki Luki, and had broken
through to a depth of twenty miles on a
front of ninety miles, capturing Idritsa.
At the same time Bagramyan's right
wing apparently spread north-west from
Polotsk to co-operate. The Germans in
the previous winter had fought hard
west of Novo Sokolniki when they were
stabilizing their front in the eastern
borderland of Estonia and Latvia :
their particular object at that point
being to cover Idritsa on the Veliki
Luki-Riga railway where it crosses the
line from Pskov to Polotsk. The former

2nd Baltic Army Takes Offensive

line was indicated as the axis of a
Russian advance towards Riga, while
the latter was a valuable line of lateral
communication on the German defensive front.

On July 14 Yeremenko, by capturing
Opochka farther north on the lateral
railway, eliminated another anchor defence centre which the Germans fought
desperately to hold. This success was

GENERAL MASLENNIKOV

Commander-in-Chief of the 3rd Baltic Army
in the summer of 1944, Colonel-General
Ivan I. Maslennikov was promoted Army
General at the end of July. He stormed Pskov
on July 23, Tartu (Estonia) on August 25.
Together with General Yeremenko of the
2nd Baltic Army he captured Riga, capital
of Latvia, on October 13.

Photo, Pictorial Press

won in typical Russian fashion by a
direct attack from the east, under cover
of a furious artillery bombardment,
while the previous capture of Idritsa
opened the way for an encircling attack
from the south, preventing retreat in
that direction. This manœuvre had
been made possible by securing in the
Idritsa fighting a crossing of the Velikaya River which formed the main
defensive position between that town

and Opochka. By these successes Yeremenko had well and truly broken
through the " Panther " position, which
Russian commentators noted as yet
another proof of the failure of Hitler's
attempt, when driven on to the defensive, to re-establish the trench warfare
conditions of the first great war. Of the
key strongholds of the " Panther " line
only Pskov and Ostrov remained, and
everywhere south of Ostrov conditions
were fluid.

From Idritsa, Yeremenko pressed
west along the Riga railway, capturing
on July 17 Sebezh, just short of the
Latvian border. Two
days later an Order of
the Day announced
that, farther north, the
3rd Baltic Army under Colonel-General
Maslennikov had also taken the offensive and had crossed the Velikaya south
of Ostrov, creating a breach twenty-
five miles deep and forty-four miles
wide. Following what was now becoming an almost routine manœuvre,
Maslennikov outflanked Ostrov and
then carried it by storm on July 21.
On the following day it was announced
that Bagramyan, who had been advancing rapidly south of the Dvina,
by-passing Dvinsk, had reached and
captured Ponovezh, an important
centre of communication in the heart
of Lithuania, thus cutting a number of
roads connecting the Baltic Republics
with East Prussia.

Maslennikov Attacks

The offensive of the three Baltic
Armies was by now well under way, and
on July 23 the last German stronghold
on the German front south of Lake
Peipus was taken, when Maslennikov
carried Pskov by storm. The capture of
Pskov removed an important block
on the Leningrad-Dvinsk railway, and
that line was further cleared when on
July 27 Yeremenko captured not only
Rezekne but Dvinsk itself. Dvinsk, for
which the Germans fought desperately,
had for some days been closely threatened, not only by Yeremenko's troops
from the east and north-east, but also
by Bagramyan's outflanking movements
to the south-west which had removed
all hope of the garrison's escaping to
the south. The capture of Dvinsk, by

SOVIET INFANTRY PASS THROUGH PSKOV

One of the oldest towns of Russia, close to the Estonian border, Pskov was carried by assault by the 3rd Baltic Army on July 23, 1944. By the capture of this last stronghold on the German front south of Lake Peipus an important block on the Leningrad-Dvinsk railway was removed. Here the newly created Red Army defeated the Germans in its first action, in February 1918.

salient formed by the Baltic Republics, when the danger of his being cut off from East Prussia and of his being pinned against the Baltic coast was so obviously growing ? Partly, it may be believed, owing to Hitler's obstinate refusal to face strategical implications ; but no doubt also in order to maintain contact with Finland and to prevent her from dropping out of the war, which was becoming likely as her situation grew more desperate and prospects of German assistance more remote (*see* Chapter 327).

Operations in Finland

In Finland, Meretskov had cleared the Murmansk-Leningrad railway line by June 29 (*see* page 3222), on which date he took Petrozavodsk. On July 5 he reached Salmi on the east side of Lake Ladoga, where the Finns fought hard in 1940 (*see* Chapter 50). A week later he had cleared the northern end of Lake Ladoga, making contact with Govorov's Army, and also occupied Suojarvi (July 13), the scene of 1940 battles and the head of a branch railway leading to the pre-1940 Finnish frontier. He had thus recovered nearly all the territory annexed by Russia under the 1940 Treaty and thereby apparently fulfilled the task set him.

opening direct communication between Leningrad and Polotsk, gave promise of markedly strengthening Bagramyan's lines of communication as soon as the railways could be restored to service.

The situation of Lindemann's Group in the Baltic States was becoming increasingly precarious, for it had suffered another blow when on July 26 Marshal Govorov took Narva, thus opening a direct road into northern Estonia from Leningrad. The Narva River had been crossed during the winter campaign, but

the defences of Narva itself resisted attack and the space between Lake Peipus and the Gulf of Finland was too narrow and marshy to admit of bypassing manoeuvres.

Why did Hitler insist on Lindemann's remaining strung out in the long narrow

GUERILLAS SABOTAGE GERMAN COMMUNICATIONS

In all the Baltic countries, as in others occupied by Germany, there were active and efficiently run underground organizations. An illicit trade union newspaper was published regularly and distributed secretly in Vilna, reporting the struggle of the partisans against the invader. Important among the guerillas' many harassing activities was the disruption of enemy rail traffic: here a freight train has been derailed by them in the Vilna area. *Photos, Planet News*

The chief military objects Govorov and Meretskov had achieved were the removal of the latent threat to Leningrad and the liberation of the Murmansk railway, while the political results were sufficiently satisfactory to allow of reasonable peace terms being offered to Finland, no longer a source of danger. (For the course of the negotiations between Finland and the Allies, *see* Chapter 327.) The Finns ceased operations on September 4, and next day the Red Army sounded the " cease fire " on the Finnish front.

This left Rendulic's Army in the Murmansk - Petsamo area in a precariously isolated position, for the Finns had undertaken (*see* Historic Document 283, page 3328) that if it did not withdraw before September 15 they would take action against it in co-operation with the Russians. The chief anxiety of the Finns was to prevent their country, if possible, from becoming a battleground for Russian and German armies. But Rendulic remained in northern Finland, and as a further proof that the Germans were not disposed to acquiesce in Finland's surrender, on September 15 they attempted to seize the island of Hogland in the Gulf of Finland. The Finns successfully beat off the attack, and the only result was to make them actively hostile to their late ally. The Hogland episode showed the German fear that, with the defection of Finland, the Russian Fleet might emerge into the Baltic—one more reason probably for their continuing to hold on to Estonia, not only as an air base but in order to deny Tallinn and other Estonian ports to the Russians.

Although Rendulic did not withdraw on the date stipulated in the terms imposed by the Allies on Finland, it was clear that, with the prospect of the Finns' co-operating with the Russians and cutting his communications with the head of the Gulf of Bothnia, his position had become impossible. The Finns were, in fact, compelled to close that route, leaving him only the possibilities of evacuating by sea from Petsamo and Kirkenes or of retreat into northern Norway. Neither was an attractive prospect, for in the one case there was shortage of shipping and the danger of attack by the British and Russian Navies, and in the other he was faced by a long march through desolate country in an Arctic winter. He was forced to take the second course, pursued by Russian troops under Meretskov's command. To check pursuit he adopted a scorched earth policy, burning Finnish villages as he withdrew. This

Finns Attack Their Late Ally

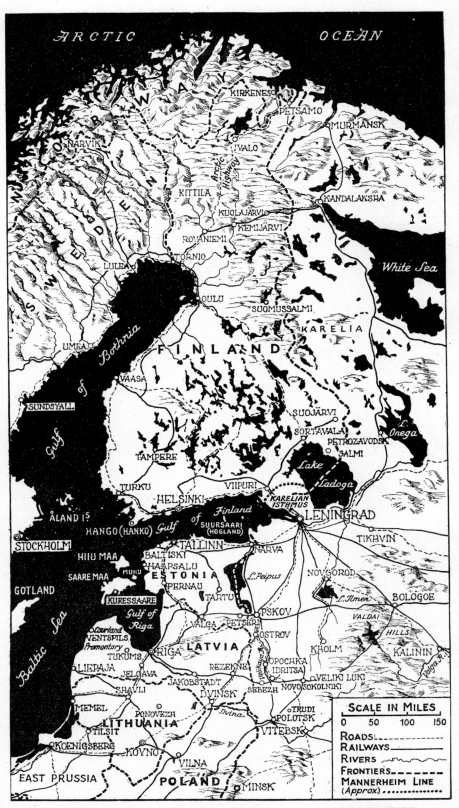

BALTIC STATES AND FINLAND CLEARED OF THE ENEMY

This map shows the scene of the successful offensives by Soviet Armies of the Baltic, Leningrad and Karelian fronts in the summer and autumn of 1944. These skilfully planned and executed operations cleared the Germans by the end of the year from Estonia, Latvia and Lithuania with the exception of a small pocket of the enemy penned in the Courland Promontory. The ' cease fire ' sounded by the Red Army on the Finnish front on September 5 did not end the fighting in that country, for the Germans were not finally driven out until the end of October and the people of northern Finland suffered much during their expulsion.

WITH GENERAL MERETSKOV'S FORCES IN KARELIA

On the Karelian front a new Russian offensive against the Finns opened on June 10, 1944, and continued against the Germans after the Finns were forced out of the war on September 5. 1. The Russians illuminated their front in Karelia during the long, dark night of the northern winter by means of rocket flares. 2. Coastal gun of the Red Banner Baltic Fleet shells Finnish fortifications. 3. Red Army troops examine armoured pill-box domes abandoned by the Finns in retreat: the domes had never served their intended purpose. 4. Soviet infantry use rubber floats to cross a lake in the Karelian isthmus.

stirred the Finns into more active co-operation with the Russians, for one of their chief objects in accepting the Allied terms had been to save their country from the effects of further war. They therefore not only attacked German detachments on the "Arctic Highway" between Petsamo and the Gulf of Bothnia, but also closed the easier inland road leading into Norway, compelling Rendulic to take the longer and more difficult coastal route.

Meretskov, pursuing from Murmansk, prevented Rendulic from making any prolonged pause at Petsamo, and on

Petsamo Liberated

October 15 he and Admiral Golovko were credited with the capture of that valuable port. Within a week, he had liberated the whole Petsamo region, including

FINNISH ARMY PURSUES THE RETREATING GERMANS
In accordance with the terms of the armistice signed on September 19, 1944, Finnish troops co-operated with the Russians in clearing the Germans from their country. The enemy in their withdrawal northwards burned the towns and villages with savage thoroughness so as to hinder pursuit. Here Finnish units pass through blasted Kittila—see map in page 3339.
Photo, Keystone

C.-in-C., KARELIAN FRONT
General Kiril Meretskov, commanding the Red Army on the Karelian Front, launched the final attack on Finland in June 1944, in collaboration with General Govorov. After the surrender of the Finns, and with their assistance Meretskov forced the Germans to retire to the north. He was promoted Marshal towards the end of October.
Photo, Pictorial Press

the nickel production area, and on October 25, after crossing the Norwegian frontier, he captured Kirkenes. Thus in ten days Germany had lost two bases from which convoys to Murmansk could most easily be attacked, and also what had become almost her last source of nickel, so essential to her war industries. The pursuit continued under arctic conditions with the Germans adhering to their scorched earth policy in its most barbaric forms, looting, burning villages and fishing boats, and leaving the native population to die of exposure and famine, except where they were

rescued by the advancing Red Army. The retreat was on the whole successfully carried through, but it added one more blot to the record of the Wehrmacht.

To return to the operations of the three Baltic armies : after the capture of Dvinsk, Rezekne and Pskov in the last days of July, the progress of the armies under Yeremenko and Maslennikov was slowed down by determined

General RENDULIC
General Lothar Rendulic was appointed C.-in-C. of German forces in Finland and Norway after General Dietl's death, announced on June 29, 1944. His retreat before the Russians from Finland into Norway was marked by a ruthless 'scorched earth' policy. He was transferred to the Eastern front in January 1945.

General LINDEMANN
Colonel-General Lindemann was C.-in-C. of the German Army groups in the Baltic Republics in the summer of 1944, until, following reports of disagreement with Hitler, he was replaced on August 30 by Colonel-General Ferdinand Schoerner. Here General Lindemann is studying a map at his headquarters.

resistance in difficult marshy country ; but Bagramyan continued to advance rapidly westwards. On July 27 he captured the important railway centre of Shavli and then struck northwards towards Riga, taking Jelgava on July 31 and thus cutting the last railway connecting Latvia and Estonia with East Prussia. Near as he then was to Riga, he did not attempt to rush its strong defences. Instead he turned north-west to capture, on August 1, Tukums, on the road leading from Riga along the southern shore of the Gulf of Riga, the only possible escape road to the south from Riga.

By that time Yeremenko had fought his way down the Dvina till he had approached Jakobstadt, where the Moscow-Riga railway crosses the river, but was then held up. Maslennikov, after fighting his way westwards round the southern end of Lake Peipus, was also checked. There was no definite pause, and heavy fighting continued in which Yeremenko and Maslennikov captured many villages, but for a time there were no advances of importance.

About August 10, after Mannerheim had become President of Finland (*see* page 3320), differences between Hitler **Hitler and** and Lindemann oc-**His Generals** curred as to the policy **Differ** to be pursued. Linde-mann, supported by other generals, advocated withdrawal, but Hitler was determined to remain in Estonia, hoping to browbeat the Finns into maintaining the struggle under Mannerheim, who had strong Germano-phile leanings. Hitler had his way. Lindemann was replaced by Colonel-General Ferdinand Schoerner who, pre-sumably in hopes of reopening commu-nications with East Prussia and a way of escape should he have to retreat, initiated a counter-offensive, in consider-able strength and with a high proportion of armour, against Bagramyan in the Shavli area. Though fierce fighting resulted, Bagramyan maintained his positions firmly and even extended the area he controlled. The pressure exer-cised by Yeremenko and Maslennikov prevented Schoerner from taking full advantage of his interior lines position, and his counter-offensive only resulted

THIS WAS THE NATIONAL HOUSE OF ART IN DVINSK
On the River Dvina in southern Latvia, Dvinsk was desperately defended by the Germans for some days before it fell, on July 27, 1944, to General Yeremenko's 2nd Baltic Army. Its capture opened direct communication between Leningrad and Polotsk, strengthening the supply lines of the 1st Baltic Army. Many of the city's buildings were demolished by the Germans
Photo, Pictorial Press

in loss of ground on their fronts also.

Maslennikov, having by August 11 captured Petseri, about 27 miles west of Pskov, then turned northwards up the west side of Lake Peipus, after August 20 attacking east and south of Tartu. Meanwhile the Germans had continued to counter-attack Bag-ramyan, especially in the Jelgava area, and on August 21 compelled him to withdraw from Tukums, a setback which was to have important con-sequences later.

On August 25 Maslennikov achieved an important success in capturing Tartu, the second largest city in Estonia and a famous ancient cultural centre, which stands on the main

FIRST BALTIC ARMY TAKE JELGAVA
The capture of Jelgava, south of Riga, on July 31, 1944, by troops of General Bagramyan's 1st Baltic Army in a quickly executed manoeuvre by tanks and infantry cut the last railway connecting Latvia and Estonia with East Prussia. Here Soviet assault troops are dislodging Germans from the battered area round the railway station, where fighting was bitter and prolonged.
Photo, Planet News

BALTIC TORPEDO-CUTTERS

Operations of the Red Banner Baltic Fleet between September 1941 and September 1944 were greatly handicapped by its being blockaded by the Germans. After Soviet advances freed the Gulf of Finland the Fleet effectively supported the Red Army, one instance being its co-operation in the capture on September 24 of the naval base at Baltiski, on the Estonian coast. Left, German A.A. boats off the Finnish coast.

Photos, Planet News

railway running from Riga to the Gulf of Finland and had been held by the Germans as a strongpoint on their line of communications. The success was brought about by skilful strategy, for Maslennikov, striking westwards along the Pskov-Riga railway, threatened the vital railway junction of Valga on the Estonian-Latvian border. To meet this threat troops were rushed from Tartu, and the Russians promptly took advantage of the resulting weakness to storm its defences.

After the capture of Tartu little news was released for some time about the Baltic front, except that fighting continued north of Tartu and that Maslennikov was pressing in on Valga from the north and south-east through difficult country. It was not till September 19 that Moscow announced that Valga had been taken and that Bagramyan, who had recently repelled renewed German counter-attacks at Jelgava, had gone over to the offensive and had broken through south-east of Riga to a depth of 25 miles on a 90-mile front.

Renewed Advances on Baltic Fronts

TWO BALTIC CAPITALS FALL

Riga, capital of Latvia, and Baltic naval base, fell on October 13, 1944, to the combined advance of the three Soviet Baltic Armies : here the Red Flag is being hoisted. Tallinn, capital of Estonia (top), was captured on September 22 by troops of Marshal Govorov's Leningrad Army : the smoke of burning buildings is seen behind the domes. *Photos, Pictorial Press*

With the Baltic front partially stabilized and operations in Finland over, regrouping had been proceeding behind the Russian lines with a view to an intensified combined attack on Schoerner's Group before it could adjust itself to the situation created by Finland's defection. For, simultaneously with Bagramyan's offensive, a new offensive was opened by Govorov north of Tartu, which in four days broke through on a front of 75 miles to a depth of 45 miles. At the same time he attacked west of Narva, and in three days advanced 37 miles. Schoerner may have already started withdrawing when Finland surrendered, but Govorov's offensive, coming immediately on top of the Hogland attempt, caught him by surprise, for it made progress at a rate which gave little indication that it was meeting well-organized rearguard opposition. Moreover there was nothing to show whether the Germans were retreating to the Baltic ports with a view to evacuation by sea, or whether their aim was to concentrate in Latvia for the defence of Riga. If the former was their intention, the speed of Govorov's pursuit defeated it. His first objective was Tallinn, and on September 22, two days after the announcement of his breakthrough, it was captured. The following day he took Pernau, an important port in the Gulf of Riga. Meanwhile farther south the three Baltic armies were maintaining the offensive, all directed towards Riga.

One of the strategic results of the defection of Finland and the failure of the Hogland attempt came in evidence when, on September 24, the Baltic Fleet co-operated with Govorov's troops in the capture of the naval base of Baltiski, 26 miles west of Tallinn. On the following day Haapsalu, the last of the Estonian ports, was captured, and by then it had become only a question of mopping up to clear the whole of Estonia. The Germans failed utterly to make an organized stand though, as usual, determined resistance was offered by isolated rearguard detachments. This, however, only added to their losses, which in Estonia alone totalled over 30,000 killed and 15,745 prisoners besides wounded.

By October 1, having cleared the mainland of Estonia, the Russians were capturing the islands which command the entrance to the Gulf of Riga. On September 30 they secured Muhu (Moon), which forms a stepping stone between the mainland and Saare Maa (Oesel), and on October 3, by a skilful landing operation, captured Hiiu Maa (Dagö), the second largest island of the group. By October 7 they had gained a footing on Saare Maa and had captured Kuressaare, the chief town and port in the island. The rest of the island was quickly overrun, except the narrow peninsula at its southern tip, where the garrison was to hold out for a considerable time longer.

Gulf of Riga Islands Captured

Meanwhile the position of the Germans in Riga, in spite of the strong ring of defences surrounding the town and the large force now concentrated there, was becoming precarious. Maslennikov, Yeremenko, and Bagramyan's right wing were all closing in on it—Bagramyan's main body was held to the Shavli area by constant, though ineffective, German counter-attacks.

The Germans must have had a considerable force between Shavli and the Baltic, based probably on Memel and Liepaja. After it had recaptured Tukums this force, although railway communication was interrupted at Jelgava, may have been able to keep open a narrow and precarious road corridor between Riga and East Prussia. But on October 8 it was announced that Bagramyan, in co-operation with Chernyakhovsky's right wing, had gone over to the offensive in the Shavli region and had broken through the German lines in the direction of Memel, advancing in four days to a depth of 60 miles. Continuing the offensive, Bagramyan closed in on Memel and Chernyakhovsky on Tilsit. Neither of these important places fell in 1944, but on October 10 Bagramyan reached the Baltic coast between Memel and Liepaja, thus finally cutting off Riga. Then on October 13 came an Order of the Day announcing that Yeremenko and Maslennikov had captured Riga.

Capture of Riga

Schoerner may have made a last-minute attempt to escape to Memel, for he fought his way out of Riga through Tukums into the Courland promontory. He may, however, have only intended to join up with the troops at Liepaja and Ventspils on the west Courland coast, whence there would be a better chance of withdrawal by sea than from inside the Gulf of Riga. In the event he succeeded in withdrawing into Courland and there successfully resisted Russian attacks. At the date of writing (November 1945) it is still not known how much of his army was evacuated by sea, or whether his position in Courland made it still impracticable for the Russians to use the port of Riga after the tip of Saare Maa was cleared on November 24, when the Germans attempted to evacuate the garrison at the cost of several ships.

This virtually brought the campaign in the Baltic Republics to an end, and considering the difficult terrain and the immense operations proceeding elsewhere, it had been remarkably successful. Although it had not achieved the complete annihilation of Schoerner's army, it bottled it up securely and prevented it from exercising any further influence of importance in the war. It had undoubtedly influenced Finland's decision to withdraw from the war, and had released the Baltic Fleet from the Gulf of Finland. Moreover, it had successfully protected Chernyakhovsky's flank from any counter-offensive attempts Schoerner might have made against it.

DVINA BRIDGE DESTROYED

As they retreated in Latvia in the summer of 1944, the enemy blew up bridges over the River Dvina, on which stand Dvinsk and Riga : here German pioneers are running as the charges they have inserted in one of them explode. This photograph was among a collection found a year later in Goebbels's files in the ruined Ministry of Propaganda in Berlin.　　*Photo, Planet News*

Chapter 330

PROGRESS TOWARDS PEACE IN THE U.S.S.R.

As here recorded by Mr. Andrew Rothstein, the year 1944 was for the U.S.S.R. one of quickening preparations for the return to peacetime conditions. While the war effort rose to its maximum, far-reaching steps were taken to accentuate the developments already beginning in 1943, and described in Chapter 292, to rebuild disorganized economy and shattered family life, and to resume cultural progress in all the Republics of the Union

IN one of its rare wartime sessions (January 28–February 1), the Supreme Soviet adopted three important measures towards reorganization and reconstruction of Soviet life and economy. It approved a Budget which provided for a slight increase in expenditure on defence (from 124·7 milliard roubles in 1943 to 128·4 milliards in 1944); for a 44 per cent increase in capital expenditure on industry, agriculture, transport, municipal enterprise and housing, and for an increase of 38 per cent in expenditure on social and cultural services. Sixteen milliards out of the 44·7 milliards provided for capital expenditure were earmarked for the reconstruction of devastated areas; and two-fifths of the estimates for social and cultural services were for education, showing a 66 per cent increase compared with 1943. Though there is no reliable basis for expressing these values in sterling, since the purchasing power of the rouble is greater than its official British equivalent in some respects (e.g. rent and essential food-stuffs) and less in others (e.g. clothing), some idea of their magnitude can be gained if it is remembered that the pre-war exchange value of the £ was about 23½ roubles.

The second measure was to reintroduce the principle, abandoned when the Union of Soviet Socialist Republics was set up in 1922, that the constituent Republics should have their own People's Commissariats, or Ministries, for Foreign Affairs, under the Union People's Commissariat for Foreign Affairs, and that they should have the right to maintain their own foreign relations and conclude their own treaties. Parallel with this was the third measure—that the constituent Republics should be entitled to their own Defence

Commissariats (again under general supervision of the Union People's Commissariat for Defence) and form and train their own national Red Armies. Moving these proposals, Mr. Molotov pointed out that they were a sign both of the vastly increased strength of the Union as a whole since 1922, and of the political, economic and cultural growth of the Union (*i.e.* constituent) Republics.

During the subsequent twelve months, all the Republics formed their Foreign Commissariats and appointed their People's Commissars for Foreign Affairs. Ukraine and Byelorussia signed agreements with the Polish Committee of National Liberation on September 9 (*see* page 3203), concerning mutual repatria-

tion of evacuees and their settlement on the land ; Lithuania followed suit on September 22. The Estonian and Latvian National Corps and the Lithuanian National Division played a prominent part subsequently in the liberation of their countries.

Economic progress, particularly reconstruction of the regions devastated by the Germans (computed this year as measuring 580,000 square miles, with a population of 70 millions) was very marked. **Steps Towards Reconstruction** In Ukraine coal mines and blast furnaces, marten ovens, chemical factories and power stations, were laboriously repaired and set going. In the ravaged countryside over 3,000 Machine Tractor Stations—almost 100 per cent of the pre-war figure—were at work by the end of the 1944 harvest, and very big livestock deliveries (1,700,000 head) were made from the eastern territories of the U.S.S.R. In the liberated Baltic Republics the land (which the Germans had once again taken from the peasantry) was restored to the small proprietors at the rate of 25–75 acres per homestead according to circumstances, and landless peasants were set up with farms from State reserves. Small factories in these Republics employing up to 10 workers were not nationalized. Kharkov, Stalingrad, and many other ruined towns saw houses rapidly built, factories of building materials created, transport restored, green boulevards laid out, municipal services re-established. Nevertheless, at the end of 1944 many millions of Soviet citizens in the ravaged areas were still living in dug-outs where their villages used to stand, or in the basements and cellars of their razed towns. The great recuperative powers of the

SOVIET WOMEN IN INDUSTRY

In the U.S.S.R. in 1944 the drive for arms proceeded side by side with reconstruction in liberated territory. Reviewing the year's victories on November 6, Stalin declared, ' The matchless labour exploits of Soviet women and youth will go down in history, for it is they who have borne the brunt of the work in factory and on farm.' Soviet women are here repairing a Red Air Force bomber. *Photo, Pictorial Press*

TRENCHES FROM WHICH THE FINNS THREATENED LENINGRAD

Although Leningrad was relieved in January 1944, the Finnish armies still held strongly fortified positions in the Karelian Isthmus, only a few miles from the city. Attacking on June 10, the Soviet General Govorov's Leningrad Army smashed the Finnish lines to capture Terijoki, five days later piercing the Finns' second lines. Despite natural advantages, the defences failed to withstand the Russian heavy artillery. Timber-revetted trenches of the Finnish lines are here seen after their capture.

Photo, Planet News

CITIZENS OF ODESSA WELCOME THEIR LIBERATORS

The recapture of Odessa, Black Sea port and third city of the Ukraine, on April 10, 1944 (see page 3081) was the occasion of great rejoicing among its people. Rumanian and German forces had occupied the city for two and a half years, but as the Red Army entered it was joined by guerillas who had lived throughout the occupation in the sewers and catacombs. Some 200,000 civilians in Odessa and the Odessa region were shot, tortured, or burned to death by the enemy

Photo, Pictorial Press

LIBERATED ATHENS GREETS THE BRITISH

Athens and its port of Piraeus were entered without opposition on October 13, 1944, by a British Commando force transported in British and Greek warships and led by Colonel Earl Jellicoe (see illus. in page 3083). They received a thunderous welcome. Later, British and U.S. transport aircraft landed at Megara, 28 miles away, with much-needed food, clothing and medicines. Athenians are here seen cheering outside the Hotel Grande Bretagne, the British H.Q. in Greece. Below, crowds welcoming the troops at the Piraeus. *Photos, British Official*

GERMAN PRISONERS FROM WHITE RUSSIA MARCH THROUGH MOSCOW'S SILENT STREETS

As the Red Armies swept forward in their great offensive in midsummer 1944—complementary operation to the Allied landings in Normandy—the defeated Germans gave themselves up in increasing numbers. Towards the end of July, south-west of Brody (see map in page 3331) Marshal Rokossovsky's 1st White Russian Army took over 17,000 prisoners in one engagement alone. A few days earlier—on July 17—some 60,000 prisoners from White Russia, including several generals and many other high-ranking officers, were marched through Moscow's silent, though crowded streets : they were on their way to Siberia. Many seemed pleased at being captured.

Photo, Pictorial Press

national economy of the Soviet Union as a whole showed themselves unmistakably, however, in 1944. Coal output

Increase in Consumer Goods

increased by over 25 per cent compared with 1943, pig iron by 29 per cent, steel by 26 per cent, heavy engineering (on which the equipment of shattered works, railways and docks depended) by 31 per cent. Output of electric power in the Urals—the main seat of Soviet war industries—was doubled during the year. The agricultural plan for 1944, issued in March, provided for further large increases in land under cultivation, and by harvest time the area under crops was nearly 20 million acres above the 1943 figure. The light industries and food supply showed marked improvement, and household consumer goods began to reappear on the market, as each of the large factories began to apply Government instructions that special auxiliary workshops should be established to utilize waste and scrap materials for production of consumer goods. One of the big engineering feats of the year was the construction of a 500-mile pipe line for the conveying of natural gas from Saratov to Moscow.

Once again Socialist emulation—voluntary co-operative and competitive effort by the workers—was decisive in securing these results. At the end of the year there were 70,000 " front

line brigades "—volunteer teams grouping some 500,000 young workers—leading this movement in the factories. In the armaments industries 80–90 per cent of the workers took part in Socialist emulation, and about 35 per cent of them were " Stakhanovites " (*see* illus. in page 2508), working with exceptional efficiency on modern machinery. About 600,000 " public inspectors," nominated by the trade unions, devoted their spare time without payment to supervision of factory canteens, bakeries, laundries, and other establishments including crêches for their children set up for war workers (apart from the actual employees or volunteers working in these establishments). More than 16 million

townspeople grew food on their allotments, as against 12 millions in 1943.

Something of the same spirit was shown in the over-subscription of the 25-milliard-rouble (about £1,060,000,000) War Loan (issued May 5, closed May 12) by more than 3 milliards (£123,000,000). The subscribers were tens of millions of individual citizens, who put themselves down for a fortnight's to a month's wages, to be deducted over five months.

Casualty figures published by the Soviet Information Bureau on June 22 gave a measure of the sacrifice in human life and suffering made by the armed forces of the Soviet Union. In three years of war, 5,300,000 officers and men were killed, captured and missing. This

STUDENTS OF WAR STUDY A PUBLIC-DISPLAY MAP

In the city of Lwow in November 1944 a crowd—including troops of the Red Army—gathers round a large-scale map of the European war theatres. Flags indicate the position of the Allied armies as they close in on the Reich from east and west. Lwow, freed by the Russians on July 27, 1944, and included in Poland before 1939, lies east of the Curzon Line.

Photo, Planet News

widening measures of State aid for the encouragement of family life, and increasing protection of motherhood and childhood. This vast law (i) instituted extra lump payments and monthly allowances—over and above the statutory nursing allowance—to mothers on birth of their third child, instead of the seventh as previously; (ii) established monthly allowances for unmarried mothers, or free maintenance of their children in infants' homes should they prefer (with retention of their full parental rights) and, at the same time, abolished their right to sue for affiliation orders and maintenance; (iii) increased maternity leave at full pay to eleven weeks (previously nine weeks), with increased rations, and prohibited night work after the fourth month of pregnancy and during breast feeding; (iv)

DE GAULLE IN MOSCOW

On December 2, 1944, General de Gaulle and Mr. Bidault, French Foreign Minister, arrived in Moscow; eight days later a twenty-year Treaty of Alliance was signed between France and the Soviet Union. (See page 3358). Here the General, with Mr. Molotov, inspects the guard of honour at the railway station. *Photo, U.S.S.R. Official*

terrible figure, it will be noted, takes no account of the wounded, or of partisan and other losses of citizens not in the armed forces.

One of the big forward-looking social measures of the year was the Edict of July 8, issued by the Presidium (Standing Committee) of the Supreme Soviet,

INTO THE SUNSHINE AGAIN

As the Red Army advanced on all fronts in 1944, peasants who had been in hiding from the Nazis (some for over two years) emerged from the forests and mountains to return to the ruins of their native towns and villages. Most travelled on foot; some had an ox-cart to carry their few belongings.

Photo, Planet News

MOSCOW HEARS OF INVASION

News of the Allied landings in Normandy was first given to the Russian people at 12.43 p.m. (Moscow Time) on June 6, 1944, when Moscow Radio interrupted a concert to broadcast General Eisenhower's first communiqué. Throughout the day, crowds gathered in the streets and at mealtimes in factory yards to listen to the latest reports of operations as they issued from public loud-speakers. *Photo, Pictorial Press*

instituted a series of special decorations —the Motherhood Medal for mothers of five or six children, all living (apart from those who had perished or disappeared during military operations in the war); the Order of Motherhood Glory for mothers of seven, eight and nine children; and the title and Order of Heroine Mother to women who had borne and brought up ten children; (v) made parents of one or two children liable to the " Bachelor Tax," introduced for single and childless citizens as a war measure in November, 1941; (vi) laid down more stringent divorce procedure.

The Suvorov Schools (named after a famous Russian Marshal) provided, under the reconstruction decree of August 22, 1943 (*see* page 2928), to train war orphans and sons of partisans with a view to their taking commissions in the Red Army, were all in operation by the beginning of 1944, as well as a number of Nakhimov and Ushakov Schools, named after famous Russian Admirals and organized to train their pupils as young naval officers. All these schools gave a full secondary education as well as specialist courses. The principle of separation of the sexes at secondary schools in the main Soviet cities was extended to many other towns, and also to vocational (trade and railway) schools. A school-leaving, or "maturity," certificate for all children finishing secondary school was re-instituted, and special distinction in this examination was rewarded with gold or silver medals and exemption from entrance examinations at universities.

In the field of more advanced knowledge an Institute of History of the Natural Sciences and an Institute of Russian Studies (under **Pursuit of** the Academy of Sciences **Knowledge** of the U.S.S.R.); Academies of Pedagogics and Medical Sciences; and a Faculty of International Studies at Moscow University, at which several distinguished Soviet diplomats were lecturers, were established during 1944.

Soviet theatres in September 1944 celebrated the 25th anniversary of their passing under public control (exercised by the national or local authorities) and thereby receiving aid from public funds. In 1917 there were 153; when the U.S.S.R. entered the war there were eight hundred, playing in the languages of forty nationalities.

The life of the Russian Orthodox Church was darkened, on May 15, by the death of the Patriarch Sergei (elected in September 1943—*see* page 2940). Alexei, 67-year-old Metropolitan of Leningrad and Novgorod, decorated with the Defence of Leningrad Medal for his work during the siege (*see* illus. in page 2933), was appointed Acting Patriarch. In September he opened the first Theological Institute of the Russian Orthodox Church established since the Revolution. In October a Council of Christian Evangelists and Baptists of the U.S.S.R. was set up: like other nonconformist (*i.e.* non-Orthodox) religious communities, it came within the purview of the Council for Religious Denominations other than the Orthodox

IN THREE CITIES LIBERATED BY SOVIET ARMS

An officer of the first Soviet unit to enter Odessa on April 10, 1944 is greeted by citizens: a special medal was struck and presented to all—men and officers of the Red Army and the Red Navy and citizens—who defended the city during the 69 days' siege of 1941 (see Chapter 182). Top, students at Lublin, Poland, help to restore their school with material supplied by Russia. Below, a street in Kiev, capital of the Ukraine, under repair. *Photos, U.S.S.R. Official; Pictorial Press*

REPAIRING THE FAMOUS DNIEPER DAM

As soon as the Germans were driven from Zaporozhe (October 14, 1943—see page 2921), clearance work began on the great dam there, source of power of the Lenin hydro-electric station and pride of the first Soviet five-year plan. Pursuing their 'scorched earth' policy, the Russians breached the dam in August 1941 as they retreated (see illus. page 1834), and the Germans damaged the structure still further. Reconstruction started in March 1944. Here workmen are riveting steel girders—some 25,000 tons were needed—across one of the gaps.

Photo, Pictorial Press

Church, created by the Soviet Government in June 1944. (One for relations with the Orthodox Church had been set up in October 1943.)

As in previous years, Stalin's very rare public statements were followed with the greatest interest. In his Order of the Day for May 1 he declared that the German armies had been mortally stricken and had been forced back to their frontiers, but "the wounded German beast must be pursued close on its heels and finished off in its own lair." This could only be done if there were "joint blows from the East dealt by our troops and from the West dealt by the troops of our Allies." After the Western front was reopened on June 6 Stalin, asked to comment by a foreign journalist, declared a week later that never before had there been a warlike enterprise "so broad in conception, so gigantic in scale, so masterly in execution."

In his review of the year, on the eve of the Revolutionary anniversary (November 6), Stalin noted that, in the course of their decisive defeats, the German armies on the Eastern Front had been reduced from a total of 257 German and satellite divisions a year before to 204 German and Hungarian divisions (180 of them German) ; 75 German divisions were held in the West of Europe, without which "our troops would not have been

IN A SMOLENSK SPINNING MILL

Immediately after the expulsion of the Germans in September 1943, new homes and factories began to spring up. Within twelve months nine power-stations and four water-projects were in operation, 113 factories restored to working order and 43 new factories built.

Photo, Planet News

able to break the resistance of the German troops and to throw them out of the Soviet Union in such a short time." Surveying the economic achievements of the Soviet people, Stalin declared that it had been made invincible by "the Socialist system born in the October Revolution." On the subject of international relations, Stalin said there were necessarily differences between the Great Powers, but "these differences do not transgress the bounds of what the interests of unity of the three Great Powers allow." This was because the alliance between them "is founded not on accidental, transitory considerations, but on vitally important and long-term interests." He gave the warning that it would be naïve to think that Germany would not attempt to restore her power and launch new aggressions, and, for the first time since

SURVEYOR WORKS IN STALINGRAD

When the last shot was fired at Stalingrad on February 2, 1943 (see Chapter 269), over half-a-million people were homeless there. Rebuilding proceeded rapidly, and by mid-October 1944 nearly 10,500 dwelling-houses had been new-built or restored. Here a Soviet surveyor and his woman assistant are at work among the ruins. (See also illus. in page 2938.)

Photo, Planet News

1941, openly spoke of Japan as an "aggressor nation" (*see* page 3287). To guard against future peril, it was necessary to disarm completely the aggressive nations, to create an international security organization equipped with the necessary minimum of armed forces, and "to oblige this organization to employ these armed forces without delay if it becomes necessary to avert or stop aggression, and to punish those guilty of aggression." Finally, Stalin emphasized that all these measures would be effective only if the three Great Powers continued to act in a spirit of accord.

Reinforced by great military victories and by economic reconstruction, the Soviet Government in 1944 displayed vigorous and considerably increased diplomatic activity. It established official relations during the year with Iceland (January), New Zealand (April), Costa Rica (May), Syria, the Danish Freedom Council, and the Polish Committee of National Liberation (July), Lebanon (August), Iraq (September), Italy ("direct relations" in March and diplomatic relations in October), Chile and Nicaragua (December). The Soviet Government simultaneously with the Governments of the U.S.A. and the United Kingdom recognized the French Provisional Government in October. It refused to attend the International Air Conference at Chicago "because," announced the Soviet News Agency (Tass) on October

29—the very eve of the Conference (*see* page 3256)—" among the nations taking part are Switzerland, Spain and Portugal, countries which for a number of years have carried on a hostile policy towards the Soviet Union." On November 4, it announced the rejection of a Swiss request for diplomatic relations (*see* page 3157).

On January 11 the Soviet Government issued a statement regarding relations with the Polish Government in London (*see* page 3212), conciliatory in tone and underlining that the adoption of the **Diplomatic** Curzon Line as the **Relations** Soviet - Polish frontier was only a rectification of an injustice imposed by the Riga Treaty of 1921. The U.S.S.R., said the statement, wanted a strong, independent Poland, and would be glad to see it a partner to the Soviet-Czechoslovak Treaty of Friendship and Mutual Assistance : such a Poland could be reborn, not by seizing Soviet territory but by restoring Poland's ancient lands, wrested from her by the Germans when they were the stronger. An agreement signed with the Czechoslovak Government (*see* page 3214) provided for the restoration of full Czechoslovak administration in territories liberated by the Red Army. A similar agreement was made with the Polish Committee of National Liberation on July 26.

A joint Protocol, signed with the British and Canadian Governments on October 8, provided that the U.S.S.R.

G. Hrapak

ON THE HIGHWAY

WORK OF THE RED ARMY'S WAR ARTISTS

In Soviet Russia the artist played an important part in maintaining war-time morale. The Red Army had its own studios and employed artists to depict specific campaigns and incidents, their work being used for public display. At the Tretyakov Gallery, Moscow, in mid-1944, a Great Patriotic War Exhibition was held which later went on tour through the Soviet Union. Here are four typical paintings by Russian war artists.

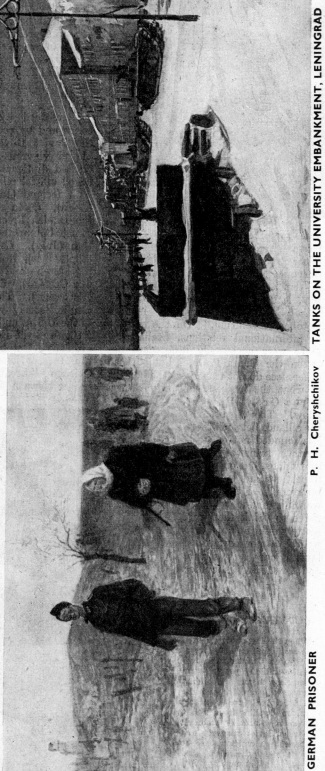

TANKS ON THE UNIVERSITY EMBANKMENT, LENINGRAD   Mikhail Platunov

Alexander Gorpenko

SPRING IN THE DONETZ

P. H. Cheryshchikov

GERMAN PRISONER

would pay 20 million U.S. dollars over six years, as compensation for the taking over of the Canadian-owned nickel mines in the Petsamo peninsula ceded by Finland to the U.S.S.R. under the armistice terms (*see* Historic Document CCLXXXIII, page 3328).

Marshal Stalin was unable to attend the Quebec Conference (*see* Chapter 339), but on its conclusion Mr. Churchill and Mr. Eden, accompanied by Field-Marshal Sir Alan Brooke, C.I.G.S., Sir Hastings Ismay, Chief of Staff to Mr. Churchill as Minister of Defence, and other military advisers journeyed to Moscow, arriving on October 9, to continue the Quebec discussions on Allied strategy with the Marshal and Mr. Molotov and their advisers. A communiqué issued on the 19th stated that at meetings held from October 9–18 " the unfolding of military plans agreed upon at Teheran was comprehensively reviewed in the light of recent events, and the conclusions of the Quebec conference on the war in Western Europe, and the utmost confidence was expressed in the future progress of Allied operations on all fronts. A free and intimate exchange of views took place on many political questions of common interest. Important progress was made towards a solution of the Polish question, which was closely discussed " (*see* page 3212). " . . . The march of events in south-east Europe was fully considered. Agreement was reached on remaining points in the Bulgarian armistice terms " (*see* Historic Document CCLXXXIV, page 3328). " The two Governments agreed to pursue a joint policy in Yugoslavia . . ." Mr. Churchill, seen off at Moscow air-field by Marshal Stalin, whom he referred to as his " friend and war comrade," described the Moscow conversations as " a council of workmen and soldiers."

During a visit paid by General de Gaulle and Mr. Bidault, the French Foreign Minister to Moscow, a Franco-Soviet Treaty of Alliance and Mutual Assistance was signed on December 10 (*see* page 3358). Like the Anglo-Soviet Treaty of May 1942, it was to be valid for twenty years and provided for automatic mutual assistance in case of German aggression.

In September and October, the Soviet Government pressed the Persian Government, with which American and British oil companies had been negotiating for concessions in Southern Persia, to grant it a concession, on terms more favourable to Persia, in the north. A Deputy People's Commissar for Foreign Affairs, M. Kavtaradze, visited Teheran for this purpose (*see* page 3060); but the Persian Government first refused and then secured a resolution from the

BRITISH EXPERTS HELP SOVIET RECOVERY
A million and a quarter tons of material—the cargoes of more than 98 per cent of the ships dispatched—reached Russia by the Arctic route during the six months ending April 1944. Here part of a mobile power station, specially designed by British engineers to follow the advancing Soviet forces, is being taken on board. These stations substantially assisted in restoring public utilities and restarting factories in areas recovered from the enemy, beginning with Stalingrad. *Photo, British Official*

Persian Parliament against the granting of any oil concessions during the war.

A Soviet delegation participated in the Dumbarton Oaks Conference (*see* page 3256). Stalin, in the speech of November 6 already quoted, called the draft statutes worked out there a " striking indication of the solidarity of the front of the United Nations."

In preparation for the end of the war, the Extraordinary State Commission for the investigation of Nazi atrocities went on with its reports on the large-scale torture and massacre of Soviet citizens, killing of Soviet prisoners of war, mass deportations to Germany, destruction and robbery of public, co-operative and private property, and destruction of historical monuments and other treasures, practised by the Germans in various parts of Soviet occupied territory. Hundreds of thousands of Soviet citizens and others testified before the Commission and its representatives. A mixed Soviet and Polish Commission investigated the massacre of 10,000 Polish officers at Katyn, near Smolensk, which the Germans in 1943 attempted to pass off as a Soviet atrocity (*see* pages 2735 and 2939 and illus. in page 2935).

The Soviet Government also appointed a special delegate to organize the repatriation of Soviet war prisoners and deported civilians; he was Colonel-General Golikov, who had been head of the first Soviet Military Mission to Great Britain in July, 1941.

During the year some important changes took place in the high authorities of the U.S.S.R. Mr. Nikolai Shvernik, secretary-general of the Central Council of Trade Unions of the U.S.S.R. for many years, became First Deputy-President (under Mr. Kalinin) of the Presidium of the Supreme Soviet—that is, assistant chief of the body which, in the Soviet Union, acts as Head of the State. His place in the leadership of the trade unions—this time as President of their Central Council—was taken by Mr. Vassili Kuznetsov. Marshal of the Soviet Union Kliment Voroshilov left the State Committee of Defence—the War Cabinet—to become chairman of the Allied Control Commission in Hungary. His place was taken by Army-General Bulganin (who had been formerly Chairman of the Council of People's Commissars of the R.S.F.S.R. —Russia proper—and, earlier still, director of one of the biggest Soviet electrical engineering works). Promotion to the rank of Marshal was accorded so several of the generals leading the victorious Red Army: to Koniev in February, Rokossovsky and Govorov in June, Malinovsky and Tolbukhin in September, and Meretskov in October.

FRANCO-SOVIET TREATY: THE CASERTA AGREEMENT

A twenty-years' treaty of alliance and mutual assistance, similar in aim to the Anglo-Soviet treaty of May 26, 1942 (see page 2107) was concluded between France and the Soviet Union on December 10, 1944. The articles are given here. The Caserta Agreement and Mr. Churchill's speech of December 26, 1944, in Athens, the main part of which appears below, had an important bearing on developments in Greece

Treaty of Alliance and Mutual Assistance between the Union of Soviet Socialist Republics and the French Republic, signed in Moscow, December 10, 1944.

1. Each of the High Contracting Parties shall continue the struggle on the side of the other Party and on the side of the United Nations until final victory over Germany. Each of the High Contracting Parties undertakes to render the other Party aid and assistance in this struggle with all the means at its disposal.

2. The High Contracting Parties shall not agree to enter into separate negotiations with Germany or to conclude without mutual consent any Armistice or Peace Treaty either with the Hitler Government or with any other government or authority set up in Germany for the purpose of the continuation or support of the policy of German aggression.

3. The High Contracting Parties undertake also after the termination of the present war with Germany to take jointly all necessary measures for the elimination of any new threat coming from Germany and to obstruct such actions as would make possible any new attempt at aggression on her part.

4. In the event of either of the High Contracting Parties finding itself involved in military operations against Germany whether as a result of aggression committed by the latter or as a result of the operation of the above Article III, the other Party shall at once render it every aid and assistance within its power.

5. The High Contracting Parties undertake not to conclude any Alliance and not to take part in any coalition directed against either of the High Contracting Parties.

6. The High Contracting Parties agree to render each other every possible economic assistance after the war with a view to facilitating and accelerating the reconstruction of both countries and in order to contribute to the cause of world prosperity.

7. The present Treaty does not in any way affect obligations undertaken previously by the High Contracting Parties in regard to third states in virtue of published Treaties.

8. The present Treaty, the Russian and French texts of which are equally valid, shall be ratified, and ratification instruments shall be exchanged in Paris as early as possible. It comes into force from the moment of the exchange of ratification instruments and shall be valid for twenty years. If the Treaty is not denounced by either of the High Contracting Parties at least one year before the expiration of this term it shall remain valid for an unlimited time, each of the Contracting Parties being able to terminate its operation by giving notice to that effect one year in advance.

Text of the Caserta Agreement signed in the presence of General Sir Henry Maitland Wilson, Supreme Allied Commander in the Mediterranean, by General Sarafis, leader of E.L.A.S., and General Zervas, leader of E.D.E.S., on September 24, 1944 :

1. All guerilla forces in Greece place themselves under the orders of the Greek Government of National Unity.

2. The Greek Government places these forces under the orders of General Scobie, nominated by the Supreme Allied Commander as G.O.C. in Greece.

3. The Greek guerilla leaders declare that they will forbid any attempt by units under their command to take the law into their own hands. Such action will be treated as a crime and punished accordingly.

4. As regards Athens no action is to be taken save under the direct orders of General Scobie.

5. The security battalions are considered as instruments of the enemy. Unless they surrender according to the order issued by the G.O.C. they will be treated as enemy formations.

6. All Greek guerilla forces, in order to put an end to past rivalries, declare that they will form a national union in order to co-ordinate their activities in the best interests of the common struggle.

Mr. Churchill, British Prime Minister, explains the presence of the British in Greece to Greek representatives assembled in Athens on December 26, 1944

Why is it we British came here ? We came with the knowledge and approval of President Roosevelt and Marshal Stalin. We also thought that at Caserta we had the invitation of all Greeks, including the commander of the E.L.A.S. army. In those days there were Germans to throw out, and it is quite true that we are in a different situation now. That is why we accepted when we were invited to come. That is why I take the pains to offer to the delegates of E.L.A.S. the statement of our position, that we consider we were invited and that we came with good hearts and full hands, with no thought in view but the restoration of Greece to her place, won by hard fighting, in the ranks of the Allies.

When victory is not so distant, why is it we cannot leave ? Since we have been here very violent and unexpected troubles have arisen, and we have been involved in them through doing what we believed was our duty. That duty we shall discharge inflexibly and faithfully to the end, but do not let anyone have in his mind the idea that Great Britain desires any material advantages from Greece. We do not want an inch of your territory ; we seek no commercial advantages save those which are offered by Greece to all the nations of the world. We have not the slightest intention of interfering with the way in which normal and tranquil Greece carries on its affairs. Whether Greece is a monarchy or a republic is a matter for Greeks and Greeks alone to decide. All we wish you is good and good for all.

What will enable us to leave Greece ? Naturally, now that all these tragic things have happened, we are bound in honour to bring this matter to a good conclusion. We must, of course, ask the acceptance and fulfilment of General Scobie's terms. We hope there may be established a broad-based Greek Government, representative of the Greek nation, possessed of sufficient armed power in a Greek national army, and with Greek police, to preserve itself in Athens until a fair, free general election can be held. . . . All we want from Greece is our ancient friendship. We thought it would be a good thing to have a talk around a table. . . . . Therefore we had a talk with M. Papandreou, who in the Lebanon, he was led to believe, was supported by all parties in Greece, and we proposed to him that there should be a conference like this.

I and Mr. Eden have come all this way, although great battles are raging in Belgium and on the German frontier, to make this effort to rescue Greece from her miserable fate and raise her to a point of great fame and repute. M. Papandreou said immediately that he would welcome such a conference, and we have all met here now in this city, where the sound of the firing can be heard from minute to minute at no great distance. The next British step was to invite the Archbishop to be chairman of this Greek conference. We do not intend to obstruct your deliberations. We British and other representatives of the great united victorious Powers will leave you Greeks to your own discussions under this most eminent and venerable citizen, and shall not trouble you unless you send for us again. We may wait a little while, but we have many other tasks to perform in this world of terrible storm. My hope is, however, that the conference which begins here this afternoon in Athens will restore Greece again to her fame and power among the Allies and the peace-loving peoples of the world. . . .

Chapter 331

TROUBLOUS TIMES IN THE BALKANS

To Greece and Yugoslavia, the two Balkan countries which had resisted German aggression, the year 1944 brought freedom again. But liberation from the forces of occupation did not mean the end of trouble and misery in them. In both countries there had been widespread destruction of the means of production and transport, and there was great scarcity of food. Both countries were rent by internal strife, which in Greece took the form of civil war. For the history of Greece and Yugoslavia and of their exiled governments in 1943, see Chapters 273 and 274

THE year 1944 began in Yugo-slavia with the Germans still more or less securely in possession of the main centres of the country, in particular the cities of Belgrade, Zagreb, Subotica and Sarajevo, the main ports like Susak, Split and Dubrovnik and the majority of the important railway centres. On the other hand the Army of National Liberation, led by Marshal Tito, was

LIAISON OFFICER
Brigadier Fitzroy Hew Royle Maclean, C.B.E., M.P. for Lancaster, was appointed Head of the British Military Mission to Marshal Tito in August 1943, before the recognition of the Marshal as a full Allied Commander. Formerly in the Diplomatic Service, the Brigadier had enlisted as a private in the Cameron Highlanders in 1941.
Photo, Associated Press

growing in strength. At that time it amounted, according to its leaders, to about 300,000 men (Mr. Churchill, in his speech of February 22, put it at more than 250,000), and by its existence and its continuous activities against German communications and supply lines it pinned down German, Hungarian and Bulgarian forces of a strength estimated by Marshal Tito on January 13 at 36 divisions, though it may be assumed that some of these were resting and re-forming after service on the Eastern Front.

The Germans made new attempts, somewhat less determined than in 1943, to put down the guerilla forces. An

offensive launched in December 1943 was followed by a second in January 1944, which resulted in the capture of Jajce, on the river Vrbas north of the Dinaric Alps, a town that had served as Tito's headquarters for a considerable time. But its recapture by the Partisans was reported on January 21. By the middle of February Tito's army won control of a large part of southern Slovenia, a territory of great strategic importance as through it or nearby ran some of the main lines of communication between the Reich and German-occupied northern Italy.

After Marshal Tito's recognition as a full Allied commander, his army received considerable help in the form of weapons, ammunition, instructors, medical and other supplies by air, and to some extent also by sea, along the long and rugged Dalmatian coast which the Germans could not effectively control in its full length. To the Chetniks under General Mihailovich, Minister of War in the exiled Yugoslav Government, no more help was given, as it had become clear beyond doubt that their leader had compromised with the Germans and that he was more concerned with fighting the Partisans, who were opposed to the centralized government of prewar times, than the enemy. There was, moreover, a steady flow to the Partisans of men who had previously served under Mihailovich (his forces were put by

Marshal Tito in May at a total of 16,000). In January Mihailovich convoked an "All-Yugoslavian National Congress," which, however, proved a failure.

Tito, on the other hand, certainly had adherents in all the national groups of Yugoslavia. His army was made up of 44 per cent Serbs, 30 per cent Croats, 10 per cent Slovenes, 5 per cent Montenegrins, the remainder consisting of Macedonians, Muslims, and foreign nationals, including two Italian divisions. It became increasingly clear that his was the only strongly organized force of resistance in Yugoslavia, an impression which gained ground even in the circles round the exiled government of King Peter II.

In March the young King arrived in London from Cairo, accompanied by his Prime Minister, Mr. Puritch. He

Marshal Tito's Supporters

TALKS BETWEEN SUBASICH AND TITO
Important discussions between Marshal Tito, President of the National Liberation Committee, and Dr. Ivan Subasich, Prime Minister of the Royal Yugoslav Government, were held from June 14-17, 1944. Subsequently, on July 7, a new Government was formed under the Premiership of Subasich which included representatives of Marshal Tito's movement. Here, Dr. Subasich (left) is lunching with the Marshal in the cave which for a time served him as headquarters.
Photo, New York Times Photos

BRITAIN AIDS YUGOSLAV PARTISANS

Britain would 'back Tito with all the strength we can draw,' announced by Mr. Churchill on February 22, 1944. 1. Tito's men guard German prisoners at Ledenice (N.W. of Cetinje) in November 1944, after a joint British-Partisan attack. 2. Yugoslav lad under instruction—in Malta—by a British soldier. 3. Partisans examine newly arrived American 'Stuart' tanks. 4. British gunners manhandling their 25-pounders aboard landing craft after raiding Loviste on the enemy-held Yugoslav coast, August 1944.

PARTISANS AND RUSSIANS LIBERATE BELGRADE

Traditional Slavonic sympathy between Yugoslavia and Russia was further cemented on October 20, 1944, when Belgrade, the capital, was freed after several days of street fighting in which units of the Yugoslav National Liberation Army joined with Marshal Tolbukhin's 3rd Ukrainian Army. Here is a scene in the newly liberated city where heavily armed Partisan troops patrolled the streets and guarded strategic points. *Photo, Pictorial Press*

had conversations with Mr. Churchill and Mr. Eden, and finally agreed towards the end of May to form a new government to be led by Dr. Ivan Subasich, a prominent member of the Croat Peasant Party who had been living for some time in the United States of America. Dr. Subasich went immediately to Yugoslavia, where he met Tito on June 14, and after a three days' conference, reached agreement with him on many questions. Back in London, Subasich, on July 7, formed a new "government of fighting unity" which included representatives of Tito's movement.

During his visit to Italy in August (*see* page 3240), Mr. Churchill talked with Dr. Subasich and Marshal Tito:

Churchill Meets Marshal Tito — "political and military questions were discussed in a spirit of entire frankness" — following which King Peter on August 25 withdrew recognition from Mihailovich by officially dissolving his headquarters, and on September 12 called on all Serbs, Croats and Slovenes to join Marshal Tito.

Meanwhile the Soviet forces on the Eastern Front were moving swiftly westwards through Rumania and Hungary (*see* Chapter 340); and the Southern Front moving northwards in Italy (*see* Chapters 302 and 338) was separated from Yugoslavia only by the narrow Adriatic Sea, dominated by the Royal Navy. A new Allied Commando Force, called Land Forces Adriatic, went into action on July 29, operating with the support of the Royal Navy and the R.A.F., obtained several footholds on the Dalmatian and Albanian coasts, and established contact with Tito's forces. During

September British troops landed by sea and air harassed the German forces as they withdrew. The main impact of Allied military power, however, came from the Russian side, in particular after the surrender and change of sides of Bulgaria. On September 28, the Russian Army, having obtained the willingly given permission of the Tito-Subasich Government, entered Yugoslavia from the east. On October 20 the capital city of Belgrade was freed after a German occupation lasting three-and-a-half years. (For military operations, *see* Chapter 340.) Soon all Serbia was free again. But a considerable part of the German armed forces from Greece, Macedonia and Albania succeeded in extricating themselves from encirclement and were concentrated in the north-west of Slovenia and in Hungary. Most of Yugoslavia, however, was free by the end of the year.

In October, Marshal Tito came to an agreement with representatives of the new Bulgarian Government (*see* page 3325) for military collaboration against "the common enemy, the German invaders," and Bulgarian troops which had been serving as occupation forces in parts of Serbia and of Macedonia helped, under the supreme command of the Red Army, to drive the Germans out.

On November 1, Dr. Subasich and Marshal Tito drew up an agreement, the principal provisions of which were (1) that King Peter II should not return to the country until the people had pronounced a decision on the subject; (2) that a Regency Council should be set up to wield the Royal power in his absence;

Regency Council Set Up

MEETING OF WAR LEADERS

Marshal Tito's forces were described by Mr. Churchill in the Commons in February 1944 as the only people doing effective fighting in Yugoslavia. Six months later, during his visit to Italy, Mr. Churchill met Marshal Tito for the first time, holding with him and Dr. Subasich conversations at which 'political and military questions were discussed in a spirit of entire frankness.' Mr. Churchill is seen here greeting the Marshal. *Photo, British Official*

GREECE AND YUGOSLAVIA

In 1944 Land Forces Adriatic, operating with the Royal Navy and the R.A.F. along the Dalmatian and Albanian coasts, materially assisted Marshal Tito's Army of National Liberation in freeing Yugoslavia. In Greece, where British and Greek regular forces landed in the Peloponnesus in early October, the Germans withdrew with very little fighting. But the country was still torn by civil strife.

(3) that a new Government should be formed composed of representatives of all the Yugoslav peoples. On November 20, accompanied by advisers, Dr. Subasich paid a visit to Moscow, where he saw Mr. Stalin, Mr. Molotov, and other Soviet statesmen. He returned to Belgrade, and two annexes to the agreement of November 1 were drawn up, the chief point of which was that elections for a Constituent Assembly should be decided upon within three months of the liberation of the whole country, a law on the elections for the Constituent Assembly to be enacted in good time. In an interview published on December 12, Marshal Tito said that the new

IN MUCH-DISPUTED SPLIT

Among the Yugoslav vantage-points fought over by Germans and Partisans was Split, on the Dalmatian coast. Tito's forces seized and held it for two weeks in September 1943, (see illus. on page 2726), recapturing it finally on October 29, 1944. Here a machine-hand removes newly printed copies of 'Free Dalmatia,' a Partisan organ printed in Split during the 1943 Tito occupation.

Photo, New York Times Photos

Yugoslavia would consist of six federal units (Serbia, Croatia, Slovenia, Bosnia-Herzegovina, Montenegro and Macedonia), each of which would have its own national government, some provinces having local autonomy within the framework of one of the federal units.

Dr. Subasich arrived in London on December 10, and negotiations for the formation of the Regency Council began.

While in Yugoslavia Marshal Tito came to the fore as an internationally recognized leader and successful warrior, in Greece no such person emerged either from the ranks of E.A.M. (Ethnikon Apeleutherikon Metapon, National Liberation Front) and its military organization E.L.A.S. (Ellenikos Laikos Apeleutherikos Stratos, Greek Popular Liberation Army), or from those of the right-wing group known as E.D.E.S.— initials representing both Ethnikos Dimokratikos Ellenikos Stratos (Greek

National Democratic Army) and Ethnikos Dimokratikos Ellenikos Syndesmos (Greek National Democratic Association), the organization behind the army.

Fighting between these two groups continued, though both also continued to attack the German occupation forces. The Allies, and in particular the British **GREECE** Government, tried hard to induce them to come to an arrangement which would ensure that they would not turn the weapons sent to them against each other, but only against the real enemy—the Germans. As a result of these appeals, in February 1944, E.L.A.S. and E.D.E.S. signed an agreement in which they undertook to cease hostilities against each other, to release all political prisoners and hostages, and to cooperate against the Germans.

son of the great liberal statesman of the First Great War, formed a government which lasted only until April 26. Next day, Mr. George Papandreou, leader of the Social Democratic Party and a man whose integrity and patriotism were highly respected in Greece (from which country he had just escaped), took office, and at once set about unifying and reorganizing all Greek political and

BRITISH TROOPS IN GREECE

Parachute troops landing in Greece (left) were aided by resistance forces. Among important airfields captured was Megara, 28 miles from Athens, taken on October 13, 1944. Next day, landing craft (below) brought British troops to the Piraeus, port of Athens, seized by Commandos twenty-four hours earlier. *Photos, British Official*

In March, trouble broke out among the Greek Government forces in Egypt. On March 31 a group of Greek Army, Navy and Air Force officers called on Mr. Tsouderos and demanded his resignation. At the Greek Government's request, they were arrested by the British. As a result, the men of the Greek warships at Alexandria and the Greek 1st Brigade mutinied and for three weeks refused to obey orders. The British naval and military authorities suppressed the mutineers, arresting a number of their leaders. Courts-martial subsequently sentenced twenty-four, including seven officers of the Brigade, to death; twenty-four, including nine officers of the Brigade, to life imprisonment, and thirty-five to imprisonment for from fifteen months to twenty years; ten were acquitted.

In the meantime, Tsouderos resigned. His Navy Minister, Sophocles Venizelos,

BRITISH AT SALONIKA AGAIN AFTER 29 YEARS
Cutting off the only escape for enemy garrisons on Crete, Rhodes and other Aegean islands, British patrols reached Salonika on November 1, 1944. Three days later, British troops landed in force, to find port installations completely destroyed, over 40 wrecks blocking the harbour and more than 2,000 mines sown in the approaches. After sweeping operations, warships escorted in a convoy on the 9th, bringing troops, stores, and transport. Here landing craft of the convoy are being unloaded.
Photo, British Official

military forces, both in Greece and out-side it. He called a conference, which met in the Lebanon from May 17-20, of delegates from all the Greek parties, including the Liberals, the Social Democrats, the Populists (Royalists), the Communists, E.A.M. and lesser resistance groups. Eleven of the twenty-five delegates came from Greece.

After lengthy and often difficult proceedings in which Mr. Papandreou as chairman showed much wisdom in bridging divergencies of opinion, the **The Lebanon Charter** conference accepted the policy he had laid down on taking office, namely : 1. Reform of the Greek Armed Forces ; 2. Unification of all guerilla forces in Greece ; 3. Suppression of terrorist activities by Greeks against their fellow-countrymen ; 4. Provision of food and medical supplies to the starving people of Occupied Greece ; 5. Full freedom for the Greek people to decide in a democratic and orderly way whether Greece should remain a Monarchy or become a Republic ; 6. Just punishment of all traitors ; and these were embodied in an agreement which became known as the Lebanon Charter.

Mr. Papandreou was then entrusted by King George with the task of forming a new Government of National Unity. He met fresh difficulties, E.A.M. representatives being unable to secure the consent of their followers in Greece to

their participation. However, on June 8 he formed a Government without them, with himself as Prime Minister, Minister of War and of Foreign Affairs. His predecessor, Mr. Venizelos, entered the Cabinet as Vice-Premier. Mr. Papandreou at once opened negotiations with E.A.M. leaders in Greece in an effort to persuade them to participate in the Government, at first without success. He visited Mr. Churchill in Rome on August 23, a step which led to the resignation of three of his ministers because, it was said unofficially, they objected to his not having previously consulted the Cabinet. On August 31, fresh delegates from E.A.M., endowed with full powers, arrived in Cairo from Greece at Mr. Papandreou's renewed invitation, and after further talks they agreed to join the Government, which was re-formed and broadened on September 2. A few days later, the Government moved from Cairo to Caserta, near Naples, in Italy, in order to be able to return to Athens immediately military developments permitted. By an agreement signed at Caserta on September 24, by Generals Sarafis and Zervas, leaders respectively of E.L.A.S. and E.D.E.S., in the presence of General Sir Henry Maitland Wilson, Allied Supreme Commander, Mediterranean, all the Greek guerilla forces placed themselves under General Scobie, appointed Allied C.-in-C., Greece (*see* Historic Document 286, page 3358).

The Germans at this time were withdrawing their forces from Greece and only weak forces remained on the mainland, though considerable bodies of troops still clung to Crete and some of the Aegean Islands, partly to hamper Allied operations, but mainly because British Naval and Air activities had prevented their timely evacuation.

Samos, from which the Germans had retired, was captured on October 6 by British and Greek troops operating from the Middle East, the Italian Fascist garrison surrendering after a brief show of opposition. Naxos surrendered to forces of the "Sacred Brigade" on October 15. Lemnos fell on the 17th, after some fighting, to a military force landed the previous day by the Royal Navy. Scarpanto was occupied on the 17th by a British naval party, which landed unopposed.

German resistance on the mainland was sporadic when, on the night of October 4-5, British and Greek regular forces, coming from Italy, began to land in the Peloponnesus, occupying the important town and harbour of Patras without opposition. Corinth was occupied on the 8th, a British Commando force liberated Athens and the Piraeus on the 13th, meeting no opposition.

Five days later Mr. Papandreou and the exiled Government landed at Heraklia from the Greek cruiser "Giorgios Averoff," and pro- **Exiled Government Reaches Athens** ceeded to Athens, followed by General Scobie. They were enthusiastically greeted by the population of the capital (*see* colour plate following page 3482), who had shown no less enthusiasm towards the liberating British forces. But these days of joy were short ; soon the tension between the old rival groups of the resistance movement became apparent again. Following the Moscow Conference (*see* page 3357), the British Foreign Secretary, Mr. Eden arrived in Athens on October 26 with Lord Moyne, Minister of State for the Middle East, for conversations with Mr. Papandreou, and was given the freedom of Athens. He said in the House of Commons on his return, " I do not believe that informed opinion in this country fully understands how complete, merciless, and dastardly has been the devastation inflicted by the German armies in Allied lands as they withdraw " with the deliberate object of bringing " to a standstill the whole life of the nation." The aim of British policy was first to send enough material help to get life running again in Greece, and then to promote a state of affairs which

STREET-FIGHTING IN GREEK CAPITAL

Difficulties soon followed liberation in Greece. On December 2 an E.A.M. demonstration in Athens was fired on by the police, and the Communists called a general strike for the next day. Following the attack by E.L.A.S. on the Anglo-Greek Naval H.Q. later on the 3rd, General R. M. Scobie, Allied G.O.C., ordered E.L.A.S. forces to quit an area round Athens by December 6. 1. E.A.M. followers surrender to British troops who had forced an entry into their H.Q. with tanks. 2. E.A.M. members and sympathizers assemble to bury victims of the December 2 shootings. 3. Mr. Papandreou, Greek Prime Minister, with General Scobie. 4. British troops pick off snipers.

ALLIED TROOPS CO-OPERATE WITH PARTISANS IN ALBANIA

Seaborne and airborne troops of Land Forces Adriatic, mainly British and supported by the Balkan Air Force, began operations on the Dalmatian coast on September 16, 1944, assisting partisans who had been organized by a British Military Mission to Albania since April 1943. Here Albanian shepherds watch Allied troops trudging along a dried-up river-bed.

the Anglo-Greek Naval H.Q. in the Piraeus was attacked by E.L.A.S. forces, three British being wounded. In defiance of the Government and General Scobie, 800 armed men of E.L.A.S. tried to enter Athens, but were disarmed by British troops, without incident.

The situation was most embarrassing for the elements of the British Army who had come to Greece as liberators and friends. It was certainly not the British intention to re-impose on the Greek people a reactionary regime they did not want. On the other hand, civil war would cause untold harm to the people of Greece, still suffering from the German occupation and retreat, and was likely to end in some sort of minority dictatorship. To prevent this development and to leave the way open for the Greek people to express their will by ballot instead of by the bullet, the British Army intervened. Its commander, General Scobie (under whom, it should be remembered, E.L.A.S. had agreed to serve by the Caserta agreement), acting under the instructions of the British Government, ordered all E.L.A.S. troops and police forces to leave a large area round Athens and the Piraeus, failing which they would be treated as enemies. They did not do so, and fighting developed more violently in and around Athens, the R.A.F. doing more machine gunning and dropping many leaflets explaining the situation. Fighting between E.L.A.S. and E.D.E.S. spread to Macedonia, and a general strike was declared in Salonika, bringing relief measures there to a standstill.

After a two-day debate in the House of Commons, in which the British Government and General Scobie received a great deal of criticism, Mr. Harold Macmillan, Minister Resident at Allied H.Q. Mediterranean, and Field-Marshal Alexander arrived in Athens for consultations with General Scobie, who, on December 12, issued the following terms to Mr. Phorphyrogenis, former E.A.M. Cabinet Minister: E.L.A.S. troops, as troops placed under his command, should move out of Attica, the province in which the capital lies; all E.L.A.S. supporters in Athens should cease resistance and hand in their arms. But the fighting

British Reactions

would allow the genuine, unfettered and peaceable expression of the political will of the Greek people as a whole.

On November 4, members of E.A.M. paraded the streets of Athens, carrying three dead bodies which they alleged were those of comrades murdered by right-wing terrorists and demanding the suppression of right-wing organizations. General Scobie announced on November 7, after conversations with Mr. Papandreou, that all guerilla forces, both E.D.E.S. and E.L.A.S., would be disbanded by December 10. This was part of an agreement accepted by all parties which provided that the Mountain Brigade and the "Sacred Brigade," which had been formed in Egypt and fought at Alamein and Rimini, should be maintained as part of a new National Army; that a special brigade of E.L.A.S. forces and another of E.D.E.S. forces should be formed, also for integration into the new army; and that the police should be reorganized.

Formation of New National Army

But mistrust between left and right wing was deeply rooted, a fact which may be more easily understood if it is remembered that for almost a decade, that is since General Metaxas seized power in 1935, the Greek people had been deprived of their democratic liberties, that this semi-fascist regime had been backed without reservation by

King George II, and that the King and his advisers were therefore considered hardened reactionaries by all the forces of the left. Fear was widespread that the King, by the force of arms, would try to have himself reinstated and that he would then suppress all the popular forces which, representing far more than the Communist Party, had formed E.A.M. The actions of the left, on the other hand, seemed to threaten all those opposed to E.A.M. with a left-wing dictatorship based on the military power of E.L.A.S.

The crisis was brought into the open when on November 29 the representatives of E.A.M. in the Government changed their minds and refused to sign the agreement they had already accepted for the disarming and demobilization of guerilla formations. When the other members of the Government, including the Prime Minister, declared that they would enforce the disarming of irregular forces as agreed, the six E.A.M. Ministers resigned and staged a protest meeting on December 2, despite a Government prohibition. The police fired on the demonstrators, almost in front of the British H.Q. E.A.M. announced that 15 had been killed, and 148 wounded, and the Communist Party called for a general strike next day. Sharp fighting broke out in the capital and elsewhere, and

MR. CHURCHILL FLIES TO ATHENS: ALL-PARTY CONFERENCE BY LAMPLIGHT

A dramatic development in the Greek internal crisis occurred on December 25, 1944, with the arrival by air in Athens of Mr. Churchill and Mr. Eden. Next day an all-party conference was opened with Archbishop Damaskinos, the Greek Primate, in the chair, and lit only by hurricane lamps, the local power station being out of action through a general strike. Here is the Archbishop at the conference, with Field-Marshal Alexander and Mr. Harold Macmillan on his left, Mr. Churchill and Mr. Eden on his right.

Photo, Associated Press

3 R³

LANDING AT WESTKAPELLE

First Admiralty statement on the Walcheren landings of November 1, 1944 (see page 3375) was given in the Commons by Mr. A. V. Alexander, the First Lord, a fortnight later. This disclosed that a Royal Marines Commando went close inshore at Westkapelle under heavy fire and—owing to bad weather —without air support. Landing-craft could beach only two at a time in the gap (see 4 above) torn in the dyke by the R.A.F. early in October. 1. Marines go ashore from a tank landing-craft. 2. Survivors from a sinking craft are picked up. 3. Light howitzer in action during the attack on Flushing.

Photos, British Official ; Associated Press

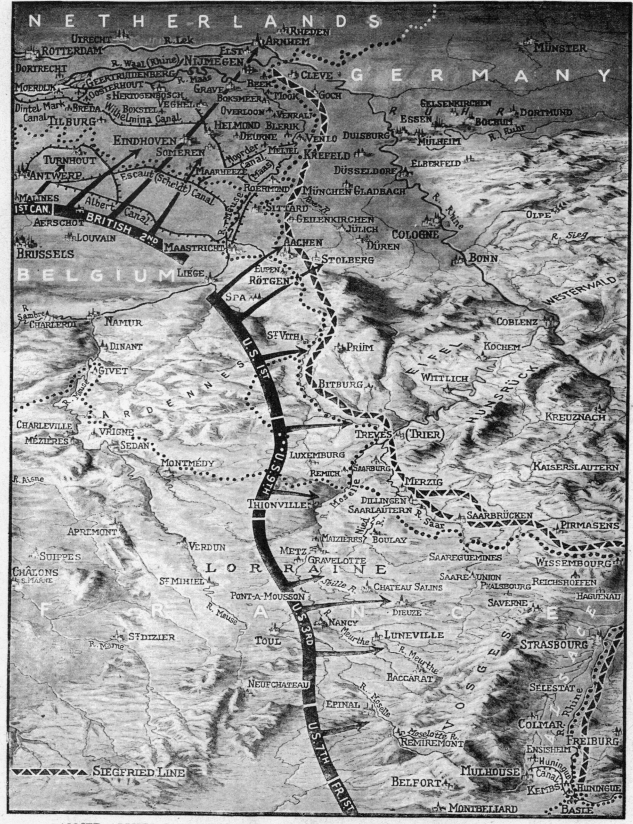

ALLIED ARMIES GROUP FOR THE ATTACK ON WESTERN GERMANY

By late September 1944 the Allied armies in France and the Low Countries were grouped approximately as shown here ; arrows indicate chief lines of attack. On October 23 the U.S. 9th Army (first brought into position on this front on October 3 after it had treed Brittany and conquered Brest) was interposed between the British 2nd and U.S. 1st Armies. Distances : Brussels to Belfort, 250 miles ; Brussels to Cologne, 120 miles.

continued, and relief measures had to be almost entirely suspended.

The House of Commons held another debate on Greece on December 20. On December 25 the British Prime Minister, Mr. Churchill, accompanied

Mr. Churchill Flies to Greece

by the British Foreign Secretary Mr. Eden, arrived by air in Athens, and invited all parties to join him in a round table conference. The conference, attended by E.L.A.S. representatives under safe conduct, met under the chairmanship of the Archbishop Damaskinos, head of the Greek Orthodox Church, a man who by his courageous stand against the German invaders and his general attitude had won a wide measure of confidence and respect in almost all Greek circles. The two British statesmen attended the opening of the conference, at which Mr. Churchill made an opening statement on the reasons for the presence of British troops in Greece (see Historic Document 287, page 3358), but later withdrew to leave the Greeks to settle their problems. Little was achieved in the way of a political rapprochement, but it was agreed that the King should be asked to nominate Archbishop Damaskinos as Regent of Greece as an essential prelude

to the solution of many problems. Mr. Churchill and Mr. Eden returned to London, and on December 31 the King of the Hellenes issued a proclamation making the desired appointment, and announcing his resolve not to return to Greece until invited.

Greece's relations were best with Turkey. Both countries were equally interested in security in the Eastern Mediterranean, both were equally determined to secure Thrace, where their common frontier runs, from every attempt by Bulgaria to separate them by gaining direct access to the Aegean. Propaganda, originating in certain Yugoslav quarters, for creating a "Greater Macedonia" which would include Salonica, Greece's second city and port, and its hinterland, led to bad feeling in Greece. On the other hand, Greek politicians tried to make a case for moving the Greek frontier farther north in the Epirus to take in some Greek communities lying on the Albanian side of the frontier—it was from this part of Albania that Mussolini launched his infamous invasion of Greece in 1940.

In Albania itself, the years 1943 and 1944 witnessed an impressive growth of the guerilla resistance movement under the guidance of a British Military Mission, led for over a year by Brigadier E. F. Davies (subsequently commander of Land Forces Adriatic)

ALBANIA

which arrived in Albania in April 1943. As in Yugoslavia and Greece, there was internal dissension among the Albanian partisans, who by the summer of 1944 numbered 20,000 trained men. British troops of Land Forces Adriatic landed in Albania on October 9, capturing Saranda that day and cutting off the German garrison in Corfu, invaded on the 13th when most of the enemy surrendered at once. On October 28 the quisling Albanian government which had been installed by the Germans after Italy's collapse in 1943 resigned. Tirana, the capital, was evacuated by the German forces on November 18 ; its actual occupation by partisans, and that of the port of Durazzo were announced three days later.

ALBANIAN PARTISAN TROOPS CELEBRATE INDEPENDENCE DAY

On November 28, 1944, for the first time since Albania's occupation by Italy in 1939, she celebrated Independence Day. It was the thirty-second anniversary of her freedom from the Turks. A partisan parade, attended by representatives from Britain, Russia, the U.S. and Yugoslavia, was held in Tirana. Here troops of the 1st Corps of partisans march past the saluting-base.

ALLIED ARMIES OF LIBERATION IN THE WEST

British, Canadian, American and French forces, with Polish, Dutch, Belgian and Czechoslovak units, and their commanders operating under the supreme command of General Eisenhower in early October 1944 in the advance on Germany from the West

Army Groups

21st ARMY GROUP under Field-Marshal Sir Bernard Montgomery.
(Chief of Staff : Major-General Sir Francis de Guingand.)

12th ARMY GROUP under Lieut.-General Omar Bradley.
6th ARMY GROUP under Lieut.-General J. L. Devers.

Armies

BRITISH 2nd ARMY under Lieut.-General Sir Miles Dempsey.
1st CANADIAN ARMY under Lieut.-General H. D. G. Crerar.
U.S. 1st ARMY under Lieut.-General C. H. Hodges. (Chief of Staff : Major-General W. B. Kean.)
U.S. 3rd ARMY under Lieut.-General George S. Patton, junior.

U.S. 7th ARMY under Lieut.-General Alexander M. Patch.
U.S. 9th ARMY under Lieut.-General William B. Simpson.
FRENCH 1st ARMY under General de Lattre de Tassigny.
ALLIED 1st AIRBORNE ARMY under Lieut.-General Lewis H. Brereton.

Other Units

BRITISH

CORPS

I under Lieut.-General J. T. Crocker.
VIII under Lieut.-General Sir Richard O'Connor.

XII under Lieut.-General N. M. Ritchie.
XXX under Lieut.-General B. G. Horrocks.

DIVISIONS

Infantry
3rd under Major-General L. G. Whistler.
15th (Scottish) under Major-General C. M. Barber.
43rd (Wessex) under Major-General G. I. Thomas.
49th under Major-General E. H. Barker.
50th (Northumbrian) under Major-General D. A. H. Graham.
51st (Highland) under Major-General T. G. Rennie.
53rd (Welsh) under Major-General R. K. Ross.

Armoured
7th (" Desert Rats ") under Major-General G. L. Verney.
11th under Major-General G. P. B. Roberts.
Guards under Major-General A. H. S. Adair.

Airborne
1st under Major-General R. E. Urquhart.
6th (including Canadians) under Major-General R. N. Gale.

REGIMENTS

Argyll and Sutherland Highlanders.
Black Watch.
Border.
Cameronians.
Cheshire.
Corps of Military Police.
County of London Yeomanry.
Derbyshire Yeomanry.
Devonshire.
Dorsetshire.
Duke of Cornwall's Light Infantry.
Duke of Wellington's (West Riding).
Durham Light Infantry.
East Lancashire.
Essex.
Gloucestershire.
Gordon Highlanders.
Green Howards.
Grenadier Guards.
Hampshire.
Highland Light Infantry.
23rd Hussars.
King's Own Royal.
King's Own Scottish Borderers.

King's Own Yorkshire Light Infantry.
King's Royal Rifle Corps.
King's Shropshire Light Infantry.
Lancashire Fusiliers.
Leicestershire.
Lincolnshire.
Manchester.
Middlesex.
Monmouthshire.
59th Newfoundland Heavy R.A.
Nottinghamshire Yeomanry (Sherwood Rangers).
Oxfordshire and Buckinghamshire Light Infantry.
Pioneer Corps.
Queen's Own Cameron Highlanders.
Queen's Royal (West Surreys).
Rifle Brigade.
R.A.F. Regiment.
Royal Armoured Corps.
R.A.M.C.
R.A.O.C.
R.A.S.C.
Royal Artillery.
Royal Berkshire.
4/7th Royal Dragoon Guards.
Royal Engineers.

13/18th Royal Hussars.
Royal Norfolk.
Royal Northumberland Fusiliers.
Royal Scots Fusiliers.
Royal Signals.
Royal Ulster Rifles.
Royal Warwickshire.
Seaforth Highlanders.
South Lancashire.
South Staffordshire.
South Wales Borderers.
Staffordshire Yeomanry.
Suffolk.
Tyneside Scottish.
Warwickshire Yeomanry.
Welch Fusiliers.
Welch.
Westminster Dragoons.
Wiltshire.
York and Lancaster.
Royal Marines (Commandos).
Special Service Troops.
Royal Observer Corps (volunteers acted as aircraft identifiers with invasion fleet).

CANADIAN

CORPS
II under Lieut.-General G. G. Simonds.

DIVISIONS
Infantry : 2nd under Maj.-Gen. C. Foulkes.
3rd under Maj.-Gen. R. F. L. Keller.
Armoured: 4th under Maj.-Gen. H. W. Foster.

BRIGADE
2nd Armoured under Brig. J. F. Bingham.

REGIMENTS

Algonquin.
Argyll and Sutherland Highlanders.
Black Watch of Canada.
British Columbia.
Calgary Highlanders.
Cameron Highlanders of Ottawa.
Canadian Grenadier Guards.
7th Canadian Recce (17th Duke of York's Royal Canadian Hussars).
1st Canadian Scottish.
Essex Scottish.
Fort Garry Horse.

Les Fusiliers Mont-Royal.
Governor-General's Foot Guards.
Highland Light Infantry of Canada.
1st Hussars.
Lake Superior.
Lincoln and Welland.
Loine Scots (Peel Dufferin and Halton).
12th Manitoba Dragoons.
North Nova Scotia Highlanders.
North Shore (New Brunswick).
Queen's Own Cameron Highlanders of Canada.

Queen's Own Rifles of Canada.
Regiment de Chaudiere.
Regiment de Maisonneuve.
Regina Rifles.
Royal Hamilton Light Infantry.
Royal Regiment of Canada.
Royal Winnipeg Rifles.
Sherbrooke Fusiliers.
South Alberta.
South Saskatchewan.
Stormont Dundas and Glengarry Highlanders
Toronto Scottish.

Dutch, Belgian, Polish and Czechoslovak Units serving with the 1st Canadian Army.

AMERICAN

CORPS
V under Major-General L. T. Gerow.
VII „ Major-General J. L. Collins.
VIII „ Major-General T. H. Middleton.
XII „ Major-General M. S. Eddy.
XV „ Major-General W. H. Haislip.
XIX „ Major-General C. H. Corlett.
XX „ Major-General W. H. Walker.

DIVISIONS
Infantry
1st under Major-General C. R. Huebner.
2nd „ Major-General W. M. Robertson.

3rd under Major-General John O'Daniel.
4th „ Major-General R. O. Barton.
5th „ Major-General R. E. Brown.
8th „ Brig.-General D. A. Stroh.
9th „ Major-General L. A. Craig.
29th „ Major-General G. H. Gerhardt.
30th „ Major-General L. S. Habes.
35th „ Major-General P. W. Baade.
36th „ Major-General John Dahlquist.
45th „ Major-General W. W. Eagles.
79th „ Major-General I. T. Wyche.
80th „ Major-General H. L. McBride.
83rd „ Major-General R. C. Macon.
90th „ Brig.-General J. A. van Fleet.

Armoured
2nd under Major-General E. H. Brooks.
3rd „ Major-General M. A. Rose.
4th „ Major-General R. N. Grow.
6th „ Major-General J. S. Wood.
7th „ Major-General R. W. Hasbrouck

Airborne
82nd under Major-General M. B. Ridgway.
101st under Major-General M. D. Taylor.
N.B.—The airborne " force " which took part in the South of France landings was under Major-General Robert Frederick.

FRENCH
DIVISIONS
1st Armoured : General Touzet du Vigier
2nd Armoured : Gen. J. P. Leclerc.
Colonial and F.F.I. units.

POLISH
DIVISION
1st Armoured : Brig.-General Stanislaw Maczek.

Chapter 332

CLOSING IN ON THE SIEGFRIED LINE

The inability of the British 2nd Army to consolidate the bridge-head seized at Arnhem by the British 1st Airborne Division (see Chapter 325) meant the abandonment for the time being of the attempt to force the lower reaches of the Rhine. But from the sea to Belfort Allied armies pushed slowly on during the autumn of 1944 towards that great water barrier. In this chapter, the clearing of the West Scheldt and this advance towards the Rhine are described by Squadron Leader Derek Adkins. Consult also map in page 3370.

IN spite of the withdrawal from the Arnhem bridge-head, a narrow corridor which included the vital crossings at Grave and Nijmegen had been established inside the defences of the northern Netherlands. The widening of this corridor met determined resistance, but it went ahead steadily. On September 24 British troops crossed the Reich frontier near the villages of Beek and Mook, patrols pushing forward into the Reichswald. By September 27 the 2nd Army had reached Maasheeze to the east, and Heesch and Nistelrode to the west. At the same time Canadian troops on the right of General Crerar's 1st Canadian Army forced a passage over the Antwerp-Turnhout canal in Belgium, defeating strong German opposition, and found Turnhout abandoned on September 25.

Although preoccupied with regrouping, the British 2nd Army under General Dempsey launched an attack on the 27th north-east of Nijmegen, which resulted in the capture of Elst and Bemmel. The enemy by now was resisting stubbornly, and during the last few days of September reacted strongly with numerous counter-attacks between the river Waal and Turnhout against Allied progress towards s'Hertogenbosch and Tilburg.

The Germans were also making a real effort to drive in the bridge-head north of Nijmegen. They lost 118 aircraft, for the loss of 16 Allied machines, in three days' vain attacks on the rail and road bridges at Nijmegen; and they failed to blow them up in a daring attempt on the night of September 28–29 made by twelve specially picked swimmers who had spent three months in Venice training for such operations. Wearing rubber skull caps, skin-tight suits and special rubber boots with two-foot-long flaps enabling them to cut through the water at a speed impossible to unaided swimmers, they entered the Waal 17 miles above Nijmegen, reached the road bridge and, with great difficulty owing to the strength of the current, affixed two charges of Hexanite fitted with delayed-

German Attempts on Waal Bridges

action fuses. They then attempted to swim upstream again to the railway bridge (see air photograph in page 3299), but after covering 6¼ miles were compelled by exhaustion to go in to the bank. Two were shot while swimming, ten surrendered. One of the charges set exploded; the other was removed just in time — and the bridge saved—by Lt. John Bridge, G.C., G.M., R.N.V.R., who dived into the river and examined the piers until he found it.

On October 1 the Germans attacked near Nijmegen. They threw large numbers of tanks and infantry into the battle, but at no point did they penetrate Allied positions.

The corridor was now some thirty miles wide, extending from Boksmeer to within four miles of s'Hertogenbosch. A further effort to clear the country of the enemy from east of the general line Deurne-Boksmeer to the Maas was frustrated by extensive minefields, added to which the marshy nature of the terrain made it difficult for armour.

But after the British 2nd Army's determined but unsuccessful attempts to relieve the 1st Airborne Division at Arnhem, the Supreme Commander's first objective was the clearance of the Scheldt estuary so that Antwerp could be opened up to support a thrust to the Rhine. A captured Order of the Day of October 7 by General von Zangen (commanding the German 15th Army) emphasized the importance

of these operations to both Germany and the Allies, who could "deliver a death-blow at northern Germany and even at Berlin itself" if in possession of Antwerp. "For this reason we must hold the Scheldt fortifications at all costs—to the last man. . . . It is a decision for the future of our people."

GERMAN 'FROG-MAN'
On the night of September 28, 1944, German saboteurs in the special equipment shown here swam down the Waal to Nijmegen in an unsuccessful attempt to blow up the bridges. Though they fixed charges to the road bridge, one of which exploded, the bridge was saved by the removal of the other charge by Lt. John Bridge, G.C., G.M., R.N.V.R. (above right).

Starting with only one bridge-head over the Antwerp-Turnhout canal, the British 1st Corps within one week made a general advance of ten miles, bringing its forward troops to within four miles of Tilburg. The Canadian 2nd Division north of Antwerp fought its way steadily forward towards Breda (captured by Polish units on October 29) against stubborn resistance and heavy artillery fire; while down the east bank of the West Scheldt other Canadians reached the isthmus connecting the island of South Beveland with the mainland. At 5 a.m., on October 6, Canadian troops farther west launched an attack across the Leopold Canal on a 6,000 yard front between Maldegem and Aarden-

burg. By midday on the 7th they had secured a bridge-head, and by the 10th one brigade, after repelling thirty counter-attacks, was firmly established on the northern side of the canal. West of Terneuzen, Canadian and British troops made an assault in barges and landing craft across the Braakman inlet on the night of October 8–9 and secured a bridge-head two miles deep on either side of Hoofdplaat. (*See* map in page 3375.)

These operations were part of the development of plans for the capture of Walcheren.

Walcheren Dykes Breached

The reduction of this heavily defended fortress presented many novel problems. On October 2 the Supreme Allied Commander warned the inhabitants of the islands of the Scheldt estuary that severe aerial bombardment of enemy troops and installations on them would be necessary, and urged them, if possible, to leave the islands or at least to move away from military objectives. Lancasters of R.A.F. Bomber Command attacked the sea dyke at Westkapelle, Walcheren, on October 3, with 12,000-lb. bombs, breaching it for 120 yards and inundating considerable areas of the

island, including the town of West-kapelle. On the 7th, the dykes on both sides of Flushing were repeatedly bombed. German strongpoints in the area were marooned, others were flooded.

On October 11 Canadian troops captured Woensdrecht and cut the road

leading from the mainland to South Beveland and Walcheren, thus isolating the enemy garrisons in the islands. Repeated attempts by the enemy to re-establish contact with the mainland failed. By the 16th the forces landed in the Hoofdplaat area had made firm

POLISH TROOPS IN HOLLAND

Polish units attached to the 1st Canadian Army pushed north from Antwerp in October-November 1944, entering Breda on October 29 (right). Eleven days later tanks of the 1st Polish Armoured Division were in Moerdijk (below) after overcoming fierce resistance from an enemy force holding out at the southern end of the demolished bridges spanning the Hollandsch Diep (mouth of the Maas and Waal). (See also illus. in page 841.) *Photos, Keystone*

contact north of Watervliet with the troops advancing from the Leopold Canal. The port of Breskens fell on the 22nd, after bitter street fighting. Schoondijke and Aardenburg were captured on the same day, Fort Frederik-Hendrik, key to the German positions south of the Scheldt, on the 25th, Cadzand on the 29th. Knocke, where the Germans south of the Scheldt made their last stand, fell on November 1.

North of Antwerp troops of the 1st Canadian Army made a new crossing of the Dutch frontier and seized Rosendaal on October 30. These successes

BRITISH TROOPS TAKE s'HERTOGENBOSCH

Foremost in the capture of s'Hertogenbosch, capital of Brabant, completed on October 27, 1944, was the British 53rd (Welsh) Division under Major-General R. K. Ross, C.B., D.S.O., M.C., which employed ' Crocodile ' flame-throwers and ' artificial moonlight ' (a device first used in Normandy, but kept secret). Here infantry and anti-tank guns are moving up towards the town ; while (below) infantry march alongside an A.V.R.E. tank carrying fascines for filling ditches. (See also illus. in page 3096.) *Photos, British Official ; British Newspaper Pool*

decisively isolated the islands where the Canadians were advancing into South Beveland. British and Canadian troops and naval ratings, landed across the Scheldt in the south of South Beveland on the 26th, took in the rear the Germans defending the east of the island against the Canadians advancing from the mainland. The two Allied groups linked on October 29, liberating Goes. Next day they were in control of the whole island and were pushing on over the causeway connecting South Beveland and Walcheren—the latter by that time was four-fifths under water.

On November 1, three bridge-heads were secured on Walcheren. Canadian troops, attacking across the causeway

Bridge-heads on Walcheren

from South Beveland, won one against desperate opposition. Under cover of a heavy bombardment from the south bank of the Scheldt, British and Canadian infantry crossed from Breskens to Flushing, much of which was in Allied hands by nightfall. A Commando force of Royal

Marines from Ostend landed at Westkapelle. Weather conditions made air support impossible ; but a naval force consisting of the battleship H.M.S. " Warspite " and the monitors H.M.S. " Erebus " and H.M.S. " Roberts," and some two hundred smaller vessels (including rocket-firing craft—*see* page 3069) bombarded coastal installations while a gun support squadron of 25 converted landing-craft went close inshore, engaging coast batteries at point-blank range.

The strength of their fire, and of that from the 11-inch guns of the enemy heavy batteries at Domburg, showed that preliminary aerial attack had been only some sixty, instead of the anticipated ninety, per cent effective, and the tank-landing craft disembarking Royal Marines and their vehicles into the breach made in the dyke by the R.A.F. on October 3— where only two could beach at a time—had a tough task. Casualties were high : Mr. A. V. Alexander, describing the operation in the House of Commons on November 15, said : " Of the 25 support craft engaged, nine were sunk, eight damaged, 172 of the crews were killed and 200 wounded ; of the 47 other major landing-

craft engaged, four were sunk and others damaged. Royal Marine Commando casualties were 37 killed, 77 missing, and 201 wounded."

But the third foothold was won, and Domburg was captured in falling snow by Royal Marines on the 3rd. Flushing, except for snipers, was occupied by the 4th, and on the 5th British and Canadian troops were fighting, sometimes waist deep in mud, over the worst terrain encountered in Western Europe towards Middelburg and Veere, both occupied on the 7th. The last German troops were taken off Walcheren on November 10. North Beveland and Tholen had been occupied without opposition on the 3rd.

The shores of the West Scheldt were clear of the enemy. Minesweeping operations had begun on November 2 when British minesweepers forced their way up the estuary under the nose of shore batteries. A narrow unbuoyed

CLEARING THE APPROACHES TO ANTWERP

The clearing of the West Scheldt was a vital part of the Allied campaign in the Netherlands in the autumn of 1944. Use of the port of Antwerp was necessary for the maintenance of supplies for the Allied armies before they could advance into Germany.

waterway was open by November 26. (*See* also illus. in page 3035.)

The situation in the Nijmegen salient remained generally unchanged until October 12, when the British 2nd Army launched an attack from its eastern flank, capturing the village of Overloon, completely destroyed in the fighting. Flail tanks (*see* illus. in page 3182) were used to overcome the minefields. Pressing slowly forward over difficult waterlogged terrain and in bad weather, General Dempsey's troops took the important communications centre of Venraij on the 18th. Four days later British forces attacked westwards from the salient towards s'Hertogenbosch and Bokstel. Although the advance was held up by destroyed bridges, s'Hertogenbosch was reached on the 23rd and

Widening the Nijmegen Salient

SERGEANT WINS V.C. FOR HEROISM NEAR NIJMEGEN

On the eastern outskirts of Overloon, south of Nijmegen, on October 16, 1944, an important position in the woods was taken as a result of the heroism of Sergeant G. H. Eardley, M.M., of the King's Shropshire Light Infantry, who, single-handed and under devastating fire, silenced three enemy machine-gun posts. He was later awarded the V.C. and is seen here having the ribbon pinned to his breast by Field-Marshal Montgomery. Left, Royal Engineers pass through Overloon, captured on October 12th, with a flail tank. *Photos, British Official*

completely liberated by the 27th; while Bokstel was freed on the 25th. Other troops cleared the banks of the Wilhelmina Canal towards Tilburg (entered on the 27th).

Meanwhile the enemy had counter-attacked south of Venraij, cutting the Meijel-Deurne road and breaking into the village of Meijel on October 27. Hard fighting continued in this area for several days, with both sides employing infantry and tanks, and it was not until November 14 that the village, heavily mined and booby trapped, was finally cleared of the enemy, thus con-

cluding for the time being operations on the eastern flank of the salient.

To the north-west of s'Hertogenbosch the British 2nd Army continued to advance towards the Maas, and by November 5 had reached the south bank of the river on a wide front stretching westwards to the outskirts of Geert-ruidenberg. The 1st Canadian Army also thrust towards the river, establishing bridge-heads over the Dintel Mark canal between Oosterhout and Ouden-bosch on the night of November 2–3, and by the 5th reaching the line of the Maas north-west of Geertruidenberg (cleared by Polish troops the same day) while other Allied troops reached the outskirts of Klundert. The only enemy strongpoint then remaining on the south bank of the Maas between s'Hertogen-

COMBINED OPERATIONS ASSAULT ON SOUTH BEVELAND

In Zeeland, Canadian forces attacking the eastern part of South Beveland met strong opposition. An amphibious assault launched on October 26, 1944, by British and Canadian troops and naval ratings crossing the Scheldt Estuary took the Germans in the rear. Initial landings were only slightly opposed. Here, a smoke-screen is being laid to cover the landings.

bosch and the sea was a bridge-head held by S.S. troops at the south end of the demolished bridges at Moerdijk. On November 8 Polish forces of the 1st Canadian Army made two gaps in the eastern side of its perimeter, through which infantry and armour passed, and by the following day this last pocket had been liquidated. Booty taken included British A.A. guns captured at Dunkirk in 1940.

After General Patch's U.S. 7th Army made contact with the U.S. 3rd Army at Sombernon on September 11 (*see* page 3251), it ceased to be part of General Maitland Wilson's Mediterranean Command, and came under the command of General Eisenhower. With French units (later to become General de Lattre de Tassigny's French 1st Army, made up of formations from the French Empire and fresh formations drafted into the army from the F.F.I.) it composed the 6th Army Group. By the date of the junction of the Allied forces from west and south, American armour had already reached the Saar basin in its thrust from Verdun (*see* page 3246). A crossing had been secured over the Meuse in the area of St. Mihiel and bridge-heads established in the Moselle valley. By September 17 Allied forces had closed to within six miles of Belfort and were in contact with the enemy, who was fighting stubbornly from prepared positions to protect the southern hinge of a withdrawal towards the Belfort gap.

While this steady progress was being made from the south, Allied armour pushed south-eastwards from Neufchâteau to occupy Nancy on the Meurthe after fierce fighting on the 15th, and forward elements immediately drove on east of the town. At the same time, the Moselle bridge-heads were persistently enlarged and considerable forces were established across the river.

Farther north, American armoured columns, having liberated the city of

Allies Invade Germany

Luxemburg on September 10, met only weak enemy rearguards and moved rapidly forward to free large areas of the Duchy. On the 11th they made the first Allied entry into Germany near Trier. Next day saw limited penetrations into the Siegfried Line here and east of Eupen (captured on the night of the 11th–12th). Maastricht, in Limburg, first large Dutch town to be liberated, was entered by American troops, supported by Dutch patriots, on the 14th. The retreating Germans had, however, blown up all the bridges in the town over the Maas. American armoured elements crossed the frontier

3377

'BUFFALO' TANKS SPEARHEADED SOUTH BEVELAND ATTACK

'Buffalo' amphibious troop-carrier comes ashore during the assault on South Beveland on October 26, 1944 (see page 3375). Officially known as 'Landing Vehicles Tracked (Armoured),' these were amphibious tanks equipped with rubberized tracks which enabled them to move both on land and water. They were first used during the New Britain landings in December 1943 (see pages 2889 and 3267). Top, infantry assembling for the attack on South Beveland. Below, armoured reconnaissance units of the R.A.F. Regt. in Middelburg, on Walcheren, taken on November 7.

DOGS AS MINE-DETECTORS
Dogs played an increasing part in the detection of mines, as the Allied armies swept towards Germany. Nearly 3,000, loaned by private owners in Britain, were taught at the War Dogs Training School in England, first, to hunt out, by scent, mock-mines near which meat had been laid. This dog indicates to a sapper of the Royal Engineers a mine he has detected on the Helmond-Venlo railway (November 1944).   *Photo, British Official*

south of Aachen in considerable strength and cut the main road to Cologne. Patrols entered Aachen on the 16th, but had to withdraw, and bitter street fighting continued.

By the middle of September the American line extended from Maastricht in the north to Belfort, near the Swiss border, in the south. Along the whole of this front the Germans showed increased resistance, for they were determined to fight for every foot of ground in an effort to upset the Allies' basic plan of reaching the Rhine before winter. The final outcome was never in doubt, but the supply difficulties presented by the lengthening line of communications from Normandy and the delay in opening the port of Antwerp slowed operations.

Heavy fighting took place in four main storm centres where bitter, at times almost fanatical, opposition was encountered. In the Aachen area General Hodges's U.S. 1st Army entered Büsbach on September 16, Höfen on the 18th, Stolberg on the 22nd, but stubborn fighting continued in the area. Other American troops made slow progress towards Geilenkirchen, some 12 miles north of Aachen. Not until October 2, following an attack launched north of Aachen between Geilenkirchen and Kerkrade, did the U.S. 19th Corps break through the main Siegfried Line defences in this area on a two-divisional front of some six miles and penetrate beyond to a depth of five miles against heavy artillery and anti-tank fire. The enemy threw in numerous and violent counter-attacks and suffered very heavy losses, but a general line was established from Alsdorf through Beggendorf to Geilenkirchen (*see* map in page 3379).

By October 10 Aachen was surrounded except for one mile-wide escape gap,

and three American soldiers went forward under the white flag with an ultimatum from their commander : "We shall take the city either by receiving its immediate unconditional surrender, or by attacking and destroying it. There is no middle course." But the German garrison refused to surrender, and on October 11 a massed air and artillery bombardment was brought down on the city, and repeated the next day, and the next. Hard fighting continued, however, and not until the evening of the 16th was the city completely encircled. American troops then closed in from the north and south, beating back repeated counter-attacks and clearing the houses street by street until, except for the last remnants of the garrison still fighting in the outskirts, Aachen fell to the U.S. 1st Army at 3.30 p.m. on October 20. The Allies had captured their first large town in the Reich.

Around St. Vith the Americans encountered further heavy and determined resistance, which slowed down their advance south-west of Prüm and necessitated the capture of many pill-boxes and the repulse of several counter-attacks from Trier. On September 28, the U.S. 20th Corps, in a strong thrust south-east of the town of Luxemburg, entered Remich.

The third centre of resistance was in the Moselle valley and south-east of Nancy, on General Patton's U.S. 3rd Army front. The strength of the position and the determination with which it was held, apart from the nature of the country, made it probably the most

Fall of Aachen

WARNINGS AND GRIM HUMOUR AS THE REICH IS ENTERED
Allied troops first crossed the German frontier on September 11, 1944. As they pushed on, hurriedly painted sign-posts pointed the way, gave information (often ironical) of the local amenities, and warned troops of likely dangers. Of the notices below, those right and left were erected by the Canadians on the Dutch-German frontier, that in the centre by the Americans.
Photos, U.S. Official ; Planet News ; Associated Press

IN AACHEN—FIRST BIG GERMAN TOWN TO FALL TO THE ALLIES

The ancient border-city of Aachen (Aix-la-Chapelle) fell to the U.S. 1st Army on October 20, 1944. The first attack was launched on October 7 when the German radio announced : ' The Battle of Germany has begun ! ' Three days later Colonel Gerhard Wilck, the German commander, was presented with a demand for unconditional surrender within 24 hours, failing which the city would be destroyed. Two U.S. lieutenants, accompanied by a private with a bedsheet as white flag (3), bore the ultimatum. The Germans gave no reply, and at 12.30 p.m. on October 11 the final assault began—with waves of Thunderbolt dive-bombers and heavy artillery fire. Last resistance ended on October 21, with the surrender in the outskirts of Colonel Wilck. 1. Americans street-fighting in the suburbs. 2. Volkssturm Grenadier goes into action with his ' Panzerfist ' (heavy anti-tank bomb) (see also illus. in page 3172). 4. The wrecked railway station. 5. An American tank fights its way into the ruined city.

CAPTURE OF METZ

Metz, formerly capital of Lorraine and famous for its perimeter defences, formed a hard core of resistance to troops of General Patton's U.S. 3rd Army as they fanned out towards the Saar in mid-November, 1944. The first outer defence to fall was Fort Verny, captured on November 13. Seven days later the city itself was entered. 1. A field gun in action during the street-fighting. 2. Major-General Anton Dunckern, Gestapo Chief of Metz, and Colonel Constantine Meyer, the military commander (right) after capture. 3. U.S. tanks knocked out during the attack on Fort Driant (see opposite page), where some of the most bitter fighting took place. 4. Germans surrender at Fort Jeanne d'Arc.

Photos, U.S. Official ; Planet News ; Associated Press

effective of all. The Americans were chiefly engaged west of Metz, where they were unable to overcome resistance from the system of linked forts six miles west of the city, the moated Fort Driant offering particularly strong opposition. To the east and north-east of Nancy they also encountered severe opposition, for the enemy was extremely sensitive to any movement in this salient and held a high proportion of his armour in the area for counter-attacks. Between Lunéville and Epinal there was fierce fighting until September 16, when American tanks took Lunéville. The same day the west half of Thionville was secured. More heavy tank fighting followed, mostly in the Château Salins-Dieuze sector. Between September 12 and 22 the enemy lost 306 tanks, and his losses went on. Their action was well supported by German artillery, but a fortunate spell of good weather enabled the Allied air forces to intervene with effect. Epinal fell, after changing hands several times, on the 25th, Dieuze on the 24th; enemy counter-attacks were checked west of Metz on the historic battlefield of Gravelotte on September 29 and repulsed with heavy losses north of Lunéville. Château Salins which, like Epinal, changed hands several times, was captured on the 29th.

The fourth area of resistance was farther south, where General Patch's U.S. 7th Army and General de Lattre de Tassigny's French 1st Army were advancing slowly and laboriously, much impeded by heavy rains, in very difficult country west of Belfort; by the end of the month the U.S. 6th Corps was within ten miles of it.

Advance Towards Belfort

During October, the U.S. 7th Army, with the French 2nd Armoured Division as its spearhead, took over in the Epinal area from the U.S. 3rd Army. Throughout the month pressure was maintained on the whole of the U.S. 3rd and 7th Army front. The French 1st Army made slow progress towards Belfort, occupying the high ground east of the Moselotte, while the U.S. 6th Corps achieved limited advances astride the Epinal-Colmar road. At the same time the U.S. 12th Corps put in an attack north of Nancy, to make a penetration of seven miles by the 10th.

Heavy fighting continued at the approaches to Metz till the end of the month, the garrison of Fort Driant still offering effective resistance. American troops forced the moat and stormed the outer defences on the 3rd and gained control of part of it on the 7th, but were compelled to withdraw after ten days' grim fighting inside the

BRITISH TROOPS LAUNCH FIRST ATTACK IN GERMANY

First full-scale British attack on German soil was directed at Geilenkirchen, a Siegfried Line strongpoint north of Aachen, on November 18, 1944 (see map in page 3379). British 2nd Army troops were switched from the Netherlands to join the U.S. 9th Army in the assault. Next day, against violent opposition, Allied forces took the town. Here U.S. infantry and British tanks advance towards Geilenkirchen. Below, the preliminary bombardment by massed British armour.
Photos, British Newspaper Pool ; Keystone

fortress. Maizières-les-Metz then became the focus of intense battle. It was captured, reduced to rubble, by the U.S. 90th Division on October 30 after three weeks of intense struggle.

Active patrolling and local attacks and counter-attacks went on elsewhere, with the U.S. 3rd and 7th Armies and the French 1st Army making slight advances against strong and sometimes fanatical resistance. On November 8 the situation on the U.S. 3rd Army front was suddenly transformed by the launching, in driving rain, of a large-scale attack north-east of Nancy. The river Seille was crossed at three points that day, and a " pincer " drive on Metz began, from Maizières-les-Metz on the north and across the Nied Française river on the south. The U.S. 95th Division, by-passing Fort Driant, was some two miles west of Metz by November 15, when the escape gap to the east had been reduced to barely eight miles. Metz, described by the German commentator, Captain Sertorius, as merely " an advanced outpost," was formally declared liberated on November 22.

The Allied front could now be divided into the following focal points:

When the news was announced to the French Consultative Assembly in Paris by its President, all the delegates rose and sang the Marseillaise, and the sitting was suspended.

Nine-tenths of the city **Strasbourg** were cleared next day **Captured** by the Americans, the inhabitants receiving the Allies with enthusiasm, and a pocket was formed to the south from which the enemy's only line of retreat was across the Rhine. The elimination of this pocket

ACROSS THE MOSELLE

On September 6, 1944, troops of the U.S. 3rd Army were reported to have established bridge-heads across the Moselle. In the following month the U.S. 7th Army, with the French 2nd Armoured Division, took over the Epinal area from the U.S. 3rd. Infantry of the U.S. 7th Army here use a hand line to cross the Moselle; while artillerymen load a 105 mm. howitzer near St. Dié (right). *Photos, U.S. Official*

first, on the Swiss frontier, where French troops on November 15 began an advance to the Rhine; second, around Metz; third, in the Aachen area, where the U.S. 1st Army launched a big attack on the 16th; and fourth, in the Maas pocket where British units were clearing the enemy west of the river.

The French 1st Army made a spectacular advance, liberating Montbéliard and a number of smaller places on **French** November 17. On the **Reach** 20th, the French **the Rhine** 1st Armoured Division reached the Rhine at a point between Mulhouse and the Swiss frontier. Belfort, entered by a Zouave regiment on the 20th, was cleared on the 21st, and the French were facing north on a line from the Rhine to north of Belfort. On that day General Eisenhower in a statement said that the Allies were attacking along the traditional routes to Germany through Aachen, Metz and Belfort, and emphasized that the offensive must be maintained at full pressure until the enemy reached breaking-point : " To get the peace, we must drive like hell." Resistance stiffened, but the French consolidated a line along the Canal de Huningue from Basle to Kembs. The enemy, however, held the west bank of the Rhine.

The French liberated Mulhouse on the 22nd, and next day an armoured column pushed north to Ensisheim, but

fierce counter-attacks forced it to withdraw. A pocket west of Belfort was eliminated and all the Belfort forts, which were very strongly held, were captured. On November 28 French troops, advancing from both Mulhouse and Belfort, secured the road between these two towns, thus cutting off an enemy pocket north of the Rhine–Rhône canal. A sudden drive by Moroccan troops, under cover of artificial fog and with artillery support, took the French into Huningue on November 30, and by December 1 the Franco-Swiss border was cleared and only one enemy bridge-head remained west of the Rhine and south of Kembs. The French 1st Army then exerted pressure north towards Colmar.

To the east of Lunéville, infantry of the U.S. 7th Army supported by French armour, advanced rapidly on a three-divisional front during November 19 and 20 in a north easterly direction, forward troops reaching the outskirts of Sarrebourg on the 20th. On the 23rd the French 2nd armoured Division reached Strasbourg after a spectacular dash through the " Saverne gap."

was then achieved by other troops of the 7th Army advancing east through the Vosges, aided by French armour and U.S. troops directed south from Strasbourg.

The U.S. 7th Army then pushed north and south. On the southward drive, U.S. troops entered Salestat by December 2, clearing it on December 5. Although seriously impeded by floods, troops of the U.S. 7th Army and the French 1st Army closed in, against fierce resistance, towards Colmar. The U.S. 7th Army forces driving north from Strasbourg by-passed Hagenau, captured only on December 11 after three weeks' heavy fighting, to reach Selz on the 12th. German resistance collapsed between Strasbourg and Selz, which was captured on the 13th.

By the time Metz was liberated, armoured spearheads of the U.S. 3rd Army were already striking towards the river Saar. They forced it near Postroff on November 24. Very heavy fighting developed all along the 3rd Army's front, especially in the north near Merzig, where it was taking place inside the German border. On

3382

December 2, U.S. troops broke into Saarlautern, first important industrial town of the Saar to be entered by the Allies. During the night of December 2–3 they seized intact the bridge across the river. By the 5th, General Patton's Army had completed the capture of Saarlautern, and was in places, on a thirty-mile front, eight miles inside the German border, and fighting its way into the Siegfried Line. In Sarreguemines the enemy was offering desperate resistance, and at Dillingen he put in a number of fierce counter-attacks, all held : in one, on December 11, 85 German infantrymen made a fanatical charge screaming "Heil Hitler" and were killed to the last man.

After the fall of Aachen, General Simpson's U.S. 9th Army, which, after clearing Brittany (*see* Chapter 314), had been brought into the line between the U.S. 1st and 3rd Armies on October 3, was moved to the northern flank of the U.S. 1st Army on October ber 23. The Aachen front remained quiet until November 2, when General Hodges's U.S. 1st Army launched a fiercely contested attack in the Hürtgen forest. The battle raged back and forth, the Americans making minor gains. November 16 brought a joint attack, aimed at Cologne, by the U.S. 9th Army (between Geilenkirchen and Eschweiler) and the U.S. 1st Army (in the Hürtgen area) : it was preceded by the biggest "obliteration" attack to that date, on Düren, Jülich, and Heinsberg, carried out by 2,320 heavy and 80 medium bombers of the British and American air forces. Fighting their way forward in rain and sleet, which made strong air support impossible, the two armies encountered stiffening resistance. Wire obstacles, booby traps, dense woods heavily mined also helped to delay the advance.

After the capture of Meijel (November 14) Field-Marshal Montgomery transferred responsibility for the Nijmegen bridge-head to the 1st Canadian Army, which had then completed the Scheldt operations, and the British 2nd Army was switched to the front north of Aachen. "This regrouping had a further object," explained the Field-Marshal later. "1st Canadian Army was required to plan the battle of the Rhineland, which was to be launched from the Nijmegen area ; British 2nd Army was to plan the subsequent assault across the Rhine."

Early on November 18, the British 2nd Army, concerting operations with the U.S. 1st and 9th Armies, attacked towards Geilenkirchen, capturing the town, reduced to rubble, next day, on

Regrouping of Allied Armies

which day also the Americans fought their way into the outskirts of Eschweiler. They cleared that town on the 22nd.

By November 24 the Germans had brought up at least twelve divisions—the bulk of their re-formed 7th Army—in an effort to stop the Allied drive on Cologne. Field-Marshal von Rundstedt issued an Order of the Day to his troops saying that if they were "rolled down by the enemy steamroller, the way into the Reich would be open." Slowly the armies pushed forward, every little

SWASTIKA IN THE DUST
Towards the end of November 1944 the French 1st Army made spectacular gains. Within a few days they penetrated the Belfort Gap, reached the Rhine, and on November 22 freed Mulhouse, where this Moroccan soldier trails a Nazi flag through the streets. The French 1st Army contained many troops drawn from the French Empire.
Photo, U.S. Official

village being hotly contested, with the enemy resisting from every house and cellar. Troops of General Simpson's U.S. 9th Army penetrated into both Linnich and Jülich on December 2. By the 14th the Allies were reported to hold a sixteen-mile stretch of the west bank of the Roer river, from Linnich to a point just north of Düren.

On its northern flank, which lay still in the Netherlands, in Dutch Limburg, the British 2nd Army began a new advance to the Maas, also on November 18. It was severely hampered by numerous minefields, intersected by anti-tank ditches and wire defences, country reduced to a bog by heavy rains, and waterlogged and collapsed roads, rather than by enemy resistance ; but by the 25th it held some sixteen miles of the west bank of

the Maas, from just south of Venlo to just north of Roermond. On December 4, General Dempsey's troops occupied Blerik, suburb of Venlo on the west of the Maas, which brought the west bank of the river from the sea to Blerik under the control of the 21st Army Group.

South-west of Arnhem, on December 3, Germans appers breached the southern bank of the Lower Rhine. Two days later the land between the Lower Rhine and the Waal was a foot under water, and the Canadians were forced to make local withdrawals. By December 6 the floods were slightly subsiding, but an area of 25-30 square miles north-west of Nijmegen was still under water. Bitter weather and the first falls of snow reduced activity along the whole Dutch front to patrolling.

Plans for a general regrouping of the 21st Army Group for the battle of the Rhineland were, however, nearing completion. Some divisions were actually on the move to their new concentration areas when, on December 16, a German counter-offensive in the Ardennes broke.

During the period covered by this chapter the Germans undoubtedly displayed remarkable powers of recovery and a fierce determination to maintain the frontiers of the Reich intact, utilizing not only the strong artificial defences of the Siegfried Line but also the defensive potentialities of the difficult terrain to the west of it. The Allies, however, although their progress was slowed down, by maintaining unrelenting pressure secured a number of important tactical objectives. They were also better able to afford the losses incurred in battles of attrition. The capture of Aachen, Metz and Strasbourg were notable successes of moral and strategic value, and by the end of the period Allied forces were within striking distance of the enemy's main defences—in places, as at Aachen, some penetration had been effected.

Strategic Gains and Losses

By far the most important strategic achievement of the period was, however, the opening of the approaches to Antwerp, for it was an essential preliminary to the launching of the decisive offensive on a maximum scale. Full use of the port had become necessary to provide a base for Montgomery's 21st Army Group and also for the northern sections of the American front, to which more than half the tonnage discharged at Antwerp was allotted. German realization of the importance of the port inspired the desperate resistance of the Scheldt defences.

Chapter 333

DEVELOPMENTS IN PILOTED WAR AIRCRAFT

Apart from the German introduction of flying bombs and rocket bombs (see Chapter 337) and the appearance of rocket- and jet-propelled aircraft both in the Luftwaffe and in the R.A.F., the mid-years of war were more notable for the development of existing air weapons than for the production of new ones. Some account of these developments in piloted aircraft, and weapons designed for use in them, is given here by Captain Norman Macmillan, M.C., A.F.C.

FIRST to be noted of the air-weapon developments of 1944 is the introduction of still heavier armaments on many aircraft. The Mosquito XVIII, for instance, carried four ·303-inch machine-guns and one 6-pounder quick-firing gun in the nose. The Americans tried a Mitchell with a 75-millimetre gun in the foremost cockpit. Rocket projectiles came into increasing use ; in the R.A.F. and Fleet Air Arm they were carried by the Hurricane, Beaufighter, Typhoon, Mosquito, Beaufort, Barracuda and Firefly.

In British aircraft rocket projectiles were carried on racks fitted under the wings, usually four on each side. The rocket propellant was cordite, contained within the stick behind the warhead. This propellant, fired electrically by the pilot, discharged the rocket. There was no reaction on the aircraft. This was important, as the recoil after firing a battery of machine-guns or

cannon caused the aircraft to slow down (sometimes by 30 m.p.h.), a disadvantage when engaging fast enemy aircraft.

Unrotating projectiles, as rockets were officially called, travelled ahead of the aircraft, firing them with a remarkably flat trajectory which made sighting comparatively easy with the normal reflector sight. The 60-lb. explosive warhead had the effectiveness of a shell fired by a six-inch gun, and a

salvo of eight R.P.s from an aeroplane was considered to be as destructive as a broadside from a six-inch-gun cruiser. Pilots could discharge the rocket projectiles in pairs, one from under each wing, or in one complete group of eight, according to the target. American rocket projectiles were mounted not on permanent racks, but in paper plastic tubes which could be dropped after the rockets had been fired. The fins of their rockets were folded, and opened when the projectile was discharged. The Thunderbolt carried six rockets, its complete installation weighing 450 lb.

Rocket projectiles were first used mainly against shipping, and attacks on Europe's coastwise traffic organized by the Germans to aid the railways, which were being increasingly dislocated by bombing, were of daily occurrence. This method of attack against unarmoured ships proved so effective that it replaced the earlier skip-bombing form of attack (in which the pilot made his bomb ricochet off the water as a boy makes a flat stone ricochet off the surface from the shore's edge). This was a distinct step forward, for skip-bombing was both difficult and dangerous for those engaged on it, because it meant approaching very low and close to the target, leaving little room for manoeuvre within the zone of hostile flak.

R.P. Attacks on Coastal Shipping

Rocket projectiles were found to be effective against certain kinds of shore targets : for example, houses used by the enemy as billets and headquarters, and for breaking down the sandbag protection erected around radar stations on the enemy-held coast, after which cannon-firing aircraft could punch their small explosive shells through the breaches to destroy or wreck the delicate electrical apparatus within. This technique was used with complete success to put the enemy coastal radar chain out of action before the invasion of Normandy.

The power of British bombers was increased during 1944 by the introduction of larger bombs. The first of these was the 12,000-lb. blast bomb, nicknamed the " factory-buster " (see page

R.A.F.'S MOSQUITO MARK XVIII
Details of the R.A.F. Mosquito Mark XVIII fighter-bomber were released in November 1944. Armed with four ·303-in. machine-guns and a 6-pdr. cannon with a firing rate of 60 shells per minute, this aircraft materially assisted Coastal Command in their war against the U-boats. Right, nose view showing armament and size of one of the 6-lb. shells. Below, in flight.
Photos, British Official

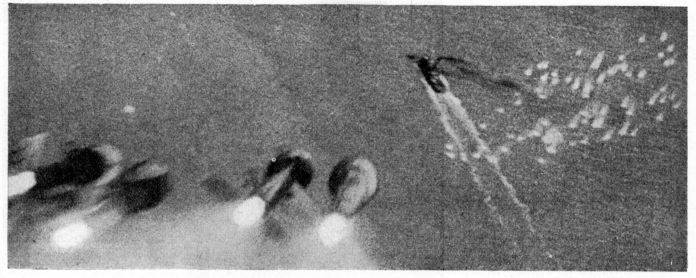

ROCKET PROJECTILES AID THE ALLIED WAR AT SEA

That R.A.F. Coastal Command had been greatly aided in its attacks on enemy shipping by the use of rocket-projectile (R.P.) aircraft since June 1943 was announced on May 28, 1944. The rocket consisted of a tube filled with cordite, the gas emitted from its tail propelling it at a great velocity. Here rockets from a R.A.F. Typhoon speed towards enemy shipping in the Scheldt in September 1944. Below, loading a Typhoon with the rockets. *Photos, British Official ; Fox*

tion of methane in petrol under pressure. The impact of landing caused a striker to fire a detonator which in turn ignited priming in a central tube and this gave enough heat to ignite thermite. The heat then generated raised the internal pressure and this forced the liquid content through a jet, where it was ignited by the burning thermite, and then issued through a hole in the bottom of the parachute container in a pressurized flame.

During 1944 the U.S. Air Forces tried radio-controlled bombers as

NEW ARMAMENT FOR B-25

The largest weapon mounted in an aircraft up to the early part of 1944 was installed in the North American B-25 Mitchell bomber. It was a 75 mm. cannon, here shown in the aircraft's nose ; above it were mounted two ·5 in. machine-guns. *Photo, Keystone*

2964). This bomb measured 17 feet 4 inches long and 3 feet 2 inches in diameter. It was, in fact, three 4,000-lb. bombs in one. Unlike the smaller blast bombs it required tail fins to steady its flight. It had a destructive effect over an area of 81,235 square yards. The Potez factory, near Albert, where it was used on March 2, still stood, gutted and a forlorn spectacle of twisted girders and windowless broken walls, almost a year later.

The first giant streamline bomb also weighing 12,000 lb. was 22 feet long and 3 feet 4 inches in diameter. It was built

Armour-Piercing 'Tallboy'

in three sections, an armour-piercing nose, the main body holding the explosive, and a stream-lined tail cone carrying four aerofoil fins set at an angle of 5° to make the bomb spin like a shell and so maintain an accurate ballistic curve from bomber to

target. (Some of the earlier heavy cylindrical bombs fell on their sides and did not explode until the delayed action fuse operated.) The 12,000-lb. A.P. bomb was first used against Le Havre on June 14, 1944, to put German E and R boats out of action. Air Chief Marshal Sir Arthur Harris called it the earthquake bomb, because it penetrated deeply before exploding, but the more usual nickname for it was the "Tallboy" (*see* pages 2964 and 3192, and illus. in page 2969).

A new British incendiary bomb (the "flying meteor") came into use in 1944. Developed by a scientific team drawn from the Ministries of Aircraft Production and Home Security, I.C.I. and Leeds University, it descended by parachute and after landing emitted for two minutes a flaming jet 15 feet long and two feet wide. It was a cylinder 21 inches long and 5½ inches wide, weighing 30 lb., and filled with a solu-

weapons of attack. Both Liberators and Fortresses were used. They were loaded with high explosive, and flown by a crew of two until the moment the radio-controlled aircraft took over, when the crew of the bomber-bomb baled out.

One Liberator laden with 21,000 lb. of high explosive was sent against flying bomb sites in Normandy, but the venture was unsuccessful, the crew losing their lives. These weapons were also directed against fortress Heligoland. On one occasion a Flying Fortress laden with explosive and minus its crew turned west and flew over England, causing warning sirens to be sounded in advance of its flight. It circled Liverpool, then headed west again, crossed Ireland, and was finally shot down into the Atlantic by fighters. It was announced at the time that this was a bomber which the crew had abandoned, and which the automatic pilot had under control without human aid.

Bombers Without Pilots

British explosives of enhanced power came into use. Some were claimed to be five times more powerful than pre-war explosives. One was R.D.X. (Woolwich Research Department formula X), previously known as cyclonite; this was the filling for some R.A.F. bombs. Many R.A.F. block-busters and some American bombs were filled with Tritonal, a mixture of T.N.T. and aluminium powder. The Americans also used an American explosive called

Pent in bombs. The most effective depth charge explosive of the war was Torpex, a mixture of T.N.T., R.D.X., and aluminium powder; it increased the distance at which a depth charge could destroy a submarine and augmented the destructive properties of mines and torpedoes.

The most notable new aircraft of the year 1944 were the R.A.F. Hawker Tempest and Gloster Meteor; the U.S.A.A.F. Super-Fortress; the Luftwaffe rocket-propelled Messerschmitt 163, and the twin-jet Messerschmitt 262.

THE R.A.F. TEMPEST

The Tempest, fast single-seat fighter, achieved outstanding success against the flying-bomb. (See Chapter 337.) Powered with a 2,400 h.p. Napier Sabre sleeve-valve engine and armed with four 20-mm. Hispano cannon, it had a span of 41 ft. and a length of 33 ft. 8 ins. Here is shown the aircraft's variable pitch 4 bladed air-screw; (top) the Tempest in flight.

Photos, British Official

The Tempest was in action during the days preceding the invasion of Normandy, and from the first against the flying bombs. It was a development of the Typhoon, with a Napier Sabre II B 24-cylinder sleeve-valve motor of 2,400 h.p., a top speed of 435 m.p.h., and four 20-millimetre Hispano cannon in the wings. For a military single-seater fighter, it had a neat and accessible cockpit layout.

Although the first Meteor squadron was formed at Manston airfield in June 1944, the Meteor did not go into

BRITAIN'S FIRST JET-PROPELLED FIGHTER

Experiments in jet-propelled aircraft were begun in Britain in 1933. In July 1945 it was disclosed that the R.A.F. Meteor, a jet-propelled fighter, had been in use since 1943, and in 1944 fought the flying-bomb. Power was two gas-turbine units; span, 43 ft.; length, 41 ft.; armament, four 20-mm. Hispano cannon; speed, in excess of 500 m.p.h. Here is a close-up of the port power-unit.

Photo, British Official

ALLIES PIERCE SIEGFRIED LINE

The Siegfried Line first came into prominence in a speech by Hitler at the Nazi Congress in Nuremberg on September 12, 1938. 'The most gigantic fortifications that ever existed,' he said, were then being built by almost half-a-million men and would extend to a depth of up to thirty miles, with 17,000 armoured turrets. After 1940, the defences were neglected in favour of those on the Atlantic coast. When the actual struggle for them began on September 11, 1944, with the entry of General Hodges's U.S. 1st Army into the Reich north of Trier, they were overcome by tactics and weapons developed after they were built. Above, a bulldozer tank of the U.S. 3rd Armoured Division carries infantry through "Dragon's Teeth" tank obstacles near Roetgen. Right, a British 2nd Army infantryman takes his ease among similar field works further north.

LAST OF THE CROSS-CHANNEL BOMBARDMENT GUNS CAPTURED

Britain's 'front-line' towns on the south coast rejoiced on September 30, 1944 at the capture of the last long-range German guns trained across the Channel (see page 3022). The first shell fired at Dover—most heavily shelled of these towns—fell on August 12, 1940, and was followed in four years of war by 2,225 which killed 107 and seriously injured 200. Soldiers of the 1st Canadian Army here examine one of the captured guns. *Photo, New York Times Photos*

THE R.A.F.'s 'GRAND SLAM' BOMB IN THE MAKING

'The most destructive lethal weapon ever made' was the official description, issued on March 3, 1945, of the R.A.F.'s newest bomb which weighed ten tons. It was a scaled-up version of the 6-ton 'Earthquake' or 'Tallboy' bomb (see illus. in pages 2969 and 2974). The new bombs, flown by Lancasters, were first reported in action on March 14, 1945, when they almost completely demolished the twin railway viaducts at Bielefeld in the Ruhr. On the right are cores for three of the 10-ton bombs before casting.

Photo, British Official

3389

3s

NEW BRITISH FLEET FORMED FOR CAMPAIGN IN THE PACIFIC

On December 10, 1944, the Admiralty stated that the British Eastern Fleet, formerly operating in the Indian Ocean and the Netherlands Indies, had been superseded by the newly created British Pacific Fleet. Commander of the powerful new naval force was announced as Admiral Sir Bruce Fraser, G.C.B., K.B.E. formerly C.-in-C. of the Eastern Fleet. Re-establishment of an East Indies Station, under Vice-Admiral Sir Arthur Power, K.C.B. (see illus. in page 3395), was also disclosed. Here the 35,000-ton battleship H.M.S. 'Howe,' Admiral Fraser's flagship, is passing through the Suez Canal on her way to the Far East.

Photo, British Official

action until August 1944, when it shot down its first flying-bomb. The Meteor mounted four 20-millimetre Hispano cannon in the nose. Her span was 43 feet, length 41 feet, and height 13 feet. She had a tricycle under-carriage with a nose wheel retracting into a housing between the rudder pedals. The short main legs folded inwards into wing housings between the engines and fuselage. The split tail-plane was set high on the fin to give ample clearance for the jets from the twin gas-turbine units. Two models of the Meteor were made. The first was fitted with Welland and the second with Derwent turbines. Both turbines had a diameter of 43 inches; the Welland weighed 850 lb., the Derwent 920 lb.

The Derwent was designed, and the first on test, within three-and-a-half months; it developed a 2,000-lb. thrust at 16,500 r.p.m., 300 lb. more than the Welland. The first Meteor to be fitted with Derwent I turbines flew in March 1944. (This model was the forerunner of the aircraft which broke the world's speed record by flying at 606 m.p.h. on November 6, 1945.)

Derwent Turbines for Meteor

The Derwent II developed a 2,200-lb. thrust; the Derwent IV gave 2,400 lb. These Rolls-Royce gas-turbine jet units work on paraffin to which one per cent of lubricating oil has been added.

In 1944 the Spitfire was still further developed, and the Mark XIV, fitted with one 2,040 h.p. Rolls-Royce Griffon motor, attained a maximum speed of 450 m.p.h. The Seafire III, the Fleet Air Arm equivalent of the Spitfire,

SPITFIRE MARK XIV WITH FIVE-BLADED AIRSCREW
Details of the Mark XIV Spitfire, used against flying-bombs and enemy fighters in north-west Europe during 1944, were released on September 8 of that year. It was powered with a Rolls-Royce Griffon engine developing over 2,000 h.p.; armament was three alternative arrangements of 20-mm. cannon and ·5-in. and ·303-in. machine-guns. The five-bladed Rotol airscrew, shown above, gave an outstanding rate of climb up to 40,000 feet. *Photo, Charles E. Brown*

powered with a Merlin motor of 1,470 h.p., and fitted with two 20-millimetre cannon and four ·303-inch machine-guns, had a top speed of about 400 m.p.h.

Perhaps nothing better illustrates the great advances made in speed during the war years than the fact that during the Moscow Conference of October 1944, Mosquitoes made twenty-one single trips between England and Moscow in eleven days, each taking only about five

hours; while during the Crimea conference of February 1945 Mr. Churchill's correspondence and his London newspaper were delivered to him every morning by Mosquito aircraft.

The power of Bomber Command's offensive was aided by the further development of British heavy bombers. The Handley Page Halifax III had Bristol Hercules XVI motors giving 1,650 h.p. The Halifax VI had Hercules 100 motors giving 1,800 h.p., providing a better take-off, faster cruising speed, a higher ceiling, and a top speed of 328 m.p.h. Maximum bomb-load grew to 14,500 lb. and range to 3,000 miles.

Heavy Bomber Development

Britain's scientific leadership during the war is further emphasized by the fact that the engine which powered America's Lockheed Shooting Star during its trial flights in January 1944 was the De Havilland Goblin gas-turbine.

The Messerschmitt-163, called the Komet, was a semi-tailless single-seater which took off under its own power, jettisoned its wheels, and landed on a retractable skid. In the air it looked rather like a huge moth, Its wing-span was 30½ ft. It was fitted with two 30-millimetre guns, and being made partly of wood, was cheap to build. The motive power was a Walter rocket unit called the HWK509, using concentrated hydrogen peroxide and a mixture of hydrazine hydrate and alcohol as fuel.

NEW SIGHTING DEVICES FOR THE R.A.F.
The Mark II D gyroscopic gun-sight for R.A.F. fighter aircraft—disclosed in August 1944—wrought revolutionary changes in R.A.F. air-combat tactics, automatically providing the pilot with the correct target, even when attacking at speeds of over 400 m.p.h. Left, dial of the Mark II D, with settings for different types of enemy aircraft. Right, Mark XIV bomb-sight, first issued to the Pathfinder Force in August 1942 (see page 2962). *Photos, British Official*

FAIREY FIREFLY AND SEAFIRE III: NEW AIRCRAFT FOR THE FLEET AIR ARM

Additions to Fleet Air Arm aircraft in 1944 included the Fairey Firefly and Seafire III, both rocket-assisted in take-off. both with folding wings, enabling more aircraft to be accommodated in carriers than hitherto. Seafire III first went into action in the Normandy invasion. Wing-span was 36 feet 8 inches; power, a single Merlin 1,470-h.p. engine, and armament, two 20-mm. cannon and 4 Browning 0·303-in. machine-guns. Fairey Firefly reconnaissance-fighter, first announced on November 7, had wing-span, 44 feet 6 inches; length, 37 feet; armament, four 20-mm. cannon; power, one 2,375-h.p. Griffon engine. 1. Ground staff unfold Firefly's wings. 2. Seafire III with wings folded. 3. Ratings attach rockets to a Seafire. 4. A Seafire takes the air.

This unit gave a maximum thrust of 3,300 lb. for a weight of 365 lb., but it consumed more than 1,000 lb. of fuel a minute at full thrust. A later unit, the HWK509C, had a smaller secondary combustion chamber, used when cruising to increase the duration of flight; in this unit the main combustion chamber gave a thrust of 3,740 lb. and the cruising chamber 660 lb. The Komet with the first unit could climb to 30,000 feet in just over 2½ minutes, and had a top speed of 550 m.p.h. The second unit gave it a top speed of 590 m.p.h., with an endurance under power of about 12 minutes. The pilots of the Komet used to give bursts of power and then shut off and glide in an endeavour to increase duration, flying in undulations somewhat in the manner of a green woodpecker.

The standard Messerschmitt-262 was fitted with two Jumo 004B axial-flow gas-turbine units. The prototype with these units first flew early in 1943, and the production model became operational in 1944. The static thrust of this unit at sea level was 1,980 lb. at 8,700 r.p.m.—the full thrust speed. At 500

FIRST GERMAN ROCKET-PROPELLED FIGHTER

The Me-163, believed to be the world's first operational rocket-propelled aircraft, appeared in 1944. It was powered with a Walter HWK509 unit, weighing only 365 lb. Death-rate among the pilots was high, and mutinies were reported. Not only was it dangerous to fly, but there were instances of its exploding while being fuelled. *Photo, Flight*

Diesel oil as fuel, four 30-millimetre cannon, and when required two bombs of 550 lb. or one of 1,100 lb. Its landing speed was about 120 miles an hour. Despite its high performance the slower Tempest fighters of 2nd T.A.F. succeeded in shooting down Me-262s, sometimes by diving on them from a superior height, and at others by continuing to fly after them even when the

Me-262 had accelerated out of sight, for often the German pilots slowed down, thinking they were safe, only to be overhauled by the Tempests, sometimes even when they had reached their airfield and were about to land.

The newest American fighter in 1944 was the Northrop Black Widow, primarily a two-seater night interceptor but also used by day. This was a fast, twin-boom aircraft, in appearance not unlike the Lockheed Lightning. But the greatest military aeronautical advance of the United States during the year was the introduction of the Boeing B-29 Super-Fortress bomber

LUFTWAFFE'S JET-PROPELLED ME-262

First German jet-propelled aircraft to be used in operations was the Me-262 fighter, which appeared about the same time in 1944 as the Me-163. It was powered with two Jumo 004B units and armed with four 30-mm. cannon. With a top speed of 525 m.p.h., it had a landing-speed of 120 m.p.h. Left, U.S. engineers examine one of the power units of a captured Me-262. Below, a Me-262 landing with tyres smoking. *Photos, Flight; Associated Press*

m.p.h. at sea level the net thrust was about 1,670 lb., and at the same speed at 20,000 feet it fell to about 1,050 lb. At 20,000 feet when flying at 500 m.p.h. this unit was equal in power to a normal propeller engine combination developing 1,400 thrust horse-power.

The Me-262 developed its top speed of 525 m.p.h. at 23,000 feet, and had a service ceiling of just under 40,000 feet. It carried over 500 gallons of light

THE BLACK WIDOW FOUGHT THE FLYING BOMBS

The U.S.A.A.F.'s twin-fuselage night-fighter, the P61 or Black Widow, came off the secret list on August 31, 1944, being announced as operating from French bases and joining in the battle of the flying-bomb. Powered with two 2,000-h.p. engines and armed with 20-mm. cannon fore and aft, its wing-span was 66 feet. It carried a crew of three. *Photo, U.S. Official*

like a two-engined plane. But the machine suffered from structural failures, fires in the air, and performance inferior to that of the British bombers. Its development was discontinued, and the Luftwaffe never caught up with British and American bomber programmes.

The Fleet Air Arm was strengthened by the addition of more Barracudas, and by the acquisition of Firefly fighters. The **New** Fairey Barracuda was **Naval** a torpedo-bomber-re- **Aircraft** connaissance, mine-laying, and dive-bomber monoplane of unusual and not very elegant design. It made an

into the war in the Far East. This 31-ton aircraft (60 tons loaded) was the biggest bomber used during the war. Powered by four 2,200 h.p. 18-cylinder air-cooled Wright Cyclone radial motors driving 16½ feet diameter four-bladed airscrews, its wing span was 141 feet, or 30 to 40 feet more than the Liberator, Flying Fortress, Stirling, Halifax and Lancaster. Its crew of 11 worked in three compartments of the fuselage, each supercharged with warmed air so that everyone could breathe comfortably and work in ordinary clothing even when flying on reconnaissance at 39,000 feet at nearly 400 m.p.h. Its ten half-inch machine-guns were electrically controlled from within the cabins, although mounted in remote turrets; from one gun station three turrets could be trained simultaneously

against one attacking fighter. These aircraft were capable of attacking targets lying more than 1,500 miles from their airfields with loads of from six to ten tons of bombs, with a maximum individual bomb size of 2,000 lb. (*See* illus. in page 3092.) In November 1945, one flew, with its gun turrets removed, non-stop from Guam to Washington, a distance of 8,000 miles.

In January 1944, the Heinkel-177 was in action for the first time over the United Kingdom. German air leaders had placed great hope in this heavy bomber as a counter to the British Halifax and Lancaster. But it proved a failure. It was designed to take four Daimler Benz engines coupled fore and aft into two double engines, and enclosed in two nacelles. This feature made this four-engined aircraft look

L.S.T. AIRCRAFT-CARRIERS

L.S.T.s (Landing Ship, Tanks) with portable landing-strips were used in the Pacific as miniature aircraft-carriers. Here a U.S. aircraft is about to land on a vessel so equipped, which could carry up to eight aircraft. *Photo, New York Times Photos*

airborne torpedo attack on April 3, 1944, on the Tirpitz when she was lying in Alten Fjord (*see* page 3070), and was used also in the Far East. With its single Merlin motor it was probably slightly under-powered, compared with many other aircraft, for the work it had to undertake.

The Fairey Firefly was a two-seater Griffon-motored naval fighter of more orthodox line, equipped with four 20-millimetre Hispano cannon in the wings. The top speed of the Mark IV Firefly was 386 m.p.h. at 14,000 feet, and this model was equipped to carry double batteries of eight rockets.

LUFTWAFFE'S ANSWER TO THE R.A.F. HALIFAX

Existence of the Luftwaffe's He-177 was disclosed by the British Air Ministry on December 22, 1943, though it had been under development since the first year of the war. Used as a long-range, high-speed bomber and reconnaissance aircraft, it was powered by four 1,500-h.p. Mercedes-Benz DB 601 engines, housed in pairs. Its wing-span was 103 feet, 6 inches; armament, 13-mm. guns in nose, dorsal, ventral and tail positions *Photo, British Official*

Chapter 334

CLIMAX OF NAVAL WAR IN THE PACIFIC

The peak of the naval fighting in Far Eastern waters was reached in 1944. Both in Britain and the United States naval construction had been largely switched to the purpose of defeating Japan, and the results showed in the growing ascendancy of the Allied fleets, particularly the U.S. fleets, which inflicted on the Japanese in October the decisive defeat of the Battle for Leyte Gulf, described in this chapter. Naval operations in the Pacific during 1943 are recorded in Chapter 263. Consult also map in page 3274

THE elimination of the Italian surface fleet and the successive sinkings of the bigger German units, permitted the Admiralty to transfer a number of ships of all kinds to the Eastern Fleet during 1944. From enemy sources there was a steady stream of reports, naming various ships which had been sent East, but these were obviously for the purpose of obtaining

C.-IN-C., EAST INDIES

A communiqué from S.E.A.C. Headquarters at Kandy, on December 11, 1944, announced the appointment of Vice-Admiral Sir Arthur Power, K.C.B., C.V.O., as Commander-in-Chief, East Indies Station, an appointment arising on the redistribution of units of the Royal Navy to form two fleets in Eastern waters.

information, and the Admiralty did not give it. But the release of various items of news culminating with that of the transfer of Admiral Sir Bruce Fraser from the Home Fleet to the Eastern Fleet on July 31 gave ample assurance to the British and American publics that affairs were moving.

In the early months of the year, only a few British units co-operated directly with the U.S. Navy in the Pacific; the Eastern Fleet as a whole confined its operations to the Indian Ocean and

the Netherlands Indies. Two of its great functions were to protect shipping in the whole of the Indian Ocean and to harry the Japanese sea supply lines to Burma, which would normally pass through the Straits of Malacca. A surprising decline in Japanese enterprise west of the Straits was observed. The first communiqué from the Headquarters of the C.-in-C., Eastern Fleet (Admiral Sir James Somerville) was published on April 10, and reported that two Japanese supply ships which had been intercepted had scuttled themselves. Carrier-borne attacks on Port Blair, Sabang, Surabaya, and Padang are described in Chapter 306; these bases were invaluable to the enemy not only for operations to westward, but also for repairing damaged ships.

In September a large Japanese convoy on its way to Burma through the Formosa Straits was attacked by rocket-firing aircraft of the U.S.A. 14th A.F. which hit fourteen supply ships and three men-of-war. The sea supply line to Burma was constantly under attack, and the enemy was forced to

rely more and more on the mountainous land route which was expensive and difficult. In the Burma campaign, also, the Royal Indian Navy did excellent work, and throughout the area the initiative was in British hands. Weather frequently made operations most difficult; a particularly heavy naval air attack against the Pangkalan Brandan oil refinery in north-east Sumatra, planned for December 20, 1944, had to be postponed until 1945 owing to weather conditions, and the secondary target, the harbour of Belewan-Deli, was taken instead (*see* page 3088).

H.M. submarines were constantly at work, largely in and around the Malay Straits, and not only took a heavy material toll of warships and merchant-men (an announcement of November 11 credited them with 45 Japanese ships) but produced indirect results by diverting Japanese warships to convoy duties. Although more spectacular events took place in the Pacific, with the U.S. Navy playing the major part, and the

Flank Attacks on Japan at Sea

COMMANDER OF THE BRITISH PACIFIC FLEET

Admiral Sir Bruce Fraser, G.C.B., K.B.E., was appointed to command the British Pacific Fleet on its formation, announced in December, 1944. In June of that year he had relinquished command of the Home Fleet on being appointed C.-in-C., British Eastern Fleet, in succession to Admiral Sir James Somerville with whom (on his left) he is here seen. Before the war he was for nearly three years Chief of Staff of the East Indies Station.

enterprise that could be desired in the Pacific theatre. The policy of "island-hopping," necessary in the early stages of reconquest but bitterly criticized by the American public and press, was supplemented by unexpected attacks far behind the Japanese lines by task forces of the U.S. fleet so that the enemy was kept continuously " on the jump " and uncertain where to mass defensive forces. At first the public failed to see any definite plan of campaign in these operations, but as more and more successes were scored, it became plain that they were a masterly scheme to pave the way for the reconquest of the Philippines, and it was realized that their plan had been determined by the range of land-based planes as there were still insufficient carriers for longer distances.

The naval difficulties were little appreciated. Distances to be covered were colossal : roughly 5,000 miles from the Philippines to the nearest U.S. dockyard at Pearl Harbor and about the same to the commercial repair facilities at Sydney. This made a fleet action a big risk even though the Americans had the finest and most numerous repair ships in any navy. The Japanese had no such facilities, and one of the first objects of the Allied plan was to put their great repair base at Truk in the Carolines out of action. Powerful task forces of the U.S. Navy, aided by hundreds of aircraft, launched an attack on Truk at dawn on February 16. The attacking forces maintained radio silence, and not until the 20th was a communiqué

Return Visit for Pearl Harbor

WITH THE EASTERN FLEET

The British Eastern Fleet, operating in the Indian Ocean, comprised British, U.S., French and Dutch units, among them H.M.S. 'Valiant' and the French battleship 'Richelieu,' (astern), here seen returning from an attack on Sabang, Sumatra. In the same operation was H.M.S. 'Queen Elizabeth' from which (right) a seaman is flinging a line, coiled up in a canister to H.M.A.S. 'Nepal', in order to pass across mails or other small articles.

Australian Fleet supporting gallantly, these flank attacks on the Japanese had a big influence on the war in the East —far larger than the public realized.

In contrast to the Japanese Navy's rapid and noticeable decline from the dash which marked its early operations, the United States Navy showed all the

AMERICAN FLOATING DRY-DOCKS IN THE PACIFIC

The U.S. naval offensive in the Pacific was greatly aided in 1944 by floating dry-docks. These were made in prefabricated sections welded together at an advanced naval base and towed as close to the combat zone as possible. Each dock had a capacity of between 56,000 and 100,000 tons. As shown here, they were large enough to accommodate two ships simultaneously. Floating machine-shops are moored alongside.

Photo, Associated Press

On January 31 a strong naval force began operations covering the first of a series of landings on the Marshall Islands on February 1. At the end of February similar tactics were employed against the Admiralty Islands, preliminary softening by air being followed by heavy bombardment by capital ships, cruisers, destroyers and rocket craft, the barrage being lifted only immediately before the actual landing. Rabaul was within an hour's flight of the Admiralties and it lost all its virtues as a base G.H.Q. for the Japanese following the Allied reoccupation of those islands.

A U.S. task force under Admiral R. A. Spruance raided the Palau Islands on March 29, and Yap and Woleai Islands on the 31st. The American communiqué of the 30th stated that " after the **Enemy Shipping in Palaus Attacked** discovery of the approach of our forces [to Palau] by enemy planes, their ships were observed fleeing the area before our units could reach attack positions"; one of the fleeing ships—an unidentified battleship—was torpedoed by a U.S. submarine, but was able to escape. At Palau five oilers were sunk; one destroyer damaged; one repair ship, 12 cargo ships and three oilers left beached, burning or damaged. Severe damage was done to a seaplane base, the docks at Babelthuap, and other buildings and installations. At Yap and

issued from Admiral Nimitz's G.H.Q. It announced that " the Pacific Fleet has returned in Truk the visit made by the Japanese Fleet to Pearl Harbor on December 7, 1941, and has effected a partial settlement of the debt." In attacks on February 16 and 17, the Americans destroyed 201 enemy planes (127 in combat); two Japanese light cruisers, three destroyers, one ammunition ship, one seaplane tender, two gunboats, two oilers, and eight cargo ships; probably sank one cruiser or large destroyer, two oilers, and four cargo ships. (Reconnaissance photographs taken later revealed that 23 ships had been sunk, six probably sunk, and 11 damaged.) Shore installations were heavily bombed. American losses were 17 aircraft, and one U.S. warship sustained moderate damage. Admiral Spruance was in over-all command of the operation; Rear-Admiral Marc A. Mitscher directed the carrier attack. The big risk taken had been fully justified by results; after that occasional air and naval visits to Truk checked reconstruction, the weightiest on April 29 and 30 when Mitscher's carrier-borne aircraft dropped 740 tons, and his warships gave the atoll a heavy shelling.

U.S. NAVY SHELLS GUAM

Ships of the U.S. 5th Fleet took part in the preliminary bombardment of the Japanese-held island of Guam, largest of the Marianas, on July 18, 1944, before the landings two days later. (See also illus. in page 3266.) Warships shelled shore installations from close range, putting A.A. guns out of action. Gunners here take cover as their ship's guns go into action.

Photo, Keystone

Japanese Fleet which followed are described in page 3093. This battle of the Philippine Sea was not in the strict sense a naval action, since the two fleets did not make contact, but it was a decisive defeat for the forces of the Japanese Navy engaged in it.

Attacks by carrier-borne aircraft and by surface vessels on Iwo Jima in the Volcano Group, Haha in the Bonins, Guam in the Marianas and other Japanese and Japanese-occupied islands far-flung in the Pacific are described in pages 3093, 3264 and 3267. The apparent impotence of the Japanese Navy against these continuous attacks, and their repeated retirement before forces which they claimed to have sunk, was presumably the reason for the extraordinary number of Japanese flag officers who continued to be reported "killed in action" (*see* page 3288); it was undeniably the reason for the dismissal of Admiral Shimada, Navy Minister, in July (*see* page 3285). Tokio radio announced on July 25 that "the times were not ripe for the Japanese fleet to fight the Allies," and on August 18 a naval spokesman declared that the Navy would not fight except to

Japanese Fleet Impotent

SAIPAN LANDINGS

Between June 10-13, 1944 a powerful U.S. task force struck at the Marianas, preparatory to the landings on Saipan on June 15. In an unsuccessful attack by enemy naval units and aircraft, 141 Japanese planes were shot down for the loss of 15 Hellcat fighters. Below, a curtain of flak covers the U.S. ships during this lively action.

Photo, New York Times Photos

R.I.N. OFF MAYU PENINSULA

At the beginning of 1944, on the Burma front, seaborne raids were launched on Arakan, seaboard strip on the Bay of Bengal. They were covered by Coastal Forces of the Royal Indian Navy which in 1943 had a total personnel of 27,000 and included sloops, a corvette, fleet mine-sweepers, trawlers, besides many useful light craft.　　*Photo, Indian Official*

Woleai, much damage was done to shore installations, and several small vessels were sunk. In the three actions, U.S. losses were 25 combat planes and 18 aircraft personnel.

Aircraft of U.S. carrier task forces also attacked and neutralized Wake Island (April 30 and May 23) and Marcus Island (May 19 and 20), before a landing was effected on June 15, under cover of Admiral Spruance's task force, on Saipan in the Marianas (*see* page 3264 and map in page 3274).

The Japanese fully understood the importance of this action—the air attacks by the Japanese on the American Fleet and by the Americans on the

defend the homeland and the inner sea supply lines (*see* page 3286).

On July 20 U.S. troops landed on Guam; on September 14 on Peleliu Island in the Palau Group (*see* page 3267). The landing on Morotai in the Halmaheras on the same

Philippines in Danger day (*see* Chapter 351) was assisted by the Royal Australian Navy, as well as by units of the R.A.A.F. Japanese strategy based on Netherlands New Guinea was completely neutralized; the Philippines were in danger and, in contrast to the early boast that no enemy had been able to set foot on the islands of Japan for a thousand years, the Premier warned the Japanese people that invasion of the homeland was not impossible.

In preparation for the assault on the Philippines, the 7th Fleet, under Vice-Admiral Thomas C. Kinkaid, was greatly reinforced to comprise a total of more than 650 ships, including old battleships, cruisers, destroyers, destroyer escorts, escort carriers, transports, cargo ships, landing craft, mine craft and supply vessels. Its task was to transport the four army divisions to be landed, to set them ashore, and to provide bombardment support. Admiral

U.S. 3rd FLEET AT PELELIU

A furious bombardment by the U.S. 3rd Fleet, in which rocket-firing close-support craft took part (below), preceded the landings by U.S. Marine and Army assault troops on Peleliu, on September 14, 1944. One of the Palau group, Peleliu was the last big Japanese stronghold in the Central Pacific, and — with Morotai — the extreme western landing before the Philippines invasion.

SUPPLIES FOR LEYTE

The Japanese in the Philippines were caught completely unawares by the U.S. landings on Leyte, central island of the group, on October 20, 1944, in the greatest amphibious operation in the Pacific to that date. (See Chapter 322.) Here a heavily laden Coast Guard manned L.S.T. noses ashore after the devastating bombardment.
Photos, Planet News; Associated Press

Halsey's 3rd Fleet, which included nearly the whole of the fast carrier and fast battleship forces in the Pacific, was to give more general cover by launching air attacks (some account of which is given in page 3093) against Formosa, Luzon, the Visayas and other strategic points. Of the vast mass of Allied ships in these fleets and their train, only two cruisers had to retire prior to the landing on October 20 on Leyte Island, which proved a complete surprise to the enemy (*see* page 3270). Once the troops were ashore, the Navy gave them invaluable support by gunfire, and also by the close watch which prevented any considerable succour

3 s²

THE DECISIVE BATTLE FOR LEYTE GULF

'One of the pivotal actions of the war' was the description given on October 27, 1944 by Mr. James Forrestal, the United States Secretary of the Navy, of the five-day Battle for Leyte Gulf which had just ended. 1. A Curtiss Hell Diver from an Essex-class carrier dropped a 1,000-lb. bomb, hitting amidships and setting on fire this enemy cruiser. 2. The Japanese 42,500-ton battleship 'Musashi' as bombs burst near her 'A' turret. Though badly damaged, she escaped, but ultimately sank. 3. The burning 10,000-ton carrier U.S.S. 'Princeton,' which was lost, hosed by a cruiser during the action. *Photos, Keystone*

reaching the defenders ; the enemy made repeated and gallant attempts to reinforce the Leyte garrison, but with little success. A special communiqué issued by General MacArthur on December 26 gave 40 or 41 transports, aggregating over 164,000 tons, as the number lost by Japan since October 20. One convoy on November 9, of four transports and fifteen destroyers, lost three transports, seven destroyers ; others on November 10 (four transports and six destroyers), December 7 (thirteen vessels) were wiped out.

The landing at Leyte at last brought the Japanese fleet to action. Relying

L.S.T.s AT TACLOBAN

Initial landings in the Philippines were made at Tacloban in northern Leyte on October 20, 1944. They were supported by the U.S. 7th Fleet with an Australian squadron. Below, the beach at Tacloban as L.S.T.s poured equipment ashore. The causeways stretching to the landing craft and enabling troops and supplies to be run straight to shore, were made by bulldozers.
Photo, Keystone

on reports that exaggerated the effect of their air attacks on the U.S. naval forces in the Pacific, the enemy determined to strike with full force at the U.S. 7th Fleet. His plan was to deliver converging attacks by two fleets.

On October 21 and 22 U.S. submarines, detecting major Japanese fleet movements northwards from Singapore, sank two heavy " Atago " class cruisers (10,000 tons) and damaged another. On October 23, carrier aircraft observed two strong naval forces moving east, one through the Sibuyan Sea, the other through the Sulu Sea. The first comprised two new battleships, three

THE PHILIPPINES

On October 29, 1944, reviewing the Battle for Leyte Gulf, Admiral Chester Nimitz, C.-in-C. U.S. Pacific Fleet, declared that it ' ranks as one of the major sea battles of World War Two in the Pacific, together with the battle of the Coral Sea, the battle of Midway, the battle of Guadalcanal, and the first battle of the Philippine Sea.' From this map the course of the long battle can be followed.

FLAGSHIP OF THE R.A.N.

The Royal Australian Navy won high praise from U.S. commanders for its part in the Leyte landings in October 1944. R.A.N. minesweepers swept Leyte Gulf; cruisers formed part of the Allied covering force; L.S.I.s carried troops. Here is H.M.A.S. 'Australia,' the flagship of 10,000 tons, which was damaged by an out-of-control enemy bomber striking the forward funnel.

Photo, Royal Australian Navy

other battleships, eight cruisers, and 13 destroyers; the second two battle-ships, two heavy cruisers, two light cruisers, and seven or eight destroyers. U.S. naval aircraft heavily attacked both forces, scoring a number of hits and severely damaging, possibly sinking, a battleship and a cruiser in the Sibuyan Sea.

Meanwhile, enemy shore-based aircraft attacked U.S. carriers lying east of the Philippines, sinking U.S.S. "Princeton" (10,000 tons) for the loss of 150 aircraft.

In the afternoon of October 23 another force of seventeen enemy war-ships, including a large aircraft carrier of the "Zuikaku" class, three light carriers of the "Ghitose" and "Zuiho" classes, two battleships, a heavy cruiser, three other cruisers and six destroyers, was sighted by naval aircraft 200 miles off Cape Engano (north Luzon) heading south. Whether this was a purely diversionary operation or was designed to provide for "mopping up" the U.S. fleet after it had been defeated and scattered by the earlier attacks is uncertain. Admiral Halsey at once concentrated a number of carrier task groups and proceeded northward at high speed to meet this new threat,

The Battle for Leyte Gulf

bringing the enemy to action on October 24. Without damage to a single U.S. ship, the 3rd Fleet sank the four carriers, one light cruiser or large destroyer, and one destroyer (another badly damaged cruiser being sunk during the night by a U.S. submarine), and damaged two battleships, three cruisers and four destroyers. The U.S. 3rd Fleet then broke off the action, and returned to assist the 7th Fleet under attack off Samar Island by the enemy force which, despite its losses in the Sibuyan Sea, had succeeded in negotiating the San Bernardino Strait. In the ensuing action most of the enemy's heavy ships were badly damaged, an 8,000-ton cruiser was sunk, and a destroyer was left adrift; a straggling cruiser was sunk by gun-fire as the enemy retired to the Sibuyan Sea, where carrier aircraft of the 3rd Fleet vigorously attacked it throughout the next day. During this phase of the battle Japan's newest battleship, the 42,500-ton "Musashi," was destroyed, together with three cruisers. Two more cruisers were so seriously damaged that they got no farther than Manila Bay, where they were subsequently sunk after persistent air attack on November 5 and November 13. Another cruiser, sheltering in Dasol Bay, suffered the same fate a few days later.

The enemy force attacked in the Sulu Sea on the night of October 23–24 to pass through the Surigao Strait and engage the 7th Fleet from the south. Every unit of this force was sunk or so severely damaged that it retired in a crippled condition. The most decisive sea battle of the Second Great War was over.

In his report of October 29, Admiral Nimitz gave Japanese losses in the second Battle of the Philippine Sea (subsequently named the Battle for Leyte Gulf) from October 22–27 as: sunk, the battleships "Huso" and "Yamashiro," four carriers, six heavy cruisers, three light cruisers, three small cruisers or large destroyers, six destroyers; severely damaged, probably sunk, one battleship, three heavy cruisers, two light cruisers, seven destroyers; escaped in damaged condition, six battleships, four heavy cruisers, two light cruisers, seven destroyers. U.S. losses were the U.S.S. "Princeton," two escort-carriers, two destroyers, one destroyer escort, and a few small craft.

A noteworthy feature of the battle is that most of the fighting was at night, enabling the Americans to reap the full advantage of an efficient radar system. The Japanese relied on searchlights and star shells, which proved less effective.

In the middle of November Tokyo stated that the British Eastern Fleet

from the Indian Ocean was operating in the Pacific, but not until December 10 did the Admiralty release the news that this fleet had been superseded by a newly created British Pacific Fleet under Admiral Sir Bruce Fraser (formerly C.-in-C., Eastern Fleet), and an East Indies Station under Vice-Admiral Sir Arthur Power. The ships of the East Indies Station operated chiefly in the Indian Ocean and were under the supreme direction of Admiral Mountbatten. The arrival in Australia of the British Pacific Fleet, which was to operate under the supreme direction of Admiral Chester Nimitz or, where appropriate, of General MacArthur, was announced at the same time. It was a strong force and included many of the newest and most powerful units of the Royal Navy, the ships specially prepared and the men specially trained. The new 35,000-ton battleship H.M.S. "Howe" was the flagship of Admiral Fraser, who declared, "Our strategy can be expressed simply. It is to find and sink the Japanese fleet. We have the strength to do it."

New Pacific Fleet Created

'ARUNTA' IN ACTION

The R.A.N. destroyer 'Arunta,' of the Tribal class, was part of the covering force in the Philippines invasion. She was later engaged in intercepting and destroying a strong enemy naval force which attempted to raid Leyte Gulf on October 25. Here 'Arunta's' guns are in action off Hollandia, Netherlands New Guinea, on April 22 (see page 3123).

Photo, Royal Australian Navy

Chapter 335

YEAR OF LIBERATION IN FRANCE

For France, 1944 was the year of liberation. That event, so impatiently awaited, dominated the whole of French internal politics—Vichy and its pseudo-government, Algiers and the Committee of National Liberation, and Metropolitan France after the invasion. The course of events, both before and after the Allied landings on June 6, is described here by Georges Gombault For the history of France in 1943, see Chapters 289 and 290

DAY by day during the first seven months of 1944, Vichy, which had never had any real existence of its own, became more and more intimately associated with the Berlin Government; it collapsed in August, when the Germans were expelled from Paris. The Committee of National Liberation moved from Algiers and installed itself in Paris as the Provisional Government of France as soon as the capital was freed. The Republic, which Pétain and Laval had suppressed in 1940, resumed its prerogatives.

At first the people of France gave themselves up to the joy of deliverance: they were full of enthusiastic gratitude to the Allied soldiers, to the French troops, and to the F.F.I. (Forces françaises de l'Intérieur, French Forces of the Interior, the combatants of the internal Resistance movement), who had given them back their country and their freedom. But they quickly realized the immensity of the destruction carried out by the enemy, and the extent of the resulting disorganization in every field. They knew they had still to suffer, and that the task of reconstruction would be enormous. But rebirth began. The end of 1944 marked the transition from occupation to independence, from acute privation imposed by the Germans to restrictions at the conclusion of which—distant as that time might be—normal life would reappear.

French Reaction to Liberation

At the end of 1943 and the beginning of 1944 the Germans, haunted by the fear of a landing and alarmed by the spirit of resistance of the French people, set out to harshen the rule of Vichy by introducing their direct agents, men who were active abettors or Nazi fanatics—Darnand, who, as Secretary of State for the maintenance of order, was virtually Minister of the Interior; Philippe Henriot, who in January was assigned the duties of Minister of Information; Marcel Déat, who was given charge of the Ministry of Labour, that is to say of the dispatch of French workers to Germany. This trio had managed to supplant Doriot, whom the Nazis continued to use for the basest police work against the patriots.

Pierre Laval looked with no good grace upon these rivals; he inferred that Hitler and Himmler were in some measure withdrawing their confidence from him. He made, however, not the least sign of concern. He even gave a cordial reception to the collaborators Berlin had sent him. He summoned all the high police officials and the heads of the gendarmerie, and requested them to carry out Darnand's orders strictly. He declared that he took full responsibility for these orders. It proved heavy: Darnand instituted courts-martial and ordered the immediate execution of those found guilty. How many patriots fell victim to these special tribunals, which were tribunals only in name and on which no magistrate sat, is not known, but they were certainly many.

The militia of which Darnand was the head (*see* pages 2902 and 2563) made no pretence at trial before killing: it systematically murdered eminent French intellectuals and democratic politicians. Victor Basch, professor emeritus at the Sorbonne, a philosopher of repute, president of the League of the Rights of Man, an old man of eighty, and his wife fell beneath the blows of Darnand's men. Georges Mandel, Colonial Minister and later Minister of the Interior in Reynaud's last Cabinets, who stood out in 1939–40 as a determined advocate of resistance, and Jean Zay, who had been Minister of Education in Léon Blum's Cabinet, were murdered on the high road. Gosse, Dean of the Faculty of Science at Grenoble, and his son, and Serlin, Senator for the Rhône, were similarly assassinated by militiamen. These were well-known persons, but numbers of obscure patriots suffered the same fate. The militia was the Gestapo's executioner; it deputized for the Gestapo when the forces of that body proved insufficient for the work it had to do.

While Darnand thus systematically decimated the forces of the Resistance, Philippe Henriot carried on wireless propaganda for Berlin: in France the former played Himmler's part, the latter that of Goebbels. Philippe

S.S. MEN REPEAT LIDICE MASSACRE IN FRANCE

Probably the most horrible atrocity perpetrated as a 'reprisal' by the Germans in France occurred on June 10, 1944 at Oradour-sur-Glane, a village near Limoges. Here S.S. troops rounded up the inhabitants, summarily shot the men, flung the women and children into the church in which they had placed time-bombs, and burnt the village. Of between 750–800 people only seven escaped. This is the church after the explosion. *Photo, Keystone*

F.F.I. DESTROY THE BARRACKS AT GRENOBLE

Grenoble was a strong centre of French resistance towards the end of 1943. Among notable acts of sabotage was the destruction of the Artillery Park on November 13–14, following the seizure of hostages by the Germans. On December 2, after an ultimatum to the Nazis had been rejected, patriots blew up the 'De Bonne' barracks—here seen after the explosion—killing 220 Germans and wounding 500.

Photo, French Official

Henriot, who had represented the department of the Gironde in the Chamber of Deputies, was a demagogue of the extreme Right. On public platforms he had specialized in the most violent attacks on the Republican regime ; he had secured attention by a certain facility in popular oratory, the wheedling manner of a juggler at a fair, and a complete absence of scruples in the means he adopted. Vichy made use of him, however, at first only in secondary

FRENCH NORTH AFRICA HAILS THE RISING TIDE

France's African Empire followed with growing interest events at home before and after the Normandy landings. General de Gaulle is enthusiastically welcomed at Bizerta on May 9, 1944, a year after its liberation. Left, members of the French National Committee of Liberation, later the Provisional Government, watch the unveiling of a huge map of France showing the Allied advance on Paris, which was displayed outside the Post Office in Algiers after the invasion.

Photos, U.S. Official

posts, and on this account Henriot became bitterly resentful against Laval, whom he privately charged with having sold himself to the Germans.

This line of attack did not prevent Henriot from himself courting German favour : they rewarded him by getting him made Minister of Information. In this capacity he spoke every day at the microphone and carried on a virulent campaign against the French patriots and against the Allies. When the landing was imminent, he called for active opposition to the British and Americans. One morning a group of

patriots killed him at the Ministry of Information. Vichy arranged a "national" funeral for him and organized a ceremony at Nôtre Dame. The people of France considered his execution an act of justice and patriotic vengeance.

The third person whose entry into the Government was secured by the Germans was Marcel Déat. He had gained favour with the Nazis by his impassioned defeatism before the war and his campaigns in the "Oeuvre" in favour of the closest collaboration with the enemy. But Pétain detested him on account of his lack of respect, and Laval feared a rival in him. Marcel Déat was certainly ambitious to play the lead ; but he had to content himself with the secondary part of Minister of Labour. In this post, however, he showed the greatest zeal. Emulating Ley, he sent to Germany all the workers he could possibly get together. Working with the small collaborationist group among the trade union leaders, Déat made use of the worst police methods to secure the labour Berlin demanded and to compel men to leave for Germany. With Laval, he was the most hated man in France.

Vichy's New Minister of Labour

During the first months of 1944 there was an appalling increase in the searches, the persecutions, the punishments inflicted by the occupying forces. The men of the Resistance were pursued by the Gestapo and by Darnand's militia ; punitive expeditions were organized by the S.S. or the militia against the Maquis ; villages were destroyed by fire and explosives, their inhabitants machine-gunned or burned alive—the episode of Oradour-sur-Glane, the village whose entire population was massacred, will live long in men's memories. Deportations to Germany multiplied.

Jewish citizens were systematically arrested in town after town, region after region, and collected in camps to be sent to Germany for extermination in gas chambers. It was a period of savage terrorism.

But it was also, for the "collaborators," a period of terrible anxiety. Pétain tried to convoke the Chamber of Deputies and the Senate, and to normalize his regime. But, called harshly to order by Ribbentrop, he did not persist. Pierre Laval tried to make use of Mr. Edouard Herriot, whom the Germans placed at his disposal for a few days. But Herriot would not lend himself to Laval's game. Inevitably these efforts of men at bay failed. Their fear grew as Allied successes mounted; it became panic in the days following June 6, once there was no doubt that the landing had succeeded. It was useless for Marcel Déat to write that the Wehrmacht had in reserve a smashing reply to Eisenhower and Montgomery—and for Jean-Hérold Paquis and the other hired spokesmen of Berlin to tell the same story on the wireless. All of them were forced to realize, after the British victory at Caen and the lightning advance of General Patton's U.S. 3rd army, that Germany, and therefore they themselves had lost the game. Then came the organization of flight. Each made his own arrangements for escaping with the German army, if not for speeding ahead of it. Vichy was dismembered, dispersed, in the dissolution of death. Vichy had ceased to exist.

Pétain, Laval, Déat, Darnand, De Brinon, Doriot, the whole paid crew of collaborating politicians, journalists and

Collaborators Flee to Germany

wireless propagandists, found themselves in Germany. But harmony did not reign among them. Laval, who had renounced power, and Pétain ceased to speak to one another, although they lived in the same castle at Sigmaringen. De Brinon constituted with Déat a sort of government committee. Darnand reorganized the militiamen who had accompanied him. Paquis broadcast from a German radio station. Thus Hitler, Himmler and Goebbels continued to find a use for their agents. But all these émigrés, traitors to their country, were well aware that they would be trapped beneath the ruins of Hitler's Reich, which was already in process of collapse. "Collaboration" came to its logical, sordid end in Germany.

After the Allied landing in North Africa, Algiers became the temporary capital of France. The French Committee of National Liberation (*see* page 2910 *et seq.*) continued to exercise the functions of a government. On April 3, the Communists entered the Ministry : Mr. Fernand Grenier, formerly deputy

IN THE WAKE OF THE ALLIED ARMIES IN NORMANDY

Among Allied leaders in the liberation of France was 42-year-old General Jacques Phillipe Leclerc, commanding the French 2nd Armoured Division which fought with the Americans. 1. General Leclerc with a French tank crew after their first battle. 2. British troops join in the Fourteenth of July celebrations at Bayeux (freed June 7). 3. Refugees in a stable near Falaise wait for transport to evacuation areas. *Photos, P.N.A.; Keystone; British Official*

for St. Denis (Paris), received the portfolio of Air, and Mr. Billoux, deputy for Marseilles, became a Minister of State.

The Provisional Consultative Assembly continued to study most carefully the problems submitted to it. There

Consultative Assembly Activities were debates on foreign policy, in which close co-operation with the Allies was advocated; on the organization of public administration in France, keen concern being shown for the restoration of freedom; on the rights to be granted to the native populations of the French colonial possessions; on the organization of the Press; and on the purging of the public service, the purge so far carried out being considered inadequate.

It was complained especially that men of Vichy continued to hold positions in

INVASION CURRENCY

French paper money, printed abroad, amounting in value to not more than £3 per head and intended for only immediate needs, was issued to Allied invasion forces. Rate of exchange in February 1944 had been fixed at 200 francs to the pound. Obverse and reverse sides of a five-franc note are shown.

the administration and the army. The authorities countered with the assertion that in many cases they had no one to put in the place of those to whom objection was taken, for Marshal Pétain's prestige was still considerable among the soldiers of the army in Africa, which had been commanded by General Weygand, and in certain civilian circles in Algeria. Little by little, however, Vichy's victims were wrested from

the hands of their intended executioners, and restrictive laws were abrogated. Justice pursued its course: eleven officers and guards of one camp, that of Hadjerat, accused of the murder or torture of patriots and republicans, were tried at Algiers during February. On March 3, four were condemned to death, two to life imprisonment with hard labour, two to twenty years' imprisonment, and two to ten years; one was acquitted. Pierre Pucheu, former Vichy Minister of the Interior, who had carried out savage measures of repression against the Resistance movement, was condemned to death by a special military tribunal at Algiers, and was executed on March 20.

The army in Africa, from which Mr. Le Troquer eliminated the most deeply compromised Vichy elements, fought bravely in Tunisia under the command of General Giraud and General Juin; a German division surrendered to one of its leaders, General Mathenet. A gradual amalgamation took place between these troops and the forces raised by De Gaulle, which had been carrying on the struggle since 1940. But the young generals of fighting France—Koenig, Leclerc, De Larminat—retained a certain autonomy.

General Giraud was Commander in Chief of this combined army, which was re-equipped by the United States. On April 10 General de Gaulle offered him the post of Inspector-General of the Army. General Giraud refused the appointment and went on the retired list. From that moment General de Gaulle exercised supreme authority over the army, while remaining President of the Committee of National Liberation.

In his capacity as head of the government, General de Gaulle broadcast several times in order to stimulate the spirit of resistance, to defend the rights of France which Vichy had sacrificed, and to make known his views on the future regime in France. He proclaimed the return of liberty and spoke repeatedly of "the force and the stability which the authority of the State and the greatness of France demanded." On June 2, in Algiers, the Committee of National Liberation adopted an ordinance by which it took the name of Provisional Government of the French Republic.

As soon as Normandy was liberated (see Chapter 311), the President of the Provisional Government proceeded thither, and he went on to Paris the moment the capital was purged of the Germans (see page 3244). On August 26 General de Gaulle laid a wreath on the tomb of the Unknown Soldier at the Arc de Triomphe, and then walked down the Champs Elysées to the Place de la

SAVED FROM SABOTAGE

Important task of the F.F.I., as the Allied armies crossed France, was the prevention of sabotage by the retreating Germans. In Paris, before the liberation, F.F.I. forces, employed as labourers in a vast German underground explosives factory and storage depot on the outskirts of the city, cut the demolition wires at the crucial moment. Among weapons saved were these U-boat torpedoes. *Photo, New York Times Photos*

Concorde, accompanied by the National Council of Resistance, by the Minister for the Liberated Regions, Mr. Le Troquer, and by others of his close associates. The people acclaimed the General in a frenzy of enthusiasm; they saluted in him the man who on June 18, 1940 had not despaired, who had called upon the French to continue the struggle by the side of Great Britain, and whose bold anticipation had now been justified by the event. From the Place de la Concorde the General drove to Nôtre Dame to attend a service of thanksgiving for the liberation of Paris. Shots were fired at him by snipers perched on the roofs of surrounding houses, on the roof of the Cathedral, and even inside it, but he walked calm and unharmed through a hail of bullets, and though there were casualties the firing did nothing to abate the joy of the Parisians.

But while the people were rejoicing it was necessary to organize public administration. First of all a Government had to be instituted.

Paris Resistance Council General de Gaulle found in Paris the National Council of Resistance, of which Mr. Georges Bidault was president, and on which Mr. Alexandre Parodi represented Algiers. The Resistance Council had given the signal for the rising in Paris. In order to meet essential administrative requirements, it had placed Secretaries-General at the head of the principal Ministries.

COMMANDER OF THE BRITISH SECOND ARMY

In January 1944, Lieutenant-General Miles Christopher Dempsey, D.S.O., M.C., returned from Italy (where he had commanded the XIII Corps of the 8th Army), to become C.-in-C. of the British 2nd Army then being formed. Five months later, he led it across the Normandy beaches and thence through France, Belgium and Holland into Germany. On October 16, 1944, H.M. The King invested General Dempsey with the K.C.B. in the field.

3 s³

COMPANY SERGEANT-MAJOR WATERS, LANCASHIRE HOME GUARD

BRITAIN'S HOME GUА

IF the Second Great War did not call forth a
remarkable contribution to British art than
which distinguished the First, with the fine fresh
of inspiration which it evoked in the memo
action pictures of the Brothers Nash, Eric Kennin
C. R. W. Nevinson, and the vivid portraiture o
William Orpen, to mention but a few, it has at
seen a vastly greater total of artistic energy an
decline of imaginative power.

The examples already given in our pages o
paintings by combatant artists who fought in
fires during the air attacks on London have s
the richness of the war record which personal ex
ence has left for future generations to contempl

COAST DEFENCE SEARCH

ECORDS for POSTERITY

Among the official artists of the First Great War who have been active in the Second, Eric Kennington has worthily exercised his eminent gift for interpreting character in his most convincing studies of the men who made our Home Guard (which was disbanded on Monday, December 31, 1945) a glory of the common people, and we are proud to include among the artistic documents of our History this selection, which so well illustrates the artist's sensitive and penetrating portraiture, from 'Britain's Home Guard,' published in 1945 by George G. Harrap & Co., Ltd., with appropriate text by John Brophy. They are reproduced here from the original blocks by kind permission of the artist and his publishers.

SERGEANT BLUETT, CORNWALL HOME GUARD

LANCASHIRE HOME GUARD

CHINA'S WAR IS OUR WAR

UNITED 'AID TO CHINA FUND
57 New Bond Street · London W1 · Tel. Mayfair 6511·5

TELEGRAPH LESS

Steering London through
daylight & blackout - faithfully

DANGER
DON'T TOUCH

IF YOU FIND ONE OF THESE TELL TEACHER OR A POLICEMAN
DO NOT TOUCH IT EVEN WITH A STICK
AND DO NOT THROW STONES AT IT

AID THE WOUNDED
red army day feb. 23

DRIVERS

Before you start!.

LOOK OUT for CHILDREN

radiolocation

TRAIN WITH THE ARMY OR WITH THE A.T.S

MEN AND WOMEN ARE URGENTLY REQUIRED TO OPERATE AND MAINTAIN RADIOLOCATION EQUIPMENT IN THE
ROYAL ARTILLERY AND ROYAL ARMY ORDNANCE CORPS.   PARTICULARS MAY BE OBTAINED FROM ANY
RECRUITING OFFICE AND IN THE CASE OF WOMEN, FROM ANY RECRUITING OFFICE OR LABOUR EXCHANGE.

stub it out

1,000 FIRES A DAY HELP HITLER

APPEALS BY POSTER

These posters with
their varying ap-
peals to British citi-
zens on the Home
Front were ex-
hibited on hoard-
ings and factory
noticeboards during
1943-44. Typical of
numerous effective
designs produced
in this period, they
continue the selec-
tions given on the
plate facing page
3027 and in pre-
vious pages.

ORDER YOUR FUEL
NOW

-but
STORE IT FOR THE WINTER

TALK LESS

YOU NEVER KNOW

COVER your HAIR
FOR SAFETY

YOUR RUSSIAN
SISTER DOES !

SALUTE THE SOLDIER
SAVE MORE   LEND MORE

General de Gaulle quickly formed his Government : he kept a number of those who had been his colleagues at Algiers, and secured the assistance of several members of the Resistance Council and other Resistance elements. Mr. Georges Bidault became Foreign Minister in succession to Mr. René Massigli, who was appointed Ambassador in London ; Mr. Parodi became Minister of Labour, Mr. Aimé Lepercq Minister of Finance. Mr. Jules Jeanneney, former president of the Senate, became Minister of State. Eight of the Ministers at Algiers went out of office, including Mr. Massigli, Mr. Henri Queuille, Minister of State, a Radical ; Mr. André Philip,

was made Minister of Agriculture, and Mr. Augustin Laurent, former Deputy, Socialist, became Minister of Posts ; Mr. Pierre Mendès-France, former Deputy, Radical, left the Finance Ministry for the Ministry of National Economy. A few weeks later, following the death of Mr. Lepercq in a motor accident on November 10, Mr. René Pleven became Minister of Finance ; his place was taken at the Colonial Ministry by Mr. Paul Giacobbi, Radical, who himself was succeeded at the Ministry of Food by Mr. Paul Ramadier, Socialist. Mr. Raoul Dautry, Minister of Armaments in the Daladier Cabinet, was appointed Minister of Reconstruction on November 24.

The Provisional Government at once found itself faced with an immense task. It had to overcome the harshest material difficulties. The country was completely disorganized, the ports destroyed and some of them still in the hands of the enemy. Many bridges had been demolished, roads destroyed, telephone and telegraph lines cut. Of France's 18,000 locomotives only 2,000 remained in use, and of her 450,000 coaches and trucks only 160,000 were fit to run. There remained 6,000 out of 18,000 lorries, and few motor cars. The shortage of tires was acute. The only motor spirit was supplied by the Allied military authorities, and civilian needs came after the exigencies of the war. The Government, during this initial period, had the greatest difficulty in making contact with the rest of France. In anticipation of this difficulty, it had appointed for each region a commissioner of the Republic, who had almost unlimited powers. But the central authority had the greatest trouble in making its instructions run in all parts of France, and in giving its initiative to the whole country. The crucial problem was, therefore, that of transport and communications. The public authorities promptly applied

Problems Facing the Government

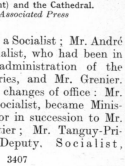

DE GAULLE IN PARIS

On August 26, 1944, twenty-four hours after arriving in liberated Paris, General de Gaulle narrowly escaped death from snipers both inside and outside the Cathedral of Nôtre Dame. His calmness under the hail of bullets was remarkable. Here, the General, cheered by the crowds, walks down the Champs Elysées on his way to the Place de la Concorde (right) and the Cathedral.
Photos, Associated Press

Minister of State, a Socialist ; Mr. André Le Troquer, Socialist, who had been in charge of the administration of the liberated territories, and Mr. Grenier. There were some changes of office : Mr. Adrien Tixier, Socialist, became Minister of the Interior in succession to Mr. Emmanuel d'Astier ; Mr. Tanguy-Prigent, former Deputy, Socialist,

FINAL STAGES IN THE LIBERATION OF THE FRENCH CAPITAL

After four years and two months, Paris was liberated in a six-day battle which began on August 19, 1944, when the National Council of Resistance and the Paris Committee of Liberation went into action with F.F.I. 50,000 strong. Six days later the French 2nd Armoured Division penetrated to the heart of the city (see page 3244). 1. A German with a white flag surrenders to members of the F.F.I. at the Chamber of Deputies, on behalf of 500 Nazis who had barricaded themselves in there. 2. Crowds in the Place de l'Hôtel de Ville crouch down to avoid snipers' bullets on August 26 (see page 3406). 3. Collaborator stripped of his trousers before being arrested by the F.F.I. 4. A French machine-gunner in action in Paris. 5. Nazi prisoners, driven away under the Eiffel Tower in U.S. jeeps, shrink from the jeers of a Frenchwoman.

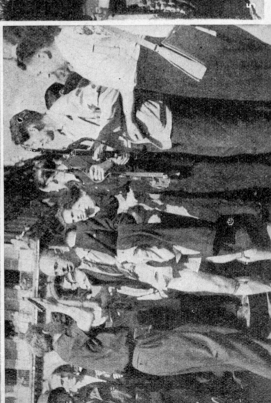

BRITISH TROOPS IN FRANCE'S FREED CAPITAL

Although Paris was cleared of the Germans by the end of August 1944 (see page 3244), acute shortage of food did not diminish, and during the severe winter of 1944-45 a large part of the population continued to be undernourished. Allied troops managed to bring in foodstuffs, but this relief was strictly governed by military needs. Right, British Army lorry delivers a welcome load of flour. Left, British soldiers at the salute in a ceremony at the Tomb of France's Unknown Soldier of the war of 1914-1918. *Photos, British Official ; British Newspaper Pool*

themselves to the task of solving it, at least in part ; temporary repairs were made, and the latter half of 1944 showed a notable improvement. The Government could communicate by telephone and telegraph with the regional commissioners and the prefects. Its authority began to function normally, and day by day the departmental or local Liberation committees lost a little more of their powers.

The Government, indeed, found itself faced by, or working alongside, the organizations of resistance : in Paris
Claims of the Resistance Movement
there was the National Council of Resistance ; in the provinces there were the Liberation committees, which in some places (though this was exceptional) gave their instructions to the prefects and sub-prefects. The Resistance made no claim to govern, but it was determined that no one should govern without it.

It argued on the strength of the part it had played as an underground movement, and that part had, indeed, been of capital importance. During the first half of 1944, in spite of increasing persecution by the enemy, the Resistance groups had redoubled their activity : carrying out their special tasks, they had multiplied acts of sabotage and of surprise destruction ; sent an increasing amount of information to London or Algiers ; stimulated propaganda by means of tracts and newspapers ; and the men of the Maquis had grown more aggressive. At the moment of the landing the F.F.I. and the F.T.P. [Francs-tireurs (or snipers) et Patriotes] harassed the enemy rear, disorganized enemy transport. During the fighting, detachments of the F.F.I. and the F.T.P., with such poor arms as they possessed, threw themselves upon the German troops. They seized Paris

before the arrival of General Leclerc's French 2nd Armoured Division.

The value General Eisenhower placed on the Resistance groups, and the position they occupied in Allied military strategy, was left in no doubt after the issue of the following statement on July 15 : " The Supreme Allied Commander has conclusive evidence that the German Forces in France have acted upon the announcement of June 7, made by the C.-in-C. of the German armed forces in the West, labelling as francs-tireurs the members of French Resistance groups. The Supreme Commander, therefore, makes the following statement : (1) The French Forces of the Interior constitute a combatant force commanded and directed by General Koenig [*see* page 3183], and forming an integral part of the Allied Expeditionary Force. (2) The F.F.I. in the Maquis bear arms openly against the enemy and are instructed to conduct their operations against him in accordance with the rules of war. They are provided with a distinctive emblem and are regarded by General Eisenhower as an army under his command. (3) In these circumstances reprisals against Resistance groups violate the rules of war by which Germany is bound. . . . (4) The Supreme Commander is determined that every effort will be made to trace the authors of any atrocities committed against members of the forces under his command. Steps to this end are already being taken. The guilty will be brought to swift justice."

The Resistance demanded that this should be remembered. Essentially a

popular movement, revolutionary in temperament, it was ardently democratic in feeling : that is why the National Council of Resistance proposed to General de Gaulle that the Republic should be solemnly proclaimed at the Hôtel de Ville in Paris. It organized repeated mass demonstrations. It drew up a programme of reforms in which the suppression of every vestige of Vichy, nationalization, the fight against " the trusts," and the merciless punishment of the Fifth Column figured prominently.

The Government, although born of insurrection, wanted to establish itself as a regular, even a moderating power. It set about diminishing the importance of the National Council of Resistance and the Liberation committees, depriving them of any semblance of official institutions. The F.F.I. and the F.T.P. were disarmed or incorporated into the army : a special section, which lasted only a few months, was created at the Ministry of War to deal with this matter. Municipal elections were held, and in each commune elected councils replaced the Liberation committees.

The Resistance movement which, during the occupation, had pursued a single aim, the liberation of the country, lost its homogeneity once that aim had been achieved. Its various organizations grouped
Revival of Parties
themselves into two main formations— the Liberation Movement, inspired by the Socialists, and the National Front, mainly Communist. Moreover, the Resistance proved to be in no sense

a party. The old parties revived, and most of the members of the Resistance rejoined them and exercised their influence within them. The political action of the Resistance proper grew less and less, and the Provisional Government progressively disengaged itself from it ; it rested mainly on an old party, the Socialists, and a new one, the M.R.P. (Mouvement Républicain Populaire, People's Republican Movement), which claimed to include those Catholics who were strongly in favour of social progress. Thus, while attaching importance to the support of the whole nation, while bringing in the representatives of the various political and spiritual groups of France, while remaining associated with the Resistance, the Government seemed to have as its axis a sort of centre formed by the M.R.P., that is to say the popular democrats, and the Socialists led by Mr. Vincent-Auriol, pending the liberation of Mr. Léon Blum, who was a prisoner in Germany.

The first act of the President of the Provisional Government was to issue a proclamation (September 10) abolishing

Women Given Franchise

the so - called *Etat français* set up by Marshal Pétain, abrogating all Vichy legislation, and affirming that France had never ceased to be a Republic. But the constitution of 1875 was not restored. General de Gaulle said on September 12 : "As soon as all national territory is liberated, and the prisoners are home, we shall lead the nation to the ballot-

box, and by the universal suffrage of all men and women re-establish the National Assembly," and that freely-elected Assembly was to have the task of producing a new constitution. There had been little agitation in France for woman suffrage, and this spontaneous inclusion of women in the prospective electors of the National Assembly, and in the actual electors of the local councils, was a striking tribute to the part they had played in the Resistance movement. Except where it was established that the prefects and sub-prefects appointed by Vichy had belonged to the Resistance and had continued in office under its orders, they were dismissed and replaced by patriots.

In each Ministry a *Commission d'Epuration* (purge commission) was set up. It examined the cases of all the officials, and submitted its recommendations to the Minister in charge. According to the degree of his offence, the official was reduced in rank, retired on pension, or dismissed without pension. These administrative punishments did not exclude the possibility of legal action. The purge went farthest in the Ministry of the Interior. The police came under that Department, and those infamous officials who had collaborated with the Gestapo could not be retained ; the renascent Republic required a dependable and loyal police.

At first, armed groups of the Resistance sought out collaborators. Sometimes, though not often, they carried out summary executions ; more often they delivered up their prisoners to

FREEDOM MEDAL

The French Provisional Government in December 1944 struck a medal for those who had distinguished themselves during the liberation of Paris. It was designed by the sculptor L. Bazor. Here are the obverse (top) and reverse sides, the former depicting a worker armed with a tommy-gun.

the special courts of justice (on which women could sit) set up by the Government to try traitors and collaborators.

Sentences were pronounced in virtue of the laws of the Republic concerning treason and intelligence or trading with the enemy. A new penalty was instituted, **Collaborators** that of national dis- **Interned** grace. It was pronounced by civil courts for a stated period or in perpetuity ; it included deprivation of civil and political rights, and could be accompanied by deprivation of property. All individuals suspected of Nazism were interned by the administrative authorities in camps in which followers of De Gaulle, democrats and Jews had been confined, notably in one at Drancy. Little by little these measures of repression were regularized, not, however, without many complaints that the purge was too slow and lenient.

Three men charged with the murder of Mr. Georges Mandel (Colonial Minister and later Minister of the Interior in Reynaud's Cabinet in 1940) were brought before the Paris Court of Justice on October 25. Mandel, after spending a

CYCLE-TAXIS FOR FOOT-WEARY PARISIANS

One of the main problems for Parisians after the liberation was transport. The Germans had left the city without petrol, the Allied military could spare little. No taxi-cabs or buses were available, and the underground system, the Metro, running only intermittently, was painfully overcrowded. Here are cycle-taxis lined up for hire. They were towed by cyclists.

Photos, Keystone ; U.S. Official

year in a Weimar concentration camp, had been brought back to the Santé Prison, Paris on July 7, 1944, as a hostage. Next day, on the pretence that he was being taken to Vichy, he was driven into the Forest of Fontainebleau and there murdered. Two of those charged, described by the prosecution as "accredited

NEW FRENCH POSTAGE STAMP

In late 1944, the French Government issued its new postage stamps. Replacing the head of Pétain was that of Liberty wearing the Phrygian cap. They were designed by Edmond Dulac, French-born British artist.

killers of the militia," were sentenced to death and executed on October 28, and the third received twenty years' hard labour.

An important problem was that of the news service. The men of the Resistance had seized the radio and had ensured a wireless service, on the initiative of Mr. Guignebert, even before Paris was liberated. The broadcasting staff was purged and the service reorganized and placed under the direction of the State.

The Vichy news agency (Office d'Information) was replaced by the France-Presse agency, which was also given an official character, pending its organization on a co-operative basis.

The newspapers were brought under regulations drawn up at Algiers. Only the daily and weekly newspapers authorized by the Ministry of Information were permitted to appear : they took over the premises of suppressed newspapers, and were given a quota of paper. Vichy and collaborationist papers were forbidden to appear : they had, indeed, gone out of existence the moment the enemy disappeared—for instance, the "Matin," the "Petit Parisien," the "Oeuvre," "Gringoire," to mention the most gravely compromised. Only those of the old papers reappeared which had ceased publication before July 1940, or, in the south, had scuttled themselves before November 1942, that is to say, before the occupation of all France. Thus, such papers as the "Populaire," "Humanité," "L'Aube," "Figaro" were seen once more in Paris. A number of underground papers came into the open, among them "Libération," "Combat," "Franc-Tireur," "Front National." The same rules were applied in the provinces, but the paper shortage greatly reduced the number of dailies, as well as the number and even the size

Purge of the Press

of pages. In many towns only a single newspaper appeared.

The censorship was maintained at first. There were protests against the exercise of political censorship, and it was brought to an end. There remained in principle only the military censorship.

A Commission composed of delegates from among newspaper editors or professional journalists, and presided over by a magistrate, carried out a purge of journalists. Only those members of newspaper staffs were allowed to carry on their profession to whom the Commission granted the card provided for by the law of 1935 regulating the journalists' profession.

The principle of freedom of the press had been affirmed ; gradually it became a reality, subject to the system of authorization. The reorganization of the cinema came more slowly. German films, naturally, were no longer shown ; films depicting the most glorious episodes of the Resistance or of the Allied campaigns took their place. A great effort to give renewed life to French film-making was made by the member of the Resistance responsible for its direction, Mr. Painlevé.

The Government not only had to substitute a régime of liberty for the despotism of Vichy, it had also the urgent tasks of assuring the food supply

LAVAL CONDEMNED TO DEATH IN HIS ABSENCE

Pierre Laval, Chief of the Vichy Government, whose property was seized by the French Provisional Government on September 4, 1944, was sentenced to death in his absence by the Court of Marseilles on October 20. Here is a copy of the death-sentence posted outside the former collaborationist Government H.Q., the Hôtel du Parc, Vichy (see illus. in page 2566). Having fled to Germany, he was described as of 'unknown residence.'

Photo, U.S. Official

of the country and of restoring its economic life. In this field it was faced with two obstacles—the disorganization of transport and the coal shortage.

In regard to transport, the Government had some success in mitigating the gravity of the crisis; but not to
the extent of restoring
Population normal food supply in
Under- the great cities. For this
Nourished reason, and because of
the insufficiency of agricultural production, and, indeed, also because of administrative mistakes, it proved impossible to assure even the insufficient rations to which everyone was in theory entitled. There was, for instance, an almost complete absence of fats. Moreover, consumers were resourceful in procuring the supplies they needed; this was the prime cause of the continued existence of the black market (considered under the occupation a laudable thing, since it diverted supplies from the enemy) to which those persons had recourse who had the means. The Government fought the black market, but as the police measures were not accompanied by any substantial improvement in the distribution of

PARIS—NOVEMBER 11, 1944
In 1944, Paris celebrated Armistice Day for the first time for five years, when Mr. Churchill and General de Gaulle took the salute from Allied forces in the Champs Elysées. It was the Premier's first visit since the city's liberation. Below, Mr. Churchill and the General, with Mr. Jules Jeanneney and Mr. Anthony Eden.
Photo, New York Times Photos

THE ASSEMBLY MEETS IN THE FRENCH CAPITAL
The French Consultative Assembly, which originally met in Algiers in November 1943 (see page 2915), held its first meeting in Paris—at the Luxembourg Palace—on November 7, 1944—with Mr. Felix Gouin as President. It consisted of 248 members, including seven women: the first time women had sat in a French Parliament. General de Gaulle, President of the French Provisional Government, arrives with Mr. Gouin for the opening ceremony.
Photo, French Ministry of Information

food, they remained largely ineffective. The Allies brought in certain quantities of foodstuffs, but these were limited by military exigencies. Various expedients were attempted in order to meet the lack of food—for example, parcels from the countryside; but beyond question a large part of the population, both in big towns and in country districts where the land was poor, continued to be under-nourished.

As for coal, the Government did not succeed in remedying the shortage. The miners who, owing to poor feeding, could not work to their full capacity, were hampered also by lack of pit props. Even after the coal had been extracted there were no trucks or barges to transport it. If a few lighters became available, the state of the locks (and in the winter ice) made the canals unusable. Finally, military needs had to have priority, since operations were still in progress. There were two main consequences: industry could not get going again, and the number of blast furnaces, factories, and other works restarted was infinitesimal; and throughout the particularly severe winter of 1944–45, homes, hospitals and schools remained unheated, and gas and electricity were strictly rationed. In November and December the situation of the country, short of food and warmth, became very bad.

The Consultative Assembly (*see* page 2915) held its fifth and last session in Algiers from July 24–26. When it met again in Paris, on November 7, its composition had been changed. Of its 248 members, 148 represented the Resistance movement in France, 60 were former deputies and senators who had voted against Pétain in 1940, 28 represented Corsican and other resistance groups outside France, and 12 represented overseas territories. The Assembly still had no control over the Provisional Government, and though bills and proposed financial measures were submitted to it, the Government was under no obligation to follow the advice it offered.

The twenty-year Franco-Soviet Treaty of Alliance and Mutual Assistance (*see* Historical Document 285, page 3358) negotiated by General
de Gaulle in Moscow in **Franco-**
December (*see* page **Soviet**
3357) was an inter- **Treaty**
national event second only in importance to the recognition of the Committee of National Liberation as the Provisional Government of France by the United Kingdom, the United States, and Soviet Russia on October 23 following the transfer by Allied Military Government of the greater part of France, including Paris, to its administration.

September 1. Dieppe, Verdun and Arras liberated. R.A.F. made night attack on Bremen. German guns bombarded S.E. England for 5½ hours. First major U.S. bombing of Philippines ; U.S. task forces attacked Bonin, Volcano and Mariana Islands. General Montgomery's promotion to Field-Marshal announced.

September 2. Lens, Douai, Bapaume, Vimy Ridge, St. Valéry-en-Caux liberated. Allies crossed Belgian frontier. 5th Army occupied Pisa (Italy). U.S. Liberators dropped 130 tons on Davao (Philippines) ; U.S. task force bombarded Wake Island. Greek Government of National Unity formed in Cairo.

September 3. Brussels, Tournai, Béthune, Abbeville, Lyons, Villefranche liberated. Heavy attacks on Brest by American bombers. Enemy cleared from Pesaro (Italy).

September 4. Antwerp, Malines, Louvain, Mons, Lille, Macon liberated. Concentrated R.A.F. night attack on Karlsruhe. M.A.A.F. made 1,800 sorties in N. Italy. Partisan rising in Czechoslovakia.

September 5. Charleroi and Namur liberated ; U.S.A. 8th A.F. heavily bombed Karlsruhe ; R.A.F. dropped over 1,000 tons on Le Havre (day), bombed Hanover, Krefeld, Maastricht (night). 8th Army closing in on Rimini (Italy). 14th Army captured Sittaung (Burma). Cease-fire on Soviet-Finnish front ; U.S.S.R. declared war on Bulgaria.

September 6. Ghent, Courtrai, Armentières, Poitiers, Châlon-sur-Saone, Cluny liberated. U.S task force attacked Palau Islands.

September 6 and 7. U.S. Liberators dropped over 250 tons on bases near Davao (Philippines).

September 7. Ypres liberated. Karlsruhe bombed by R.A.F. (night). Organized evacuation from London ceased.

September 8. Liége, Beaune, Le Creusot, Besançon liberated. 1,500 U.S. aircraft attacked Ludwigshafen, Karlsruhe, Kastel (Germany). Concentrated R.A.F. night attack on Nuremberg. First rockets fell in London. Red Army captured Varna and Ruschuk (Bulgaria). Targets in Yugoslavia heavily bombed by Allied aircraft. Japanese capture of Lingling (Hunan, China) announced. Enemy convoy (32 ships and 20 sampans) wiped out by air attack off Mindanao (Philippines). Bulgaria declared war on Germany.

September 9. 1,500-1,750 U.S. aircraft attacked Mannheim, Ludwigshafen, Mainz, Düsseldorf, the Ruhr ; R.A.F. made night attack on Munchen-Gladbach. Cease-fire on Soviet-Bulgarian front.

September 10. Enemy resistance in Ghent and Ostend ceased ; city of Luxembourg liberated. Canadian assault on Le Havre began. 1,600-1,850 U.S. aircraft attacked Gaggenau, Nuremberg, Ulm (Germany). Naval bombardment of Rimini (Italy) begins.

September 10-11 (night). Ventimiglia area bombarded from the sea.

September 11. U.S. 1st Army crossed Luxembourg-German frontier. British 2nd Army crossed Belgian-Dutch frontier. U.S. 7th Army from S. France joined U.S. 3rd Army from west. First major air engagement over Germany ; 133 German fighters shot down. Bomber Command dropped 286,000 incendiaries on Darmstadt. 2nd Quebec Conference (to 16th).

September 12. Le Havre garrison surrendered ; Bruges, Eupen, Malmédy liberated ; over 2,000 U.S. aircraft from Britain and Italy attacked targets in Germany. Bomber Command showered 400,000 incendiaries on Frankfort-on-Main, 200,000 on Stuttgart ; 25 aircraft lost out of more than 1,400 (night). Armistice signed between Rumania and Allies.

September 13. Neufchâteau, Vittel, La Rochelle liberated ; for sixth successive day 1,000 U.S.A. 8th A.F. heavy bombers attacked targets in Germany ; Bomber Command Lancasters attacked Osnabrück, Münster, the Ruhr ; Mosquitoes bombed Berlin for fourth night in succession. Dover heavily shelled by cross-Channel guns. Red Army captured Lomza. R.A.F. heavy bombers made attack on aerodromes near Athens.

September 13-14 (night). German cross-Channel guns shelled S.E. England for ten hours. Red A.F. bombed Budapest.

September 14. Maastricht liberated. Red Army captured Praga ; Red A.F. bombed Budapest. U.S. forces landed on Peleliu (Palaus) and on Morotai (Halmaheras).

September 15. Nancy liberated. Aachen hemmed in on three sides. 800 aircraft of Bomber Command attacked Kiel (night). Dover shelled for 8½ hours. Germans repelled in attempt to occupy Hogland I. (Finland). U.S.A. 15th A.F. attacked Athens aerodromes. French fleet returned to Toulon. Russian-based R.A.F. hit " Tirpitz " with 12,000-lb. bomb.

September 16. Lunéville liberated (France). Bisbach occupied (Germany). Land Forces Adriatic began landings on Dalmatian coast. Red Army spearheads crossed Polish-Czechoslovak frontier.

September 17. Allied 1st Airborne Army landed at Eindhoven, Nijmegen, and Arnhem (Netherlands) ; Dutch Government in London called on railwaymen to strike. Canadians launched all-out assault on Boulogne. American landing in Angaur (Palaus).

September 18. British 2nd Army liberated Valkenswaard, Aalst and Eindhoven (Netherlands). Bisbach (Germany) cleared. Bomber Command Lancasters dropped over 420,000 incendiaries on Bremerhaven. Red Air Force bombed Budapest (Hungary). U.S.A. 14th A.F. attacked shipping in Formosa Straits at night. Carrier-borne aircraft of Eastern Fleet attacked Sigli (Sumatra).

September 18 and 19. Two heavy U.S. air attacks on Manila area ; 357 Japanese planes destroyed, at least 40 ships sunk for loss of 11 U.S. aircraft.

September 19. All organized resistance in Brest ceased. 700 U.S.A. 8th A.F. heavies bombed railyards and industrial targets in Germany ; U.S.A. 9th A.F. bombed Eschweiler, Düren and Mezenich (enemy supply centres for Arnhem area). R.A.F. made concentrated attack on Rheydt and Munchen-Gladbach (night). Luftwaffe made night attack on Eindhoven. Red Air Force bombed Budapest. Greek troops of 8th Army occupied Rimini airfield (Italy). Armistice signed between Finland and Allies.

September 20. Nijmegen liberated.

Dover guns shelled German cliff-top positions. Bomber Command dropped 3,000 tons on Calais. U.S.A. 15th A.F. attacked targets in Hungary and Czechoslovakia. Concentrated U.S. air attack on Manila (Philippines). U.S. Naval bombardment of Ventimiglia.

September 21. Terneuzen liberated. R.A.F. bombers from Italy made sixth trip to drop arms and supplies to Polish Home Army in Warsaw. Rimini captured by 8th Army (Italy).

September 22. All organized resistance in Boulogne ceased. Americans captured Stolberg (Germany). U.S.A. 8th A.F. attacked Kassel area. Red Army captured Tallinn (Estonia).

September 23. Powerful R.A.F. Lancaster forces made night attack (over 3,500 tons) on Münster, Neuss, and Bochum ; Dortmund-Ems Canal breached (Germany). Red Army captured Pernau (Estonia). Republic of San Marino declared war on Germany. Solta, last Dalmatian island in enemy hands, cleared. U.S. aircraft attacked Visayan Is. (Philippines) ; 22 Japanese ships sunk, 15 others probably sunk.

September 24. British troops entered German territory. Soviet forces captured Baltiski (Estonia). 500 Italian-based U.S. Liberators bombed aerodromes round Athens and Salonika railyards. Caserta Agreement signed between Allies and Greek guerilla leaders.

September 24-25 (night). Allied Corridor between Eindhoven and Nijmegen cut near Veghel by S.S. troops and tanks.

September 25. Position in Eindhoven-Nijmegen corridor restored. Canadian troops began all-out attack on Calais. Over 1,200 U.S.A. 8th A.F. heavies with fighter cover attacked Frankfort-on-Main, Coblenz and Ludwigshafen. Salvoes of shells fired across the Channel at Dover. Red Army captured Haapsalu (Estonia). British troops crossed the Rubicon (Italy).

September 26. Turnhout liberated. Over 1,600 U.S. aircraft attacked Osnabrück, Hamm, and Bremen. 4,000,000 " surrender " leaflets dropped on German troops in French ports and in Netherlands ; strong Luftwaffe formations met over Nijmegen. R.A.F. dropped 3,500 tons on Calais. Powerful R.A.F. night attack on Karlsruhe. Heaviest enemy cross-Channel shelling of the war. U.S. Super-Fortresses bombed targets in Manchuria.

September 27. British 1st Airborne Division withdrawn from Arnhem ; Luftwaffe attacked Nijmegen bridge. Over 1,100 U.S.A. 8th A.F. heavies, strongly escorted, bombed Cologne, Ludwigshafen, Kassel and Mainz.

September 28. British 2nd Army captured Elst. Remich (Luxemburg) liberated. Over 1,000 U.S.A. 8th A.F. heavies attacked Kassel, Magdeburg and Merseburg. Australian-based U.S. Liberators bombed Balikpapan (Borneo).

September 28-29 (night). Attack by German swimmers on Nijmegen bridges.

September 29. Canadians overran Cap Gris Nez long-range guns. Mainland of Estonia completely liberated.

September 30. " Hellfire Corner " celebrated end of four years' shelling. Red Army entered Yugoslavia ; captured Muhu (Moon) I. (Estonia). 8th Army captured Savignano (Italy).

Chapter 336

THE BATTLE OF THE ARDENNES

In December 1944, while the Allied armies were building up for the advance across the Rhine, the last great German effort in the West materialized with the breakthrough in the Ardennes of strong forces under Rundstedt's command. They penetrated fifty miles into the Allied lines, but were halted short of the Meuse, and in six weeks were driven back into Germany. Previous operations in the West are described by Derek Adkins in Chapter 332

WHILE Allied plans were being completed in early December for the Battle of the Rhineland, the enemy, too, was making ready for battle. The severe attrition he had experienced during the previous two months had not prevented the re-equipment of his strategic reserve, and it was known in November that the 5th Panzer Army of five divisions was refitting east of Cologne and that the enemy's defensive system had been laid out with special emphasis on the direct approaches to the Ruhr via the Aachen gap and the Saar.

The Allies, on the other hand, were determined to give the Germans no chance to recover from the blows already delivered. The immediate object of the winter campaign was therefore to maintain the offensive pressure on the enemy with a view to dealing him a decisive blow as soon as possible. This inevitably demanded that some sectors of the front should be held with comparatively weak forces in order to gather sufficient strength at the vital points of attack.

The 75-mile front between Monschau and Trier was held by only four divisions of the U.S. 1st Army, and it was here that the German armies of the west made a last desperate effort to stave off disaster. Under the command of Field-Marshal von Rundstedt acting on the direct orders of Hitler, the attack was launched on December 16 with a force that reached twenty-four divisions, of which no fewer than ten were armoured. In his order of the day to the soldiers of the western front, Rundstedt declared: "Your great hour has struck . . . . Everything is at stake. You have a sacred duty to give everything to achieve the superhuman for the Fatherland and our Fuehrer."

The full weight of the German counter-offensive in the Ardennes was not immediately realized. Extremely bad weather, including fog, which continued for days, had prevented satisfactory air reconnaissance, and had enabled the German concentration to be carried out with a high degree of secrecy in a sector where higher ground afforded reasonably sound going, and hilly wooded conditions gave concealment.

When the blow fell, eight panzer divisions broke through the American 8th Corps line on a 40-mile front, and some of the U.S. 1st Army's forward positions were overrun, particularly in the neighbourhood of Honsfeld, south of Monschau, and near Vianden and Echternach to the north and north-east of Luxemburg. Parachutists were also dropped behind the American lines, while diversionary attacks in other sectors and considerable air and artillery support assisted the main offensive. The Allied tactical air forces were engaged almost continuously against the Luftwaffe which was up in strength trying to ward off the attacks on German armour, transport, and lines of communication, and on December 17 a total of 98 enemy aircraft was shot down, nine were probably destroyed, and 47 were damaged on this front alone, for the loss of 29.

By the 19th the full implications of the German attack were established. It was clear that Rundstedt was aiming at the Meuse and intended also to develop separate thrusts in the direction of Mon- **Enemy's Objectives** schau and Malmédy, towards St. Vith by a converging pincer movement, into Luxemburg from the frontier area of Vianden, and into central Luxemburg from near Echternach. The enemy's forces consisted of the 6th S.S. Panzer Army, whose objectives were Liége, Namur, Brussels, Antwerp and then the sea, and the 5th Panzer Army, making a sweep on its left, with the re-formed German 7th Army in support. Rundstedt hoped in this way to split the Allied forces in two and halt the Allied advance to the Rhine.

General Eisenhower reacted promptly and decisively. All available reserves in the 12th (or Central) Army Group were used to strengthen the northern and southern flank of the penetration, while the British XXX Corps of the 21st (Northern) Army Group was deployed to hold a general line from Liége

RUNDSTEDT LED THE GERMAN ATTACK IN THE ARDENNES
Last important counter-offensive mounted by the Germans in Western Europe opened in the Ardennes on December 16, 1944. The attack, initially concentrated against four divisions of the U.S. 1st Army, between Monschau and Trier, was personally ordered by Hitler and was commanded by Field-Marshal Gerd von Rundstedt, then Supreme German Commander on the Western Front Here, at his headquarters, Rundstedt (extreme right) discusses tactics with Field-Marshal Model (extreme left), commanding the German 'A' Army Group.

GERMAN ARDENNES OFFENSIVE OPENS

Scout-car of an enemy reconnaissance unit pauses at a signpost in the Recht area during the first days of the battle. Right, behind the cover of a captured American half-tracked vehicle, a German officer gives the order to advance. Both these photographs are excerpts from a German film which fell into Allied hands.

whom were men of the 1st, 2nd, 4th, and 99th Divisions. Monschau was lost, but was recaptured by the 18th, while near Echternach there was very hard fighting in which the town changed hands more than once. A deep penetration, however, was made towards Liége, reaching Stavelot, and fierce fighting took place in this area. Allied resistance stiffened and successful counter-attacks ended with the recovery of Stavelot and Malmédy, announced on December 22. Two columns moving on St. Vith were held east and south of it for several days by a gallant stand of the U.S. 7th Armoured Division. But the Germans, employing twenty divisions, eight of them tank divisions, continued their thrust due west, two tank spearheads reaching Celle, only four miles from Dinant on the Meuse, and Ciney on December 24. Here they were halted with the aid of British armour and infantry and by noon next day the threat to the Meuse had been warded off. The enemy's tanks began to run out of fuel— seventeen were found abandoned for lack of petrol at Celle alone. Major air attacks on enemy concentrations in the St. Vith area played a big part—on December 23 and 24, between St. Vith and Bastogne, 864 motor vehicles were

ENEMY SPEARHEADS

Along a Belgian road blocked by abandoned American transport, leading files of a German infantry section move up in support of their forward units. This is another cut from a captured enemy film taken in the initial stage of Rundstedt's offensive in the Ardennes.

to Louvain, west of the Meuse, with patrols forward along the western bank of the river between Liége itself and Dinant. The Corps was thus suitably placed to prevent the enemy from crossing the river, and could cover the routes from the southeast leading into Brussels. The U.S. 1st and 9th armies (which were on the northern side of the German salient and therefore remote from the Central Army Group axis) were placed temporarily under Field-Marshal Montgomery's command. General Bradley co-ordinated the effort from the south. The U.S. 82nd and 101st Airborne Divisions, which had formed part of the Airborne Army landed in the Netherlands in September (see page 3297), were brought up to retard the momentum of the enemy thrust, the 101st, reinforced by armour and artillery from elements of the U.S. 10th Armoured Division, holding the important centre of Bastogne.

Monschau and Echternach, the extreme points at the base of the penetration, were stubbornly held by American infantry moved in from the north and south, outstanding among

CAPTURED TIGER TANK
Fierce fighting in the Ardennes raged round Stavelot and Malmédy, near the Belgian-German frontier, during mid-December 1944. Above, a German Mark 6 Royal Tiger tank being examined by U.S. troops. It was abandoned on the road near Stavelot in almost perfect condition (note the white flag), having run out of petrol. Right, the town of Malmédy, bombed in error by the U.S.A.A F. while occupied by Allied forces.

Laroche, and also surrounding Wiltz to the south-east. On the north of the salient the enemy advanced up the Ourthe valley to Hotton and Grandménil, where very heavy fighting took place, the recapture of Grandménil being announced on December 28, when the liquidation of a large enemy force at Celle was also reported.

Meanwhile, at Bastogne, the encircled 101st Airborne Division, under its Deputy Commander Brig.-General

destroyed and 332 damaged. In ten days from December 16 the U.S.A. 9th Air Force, flying nearly 9,000 sorties, destroyed or disabled 571 tanks and armoured cars, 3,521 lorries, more than 685 railway wagons, and shot down 362 aircraft for the loss of 172. The Tactical Air Forces, however, were hardly able to operate until December 23 when the weather cleared, but in

three days from the 24th to 26th over 14,000 sorties were flown.

Farther south, the Germans found Bastogne strongly held. They by-passed it and surrounded it, cutting the roads from it to Libramont, St. Hubert and

A. C. McAuliffe, was holding out with a gallantry that was to win for it in March 1945 the first Presidential Citation in U.S. military history for an entire division. That Citation tells the story in the following words :
"The 101st Airborne Division and attached units distinguished

U.S. 101st Airborne at Bastogne

themselves in combat against powerful and aggressive enemy forces, composed of elements of eight German divisions, during the period from December 18 to December 27, 1944, by extraordinary heroism and gallantry in defence of the key communications centre of Bastogne, Belgium. Essential to a large-scale exploitation of his break-through into Belgium and northern Luxemburg, the enemy attempted to seize Bastogne by attacking constantly and savagely with the best of his armour and infantry. Without benefit of prepared defences, the facing division and attached units maintained a high combat morale and an impenetrable defence, despite extremely heavy bombing, intense artillery fire, and constant attacks from infantry and armour on all sides of their completely cut off and encircled position. This masterful and grimly determined defence denied the enemy even momentary success in an operation for which

U.S. FIELD ARTILLERY IN LUXEMBURG
The Luxemburg town of Echternach, completely surrounded by the enemy and changing hands several times, was the scene of an heroic stand by General Patton's forces during the earlier stages of the Ardennes attack. Below, a 155-mm. self-propelled field-gun of the U.S. 3rd Army in the ' ready fire ' position on the outskirts of the town. These guns were brought up to demolish German strongpoints across the river Sure in Germany   *Photo, P.N.A.*

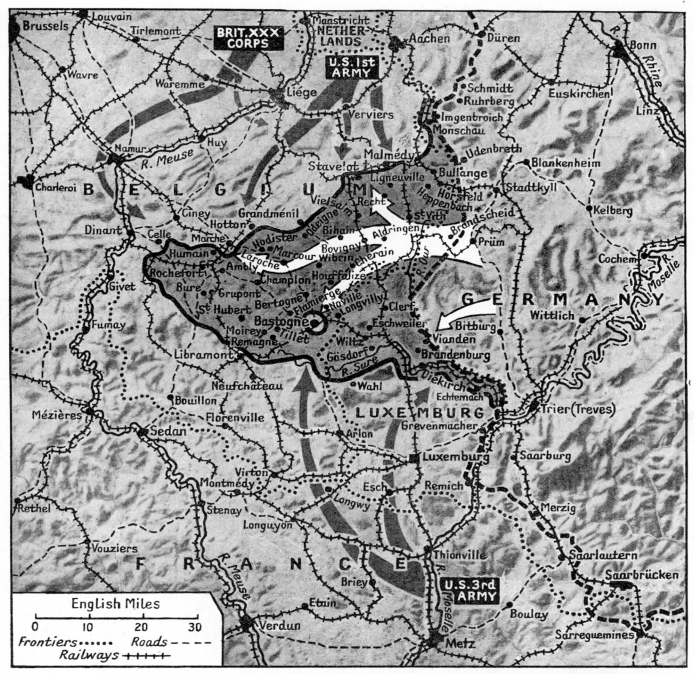

WEHRMACHT'S LAST BLOW ON THE WESTERN FRONT

The area in the Ardennes overrun by the Germans in their offensive launched on December 16, 1944 is here indicated by dark shading. Principal lines of the enemy thrust are shown by the white arrows. Penetration of the Allied positions did not in the main exceed 50 miles, but armoured units reached Celle and Ciney. Allied movements are indicated by grey arrows.

he paid dearly in men, material and, eventually, morale. The outstanding courage and resourcefulness and undaunted determination of this gallant force is in keeping with the highest traditions of the service." Presenting the Citation General Eisenhower said, "You were given a marvellous opportunity, and you met every test."

Bastogne was relieved by the 4th Armoured Division of the U.S. 3rd Army after a stand that, together with the strong resistance farther north, especially west of Stavelot, narrowed the German front and denied Rundstedt sufficient elbow-room to maintain the

weight and range of his attack on an adequate scale, particularly when, after the 23rd, the Tactical Air Forces were able to operate effectively against his troop concentrations, armour, transport and supply columns.

Between December 18 and January 6 the Motor Transport Service of the U.S. Transportation Corps, at the height of the crisis of the German counter-thrust near Bastogne, trans-

ported 67,236 troops and 10,800 tons of supplies an average distance of 100 miles from the Mourmelon district to the vicinity of Bastogne. That work was done by 220 two-and-a-half ton trucks and 162 ten-ton semi-trailers, and its success played a large part in putting the finishing touches to the smashing of the German assault.

The arrival of the 4th Armoured Division at Bastogne was part of the

U.S. TROOPS HASTILY IMPROVISE DEFENCES

The German counter-blow in the Ardennes took the U.S. 1st Army by surprise, and rapidly erected road-blocks had to be contrived in an attempt to delay the forward surge of the enemy's overwhelming numbers. Left, U.S. engineers in a forward position use a telephone-pole 'dibble' to bore holes in a roadway for explosive charges. Right, an improvised road block during the earlier stages of the enemy advance, with a 90-mm. gun in the background. Even 'Christmas trees' were employed. *Photos, U.S. Official ; Planet News ; British Official*

movement of the U.S. 3rd Army which, bringing its full weight to bear on the southern flank of the salient, turned the tide in the Ardennes battle. "This change from an offensive across the Saar to a general attack in southern Luxemburg was a brilliant military achievement, involving corps and army staff work of the highest order," says General Marshall in his report to the U.S. Secretary of War. "Elements of the U.S. 5th Division, which were fighting in the Saar bridge-head on the morning of December 20 moved sixty-nine miles and were in contact with the

enemy north of the Sauer [Sure] river by nightfall." At the same time the 6th (Southern) Army Group added twenty-five miles to its already extended front by taking over the line as far north as Saarbrücken.

On December 29 S.H.A.E.F. reported enemy withdrawals north of Rochefort,

and on the following day the recapture of that town was announced. The U.S. 3rd Army, attacking with twelve divisions (about 180,000 men) launched a fresh attack between St. Hubert and Bastogne early on December 30 and also made a thrust north of Bastogne towards Houffalize, the key centre of the entire enemy position in the Ardennes. On January 2, 1945 it was announced that both Moirey and Remagne had been captured, and Remagne lost again. Next day St. Hubert was reached but was not held.

The waist of the German bulge had now been narrowed to fifteen miles, for on the north flank of the salient progress had also been made between Marche and Hotton, and on January 3 the U.S. 1st Army opened a new attack on a front east and west of Grandménil just north of the Laroche–St. Vith road, taking 1,300 prisoners. On the south flank the Germans threw in another armoured division, bringing their estimated total strength in the salient to 23 divisions, and made repeated counter-attacks around Bastogne but failed to break through. On the northern flank, Odeigne, only two miles from the main cross-roads south of Grandménil, was occupied on the 6th, and British forces were four miles south of Hotton. Correspondents reported that the Ardennes salient had been reduced to half its original area.

The enemy was now being attacked from north, south and west. On

LUFTWAFFE ATTACKS ALLIED AIRFIELDS

On January 1, 1945, the Luftwaffe came up in strength for the first time since the Normandy landings to deliver a surprise attack on Allied airfields in Belgium and Holland. Though they destroyed a number of aircraft on the ground, their own losses were heavy, totalling over 300 planes and well over 100 pilots. Here a blazing U.S. fighter is being hosed by Brussels firemen.

HEROIC U.S. DEFENCE OF BASTOGNE

Between December 18 and 27, 1944, the U.S. 101st Airborne Division, under its deputy commander, Brigadier-
General A. L. McAuliffe (3), at Bastogne, in Belgium,
made a most gallant stand that won the first Presidential
Citation in U.S. military history for an entire division
(see page 3416). 1. Guns of the 969th U.S. Field Artillery
prepare for action during the siege. 2. Major-General
Maxwell Taylor, commanding the Division, who flew
from Washington to lead the final phase of the battle.
4. Supplies are flown in to the hard-pressed garrison
by low-flying C-47 transport aircraft. 5. Transport of
the U.S. 3rd Army in the main square of Bastogne
after the defenders had been relieved.

BRITISH AND U.S. FORCES MEET AT LAROCHE

By early January 1945, the Allies had begun to reduce the German salient in the Ardennes. The key road-centre of Laroche, on the Ourthe river, fell on January 11 to U.S. forces fighting under Field-Marshal Montgomery. Left, British and American patrols meet in the town. Right, a British tank, courageously driven through blazing vehicles and exploding ammunition, makes a way for the ambulances. *Photos, British Newspaper Pool*

January 7 American tanks cut the Laroche–St. Vith road in three places between Laroche and Vielsalm, and by the following day the American hold had been widened to about ten miles to include the cross-roads of the north–south road from Grandménil to Houffalize.

To the west the east bank of the river Ourthe was cleared as far as Marcour (four miles north-north-west of Laroche) and by the **'Laroche Gap'** 8th more ground had **Retaken** been gained, against very stiff opposition, on the way to Laroche, entered by American troops on the 10th and cleared without much resistance next day. On the 11th also British and American troops fighting side by side stormed the "Laroche gap," a narrow gorge through which the Ourthe flows, in the almost vertical walls of which German troops had dug themselves in. On the south flank, Tillet was captured

on the 10th, and a strong enemy pocket south-east of Bastogne was wiped out on the 11th. Fierce German counter-attacks were repulsed.

The enemy was now withdrawing from the head of the salient, but in good order. A new phase of bad weather, however, prevented the Tactical Air Forces from attacking the concentrations of enemy transport moving eastward. Bure, Ambly, and Hodister were recovered on the 10th,

and at St. Hubert on the 12th troops of the U.S. 3rd Army met British troops striking from the north.

British forces took Champlon on January 14 and advanced towards Houffalize, meeting troops of the U.S.

SNOW CHANGES THE FACE OF THE ARDENNES

Almost throughout the Ardennes counter-offensive, operations were hampered by bad weather, including heavy falls of snow which necessitated drastic alterations in camouflage, tactics and equipment. Right, toboggans being used by U.S. troops to carry supplies up the line and bring back wounded. The snow was too deep for jeeps to be driven with safety. Below, a U.S. infantry patrol, wearing snowsuits, advances over a hill near Wahl in Luxemburg. *Photos, U.S. Official ; Keystone*

3rd Army which had moved up from the St. Hubert area. The U.S. 101st Airborne Division thrusting north from Bastogne also threatened Houffalize. A third contact between forces from north and south of the salient occurred at Bertogne, the scene of very heavy fighting, the Germans launching three powerful counter-attacks in that area during the night of January 13-14.

Troops of the U.S. 1st Army launched a strong attack on January 13 on a nine-mile front between Stavelot and Malmédy. It met powerful resistance.

BRITISH TROOPS GO IN

The German salient in the Ardennes was declared to be no more than ten miles wide by January 9, 1945, British and U.S. forces under Field-Marshal Montgomery pushing the enemy back steadily. By January 12 a link-up between the U.S. 3rd Army, pressing in from the south, and Montgomery's men from the north, was reported at St. Hubert at the tip of the salient. Here, British tanks and infantry are seen moving up to go into action on the northern flank of the salient.

Other American forces cut the Houffalize–St. Vith east of Houffalize on the 14th. Houffalize itself fell to the U.S. 1st Army on the 16th, after German troops had pulled out. Dispatches from the front said : " With the entry of Allied troops into Houffalize the episode of the German invasion of the Ardennes is virtually finished." But hard fighting still remained to be done before the salient was eliminated. German resistance was strong at Cherain, Bovigny Recht, and north of Bastogne. By the 19th troops of the U.S. 1st Army had fought their way to within four miles of St. Vith against bitter opposition.

The 3rd Army opened a new attack on the 17th, across the river Sure, occupying Diekirch in Luxemburg and reaching the German frontier at several points on January 19. On the 21st, advancing against very light opposition, it retook a number of towns and villages, including Brandenburg. Next day it took Wiltz and Eschweiler. On the 23rd St. Vith was captured by the U.S. 18th Airborne Corps and tanks of the U.S. 7th Armoured Division (U.S. 1st Army) and all but a fraction of Belgian soil was again free ; and patrols of the 3rd Army entered Vianden in Luxemburg. Captain Sertorius, the German

military commentator, admitted in a broadcast that the Ardennes front had " ceased to be a salient." But enemy rearguard resistance stiffened in an endeavour to cover the retreat of the main German forces into the Reich.

Aldringen fell on the 25th. On the 26th the 3rd Army, fighting in bitter cold and driving snow, cut the " skyline drive " on the St. Vith–Diekirch road in several places, **U.S. Armies Take the Offensive** and recaptured a number of villages. Two counter-attacks north-east of Wiltz were repelled by the U.S. 80th Infantry Division. In a surprise attack made in a blizzard without artillery preparation at 4 a.m. on January 28, the U.S. 1st Division overran a number of German dugouts—many of their inmates were still sleeping—to capture Heppenbach and other places some seven miles north-east of St. Vith. Next day they took Bullange, a major enemy communications centre during the offensive. The 3rd Army gained control of almost the whole St. Vith–Diekirch road and recaptured Clerf on the 28th. January 30 saw a steady advance of U.S. 1st and 3rd Army troops on a forty-mile front between Monschau and Echternach, the extreme points at the base of Rundstedt's Ardennes wedge, and on February 5 it was announced that the U.S. 1st Army had reverted to General Bradley's command.

AFTER HOUFFALIZE THE 'WEDGE' BECAME A 'BULGE'

With the fall of Houffalize to the U.S. 1st Army under Field-Marshal Montgomery on January 16, 1945, the enemy Ardennes salient was reduced to little more than a 'bulge.' Here a half-tracked vehicle of the 2nd Armoured Division crosses the river Ourthe over a temporary bridge which linked forces of the U.S. 1st and 3rd Armies in the Houffalize area the following day

The offensive was a complete military defeat for Germany. The 6th Panzer S.S. Army broke itself against the northern shoulder of the salient, while

Dietmar on Ardennes Battle

the 5th Panzer Army spent its drive in the fierce battles which centred on Bastogne. General Dietmar, in an interview with a B.B.C. correspondent after the German surrender, said of the Ardennes offensive, which had been mounted by Hitler, that the intention was to cross the Meuse and swing northwards so as to cut off all the Allies beyond the river. But the operation was poorly prepared, and the 6th S.S. Panzer Army, the mainstay of the attack, was grossly mismanaged by Sepp Dietrich, who had been placed in command of it by Hitler. The resistance was much too tough and well-organized for the Germans. And when Rundstedt went to Hitler to report this, and to propose that they should be satisfied with the gains they had made and should call a halt to the operation, Hitler flew into a temper and sacked Rundstedt, making him the scapegoat for the faults of the party men, who, in the opinion of 90 per cent of the officers of the German Army, were responsible for the Wehrmacht's collapse. "We not only lost the Ardennes battle," said Dietmar, "but we threw away the reserves we ought to have been cherishing for use elsewhere."

Enemy losses in December and January, mainly in that battle, numbered 110,000 dead and 110,000 prisoners, and to launch this battle

the Reich had been stripped of strategic reserves. "Possibly more serious," said General Eisenhower, "was the widespread disillusionment ensuing from the failure to seize any really important objective and the realization that this offensive for which every effort had been brought to bear and on which such great hopes were pinned, had in no sense achieved anything decisive."

The enemy drove more than fifty miles into the American lines, making use of American tanks, lorries and other vehicles in which troops, in American uniforms, did their utmost to disrupt Allied communications. But the Allied troops defending the critical "shoulders" of the salient held. This limited the breadth, and therefore the depth, of the enemy advance, and it remained possible to cover by artillery fire all the important supply roads between base and tip of salient. The Germans delayed the main Allied offensive by some six weeks, but they failed to reach even their first objectives, Liége and Namur.

"The battle of the Ardennes was won," said Field-Marshal Montgomery, "primarily by the staunch fighting qualities of the Ameri-

Montgomery's Praise of Americans

can soldier, and the enemy's subsequent confusion was completed by the intense air action which became possible as weather conditions improved . . . Regrouping the U.S. 1st and 9th Armies, assisted by British formations, made possible the rapid formation of a reserve corps of four U.S. divisions under General Collins. The action of this corps, co-ordinated with the drive from the south by General Patton's U.S. 3rd Army, pinched the enemy forces out of the salient and began the bitter struggle which was to push them out of the Siegfried Line."

As soon as the enemy had been pushed back from the salient, Field-Marshal Montgomery ordered the British divisions which had shared in the Ardennes battle north to the concentration areas that had been made ready in December for the launching of the battle of the Rhineland.

U.S SEVENTH ARMOURED DIVISION TAKES ST. VITH

Outstanding among the heroic episodes of the Ardennes counter-offensive was the unsuccessful stand in its first days of the U.S. 7th Armoured Division at St. Vith, vital road junction five miles from the Reich border. The town was retaken by tanks of the 7th Armoured Division and the U.S. 18th Airborne Corps on January 23. Here infantry are dug in along one of the ruined snow-covered streets.   *Photos, L.N.A.; Associated Press*

BRITISH AND AMERICAN PATROLS MEET IN THE ARDENNES

British and American forces—in some areas fighting side by side—had made considerable progress in reducing the enemy's salient in the Ardennes by the middle of January 1945 (see page 3420). South-west of Laroche, on January 11, units of the British 2nd Army approached Champlon, meeting-place of six roads and last major cross-roads in the western part of the salient to remain in enemy hands. Here a British reconnaissance patrol links up with Americans. The British patrol wears snow camouflage.

Photo, British Official

'BUSINESS AS USUAL' AS FLYING-BOMBS FELL ON LONDON

Germany began her 'reprisal weapons' attack on England on June 13, 1944, when the first flying-bombs (V1) flew in over Kent. Between that date and September 4, an estimated total of 8,070 was launched against Southern England. Despite the onslaught, trams, trains, and buses continued to run normally. Here, people in Fleet-street on June 30 are going about their business as usual as a V1, which killed 25, crashed in Aldwych nearby. The smoke of the explosion rises above St. Dunstan's-in-the-West.

Photo, Daily Mirror

RESCUE SQUAD IN ACTION AT A V1 'INCIDENT'

London scene, typical of all too many during the earlier stages of the flying-bomb attacks on the capital in the summer of 1944. A woman victim is being removed by a Civil Defence light rescue squad after a V1 had crashed on St. John's Hill, Battersea, on June 17. The wrecked bus is partially obscured by the dust-cloud peculiar to these incidents. The moral effect of the onslaught on the public was greater than that of the earlier 'Blitzes'—largely owing to the fact that the V1s were mechanically controlled.

Photo, George Rodger

LONDON CHILDREN EVACUATED FROM V1 PERILS

Because of the V1 attacks on London, the Government's evacuation scheme was reopened on July 1, 1944, when schoolchildren left for the Midlands and the North. The scheme included children from 5–16 ; expectant mothers ; and the aged and infirm. It was estimated that some 100,000 children, evacuated earlier (see page 554), had returned to the capital since 1941. Organized evacuation was suspended on September 7 when the worst of the flying-bomb attack was over. Here a party of schoolchildren, with teachers, line up at Marylebone Station.   *Photo, Hans Wild*

Chapter 337

GERMAN "REPRISAL WEAPONS" IN ACTION

Of several self-propelled projectiles which the Germans were developing, and which they called " reprisal weapons," only two became effective during the Second Great War—the flying-bomb (V1) and the rocket-bomb (V2). The construction, mechanism, and effects of these revolutionary missiles and the successful counter-measures employed against the V1 are described in this Chapter by Captain Norman Macmillan, M.C., A.F.C.

IN 1942 Hitler diverted large German scientific and industrial resources to a robot weapon programme, and early in 1943 intelligence sources in touch with the foreign slave workers employed in German secret factories passed information to the British Government that Germany was preparing a long-range weapon to bombard London. It was thought that this was a rocket. Information from agents narrowed down the area wherein the technical development was proceeding. Flight-Lieutenant Maurice Briggs, D.S.O., D.F.C., D.F.M. (who was killed in an air crash at Calgary airport on May 10, 1945), was reported in *The Times* to have been the pilot who discovered the exact location of the Peenemunde research establishment.

One air photograph, taken on November 8, 1943, disclosed a small aircraft ready on a launching
Evidence from Photographic Reconnaissance
ramp (*see* page 2971); another showed dark streaks near the ramp which might have been caused by the discharge of hot gases, and these gave the Allies positive evidence of the nature of the weapon under construction: it was a diminutive jet-propelled aircraft, possibly intended for use as a flying-bomb or an artillery target-plane.

During their development work on the flying-bomb (which the aircraft proved to be) German scientists failed

to solve all their problems without a test pilot. Because the fuselage diameter was only 2 feet 8½ inches, the pilot had to be small. Fraülein Hanna Reisch (who had gained publicity in 1938 by flying a Focke-Wulf helicopter inside the Deutschlandhalle in Berlin) made the required test flight. Despite the special landing gear fitted to this test flying-bomb, she was seriously injured when landing at about three miles a minute. For her bravery she received the Iron Cross First Class.

Robot weapons were called by the Germans *Vergeltungswaffen* (literally reprisal weapons), a name foreshortened for the flying-bomb, officially the FZG–76, to V1, and for the rocket-bomb, officially the A–4, to V2. The operational employment of these weapons was retarded for many months by a bombing attack on Peenemunde, made on August 17, 1943 (*see* page 2964 and illus. in page 2658), when General von Chamier-Glisenski was killed, together with many of his assistants in the building where they lived.

Allied air reconnaissance discovered curious large ferro-concrete structures,

presumably intended for the launching of robot missiles, at Watten, in the Pas de Calais, and in September 1943 these were heavily bombed. Reconnaissance aircraft also discovered that about 100 smaller structures were being erected behind the French coast between Le Havre and Calais, all pointing towards London. The enemy had made the fatal mistake of omitting to camouflage them, and bombing destroyed all these permanent sites. The official communiqués described these operations as " attacks on military installations." During the winter of 1943–44 British newspapers hinted that " the military installations " were sites for firing rockets, but no official statement was made.

Air attack forced the Germans to build smaller, movable launching structures which could be
quickly assembled and camouflaged, but
Allied Air Attacks on 'Robot' Targets
these were less efficient for the rapid and accurate discharge of the robot missiles. These, too, were bombed, but being small they were difficult to hit. By the first week in July 1944 about 50,000 tons

R.A.F. BOMB V-WEAPON LAUNCHING SITE IN FRANCE

That Germany was preparing an onslaught on Southern England by robot weapons was known to British Intelligence over a year before the attack was launched. Left, R.A.F. air photograph of an enemy concrete structure in the Pas de Calais, intended for V-weapon projection. Right, the same site, heavily pocked with bomb craters, after an attack by heavy bombers on the night of June 27-28, 1944. *Photos, British Official*

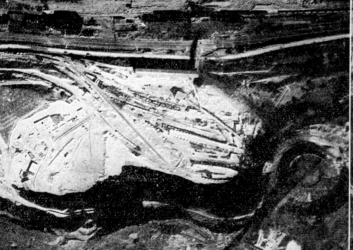

INVENTED V1 RANGE-FINDER
A range-finder, devised by Professor Sir Thomas Merton, Scientific Adviser to the Ministry of Production since 1942, and costing only a shilling to make, helped R.A.F. night-fighters to solve their biggest problem of the flying-bomb attacks (see page 3429.) *Photo, Navana*

A.A. Command were disposed for the protection of the British ports whence the invasion fleets were to sail to the Normandy coast, for it was thought that the Luftwaffe, despite its depletion, might make desperate attacks on these ports when the invasion of western Europe began. Meanwhile, in south-eastern England, men were waiting and watching for the opening of a form of bombardment which the world had never before seen.

At Dymchurch, in Kent, two members of the Royal Observer Corps spotted a strange aircraft approaching at a few

of bombs had fallen on the launching sites in France and the experimental station at Peenemunde, and it was estimated that these Anglo-American counter-measures delayed the attack for six months and considerably reduced its volume when it came. Thanks to this delay the Allies landed in Normandy before the robot assault began.

Immediately before the Allied landings on June 6, 1944, most of the guns of

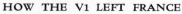

HOW THE V1 LEFT FRANCE
At a launching site in the Pas de Calais (1), a flying-bomb is wheeled to its launching ramp. Under the full length of this runs a conduit into which a spragged piston (2) is fitted. Projecting through the central slot in the camouflaged ramp (3) the sprag engages the V1 and, when the piston is propelled up the conduit, carries the missile along the rails to the end of the ramp whence the flying-bomb continues under its own power. The launching is operated by a compact starter mechanism (4).

minutes past four in the morning of June 13, 1944. Instantly they identified it, plotted its course, and reported within 35 seconds, repeating the code word

"Diver" three times. Their signal set into immediate operation the Diver Plan of defence. From H.Q., Air Defence of Great Britain, orders flowed out to the units concerned.

The Diver Plan had been prepared on the thesis that the bombs would fly at about 6,000 feet and at about 200 m.p.h. It was soon found, however, that they flew between 800 and 2,500 feet at an air speed of about 360 m.p.h. Their speed over the ground varied with the wind from about 320 to 400 m.p.h. They were thus a difficult target for the heavy A.A. guns, and the first flying-bomb shot down from the ground fell to a sergeant gunner firing twin Lewis guns from the flat roof of a house on the south coast.

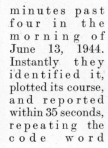

had to invent new tactics, for the standard fighter air drill did not produce good results against the robot planes. The most effective attack was found to begin with a dive at an acute angle from astern, thus increasing the fighter's speed temporarily. The fighters' scores then rose rapidly and their casualties from exploding bombs decreased.

Because of the speed of the V1, standing patrols of 30 to 40 fighters flew continuously by day and night. In the dark, pilots found it difficult to determine the bomb's range, until a range-finder, invented by Professor

SHOT DOWN 60 V1s

Squadron-Leader Joseph Berry, D.F.C., was the top-scoring R.A.F. pilot against the flying-bombs : his maximum in one night was seven. For this he was awarded a bar to his D.F.C. He was killed on October 2, 1944 over the Netherlands.
Photo, Planet News

robot's wing and tip it up, sometimes making it dive to a premature crash, at others causing it to turn in its course. Sometimes, the delicate gyro mechanism controlling the bomb recovered, and the manoeuvre had to be repeated two or more times. The fighter's wing and the flying-bomb's wing never touched, as a pad of air, due to speed, was formed between the two rapidly moving surfaces. Squadron-Leader J. Berry, D.F.C., (later killed), flying a Tempest from Manston

OVER THE CHANNEL TO LONDON

With its propulsion unit in full blast and emitting its characteristic rumbling roar, the flying-bomb leaves its ramp (5) and heads for London, streaking across the English Channel at over 350 m.p.h. (6). [This remarkable photograph was taken from a pursuing R.A.F. fighter.] Close to the Law Courts—its pre-determined range reached—the V1 dives to earth (7), and explodes in a billowing cloud of black smoke off Drury Lane (8). This incident occurred on August 3, 1944.
Photos, British Official ; Associated Press

Guns were deployed into their Diver Plan positions close to London, leaving the defences of the country between them and the sea to fighter aircraft. The London gun barrage went into action. Londoners felt, not without reason, that the bombs shot down were exploding among them.

The brunt of the defence meanwhile fell on pilots flying single-seater Mustang, Spitfire and Tempest fighters. They used a special fuel, Iso-Octane, which produced 20 per cent more power from their engines and thus increased their speed. Even so, the flying-bomb was faster than the fighters at that low height. Pilots found they

Sir Thomas Merton, and costing about one shilling to produce, solved their problem.

First a Polish pilot, and after him others, found they could fly alongside a V1 and put a wing-tip under the

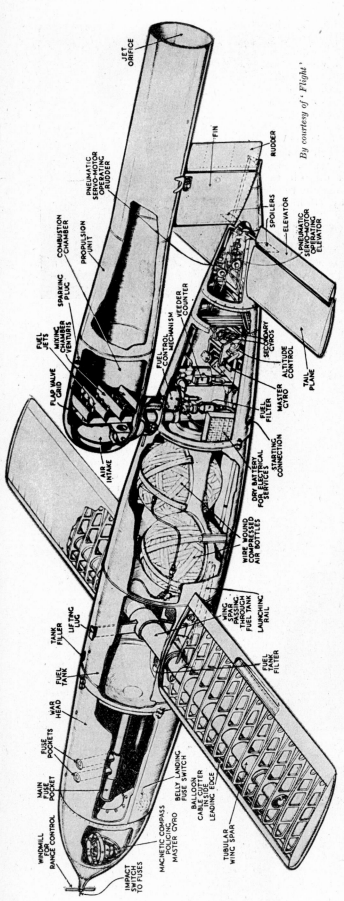

JET
ORIFICE

FIN

PNEUMATIC
SERVO-MOTOR
OPERATING
RUDDER

RUDDER

SPOILERS

ELEVATOR

COMBUSTION
CHAMBER

PROPULSION
UNIT

SPARKING
PLUG

PNEUMATIC
SERVO-MOTOR
OPERATING
ELEVATOR

FUEL
JETS

MIXING
CHAMBER
VENTURIS

VEEDER
COUNTER

FUEL
CONTROL
MECHANISM

TAIL
PLANE

SECONDARY
GYROS

FLAP VALVE
GRID

ALTITUDE
CONTROL

MASTER
GYRO

FUEL
FILTER

STARTING
CONNECTION

AIR
INTAKE

DRY BATTERY
FOR ELECTRICAL
SERVICES

WIRE WOUND
COMPRESSED
AIR BOTTLES

WING
SPAR
PASSING
THROUGH
FUEL TANK

LAUNCHING
RAIL

TANK
FILLER

LIFTING
LUG

FUEL TANK
FILTER

FUEL
TANK

WAR
HEAD

FUSE
POCKETS

MAIN
FUSE
POCKET

WINDMILL
FOR
RANGE CONTROL

MAGNETIC COMPASS
POLICING
MASTER GYRO

BELLY LANDING
FUSE SWITCH

BALLOON
CABLE CUTTER
INSIDE
LEADING EDGE

TUBULAR
WING SPAR

IMPACT
SWITCH
TO FUSES

By courtesy of ' Flight '

'REPRISAL WEAPON ONE' had several wing variations. In two models seen over England, one had 16-foot span wings, tapering in plan from the body to cut-back wing tips, and the other (see illustration) had parallel-chord 17½-foot span wings. Sharp steel strips were fitted inside the wings' leading edges to cut balloon cables. No model had ailerons.

Other dimensions appeared to be standardized. Fuselage : length 21 ft. 10 in., and maximum diameter 2 ft. 8½ in. Propulsion unit : 11 ft. 3 in. long and 1 ft. 10½ in. maximum diameter. The jet tube projected behind the rudder, and the overall length was 25 ft. 4½ in. Tail plane span : 7 ft. 5 in.

Construction was almost entirely of mild-steel sheet, but the nose section, containing the magnetic compass, was of duralumin to reduce compass deviation. Gross weight was 4,700 lb., made up thus : shell, about 1,800 lb., explosive 1,870 lb., and fuel about 950 lb., with tankage for about 130 gallons.

THE propulsion unit was a simple welded-steel casing mounted above the rear of the fuselage on a front fork and on the fin aft. Air, compressed at very high initial pressure and contained in two wire-reinforced spherical bottles, forced fuel from the tank through pipes running up the front support of the 'engine.' This fuel was sprayed into the combustion chamber through nine atomizer jets arranged in three rows of three between a venturi grill. Three compressed-air jets for starting the engine were mounted above the topmost fuel jets. In front of the jets was a square 'honeycomb' of non-return valves made of 126 double leaves of pen-nib steel, with each double leaf pressing its two inner edges together. In front of this honeycomb was the circular air intake.

The fuselage contained six sections for the compass, warhead, fuel tank, air bottles, gyroscopes and controls, and servo-motor. Under the fuel tank centre-section a fore-and-aft launching rail with thick metal sides tapered from front to rear.

Flying-bombs came from their assembly shed to the launching

VERGELTUNGSWAFFE EINS (FZG-76)—THE V1 OR FLYING-BOMB

ramp on a trolly. A derrick travelling on rails, one on either side of this ramp, lifted them on to the ramp by the lug above the wing spar.

A detachable panel in the fuselage section containing the gyroscopes could be removed to adjust the control mechanism. The gyroscopes were driven by compressed air from the air bottles in the adjoining section. Bearings from the repeater compass in the nose were used to maintain the course through the master gyroscope, which controlled both yaw and pitching movements, while two secondary gyroscopes controlled the rates of any such movements. Gyroscope movements actuated valves in two small air motors in the tail section, whose double-acting pistons operated the rudder and elevator through links. A pre-set aneroid barometer controlled the height of flight, and an air log set to the estimated distance governed range. After fuel and compressed air were turned on, the propulsion unit was started by the sparking plug from an external circuit. When the unit warmed up, the internal heat of the combustion chamber ignited each charge automatically, and the connexion to the sparking plug could be removed.

LAUNCHING was controlled from a blast-proof concrete control-house about 30 yards from the upward inclined ramp, and was effected by a piston driven by compressed air within a cylinder that ran the full length of the ramp. A sprag on the piston projected through the upper wall of the cylinder and engaged with the launching rail of the flying-bomb. At the end of its run the flying-bomb rose abruptly into the air, and climbed to its pre-set height before flying level. The piston, ejected from the mouth of the cylinder, fell sometimes 300 yards away, and pistons were collected at the end of a day's shoot. But all V1s did not start successfully ; traces of explosive violence shown around the end of ramps on air reconnaissance photographs were almost certainly due to misfires.

Launching speed was about 185 m.p.h., and had to exceed 170 m.p.h. to open the air valves and commence the normal operational cycle of the engine. The main force propelling the flying-bomb came from gas pressure (formed by the mixture or fuel and air burning within the combustion chamber) closing the air valves and exerting a thrust of about 600 lb. against them. The pressure, meeting no resistance rearwards, was exhausted by the discharge of the gas from the narrowing tube, in a jet which provided a lesser propulsive force. The valves opened to admit air when the pressure within the combustion chamber fell below the external pressure at the air intake ; fuel was simultaneously drawn from the jets, and the cycle was repeated. Frequency of firing depended upon the length of the unit ; in the V1 it was about 45 cycles a second. This simple engine developed about 600 h.p. for about one-fourth the weight of an equal-powered piston petrol engine, but used about eight times as much fuel, consuming roughly a gallon a mile.

DURING flight the air log was rotated backwards by a calibrated airscrew of about 12 inches diameter mounted in front of the fuselage nose. When the estimated range had been flown and zero reached on the log, detonators attached to the tail plane were electrically fired. These forced down two control tabs and made the bomb commence to dive. The warhead had (1) a sensitive impact fuse ; (2) a universal mechanical fuse with one switch at the nose and another under the warhead to detonate if the flying-bomb should glide into the ground ; and (3) a clock fuse to explode the bomb after two hours in the event of the others failing.

A few V1s carried small radio transmitters and German receiving stations plotted the course of their flight to check shooting. Heinkel bombers carried one flying-bomb on their backs. At the launching position, the V1 propulsion unit was started as on the ground. The bomber pilot then headed towards the target and the flying-bomb was released.

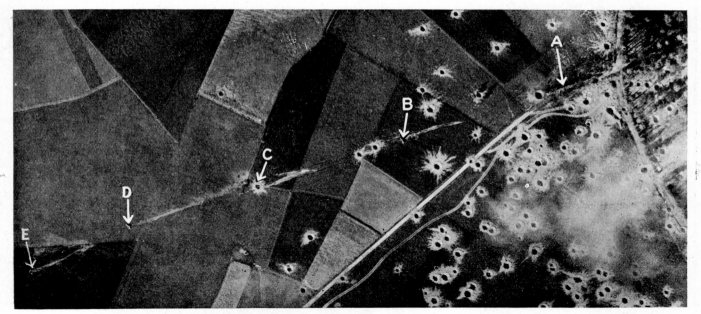

NOT ALL THE FLYING-BOMBS LEFT FRANCE

Before the battle of the V weapons began—as well as afterwards—bombers of the Allied air forces heavily plastered launching sites in France. Here is one after an attack in July 1944. A is the launching ramp surrounded by bomb craters, B, C, D, and E are flying-bombs which had dived to earth prematurely, immediately after being launched—a frequent occurrence. Streaks behind these bombs show where they had slid along the ground. *Photo, British Official*

aerodrome, Kent, was the top-scoring pilot; he shot down 60 flying-bombs, all but three between sunset and dawn, and reached a maximum of seven in one night. Britain's first twin-jet fighter, the Meteor, shot down its first flying-bomb on August 14, 1944. Two American Airacomet twin-jet fighters were tested experimentally against them.

During the defence reorganization to meet the unexpected conditions of the attack, London suffered heavily.

The knowledge that no man guided the V1 seemed to arouse in the minds of those who heard it a curious apprehension that the blind missile was aimed at each one personally—until the weapon passed overhead with its engine still thrumming. The feeling of suspense was increased when the engine stopped—either through shortage of fuel, or through the action of the range-controlling mechanism—and the robot began to glide or dive almost noiselessly to the contact explosion of its 2,000-lb. warhead. Because it had little penetrative power, the flying-bomb warhead caused lateral blast damage greatly in excess of H.E. bombs of similar weight.

The psychological effect of this attack, which continued with short intermissions until the first week in September, exceeded that of the attack by manned aircraft of 1940–41. Londoners were weary from almost five years of war and black-out. The time

Psychological Effect of V1 Attack

between the sounding of the alert and the arrival of the bomb was shorter than that between the alert and the arrival of aircraft. Sometimes bombs were overhead before the sirens sounded. A Cabinet instruction, subsequently cancelled, was issued not to sound the sirens when only one bomb entered a warning area. Perhaps fortunately, the peculiar sound of the flying-bomb, whose reaction propulsion engine, functioning at about 50 impulses a second, made a regular purring note like that of an enormous motor-cycle, was unmistakable above the subdued din of London's lessened wartime traffic; this acted as a warning to people in the streets to take cover.

R.A.F. WING-TIP TACTICS AGAINST THE V1

One of the most effective methods adopted by the R.A.F. against flying-bombs was for fighter-pilots to fly alongside and tip them over with their wings. Several important targets were saved in this way. These photographs, taken from the ground, show a Spitfire approaching a V1 and edging into position (left) and tipping it over (right). *Photos, British Official*

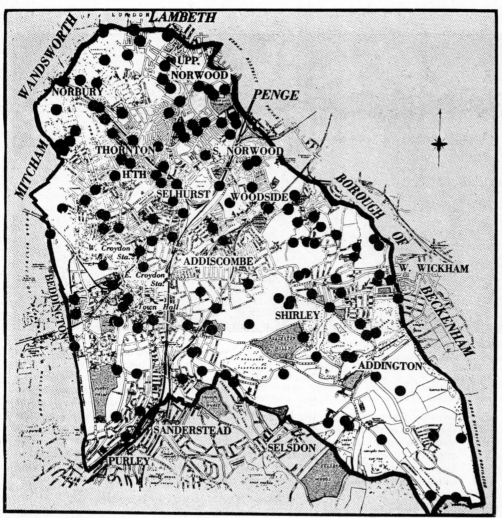

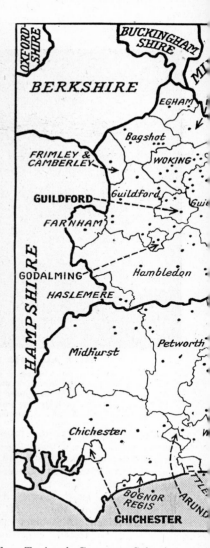

The round-the-clock continuity of the attack induced great nervous stress to which, however, people rapidly adjusted themselves. The frequency of alerts made the authorities cut the warning from eight to five wails of the siren.

The recurrent alarms dislocated work because the great danger from flying glass and debris made it necessary for workers to take cover at each alarm. Trams, trains and omnibuses continued to run normally throughout the attacks. Seventy-eight bus workers of the London Passenger Transport Board were killed, and 1,410 injured. Croydon was the worst-hit borough. Eight bombs dropped there in one day, and 15 during one week-end. Seventy-five per cent of its houses were damaged in greater or less degree. No London borough escaped damage, Wandsworth being most severely hit.

To the end of August, flying-bomb damage was reported to 149 schools (including Archbishop Tenison's Grammar School, dating from 1685), 111 churches (among them St. Bartholomew's, Smithfield, London's oldest parish church), 98 hospitals (the Royal Free Hospital in Gray's Inn Road was one which received a direct hit), and 112 public houses.

Serious Flying-Bomb Incidents

One flying-bomb destroyed the Guards Chapel at Wellington Barracks in Birdcage Walk, on Sunday, June 18 : among those killed was Colonel Lord Edward Hay, commanding the Grenadier Guards, and the Rev. R. H. Whitrow, Chaplain to the Brigade of Guards. A V1 which fell in Aldwych about 2 p.m. on June 30 killed 25 ; another, on July 6, hit a surface shelter at Chalk Farm, killing 24 ; another in Lewisham High Street on July 28 killed 56.

A.A. guns were redeployed from their first position close to London until 800 heavy and 2,000 light A.A. guns, with 20 American batteries (one-eighth of the heavy guns) were concentrated along a belt stretching inland about 20 miles from the south-east coast. Siting was

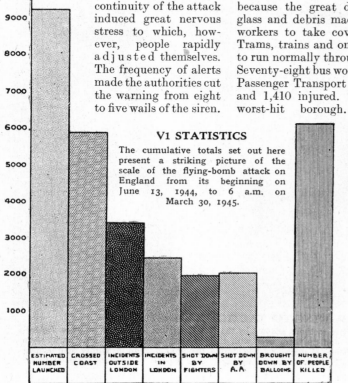

V1 STATISTICS

The cumulative totals set out here present a striking picture of the scale of the flying-bomb attack on England from its beginning on June 13, 1944, to 6 a.m. on March 30, 1945.

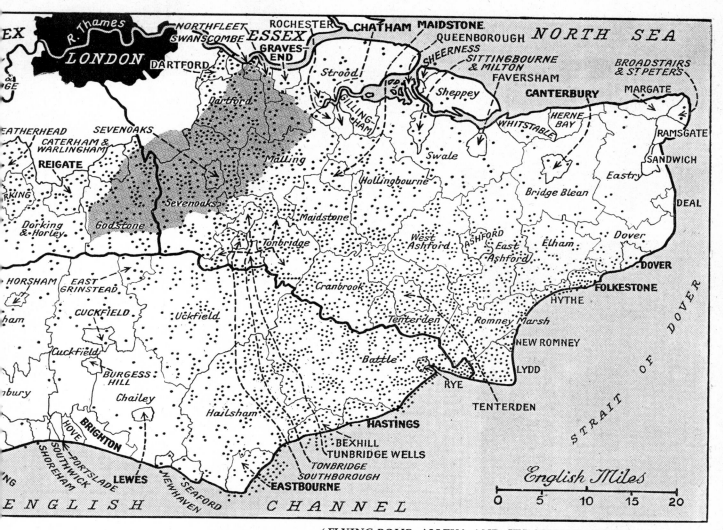

'FLYING-BOMB ALLEY' AND ITS NEIGHBOURHOOD

Attacks by flying-bombs were confined mainly to London and the south-eastern counties. 'Flying-bomb Alley' was roughly the area in the triangle with its apex in London, its base between Bexhill and Folkestone. This map shows exact points at which flying-bombs fell outside the London Defence Area from June 13–August 8 when the peak of the attack had passed. Shaded portion indicates position of the balloon barrage screening London. Left, points at which flying-bombs struck Croydon from June to September 1944.

speeded up by the use of portable gun platforms (invented by Brigadier John Burls, O.B.E.) instead of concrete emplacements. These platforms were made from 22,500 wooden sleepers and 35 miles of railway track rails. Each battery moving in found its telephone and radio communications already laid by G.P.O. engineers and the Army; 30,000 fir poles with 200,000 bobbins carried 3,500 miles of wire.

Five hundred searchlights, operated by 20,000 personnel, helped night fighters to spot the bombs and indicated the line between the gun belt and the fighter zones now across the Channel ahead of the guns and between the guns and balloons.

Anti-Flying-Bomb Tactics

But sometimes fighter pilots engrossed in the chase ran into the gun-belt, which made vigilance and quick control of gunfire necessary.

£2,000,000 were spent in two months and a half to house 59,000 gunners and members of the A.T.S. who operated predictors and signals. Batteries were re-equipped with later type American radar with greater detection range, and faster predictors, which improved shooting precision. Two young lieutenant-colonels, one of whom was a solicitor before the war, worked out a new drill for engagement of the robots which, as the record shows, proved increasingly effective. During their first week round London the guns had shot down 16 per cent of the V1s entering the gun belt. In the first week after redeployment to the coast the score rose to 17 per cent,

ROOF-SPOTTERS GIVE THE WARNING

Problem for London's Civil Defence during the flying-bomb period was the issue of warnings. Klaxon horns were used to notify 'Immediate Danger' in many offices and railway stations. The red-painted dustbin, here being hoisted by a roof-spotter, indicated 'V1 Approaching.'

DESTRUCTION OF HISTORIC BUILDINGS

In London, buildings of historic and other interest suffered severe damage from flying-bombs. 1. The Guards' Chapel at Wellington Barracks, almost completely destroyed during Sunday morning service, on June 18, 1944. 2. The Dutch Garden in Staple Inn, Holborn—one of the Inns of Chancery from Henry V's time to 1884—before it was struck by a V1 on August 29, 1944, and (3) afterwards.

Photos, Planet News ; Fox

in the second to 24 per cent, in the third to 27 per cent, in the fourth to 40 per cent, in the fifth to 55 per cent, in the sixth to 60 per cent, and in the last week to 74 per cent. The guns destroyed 1,551 flying-bombs, their most potent weapon being the 3·7-inch heavy gun. The fighters of A.D.G.B. destroyed more than 1,900. Tempests brought down 578, Spitfires over 300.

Balloons were rushed from all over Britain to aid the defence. The first curtain of 500 balloons was raised in five days. Roads had to be cut by bulldozers to get the winches to some of the sites. Another 500 balloons quickly followed, and then the remainder, until some 2,000 of the 2,400 balloons in Balloon Command screened London. Flying well below their maximum altitude, they were able to lift two and three cables instead of one. To catch the small-span robots, whose wing-

spread varied from 16½ to 18 feet, the balloons were flown so close to one another that their cables sometimes became entangled. Women factory workers, including girls of 14 and women of 68, toiled to produce more balloons with the utmost speed to maintain the curtain. Balloon Command brought down 278 flying-bombs ; some fell near the balloon crews and caused casualties among them.

From June 13 to September 4, 1944, the enemy launched flying-bombs, sometimes singly and sometimes in waves, against England ; the total was estimated at 8,070. Twenty-nine per cent reached the London defence area, 25 per cent were erratic or inaccurate (some diving into the sea), and 46 per cent were brought down by the triple defences. On two days the rate of

Scale of
V1 Attack

OPENING OF LONDON'S DEEP SHELTERS

Early in July 1944 the Government opened London's deep shelters, construction of which had been ordered in 1941 (see page 3022). Four were north of the Thames and four south, each being staffed by 48 wardens, aided by 120 other volunteers. All public shelters closed on May 6, 1945. Below, left, 'cross-roads' in a deep shelter. Right, bedtime in the deep shelter at Stockwell.

Photos, Sport & General ; New York Times Photos

BALLOON BARRAGE THAT SCREENED LONDON

To defeat the flying-bomb, a gigantic balloon barrage was raised in the south-eastern counties as a protection for London (see map in pages 3432–33). Some 2,000 balloons were eventually employed in what was the greatest barrage ever put into the air : it brought down 278 V1s. Here a section of it flies just above a layer of low-lying cloud. *Photo, British Official*

assault exceeded 200, but the average rate was about 100 a day. On August 28 a defence record was created when 97 were destroyed out of 101 launched. During the last fortnight of the attack, only 45 per cent of the bombs launched crossed the English coast, and towards the end of the attack only nine per cent reached London. Some bombs fell in Norfolk and one strayed as far as Northampton.

Throughout the course of the attack, tactical aircraft attacked trains carrying flying-bombs to their launching sites, and many were thus destroyed or damaged. In July 1944 Bomber Command dropped 12,000-lb. bombs on caves at St. Leu d'Osserat, 30 miles north-west of Paris, then used as a flying-bomb store. Before the Pas de Calais launching sites were overrun by the Allied armies,

Help from Bomber Command

the Allied air forces had dropped about 100,000 tons of bombs upon them. From August 1943 to September 1944 inclusive, Bomber Command dropped 64,522 tons on V-weapon targets ; the U.S.A. 8th A.F. dropped 51,512 tons on these and tactical targets.

During the conquest of the Cotentin Peninsula in June, launching sites alined towards Bristol were overrun before they could be used. When the Canadians surrounded Calais on September 6 they overran the launching sites used to attack London. The British and U.S. air forces had then lost 450 aircraft, and about 2,900 pilots and other air-crew categories in V1 counter measures. Casualties among the civilian population were 5,682 killed and 18,578 seriously injured. No fewer than 23,000 houses were destroyed, 1,104,000 were damaged, many of them only slightly.

ACK-ACK DEFENCES TOOK A HEAVY TOLL

Anti-aircraft defences, skilfully deployed in south-eastern England, accounted for no fewer than 1,551 flying-bombs. 1. Their most potent weapon was the 3·7-inch heavy gun (equipped with radar), here seen in action. 2. A.T.S. telephonists in an operations-room of the A.A. defences : they maintained minute-by-minute contact with the gun-sites. 3. A light Bofors detachment runs to stations as a V1 is signalled. *Photos, British Official ; Planet News*

T 2

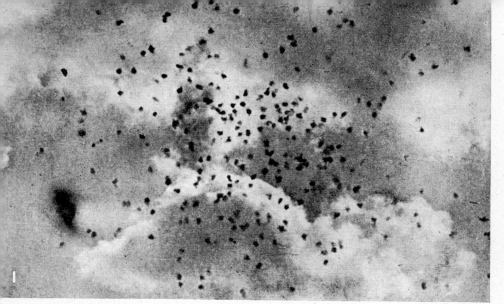

BRITISH COASTAL BATTERIES IN ACTION AGAINST V1s

1. Pattern of exploding rockets made by ' Tonsil,' the Royal Navy's anti-flying-bomb rocket-firing battery, installed between Hythe and Dymchurch, Kent, on July 19, 1944, which made its first ' kill ' the following day. 2. ' Tonsil ' in action. Originally consisting of ten, it was later enlarged to 20 projectors firing 400 rockets at once. 3. A V1 (on left) shot down at night in the dazzling pattern of blazing guns and tracer shells. *Photos, British Official; Fox*

After the main attack was over a few flying-bombs arrived from the east; these were found to have been launched from specially adapted Heinkel 111 bombers. Most of these robots arrived at night, for the Heinkels dared not face Britain's day fighters, and one such attack occurred at daybreak on September 5. Bomber Command attacked the Heinkels' aerodromes, fighters patrolled the Belgian and Netherlands coasts at night, and guns were deployed in the Thames Estuary.

An occasional aircraft-launched flying-bomb continued to arrive in England; but at nine o'clock in the evening of September 8, 1944, direct transmission of the chimes and hour bell of Big Ben was resumed by the B.B.C., an indication that the first battle of the robots had been won, for Big Ben time signals had been transmitted from recordings since June 16, 1944, lest their sudden cessation should betray the destruction of the Clock Tower at Westminster.

During September, the V1 attack was switched against continental targets from launching sites in the Zutphen–Meppel–Almelo triangle in the Netherlands, an area too distant to include London within the 150 miles range of the flying-bomb. Antwerp was the main target. General Marshall, Chief of Staff of the U.S. Army, in his report covering operations on the Western Front, says, " By November 27 the port of Antwerp was in operation, but under heavy fire of the vicious German V weapons which fell at one time at the rate of one every $12\frac{1}{2}$ minutes and caused thousands of Allied civilian and military casualties and cast grave doubts for a time as to the advisability of continuing the operation of the port," but " after the port of Antwerp became operational, it handled an average of over 25,000 tons of stores daily, despite the V bombs," and the Allies were, as had been hoped saved the necessity of re-opening the shattered ports farther west.

V Weapons on Continental Targets

A.A. gunners of the U.S.A. 9th A.F. claimed the destruction of 62 per cent of the many hundreds of flying-bombs aimed at Antwerp between October 1944 and March 1945. This percentage presumably referred to V1s passing through the American gun-belt, for British batteries—including some with mixed personnel—also manned the continental flying-bomb alley, and many bombs were shot down by their radar-controlled guns. A Civil Defence unit voluntarily recruited from the British Civil Defence forces (see page 3024) also helped to deal with the effects of

(Continued on page 3439)

MISSILE THAT OUTWITTED CONTEMPORARY METHODS OF DEFENCE—THE GERMAN V2 ROCKET-BOMB

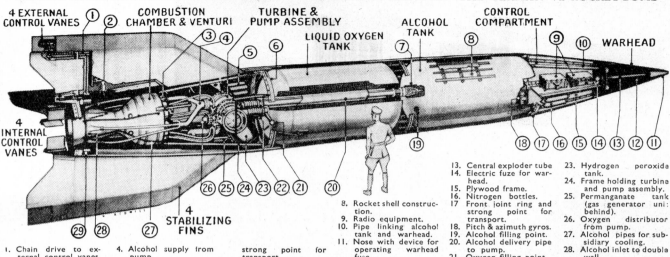

1. Chain drive to external control vanes.
2. Electric motor.
3. Burner cups.
4. Alcohol supply from pump.
5. Air bottles.
6. Rear joint ring and strong point for transport.
7. Servo-operated alcohol outlet valve.
8. Rocket shell construction.
9. Radio equipment.
10. Pipe linking alcohol tank and warhead.
11. Nose with device for operating warhead fuse.
12. Conduit carrying wires to 11.
13. Central exploder tube.
14. Electric fuze for warhead.
15. Plywood frame.
16. Nitrogen bottles.
17. Front joint ring and strong point for transport.
18. Pitch & azimuth gyros.
19. Alcohol filling point.
20. Alcohol delivery pipe to pump.
21. Oxygen filling point.
22. Concertina connexions.
23. Hydrogen peroxide tank.
24. Frame holding turbine and pump assembly.
25. Permanganate tank (gas generator unit behind).
26. Oxygen distributor from pump.
27. Alcohol pipes for subsidiary cooling.
28. Alcohol inlet to double wall.
29. Electro hydraulic Servo motors.

THE ingenious Vergeltungswaffe Zwei (A4) was 46 feet long and 5 feet 6 inches in diameter, and weighed about 12 tons gross. It was driven by the product of combustion of a mixture of alcohol and liquid oxygen ignited in a combustion chamber into which the two fuels were pumped at pressure from separate tanks (containing 7,500 lb. and 11,000 lb. respectively). The pumps were driven by a turbine actuated by superheated steam derived chemically from the mixing of concentrated hydrogen peroxide with calcium permanganate solution. The fuel carried within the rocket weighed over 8 tons.

A rocket to be fired was hoisted upright on its four stabilizing vanes by trucks carrying special elevating gear. The vanes rested either on a steel plate 12 feet square, or on any suitable reinforced level ground. When the pumps had forced the alcohol and oxygen into the combustion chamber, it was ignited by electric cable (see 4 in page 3438), thereafter burning automatically at a temperature of about 3,000 degrees centigrade. The resultant gases rushed through a venturi to emerge from the orifice at the rear of the rocket as a hot jet with a thrust of about 26 tons, which lifted the rocket vertically into the air.

Although initial speed was comparatively slow, acceleration was very rapid as height increased and weight decreased with the burning of the fuel. The rocket exhausted all its fuel in about one minute, and then weighed about 3½ tons.

The stability and direction of the rocket's flight were governed by four control tabs on the vanes, and four internal control vanes symmetrically disposed behind the jet orifice, deflecting under the influence of internal gyroscopes. These caused the rocket to curve away from the vertical to an angle of about 45 degrees, by which time a speed of about 3,000 m.p.h. was attained.

Because the range of the V2 was determined by the combination of speed and angle of flight, the accuracy of aim at the target, London, was decided at the moment propulsion ceased. In the early models fired at London the fuel was cut off by remote radio control from the ground. In later models a self-contained integrating accelerometer measured the velocity during flight and diminished or cut off the fuel supply, according to its preselected setting, to reduce or stop the thrust.

WHEN propulsion ceased the missile followed the same parabolic flight path as a shell fired from a gun elevated to the same angle. The rocket rose to a height of about 60 miles to achieve its range of about 200 miles. During the descent, friction against the atmosphere raised its temperature to about 600 degrees centigrade, when it glowed a dull red in the dark. This heat sometimes caused the rocket to explode in flight, despite the use of explosive insensitive to heat. In the denser lower air its speed fell to about 2,000 m.p.h., almost three times the speed of sound (743 m.p.h.).

The warhead contained about a ton of high explosive, and had three fuzes, two in the front and one in the rear of the charge. The internal mechanism of the V2 is illustrated in the annotated diagram above.

ROCKET-BOMB STATISTICS

The first rocket-bomb (V2) fell on England on September 8, 1944. The diagram below shows the number which landed each week from that date until March 1945, each column indicating, also, how many fell inside and outside the London Defence Area. Figures at the top of the columns show the number of people killed in each 7-day period.

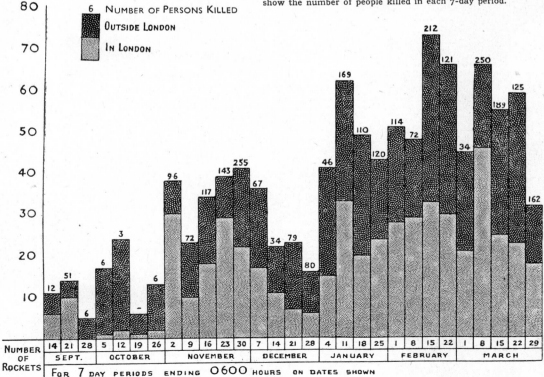

HOW V2 WAS FIRED

To test the accuracy of German-supplied data about the performance of the rocket-bomb, experiments were carried out at Cuxhaven early in October 1945, when the projectiles were successfully fired into the North Sea by Royal Artillery experts of the B.A.O.R. 1. A rocket on its trailer; and (2) being raised into position. The powerful elevating mechanism is seen just above the trailer's rear wheels. 3. In the vertical firing position; the servicing platform is at the top. 4. Just before the take-off: note firing cable on left. 5. The charge is fired. 6. In full flight.

Photos, British Official

WHERE THE FIRST V2 FELL IN ENGLAND

First rocket to land in Britain fell at seven o'clock on the evening of September 8, 1944, at Staveley Road, Chiswick, London (here seen shortly afterwards), where it destroyed eight houses and damaged fifty others. Two people were killed and 10 injured. The average number of casualties in the V2 bombardment, it was officially announced, was 2·7 killed and 10 injured per rocket. In all, 1,050 rockets reached Britain in the six and a half months of the attack.

Photo, News Chronicle

the bombardment in Antwerp, where a flying-bomb density about six times as heavy as that on Croydon fell. Only about five per cent of the missiles launched fell within the actual port area, whose activity continued unchecked. The civil population largely evacuated Antwerp, yet about 5,000 were killed and 21,000 wounded there. Liége suffered from flying-bombs during Von Runstedt's counter-offensive in the Ardennes in December 1944. About half the houses in Liége and Antwerp were reported to have been destroyed. Brussels also received an intermittent bombardment.

The flying-bomb battle over, the attack by rocket-bombs began, for the V2—*Vergeltungswaffe Zwei*—had a range of about 200 miles, and could be fired in the direction of London from launching sites in The Hague–Amsterdam area of the Netherlands. The first V2 known outside Germany fell in a swamp near Kalmar, south-east Sweden, on June 13, 1944, and was brought to Britain in August by Lieut.-Colonel Keith N. Allen in an unarmed and unescorted Dakota of the U.S.A.A.F. (*see* page 3156). British experts had therefore already examined parts of the V2 weapon some weeks before the first rocket-bomb to reach England fell at Chiswick in the evening of September 8, 1944, killing two people and seriously injuring ten, destroying eight houses,

Reprisal Weapon Two

damaging 50, and affecting water and gas mains.

The defence organized against the flying-bomb was useless against the rocket-bomb. Current radar could detect it in flight, but that was all. This weapon took but five minutes to travel from the launching sites, first in Walcheren and later, after Walcheren was captured, near The Hague, to its impact in England. Travelling faster than sound, it could not be intercepted by aircraft. Its warhead contained the same weight of explosive as the flying-bomb, but its effect was different, for this was a penetrating bomb whose sharp-pointed nose bored deep into the ground or through buildings. Gunfire was useless against it. It arrived unheralded either by its own noise or the sound of the sirens. The shock-wave of its passage through the atmosphere followed the explosion of its warhead, and sounded like the rumble of a heavy thunderstorm.

Interdiction aircraft were employed to bomb and shoot up the launching sites and to attack the trains and special trucks that carried the bombs from factory or store to the launching area. British and American fighter and bomber aircraft, combining in this

work, reduced the weight of attack. But these launching sites were very small, and therefore much more difficult to discover than those used for the flying-bomb. The 12-ton A-4 rocket could be stood upright on its stabilizing vanes on a steel plate about 12 feet square, or, indeed, on any piece of reinforced level ground. The buildings used by the launching parties were small and carefully camouflaged.

Not all the rockets took off successfully. Dutch people who lived near the launching sites said that some fell back near their starting-point, when they took 12 minutes to explode. Many Dutch houses were damaged both by the concussion of discharge and by the explosions of the duds.

During the rocket bombardment the Government remained reticent about the attack, to prevent the enemy from learning where the V2s fell; it was mentioned for the first time by Mr. Churchill on November 10, after Walcheren was in Allied hands. The rigid exclusion from the Press of reference to the V2 did not, however, prevent persons hundreds of miles from the area learning quickly that mysterious explosions were occurring in London. When the atmospheric conditions were

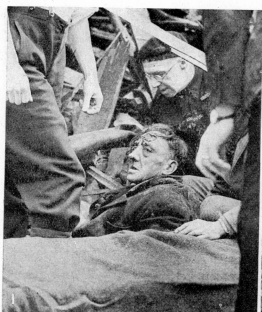

RESCUE WORKERS AGAIN PROVED THEIR WORTH

The attack by V weapons put a new strain on the Rescue Service of London's Civil Defence. One of the worst incidents with which they had to deal was at Smithfield Market on March 8, 1945, when 110 people were killed.　1. A casualty is removed at Smithfield.　2. Many dogs were trained to detect buried victims : here an Alsatian is at work.　3. Rescue-workers assist an injured woman extricated from the top floor of a damaged building.

Photos, Planet News : Central Press

favourable, persons on the east coast of England saw what must have been rocket-bombs soaring like ragged comet's tails into the sky. Aircraft pilots in flight saw man-made meteors flashing upwards into the stratosphere.

There were five major tragedies in London. One Saturday noon in November a rocket fell on a large multiple store in New Cross. Both store and the road outside were crowded with shoppers, mostly women and children. 160 persons were killed and 108 seriously injured. Another which fell in Mackenzie Road, Islington, in December killed 68, seriously injured 99. During March 1945 one destroyed a block of flats and partly destroyed two others in Hughes Mansions, Stepney, killing 131, severely injuring 49. At Smithfield Market, one lunch time, another killed 110, badly injured 123 ; while a third destroyed two blocks of flats and several houses in Folkestone Gardens, Deptford, when 52 died and 32 were injured.

Seven U.S. soldiers were killed when a V2 fell about midnight in Duke Street, W.1. A taxicab was blown into a window of a shop without trace of its occupants being found.

The rockets were aimed towards London, but there was little precision about their direction. Many did not score even outers on the world's biggest target. Some fell in Essex, Hertfordshire, and Kent. Some burst in the air when they met the friction of the lower atmosphere. One fell in the garden of a house in Northumberland Avenue, Hornchurch, and did not explode, but the earth tremor it caused damaged four houses.

Damage Caused by Rocket-Bombs

Forty-five churches and chapels were destroyed or damaged, most noted among them being Whitefield's Tabernacle, Tottenham Court Road ; and thirty-five hospitals, including the Central London Eye Hospital at St. Pancras.

During one week in February 1945, when 71 rockets fell, the V2 attack reached its maximum. Seventeen rockets in 24 hours was its greatest density. During the seven months of the rocket attack London received about half of the 1,050 V2s that fell on England. Carrying a total of about 1,000 tons of high explosive, these ingenious and costly missiles killed 2,754 persons and seriously injured 6,523. The last V2 rocket-bomb fell at Orpington, Kent, on March 27, 1945, this second ordeal ending only when the victorious advance of the Army of Liberation on the Continent of Europe cut the railways delivering these weapons to the launching sites near The Hague.

Chapter 338

BRITISH DOMINIONS IN COUNCIL

The outstanding event in the British Empire during the year 1944 was the meeting of Prime Ministers of the Dominions in London in May. The unity of purpose and sense of comradeship felt and proclaimed there continued to find practical expression in all the self-governing units of the Empire, in contributions to the joint war effort and in internal developments in harmony with their common way of life. For Dominion events in 1943, see Chapter 280

ON January 25, 1944, Mr. Attlee, Deputy Prime Minister of Great Britain and Leader of the House, announced in the Commons that definite arrangements had been made for a meeting of the Prime Ministers of the Dominions within the next few months —their first meeting during the war. This important gathering took place at the beginning of May. Mr. Mackenzie King of Canada and Mr. Peter Fraser of New Zealand arrived in England by air on April 27 ; Field-Marshal Smuts of South Africa, accompanied by Sir Godfrey Huggins of Southern Rhodesia, arrived on the 28th ; Mr. John Curtin of Australia, accompanied by Lieut.-General Sir Thomas Blamey, Australian C.-in-C., and Sir Frederick Shedden, Secretary of the Australian Advisory War Council, arrived on the 29th.

Inaugurating the conference on May 1, Mr. Winston Churchill said, " This meeting is undoubtedly one of the most important events that have taken place since the outbreak of the war."

The importance of such a meeting for the British peoples needed no emphasis ; but in so far as unison of the countries remaining voluntarily within the Empire was of good augury for the world, and for the formation ultimately of a world organization, this meeting was of special significance for the whole world too.

" A wide variety of important matters " concerning the conduct of the war and affecting the Commonwealth were discussed—among them armistice **Dominion Premiers Confer** terms ; the future organization of public law ; the improvement of arrangements for inter-Commonwealth consultation on defence, foreign affairs and economic progress ; Colonial welfare and development ; trade within the Commonwealth ; problems of migration, transport, and educational development.

Every meeting was attended by the Prime Ministers of Great Britain, Canada, Australia, New Zealand, and South Africa, and by Mr. Attlee and Lord Cranborne, Secretary of State for the Dominions. Mr. Eden, the Chiefs of Staff, Sir Godfrey Huggins, Sir Firoz

Khan Noon and the Maharajah of Kashmir (the Indian representatives in the War Cabinet) attended when problems affecting their departments or countries were discussed. Mr. Curtin, Mr. Fraser, Mr. Mackenzie King and Field-Marshal Smuts also attended meetings of the British War Cabinet during their stay in London.

All the Empire statesmen spoke at the concluding session on May 16. Some idea of the sense of comradeship which made the meeting memorable to all who took part in it, and of the essential unity of method and purpose it revealed, can be gathered from these short quotations :

Mr. CHURCHILL · " We have found pleasure in meeting men whose companionship is a comfort, whose comradeship is strong as a rock."

Mr. MACKENZIE KING : " We shall return to our countries more impressed than ever with the magnitude and complexity of the problems which confront the world today, but also with our hopes heightened and with

a profound appreciation of the courage and resolution with which they are being faced."

Mr. CURTIN : " I count myself happy to have taken part in these discussions. . . . I believe that the episode through which we are passing has hastened the evolution of our association, has strengthened it and given much acceleration and greater speed to our complete fraternization . . . the greatest confraternity of governmental relations the world has yet witnessed."

Mr. FRASER : " I am most deeply gratified with the spirit of mutual understanding and co-operation which has throughout pervaded the discussion. . . . I repeat and renew solemnly but with great pride the pledge given by our late Prime Minister, Mr. Savage, in 1939 : ' Where Britain goes, we go : where she stands, we stand.' "

Field-Marshal SMUTS : " I have attended many of the Imperial Conferences of the past, but I cannot

COMMONWEALTH PREMIERS SEE INVASION PREPARATIONS
After the Dominions Conference, which opened in London on May 1, 1944, Mr. Churchill and his fellow Prime Ministers made a 60-mile tour of southern England to inspect troops then awaiting orders for the invasion of Europe. Here are Field-Marshal Smuts (South Africa), Sir Godfrey Huggins (Southern Rhodesia), Mr. Churchill, and Mr. Mackenzie King (Canada), at Invasion H.Q., Droxford, Hampshire. (See also illus. in page 3105.) *Photo, British Official*

AIRCRAFT FOR RUSSIA FERRIED ACROSS CANADA

Between October 1, 1941 and April 30, 1944, the United States sent 6,430 aircraft to the Soviet Union. They flew across Canada to the U.S. air base at Fairbanks, Alaska, whence they were flown by Russian pilots to Siberia. Here dozens of newly-arrived fighters on the runway at Ladd Field, Fairbanks, wait to take-off for Russia. Left, control tower at one of the Canadian airfields on this Trans-continental ferry route.

The most striking phrases of the statement issued jointly by the Prime Ministers of the Commonwealth at the conclusion of the conference on May 18 (*see* Historic Document 289, page 3455) were: "In a world torn by strife we have met here in unity. That unity finds its strength, not in any formal bond, but in the hidden springs from which human action flows"; and it was imbued by that spirit that the Empire statesmen returned to their own lands.

Canada was in 1944 the scene of another momentous conference between Mr. Churchill and Mr. Roosevelt—the think of one which has had a character like the present. . . . We have discussed questions of war, questions of international affairs, matters that go to the root of our own society and of all the nations, and it has all been done in an atmosphere, in a spirit of comradeship, friendship, and understanding such as I have never experienced before. I go back to my country with a renewed feeling of strength, courage and good cheer to meet the heavy tasks that lie ahead."

Sir FIROZ KHAN NOON: "This meeting has shown us that in the wider policy of the Commonwealth there are no differences at all between the Dominions and ourselves, or His Majesty's Government in the United Kingdom and ourselves."

Sir GODFREY HUGGINS: "I rejoice in the spirit of unity displayed at this conference, and if there is no relapse when fear departs, this Commonwealth and Empire which, with courage, enterprise, and self-discipline has saved the world from barbarians, will remain in the lead and help to return this sorely stricken world to days of peace."

FROM GOOSE BAY THE NEXT STOP WAS BRITAIN

One of the world's largest wartime air bases was at Goose Bay, Labrador, last stopping-place for thousands of aircraft flying from Canada to Britain. The Canadian Government, who built it secretly during 1941-42, acquired it from Newfoundland in October 1944 on a 99-years' lease. Here, beneath the wing of a Flying Fortress making ready for the Atlantic flight, is the typical Labrador landscape of scrub, spruce and mountains.

Photos, Black Star ; U.S. Official

COMMANDER OF THE NEW ZEALAND SECOND DIVISION

Lieutenant-General Sir Bernard Cyril Freyberg, V.C., K.C.B., K.B.E., C.M.G., D.S.O. and three Bars, returned to active service to take command of the New Zealand 2nd Division in 1939. This was one of two New Zealand divisions serving overseas and won great distinction in North Africa (see in particular page 2631), afterwards spearheading the Allied offensive in Italy, notably at Cassino (see page 3051). In 1941 he was C.-in-C in Crete (see Chapter 159). This portrait is by Captain Peter McIntyre, N.Z. Official War Artist. *By courtesy of the New Zealand Government*

NIGHT SEARCH
FOR
V I VICTIMS

On August 23, 1944, be-
neath floodlights, rescue
squads toil to unearth
casualties in a block of
flats at Paddington ripped
apart by a flying-bomb.

H.M. THE KING ENTERTAINS PRIME MINISTERS OF THE BRITISH COMMONWEALTH

The conference of Prime Ministers of the British Commonwealth opened in private session at No. 10, Downing Street on May 1, 1944. In the evening Mr. Winston Churchill and the four Dominions Premiers were entertained to dinner at Buckingham Palace by the King and Queen. Here, left to right, are : the Rt. Hon. Peter Fraser (New Zealand) ; the Rt. Hon. John Curtin (Australia) ; Mr. Churchill ; H.M. The King ; the Rt. Hon. W. L. Mackenzie King (Canada) ; and Field-Marshal the Rt. Hon. Jan C. Smuts (South Africa), at the Palace.

Major JOHN K. MAHONY
(Westminster Regiment of Canada)

This officer was ordered, on May 24, 1944, to establish a bridge-head across the river Melfa in Italy under heavy fire. This achieved, the enemy counter-attacked fiercely, inflicting heavy casualties. Though wounded and in great pain, Major Mahony rallied his men to hold the position, for which he was awarded the V.C.

Major PAUL TRIQUET
(Royal 22me. Regiment)

In Italy on December 14, 1943, Captain Triquet was given the task of securing Casa Berardi. All the company officers and fifty per cent of the men were killed or wounded. With ' superb contempt ' for the enemy he encouraged his men to drive off counter-attacks, crying ' Never mind them, they can't shoot ! ' He was awarded the V.C.

Private ERNEST A. SMITH
(Seaforth Highlanders of Canada)

In October 1944 Private Smith distinguished himself during the crossing of the Savio (Italy), where by his bravery—which won him the V.C.—he materially helped to consolidate a vital bridge-head. Fighting alone against enemy tanks and infantry, he killed four and routed the rest, all the while tending a wounded comrade.

Hon. Major JOHN W. FOOTE
(Royal Hamilton Light Infantry)

The only Empire Army Chaplain to win the V.C. in this war, Major Foote on August 19, 1942, during the Dieppe landing, ' exposed himself to an inferno of fire and saved many lives by his gallant efforts.' Refusing to leave the wounded, he was not liberated until April 1945. His award was announced nearly a year later.

second they held in Canada. Mr. Churchill arrived by sea on September 10, and met the President next day at Wolfe's Cove. Marshal Stalin was not present : he sent a message saying that, with the Soviet offensive developing on an increasingly broad front, he could not leave the direction of the army for even the shortest period.

" This is a conference to get the best we can out of the combined British and U.S. war efforts in the **CANADA** Pacific and in Europe. We are working in cognisance with the situation in China, the Pacific, and in Europe, co-ordinating our efforts with those of our Allies, particularly the Chinese and the Russians," said Mr. Roosevelt. Mr. Mackenzie King ; Sir William Glasgow, High Commissioner for Australia in Canada ; Mr. A. M. Firth, Acting High Commissioner for New Zealand ; Mr. Richard Law, British Minister of State ; Mr. Anthony Eden, British Secretary of State for Foreign Affairs ; Sir Alexander Cadogan (who arrived in Quebec on September 14 from the conference at Dumbarton Oaks, *see* page 3256), and the Combined Chiefs of Staff, took part in the meetings. Prime Minister and President issued a joint statement on its conclusion on September 17 simply stating that agreement had been reached on all points. The scope and direction of that agreement was unfolded in the ensuing months by strategic developments in Europe and the Pacific.

Nearly four hundred representatives of 44 nations attended the second meeting of the Council of United Nations

Relief and Rehabilitation Administration held in Montreal from September 17–26. Mr. Lehman, Director-General, announced detailed plans for the repatriation of the masses of men and women who, as the Allies advanced, would be released from Germany whither they had been deported for forced labour. He also reported that Argentina would provide 200,000 short tons of wheat, that Sweden was contributing

300,000,000 crowns to the Administration funds, and that the U.S.S.R. had invited an U.N.R.R.A. mission to go to Moscow. The committee on policy approved the proposal made by the United States that relief in the form of medical aid and care of displaced persons should be extended to Italy up to $50,000,000 (£12,500,000).

Civil aviation within the British Commonwealth was discussed between

CANADA'S DEFENCE MINISTER IN BELGIUM

In October 1944 the Canadian Minister of National Defence, Colonel J. L. Ralston, visited Canadian troops behind the lines in Europe. He is seen in Ghent with men of the Canadian Base Reinforcement Group. Finding reinforcements inadequate to replace the heavy casualties, he advocated, on his return home, that drafted men should be compelled to serve overseas, and resigned as a result of the opposition in Canada to this proposal. *Photo, Canadian Official*

representatives of the United Kingdom, Canada, Australia, New Zealand, India, Newfoundland, South Africa, and Southern Rhodesia at Montreal between October 23 and 29. The meeting concluded unanimously that it was desirable to develop two routes—one east–west, the other west–east—which would connect the different parts of the Commonwealth and provide a complete system of Empire communications ; to create a standing Commonwealth Air Transport Council ; and to join other nations in forming an effective international air authority that would foster air development in consonance with the ideals of world security. At the conclusion of the meeting, its members left Montreal for the Civil Aviation Conference at Chicago (*see* page 3256).

Mr. Mackenzie King, addressing a joint session of both Houses of Parliament in London on **Canada's War Effort** May 11, paid tribute to the endurance of the British people, and then went on to talk of Canada's war effort. Its most significant aspect was that it was voluntary. Out of a population of 11,500,000, three-quarters of a million were in the armed forces. Canada's pre-war production had been doubled. Since the war began Canada had supplied Britain with war material and supplies worth nearly £900,000,000, almost half of it an outright contribution. The several aspects of the war effort had been paralleled in Australia, New Zealand and South Africa, and all

these efforts owed their inspiration to a common source—the love of freedom and the sense of justice which had been nurtured and cherished in Britain as nowhere else in the world. The voluntary decisions by Britain and the various dominions were a supreme evidence of the unifying force of freedom.

Next day Mr. King made a sixty-mile tour with Mr. Churchill, Field-Marshal Smuts and Sir Godfrey Huggins among the British troops preparing for the invasion ; and on the 17th he visited Canadian troops in Britain.

Air development inside Canada was foreshadowed when on March 17 the Minister of Munitions and Supply, Mr. C. D. Howe, announced that within a year after the end of the war internal air transport was to be entirely separate from surface transportation, and would be directed by a new Board (set up by an Act of August 2) which would advise the Government on ways of developing the rapid and well-planned expansion of air transport. On August 1 Mr. King announced in the House of Commons that Canada had incurred an expenditure of $120,000,000 (£27,000,000) in taking over airfields built by the United States in the north-west and north-east. The Government considered it undesirable that any other country should have an investment in permanent improvements inside Canada. Among the airfields taken over were those of a route which had been kept secret until this announcement—the Hudson Bay route to Europe, for fighter planes. Little

DRIED EGGS FOR BRITAIN
Among Canada's wartime exports, which played an important part in keeping Britain supplied with food, were dried eggs. In this Canadian dehydrating plant, millions of eggs were rendered into powder and packed into cartons for shipment overseas. (See also illus. in page 2111.) Dried eggs were introduced to prevent wastage and save shipping space. *Photo, Paul Popper*

used in the war, it was not likely to be of any value in peace-time.

On October 22 it was revealed that Canada had acquired from Newfoundland on a 99 years' lease the Goose Bay airport in Labrador, the last North American stopping point on the " great circle " route to Europe, built secretly by the Canadian Government during 1941–42 and opened in mid-1942.

The Mutual Aid Act of 1943 was renewed for a further year on July 13, and its scope was extended to cover the provision of relief supplied to U.N.R.R.A. **Mutual Aid Act Renewed** Mutual Aid agreements were made with the United Kingdom and Soviet Russia on February 11, with Australia on March 9, with the French Committee of National Liberation on April 14, and with India on November 27. Food represented a considerable part in Canada's aid to Britain—she undertook to supply 125,000,000 lb. of cheese in the year ending April 30, 1945, nearly 90,000,000 eggs in 1944, and a minimum of 50,000,000 lb. of beef in 1944 and in 1945. To India she agreed to send mainly railway equipment, including 292 locomotives—a clear indication of her growing industrialization and need of outlets for her manufactured products.

An Act to provide family allowances of 5 to 8 Canadian dollars (22s. 6d. to 36s.) a month for persons with incomes

U.N.R.R.A. DISCUSSES RELIEF PROBLEMS AT MONTREAL

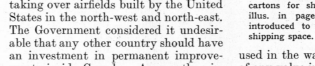

Representatives of 44 nations attended the second meeting of the Council of the United Nations Relief and Rehabilitation Administration, held at Montreal in September 1944. Below, the conference of almost 400 delegates is addressed by Mr. Herbert H. Lehman, the Director-General, who announced detailed plans for the Administration's work, declaring, 'The need is tremendous; its urgency grows apace with the rising tide of liberation.' *Photo, U.S. Official*

WAR CABINET MEETS AT CANBERRA

Australia's General Election in August 1943 returned Labour to power again with an effective majority (see page 2803). Membership of the War Cabinet—seen at their first meeting after the election—remained unchanged. Left to right : J. A. Beasley (Supply and Shipping) ; Dr. H. V. Evatt (Attorney General and External Affairs) ; F. M. Forde (Army and Deputy Premier); John Curtin (Premier and Minister of Defence) ; Sir Frederick Shedden (Secretary to the War Cabinet) ; J. B. Chifley (Treasurer) ; N. J. O. Makin (Navy and Munitions) ; A. S. Drakeford (Air) ; and J. J. Dedman (War Organization of Industry).

below 1,200 dollars (£270) was passed on August 11, to come into effect on July 1, 1945. Its cost was estimated at $200,000,000 (£45,000,000) annually. Other important acts passed during the year were for the insurance of war veterans, to establish an Exports Credit Insurance Corporation, and to establish an Industrial Development Bank.

General elections were held in four provinces. In Alberta, where Mr. William Aberhart, creator of the Social Credit Party and Premier since 1935, died, aged 64, on May 23, the Social Credit Party was re-

Provincial Elections turned again on August 9 with a larger majority than it had had since it came into power. Liberal governments were defeated in two provinces. In Saskatchewan, the Co-operative Commonwealth Federation, the Socialist-Labour party of Canada, gained a sweeping victory on June 15 : polling 208,891 votes, it secured 47 seats (against 10 in the previous House) ; the Liberal Party, with 134,295, secured only 5 seats (against 33 previously). The Progressive Conservatives, with 44,156 votes, failed to win one seat. The success of the C.C.F. in this first provincial election they had won was at least in part due to a promise that farmers would be exempted from socialization : the Federation's election manifesto promised that " a C.C.F. government will guarantee that every honest and industrious farmer is enabled to keep the title of his farm and pass it on unencumbered to his children."—a complete revocation of the party's

former declaration that once it got into power no more land would be handed over to private ownership and farmers would not be allowed to leave their property by will.

In Quebec, on August 8, in the first election at which women voted, the Union Nationale party won 47 seats, while the Liberals secured only 37 (they had held 59 in the previous parliament). The vote—1,295,052, representing 70 per cent of the electorate—was the heaviest since Confederation. The ultra-nationalist and anti-British Bloc Populaire Canadien, formed in 1942, put up 80 candidates, but polled only 188,839 votes which secured four seats.

In New Brunswick, the Liberal Government was returned with an increased majority on August 28, gaining 36 seats against a previous 28, while the Progressive Conservatives fell from 19 to 12. The C.C.F. with 41 candidates (27 lost their deposits) won no seat.

Though the question of conscription for overseas service was not emphasized in the Quebec elections, it formed the background of the campaign, for it was in this province that opposition to

AUSTRALIAN HEROES RETURN IN TRIUMPH

Melbourne welcomes the heroic 17th Brigade of the Australian Imperial Force on their return home in April 1944, as the men in their ' digger ' hats march by. The 17th Brigade, part of the famous Australian 6th Division, saw service in Palestine, Libya, Greece, and Syria, and later in the arduous New Guinea campaign. *Photo, New York Times Photos*

conscription was strongest, and the party which won—the Union Nationale —was opposed to compulsory military service. Canada's total war casualties to the end of May (that is, before the invasion of Normandy), were : Army, killed 5,483 ; presumed dead, 202 ; missing, 1,430 ; prisoners or interned, 3,629 ; wounded, 10,839. Air Force : killed, 4,566 ; missing, 2,906 ; presumed dead, 4,517 ; prisoners, 1,479 ; seriously wounded, 829. Navy : killed, 980 ; other dead, 166 ; missing, 329 ; prisoners, 8 ; wounded, 184. The strength of the forces was given in Ottawa on October 25 as : Army, 470,000 : Navy, 90,000 ; Air Force, 204,000–764,000, against a pre-war total of 10,200.

Canada had two corps overseas, one of which formed part of the 8th Army in Italy. The second was the backbone of the 1st Canadian Army, completed by units from British and other Allied forces, and commanded by the Canadian Lieut.-General H. D. G. Crerar, who set up his headquarters in France on July 18, 1944. That army, the first independent Canadian army ever sent abroad, was a source of great pride to Canada ; but the problem of how to maintain its strength produced the major internal crisis of the year.

Opinion in the country favoured the continuance of the voluntary principle for overseas service— **Crisis over Overseas Service** arguing from the fact that all but seven per cent of the 975,000 men who had entered the three services during the war had so volunteered. Towards the end of the year, however, Colonel J. L. Ralston, Minister of National Defence, came back from a visit to Canadian troops in the European theatres of war. He had found reinforcements inadequate to meet the need for trained infantry caused by the high rate of casualties in the operations of the 1st Army ; and he advised the Government to exercise its powers under the National Resources Mobilization Act of 1940 to compel drafted men to go overseas. His advice was rejected, and he resigned on November 2. He was succeeded by General McNaughton, who in December 1943 had returned from London (where he had been Chief of Staff of Canadian Military Headquarters) to take up the post of C.-in-C., Canadian Forces.

General McNaughton hoped to meet the requirements of the military situation by voluntary means ; but when Parliament, prorogued on August 14, reassembled on November 22, it was informed that an Order in Council had been issued authorizing the Minister of Defence to send 16,000 drafted men

overseas between December 1944 and February 1945. The Minister of Defence for Air resigned, there were demonstrations of drafted men in Quebec and in British Columbia. On November 27, Mr. Mackenzie King, having asked Colonel Ralston whether he was prepared to form an alternative government and been met with a negative, tabled a motion that " the House will aid the Government in its policy of maintaining a vigorous war effort." A stormy session lasting thirteen days followed ; but the Government got its vote of confidence by 141 to 70 after the words " its policy of " had been deleted from the motion.

Representatives of Australia and New Zealand met at Canberra from January 17–21 to dis- **AUSTRALIA** cuss problems of mutual interest. The delegates found remarkable unanimity in their views, and drew up an agreement of 44 clauses which Dr. Evatt, Australian Minister for External Affairs, described as " a Pacific charter of permanent collaboration and co-operation." Within the framework of a general system of world security, Australia and New Zealand proposed to set up a regional defence zone based on their two countries and stretching through the arc of islands north and north-east of Australia to western Samoa and the Cook Islands. War occupation of territory was declared to be no basis for territorial post-war claims, and no change in the control or sovereignty of the Pacific Islands should be effected except as a result of an agreement in which Australia and New Zealand concurred. A permanent secretariat was to be set up to promote continuous collaboration. The Australian Cabinet formally ratified the Agreement on January 25.

Mr. Curtin journeyed to the Empire Conference by way of the United States, where he conferred with President Roosevelt, Mr. Cordell Hull, Lord Halifax and other American and British leaders. He returned by way of Canada, where he attended a meeting of the war committee of the Canadian Cabinet, and on June 1 addressed a special joint session of the Senate and the House of Representatives at Ottawa, emphasizing the necessity of the United Nations, and particularly for the continued collaboration in peace of Britain, the United States, Russia and China. Referring to the rallying of the Dominions to Britain's side, he asked, " If the heart should be entirely destroyed, how could the nether limbs survive ? " Before returning home, he met Mr. Roosevelt again in Washington on June 5.

To strengthen its position for dealing with post-war problems, the Federal Government was anxious to retain, at any rate for a period after the end of the war, powers over the State governments similar to those it had been given during the war, and on March 23 the Senate passed by 19 to 17 the Constitution Alteration (Post-War Reconstruction) Act which authorized the holding of a referendum to grant the Commonwealth Government for five years after the close of hostilities powers to carry out an Australia-wide policy of post-war reconstruction in fourteen specified ways, covering employment, production and distribution of goods, control of overseas exchange, air transport, introduction of uniformity in railway gauges (these varied from State to State, which made inter-State communications difficult), and the care of ex-servicemen and their dependents. Voting in the referendum, held on August 19, was compulsory, and had to be for or against all fourteen powers. The Government's request was rejected, the civilian vote giving 2,110,270 against, 1,744,984 for, the Service vote 195,148 against, 218,452 for. South and Western Australia showed small majorities for the Government.

An Unemployment and Sickness Benefit Act, passed on March 30 to come into force on **Social Welfare Measures** January 1, 1945, provided weekly benefits of from 15s. to 25s. with additional allowances for dependents, payable for an unlimited period provided the person was available for and willing to work, and during continuance of temporary incapacity for sickness subject to a doctor's certificate and proof of loss of earnings up to the amount of the benefit. These allowances were payable from the National Welfare Fund. In introducing the bill on February 10, Senator Fraser, Minister for Health and Social Service, stated that it was the Government's considered opinion that a contributory insurance scheme would impose an undue burden on the lower paid members of the community ; the cost of benefits met from general revenue was spread more in accordance with ability to pay. The Pay-as-You-Earn method of collecting income tax, with cancellation of 75 per cent of the tax for 1943–44, was introduced in March.

General elections held in Queensland (April 15), South Australia (April 29), and New South Wales (May 27) resulted in very little change of representation, the Labour Party maintaining its lead in the first and last, the Liberal-Country Party in the second.

ROYAL NAVY BASE IN AUSTRALIA

H.M.S. 'Golden Hind,' Royal Naval barracks and British Pacific Fleet transit camp, first set up in 1944 on Warwick Farm, one of Sydney's racecourses (1), was afterwards moved to Hargrave Park. 2. Admiral of the Fleet Lord Keyes, who was on H.M.A.S. 'Australia' in the Philippines landings (October 1944), here visits a Sydney dockyard. 3. The Captain Cook dry dock at Sydney under construction. Large enough to take the liner 'Queen Mary,' the dock cost £A9,000,000 and was opened by the Duke of Gloucester on March 24, 1945. *Photos, British and Australian Official ; L.N.A.*

Mr. Forde, Acting Prime Minister, announced in the House of Representatives on November 22 that all inter-State air lines in Australia would be taken over by the Commonwealth Government, a Government-owned statutory authority being created for the purpose.

V.C. AND BAR

First man in this war—and the third in history—to be awarded a bar to his V.C. was Captain Charles Hazlitt Upham, a New Zealander born in 1908. Award of the V.C. was for bravery in Crete in May 1941, and of the bar for courage in the Western Desert in July the following year. (See opposite page and illus. in page 1630.)
Photos, Planet News ; New Zealand Official

Australian industry was considerably re-oriented during the year. Plants were turned over from making tanks to making small craft and locomotives, from the production of Bofors A.A. guns, 25-pounder gun-howitzers and small arms to 25-pounder pack howitzers for use in the New Guinea jungle, the 17-pounder " tank buster," the 4-inch naval gun for merchant ships, and the 25-mm. cannon for aircraft. Some firms were released from munition making in order to produce new types of agricultural, food-processing and canning machines, and composite machines for large-scale vegetable production which would cultivate the ground, sow seed, and distribute fertilizer in one operation.

By the end of October, except for skeleton supply units, all U.S. Army and Navy personnel who had been stationed in Australia had left. Their withdrawal gave Mr. Curtin occasion to say, " Now that the bulk of U.S. forces have moved from the mainland of Australia I offer to them and their great Commander-in-Chief the deep gratitude of the Australian Government and people. We will never forget the feeling of deep relief which swept the country when the U.S. forces arrived early in 1942." The first contingent of Canadian troops to arrive in Australia landed at Sydney on September 27 ; and on December 11 the Acting Prime Minister stated that at the request of the United Kingdom Government the Commonwealth Government had undertaken to provide by June 1945 facilities, services and supplies for the new British Pacific Fleet based on Sydney, at an estimated cost of

£A21,000,000. On the same day Admiral Sir Bruce Fraser, commander of this fleet, arrived in Melbourne.

Australia made even greater contributions than she had done in previous years to the feeding of the United Kingdom. Meat rationing, expected to save 150,000 to 200,000 tons in the year, was introduced on January 17. Speaking at Perth on October 19, Mr. Curtin gave the following estimates for Australian food production in 1944 : meat, 1,035,000 tons, of which Britain and the British forces would receive 178,000 tons, U.S. forces 158,000 tons ; butter, 145,000 tons—Britain and British forces, 47,000 tons, U.S. forces 9,000 tons ; cheese, 34,000 tons—10,000 tons to Britain and 8,500 to British forces ; milk, 11,000,000 gallons (condensed and dried) for Britain and the British forces.

Australian Help for Britain

Under reciprocal lease-lend, Australia provided ninety per cent of the food needed by the U.S. forces in the southwest Pacific as well as clothing and other supplies of all kinds, reaching a value of £A100,000,000 during the year—one-sixth of the country's total war expenditure. To meet the Allied food requirements, manpower was reallocated over a period of fifteen months ; 20,000 were specially released from the forces, 20,000 from munitions, to which were added

NEW ZEALAND'S PREMIER WITH HIS COUNTRYMEN IN ITALY

The Rt. Hon. Peter Fraser, Premier of New Zealand, in May and June 1944 visited the famous New Zealand 2nd Division in forward positions in Italy. On June 10 he went to Rome (freed only six days before), being the first member of any United Nations Government to enter the Italian capital since its liberation. Above, Mr. Fraser among the monastery ruins on Monte Cassino, captured only a few days previously (see Chapter 302). Below, addressing troops in the area.

SOUTH AFRICAN V.C.

Lieut. Gerard Ross Norton, M.M., attached to the Hampshire Regiment, won the V.C. when, during an attack in August 1944 on Monte Gridolfo, a strongpoint on the Adriatic sector of the Gothic Line in Italy, he captured two enemy machine-gun posts single-handed, killing or taking prisoner the crew of 18. *Photo, British Official*

30,000 routine discharges from the forces ; 30,000 women were diverted to war industries. The reduction in the strength of the armed forces was made possible by the reduction of field defences no longer considered necessary.

An announcement by General Mac-Arthur in January 1945 made it known that the Americans had withdrawn from New Guinea and the Solomon Islands in the previous November, and all operations there had been taken over by Australian forces. The Department of External Territories was already administering the recaptured parts of Papua and New Guinea.

Lord Gowrie, the Governor-General, left Australia in September. He had represented the Crown in the continent for sixteen years—as Governor of South Australia and of New South Wales before he became Governor-General. Sir Winston Duggan, Governor of Victoria, was sworn in as Acting Governor-General until the arrival of the Duke of Gloucester, who reached Sydney on January 28, 1945.

On his way to the Empire Conference, Mr. Peter Fraser called at Honolulu, where he met Admirals Nimitz and Ghormley **NEW ZEALAND** and discussed the Pacific campaign, and at Washington, where he conferred with members of the U.S. Cabinet on war and post-war policy in the Pacific. While he was in Europe, he went to Italy, where he visited the New Zealand 2nd Division, talking with its commander, Lieut.-General Freyberg, and touring the front, including the Cassino sector. In England he saw General Eisenhower and visited the assembled invasion forces.

New Zealand, like Canada and Australia, found herself faced with great manpower difficulties during 1944. At the beginning of the year the Governor-General, Sir Cyril Newall, in the speech from the Throne to the new Parliament which assembled on February 22, said that she had two divisions overseas— the 2nd, under the command of Lieut.-General Sir Bernard Freyberg which, after fighting with great distinction in North Africa, was the spearhead of the offensive in Italy ; and the 3rd in the Pacific under the command of Major-General Barrowclough, which had given a good account of itself at Vella Lavella (*see* page 2886 and illus. in page 2816), the Treasury Islands (*see* page 2674 and 2886), the Nissan Group and elsewhere.

The total number of persons in the Services on July 31 was 114,022, of whom 61,068 were overseas, including 6,589 women at home and 882 abroad. Total casualties to that date were 31,607—killed 8,065, wounded 15,330, missing 963, prisoners 7,249 (compared with a total of 58,004 in the war of 1914–18).

Food production declined as a result of the strain on manpower, and, on the combined advice of the British and American Chiefs of Staff, it was decided in April to release selected men from the army for work on farms. By September, it was agreed that New Zealand could no longer maintain two divisions overseas, a large air force, and a naval contribution, and at the same time produce the food and raw materials urgently needed for Britain and for the Allies in the Pacific. In the light of the decisions taken at the Quebec Conference it was decided to keep the 2nd division in Italy until the conclusion of hostilities in that country, using the personnel of the 3rd Division for posting to the 2nd as necessary.

Meat was rationed from March 6, with an anticipated saving of 50,000 tons of meat annually, which would be used to maintain supplies to Britain. Coupons had to be surrendered for meat meals in restaurants. The British Minister of Food announced in London on August 3 the conclusion of a four-year agreement covering the sale to Britain of all exportable surpluses of New Zealand butter, cheese, and meat at prices agreed for two years.

To a New Zealander fell the honour of gaining the only double Victoria Cross of the Second Great War, Captain Charles Hazlitt Upham. The V.C. was conferred on him for conspicuous bravery in Crete in May 1941. He won it again in the attack on El Ruweisat Ridge in the Western Desert on the night of July 14–15, 1942. Twice wounded, once when crossing open ground to inspect his forward sections, again when he destroyed unaided a truckload of German soldiers with hand grenades, he insisted on remaining to take part in the final assault, during which he led his company against fierce resistance to capture two strongpoints, himself destroying a German tank and several guns and vehicles with grenades. His arm was broken, but he went on until his men had consolidated the vital position they had won under his leadership. He was wounded a fourth time, and being then unable to move he was taken prisoner. He was liberated from a German prisoner-of-war camp in April 1945. The second award was announced during the following September.

NEW GEORGIA SCOREBOARD

Formed in 1937, the Royal New Zealand Air Force contributed a full share of pilots and aircrews to the Empire's air-war effort, no fewer than 18 squadrons serving in the Pacific alone. Here one of the ground-staff brings up to date the scoreboard of Japanese 'kills' by a New Zealand fighter wing on New Georgia in the Solomons, in 1944. *Photo, New Zealand Official*

On his flight to England for the Empire Conference, Field-Marshal Smuts spent two-and-a-half days in Cairo, where he saw General Sir Bernard Paget, C.-in-C., Middle East. On the eve of the invasion, he visited British and Canadian troops of General Montgomery's forces, in company with Mr. Winston Churchill, whom he also accompanied to Normandy on June 12. While in Europe he spent three days with South African troops in Italy, and on the return flight to South Africa he broke his journey at Algiers to consult with General Sir Henry Maitland Wilson, Allied C.-in-C., Mediterranean.

Shortly after his return to South Africa, Smuts spoke in a broadcast on July 13 of the South African forces abroad. He said that the South African 6th Armoured Division had been foremost in the Allied 200-mile advance in Italy. It had been the spearhead on the left flank of the 8th Army and had earned the highest tributes from Allied commanders. South African engineers had done magnificent work, and the South African Air Force comprised a very large part of the Tactical Air Force which had driven the Luftwaffe from the Italian skies and patrolled the Mediterranean shores from Algiers to Alexandria, the Atlantic coast from West Africa to Cape Town, and the Indian Ocean from Cape Town to the Red Sea.

The Indian Pegging Act of 1944 forbade the acquisition of property by Indians in recognized European areas. It was almost at once suspended, and in Natal, where most of South Africa's 200,000 Indian settlers were concentrated, a Provincial Board of Control was appointed to divide the towns into three areas : prohibited, restricted, and exempted. The resulting Residential Property Regulation Ordinance drawn up by Natal Provincial Council provoked a storm in the Indian Legislative Assembly in Delhi, which on November 6 passed a motion recommending the recall from his post of the Indian High Commissioner to South Africa, and the enforcement of economic sanctions. In the following month, Field-Marshal Smuts advised the Acting Governor-General to withhold his consent to the Ordinance, which had caused trouble in Durban as well as in Delhi, and the Pegging Act was continued in force pending some new arrangement.

A White Paper setting out a scheme of social security to include Europeans, Asiatics and Coloured people, with a separate scheme for the Bantu population living in reserves, was presented to Parliament in February. It was estimated that it would cost initially £25,000,000 a year, rising to £98,000,000 by 1955, an expenditure which would require an increase of the national income by at least 50 per cent.

Colonel Deneys Reitz, High Commissioner for South Africa in London since 1943—once a member of the famous first Commando from Pretoria which, during the South African War of 1899–1902, penetrated right down to the coast of Cape Colony under the leadership of Smuts—died after a brief illness on October 19, at the age of 62. The Hon. George Heaton Nicholls, Administrator of Natal, was appointed on November 21 to succeed him.

On April 27 the Governor of Southern

RHODESIA'S SQUADRON

South African airmen, flying from Britain and playing an important part in the bombing of Germany, were joined in 1943 by the Rhodesia Squadron. Here is a Lancaster bomber of the squadron, ' S for Sugar,' whose fuselage is being embellished with a bomb—her twenty-first—indicating that she had raided Germany 21 times.

Photo, Empire Tea Bureau

Rhodesia appointed a commission of four to enquire into all aspects of trade by and with the natives of the colony. Possible developments to be considered were the formation of a central board of cooperative organizations in each reserve, and the creation of model towns connected with large European centres by good roads, but self-contained and with their own shops, banks, amusements and other amenities. The setting up of a Department of Trade and Commerce was announced on August 25. **SOUTHERN RHODESIA**

Colonel Oliver Stanley, British Colonial Secretary, announced on October 18 the establishment on a permanent basis of a standing Consultative Central African Council covering Northern Rhodesia, Southern Rhodesia, and Nyasaland, and the setting up of a permanent Inter-Territorial Secretariat " to deal with communications, economic relations, industrial development, research, labour, education, agricultural, veterinary and medical matters, currency and other matters agreed between the three governments." But it was still, he said, impracticable, for many reasons, to follow Southern Rhodesia's proposal for the amalgamation of the three territories—one reason being the difference in their African policy.

FIELD-MARSHAL SMUTS AT ALEXANDRIA

On his way to London in October 1943 (see page 2806) Field-Marshal Smuts, South Africa's Prime Minister, Minister of External Affairs and Minister of Defence, visited Middle East H.Q. He is here on the bridge of the South African mine-sweeper ' Langlaate ' in the harbour of Alexandria. On the right is Admiral Sir John D. Cunningham, K.C.B., Naval C.-in-C. Levant.

Photo, British Official

BRITISH PREMIERS PROCLAIM THEIR UNITY OF PURPOSE

The joint statement issued by the Prime Ministers of the United Kingdom and the
self-governing Dominions at the close of the first Imperial Conference held during
the war is given below. Extracts from speeches made by Mr. Curtin and Mr. Fraser
when the Freedom of London was conferred on them are also given

The following statement was issued on May 18, 1944, outlining the results of the Imperial Conference :

AT this memorable meeting, in the fifth year of the war, we give thanks for the deliverance from the worst perils which have menaced us in the course of this long and terrible struggle against tyranny. Though hard and bitter battles lie ahead, we now see before us, in the ever-growing might of the United Nations, and in the defeats already inflicted on the foe, by land, by sea, and in the air, the sure presage of our future victory.

To all our Armed Forces who in many lands are preserving our liberties with their lives, and to the peoples of all our countries whose efforts, fortitude, and conviction have sustained the struggle, we express our admiration and gratitude. We honour the famous deeds of the forces of the United States and of Soviet Russia, and pay our tribute to the fighting tenacity of the many States and nations joined with us. We remember the prolonged, stubborn resistance of China, the first to be attacked by the authors of world-aggression, and we rejoice in the unquenchable spirit of our comrades in every country still in the grip of the enemy. We shall not turn from the conflict till they are restored to freedom. Not one who marches with us shall be abandoned.

We have examined the part which the British Empire and the Commonwealth of Nations should bear against Germany and Japan, in harmony with our Allies. We are in cordial agreement with the general plans which have been laid before us. As in the days when we stood all alone against Germany, we affirm our inflexible and unwearying resolve to continue in the general war with the utmost of our strength until the defeat and downfall of our cruel, barbarous foes has been accomplished. We shall hold back nothing to reach the goal and bring to the speediest end the agony of mankind.

We have also examined together the principles which determine our foreign policies, and their application to current problems. Here, too, we are in complete agreement.

We are unitedly resolved to continue, shoulder to shoulder with our Allies, all needful exertions which will aid our Fleets, Armies, and Air Forces during the war and thereafter to make sure of an enduring peace. We trust and pray that the victory, which will certainly be won, will carry with it a sense of hope and freedom for all the world. It is our aim that, when the storms and passions of war have passed away, all countries now overrun by the enemy shall be free to decide for themselves their future form of democratic government.

Mutual respect and honest conduct between nations is our chief desire. We are determined to work with all peace-loving peoples in order that tyranny and aggression shall be removed or, if need be, struck down wherever it raises its head. The peoples of the British Empire and Commonwealth of Nations willingly make their sacrifices to the common cause. We seek no advantages for ourselves at the cost of others. We desire the welfare and social advance of all nations and that they may help each other to better and broader days.

We affirm that after the war a world organization to maintain peace and security should be set up and endowed with the necessary power and authority to prevent aggression and violence.

In a world torn by strife we have met here in unity. That unity finds its strength, not in any formal bond, but in the hidden springs from which human action flows. We rejoice in our inheritance of loyalties and ideals, and proclaim our sense of free association to one another. Our system of free association has enabled us, each and all, to claim a full share of the common burden. Although spread across the globe, we have stood together through the stresses of two world wars, and we have been welded the stronger thereby. We believe that when victory is won and peace returns, this same free association, this inherent unity of purpose, will make us able to do further service to mankind.

> WINSTON S. CHURCHILL, Prime Minister of the United Kingdom of Great Britain and Northern Ireland.
> W. L. MACKENZIE KING, Prime Minister of Canada.
> JOHN CURTIN, Prime Minister of the Commonwealth of Australia.
> PETER FRASER, Prime Minister of New Zealand.
> J. C. SMUTS, F.M., Prime Minister of the Union of South Africa.

Speech made by Mr. John Curtin on May 10, 1944, at the Guildhall on receiving the Freedom of London.

THE crucial issue in the world today is that freedom is at stake. . . . Among the people of this country, which is the cradle of democratic liberty, there is a keen perception of the innate nature of the struggle. That perception is as clearly realized by the men and women of the Dominions as it is here. No blows were struck at Australia when Germany marched into Poland, but Australia knew that . . . the attack on Poland was as much Australia's business as if Sydney itself had been bombarded by the Nazis. A pledge of honour had been given to Poland by Great Britain. . . . And therefore in support of the word of Britain, Australia declared itself at war with Germany. . . .

Some years have passed since the conflict commenced. In all the theatres the struggle is still raging furiously. Nations have been subjugated, their institutions destroyed, their status reduced to that of helots in the service of those who conquered them. . . . We shall go on until such time as it will be impossible for malignant forces to reincubate the conditions which will compel the world to resort to war. . . .

We know how we commenced the struggle—unready, ill-prepared, believing that war was too dreadful a thing for civilized Governments to attempt again. But it came, and we were well behind the mark. We had to overcome ill-equipment, unreadiness, and all the handicaps. . . .

Having withstood for ourselves the attack which the enemy has made upon us, we hold out the prospect of early liberation to the nations ground under the oppressor's heel.

Speech by Mr. Peter Fraser on May 10, 1944, at the Guildhall on receiving the Freedom of London.

YEARS ago, in 1841, Lord Macaulay wrote, " When some traveller from New Zealand shall, in the midst of a vast solitude, take his stand on a broken arch of London Bridge to sketch the ruins of St. Paul's . . . " Well, there are New Zealanders here today, men who have sterner work than sketching St. Paul's, however fine that task may be. . . . I came here in 1939 marvelling then at the dignity and calmness of the people of Britain. . . Back here in 1941 I saw what they had gone through. . . I never heard throughout the whole of England or Scotland one whimper, one complaint, one sign of shrinking courage. . . . When at one munition factory I saw half the factory devastated, and the men, women, boys, and girls carrying on as if nothing had happened a few yards away, I felt that here was a people unconquered and unconquerable. . . .

It required no appeal from the Mother Country when the hour finally came to take a stand for freedom. In New Zealand we waited there in the Cabinet room in Wellington, some hoping against hope that war would not be declared ; but when the word did come that the United Kingdom was at war, then within three minutes New Zealand was at war also beside the Mother Country. . . . At that time we did not know what the end would be. . . . Today we have no doubt at all that it is only a question of when the victory will come. . . .

Chapter 339

ALLIED FORCES BREAK THE GOTHIC LINE

The advance on Rome, described in Chapter 302, was followed by a strenuous campaign northward across central Italy which, beginning with tremendous impetus, was slowed down by dogged enemy resistance, the withdrawal of trained men from Alexander's armies for service in other fields, and the gruellingly difficult nature of the country. By the end of September, to which this Chapter by Derek Adkins carries the campaign, the Allies had pierced the Gothic Line, strongest defence barrier across the peninsula

ALTHOUGH the fall of Rome on June 4 had great moral, political and psychological values, the liberation of the Italian capital was not the prime object of Field-Marshal Alexander's campaign, which was to destroy the hostile armies that he was engaging along the whole length of their line as they escaped northwards. The retreat of General von Mackensen's 14th Army into Tuscany was, in fact, rapid and at first disorderly in spite of the reduction of strength of Alexander's forces in Italy by the withdrawal of trained men in preparation for the landing in southern France (*see* page 3244) scheduled for August : between the middle of June and the end of July more than a division a week was taken for this purpose.

Eleven of the fourteen bridges over the Tiber in Rome were captured intact, although they were all prepared for demolition ; all the bridges between Rome and the sea were destroyed. By June 5 troops of the 5th Army were well across the river. To the east, French troops of the 5th captured Tivoli that day, while the main forces of the 8th Army made steady progress in the direction of the Rome–Pescara road, capturing Subiaco on the 7th.

The South African 6th Armoured Division, at that time attached to the 8th Army, was directed to pass northward along Highways 4 and 3 through the sector of the line held by the French. In spite of demolitions and some opposition from enemy rearguards, the Division took Civita Castellana on the 8th and passed through Viterbo on the 9th, shortly after its capture by an American armoured formation of the 5th Army. The South Africans then pressed on to the north and, in the area of Montefiascone, south-east of Lake Bolsena, had a successful action on June 10 when they captured 21 enemy guns of 75 mm. and 88 mm. calibre, four tanks, and four S.P. guns, besides killing some 300 Germans. Montefiascone, an important road junction, fell to them on the 11th—and the Allies were nearly halfway from Rome to Florence.

In the Adriatic sector (on the extreme right flank of the 8th Army), which had been quiet for five months,

the enemy began to withdraw as a result of Allied successes to the west. The Allies, moving forward against little opposition, occupied Tollo on the 8th. Two days later Indian troops captured Pescara while other forces occupied Chieti.

On the Tyrrhenian sector of the 5th Army, American armoured formations reached Lake Bracciano and took the town of that name on June 7. Field-Marshal Kesselring's former H.Q., an elaborate, tunnelled, underground structure, three miles south-east of Civita Castellana, was captured the same day. So also was the important naval base and port of Civitavecchia. Although extensively damaged by the enemy before he evacuated it, Civitavecchia was rapidly restored to use by a naval port party which was at work there by June 9. The channels were swept clear of mines, and the first convoy was accepted on the 11th. The port cleared 3,000 tons on June 15, the average daily rate of discharge then rising to something like 4,000 tons, on

Kesselring's Former H.Q. Captured

Pte. G. A. MITCHELL

Private George Allan Mitchell, of the London Scottish Regiment, was posthumously awarded the V.C. for outstanding bravery on the Damiano Ridge, south of Cassino, in January 1944. In leading his section, he 'displayed courage and devotion to duty of the very highest order.' He was killed by a German prisoner.

Maj. W. P. SIDNEY

Awarded the V.C. for 'superb courage and utter disregard of danger,' near Carroceto, in the Anzio beach-head in February 1944, Major William Philip Sidney, of the Grenadier Guards, though single-handed and wounded, drove off enemy counter-attacks 'with vitally far-reaching consequences on the battle as a whole.'

Capt. R. WAKEFORD

During the attack on Cassino in May 1944, Captain Richard Wakeford, of the Hampshire Regiment, materially assisted in the capture of two important positions, though wounded in the face, both arms and legs, and under heavy fire. For his courage, 'beyond all praise,' and disregard of his injuries he was awarded the V.C.

Flr. F. A. JEFFERSON

Serving with the Lancashire Fusiliers during the attack on the Gustav Line, in May 1944, Fusilier Francis Arthur Jefferson was awarded the V.C. for 'supreme gallantry.' Single-handed he ran into the open, destroyed one German tank with his P.I.A.T., and drove off another, defeating a counter-attack threatening to become decisive.

Sgt. M. W. ROGERS

Sergeant Maurice Wyndham Rogers, of the Wiltshire Regiment (Duke of Edinburgh's), lost his life in a gallant action in Italy which won him the V.C. Armed with a tommy-gun, he penetrated the German defences single-handed, drawing on himself nearly all the enemy's fire. Running towards another enemy post he was killed.

Photos, British Official ; News Chronicle ; Central Press ; Daily Mirror

one day the figure of 6,000 tons being reached. Tarquinia, 12 miles north on Highway 1, fell on the 9th.

German losses in Italy in one month since the combined attack by the 5th and 8th Armies launched at Cassino on May 11 were estimated at 70,000 (of whom over 25,000 were prisoners), in addition to the wounded captured in Rome, amounting to some thousands. The German 14th Army had disintegrated, the formations of which it was originally composed—the 68th, 362nd and 715th

German Losses

ADVANCE FROM ROME

Troops of the 5th Army, advancing north of Rome against a crumbling enemy, occupied the important naval base of Civitavecchia on June 7, 1944. Right, U.S. engineers blast wrecked shipping intended to hamper the Allies in their use of the port. Below, units of the South African 6th Armoured Division with recce-carriers enter Orvieto, captured June 14.
Photos, British and U.S. Official

Infantry Divisions, the 4th Parachutist and 3rd Panzer Divisions—having been virtually destroyed. Three new divisions were, however, identified: the 356th, which appeared south-east of Lake Bolsena from northern Italy, the 28th Luftwaffe Field Division rushed from Denmark, and the 162nd (Turcoman) Infantry Division, composed of Russian prisoners from various Central Asian territories under the command of German officers and N.C.O.s. The disorderly retreat of the German 14th Army endangered also the German 10th Army, retreating in better shape east of the upper reaches of the Tiber.

FALL OF PERUGIA

On June 19, 1944, 15 days after the fall of Rome, British troops of the 8th Army entered Perugia (below), historic capital of Umbria a hundred miles to the north, against heavy resistance. First to enter the city were units of the Brigade of Guards, who had to make their way in bad weather through dense minefields.
Photo, British Official

3457

SIENA FALLS TO FRENCH TROOPS OF THE FIFTH ARMY

On July 3, 1944, French troops under General Alphonse Juin took Siena, last stronghold before Florence. Though fighting in the approaches was intense, the accuracy of French artillery fire spared the city's historic monuments. Left, a mounted Moroccan Goum, of France's overseas troops, moves up towards Siena. Right, General Juin, Field-Marshal Alexander, and General Mark Clark at a 'Quatorze Juillet' celebration in the freed city. *Photos, British Official*

(The 10th Army itself had, however, suffered heavy losses earlier, particularly in the Hermann Goering Division.)

The enemy continued to withdraw on the Adriatic flank, where he depended more on demolitions and mines than on rearguards to cover his movements. Every tower which might serve as an observation post was blown up. On June 12 patrols moving down the river Pescara reported Popoli on Highway 5 clear, and on the 15th the old walled town of Aquila was entered without opposition. By the 16th the Allied forces entered Teramo, where they made contact with Italian partisans who had saved all bridges over the Tordino.

Walled Town of Aquila Taken

In the mountains east of Lake Bolsena, the Germans had rallied and put up a fierce resistance, but after being held up south of Narni a British armoured division broke through on June 13 to penetrate to the town itself, after which the advance continued north-eastwards on a two Corps front. To the right of this division, an Indian division thrust north, and by the 15th the Corps of which these two divisions formed part had reached Terni with its railway and road junctions, steel works and hydro-electric plant. The advance towards Perugia continued apace: the enemy was withdrawing so fast in this area that Allied troops were able to maintain only slender contact with him. Todi, on the left flank, was taken on June 15, Foligno, on the right, next day. Assisi, ten miles east of Perugia, and the birthplace of Saint Francis, was captured intact on the 18th. On June 19 Perugia itself was taken after heavy resistance: elements of the Brigade of Guards had fought their way into the outskirts on the 18th.

Enemy positions to the west of this advance were overrun by an armoured division, with an infantry division on its right flank, which broke through Bagnoregio on June 13, inflicting many casualties on the enemy and taking numerous prisoners. The following day armoured and infantry divisions cleared

THERE WAS SAVAGE FIGHTING AT CHIUSI

After some of the bitterest fighting in the campaign, South African troops of the 8th Army on June 26, 1944 finally captured Chiusi, west of Lake Trasimene, from which they had been driven some days previously. On June 29, Castiglione del Lago, on the shores of the lake, fell to forces of the same army. Below, left, South Africans in ruined Chiusi. Right, mopping-up operations in Castiglione del Lago. *Photos, British Official*

the east shore of Lake Bolsena and reached and passed through Orvieto. By the 20th Allied troops of the 8th Army had entered Chiusi.

On the 5th Army front, French and American troops cleared the road west of Lake Bolsena throughout its length on June 14 : they encountered delaying positions as they approached the lateral road running from Orvieto to the coast, and counter-attacks forced them to give some ground, but after making contact with an Imperial armoured division on their right, the French troops forced the enemy position and advanced to take Acquapendente on the 15th.

Along the Tyrrhenian coast, American troops of the 5th Army encountered staunch resistance in the area of Orbetello. They took Albinia on the 13th and crossed the Albinia–Manciano road, to meet determined opposition from the 162nd (Turcoman) Division at Magliano next day. On June 16 they occupied Grosseto, centre of an extensive system of airfields, where all bridges across the Ombrone had been blown up.

North of this town, on a front running eastwards to Lake Trasimene (reached by British troops of the 8th Army on June 19), the enemy again attempted to hold up the pursuit. Kesselring had received further reinforcements, particularly on the west coast, including the 26th Panzer Division, the 19th Luftwaffe Field Division (from Belgium), and part of the 16th S.S. (Reichsfuehrer) Division from the Balkans. Elements of seven divisions were identified in the Lake Trasimene area, where the enemy's resistance was officially described as greater than that of " Caius Flaminius, the Roman Consul over whom Hannibal gained such a sanguinary victory on this ground in 218 B.C." The enemy recaptured Chiusi on June 22, and bitter fighting continued for its possession until it was finally secured by the 8th Army on the 26th.

Bitter Fighting near Lake Trasimene

Simultaneously with the operations on the mainland, the Allied High Command attacked the island of Elba, where the enemy maintained a base for U-boats and E-boats and had useful observation posts only fifteen to twenty miles from the nearest point on the coast of Tuscany occupied by the advancing 5th Army. The conquest of the island was entrusted to a detachment of the French B Army commanded by General Jean de Lattre de Tassigny. British, French and American warships and aircraft took part in the operation, which was preceded by a violent bombardment ; the landings were made in

EIGHTH ARMY TROOPS IN CENTRAL ITALY

In July 1944 the Germans stiffly resisted the Allied advance in the mountain approaches to Florence. 1. British patrols mop up at the important road junction of Umbertide (15 miles north of Perugia), which fell on July 6. 2. New Zealanders pursue the enemy through vineyards south of Arezzo. 3. Units of The Rifle Brigade on patrol near the Arno : the rear files carry a ' Walkie-Talkie ' radio.
Photos, British Official

the early hours of June 17 on the south, central and south-east sections of the island by French assault troops, Commandos and Colonial troops led by General Henri Martin. The main opposition was in the Golfo di Campo, dominated by powerful enemy batteries on Capo d'Enfola on the north side of the island, and the landing there was effected with somewhat heavy casualties.

By 7.30 a.m., however, a large number of troops was ashore. The main advance was directed across the island at Portoferraio, while Goumiers worked

French Recapture Elba east along the road which runs the length of the south coast. By June 18 the assault beaches had been cleared, unloading both of stores and vehicles was proceeding satisfactorily, and Portoferraio was occupied by Senegalese troops with the support of artillery and naval gun fire. All organized resistance on the island ceased at 10.30 a.m. on the 19th. A special communiqué from Allied Headquarters stated, "The vigorous and rapid advance of the French forces prevented the evacuation of all but a small portion of the enemy garrison, and 1,800 prisoners, most of them Germans, were captured. A large quantity of material has also been abandoned by the enemy." On the night of June 19–20, German commando troops landed on the northeastern tip of the island, but they were at once engaged, and re-embarked after suffering losses without having achieved

U.S. 'JAPANESE' TROOPS

Troops of many origins in America's fighting forces included men of Japanese ancestry from the Hawaian Islands and elsewhere. Fighting in Italy with the 5th Army was the 442nd Infantry Regiment composed of Japanese Americans, which captured Follonica on June 24, 1944. Below, General Mark Clark, commanding the 5th Army, inspects troops of Japanese origin in Italy.

Photo, New York Times Photos

their object— the rescue of the remnants of the garrison not rounded up by the French.

On June 24 Americans of the 5th Army captured the small port of Follonica, where the 442nd Infantry Regiment, composed of Americans of Japanese descent, fought with distinction.

The following day patrols pushed ahead and entered Piombino, reported clear of the enemy. Capable by normal peace-time methods of discharging some 700 tons a day, Piombina was cleared and worked up by Allied transportation personnel to handle 4,000 tons a day. On the 27th San Vincenzo fell after bitter street fighting in which the Germans had to be driven from house after house converted into strongpoints.

Inland, the Americans steadily ousted the enemy from his positions along the roads between Grosseto and Siena and from Follonica eastwards. They captured Massa Marittima on June 25. Montieri, completely destroyed by the enemy to block the road to Allied tanks, fell on the 26th after

NORTHWARDS THE GATEWAY TO FLORENCE

This was the hilly type of country, thickly terraced with vines and assiduously cultivated, and most favourable to the defence, through which British and Indian troops of the 8th Army fought their way for three weeks to capture the medieval Tuscan city of Arezzo on July 16, 1944. Arezzo, which lies some 40 miles south-east of Florence in the upper Tiber valley, dominates the junction of the Tiber and Arno valleys and controls the Rome–Florence railway. *Photo, British Official*

eighteen hours' bitter fighting. South of Monticiano, the U.S. 1st Armoured Division encountered the German 504th Tank Battalion, rushed from Poitiers. Monticiano itself was captured on the 28th only after the enemy had been driven from strong defensive positions.

The French meanwhile were slowly pushing forward over the difficult and mountainous country to the west of Lake Trasimene, fighting against tenacious opposition along the general line of the upper Orcia, until by July 1 leading elements were within five miles of Siena. That historic city was taken by French troops under General Juin on the 3rd. They had encountered stiff resistance as they approached, but the Germans, threatened on their left

flank by the advancing 8th Army, pulled out of Siena itself without street fighting, and the city was found absolutely undamaged with all its art treasures, buildings and picturesque streets and squares intact.

Troops of the 8th Army were advancing up both shores of Lake Trasimene. On the 29th South Africans entered Castiglione del Lago, halfway up the western shore, Acquaviva, on the road from Chiusi to Siena, and other villages, while other 8th Army troops, including

the British 78th Division, gained ground east of the lake and north of Perugia, undergoing heavy fighting in the process. On June 30 they occupied Corciano, Magione and other small towns. Three days later columns advancing on either side of the lake made contact north of it on the road to Arezzo.

A British armoured car regiment probing into the mountains north-east of Foligno (captured June 16—*see* page 3458) advanced to take Camerino, a small city boasting an archbishopric and a university. Between this sector and the Adriatic, progress was swift, and Allied troops advanced for the most part without making contact with the enemy. They reached Ascoli and crossed the river Tronto on June 18. Grottammare was taken on the 20th, and on the 21st Pedaso and Fermo were captured by *Alpinis* of the Italian Corps of Liberation, who had been secretly switched from the central to the Adriatic front and had been responsible for the remarkably rapid Allied progress in that sector. On the 22nd, however, the Allied forces in the coastal sector came up against enemy resistance. After several days during which Allied activity was reduced to patrolling, and enemy artillery and mortar fire was particularly strong, the Germans abandoned the line of the Chienti river. Allied troops crossed it in many places on June 30 against slight opposition. Next day Macerata, capital of the Marches province, fell, the Potenza river was crossed, and Recanati captured,

GOTHIC LINE WAS ENEMY DEFENCE
Main German defence in central Italy was the Gothic Line, stretching from Pisa to Rimini. On September 12, 1944, dispatches from Allied H.Q. stated that the whole line had been strongly developed, the Futa Pass, on the road to Bologna, being more strongly fortified and held than had been Cassino. Here, Todt-workers in Italy prepare for its camouflage-cover a strongpoint embedded in rocky terrain.
Photo, Associated Press

although heavy rains and extensive demolitions hampered the advance all along this sector of the front.

After the enemy positions in the Lake Trasimene area had been successfully overcome, the German armies made a further stand covering the approaches to the line Leghorn–Arezzo – Ancona, launching frequent and vigorous counter-attacks in order to gain time for the strengthening of the so-called Gothic Line. This ran across the country from Pisa to the Futa Pass, north of Florence, and on to Rimini, along the 5,000–6,000-foot peaks of the Apennines, here constituting the most formidable mountain barrier across Italy and reinforced with numerous steel and concrete fortifications built by the Todt organization among the peaks, steep valleys and ravines. A complete Slovak division, many German labour battalions, and more than 250,000 conscripted Italians were reported to be employed on the construction of these fortifications.

The American Corps in the coastal sector came up against the stiffest resistance the 5th Army had had to encounter since the advance north of Rome. **Fanatical Defence of Rosignano** After making rapid progress on Highway 1, they captured Cecina on July 1, where there was house-to-house fighting in the heavily mined streets. Crossing the Cecina river, forward American elements on the 4th reached Rosignano, which became the focus of violent fighting, the German garrison holding out with fanatical determination until driven from the last house on July 7.

A few miles inland, on July 3, the Americans recaptured after six consecutive attacks, and held, Casole d'Elsa, first taken on June 27, but lost again. Counter-attacks at Montecatini and

GERMANS USE MINIATURE TANKS
It was disclosed on February 29, 1944 that in the German counter-attacks on the Anzio beach-head a fortnight previously the 309th Panzer Grenadiers had made use of miniature 'Goliath' tanks. These carried about 110 lb. of explosive, were directed by radio from a distance, and detonated by remote control. None reached the Allied lines. Here a 'Goliath' is serviced for action. (See also page 3167).
Photo, Associated Press

ROYAL CANADIAN NAVY'S PART IN THE BATTLE OF THE ATLANTIC

At the outbreak of the war the Royal Canadian Navy comprised six destroyers, five minesweepers, a training-ship, a ketch, and a couple of tugs, with a personnel of 1,800. By the middle of 1944—ranking third in naval strength among the United Nations—it included 330 fighting vessels and 100 special service ships, served by 90,000 officers and ratings. Much of the R.C.N.'s war service was in the Battle of the Atlantic, in the ceaseless struggle against U-boats. Here H.M.C.S. 'Prince Robert,' the first Canadian anti-aircraft cruiser, attacks an enemy submarine with depth charges.

EIGHTH ARMY PATROL IN FLORENCE

Photo, British Official

Although the Germans drew out of Florence on August 11, 1944, it was not till ten days later that Allied H.Q. announced the city's complete liberation. Main damage caused by enemy demolition was found to be the destruction of the city's bridges other than the famous Ponte Vecchio. Before their entry into Florence, British troops of the 8th Army on the south bank of the Arno were in secret contact by telephone with Italian partisans inside the city who, at great risk, smuggled a cable across the river. Here, a British patrol passes the Palazzo Vecchio (on right).

GERMAN DEMOLITIONS HELD UP PROGRESS IN THE APENNINES

The apparently slow progress of the Allied 5th and 8th Armies in Italy was caused as much by demolitions, carried out as the Germans retreated, as by the resistance of the actual enemy himself. This was especially so in the Apennines where the German forces took full advantage of the hilly terrain intersected by zig-zag, ribbon-like roads. Allied sappers are here repairing the cliff wall at a hair-pin bend on Route 67 in the Apennines during October 1944.

BOMBARDING THE GOTHIC LINE

Photos, British Official

By the autumn of 1944 the Allied air forces had virtually swept the Luftwaffe from Italian skies. This meant that British heavy A.A. regiments could turn to ground targets, for by means of an adjustable fuse in the nose of a 3·7-inch shell the heavy A.A. guns could be used as field artillery. Above, 3·7-inch A.A. guns of the Royal Artillery in action against the Gothic Line. Below, British troops of the 8th Army manoeuvre a U.S. 166-mm. ' Long Tom ' gun across a Bailey bridge over the Sieve River at Borgo San Lorenzo, on the mountain road to Faenza, near the Gothic Line.

south of Volterra were repulsed on the 4th. Heavy enemy traffic moving west from Poggibonsi showed that Kesselring was bringing up more reinforcements to cover Leghorn. On July 9, the Americans drove a wedge into the enemy positions between Poggibonsi and the sea, taking Volterra and driving four miles north of it. In a fighting advance on the night of July 13-14, American and French troops of the 5th Army made the most significant gains of a fortnight, capturing the important heights between the Cecina and Arno rivers. The American columns took Chianni and Peccioli in the Era valley; while the French, who had taken San Gimignano on the 13th, celebrated Bastille Day by seizing the important road junction of Poggibonsi, halfway between Arezzo and Leghorn.

Bitter fighting continued on both sides of the Chianna valley. British troops seized Monte Castiglione on **Allies Cross the Arno** July 8, repulsing three savage counter-attacks on its reverse slopes. On the 15th, the enemy evacuated positions covering Arezzo, which fell at 9 a.m. on July 16 to British and Indian troops of the 8th Army, the enemy having pulled out during the previous night. Arezzo, gateway to Florence, was a key communications centre of the German line in Italy, dominating the junction of the Tiber and Arno valleys, controlling the Rome–Florence railway, and lying at the intersection of Highways 69 and 71.

BRAZILIAN TROOPS IN ACTION

It was officially announced on July 18, 1944, that a Brazilian Expeditionary Force, under General J. B. Mascarenhas Morais, had arrived at Naples. It was reported in action for the first time with the 5th Army in mid-September, during the attack on the Gothic Line. Below, a Brazilian anti-tank gun is hauled across the only bridge left over the Serchio. *Photo, British Official*

ADVANCE TOWARDS FLORENCE AND THE GOTHIC LINE

On August 3, 1944 South African troops and a Guards Division of the 8th Army captured Impruneta, south of Florence, after a strong defence by the enemy. Here British tanks move through the town. Below, British sappers erect a Bailey bridge across the Arno at Pontassieve, around which much fighting took place during August. It lies in the approaches to the Gothic Line.
Photos, British Official

It was found badly damaged, but the old cathedral, the town hall and the bishop's palace were intact. Next day British Guards and South African tanks made a first crossing of the Arno four miles to the north-west over a bridge which they captured intact. On the 18th, the Allies reached Montevarchi and crossed the river on a six-mile front.

In the Adriatic sector, Polish troops under General Anders, who had taken over on the Pescara river from an Indian division, and the Italian Corps of Liberation pursued the retreating enemy to his defensive line north of the river Musone, capturing Osimo on July 2. To ward off the threat to Ancona, the Germans counter-attacked

OPERATIONS IN THE GOTHIC LINE—

The German-styled Gothic Line ran through the Apennines, roughly from Pisa to Rimini. On September 2, Allied H.Q. announced that the 8th Army had broken through the 'elaborately prepared defences' on a 20-mile front. 1. Panorama from Monte Castiglione, captured July 8, showing the 4,000-foot high Alpi di Catenaia, an outpost of the Line. 2. Dug-in tank turret used by the enemy as a

—MAIN ENEMY DEFENCE IN CENTRAL ITALY

strongpoint in the 8th Army's sector. In the background is a Churchill tank.   3. British 'Sexton' 25-pdr. self-propelled gun fords the River Foglia, first obstacle to the 8th Army's advance.   4. One of the many well-prepared infantry positions in the Line.   5. Lt.-Gen. Sir Oliver Leese, C.-in-C. 8th Army, watches the fighting.   6. Rimini, whose capture on September 21 turned the Gothic Line.   *Photos, British Official*

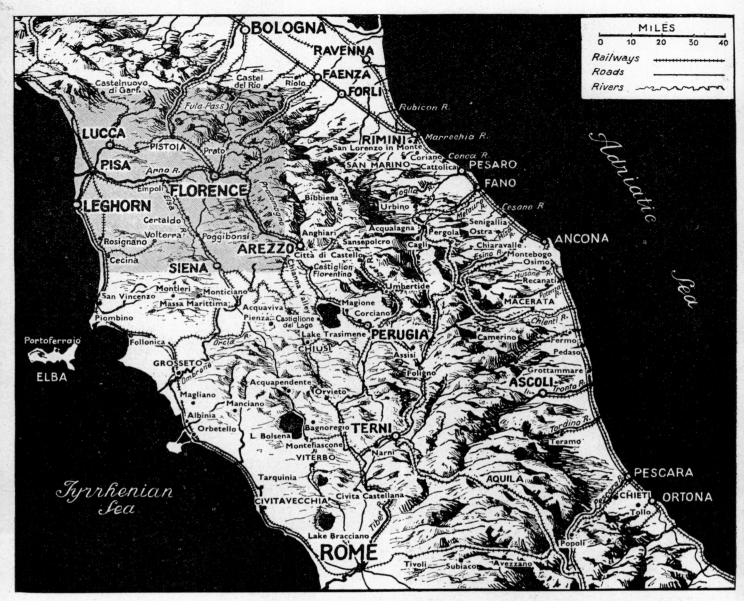

ALLIED ADVANCE FROM ROME TO RIMINI

This map shows the ground conquered by the Allied 5th and 8th Armies in Italy from the fall of Rome on June 4, 1944 to the capture of Rimini on September 21, the Futa Pass on the 23rd, and the penetration of the Gothic Line, last of the enemy's major defence works in the peninsula. The area around Florence which is shaded here is shown on a larger scale in page 3472.

strongly, but vainly. The Allied advance continued, and Ancona came under Polish fire on the 16th. Poles and Italians launched a strong attack on the last German positions before the port on the 17th, gaining control of Montebogo, a key position giving observation over the port. Next day the Poles captured Ancona, the only large port between Bari and Venice. They took 2,000 prisoners and virtually destroyed the German 278th Division. The harbour was blocked with sunken shipping, including the King of Italy's yacht.

In the west, the Americans in the Era valley, also fighting against very determined resistance, advanced to capture Pontedera at the junction of the Era and the Arno on July 18, thus cutting the Pisa–Florence road and dividing the German forces south of the Arno. Leghorn fell next day in torrential rain to a surprise thrust from high ground to the east by the American 34th Division. The port, third largest in Italy, was found completely wrecked. The dock area, said dispatches, presented "the most complete picture of desolation that the 5th Army had seen since the start of the offensive on the Garigliano." The quays had been destroyed by charges placed every few feet, all cranes and warehouses had been blown up, roads and bridges were heavily

mined, sixteen ships had been sunk in the harbour approaches. U.S. engineers and British harbour experts, however, immediately set to work to get the port into usable condition.

Patrols reconnoitring in the direction of Pisa came up against strongpoints on the Fosso d'Arno, a canal linking the Arno with the sea and draining the marshland in the area. Pisa's outskirts were probed on July 22 and found to be strongly defended, but by the 23rd Allied troops were firmly established along the south bank of the river for 25 miles from its mouth, and held the southern suburbs of Pisa. All the bridges had been blown up, the crossings were under constant fire from the Monti Pisani, and it was not until September 2 that the city was liberated. Its famous Leaning Tower

Pisa's Monuments Damaged

was found intact, but others of its monuments had suffered badly, in particular the Campo Santo.

To the south of Florence, the French made steady progress, occupying Certaldo on July 19, Tavernelle on the 22nd, by which date both the 5th and 8th Armies were within 15 miles of Florence. The 8th Army met very strong resistance as it moved along the Arno and its tributary the Pesa. Fighting continued fiercely round Montevarchi, and heavy rain also hampered progress; but by July 19 Radda, a small town in the valley of the Pesa, was reached and secured. Monte San Michele was captured and Montevarchi cleared on the 20th.

British troops were probing the slopes of Pratomagno, the 3,700-foot high mountain mass round which the

Allies Approach Florence

Arno makes a great bend, by the 23rd. New Zealanders, who had taken over from the French, advanced against strong opposition from the German 4th Parachute Division, capturing San Casciano on the 27th. South African troops cleared Mercatale on the same day. Indian forces fought their way into the outskirts of Empoli, 16 miles west of Florence, on the 29th, but failed to take it, and by next day had cleared most of the country between the Pesa and Elsa rivers to their confluence with the Arno. In the heights five miles south-west of Florence, the New Zealanders were fighting hard against successive enemy counter-attacks with Tiger tanks and motorized infantry, the enemy suffering heavy losses from British and New Zealand artillery and the fighter bombers of the Desert Air Force.

Farther east, in the valley of the upper Tiber, other Indian troops of the 8th Army drove the enemy from the stubbornly defended Città di Castello on July 22, to find this important road junction, from which a number of roads radiate towards the main chain of the Apennines, heavily mined. By the 25th they reached the vicinity of Sansepolcro. Anghiari, across the valley, was captured on the 29th.

Along the Adriatic, the Poles reached and crossed the Esino river south of Chiaravalle on July 19. Next day they were across on a fifteen-mile front. They encountered strong resistance round Ostra, which they took only on the 27th. On the 28th they crossed the Misa river and entered Senigallia where they again had to fight hard before securing the town on August 5. By the 11th, they had pushed forward and secured a bridge-head over the Cesano river, two miles from the coast.

Meanwhile, the Allied forces were advancing slowly but steadily on Florence. The German radio announced on July 1, when the Allies were forty miles away, that Hitler had declared

Enemy Defence of the Arno

Florence an open city, "so that its irreplaceable art treasures may be preserved," and on August 1 the Germans declared that there was "not a German soldier in Florence." But resistance south and south-west of the city grew in intensity as the Allies came nearer. Five enemy divisions, including the 4th Parachute and 3rd and 29th Panzer, were spread in a wide semi-circle covering the approaches from the south, and the north banks of the Arno and its tributary the Pesa were strongly held.

Indian troops took Castiglione, eight miles south-west of Florence, and crossed the Pesa on August 1; New Zealanders passed Giogoli, four miles from the centre of the city, other Allied troops took Impruneta, and British

THE BRITISH CROSS THE RUBICON

Troops of the 8th Army on September 26, 1944 reached the outskirts of Bellaria, eight miles north of Rimini at the mouth of the Rubicon—the river famous in history because Julius Caesar crossed it in 49 B.C., thereby starting the Roman Civil War. Below, British infantry cross the Rubicon, heading for Savignano. *Photo, British Official*

patrols took Incisa on the 3rd. On the 4th British troops took Bagno a Ripoli and Rignano, while South Africans and units of a British Guards Division captured Galluzzo and pressed forward into the southern outskirts of Florence. Reconnaissance patrols found that the Germans had destroyed five of the six bridges over the Arno. Only the Ponte Vecchio, rebuilt in 1345, remained; but the houses at either end of it, many of them dating from medieval times, had been demolished to create road blocks.

By August 5, the south bank of the Arno, including the suburbs of Florence, was in Allied hands from Montelupo

Germans Draw Out of Florence

(still held by the enemy) to a point four miles east of the city's boundaries. An enemy communiqué stated that German forces had withdrawn in the area north of Florence; but Allied headquarters said that enemy troops were posted along the northern bank of the Arno within the city limits, snipers were firing across the river and were directing mortar and 88 mm. gunfire into the south side of the city. There was a pause in the operations, until August 11 when at 2.30 p.m. the Germans drew out, carrying with them all copper cabling from the electric trams, all medical and surgical equipment from hospitals

SOUTH AFRICAN COMMANDER

The South African 6th Armoured Division—commanded from 1943 to 1945 by Major-General W. H. Everard Poole, D.S.O.—played a distinguished part in the Italian campaign. Here General Poole (left) is accepting the present of a sporting rifle from Lieutenant-General Mark W. Clark, U.S. Army, whose appointment as Allied C.-in-C. Italy in succession to Field-Marshal Alexander was announced on November 26, 1944.

and private practitioners, all machinery from the principal factories, and much loot.

Officers of A.M.G. and food and medical supplies were immediately sent across the river, but no troops. Sniping by Republican Fascist Blackshirts, supported by German tank and mortar units, was encountered in the northern outskirts of Florence, and scores of civilians were killed and injured when German artillery shelled the city on August 20; but on August 21 Allied headquarters announced that Florence was completely liberated, and that Allied patrols were pushing on beyond the city. Though the damage done in Florence was serious, it was much less than had seemed at one time likely. The city's movable art treasures had been dispersed about the countryside, and many of them, found by the advancing Allied forces in villas and farmhouses lying to the south of the city, were at once placed in the competent care of the Monuments, Fine Arts and Archives Sub-Commission of the Allied Forces.

East of Florence, and in the upper valleys of the Arno and the Tiber, British, Indian, New Zealand and South African troops continued to gain ground. Rufina, north-east of Pontassieve, was evacuated by the enemy on August 28. Bibbiena, on the upper Arno, a strong outer bastion of the Gothic Line, was captured on the 29th. The main fighting had, however, now shifted to the Adriatic coastal sector, where the Italians liberated Pergola (August 19) and Cagli (23rd), and the Poles crossed the river Metauro (August 23). The Italians entered the important road junction of Acqualagna on the 24th. Urbino, birthplace of Raphael, was captured on the 29th, on which day Polish troops reached the river Foglia at several points, encountering there afresh their old stubborn enemy of Cassino, the German 1st Parachute Division (see Chapter 302). By the 31st the Poles, supported by gunfire from H.M. destroyers offshore, held half Pesaro, and tanks and infantry had crossed the Foglia at several points.

THROUGH THE MOUNTAINS TO FLORENCE

The ancient city of Florence was one of the main objectives of the Allied Armies pushing northwards from Rome during the late summer of 1944. This map gives some idea of the difficulty of the country surrounding the city—which accounted for the conquering armies' slow approach. Though Siena fell on July 3, Florence was not completely liberated till August 21. (See also map in page 3470.)

A communiqué issued from General Sir Henry Maitland Wilson's Mediterranean headquarters (moved from Algiers to Italy on June 30) on September 2 said: "The full significance of the recent fighting in the

Allied Drive into the Gothic Line

Adriatic sector can now be revealed. Moving swiftly and secretly from distant concentration areas into position, troops of the 8th Army started from south of the Metauro river on August 26 and have fought their way forward over fifteen miles of most difficult country, with an increasing tempo of battle against stiffening resistance, driving the enemy back to the final prepared positions of the Gothic Line and inflicting heavy losses on him. Without pausing, the 8th Army launched a series of powerful attacks against the Gothic Line, and have now broken through the enemy's elaborately prepared defences on a twenty-mile front to a depth of three–four miles. Throughout this operation the 8th Army have been ably assisted by the Desert Air Force. Thus the last known enemy prepared defence line south of the river Po has been successfully breached. . . . The advance continues."

As the fighting approached, the tiny republic of San Marino mobilized its 300-men army and erected along its borders large signs with the words "Neutral—Keep Out" in four languages. The Poles captured Cattolica, and Canadians crossed the river Conca, on September 3. Opposition grew stronger—more German parachute troops were fighting as infantry, and the 26th Panzer Division came into the line. Destroyers of the Royal Navy bombarded transports and troop concentrations in the Rimini area; and prisoners from the German 356th Infantry Division, brought to the Adriatic front to reinforce the 98th Division, captured on September 17, said that their journey through San Marino (whose notices the enemy ignored) had been a nightmare of bombing and strafing.

Heavy rain and violent thunderstorms broke over the whole 8th Army front on September 9, but fierce fighting with heavy casualties on both sides continued. British and Indian troops stormed Passano and Sansovino, Canadians fought into Coriano, and a large part of the Coriano–Sansovino ridge guarding the approaches to Rimini was cleared on the 13th in one of the bitterest battles of the Italian campaign with merciless hand-to-hand fighting in booby-trapped villages. Canadian tanks and infantry, overcoming bitter opposition, crossed the Merano river on the 14th, coming within a mile of Rimini airfield, taken on the 19th by Greek troops (whose presence with the 8th Army was announced for the first time).

British and Indian troops crossed the Ausa on the 18th. Canadians advancing up the slopes of the mountains in the north-east corner of San Marino encountered stubborn opposition from the German 1st Parachute Division. (The republic after its occupation by the 8th Army declared war on Germany on September 23.) On September 20 Canadians broke through the San Fortunato ridge, capturing San Lorenzo in Monte, and the Greeks came to within 2,000 yards of the outskirts of Rimini. On the 21st, Rimini fell, after nearly a month of bitter fighting, to Greek infantry supported by New Zealand armour. The Allied forces cleared the deserted town of German snipers and crossed the river Marecchia just north of it.

Fall of Rimini

After capturing Pisa on September 2 (*see* page 3470), the 5th Army bypassed the Monti Pisani to occupy Lucca on the 6th. Farther inland on the same day, Americans entered Prato (not cleared, however, till the 10th). Advanced elements of the South African 6th Armoured Division, now fighting with the 5th Army, captured Pistoia on the 10th. Ponte a Moriano, on the river Serchio north of Lucca, fell on the 14th. Viareggio on the coast was captured on the 16th. In the central sector operations were mainly directed to the capture of the Futa Pass, some 22 miles north of Florence. American,

British, South African, and Brazilian troops (the last in action for the first time and showing considerable aggressive ability) were engaged in fierce fighting on a wide sector in the mountains north and east of Florence. The Pass itself was occupied by Americans on September 23 after a ten days' intense struggle.

With its capture, following the fall of Rimini, Allied headquarters announced that the whole Gothic Line between the Pass and the Adriatic had been broken. Heavy fighting continued in the narrow coastal gap leading to the valley of the Po, and British and American troops went on to cross the river Rubicon on September 26—an event which led General Maitland Wilson, in a message of congratulation, to say, " I hope that the crossing of the Rubicon will lead, as with a famous commander in the past, to a decisive victory and the destruction of Kesselring's army." But torrential rains began all along the line, and major operations in Italy were at an end until the following spring.

It was of course disappointing that Kesselring's defeat at Cassino in May could not be exploited fully. Yet the greatest credit must be given to Alexander's armies, so much reduced in strength and of such heterogeneous composition, for the relentless pressure they exercised—all the more because it must have been widely realized that the transfer of formations to other theatres meant that a campaign which earlier seemed likely to be crowned by a sweeping decisive victory had been given what was mainly a diversionary object.

How successfully that important object was achieved should be understood : Kesselring was compelled to fight at heavy cost to protect the produce of the Lombardy plain and of the factories of northern Italy, expending not only his original force but drawing reinforcements from other theatres. The expenditure of labour and war material to which he was put alone justified a diversionary campaign in view of the major Allied operations elsewhere. Future historians may question whether the Italian campaign as originally conceived was good strategy ; but its value eventually as a diversionary operation there can be no doubt.

GERMAN OUTPOST IN THE FUTA PASS

Important keypoint in the Gothic Line defences was the Futa Pass in the Etruscan Apennines, on the highway between Florence and Bologna, which fell to U.S. troops of the 5th Army on September 23, 1944. This captured turret of a German Tiger tank, mounted in concrete, had been an enemy outpost covering the road leading to the Pass. *Photo, British Official*

October 1. British 2nd Army repulsed fierce attack N. of Nijmegen. Germans at Calais surrendered unconditionally; U.S. 7th Army captured Rembervillers near Belfort Gap. 5th Army took Monte Capella (Italy).

October 2. U.S. 1st Army broke through Siegfried Line between Aachen and Geilenkirchen. U.S.A.A.F. heavily attacked Kassel, Hamm, Cologne.

October 3. R.A.F. Lancasters breached sea-dyke at Westkapelle (Walcheren). U.S. 1st Army took Ubach. U.S. 3rd Army stormed Fort Driant (Metz) outer defences. Sixty-hour truce began at Dunkirk. Polish Home Army in Warsaw surrendered after 63 days. Russians captured Hiiu Maa (Estonia). Malta blackout lifted.

October 4. U.S.A. 15th A.F. bombed Munich. R.A.F. attacked U-boat pens at Bergen (Norway). Russians took Bor and Vladimirovac (Yugoslavia). Land Forces Adriatic entered Patras (Greece), landed in Albania. 14th Army cut Tiddim (Burma) in enemy's rear.

October 4-5. British and Greek regular troops landed in Greece.

October 5. U.S.A. 8th A.F. heavily bombed Cologne and Rheine. R.A.F. attacked Wilhelmshaven and Saarbrücken. Flying-bombs over London after five-day lull. Russians landed on Saare Maa (Estonia); freed Panchevo (Yugoslavia).

October 6. Canadians established bridge-head across Leopold Canal. Gen. Patton's troops advanced through Fôret du Parroy, east of Lunéville. U.S. 7th and French 1st Armies closed in on Le Thillot (Vosges). Heavy U.S.A.A.F. attacks on Harburg, Hamburg, Berlin. Russians entered Hungary. Vyssi Kormarnik (Czechoslovakia) liberated by Czech 1st Army. Samos occupied by British and Greek troops.

October 7. R.A.F. and U.S.A.A.F. made heaviest daylight attacks of the war on Germany, including the Ruhr. R.A.F. bombed dykes at Flushing; floods cut Walcheren almost in half. Kembs dam (Alsace) collapsed under direct hits by R.A.F. 8th Army crossed Fiumicino (Italy). Russians captured Kuresaare (Estonia). Dumbarton Oaks Conference ended.

October 8. U.S. 1st Army encircled Aachen. Walcheren under Canadian artillery fire. Russians broke into Central Lithuania. Finns captured Kemi, last occupied port. Corinth occupied by British and Greek troops. U.S. forces landed on Garakayo (Palaus). Japanese took Foochow (China). West Africans captured Mowdok (Arakan, Burma). Death of Wendell Willkie.

October 9. U.S. 1st Army captured Schaufenberg. British and Canadian troops established bridge-heads west of Terneuzen (Netherlands). U.S. 3rd Fleet attacked Ryukyu Islands for the first time. Removal of Direction Signs Order (1940) revoked in Britain. Mr. Churchill and Mr. Eden arrived in Moscow.

October 10. Americans demanded surrender of Aachen within 24 hours. Russians reached Baltic Coast, cutting German escape route between Libau, Windau and Riga. Land Forces Adriatic took Saranda (Albania). U.S. forces landed on Bairokaseru (Palaus). U.S.A.A.F. attacked Balikpapan (Borneo) oil refineries. Weather reports published in Britain after two (instead of ten) days' delay.

October 11. Canadians took Woensdrecht and cut off Germans in Scheldt islands from mainland. R.A.F. again bombed Walcheren. On expiration of ultimatum, Americans began mass-bombarding and dive-bombing Aachen. Russians captured Cluj, capital of Transylvania, and Szeged (Hungary). 8th Army entered San Lorenzo (Italy).

October 11-13. Heavy U.S. carrier-borne attacks on Formosa, 397 enemy planes destroyed, 27 ships sunk, 62 ships damaged for the loss of 66 U.S. aircraft.

October 12. Aachen suburbs entered. British 2nd Army captured Overloon (Holland). British-based Mosquitoes attacked targets in Czechoslovakia and Yugoslavia. Russians reached Baltic coast above Memel.

October 13. Athens and the Piraeus liberated. Russians freed Riga. U.S. troops cleared Gesso (Italy). Land Forces Adriatic liberated Corfu.

October 13-15. U.S. task force attacked Formosa day and night.

October 13-16. U.S. carrier-borne attacks on Philippines.

October 14. R.A.F. Lancasters and Halifaxes dropped 4,500 tons of bombs on Duisburg, dropping a further 5,000 by night. U.S.A. 7th Air Force raided Iwo Jima (Volcano Islands).

October 14-15. China-based Super-Fortresses raided Formosa.

October 15. R.A.F. Lancasters attacked Sorpe Dam (Ruhr) and Wilhelmshaven. Russians took Petsamo (Finland). Germans on Naxos (Aegean) surrendered. Hungary asked for armistice. U.S.A.A.F. again bombed Balikpapan (Borneo) and Mindanao (Philippines). Allied aircraft bombed Tiddim.

October 16. British 2nd Army patrols crossed Lower Rhine, west of Arnhem. Aachen encircled. Americans withdrew from Fort Driant. 8th Army gains on Piociatello river and Via Emilia (Italy). Szalasy seized power in Hungary. U.S.A. 14th A.F. sank shipping at Hongkong. China-based Super-Fortresses made third attack on Formosa.

October 17. Centre of Aachen entered. Lemnos taken by Allies; Scarpanto (Dodecanese) occupied by forces of Royal Navy. Fusion of F.F.I. with French regular army.

October 18. British 2nd Army took Venraij (Netherlands). Bonn heavily attacked by R.A.F. Russians entered Slovakia on a 170-mile front. Hitler and Himmler announced formation of Volkssturm. Greek Government of National Unity in Athens. U.S.A.A.F. attacks on Leyte.

October 19. Russians took Eydtkuhnen (E. Prussia). 8th Army entered Cesena (Italy). 14th Army recaptured Tiddim (Burma). Death of Col. Denys Reitz, High Commissioner in London for S. Africa.

October 20. U.S. troops landed on Leyte (Philippines) in strength. Aachen captured. Russians cleared Belgrade; captured Debrecen (Hungary). 8th Army in Cesenatico, near Rimini. British Land Forces Greece took Thebes. 14th Army occupied Haka (Burma).

October 21. 8th Army drove enemy back to Savio River; Cesena cleared. Tito's forces took Dubrovnik. Red Army captured Baja (Hungary). Royal Navy shelled Nicobar Islands.

October 22. Canadians captured Breskens (Holland). Red Army occupied Nyireghaza (Hungary), crossed the River Sava, near Belgrade. 8th Army entered Cervia. Mr. Churchill home from Moscow.

October 23. De Gaulle Government recognized by Great Britain, U.S. and U.S.S.R. R.A.F. gave Essen its heaviest raid to date. Soviet forces crossed East Prussian border.

October 23-25. Great sea-air battle off Leyte: Japanese navy virtually destroyed.

October 24. British 2nd Army heavily engaged in s'Hertogenbosch. 5th Army took Monte Belmonte (Italy). U.S. 6th Army progressed on all sectors on Leyte.

October 25. Fort Frederik-Hendrik, south of Scheldt, freed. Russians completed clearance of northern Transylvania; entered Norway and captured Kirkenes. China-based Super-Fortresses bombed Omura (Japan).

October 26. British and Canadians landed on South Beveland. Red Army took Munkacevo (Munkács) and many other towns in Ruthenia. All east coast of Leyte in U.S. hands. Death of Dr. Temple, Archbishop of Canterbury.

October 27. Tilburg, Bergen-op-Zoom, s'Hertogenbosch liberated. Russians freed Uzhorod, capital of Ruthenia. U.S. landing on Samar (Philippines). Sweden to recognize De Gaulle Government.

October 28. R.A.F. bombed U-boat pens at Bergen, made heaviest attack to date on Cologne. S.S. troops occupied Banska Bystrica (Czechoslovakia). Polish troops of 8th Army took Predappio, birthplace of Mussolini. Allies and Bulgaria signed armistice. Recall of Gen. Stilwell announced in Washington.

October 29. Canadians freed Goes (S. Beveland); Poles liberated Breda. R.A.F. bombed Tirpitz off Trömso. Tito's troops captured Split (Dalmatia). Aircraft of U.S. 3rd Fleet attacked Manila harbour.

October 30. Canadians captured Rosendaal (Netherlands). U.S. 3rd Army took Maizières-les-Metz (France). Organized resistance ceased on Leyte.

October 31. Poles crossed river Mark (N.W. of Breda); British reached Maas and established bridge-head. Daring R.A.F. raid on Gestapo H.Q. at Aarhus (Denmark). Gen. A. C. Wedemeyer, succeeding Gen. Stilwell, arrived in Chungking.

Chapter 340

CLEARING THE ENEMY FROM THE DANUBE

Soviet advances in the north during the summer of 1944, described in Chapters 318 and 329, were matched by others as striking in the south, which are the subject of this chapter. The Germans were driven out of Rumania and Bulgaria, and from the greater part of Hungary, in the course of the campaigns recorded here by the Military Editor, Major-General Sir Charles Gwynn

DURING the summer of 1944 the Rumanian front remained virtually stabilized on the line established in the spring (*see* page 3081). Jassy, Kishinev and Benderi were still in German hands, but Von Kleist, in spite of many attempts, had failed to drive the Russians out of the bridge-heads they had established across the Dniester in rear of his position. He had strengthened his defences but had not been reinforced, and he had to depend largely on Rumanian troops of doubtful reliability. On August 20 the Russians resumed the offensive, and clearly had made ample preparation for it in spite of the demands of their main front in Poland. Presumably the chief reasons for postponing the offensive so long were to avoid opening a new front until the main offensive in Poland showed signs of losing its momentum, and to allow time for Rumania to become fully convinced that she had little to fear from Germany if she deserted an ally who had so ruthlessly sacrificed her armies and interests. Russia's assurance, given in April, that she had no designs against Rumania and had only entered Rumanian territory as a military necessity in her war with Germany (*see* page 3321), was clearly a move in diplomatic warfare.

It was quickly apparent that both from the military and political standpoint the offensive had been skilfully timed. Following a devastating artillery and air bombardment, in three days infantry and tanks broke through the German defences. On August 22, General Malinovsky, who had taken over command of the 2nd Ukrainian Army from Marshal Koniev, captured Jassy. General Tolbukhin, who had replaced Malinovsky in command of the 3rd Ukrainian Army, attacked simultaneously, and breaking out of his bridge-head south of Benderi on a wide front on August 23 captured that town and also Akkerman, on the west side of the Dniester estuary, securing possession of the train ferry there. Next day the two commanders in conjunction took Kishinev, the capital of Bessarabia, and Malinovsky secured Roman and Bacau on the railway that runs along the west bank of the Seret.

Jassy Captured

Tolbukhin's operation with Malinovsky in the capture of Kishinev meant that Von Kleist's positions had been shattered along the whole line, and that the Russian armies were free to advance in an unbroken front or to diverge towards particular objectives. The military victory was outstanding, and it brought about the political results for which diplomatic influences had prepared the way (*see* page 3322).

It was soon apparent that King Michael had carried the bulk of his army with him, for when Tolbukhin reached the Galati line on which the Rumanians might have rallied, he encountered little serious opposition. This historic gateway into Rumania between the Carpathians and the marshes of the Danube delta is potentially one of the strongest positions for strategic defence in Europe. Protected on one flank by the Black Sea and marshes, and on the other by the Seret and the Carpathians, the gap can be attacked only across the main stream of the Danube—an almost impossible operation until the fortresses of Galati and Ismail have been captured.

These fortresses have stood notable sieges in the past, but on this occasion they offered little resistance, Tolbukhin capturing Ismail by storm on August 26 and Galati the following day. Malinovsky, the axis of whose advance had been directed south-west and west across the Seret and the Carpathian foothills, met with equal success. His immediate objectives were to secure the Ploesti oilfields before they could be sabotaged and to reach Bucharest as soon as possible in order to strengthen the new Government's position and to anticipate the reactions of the Germans and pro-Axis elements. Sending his tanks in advance, he overran all attempts at

Ismail and Galati Fall

SECOND UKRAINIAN ARMY CAPTURES JASSY

On August 22, 1944, it was announced that the 2nd Ukrainian Army, under General Malinovsky, had in three days' fighting penetrated the powerful German defences and captured Jassy, second city of Rumania, on their way towards the Galati Gap and the Ploesti oilfields. Here Rumanians surrender to their Russian captors in one of Jassy's rubble-strewn streets.

resistance. On August 30 he took Ploesti and on the following day he entered Bucharest.

The speed and power of this thrust had proved irresistible. At Focsani the Germans made a stand before, after some sharp fighting, they were overpowered (August 27). But their main attempt to halt the Russian advance was at Buzau, about forty miles short of Ploesti. Here they had time to bring up two mechanized divisions and a large amount of artillery, in part anti-aircraft guns from the Ploesti defences. It was quite a strong force, and with the ground favourable to defence it might have caused considerable delay. But admirable co-ordination of tank, artillery and air power in an attack delivered with great determination achieved rapid success.

Apart from the political objects gained, the Red Army had inflicted disastrous losses on the enemy. In the

Huge German Losses

five days August 20 to 25, Axis losses amounted to 205,000 killed or captured, 200 planes, 664 tanks and self-propelled guns and over 3,000 guns of various calibres. Of the 30 German divisions Von Kleist is believed to have had under his command, including reserves and the garrisons of Ploesti and other centres, about half were totally lost.

While Malinovsky was dealing with the situation inland, Tolbukhin, having crossed the Danube, was given the task of securing possession of the ports on the coast in co-operation with units of the Black Sea Fleet—their capture and the shipping in them would greatly improve communications in further operations. The Sulina mouth of the Danube

was cleared on August 28; naval detachments captured Sulina and other Soviet forces took Tulcea forty miles upstream. On the following day Constanza was taken by a combined operation.

There remained, however, Bulgaria to be dealt with. She had not been at war with the Soviet Union, only with the western Allies, from whom she was now attempting to secure favourable armistice terms. But she was still harbouring many Germans, German shipping and aircraft were using her ports and airfields, and her troops were actively co-operating with the Germans in Yugoslavia (see page 3324). Apart from political considerations, this was a situation which could not be tolerated on military grounds, and the resulting exchanges are described in page 3325. The Soviet Union declared war on Bulgaria on September 5, and Tolbukhin crossed the frontier between Giurgiu and the coast on the 8th, occupying Varna and Ruschuk; but active operations ceased on the 9th following Bulgaria's declaration of war against Germany on the 8th. Forces under Tolbukhin (whose promotion, together with that of Malinovsky, to Marshal of the Soviet Union was announced on September 12) passed through Sofia on September 16 on their way to the Yugoslav frontier. After some hesitation, Bulgarian troops which had been co-operating with the Germans in the Morava valley against Marshal Tito turned against their former allies. Thereafter they took part in Russian operations in this region, designed to assist Tito's partisan armies and to interrupt the communications of the German forces in Greece and Yugoslavia.

FIELD-MARSHAL VON KLEIST
Berlin announced on March 21, 1944, that Field-Marshal von Kleist was directing operations in south Russia. No mention was made of Field-Marshal von Manstein, up till then in supreme command on this front. At the opening of the Danube campaign described in this chapter Von Kleist was reported to have 30 divisions under his command. *Photo, Planet News*

Little news of these operations was, however, given and Malinovsky for a long time was to hold the stage. His lightning exploitation of the original break-through had already had far-reaching results. His capture of the Ploesti oilfields had not only deprived the Germans of their main source of natural oil—incidentally forcing them to rely on synthetic production, far more vulnerable to air attack—but had also secured a convenient source of

FALL OF BUCHAREST
One of Moscow's biggest salvos proclaimed on August 31 the entry into Bucharest of troops of the 2nd Ukrainian Army ' as the result of a swift offensive.' The Soviet attack on the Rumanian capital was spear-headed by armour of the 4th Guards Corps under Lieutenant-General Kravchenko. Red Army tanks are here seen moving up through Bucharest on their way to the front. They were given a warm welcome.
Photo, U.S.S.R. Official

WITH YUGOSLAVIA'S LIBERATION ARMY

The Soviet High Command announced on September 30, 1944, that the Red Army had entered Yugoslavia, south of Turnu Severin. Two days later Marshal Tito's H.Q. disclosed that the Russians and the Yugoslav Army of National Liberation had linked up some eighty miles from Belgrade. Here, Yugoslav troops enjoy an open-air meal provided by the people of Brus.
Photo, Planet News

fuel for his own use, for the wells and refineries had not been completely sabotaged. His arrival in Bucharest definitely determined the attitude of Rumania. On September 12 she accepted the armistice terms offered by the Allied Powers, and undertook to wage war against Germany and Hungary under Soviet command. Already Rumanian troops had actively

co-operated, but this agreement regulated the situation pending the beginning of a more ambitious campaign directed against Hungary and the southern flank of Germany's eastern front.

Leaving a force to complete the annihilation of remnants of Von Kleist's army, surrounded and still holding out in the Kishinev position, Malinovsky organized his army in three main groups. The northern group was directed west towards northern Transylvania and the eastern tip of Slovakia, in pursuit of parties of Germans that had been holding the foothills of the

SOVIET FORCES ENTER BULGARIA

News that the Red Army had crossed the Dubruja frontier into Bulgaria without opposition was put out from Moscow on September 8, 1944. Among places captured was Varna, Bulgaria's largest seaport, which fell to the 3rd Ukrainian Army and the Soviet Black Sea Fleet. Below, left, Russian supplies stream over a pontoon bridge across the Danube. Right, Soviet motor-boat patrols enter Varna harbour.
Photos, Pictorial Press

THE RED ARMY SWEEPS THROUGH HUNGARY

An Order of the Day on October 11, 1944, stated that troops of the 2nd Ukrainian Army under Marshal Malinovsky had captured Cluj, capital of Transylvania; forced the River Tisza, and occupied Szeged, Hungary's second largest city, 90 miles S.E. of Budapest. Here, Red Army forces cross the Tisza. Below, Soviet troops enter Szeged. *Photos. Planet News; Pictorial Press*

Carpathians on Von Kleist's left. This was particularly difficult country and it was held by a considerable German force that had not been heavily involved in the defeat; progress was therefore slow in the face of determined rearguard resistance.

The central group struck across the southern Carpathians where they merge into the Transylvanian Alps, and here resistance was weaker and the going less difficult. By September 4 the mountain passes had been forced, and the important railway centre of Brasov captured. The southern group, formed by the reinforcement of the spearhead that had reached Bucharest, was the strongest and most mobile. Its line of advance lay along the north bank of the Danube, and by September 3 it had cleared a forty-mile stretch of the Danube between Giurgiu, an important river port south-west of Bucharest, and Oltenita. But it was the capture of Craiova and Pitesti on September 5, and of Turnu Severin at the east end of the Iron Gate on the following day that proved how completely and rapidly Rumania proper had been liberated.

The question remained, however, whether the Germans, reinforced and with the aid of Hungarian troops, would be able to hold Transylvania and prevent Malinovsky's armies reaching the Hungarian plain. The country was difficult, lending itself to defence, and Malinovsky's lines of communication were rapidly lengthening. In particular the spurs of the Transylvanian Alps which reach the Danube at the Iron Gate appeared to be a formidable obstacle to the further advance of his main group.

Russian Threat to Hungary

Russian pressure was, however, being exerted on so wide a front that the Germans were left in doubt where to concentrate. Their tendency appears to have been to hold firmly in the north, possibly in order to retain the passes over the northern Carpathians and to maintain a wedge between the Russians in Poland and those in Transylvania; for at this time Malinovsky's central group was making marked progress and swinging north-west towards the valley of the upper Maros, threatening Cluj, an important centre

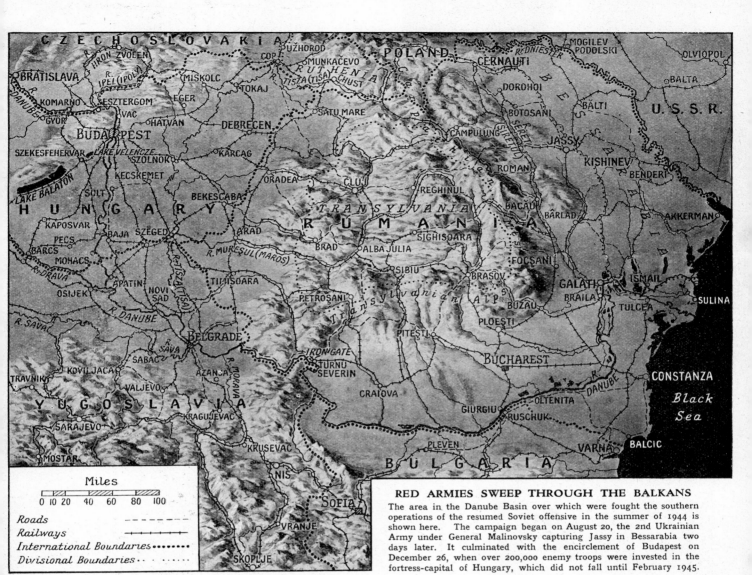

RED ARMIES SWEEP THROUGH THE BALKANS
The area in the Danube Basin over which were fought the southern operations of the resumed Soviet offensive in the summer of 1944 is shown here. The campaign began on August 20, the 2nd Ukrainian Army under General Malinovsky capturing Jassy in Bessarabia two days later. It culminated with the encirclement of Budapest on December 26, when over 200,000 enemy troops were invested in the fortress-capital of Hungary, which did not fall until February 1945.

of railway communication and capital of Transylvania. By September 11 it had captured Sighisoara (Segesvar) and Alba-Julia in the Maros valley; heavy fighting took place in this area.

If the Germans were confident that Malinovsky's southern group could be held up by weaker forces at the Iron Gate defile, they were badly mistaken, for by a brilliant advance over the mountains the position was turned and the Russians emerged in the plain beyond, capturing Timisoara (Temesvar) on September 19 and Arad on the 22nd. Spreading south-west of the former town, the left wing of this group entered Yugoslav territory on the north bank of the Danube, closing in towards Belgrade and to the lower reaches of the Tisza, the tributary of the Danube which forms the chief obstacle to an advance westwards across the plain of Hungary. The

Russians Reach Yugoslavia

right wing of this group advanced north-west from Arad, and on October 6 captured Bekescaba and other towns across the Hungarian frontier. By this time the Russians had joined Tito's troops on both banks of the Danube, for on September 30 Tolbukhin's advanced guards had made contact with them south of Turnu Severin, and Malinovsky was now co-operating with them north of Belgrade.

The pressure exercised by Malinovsky's central group towards Cluj, threatening the German main line of supply for their northern forces, had been largely instrumental in bringing about a favourable situation for a further advance into Hungary, for it had compelled the Germans to throw their reserve Armoured Division into the fight. They were therefore unable to stop the Russian southern group, the right wing of which swung northwards towards Debrecen and farther to the west of it. With their rear thus

threatened, the Germans could not maintain the fight at Cluj, which fell to the Russians on October 11.

The left wing of Malinovsky's south group, thrusting west, crossed the Tisza and took Szeged on the same date. Continuing its advance westwards, it reached the east bank of the Danube in the neighbourhood of Baja on October 21, but it made no attempt to cross the river pending developments on other sectors of the front.

Malinovsky Crosses the Tisza

In the mountainous country to the north, progress was slow, resistance was stubborn, and exceptionally heavy autumn rains increased the difficulties of the terrain. But on October 18 it was announced that General Petrov's 4th Ukrainian Army had crossed the Carpathian passes from the north and had entered Slovakia on a 170-mile front, thus threatening the rear of the Germans in northern Transylvania

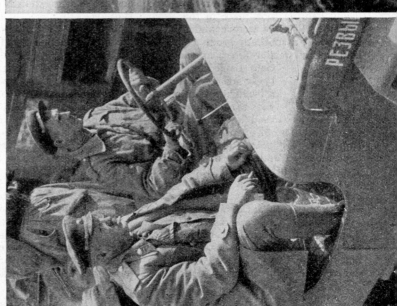

RED ARMY OVERCOMES NATURAL AND ARTIFICIAL DEFENCES IN THE CARPATHIANS

The Russian advance into the Balkans was so skilfully conceived and carried out that even the natural defences of the Carpathians provided little assistance to the enemy. 1. Red Army Mountain Pack Mortar Regiment crosses a river in the Carpathian foothills. 2. Anti-tank obstructions in the enemy's main Carpathian defence-line—called the 'Arpad Line' after the ancient Magyar hero—mistakenly believed by the Germans to be impregnable. 3. General Petrov, commanding the 4th Ukrainian Army, tours a combat area in a jeep. His troops had by October 18 crossed the Carpathian passes in the north and entered Slovakia on a broad front. 4. Advanced observation post of the 4th Ukrainian Army in the Carpathians.

Photos, Planet News

2

and holding out an early prospect of joining hands with Malinovsky's northern group. Malinovsky's central group also had considerable success, capturing Debrecen on October 20. The Germans lost heavily in these encounters and were induced to concentrate their reserves in north-east Hungary in hopes of holding the line of the upper Tisza. After reaching Baja, Malinovsky therefore swung his left wing northwards, clearing the east bank of the Danube, with the intention of penetrating between Budapest and the Germans in the Tisza valley.

Meanwhile Tolbukhin's armies and the Bulgarians south of the Danube had since the beginning of October been active. Their objectives were first to gain possession of the Morava valley, through which ran the main line of communication and retreat of the German troops in Greece and southern Yugoslavia, and then to advance on Belgrade. Tolbukhin's main army operated in the northern part of the Morava valley while the Bulgarians, stiffened with Russian troops, turned south along the valley, operating towards Skoplje, through which an alternative line of German communication ran north-west. By the middle of the month the Nis–Belgrade railway had been cut by the Russians and, after surrounding a German force south-east of Belgrade, Soviet advanced guards were fighting in the suburbs of the city. The Bulgarians had also captured Nis and had penetrated southwards as far as Vranje. After annihilating the force surrounded to the south-east Tolbukhin, in co-operation with Tito's troops, on October 20 completed the capture of Belgrade. (*See illus. in page 3361.*)

Belgrade Captured

It would seem that about this time Tolbukhin must have begun to move the main body of his forces across the Danube, relieving Malinovsky's troops which had been clearing Yugoslav territory north of the river, although part of his force continued to advance along the south bank, crossing the Sava on October 22. On October 28 Apatin, on the east bank of the Danube a short distance above the mouth of the Drava, was captured, and the Bulgarians were making good progress in the south, capturing Skoplje, virtually their final objective, on November 15.

Petrov's army and Malinovsky's northern group were also making steady if slow progress. The former captured Uzhorod, capital of Ruthenia, on October 27, and the latter completed the clearance of northern Transylvania by capturing Satu Mare on the Hungarian

3481

FALL OF BELGRADE
The capital of Yugoslavia was finally freed on October 20, 1944, by troops of the 3rd Ukrainian Army co-operating with the Yugoslav National Army of Liberation. The victorious Russian units were later given the name of 'Belgrade' divisions. Above, shattered enemy equipment strews the road to Belgrade. Right, Soviet sappers mine-detecting in the capital.
Photos, Pictorial Press; Planet News

frontier (October 25). Malinovsky's central group had also reached the upper Tisza in the Tokaj region about the same date.

Main interest was, however, centred on the wheel northwards of Malinovsky's left between the Tisza and the Danube which had started after reaching the Danube at Baja (October 21), for as it progressed it cleared the crossing of the middle Tisza and was beginning to

UZHOROD CAPTURED
Capture of Uzhorod, north-Carpathian capital of Ruthenia and described as 'a big communications centre and an important stronghold in the enemy's defences,' on October 27, 1944, virtually completed the clearance of Ruthenia. It is 170 miles north-east of Budapest. Below, Red Army officers inspect an emergency bridge at Uzhorod—erected in 48 hours.

LITTLE SHIPS FOUGHT ON THE DANUBE

A prominent part in the initial stages of the Soviet campaign in the Danube Basin was played by the Russian Black Sea Fleet which assisted in the capture of Constanza (August 29) and Varna (September 8). Later, monitors attached to the fleet operated right up the Danube as far as Budapest in support of the Red Armies. Above, Soviet monitors in Rumanian waters. Below, units of the German Danube Flotilla on patrol. *Photos, Pictorial Press; Associated Press*

ing Budapest from the east and was well on his way to clear the whole of Hungary east of the Danube, Tolbukhin again suddenly stepped into the limelight. On November 29 it was announced that his army had crossed the Danube north of the Drava, and had broken through the German defences on its right bank to a depth of 25 miles on a 90-mile front. It was just over a month since Malinovsky had reached the river here and then turned north along the east bank. It is clear, therefore, that during that period Tolbukhin had transferred his army across the river from Belgrade and, cutting the corner of its sharp bend, had regrouped to cross it again; thereby avoiding the obstacles formed by the tributaries on the right bank and securing closer contact with Malinovsky.

This new crossing in face of opposition had been a daunting project, for the ground was marshy and intersected by canals and minor channels of the river. Once again, however, the Germans, apparently deeming the river impassable, were caught by surprise and with inadequate forces. The Russians, as on many previous occasions, showed themselves to be past masters in the art of crossing great rivers. Footholds on the west bank were gained by the surprise crossing of small parties, and although the Germans made fierce local counter-attacks they failed to stop the flow of reinforcements. The first crossings were made in boats and rafts in the neighbourhood of Apatin, and some high ground was seized which covered the crossing of guns and heavy mortars. There was, however, a stretch of swampy ground on the west bank which checked progress, and a particularly violent fight took place to secure a dyke which, as it provided the only firm passage, was strongly held and entrenched. Russian infantry were for a time held up till guns and mortars blasted a way for them, but once firm ground was reached the bridge-head was rapidly expanded, and the important towns of Mohacs and Pecs were captured.

Having broken through the crust of the German defences, Tolbukhin drove rapidly in three directions. His left pressed forward in co-operation with Tito's troops to secure a front between the south end of Lake Balaton and the Drava, and on December 7 captured Barcs, an important place on that river. His centre struck towards the railway from Budapest which skirts the east side of Lake Balaton, and within a week the whole of the east side of the lake was cleared. His right at the same time swung north, and cleared the right

New Surprise Crossing of the Danube

menace Budapest. By November 1 Kecskemet, halfway between the two rivers, was reached and three days later Szolnok, where the main railway to Budapest crosses the Tisza, was captured. As the advance proceeded the east bank of the Danube was steadily cleared, and on November 14 an important German bridge-head at Solt south of Budapest was liquidated. Round Pest, the part of the city on the east bank, the Germans had constructed a heavily fortified defensive zone and had brought up reserves to hold it in strength. Malinovsky closed on this position from the south-east, but, evidently judging that he was not yet in a condition to drive home the attack, continued his advance northwards in order to cut the communications between

the city and the German forces in north-east Hungary. On November 25 he captured Hatvan, on the railway running north-east from Pest, and on November 30 Eger, an important centre still farther north-east. The Germans opposing Malinovsky's north and central groups and in eastern Slovakia were thereby forced to rely for their communications on the railway running to Bratislava on the north side of the Danube and on those that followed circuitous routes through Slovakia. To protect these lines they had been fighting hard at Cop till it was captured on November 23, and even more fiercely at the important town and railway junction of Miskolc which they did not lose till December 3.

While Malinovsky was thus threaten-

THIRD COMMANDER OF THE EIGHTH ARMY IN ITALY

Lieutenant-General Sir Richard Loudon McCreery, K.C.B., D.S.O., M.B.E., M.C., was on November 3, 1944 appointed to command the 8th Army in succession to Lieutenant-General Sir Oliver W. H. Leese (see plate facing page 3026). As commander of X Corps, he planned and executed the brilliant crossing of the Garigliano in January 1944. Previously he had commanded the Corps on the Salerno beaches and during the long, difficult advance to Cassino. In 1942-43 he was chief of staff to General Sir Harold Alexander in the Middle East.   *Photo, British Official*

5ᵀᴴ ARMY

1ˢᵀ ARMY

21ˢᵗ ARMY GROUP H Q

8ᵀᴴ ARMY

ARMY FILM AND PHOTOGRAPHIC UNIT

PARACHUTE REGIMENT

A·A· ARTILLERY

R·C·A·F OPERATIONAL WINGS

14ᵀᴴ ARMY

CANADIAN PARACHUTE WINGS

ALLIED COMBINED OPERATIONS

AIR-SEA RESCUE

NAVY FIRE FIGHTERS

INSIGNIA OF ALLIED FORCES ON MANY FRONTS

These 'flashes' and badges were worn by British, Dominion and Allied units in far-flung campaigns. They include those of the 8th Army, victors in the Desert and, later, with the 5th Army (also shown) in Italy; the glorious 14th Army of Burma; the ubiquitous A.A. Artillery, Parachute Regiment and Air-Sea Rescue ; and Field-Marshal Montgomery's 21st Army Group H.Q. in North-West Europe to which the Germans made their first unconditional surrender on German soil on May 4, 1945.

BRITAIN'S SECRETARY OF STATE FOR WAR, 1942-45

The Rt. Hon. Sir James Grigg, K.C.B., K.C.S.I., M.P., on whom fell the responsibility to Parliament for the military side of the Normandy invasion, was appointed Secretary of State for War on February 22, 1942, in succession to Capt. David Margesson. This marked the first occasion in the history of the Civil Service on which a Permanent Under-Secretary was appointed to succeed his former political chief. During the First Great War Sir James served with the Royal Garrison Artillery (1915-18). He was Principal Private Secretary to successive Chancellors of the Exchequer from 1921-30, Chairman of the Board of Inland Revenue (1930-34), and Finance Member of the Government of India (1934-39).

From the portrait by Eric Kennington in ' Britain's Home Guard,' by John Brophy. By permission of Sir James Grigg ; the artist ; and Messrs. George G. Harrap & Co., Ltd., the publishers

IN GREECE AND THE NETHERLANDS THEY HAIL FREEDOM

Freed from Nazi enslavement following the Allied landings on the Continent in the summer of 1944, liberated Europe rejoiced. In Athens (entered by British troops on October 13) vast crowds gathered in Constitution Square (above) for the broadcast speech by the Greek Premier, Mr. George Papandreou, on his return from exile. In beflagged Eindhoven (below) Netherlands youngsters sang and danced in the streets after their liberation by troops of the British 2nd Army on September 18. On the 19th the Luftwaffe bombed the town at night, killing 65 civilians and wounding 150.

Malinovsky closed in on the city, but was unable to make much progress in its suburbs. From Vac, however, he turned west towards Bratislava, and securing crossings over the Ipel was able to reach the Hron in spite of strong opposition, thereby compelling the Germans fighting to the north of Miskolc to rely entirely on communication leading through Slovakia.

That was the general situation when on December 24 Tolbukhin struck again and broke through the German line at the north end of Lake Balaton, capturing Szekesfehervar. Exploiting his break-through rapidly he pressed north, cutting the railways running west from Buda, and joined hands with Malin-

BOMBING BUDAPEST

On September 13, 1944, for the first time since 1942, long-range bombers of the Red Air Force struck at the Hungarian capital. On October 21, aircraft of the U.S.A. 15th A.F. successfully bombed airfields, motor and rail targets in the Budapest area. Above, a Russian bomber over Budapest. Right, B-17 Flying Fortresses of the U.S.A. 15th A.F. bomb the Szob railway bridge, north of the capital, in October.

Photos, U.S.S.R. & U.S. Official

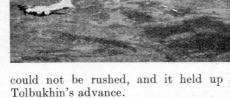

bank of the Danube with assistance from armed launches which had been brought up from the lower Danube. It was clear that this thrust enabled him to co-operate with Malinovsky's troops on the east bank, helping the latter to secure bridge-heads across the river.

Having in this manner secured protection on his left and centre and cut the communications connecting the German groups at the northern and southern ends of Lake Balaton, Tolbukhin was able to concentrate the weight of his army on his right and to threaten Budapest with encirclement. Moreover his left constituted a threat to the Hungarian oilfields west of Lake Balaton, the last source of natural oil still in German possession, and to meet this threat the Germans were compelled to keep strong forces south of the lake. On this front at least one division transferred from Italy was identified.

Budapest Threatened

The main German effort was, however, directed to preventing the encirclement of Budapest, and all available reinforcements were rushed up to hold a strong line between the north end of Lake Balaton and the Danube south of Buda. In the centre of the line the large town of Szekesfehervar provided a strong defensive pivot, and between that place and the Danube Lake Valencze formed a considerable obstacle. This position could not be rushed, and it held up Tolbukhin's advance.

Malinovsky now took up the running. Crossing the Danube south of Baja, his forces joined those of Tolbukhin at Lake Valencze on December 9, enabling the latter to concentrate between Lake Balaton and Szekesfehervar. Simultaneously he renewed his offensive on the east bank and breaking through the German defences north-east of Budapest reached the Danube on a wide front extending as far north as Vac (captured December 9), where the river turns west towards Bratislava. Thus the encirclement of Budapest to the east was complete, and the garrison of Pest had to rely on the bridges to Buda over the river for communications.

ovsky at Esztergom opposite the mouth of Hron on December 26. The encirclement of Budapest was therefore completed and the Germans had thereafter to pay the penalty for the criminal error of tying up a field army of over 200,000 men in defence of a fortress.

Withdrawal had been too long postponed and the fate of the army was sealed, though its complete destruction was not accomplished until the middle of February. The events which led up to that achievement and subsequent operations in Hungary will be described in later chapters, since they merge into the strategic developments which took place on the Eastern front in 1945, to which the 1944 campaign in the Danube valley was only an important prelude.

APPROACHING BUDAPEST

The struggle for the Hungarian capital was a long and bloody one. On Dec. 9, 1944, Moscow announced that Marshal Malinovsky of the 2nd Ukrainian Army had broken through the city's defences on both the north and south and enveloped it from three sides. On the same day it was reported that Szalasy's Fascist Government had left for Sopron on the Austro-Hungarian frontier. But it was not until Dec. 26 that the 3rd Ukrainian Army, advancing from the west, reached the Danube, captured Esztergom and completed the investment of the city. 1. Ragged and dejected German prisoners taken south-west of Budapest. 2. 'Special task cannon' used by the Russians on the approaches to the city. 3. German anti-aircraft gun employed against Red Army tanks in the suburbs. 4. Heavy tanks of the 2nd Ukrainian Army on the outskirts of the Hungarian capital.

November 1. British landed at Flushing and Westkapelle (Walcheren) ; Canadians entered Knocke-le-Zoute, liberated Sluis. Kecskemet (fifth city of Hungary) fell to Red Army. British patrols reached Salonika. Britain's Home Guard stood down. Civil Aviation Conference opened at Chicago.

November 2. Royal Navy minesweepers cleared a channel in Scheldt. Royal Marine Commando took Zoutelande, near Flushing. U.S. 1st Army attacked in Hürtgen Forest. U.S.A.A.F. heavily bombed Leuna oil plants. Major R.A.F. raid on Düsseldorf. Tito's forces liberated Zara (Dalmatia). British 36th Division took Mawlu (N. Burma).

November 3. Domburg (Walcheren) fell to Royal Marines. N. Beveland occupied. Canadians captured Heyst. U.S.A. 20th A.F. attacked Rangoon. Lt.-Gen. Sir Oliver Leese transferred to S.E.A.C.; Lt.-Gen. McCreery to command 8th Army.

November 4. Flushing cleared except for snipers. Red Army took Szolnok, S.E. of Budapest. British troops landed near Salonika. Aircraft of U.S. 3rd Fleet attacked Manila, destroying 440 enemy planes. Death of Field-Marshal Sir John Dill in Washington.

November 5. Polish troops liberated Geertruidenberg (Holland). U.S. 24th Division on Leyte captured Pinamopon. India-based U.S. aircraft bombed Singapore and Sumatra without loss. Lord Moyne assassinated in Cairo.

November 6. R.A.F. gave Gelsenkirchen its heaviest attack to date (by day). British patrols in Greece reached Yugoslav border. Tito's troops freed Bitolj (Monastir). In Moscow speech, Stalin described Pearl Harbor attack as work of " aggressor " nation.

November 7. British and Canadians occupied Veere and Middelburg (last German stronghold on Walcheren) ; Willemstad (W. of Moerdyk) captured. Indian troops of 5th Army took San Ruffillo on Florence–Forli Road. President Roosevelt elected for 4th term.

November 8. R.A.F. heavily attacked Homberg oil plant. More flying-bombs launched against England from over North Sea. 5th Army negro troops captured Fabbiani and Basati (Italy). Mr. Félix Gouin re-elected President of French Consultative Committee.

November 9. All enemy resistance on Walcheren ended. U.S. 3rd Army captured Cheminot, S. of Metz. 8th Army occupied Forli. 14th Army took Fort White. Chinese crossed Irrawaddy (Burma).

November 9-10. U.S. dive-bombers heavily attacked Japanese convoy off Leyte, sinking 3 transports, 7 destroyers.

November 10. U.S. 3rd Army captured Louvigny, the "Côte de Delme," and Château-Salins. Cologne and Frankfort heavily bombed by U.S.A. 8th A.F.; R.A.F. struck at Hanover. Mr. Churchill announced that Germans were using rocket-bombs against Britain.

November 11. U.S. 7th Army cleared the Fôret de Mortange (Lorraine). Powerful attack by R.A.F. on Harburg, near Hamburg. In Italy 8th Army took Gambellara, near Ravenna. U.S.A. 20th A.F. bombed Omura aircraft works on Kyushu (Japan) ; also Nanking and Shanghai.

November 11-12 (night). In Italy 8th Army troops captured Gavello, keypoint in German defences north of Forli.

November 12. The " Tirpitz " sunk by R.A.F. 12,000-lb. " Earthquake " bomb in Tromsö Fjord (Norway). Carrier-based U.S. aircraft heavily attacked Manila harbour. Soviet armies in Hungary captured Mezökövesd and Monor. Volkssturm took oath. British naval forces near Lister Fjord (Norway) sank 10 of 11 ships in enemy convoy. Sir Oilver Leese arrived at H.Q., S.E.A.C.

November 13. U.S. 3rd Army forced Moselle, S.W. of Thionville, capturing garrison in Uckange area. U.S. troops occupied Fort Verny, first of powerful Metz fortresses to fall. Poles captured Bagnolo, cleared Monte Casole (Italy).

November 14. British 2nd Army occupied Meijel. Russians captured Nagykata (Hungary). Indian troops of 5th Army took Monte San Bartolo ; Montone River crossed at several points.

November 15. In Lorraine, U.S. 3rd Army occupied Forts Hubert and Jussy (Metz). M.A.A.F. attacked Linz and Innsbruck areas. French 1st Army launched strong attack on Doubs River in Belfort sector. Red Army took Jaszbereni and Mende (Hungary). Bulgarian and Tito forces seized Skoplje (Yugoslavia). R.A.F. attacked Mergui (S. Burma).

November 16. Over 2,300 Allied bombers carried out "obliteration" raids on Düren, Jülich and Heinsberg, near Aachen. Russians took Jaszarokszallas, Vamösgyörk, Gyömrö (Hungary). In Italy British and Indian forces captured Modigliana, S.W. of Faenza. Japanese strongpoint of Kalemyo (Burma) fell to 11th E. African Division.

November 17. U.S. 3rd Army occupied sector of Maginot Line in Thionville area. French 1st Army freed Montbéliard, near Belfort. Widespread Allied air attacks from Düren and Jülich, through Saar, to Colmar and Mulhouse. Red Army took Füzesabony (Hungary). Poles captured Monte Fortino, S. of Faenza. On Leyte, enemy troops in Limon area encircled.

November 18. Powerful assault by British 2nd Army N. and S. of Geilenkirchen. U.S. 3rd Army overran Forts Kellermann, St. Lorraine and Julien (Metz). Widespread Allied air attacks on S. Germany by day and night. Red Army took Tiszaluc (Central Hungary).

November 19. Geilenkirchen captured by British and U.S. forces. Metz completely surrounded. U.S. 7th Army took Gérardmer. In Holland, British troops crossed Deurne canal, N. of Meijel. Gen. Eisenhower appealed to U.S. for more ammunition.

November 20. U.S. 3rd Army reached centre of Metz, liberated Dieuze. French 1st Armoured Division reached Rhine between Mulhouse and Swiss frontier.

November 20-21 (night). Heavy R.A.F. raids on Hanover (twice) and Coblenz.

November 21. Germans in retreat on entire U.S. 7th Army front. Belfort cleared, Sarrebourg liberated. R.A.F. heavily bombed Aschaffenburg, S.E. of Frankfort. Albanian patriots freed Tirana and Durazzo. 8th Army took Castiglione,

near Faenza. On Chindwin E. Africans occupied Indainggyi and Indainggale. U.S. task force bombarded Matsuwa (Central Kuriles). U.S.A.A.F. bombed Nagasaki and Omura (Japan).

November 22. French 1st Army liberated Mulhouse ; French 2nd Armoured Division liberated Saverne. British troops entered Hoven, Siegfried Line strongpoint. Americans took Eschweiler. Metz formally proclaimed defeated.

November 23. U.S. troops reached the Roer, west of Jülich. French 2nd Armoured Division entered Strasbourg. Red Army finally captured Cop (Czechoslovakia), took Tokaj (Hungary). Finnish Lapland cleared of enemy. Tito's forces liberated naval base of Tivat (Dalmatia). Macedonia declared free of enemy. U.S. troops on Leyte crushed enemy bastion at Limon.

November 24. U.S. 3rd Army gained new bridge-head across Saar, S. of Saarbrucken. Russians completed mopping-up of Saare Maa (Esthonia). In Italy 8th Army occupied Castelaccio, S. of River Marzeno. Saipan-based Super-Fortresses heavily bombed Tokyo. Polish Premier, Mr. Mikolajczyk, resigned.

November 25. Strasbourg completely cleared. U.S.A. 8th A.F. bombed oil-plants at Merseburg and Leipzig (day) ; R.A.F. attacked Nuremberg (night). Red Army captured Hatvan (Hungary).

November 26. R.A.F. bombed V2 launching sites in Holland. Waterway to Antwerp opened. U.S. 1st Army took Weisweiller. U.S.A.A.F. heavily bombed Misburg, near Hanover. R.A.F. raided Munich with 12,000-lb. "factory-buster" bombs (used for first time on Germany). Bonomi Government resigned (Italy). F.-M. Alexander appointed Supreme Allied Commander, Mediterranean; Lt.-Gen. Clark Allied C.-in-C. Italy.

November 27. U.S. 7th Army freed Molsheim and Mutzig, near Strasbourg. Heavy R.A.F. attacks on Rhineland and Berlin. Tokyo bombed by Super-Fortresses from Saipan (Marianas). Maj.-Gen. Patrick Hurley became U.S. Ambassador to China. Mr. Cordell Hull resigned.

November 28. R.A.F. attacked Nuremberg in great force. French 1st Army secured road between Mulhouse and Belfort. U.S. naval units bombarded port of Ormoc (Leyte).

November 29. U.S.A. 8th A.F. heavily bombed Misburg and Hamm. R.A.F. attacked Dortmund, Essen, Neuss and Duisberg. Russians forced Danube's west bank on 90-mile front, captured Mohacs and Pecs. 5th Army took Monte Castellaro, S.E. of Bologna. U.S.A.A.F. raided Tokyo by night for first time.

November 29-30. R.A.F. bombed Hanover. M.A.A.F. attacked Linz, Munich, and Innsbruck areas (night).

November 30. U.S. 1st Army took Grosshau and Lammersdorf. French 1st Army captured Huningue. Announced that Antwerp was open to Allied shipping. Big U.S.A. 8th A.F. raid on oil plants in Leipzig area. R.A.F. heavily bombed Duisburg by night. Red Army took Eger and Szikszo (Hungary). 14th Army occupied Paungbyin (Burma). Mr. Arciszewski formed new Polish Cabinet (London).

Chapter 341

ALLIED STRATEGIC DEVELOPMENTS IN 1944

Allied strategy in Europe for 1944 was settled at the Teheran Conference in November 1943 (see page 2645), and it envisaged for the first time a synchronized and co-ordinated offensive against Germany and her satellites with a view to achieving, if possible, decisive results in the course of the year. Strategy in the Pacific was settled at the First Quebec Conference (see page 2799). The Military Editor, Major-General Sir Charles Gwynn, shows how effectively the plans made were carried out. For Allied strategy in 1943, see Chapter 297

SINCE the reopening of a major front in the west was an essential part of the Teheran plan, involving an immense amphibious operation, the main blows could not be struck until the summer. Meanwhile the great Russian offensive which had started with the battle of the Kursk salient in the summer of 1943 was to run its course and be maintained until it was brought to a standstill by spring thaws and lengthening communications. In Italy also the offensive would be renewed early in the year, which it was hoped would enable the bombing offensive from the south to be carried out at shorter range, and might drive the Germans completely out of Italy. Invasion of southern France to synchronize with the landing in the west was also an element in the plan. It appears to have been thought probable that, if Kesselring were defeated and driven out of his Cassino defence, the Germans would not make a determined effort to retain their hold on the country. In any case the harder they fought in Italy, the greater would be the diversion of their war potential from the decisive fronts.

The Cassino offensive opened early in January (*see* Chapter 302), but met with no success, and the landing at **Failure of First Cassino Offensive** Anzio behind Kesselring's front later in the month failed to dislodge him. It did, however, give an indication of Germany's determination not to withdraw from Italy, and it compelled the Germans to reinforce their army there. Bitter fighting continued, but the Italian front remained virtually stabilized until the middle of May.

The Russian winter offensive (*see* Chapters 305 and 310) was, however, carried through with notable success, and by the beginning of May, when it was brought to an end, it had gained a favourable starting line for the summer offensive. In the north Leningrad had been liberated and the Germans had been forced to withdraw into Estonia and Latvia. On the White Russian front they still held a strong position in the corridor between the Dvina and the Upper Dnieper and along the line of the latter

river; but Vitebsk, the important hedgehog centre which was the northern bastion of this sector, had been outflanked on the north, and at its southern end Rokossovsky had driven a wedge across the Dnieper where it is joined by the Beresina north of the Pripet Marshes.

South of the marshes the Russians had cleared the whole of the Ukraine and were well across the pre-1939 Polish frontier; Lwow was threatened and the main Lwow–Odessa line had been cut. Farther south they had crossed the middle Dniester into Bessarabia and had advanced across the Prut and Seret, gaining a footing on the eastern slopes of the Carpathians, thus completely severing the direct communication between the Germans in Poland and those covering the gateway to Rumania. This latter group, including a strong Rumanian contingent, blocked the Carpathian passes and occupied a strongly entrenched position between the mountains and the lower Dniester, across which the Russians had secured only minor footholds. The recapture of the Crimea—the final achievement of the Russian winter offensive—had, however, further undermined Rumanian willingness to continue the struggle.

Thus by the middle of May the stage was set for the main summer offensive, although the Allies were not yet ready to start. Preparations in England for the great amphibious operation were complete, but the date had still to be decided, and on the Russian front regrouping and strengthening of lines of communication was being carried out. Nevertheless, on all fronts the Germans held strong positions to meet the onslaught, and on none of them could success be guaranteed.

The attack in the west in particular had much of the nature of a gamble, for there was no precedent for an amphibious operation on the scale which the situation required. The German coast defences were exceedingly strong and were backed by substantial mobile forces ready to counter-attack any force that effected a landing before it could be deployed in adequate strength. Moreover, failure would almost certainly

entail a disaster which might change the whole course of the war. Premature action had therefore to be avoided even if it meant delay, though it was found later that the secret weapons, to the production of which the Germans had devoted so much of their industries, were no wild-cat scheme, and if they had matured in time the attempt to reopen the western front might have become impracticable; had it failed, almost certainly it could not have been repeated.

The main weakness of the enemy situation was the immense perimeter the Germans had to hold with depleted forces, and the numbers of troops they had to **Enemy's Main Weakness** retain as armies of occupation in conquered territories, where underground resistance was steadily becoming more formidable. In the circumstances it is amazing that the Germans, while they still had time, did not contract their perimeter by abandoning Estonia and Latvia, Italy and possibly Norway, for it must have been obvious that their fate depended on their ability to deal with the threat in the West.

Unwillingness to cut their losses, fear of the potentialities of sea power and fear of providing the Allies with new bases from which the air offensive might be intensified all contributed to their decision not to make any voluntary withdrawals. To hold their perimeter they were compelled increasingly to water down the quality of their armies with men of low physical categories and by conscripting foreign elements from occupied countries and prisoners—and even with that, many of their formations could not be maintained at their nominal establishment.

On May 11 the Allied offensive opened with a resumption of the attack on the Gustav line, from Cassino to the Tyrrhenian as a curtain-raiser (*see* page 3052). This time it was successful; the Gustav and Hitler lines were broken and the Anzio landing finally justified its strategic purpose when a breakout from the bridge-head struck the main line of retreat of Kesselring's defeated armies. Rome was occupied on June 4, but in difficult country Kesselring was able to delay pursuit and extricate the remains of his army, which rallied where the Apennines cross Italy.

Field-Marshal Alexander, now Allied Commander-in-Chief Italy, was left with a curiously mixed force composed of many nationalities and several colours. Some of his best formations had been withdrawn to take part in the western offensive. He was to lose more in order to provide an army for the invasion of southern France, and consequently had not sufficient strength to exploit his initial victory to the full. The Germans were, however, compelled to reinforce Kesselring just at the time they could least spare troops. They would probably have been wiser to order Kesselring to abandon Italy and to continue his retreat to the Alpine passes, although that would have meant the loss of the war industries of northern Italy and the rich plains of Lombardy.

The Italian curtain-raiser had breached one of Germany's defensive walls; but that feat sank into comparative insignificance when, on June 6, her western wall was penetrated in Normandy (*see* Chapter 311). Not a moment too soon, for Hitler's secret weapons, in spite of the bombing offensive which had seriously delayed their development, were almost ready. As has often been the case, however, the seriousness of the situation induced the Germans to use their secret weapons prematurely before they could be employed on a scale to produce decisive results. The damage they caused was undeniably heavy and hard to bear (*see* Chapter 337), but the strategic consequences of their use were definitely detrimental to Germany. Not only had the diversion of war industry and scientific research been at the expense of the Luftwaffe, which might have played a much greater part in resisting the Allied landing, but the necessity of protecting V1 bases in the Pas de Calais seriously affected the strategical disposition of the German armies. Even after the Normandy landing had been effected, the expectation of an attempted landing in the Pas de Calais persisted. The 15th Army in that department was eventually in part thrown into the struggle in Normandy, but too late and only with the result that it was left too weak to resist the great drive of Montgomery's 21st Army group into Belgium (*see* Chapter 320) or to protect the V1 bases, to the defence of which it had been tied.

The successful landing in Normandy undoubtedly sealed the fate of Germany, and it gave the signal to the Russians to resume the offensive. On June 23,

Importance of Reopened Western Front

ELEVEN MONTHS' PROGRESS IN THE ITALIAN CAMPAIGN

The advance of the Allied 5th and 8th Armies up the Italian peninsula was always hampered by the immense natural difficulty of the terrain, some indication of which is given here. Far-reaching enemy demolition and mining combined with bad weather to retard progress still more. In such circumstances the gains made from the fall of Naples (Oct. 1, 1943) to the penetration of the Gothic Line north of Florence (September 1944) constituted a major military achievement.

when the success of the landing was clearly established, they struck (*see* Chapter 318), and in five days on the White Russian front inflicted what was probably the heaviest defeat the Germans had up till then sustained. The timing of this offensive was admirable, for while it avoided the danger of the Red Army's finding itself committed if the landing in Normandy failed, on the other hand it prevented the Germans from transferring reserves to the west at a critical time.

It is probable that, relying on the strength of their defences on this sector

of their front, the Germans expected that the Russian offensive would be renewed south of the Pripet marshes; and they may have envisaged in that case the possibility of staging a counter-stroke to the west of the marshes with the forces they had in East Prussia. If so, the Russian offensive north of the marshes completely upset their plans, and its progress soon threatened East Prussia so directly as to eliminate the possibility of using it as a base for a counter-offensive. By the third week of July the 2nd and 3rd White Russian Armies were checked within a short

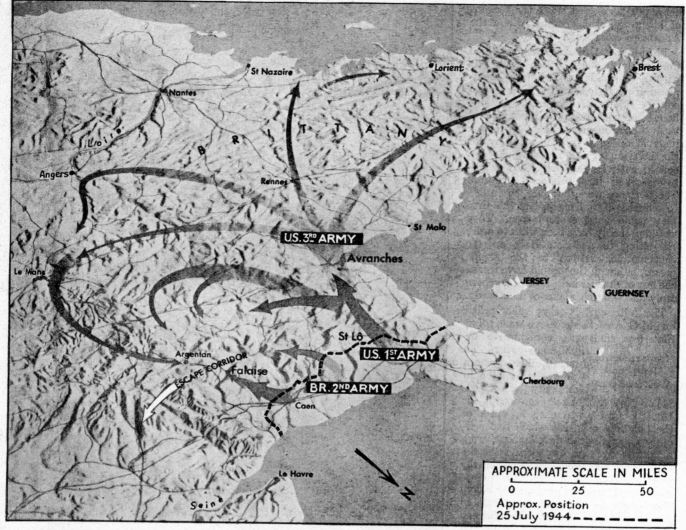

Map labels: St Nazaire, Lorient, Brest, Nantes, Loire, BRITTANY, Angers, Rennes, St Malo, US. 3RD ARMY, Avranches, JERSEY, GUERNSEY, Le Mans, St Lô, US. 1ST ARMY, Argentan, ESCAPE CORRIDOR, Falaise, BR. 2ND ARMY, Caen, Cherbourg, Le Havre, Seine

APPROXIMATE SCALE IN MILES
0   25   50
Approx. Position
25 July 1944 ‒ ‒ ‒ ‒ ‒ ‒

HOW ALLIED STRATEGY TRAPPED THE ENEMY AT FALAISE

The narrowing of the Germans' escape corridor from the Falaise 'pocket' in August 1944,
following the break-out of the Allied armies from the Normandy beach-heads, is clearly shown here.
It was through this corridor that a small part of the German 7th Army escaped, most of it being
mopped-up inside the 'pocket' (see page 3184). The Falaise–Argentan gap was finally sealed
by the French 2nd Armoured Division on August 19 when they met the Canadians at Chambois.

distance of the frontiers of East Prussia,
but to the north of them the three
Baltic Armies had also gone over to
the offensive, penetrating far into
Lithuania and breaking through the
strong defence line on the Latvian and
Estonian frontiers.

The German forces in these Baltic
States were therefore already threatened
with isolation from East Prussia, but
Russian Hitler, always unwilling
to surrender territory
Advances and probably fearing
that if Finland were
left unsupported she would drop out
of the war, would not sanction a withdrawal. Meanwhile Rokossovsky's 1st
White Russian Army, which had
taken an important share in the break-
through, had advanced on both sides
of the Pripet marshes and was rapidly

approaching the Vistula, capturing
many important towns in spite of
growing German resistance. Moreover,
when he had come into line with the 1st
Ukrainian Army (now under Koniev's
command), that army, too, renewed its
offensive. By-passing Lwow for the
moment, it captured Przemysl, crossed
the San and secured a bridge-head over
the upper Vistula about the same time as
Rokossovsky reached the middle stretch
of that river. On Koniev's left the 4th
Ukrainian Army from the Crimea also
appeared, and operating in the northern
slopes of the Carpathians still further
interfered with the communications
between the Germans in Poland and
those in Rumania.

But the Russian main offensive, with
greatly lengthened lines of communication, began in August to lose its

momentum; and the Germans, again
showing their capacity for rapid recovery, succeeded in rallying on the line
of the Vistula. They fiercely resisted
Rokossovsky's attempts to capture
Praga opposite Warsaw. Behind the
screen thus formed they rushed in
reserve formations to crush the Polish
rising in Warsaw itself, which, encouraged by Rokossovsky's approach,
had started prematurely and without
full agreement with the Russians. The
defeat of this gallant effort of the Poles
gave rise to bitter recrimination.

It is not yet fully known to what
extent the landing in Normandy diverted German formations from the
eastern front and paved the way for the
great Russian offensive. Two armoured
divisions, it is believed, were withdrawn, and certainly reinforcing drafts
from depots in Germany were sent to the
western front. Similarly, it is impossible
to say to what extent the Germans'
efforts to re-establish their eastern front
involved the employment of reserves

drawn from Norway and elsewhere which might otherwise have been sent to the western front.

Obviously, however, the landing in Normandy must have had many of the effects of the opening of a "second front" which the Germans had always dreaded. Just at the time that they may have had hopes of stabilizing the eastern front came the break-out from the Normandy bridge-head on July 27. Suddenly all prospects of a respite vanished, and in August their western front collapsed as rapidly as their eastern front had done in July. The battle of Normandy and the landing in southern France shattered two of their western armies, and the third, depleted, was in no condition to check Eisenhower's advance north of the Seine. By the end of September almost all France and Belgium had been liberated, the German frontier had been crossed in places, and only the Siegfried Line and the Lower Rhine remained as a barrier to invasion in force (see Chapter 332).

The loss of France and Belgium meant a serious reduction of food supplies and of the products of war industries; moreover, it enabled the Allied air offensive to become even more crushing and less costly. But the barrier effectively staved off complete immediate collapse, for the Allied offensive, with limited port facilities and lengthening communications, had lost momentum.

The Germans were beaten; but the knock-out blow had still to be delivered. Their resistance stiffened, and it soon became apparent that with winter approaching the final blow could hardly be struck before the following summer. Meanwhile, the approaches to Antwerp had to be cleared, and it was imperative that pressure on the Germans should be maintained and a good starting line for the great final offensive should be secured. The attempt on Hitler's life in July (see page 3168) had shown that a large section of the Wehrmacht commanders realized the desperate situation Germany was in; but the subsequent purge, and the signs of German recovery from the disorganization which followed disastrous defeat in both the east and the west, proved that the final invasion of Germany would be no easy move. It was clear that no matter how anxious his military chiefs were to avoid having to fight the final battle on their own soil, Hitler was prepared to accept its ruinous consequences, either because he still believed in the efficiency of his secret weapons, or

Enemy Resistance Stiffens

because he intended in his fanaticism that the Reich should be destroyed with him.

Although the allied main offensives on both fronts had by September exhausted their momentum, Russia was still capable of delivering heavy blows. As early as the third week in August Malinovsky's 2nd and Tolbukhin's 3rd Ukrainian Armies had resumed the offensive and inflicted a shattering defeat on Von Kleist's armies on the Rumanian front (see Chapter 340). It is evident that diplomatic influences had also been at work, and King Michael carried out a coup d'état in Bucharest to throw off German control the moment the result of the first battles was known.

Following up victory with great speed Malinovsky overran the Ploesti oilfields and entered Bucharest before the Germans could react, while Tolbukhin crossed the lower Danube and held a pistol at the head of Bulgaria. By the middle of September both Rumania and Bulgaria had not only cut themselves adrift from Germany, but were actively fighting on the side of the Allies. Malinovsky rapidly cleared southern Rumania, although the Germans retreating across the Carpathians continued to fight stubborn rearguard actions in northern Transylvania. The way had been opened, however, for Malinovsky to advance into Hungary; and both he and Tolbukhin were able to join hands with Marshal Tito's partisan armies, which, ever since the collapse of Italy, had compelled the Germans to maintain some 20 German divisions in Yugoslavia.

Malinovsky soon reached the Danube, but then wheeled northwards to interpose between the Germans in Transylvania and the strong force holding Budapest; while Tolbukhin co-operating with Bulgarian and Yugoslav troops liberated Belgrade and cleared north-eastern Yugoslavia. The Germans fought hard to hold Budapest and the line of the Danube, but their Transylvanian force was slowly pushed back into eastern Slovakia, where it was also attacked by the 4th Ukrainian Army crossing the Carpathians from the north.

Germans Try to Hold Budapest

ALLIED ARMIES CLOSE IN ON THE REICH

Shaded sections of this map show the considerable areas reconquered by the Allies from the launching of the Normandy invasion in 1944 until January 1945 when the Ardennes counter-offensive had been defeated. Allied armies of the west had cleared France, Belgium, Luxemburg, taken two-thirds of Italy, and freed Greece; while the Russians had liberated most of the Balkans and were closing in on the Reich from the east. *By courtesy of the Daily Mail*

It looked at one time as if the Russian offensive would be brought to a halt by lengthening communications and bad weather, but on November 29 Tol-

Russians Reach Lake Balaton

bukhin, having crossed to the north bank of the Danube, recrossed it again north of its confluence with the Drava and quickly overran all the country east of Lake Balaton. Between the north end of that lake and Budapest, the Germans fought hard; but Tolbukhin, with the assistance of Malinovsky, broke through their lines and completed the encirclement of Budapest by the end of the year. The Germans had thus lost the protection the Danube afforded against the invasion of Austria and southern Germany from the east, and were threatened with a disaster which the defection of Hungary would complete.

On their northern flank, the Russians had also maintained a vigorous offensive against the Germans in the Baltic States, and compelled their withdrawal towards Riga and ultimately into the Courland promontory, thus leaving Finland unsupported (*see* Chapter 329). In August she therefore sued for peace (*see* page 3320) and when in consequence the German Army on the Murmansk front started to retire into Norway she actively co-operated with the Russians. By the end of the year, in the east the stage was set for a renewal of the offensive on the Vistula front and against East Prussia, but in the west Von Rundstedt's Ardennes counter-attack in December (*see* Chapter 336) disturbed the Allied plans for a simultaneous offensive.

On the whole, however, it may be claimed that the strategy of the Allies in 1944 was admirably co-ordinated and achieved results which would fully have justified German unconditional surrender under a saner leadership.

The reopening of the western front, an outstanding feat of intimate collaboration between Allies, had accomplished all that might reasonably have been expected, and the Russian offensive had lacked nothing of skill and energy. Germany's power of recovery in desperate circumstances was undoubtedly remarkable; but the defeats she had suffered and the defection of her satellites (*see* Chapter 327) left her in a hopeless position; unrelenting pressure on all fronts had effectively prevented her from exploiting the advantages of interior lines, but her own strategic errors had contributed not a little to this.

Although in 1944 operations in Europe continued to have priority over the offensive against Japan, yet the latter proceeded with remark-

Operations in the Pacific

able success. The plan followed was that Admiral Nimitz's task force and the main American Fleet should aim at securing bases in the islands of the central Pacific from which the Japanese home islands might be brought within range of bombing attacks. Nimitz's operations

ALLIED ADVANCE IN SOUTH-WEST AND CENTRAL PACIFIC

This spherical projection in relief shows the relative positions of the principal Allied landings on Japanese-occupied territory in the Pacific during 1944, with the dates on which they were carried out. First landings in the Philippines are shown opposite. As with preparations for the Normandy invasion, each advance northward towards Japan was preluded by heavy air attack.

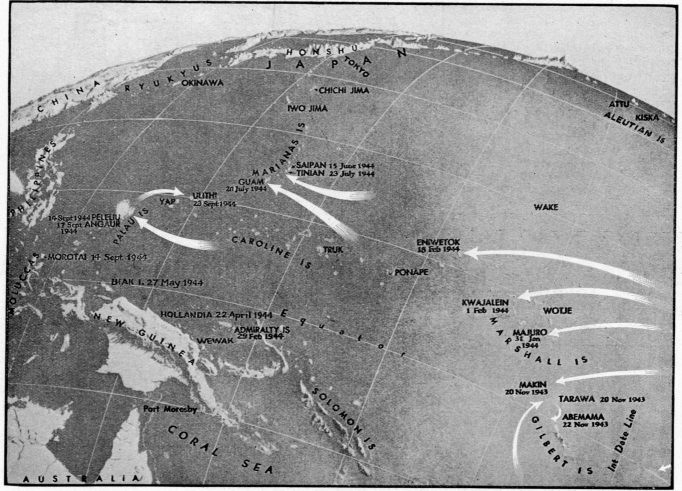

might also induce the Japanese Navy to risk decisive encounters. General MacArthur's American and Australian troops in the south-west Pacific were to continue their advance along the northern coast of New Guinea, destroying or by-passing the Japanese bases there in a series of land and amphibious operations, thus securing a line of approach to the Philippines.

The operations of both Admiral Nimitz and General MacArthur were bound to make immense demands on shipping, and in consequence it was considered that the reconquest of Burma and major operations in the south-east Asia zone would have to await release of shipping following the defeat of Germany. It was still held at the beginning of the year 1944 that the reconquest of Burma could not be effected without amphibious operations on a major scale. It was, however, intended to proceed with General Stilwell's operations to reopen communication with China by the Burma road, to develop communications across the frontier mountains and to build up a great air transport force, in order to exploit the tactics General Wingate had indicated with a view to gaining a footing in northern Burma. The offensive in the Arakan district was also to be renewed with the recapture of the airfields at Akyab as the immediate objective.

In the event these plans were upset by the Japanese attempt to invade India and to interrupt General Stilwell's communications (see Chapter 299). Lord

Invasion of India Repelled

Louis Mountbatten's forces both in Arakan and Manipur were temporarily thrown on the defensive, but first in Arakan and later in Manipur the Japanese were disastrously defeated by counter-offensives. The British force surrounded at Imphal was reinforced by air, and by the beginning of the monsoon season in June had been relieved. With desperately inadequate communications, the Japanese were decisively defeated, forced to retreat and were vigorously pursued, in spite of what had always been considered to be prohibitive monsoon conditions. With the approach of the dry season the offensive both on Stilwell's front and from Manipur made rapid progress, and a footing in the dry region of north Burma was gained. By the end of the year the forces under Sultan (successor to Stilwell) had taken Bhamo, and the main army with easy country ahead was approaching Mandalay (see Chapter 345). In this theatre therefore progress well in advance of expectations was made.

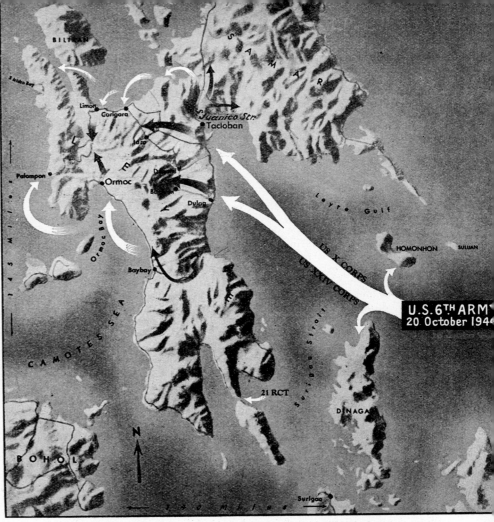

AMERICANS BEGIN RECOVERY OF THE PHILIPPINES

General MacArthur planned his reconquest of the Philippines to begin on December 20, 1944. So advanced were preparations, however, that he was able to land there exactly two months earlier. Principal troop and naval movements in the invasion of Leyte, first of the Philippine Islands to be recovered, are indicated here. [Note : RCT denotes Regimental Combat Team.]
With the exception of the map in page 3489, all maps in this chapter are adapted from the Biennial Report of the Chief of Staff of the U.S. Army to the Secretary of War, July 1, 1943–June 30, 1945.

In the Pacific theatre progress also exceeded expectations, although original plans, with some modifications, were closely followed. Admiral Nimitz in succession captured bases in the Marshall Islands and in the Marianas, by-passing the Japanese stronghold at Truk in the Carolines which, however, under bombing attack ceased to be usable as a naval base (see Chapter 322). Guam and Saipan in the Marianas were the most important islands captured; they provided invaluable advanced naval and air bases. From the latter, before the end of the year, Tokyo came under bombing attack (see page 3094). Air bases were also secured in the Palau Islands in September from which air co-operation with MacArthur's advance to the Philippines could be given.

MacArthur's operations were even more sensational. By September he not only controlled the whole northern coast of New Guinea (see Chapter 309), but had made a landing on Morotai in

the Halmahera group, halfway between New Guinea and the Philippines (see Chapter 351). The Japanese then concentrated for the defence of Mindanao, the great island at the southern end of the Philippines, but, instead of landing there as the Japanese had expected, MacArthur by-passed it, and in October effected a surprise landing on Leyte in the centre of the Philippine Archipelago (see page 3270). The Japanese fought desperately to hold the island but lost many convoys attempting to reinforce the garrison. Even more disastrous for them was the defeat of their navy (see page 3401) which suffered far more ruinous losses than off Saipan (see page 3093) in attempts to intervene.

Thus, by the end of the year, Japan's home islands were no longer immune to attack, and sea communications with her outlying detachments had either been interrupted or greatly endangered. Only in China was the situation still precarious.

Chapter 342

END OF NAVAL WARFARE IN THE WEST

The Royal Navy's work in the west during the last months of the war was to a large extent divided between support of ground forces in the Mediterranean and continued watchfulness against submarines, whose activities increased considerably in January and February 1945. The capitulation of Germany on May 7 brought the surrender of the U-boats, and the end in the west of active warfare at sea as well as on land

THE disappearance from the seas of nearly all sizable German surface ships robbed the last stages of the naval war in the West of much of its dramatic interest, but of none of its hard work.

In the Mediterranean area there was plenty to be done in mopping up enemy positions, dealing with small craft and submarines, and co-operating with the Army in its slow advance in Italy. The Adriatic was still lively. Its waters afforded the best opportunity for the German "human torpedoes," and Allied ships were frequently attacked by these, although with little success. The Yugoslav irregulars having made the roads in Dalmatia impracticable for small parties, enemy supplies had to be sent by sea, where they were under constant attack by Allied small craft and aircraft. Tito's guerillas had to be supported and supplied, and this work was exciting. Italian feeling against the Germans was growing more bitter, but helpful as the partisans were behind the enemy lines, they could not make any effective move against the naval bases.

The Navy in Italian waters not only worked on the flanks of the Army but

went ahead, wherever possible, constantly attacking the coastal roads and railways in spite of the heavy shore batteries. In the Gulf of Genoa and on the Franco-Italian frontier the British, American and French Navies worked in harmony with excellent effect. Usually France supplied the heavier metal in the shape of cruisers, but her so-called flotilla leaders, later classed as light cruisers, proved particularly useful. British and American destroyers and light coastal craft sometimes worked with the French, sometimes independently.

The enemy was given full credit for his enterprise, but when his sorties obviously had little or no chance of success, they were naturally restricted, and it was seldom that there was a target like the one on March 17, when H.M. destroyers "Lookout" and "Meteor" sank two out of three German destroyers which had ventured as far afield as Corsica. The last German sortie, by fast German patrol craft, was against the Riviera: two were sunk after they had bombarded and fired torpedoes against the shore. By the end of April, Spezia, Genoa and Venice were in Allied hands, and the

German Navy had no further shelter in the Mediterranean.

Among the Dodecanese Islands, a fleet of seven 70-foot Naval launches harried the enemy by night, hiding by day under camouflage nets in little creeks. After the loss of these islands (*see* Chapter 293), Captain H. C. Legge, D.S.C., R.N., commander of this force, set up his headquarters in secret on the tiny Turkish island of Kastelrosso (*see*

Attacks on the Dodecanese

COMMANDED 'GLOWWORM'

Posthumous award of the Victoria Cross to Lieutenant-Commander Gerard Broadmead Roope, R.N., Commanding Officer of H.M. destroyer 'Glowworm,' was announced on July 10, 1945. On April 8, 1940, the 'Glowworm' had fought a single-handed duel at point-blank range with the 10,000-ton German cruiser 'Admiral Hipper,' then, battered and blazing, rammed her. (See also illus. in page 821.)

map in page 2942) which lies a few miles from the coast and was the one island in the area not under German domination, in February 1944. His 14-knot Harbour Defence Motor Launches— originally intended for anti-submarine patrol in sheltered waters—were the smallest and slowest vessels in Britain's coastal forces. Within a short time he had recaptured Tilos and Nizyros. From these bases, they not only attacked enemy

SAILED WESTERN ATLANTIC WITHOUT BOW OR STERN

Seamanship of a very high order saved the 5,500-ton cruiser H.M.S. 'Argonaut' after she had been hit by a salvo of torpedoes from a U-boat in the western Atlantic early in 1943. Although her bow and stern, including the rudder and two of her four screws, were blown away, she was navigated safely, via Bermuda, to the U.S. Navy Yard, Philadelphia, where she is seen undergoing repairs.

Photo, Official U.S. Navy

shipping (on one occasion sinking a vessel in which the German Chief of Naval Staff and several other persons of military importance were lost), but also landed raiders from British Commando units and the Greek "Sacred Brigade," who smashed enemy strongpoints and communications and kept the enemy garrisons painfully on the alert : in April 1945 alone these little ships landed 45 raiding parties on the various islands. After the surrender of the German troops on the islands, signed by General Wagner on Symi on May 9, two of these launches worked in the area as minesweepers, entering waters and harbours inaccessible to larger vessels ; they swept a total of ninety mines off Leros alone.

It was revealed after the war that the British and Greek troops evacuated from Samos (see illus. in page 2946) were evacuated through

Turkish Ships for Royal Navy

Turkish territory. Turkey also placed at the disposal of the Royal Navy two destroyers and four submarines which were building in British yards when war broke out. One destroyer, the "Muavenet," was commissioned as H.M.S. "Inconstant," her sister ship the "Gayret" as H.M.S. "Ithuriel." Of the submarines, commissioned as P 611, P 612, P 614 and P 615, the last was sunk by a U-boat off Freetown on April 18, 1943 ; the others survived the war, and were returned to Turkey. So also was the "Inconstant." The "Ithuriel" struck

a mine and was so badly damaged that she was sold for breaking up, H.M.S. "Oribi" being handed to Turkey instead.

The German policy of hanging on to the French naval bases, and maintaining in them "fleets in being" of small craft for attacks on the Allied sea lines of communication, demanded constant air raids which did immense damage to French property, but the potential harm of the ships was not sufficient to justify any diversion of effort, and the Germans were still in possession of St. Nazaire, Lorient, La Rochelle and Dunkirk at the time of the surrender.

The U-boats worked more and more from the north, and their main bases were moved to Norway. Early in the year their operations in the open were still on a small scale ; those which were not being re-equipped were largely employed in narrow waters against Allied supply lines, but they were preparing for further effort, and showed enterprise. In January, when some contrived to get through the boom across the Clyde estuary, torpedoing and damaging an escort carrier and sinking a tanker off Ailsa Craig, at least one was destroyed.

As January progressed they became more active, bringing new devices into use, although the losses to Allied shipping were very little more than in the previous month and the counter-measures to the new methods were most effective. In February more submarines were destroyed than in January,

U-BOAT DEVICES

Intensified Allied warfare against the U-boats compelled the Germans to improve the equipment of their underwater craft. 1. Gyroplane attached by cable to a U-boat to increase field of observation. 2. Compact stowage of the gyroplane aboard the parent submarine. 3. 'Schnorkel' apparatus (see diagram in page 3035) which, erected vertically, enabled a U-boat to charge its batteries while submerged.

but the enemy made great efforts to speed the pre-fabricated construction of a new fleet, with the assembling done principally at Hamburg, Bremen and Kiel; those cities became the targets of constant air attacks which greatly reduced the output. The shortage of certain materials was becoming acute despite German ingenuity in evolving substitutes, and some of the 750-ton submarines were converted to carry cargo in the hope of getting materials from Japan. Very few got through, and a number were found tied up in Eastern waters after the surrender in the Far East.

Protective pens of colossal strength had been built for both E-boats and submarines, and these resisted all

U-Boat Devices

ordinary bombs, even the rocket-propelled bomb which was evolved by the Royal Naval Scientific Service especially to attack them. The " growler " gear (*see* page 3035) which permitted U-boats to charge their batteries submerged, but gave the personnel a terrible time, improved torpedoes and wind-driven helicopters to increase the submariner's vision undoubtedly helped them to secure results, although not nearly as great as their propaganda suggested. In February submarine U 1063, testing the very latest devices with a special crew of experts, sank near Bergen and drowned them all.

In March submarine activities were intensified but fewer ships were sunk;

ROYAL NAVY 'HEDGEHOG' TOOK TOLL OF U-BOATS

Details were withheld till November 1945 of one of the earliest and most successful anti-U-boat devices used by the Royal Navy. This was the 'Hedgehog'—a 24-unit battery of projectiles mounted in the bows of destroyers : it obviated the blind run-in for a depth-charge attack during which the U-boat often took successful evasive action. Each unit contained a 58-lb. explosive charge.
Photo, British Official

the bombing and mining of bases produced excellent results, and to improve defensive measures the Admiralty created the new post of Assistant Chief of Naval Staff for U-boat Warfare and Trade, to which Rear-Admiral J. M. Mansfield was appointed.

The Baltic was also active, although the badly crippled Russian Navy was unable to take as big a part as had been hoped. From January the Russian armies worked steadily along the coast, where German warships of all types gave considerable support to their own forces.

On January 26, Marshal Rokossovsky's Army reached the Gulf of Danzig, cutting off East Prussia from central Germany. All available German shipping and many warships rushed refugees to the

German Warships Assist Army

west, even submarines being used to carry Nazis of high rank. A very heavy toll was taken, principally by aircraft and airlaid mines in their track, and the Royal Air Force co-operated most effectively with the Red Air Force. Large numbers of German naval personnel, for whom there were no available ships, were drafted into the Eastern Army ; they gave a certain amount of trouble over discipline, and there was a great deal of friction with the regular army. At different times the pocket battleships " Admiral Scheer " and " Lützow," and the big cruisers " Prinz Eugen " and " Admiral Hipper " were co-operating with the army. Many warships assisting the Wehrmacht were damaged and were sent to Denmark for repairs.

On the refugee service the " Strength Through Joy " cruising liners " Wilhelm Gustloff " and " Robert Ley " were both sunk with heavy loss of life—as an example of overcrowding, the 13,882-ton " Monte Rosa " carried no

REPAIRING SCAPA FLOW'S STEEL NET-BOOM DEFENCES

One of Britain's most carefully guarded naval bases was at Scapa Flow. The defences—impregnable during the First Great War—were rendered U-boat-proof after the sinking of the battleship ' Royal Oak ' on October 14, 1939. Among the ruses adopted to mislead enemy air reconnaissance was a ' fleet ' of dummy wood-and-canvas warships. Below, workmen overhaul the multiple-strand steel net-boom defences.
Photo, British Official

THE U-BOATS SURRENDER

Handing over of Germany's submarines began on May 10, 1945, when the U 249 gave herself up to the Royal Navy at Portland, Dorset. 1. The U 858, first to surrender to the U.S. Navy, arrives off the New Jersey coast on May 14. 2. One of a convoy of U-boats escorted by the Navy from Norway to Loch Eriboll, Scotland. 3. Royal Marine guard watches a U-boat surrender at Wilhelmshaven. 4. U-boats at Loch Ryan before being blown up in Operation 'Deadlight.'

Photos, British Official ; Central Press ; Associated Press

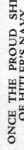

ONCE THE PROUD SHIPS OF HITLER'S NAVY

After the German surrender, ships of the German Navy still seaworthy were distributed among the navies of Great Britain, the U.S., and the U.S.S.R. Many of the heavier vessels, however, had been badly damaged by Allied bombing of enemy and enemy-occupied ports. 1. The 6,000-ton cruiser 'Köln' lying wrecked at Wilhelmshaven. 2. The cruiser 'Admiral Hipper' (10,000 tons), blasted on April 9, 1945 in the R.A.F. raid on Kiel. 3. Also damaged in the same raid on Kiel was the capsized 'Admiral Scheer' (10,000 tons). In the foreground are prefabricated U-boat bows. 4. The 6,000-ton cruiser 'Nürnberg', later awarded to the Red Navy. 5. The 26,000-ton battleship 'Gneisenau'—which in 1942 made a daring dash through the English Channel—lying scuttled at Gdynia. 6. The 13,040-ton 'Schleswig-Holstein,' built in 1906 and converted to a Cadet Training ship in 1936, was wrecked by Allied bombs, also at Gdynia.

less than 12,000 refugees. As the Russians advanced a large number of senior German officers and Nazi officials crossed to Sweden for internment, often in most inappropriate vessels of which a number were sunk.

Gdynia fell on March 28 and Danzig two days later, the last practicable German naval base on a long stretch of coast. Forty U-boats, complete or completing, were captured, virtually undamaged, at Danzig. In both ports the harbour installations were destroyed as completely as possible and the channels blocked by scuttled ships. In Gdynia the battleship "Gneisenau" was used for this purpose; she had not been to sea since her dramatic escape from Brest (*see* page 2122).

To help the Russians the R.A.F. and U.S.A.A.F. made constant raids on the bases and ports on the western Baltic, sinking or putting out of action many German warships **Baltic Ports** and making a special **Bombed** target of the shipbuilding yards. In a particularly heavy raid on Kiel on April 9 the battleship "Admiral Scheer" was sunk and the cruiser "Admiral Hipper" badly damaged in dry dock; Krupps's Germania Yard and the naval dockyard were put completely out of action. On April 16 the R.A.F. bombed Swinemünde and sank the pocket battleship "Lützow." Early in May the German Government attempted to save Kiel and Flensburg by broadcasting a radio notice that they were "open towns," but it had little effect. All the time Russian aircraft, submarines to a lesser extent, and occasionally surface ships were taking a heavy toll of German transports, but their method of estimating mercantile tonnage by displacement, normally used only for warships, made the picture very confusing.

In the North Sea the great object of the German Navy, employing principally submarines and E-boats, was to interrupt the flow of munitions and military supplies to the ports which the Allies had opened, principally Antwerp. In the estuaries and narrow waters the enemy also used their "Linsen" radio-controlled explosive motor-boats whose crews took them into position for attack and then abandoned them to be guided by wireless. Their explosion was most effective when they did hit their target, but a large number missed or were blown up before they reached it.

In the early part of the year the E-boat and U-boat attacks, frequently backed by aircraft but not to the extent that was expected, caused great damage, but the Fleet Air Arm and Coastal

Command co-operated in providing an air umbrella and helped, in collaboration with the light coastal forces led by 35-knot steam gunboats and stiffened with frigates, corvettes and other small craft, to beat off a number of E-boat attacks at night.

During this period German propaganda attempted to make the E-boats take the place of the submarines in popular favour and gave a number of thrilling accounts of successful actions against superior British forces, generally on the English coast. These accounts were nearly always entirely false; generally speaking, it was possible to intercept the formations and only occasional excursions right across the North Sea succeeded in laying mines or attacking coastal convoys.

Midget submarines were also employed, right into the Thames Estuary according to the German wireless, but as a rule they were confined to coastal waters where 81 were sunk, captured or probably sunk in about two months and nearly a hundred were fought with uncertain results.

When Germany capitulated, about a hundred midget submarines were captured in different bases and afforded opportunity for study. The "Biber" type was 29 ft. 6 ins. long with one man, carrying two modified electric torpedoes under dropping gear; while the "Seehund," 39 feet long, was more elaborate and had a crew of two.

GERMAN MIDGET U-BOATS

1. Two-men midget U-boats seized at Kiel; awaiting assembly, they had arrived in sections. Towards the close of the war the Germans made extensive use of these weapons. 2. 'Molch'-type one-man 'human' torpedo, 46 feet long and carrying a single torpedo. It was captured on Skaelland Island, off Denmark, trial station for Nazi secret weapons. 3. Danish experts examine a 'Biber'-type 29-feet long midget U-boat which carried one man and two torpedoes. (See also illus. in pages 2847 and 2859.)

U.K. 'FROGMEN'

Frogmen ' of the Royal Navy and Royal Marines executed one of the most hazardous operations of the war. This was the clearance of underwater defences on the Normandy beaches just before June 6, 1944. 1. ' Frogman ' ready for action. 2. ' Frogmen ' paddle a canoe used in approaching an objective. 3. ' Frogmen ' training in a London swimming bath. (See also illus. in page 3373.)

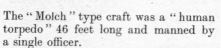

The " Molch " type craft was a " human torpedo " 46 feet long and manned by a single officer.

Submarines of normal design also reappeared in the North Sea, both attacking the supply routes and on passage, but their casualties were heavy. As more liberated ports were cleared of the ships scuttled by the enemy and had their cranes and other facilities replaced, the supply lines were distributed as widely as European internal communications permitted and attack became more difficult.

Norwegian waters became the scene of more and more naval activity as the year progressed. Submarines in the open Atlantic used Norwegian bases rather than German, while a big effort was made to evacuate at least part of the large German army in Norway for the defence of the Fatherland. The Norwegian Navy took a particularly enthusiastic part in attacking this transport line, while the Home Fleet repeatedly provided task forces of escort carriers, cruisers and destroyers which worked with the co-operation of Coastal Command in bombing shipping at sea and in the ports. The R.A.F. also worked against transports in the Skager Rak and Kattegat, both by bombing and minelaying, and destroyed many. Small craft of the Norwegian Navy smuggled in a large number of men from Commando units and volunteers who blew up railways, power stations, etc., and set fire to German depots.

Although the situation was eased when Turkey's declaration of war on Germany and Japan (from March) opened the Dardanelles route to southern Russia, the munitions service to the Murmansk and White Sea was still very important and the convoys were still constantly attacked from Norway, both by submarines and aircraft. British escort carriers became very conspicuous in these convoys and were frequently chosen as flagships, backed by 6-inch gun cruisers, British, Canadian and Norwegian destroyers, corvettes, sloops, frigates and minesweepers. In spite of the fact that some of the attacks were particularly heavy, more convoys got through without damage.

As many German warships as possible were spared to defend the north-west coast of Germany and to protect the vessels of all kinds which were withdrawing key personnel from the countries reoccupied by the Allies. Apart from the purely naval bases, Bremen and Hamburg were of great importance in these efforts, and when they were successively attacked in April the Navy assisted in their defence, both on land and sea, but eventually both ports were overrun. In the defence of Hamburg the Navy was particularly active and destroyers even fought tanks. Heligoland was prevented by intensive bombing from rendering any assistance.

German Navy Defends Home Ports

Some time before the surrender there were signs of a breakdown of morale in certain sections of the German Navy. Attempts were made to start peace movements in Hamburg and Bremen

RED ARMY PATROLS IN THE CARPATHIAN MOUNTAINS

Well-equipped Red Army mortar-crews probing the rock-strewn Carpathian mountains in northern Hungary during the Soviet offensive in the Danube Basin which opened in the late summer of 1944 (see Chapter 340). By October 18 General Petrov's 4th Ukrainian Army had crossed the Carpathian passes from the north and had penetrated eastern Slovakia on a front of 170 miles. It was thus gravely menacing the rear of the enemy in northern Transylvania and threatening to join with Marshal Malinovsky's 3rd Ukrainian Army. *Photo, Pictorial Press*

GERMAN CRUISER 'PRINZ EUGEN' SURRENDERS TO BRITISH FORCES

On May 7, 1945, 21st Army Group H.Q. announced that the German heavy cruiser 'Prinz Eugen,' of 10,000 tons, and the cruiser 'Nürnberg' (see illustration in page 3496)—both at Copenhagen—and 160,000 tons of merchant shipping, partly in Danish harbours, had surrendered to Field-Marshal Montgomery's forces. The 'Prinz Eugen' was subsequently allocated to the U.S. Navy which in March 1946 scheduled her for atomic bomb experiment. Above, Danish troops guard her as she lay at her moorings in Copenhagen harbour.   *Photo, Associated Press*

ROCKET-SHIPS SUPPORTED ALLIED INVASION OPERATIONS

Though experiments had been made as far back as April 1943, the Landing Craft Tank (Rocket) was not mentioned by the Admiralty until September 1944. It was then disclosed that these craft had assisted at the landings in Sicily, at Reggio, Anzio and Nettuno, in Normandy and in the south of France. They were also used in the Pacific. Fire was said to equal a salvo from thirty regiments of artillery or thirty cruisers each mounted with twelve 6-inch guns. Here is a close-up of rocket equipment. (See also page 3069 and illus. in pages 3275 and 3399.)

3 X

Photo, *British Official*

MR. CHURCHILL CROSSES THE RHINE INTO GERMANY

The British Prime Minister was present at Field-Marshal Montgomery's H.Q. when Allied troops forced the Rhine on March 24, 1945. In a message to 21st Army Group he declared : 'British soldiers ! It will long be told how, with our Canadian brothers and valiant United States Allies, this superb task was accomplished. Once the river line is pierced and the crust of German resistance is broken, decisive victory in Europe will be near.' Next day he crossed the Rhine to visit newly-won areas on the east bank, afterwards cruising in a Buffalo well within range of enemy artillery. Here, Mr. Churchill lunches with Field-Marshal Montgomery and Field-Marshal Sir Alan Brooke, C.I.G.S., on the bank of the wide river.

and crews of some small craft took their ships into Sweden for internment (several were stopped and sunk on the way). Plans to scuttle merchant ships were checked in April by General Eisenhower's wireless warning that if there were no ships there would be no food for Germany.

On April 30, just before his death, Hitler appointed Admiral Doenitz his successor as Fuehrer; twelve months previously that appointment would probably have caused a great change in Germany's naval effort, but it was then too late to have any effect.

On May 5 the German armed forces on the Western Front surrendered. Doenitz sent wireless orders to all U-boats to cease hostilities and return to their bases. Many captains were only too glad to obey, but others carried on the campaign. Next day all naval vessels were ordered to abstain from any act of war and were prohibited from scuttling themselves by the new Fuehrer. The unconditional surrender of all German land, sea and air forces was signed on the 7th (*see* Chapter 355).

Field-Marshal Montgomery lost no time in sending a special message of thanks to the Royal Navy for its part.

Montgomery Thanks the Royal Navy "Throughout our long journey from Egypt to the Baltic, any success achieved by the British Army has been made possible only by the magnificent support given us by the Royal Navy. With unfailing precision we have been put ashore, supported and supplied."

On May 8 the Admiralty issued wireless surrender orders to the German fleet. All German and German-controlled warships, auxiliaries, merchant and other craft at sea were to report their position in plain language to the nearest Allied wireless station, when they would be given orders to proceed to such ports as might be selected. There they were to remain until further orders were received. All ships in port were to stay there. Submarines at sea had to surface and fly a black flag or pennant, to report their position in plain language and then proceed on the surface to a named port.

All armed ships, in port or at sea, were to train their guns fore and aft, remove the breech blocks and unload all torpedo tubes. Those in port were to land all ammunition, explosives, torpedo warheads and portable weapons; but minesweepers and salvage vessels, similarly disarmed, were to fill up with fuel and fit themselves for service under Allied direction. Boom defences in ports and harbours

SURRENDERED E-BOATS IN BRITISH WATERS
Early in 1945 German propaganda tried to make the E-boat replace the U-boat in popular favour with the people. But accounts of E-boats' successes were largely exaggerated. Above, Rear-Admiral F. Bruening, Commander of Germany's 'Little Ships' operating from Netherlands bases (left), is piped ashore at Felixstowe on May 13 to surrender his forces to Commander McGowan, R.N. (centre). Below, surrendered E-boats of the latest type with their German crews at Portsmouth in June. *Photos, Planet News; Central Press*

were to be kept open, demolition charges and controlled minefields to be rendered ineffective and all naval personnel were to remain on board their ships or in their establishments until further orders were given.

Isolated units of the fleet refused to acknowledge the surrender for some time: on May 9 a German ship in the Baltic shot down an Allied plane.

On May 10 U 249 surrendered at Portland, the first of a steady stream of submarine surrenders to the Royal Navy. The last attacks were on May 7, eight hours after the surrender, when U-boats attacked a convoy bound for

Belfast and sank the steamer "Avondale Park" while the Norwegian "Sneland I" was sunk in the Forth on the same day. Until it was considered that all the U-boats had been accounted for, the Atlantic convoy and air patrol was continued, the last convoy arriving at Loch Ryan (south-west Scotland) on June 3.

A total of 866 German and Italian commissioned submarines was destroyed by the Allies: an average of nearly three a week throughout the war in Europe. Of 1,174 U-boats commissioned after the Germans restarted building them before war, at least 781 were destroyed.

The two outstanding months of the war were May 1943, when 46 U-boats were sunk, and April 1945, while the Germans were evacuating the Baltic ports, when 65 were sunk. Over 300 were destroyed within 500 miles of the United Kingdom, an area equivalent to about one-fifth of the north Atlantic Ocean. Over 500 were killed by British forces, or Allied forces under British control. A hundred were found in more or less damaged condition at Kiel. Another 170 surrendered intact, 67 of them at sea. Seventy of the 1,600-ton "Schnorkel" type, in which Doenitz had placed such faith, were destroyed, and over two hundred were captured before commissioning.

The U 963 scuttled herself off the Portuguese coast on May 20; her commander, Captain Wentz, stated that he did not know of the surrender. He and his crew of 47 were interned, Captain Wentz and his second-in-command being later handed to the British authorities. On July 10, U 530, somewhat damaged, surrendered to

Argentina at Mar del Plata; considerable excitement was caused by a rumour that she had been carrying Nazi leaders and had landed them on a lonely part of the South American coast. Her commander, Captain Otto Wermuth, said she had sailed from a German port on February 19. U 977 surrendered at the same port as late as August 17; she had left Kiel on April 13, disembarking some Germans at Christianberg (Norway), from which she sailed on May 2.

Of the German submarines which surrendered, ten each were allocated to the Soviet Union, the United Kingdom, and the United States for experimental purposes. The rest were towed out to sea and sunk in the Atlantic— by firing explosive charges fitted to the U-boat, by shell fire, or by bombing or torpedoing from the air. This operation, known as "Deadlight," began on November 25, 1945.

In Germany and the occupied countries of Europe the Royal Navy took a prominent part in receiving the sur-

render. Detached forces took possession of many areas, usually with very little trouble from direct opposition, although there was plenty of trickery and more than one German commander had to be arrested. A lieutenant of the R.N.V.R. and five ratings took possession of Kiel on May 10, the White Ensign being hoisted over the Canal on the same day. Rear-Admiral Muirhead-Gould, British Naval C.-in-C., N.W. Germany, received the surrender of Heligoland. On May 9 H.M.S. "Birmingham" led a force of cruisers and destroyers, under the command of Captain Herbert Williams, to Copenhagen, where the last two effective German warships, the cruisers "Prinz Eugen" and "Nürnberg" had surrendered to Field-Marshal Montgomery on the 7th. Aircraft rounded up a number of German war and merchant ships at sea, including the hospital ship "Freyberg," which the British had been accused by the German propaganda machine of sinking against International Law in 1944.

The signing of the surrender did not end the Royal Navy's duties in Europe. First, it had to enforce the terms laid down at Berlin (July 17–August 1,

Royal Navy Receives Surrenders

PREFABRICATED U-BOATS SEIZED AT HAMBURG

On May 3, 1945—three days before hostilities ceased in Europe—Hamburg, second city in Germany and largest port on the Continent, surrendered to the British 2nd Army. Half of the city's buildings had been destroyed, 50 merchantmen, 19 floating docks and many other ships lay sunk in the harbour. Below, some of the prefabricated U-boats found in various stages of construction on the stocks in the Blohm and Voss shipyards. *Photo. Associated Press*

1945), that German dockyards and installations classified as "essentially warlike" were to be rendered absolutely useless, that various naval assets were to be regarded as potential reparations, that certain unspecified ships might be distributed among the Allies, that coastal batteries were to be blown up, and that the whole of Germany's naval personnel was to be disbanded except those engaged in minesweeping. Some argument developed among the Allies

MINESWEEPERS START TO MAKE THE SEAS SAFE AGAIN

1. H.M.S. 'Foam' (nearer camera) and H.M.S. 'Bramble' on minesweeping duty from a Scottish naval base. In the background is one of H.M. escort-carriers. 2. Paying out the buoyant magnetic cable from the stern of a British minesweeper before sweeping a German-laid minefield. Trailed in lengths of 500 yards, these electrically-charged cables rendered magnetic mines harmless. 3. Firing mechanism of German magnetic mine with covers removed.   *Photos, British Official ; Associated Press*

over interpretation of certain sections.

The surviving German warships were distributed in January 1946 as follows : to the Soviet Union, the battleship **Distribution of German Warships** "Hessen" (13,000 tons), built in 1903 and converted into a wireless control target ship ; the cruiser "Nürnberg" (6,000 tons), ten destroyers and seagoing torpedo boats, ten submarines, thirteen depot ships including the "Otto Wunsche," and 507 other units ; to the U.S.A. the cruiser "Prinz Eugen" (scheduled by its new owner for atomic bomb experiment), seven destroyers and seagoing torpedo boats, ten submarines, twelve depot ships and 560 other units ; to Great Britain, thirteen destroyers and seagoing torpedo boats, ten submarines, 21 depot ships, and 612 other units. Great Britain transferred to France in February the eight destroyers (of four different types) she received, and two of her allotment of submarines (for experimental purposes).

Flag officers were appointed for Kiel, Wilhelmshaven and Hamburg in May and in charge of naval affairs in Holland, Denmark, Norway and Belgium. Naval officers carefully examined the German Navy's documents and questioned personnel. Soon after the surrender one German officer prisoner stated that he had been commissioned to stand by with a specially fitted submarine for the escape of Hitler, but that his ship had been wrecked. Later, in Japan, they told the story of Hitler's not trusting the Germans and of a submarine having left Yokohama to collect him on March 5 and disappearing with all hands.

One of the first things to be done was to get from the Germans complete plans of all the minefields, admitting the difficulty in stating the exact position of those laid by aircraft. Many of the defensive fields were well designed but were declared by the Germans to be unsweepable. But the Royal Navy, employing divers in conditions of great danger, immediately started to clear them with success. Very soon, except for an occasional mine, the seas were again free.

British naval casualties in the course of the war numbered nearly 51,000 killed and missing (excluding Dominions naval losses and losses of the Royal Marines)— 20,000 more than in the war of 1914-1918. Nearly 15,000 awards for gallantry were made to officers and men of the Royal Navy, including the Dominions Navies, the Royal Marines and the Reserves. Among these were 23 awards of the Victoria Cross and 29 of the George Cross. Total losses of H.M. ships and craft of all sizes and sorts from September 3, 1939 to August 31, 1945, numbered 3,282. This figure included three battleships, two battle cruisers (one-third of British capital ship strength at the outbreak of war), five fleet carriers, 23 cruisers, 134 destroyers and 77 submarines. Early in the war, it was decided not to proceed with the battleships "Lion" and "Temeraire" of the 1938 programme, and "Conqueror" and "Thunderer" of the 1939 programme, as none of these could be completed before 1944 ; at the end of the war one battleship, the 42,500-ton "Vanguard," was nearing completion.

VICTORY IN EUROPE

Below is the text of the broadcast in which at 3 p.m. British Double Summer Time on
May 8, 1945, Mr. Winston Churchill announced the end of the fighting in Europe.
Later in the same day, H.M. the King broadcast a message of thanksgiving

Mr. Churchill, Prime Minister of the United Kingdom, announces the end of the war in Europe :

YESTERDAY morning at 2.41 a.m. at headquarters, General Jodl, the representative of the German High Command, and Grand Admiral Dönitz, the designated head of the German State, signed the act of unconditional surrender of all German land, sea, and air forces in Europe to the Allied Expeditionary Force, and simultaneously to the Soviet High Command.

General Bedell Smith, Chief of Staff of the Allied Expeditionary Force, and General François Sevez signed the document on behalf of the Supreme Commander of the Allied Expeditionary Force, and General Susloparov signed on behalf of the Russian High Command.

Today this agreement will be ratified and confirmed at Berlin, where Air Chief Marshal Tedder, Deputy Supreme Commander of the Allied Expeditionary Force, and General de Lattre de Tassigny will sign on behalf of General Eisenhower. Marshal Zhukov will sign on behalf of the Soviet High Command. The German representatives will be Field-Marshal Keitel, Chief of the High Command, and the Commanders-in-Chief of the German Army, Navy, and Air Forces.

Hostilities will end officially at one minute after midnight tonight (Tuesday, May 8), but in the interests of saving lives the " Cease fire " began yesterday to be sounded all along the front, and our dear Channel Islands are also to be freed today.

The Germans are still in places resisting the Russian troops, but should they continue to do so after midnight they will, of course, deprive themselves of the protection of the laws of war, and will be attacked from all quarters by the Allied troops. It is not surprising that on such long fronts and in the existing disorder of the enemy the commands of the German High Command should not in every case be obeyed immediately. This does not, in our opinion, with the best military advice at our disposal, constitute any reason for withholding from the nation the facts communicated to us by General Eisenhower of the unconditional surrender already signed at Rheims, nor should it prevent us from celebrating today and tomorrow (Wednesday) as Victory in Europe days.

Today, perhaps, we shall think mostly of ourselves. Tomorrow we shall pay a particular tribute to our Russian comrades, whose prowess in the field has been one of the grand contributions to the general victory.

The German war is therefore at an end. After years of intense preparation, Germany hurled herself on Poland at the beginning of September 1939 ; and, in pursuance of our guarantee to Poland and in agreement with the French Republic, Great Britain, the British Empire and Commonwealth of Nations, declared war upon this foul aggression. After gallant France had been struck down we, from this island and from our united Empire, maintained the struggle single-handed for a whole year until we were joined by the military might of Soviet Russia and later by the overwhelming power and resources of the United States of America.

Finally almost the whole world was combined against the evil-doers, who are now prostrate before us. Our gratitude to our splendid Allies goes forth from all our hearts in this island and throughout the British Empire.

We may allow ourselves a brief period of rejoicing ; but let us not forget for a moment the toil and efforts that lie ahead. Japan, with all her treachery and greed, remains unsubdued. The injury she has inflicted on Great Britain, the United States, and other countries, and her detestable cruelties, call for justice and retribution. We must now devote all our strength and resources to the completion of our task, both at home and abroad. Advance, Britannia ! Long live the cause of freedom ! God save the King !

Message from H.M. the King to his peoples broadcast on May 8, 1945 :

TODAY we give thanks to Almighty God for a great deliverance.

Speaking from our Empire's oldest capital city, war-battered but never for one moment daunted or dismayed—speaking from London, I ask you to join with me in that act of thanksgiving.

Germany, the enemy who drove all Europe into war, has been finally overcome. In the Far East we have yet to deal with the Japanese, a determined and cruel foe. To this we shall turn with the utmost resolve and with all our resources. But at this hour, when the dreadful shadow of war has passed from our hearths and homes in these islands, we may at last make one pause for thanksgiving and then turn our thoughts to the tasks all over the world which peace in Europe brings with it.

Let us remember those who will not come back, their constancy and courage in battle, their sacrifice and endurance in the face of a merciless enemy : let us remember the men in all the Services and the women in all the Services who have laid down their lives. We have come to the end of our tribulation, and they are not with us at the moment of our rejoicing.

Then let us salute in proud gratitude the great host of the living who have brought us to victory. I cannot praise them to the measure of each one's service, for in a total war the efforts of all rise to the same noble height and all are devoted to the common purpose. Armed or unarmed, men and women, you have fought, striven, and endured to your utmost. No one knows that better than I do ; and as your King I thank with a full heart those who bore arms so valiantly on land and sea, or in the air ; and all civilians who, shouldering their many burdens, have carried them unflinchingly without complaint.

With those memories in our minds, let us think what it was that has upheld us through nearly six years of suffering and peril. The knowledge that everything was at stake : our freedom, our independence, our very existence as a people ; but the knowledge also that in defending ourselves we were defending the liberties of the whole world ; that our cause was the cause not of this nation only, not of this Empire and Commonwealth only, but of every land where freedom is cherished and law and liberty go hand in hand. In the darkest hours we knew that the enslaved and isolated peoples of Europe looked to us ; their hopes were our hopes ; their confidence confirmed our faith. We knew that, if we failed, the last remaining barrier against a world-wide tyranny would have fallen in ruins. But we did not fail. We kept our faith with ourselves and with one another ; we kept faith and unity with our great allies. That faith and unity have carried us to victory through dangers which at times seemed overwhelming.

So let us resolve to bring to the tasks which lie ahead the same high confidence in our mission. Much hard work awaits us, both in the restoration of our own country after the ravages of war and in helping to restore peace and sanity to a shattered world. . . .

There is great comfort in the thought that the years of darkness and danger in which the children of our country have grown up are over and, please God, for ever. We shall have failed, and the blood of our dearest will have flowed in vain if the victory which they died to win does not lead to a lasting peace, founded on justice and established in good will. To that, then, let us turn our thoughts on this day of just triumph and proud sorrow ; and then take up our work again, resolved as a people to do nothing unworthy of those who have died for us and to make the world such a world as they would have desired, for their children and for ours. . . .

Chapter 343

BRITAIN CELEBRATES VICTORY IN EUROPE

Removal of war restrictions, planning for post-war changes, already well advanced in 1944 (see Chapter 300), proceeded in Britain during the early months of 1945 despite the shadow cast over life in south-east England by the continued arrival of rocket-bombs, the enemy's last piece of frightfulness. Victory in Europe was celebrated with sober rejoicing, and heartfelt tributes were paid to Mr. Winston Churchill, whose popularity had never been greater

For London, Essex, Hertfordshire and Kent the beginning of 1945 remained peculiarly unpleasant : rockets (V2s) were arriving in increasing numbers. During one week in February—the worst of the visitation—71 fell (the highest number in twenty-four hours was 17). They came from the Netherlands, from the neighbourhood of The Hague, and not until the advancing Canadians cut the supply lines from Germany did they cease, the last falling on March 27 at Orpington in Kent, killing one, injuring 23. (Further details of the V2 attacks are in Chapter 337.)

R.A.F. Balloon Command, which had contributed to the defence of cities, towns and industrial buildings against air attack, and of London against flying-bombs (*see* page 3434), was disbanded in February, though a nucleus was retained in the United Kingdom, and detachments were still serving overseas. In September 1939, Balloon Command was responsible for 600 balloons ; at the end of the 1940-41 blitz, for 2,400. By 1943, over a thousand balloon sites were staffed by the W.A.A.F. Balloons were flown over the Sicilian, Italian and Normandy beaches during the Allied invasions, in defence of the Suez Canal, the Persian Gulf and Ceylon, and, in co-operation with the Royal Navy, helped to defend convoys at sea and naval establishments ashore.

The ban on handbells (which were to have been used as warning in case of a gas attack) and on the use of whistles worked otherwise than by mechanical power was raised on January 18. Firewatching was suspended throughout the country on March 24. Persons evacuated in 1940 from parts of East Anglia were allowed to return on March 28. All dim-out restrictions, except in a five-mile coastal belt, were removed on April 23, and next day the light at the top of the Clock Tower at Westminster was once more illuminated when the House of Commons was sitting after dark. Big Ben itself was illuminated again from April 30.

April 13 brought the stand-down, and the first intimation of the existence, of a British "underground" force,

Restrictions Removed

established before the underground movements came to birth in France, Belgium, the Netherlands and Norway, and so secretly organized that many of its members (all citizens going about their ordinary jobs) never knew the identity of any of their fellows. On May 2 came the stand-down of the Civil Defence Services and the Royal Observer Corps ; the discontinuance of the air raid warning system ; the closing of all public and communal A.R.P. shelters ; and an official invitation to some half million evacuated Londoners to return to their homes, if these were still habitable. Those whose homes had been destroyed were advised, if possible, to remain away until there was more housing room in the metropolis. News announcers of the B.B.C., who had, as a protective measure of identification, given their names at the beginning of the bulletins since May 1940, ceased to do so on May 4. Hull and Grimsby became "return home" areas on May 6.

On that day also General Eisenhower, Supreme Allied Commander in Western Europe, sent a message to Mr. Churchill saying, "I note a report to the effect that England has found it possible officially to abolish her defences against air raids. No event of this war gives me greater personal satisfaction, nor stands as a brighter symbol of Nazi defeat. One of the highlights of the history of this conflict will be the stamina, courage and determination displayed by the British population in the performance of its indispensable duties under the constant threat of the most terrifying weapons the enemy could devise."

No statistics can express the moral and physical strain to which the people of Britain, and especially those of London and the south-eastern counties, were exposed by enemy action during the long course of the war in Europe—in particular the all-night raids by piloted craft during the "blitz" period of 1940-41, and the twenty-four-hour danger from flying-bombs and rockets between June 1944 and March 1945 ; but the figures of total civilian casualties during the war given by Mr. Herbert Morrison, the Home Secretary, to the House of Commons on April 21 tell their own tale : 60,585 killed (26,920 men, 25,392 women, 7,736 children, 537 unidentified) ; 86,175 injured and detained in hospital (40,736 men, 37,816 women, 7,623 children). Of these totals,

Civilian War Casualties

FAREWELL PARADE OF BALLOON COMMAND

Sir Archibald Sinclair, Secretary of State for Air, on February 6, 1945, announced the disbandment of R.A.F. Balloon Command, though balloons would still fly under other Commands. Their number had increased from 600 in September 1939 to 2,400 at the end of the air attacks on Britain. Here Sir Archibald addresses a stand-down parade at Stanmore, Middlesex.

WESTMINSTER'S BEACON SHINES AGAIN
On April 24, 1945, the lantern surmounting the Clock Tower at Westminster—indicating, it illuminated, that the House of Commons is sitting after sunset—showed its light for the first time for five years, seven months and 23 days. In switching it on, the Speaker said: 'I pray that this light may be a beacon of fresh hope in a sadly torn and distracted world.' *Photo, G.P.U.*

other ranks, 10s., in the case of officers from 25s. for the lowest ranks to 75s. for Admirals of the Fleet, Field-Marshals, and Marshals of the R.A.F. for each complete month of service. Women were to receive two-thirds of the corresponding male rates except in the case of doctors, who were to receive the same rate if receiving the same pay as their men colleagues.

These gratuities were expected to cost two hundred million pounds sterling (in addition to the five hundred million pounds allowed under the earlier scheme).

On March 8, the war gratuities scheme was extended to Civil Defence personnel at three-quarters of the rates for the armed forces. **Women's Land Army and War Gratuities** The Women's Land Army, however, was specifically excluded, and this led to a good deal of criticism of the Government, which argued that it could not justify the extension of such benefits to classes employed under the recognized conditions of their industry or profession and receiving industrial or professional rates of pay. Lady Denman, who organized the Women's Land Army in the 1914–18 war, and had been honorary Director of the Women's Land Army in the Second Great War

NO GRATUITY FOR W.L.A.
There was strong criticism of the Government's exclusion of the Women's Land Army from the War Gratuities Scheme. On May 16, 1945, it was decided to concede training facilities to W.L.A. members wishing to take up careers. Below, W.L.A. girls engaged on the strenuous work of ' ditching ' in Surrey. *Photo, Fox Photos*

the London region suffered 29,890 deaths, 50,497 injured. The 79 London tube stations, made available as shelters in September 1940, were closed for this purpose on May 6. Shelterers had spent a total of forty million nights in them ; other shelterers during day and night alerts numbered ten million ; 7,600 three-tier bunks had been installed ; 5,000 tons of refreshments were served ; 2,000 first aiders, canteen workers, doctors, and other paid and voluntary helpers had been employed in them. German air attacks on the United Kingdom caused damage exceeding a thousand million pounds sterling in value ; payments by local authorities for the repair of houses up to the end

of 1944 already totalled over a hundred million pounds.

In February the Chancellor of the Exchequer, Sir John Anderson, announced a scheme of gratuities to men and women demobilized from the armed forces, in addition to the 56 days' paid leave and payment of post-war credits (plus resettlement grants up to £150 for those wishing to restart business on their own account) already in operation under a scheme announced in February 1942. Officers and men with at least six months' approved war service (to be assessed on total period or periods of war service on full pay since September 3, 1939) were to receive, in the case of ratings and

3508

since its inception, resigned her post as a protest. The Government finally conceded (May 16) specialized training to W.L.A. members wishing to make a career in agriculture, and free training to those not wishing to take up agriculture, and made a contribution of £170,000 to the fund raised by the W.L.A. to help its members in resuming their former occupations. It also allowed them, after six months' service, to retain one greatcoat, one pair of shoes, and one shirt on demobilization : a rather sketchy outfit in which to appear in the streets, was the sarcastic comment of some of these girls.

With consideration of demobilization plans went consideration of many other post-war factors. In the fuel and

Fuel and Power Reports

power industry, a national ballot taken at the end of October 1944 approved by 430,630 votes to 39,464 the amalgamation of the district unions affiliated to the Mineworkers' Federation into one national union, to be known as the National Union of Mineworkers, a decision which came into effect on January 1, 1945. An act was passed to continue the Ministry of Fuel and Power after the war. A panel of engineers appointed by the Ministry in November 1943 to review the Brabazon committee's con-

FROM BRITAIN'S LARDER

That the Ministry of Food had sent or agreed to release 900,000 tons of food from Britain's stocks to liberated Europe was announced to the House of Commons on March 28, 1945, by Mr. Attlee. Below, foodstuffs being checked at the Central Depot which received stocks from 'dumps' laid down to provide emergency supplies in case of invasion. *Photo, British Official*

ST. PAUL'S SERVICE FOR PRESIDENT ROOSEVELT

A congregation of over 3,000 attended a service in memory of President Roosevelt at St. Paul's Cathedral on April 17, 1945. The ceremony was conducted in the Chapel of St. Michael and St. George, and among those attending it were the King and Queen, Princess Elizabeth, Queen Wilhelmina, King Haakon of Norway, the exiled Kings of Greece and Yugoslavia, Mr. Churchill and the Cabinet. *Photo, G.P.U.*

clusions on the Severn Barrage scheme (issued in 1933) reported that the scheme was practicable from an engineering point of view, and would be economically justified : in the first fifteen years the estimated saving in coal would be 985,000 tons, and the scheme would continue to justify itself provided the price of coal did not fall below an average of 49s. 1d. a ton.

The Reid Technical Advisory Committee on Coal Mining, consisting of mining engineers, and appointed by the Government in October 1944, issued a report in March declaring that nothing less than the rebuilding of the industry without delay was required. It considered vitally necessary the comprehen-

sive reconstruction of a large number of the existing mines, both on the surface and underground, with new large-scale sinkings in some districts, and it recommended that the industry should be reorganized on a coalfield or area basis, with all pits in each area merged into " one compact and uniform command of manageable size with full responsibility, financial and otherwise, for the development of the area "; and that a central authority should be created with statutory powers to ensure the formation of such units, stimulate reorganization plans, and conserve the country's coal resources. A number of the mines in private ownership were, in the Committee's opinion, " too small for the

AIR RAID DEFENCES GO

On May 2, 1945, the Civil Defence stood down and raid shelters were closed. 1. Workmen demolish a surface shelter outside St. Paul's Cathedral. 2. Timber from bombed houses at a White City dump is carried away to relieve fuel shortage. 3. Soldiers help in delivering London's coal. 4. Over two tons of rubbish were found when this emergency water-tank at Worcester was drained.

requirements of the best mining practice," and this fact, with the haulage system in use, the conservatism of British employers and mining engineers, and the perpetual financial embarrassment of the industry, accounted for the much lower relative increase in output in Britain compared with some other countries. The report also made specific technical proposals.

Proposals for setting up two finance corporations were announced by the Chancellor of the Exchequer in January. One, the Finance Corporation for Industry Limited, with a capital of £25,000,000 and borrowing powers of another £100,000,000, was to provide temporary or longer period finance for industrial businesses in Britain for their quick rehabilitation and development in order to assist employment. Its capital was to be subscribed in about equal parts by consortiums of the insurance companies and the invest-ment trust companies and the Bank of England; the loan capital would be supplied by the clearing banks and the Scottish banks. The other, the Industrial and Commercial Finance Corporation Limited, with a capital of £15,000,000 and borrowing powers of £30,000,000, was to supply medium and long-term capital for small and medium-sized businesses in Britain. Both capital and loan capital would be subscribed by the clearing banks and

Scottish banks, with a token subscription from the Bank of England.

Sir Frank Newson-Smith, Lord Mayor of London in 1943–44, became chairman of two committees, the first to assist the Minister of Labour in helping young men and women in the forces to make good the loss of opportunities of training and experience in business life due to their war service ; the second to consider the setting up of an advisory service throughout the country to give guidance, before they parted with their money, to ex-service men and women wanting to start in business for themselves. The Appointments Department of the Ministry of Labour was also reorganized to create a specialized service on the lines of the Employment Exchange service, but to meet the needs of those seeking higher appointments (*i.e.* above the level of foreman and clerk). Plans for a policy which would mean increased employment in forestry were foreshadowed by the Chancellor of the Exchequer in February.

Plans for Post-War Employment

An act received the royal assent on March 7 which continued, from a day to be appointed, the wartime obligation on cyclists to carry a red rear light together with a red reflector and a white patch. An act of March 28 re-enacted the Trade Boards Acts, renaming the boards Wages Councils, and provided for the establishment of new Councils by order of the Minister of Labour, to consist of equal numbers of employers' and workers' representatives with up to three independent persons.

Pending the introduction of a new comprehensive social security plan, the Ministry of National Insurance, set up under an act passed on November 17, 1944, took over on April 1 from the

WORLD TRADE UNION CONFERENCE IN LONDON

A World Trade Union Conference was held in the County Hall, Westminster, from February 6–18, 1945, with some 240 delegates, mainly from Allied countries. The Chairman of the T.U.C. General Council, Mr. George Isaacs, M.P. (seen above, standing) ; Mr. M. V. Kuznetsov (U.S.S.R.), and Mr. R. J. Thomas (U.S.A.) presided in turn. At a second meeting in Paris a World Trade Union Federation was formed on October 3, with Sir Walter Citrine as President.

Ministry of Health, the Welsh Board of Health, the Scottish Health Department, and the Ministry of Labour and National Service the administration of existing social insurance schemes ; and from the Home Office its duties in connexion with the Workmen's Compensation Acts. On April 1 also the Education Act of 1944 came into force.

An act of February 15 introduced reforms in local government elections : it provided for the automatic extension of the local government franchise (previously confined to ratepayers and their spouses) to all persons qualified by residence as Parliamentary voters ;

abolished the qualification (established in 1918) of the husband or wife in relation to business premises occupied by the spouse ; and decreed the resumption of local government elections (suspended since the outbreak of war) during 1945 and 1946.

Anticipation of the end of the Coalition Government grew steadily. The Labour Party at its annual conference held on December 12–15, 1944 (postponed from the previous Whitsuntide owing to the curtailment of railway traffic at the time of the invasion of Normandy), declared that " participation in the Government should continue just as long as in the opinion of a party conference it is necessary in the national interest "; at the next election the Labour Party would go before the country with " a practical policy based upon socialist

Labour Party's Intentions

TEMPORARY HOUSES FOR THE BOMBED-OUT

Erection of temporary dwellings—intended to last ten years—began in 1944 in London (see illus. in page 3025), where bomb-damaged houses totalled over 800,000. On December 7, 1945, Mr. Aneurin Bevan, Minister of Health, stated that temporary houses were being put up at the rate of 500–600 a week. Left, specimen house prefabricated in the U.S.A. and erected in Britain. Right, Nissen-type dwellings in Brixton, London. All types had newest kitchen and bathroom fitments, and were popular with those who lived in them.

3 x ²

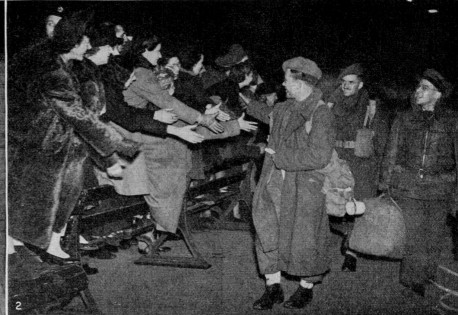

HOME CAME THE WARRIORS FROM OVERSEAS

Seven days' home leave for troops of the British Army of Liberation serving in France, Belgium and Holland—which was decided by ballot—began on January 1, 1945. To be eligible, soldiers had to have served abroad for six months. Special trains transported them from the disembarkation ports. 1. Improvised time-table at a London terminus. 2. Welcome for B.L.A. men. 3. 14th Army man returns home after three years in Burma.

Photos, Fox Photos ; G.P.U. ; Keystone

principles and invite the electors to return a majority pledged to support a Labour Government to implement that policy." The Liberal Party Assembly, held in London on February 1–3, 1945, reaffirmed that Party's independence and determination to put forward enough candidates at the coming election to give it the possibility of a sufficient number of members to enable it to form a Government without commitments to any other Party.

Addressing the Conservative Party Conference on March 15 for the first time since he became leader of the Party four-and-a-half years before, Mr. Churchill said, "When I became Prime Minister nearly five years ago, I promised nothing but blood, toil, tears and sweat, and on that I received from the House of Commons a vote of confidence of 397 to 0. From the nation I received such aid and trust as no politician in our history has ever enjoyed before. The other day after this long period of terrible events with all their ups and downs, with all their changes and perplexities, that figure of Parliamentary confidence rose to 413 to 0.

Churchill Addresses Conservatives

"But the Parliament is nearly ten years old. It has lived almost double its constitutional span and the Executive Government must refresh itself by direct contact with the electorate. Should the war in Europe end before

the summer ends or even sooner, as it might well do, we shall have reached a considerable milestone on our journey and war conditions will no longer prevent, as they have hitherto prevented, the holding of a General Election. And here I regret to say that the public declarations of our Labour and of some of our Liberal colleagues and of the party organizations which they represent leave us in no doubt that they will feel themselves bound to resume their full liberty of action, and thus bring this famous coalition to an end. We must prepare ourselves for the loss of many loyal and capable fellow-workers in the Administration and the full clash of party principles and party interests inseparable from an appeal to the judgement of the people.

"It will fall to us as the largest party in the existing House of Commons to arrange for a General Election which will be conducted with British fair play, and I trust with a minimum of party and personal rancour, and above all with the least possible injury to the underlying unity of the nation in serving the national cause. Nevertheless we cannot blind ourselves to the fact that the strength of His Majesty's Government which has borne us thus far through the struggle will be seriously weakened. Should we be successful in the election, a very heavy burden will fall upon our shoulders. The gap has to be filled, the

job to be finished ; and I am here to tell you that we must brace ourselves and summon all our energies in order that if, as I believe, the nation places its faith in us, we shall not be found unequal to the gigantic toils that lie ahead."

The policy of the Coalition Government towards Greece was strongly criticized, both inside the House and outside it, and on January 19 Mr. Eden, after a statement in Parliament on the situation in that country, asked for a vote of confidence—accorded by 340 votes to 7. After the Crimea Conference (*see* Chapter 348,) there was a three-day debate on foreign policy in general at the conclusion of which (March 1) Mr. Churchill moved : " That this House approves the declaration of joint policy agreed to by the three great Powers at the Crimea Conference and in particular welcomes their determination to maintain unity of action not only in achieving the final defeat of the common enemy but, thereafter, in peace as in war." That motion secured the vote of 413 to 0 referred to by the Prime Minister in his address to the Conservative Party.

In the first days of January, Mr. Churchill visited France, where he met General Eisenhower, Field-Marshal **Churchill in Athens Again** Montgomery and General de Gaulle. He spent four days at Malta with President Roosevelt before they proceeded to the meeting with Marshal Stalin at Yalta in the Crimea, and at the conclusion of that Conference visited Athens a second time, in the company of Mr. Eden and Field-Marshal Alexander. There he addressed a wildly enthusiastic crowd of 25,000, issuing a stirring call for the unity of all Greeks and the cessation of party strife. Next day (February 15) he received the freedom of the city. He then went to Egypt to discuss the Far Eastern war with President Roosevelt, arriving back in England on February 19.

This was his last meeting with the great American President, who died on April 12. Speaking with emotion, Mr. Churchill said to the House on April 13, " The House will have learned with the deepest sorrow the grievous news which has come from across the Atlantic and conveys to us the loss of the famous President, whose friendship for the cause of freedom and for the causes of the weak and poor has won him immortal renown." On his motion, the House adjourned for the rest of the day. In a personal message to Mrs. Roosevelt, Mr. Churchill declared that he had lost " a dear and cherished friendship forged in the fires of war."

Four days later, moving an address to H.M. the King to convey the deep sorrow with which the House had learned of the death of the President of the United States, Mr. Churchill said that he had exchanged over 1,700 messages with him, had had nine meetings—Argenta, three at Washington, Casablanca, Teheran, two at Quebec, and Yalta—in all about 120 days of close personal contact. " I conceived an admiration for him as a statesman, as a man of affairs, and as a war leader. I felt the utmost confidence in his upright, inspiring character and outlook, and a personal regard—affection, I must say—for him beyond any power to express. His love of his country, his respect for its constitution, his power of gauging the tides and currents of its mobile public opinion—all this was evident, but added to this were the beatings of that generous heart, always stirred to anger and to action by spectacles of aggression and oppression by the strong against the weak. **Premier's Tribute to Roosevelt** It is a loss indeed, a bitter loss, to humanity that those heart-beats are stilled for ever. . . . In Franklin Roosevelt there died the greatest American friend we have ever known, and the greatest champion of freedom who has ever brought help and comfort from the new world to the old."

In the first week of March, Mr. Churchill visited the Western Front, inspecting units of the 1st Canadian Army and the U.S. 9th Army. He also went over parts of the Siegfried Line. His visit was the first occasion a British Prime Minister had set foot in Germany since Mr. Chamberlain went to Munich in 1938, and the first time he himself had been in the Reich since 1931. To the 51st (Highland) Division in Germany, he said, " You are now in the midst of victorious battles. Your struggle in the north has enabled great advances to be made in the south, and soon we shall be across the Rhine. Far away on the other side the gallant Russians are pressing on. Anyone can see that one good

BRITISH MOBILE GUN FOR CROSS-CHANNEL SHELLING

This 18-inch mobile gun, on the Southern Railway in the Dover area, was used to bombard the French coast and shell enemy shipping in the Channel. When not operating it was housed in a disused tunnel. Originally a naval gun, it was radar-controlled, had a range of 25 miles and fired a shell weighing over a ton. The recoil was absorbed by the train attached.

Photo by courtesy of the Southern Railway

David Lloyd George, the great Prime Minister of the 1914–18 war, created an earl in the New Year honours, died on March 26 at the age of 82 without, on account of illness, taking his seat in the House he had so vigorously attacked in his younger days. Admiral Sir Bertram Ramsay, Naval C.-in-C. and architect of the Navy's part in the invasion of Normandy, was killed on January 2 when the plane in which he was travelling to a conference in Belgium crashed after leaving a Paris aerodrome.

Death of David Lloyd George

The " good strong heave all together " took place, and on May 2 the Prime Minister announced that Field-Marshal Alexander had on April 29 received the unconditional surrender of all German forces in Italy at Caserta, to come into effect at 12 noon Greenwich Mean Time on May 2. The number of troops concerned in this surrender was nearly a million. This triumph " brings to a conclusion the work of as gallant an army as ever marched, and brings to a pitch of fame the military reputation of a commander who has always, I may say, enjoyed the fullest confidence of the House of Commons," said Mr. Churchill.

Two days later, Supreme Headquarters Allied Expeditionary Forces issued a special announcement : " Field-Marshal Montgomery has reported to the Supreme Allied Commander that all enemy forces in Holland, North-west Germany, and Denmark, including Heligoland and the Frisian Islands, have

MR. CHURCHILL BROADCASTS— Official announcement of the end of hostilities in Europe was made by Mr. Churchill in a broadcast from 10, Downing Street, at 3 p.m. on May 8, 1945 (see Historic Document CCXCII, page 3506). The speech

SALUTE TO ROYAL FAMILY

In the early afternoon of V.E. day (May 8, 1945), crowds swarmed outside Buckingham Palace, shouting, ' We want the King.' In response to the cheers, Their Majesties, with the Princesses, appeared on the balcony. Later, the Royal party reappeared, this time accompanied by Mr. Churchill (top). The second photograph shows the Queen on a Victory visit to Stepney on May 9.   *Photos, P.N.A. ; L.N.A.*

strong heave all together will end the war in Europe, beat down tyranny, and open the path to peace and the return to the homeland." Mr. Churchill was in Germany again (*see* illus. in page 3502) for the Allied crossing of the Rhine on March 24 (*see* Chapter 357). Next day he too crossed the Rhine to visit Allied troops in the bridge-heads won on the east bank, and, to the intense anxiety of the military commanders, cruised on the river in a *buffalo* well within range of the enemy's artillery.

surrendered to the 21st Army Group, effective at 8 a.m. May 5 (British Double Summer Time). This is a battlefield surrender involving the forces now facing the 21st Army Group on the northern and western flanks." The first British victory salvo of the war (twenty-one salvos from twenty-four guns) was fired at 3 p.m. on May 5 at Field-Marshal Montgomery's headquarters on Lüneburg Heath by the 160th (City of London) Heavy A.A. Regiment. By May 5, the whole of Germany, except for a small area of less than four thousand square miles, was in Allied occupation. The Red Flag flew in Berlin, the Stars and Stripes in Munich and Nuremberg, the Union Jack in Hamburg. War in Europe ended with Germany's unconditional surrender at Rheims to the three major Allies at 2.41 a.m. on May 7 (ratified next day in Berlin at 16 minutes after midnight).

Immediately May 8 was proclaimed V.E. (Victory in Europe) Day, and broadcasts by both H.M. the King and the Prime Minister **Victory in** were announced for **Europe** that momentous occasion of relief and rejoicing to the British people. In his broadcast, Mr. Churchill announced the end of the war in Europe : " Hostilities will end officially at one minute after midnight tonight, Tuesday, May 8. But in the interest of saving lives the ' cease fire ' began yesterday to be sounded all along the front."

—END OF WAR IN EUROPE

was relayed by loud-speaker to crowds in many parts of the country. Below are some of the 60,000 listeners in Trafalgar Square, London. After the broadcast, Mr. Churchill drove through cheering crowds to the House of Commons. *Photo, Planet News*

BONFIRES FOR VICTORY

Bonfires were a feature of Britain's V.E. day celebrations. Here happy crowds dance round one in the East End of London. Youthful villagers of Eynsford, Kent (top), bring in the logs and brushwood for the evening conflagration. In many places fireworks mysteriously appeared, and Hitler effigies were burned, while searchlights combed the skies—but not for enemy planes.
Photos, L.N.A.: Sport & General

Immense crowds gathered in Whitehall, surging round the Prime Minister's open car as, after broadcasting, he left Downing Street to go to the House of Commons. Just before 6 o'clock he came out on to the balcony of the Ministry of Health (*see* illus. in pp. 3520-3521), and to the happy but orderly and disciplined crowd below said in response to the ovation that met him, " This is your victory "—words echoed back from the hearts of the thankful people of Britain to their great war leader.

December 1. U.S. 9th Army captured Wiez; 3rd Army reached the Saar River at three points in the Merzig area. French 1st Army freed Franco-Swiss border. Russians forced the River Ondava (Slovakia), capturing Trebisov. Crete liberated. British occupied Pinwe (Burma).

December 2. U.S. 9th Army troops entered Linnich and Jülich; 3rd Army entered Saarlautern; 7th Army entered Selestat. R.A.F. heavily attacked Hagen (Ruhr). Red Army captured Kaposvar, Dornbovar and Paks (Hungary). E. Africans raided Kalewa (Burma). New Government in Rumania. E.A.M. ministers resigned from Greek Government.

December 3. German sappers breached bank of Rhine S.W. of Arnhem. U.S. 3rd Army freed Sarreunion. Russians captured Miskolcz (Hungary). Saipan-based Super-Fortresses bombed Tokyo.

December 4. British 2nd Army troops cleared W. bank of the Maas; Blerik liberated. U.S.A. 8th A.F. bombed Kassel and Mainz; R.A.F. attacked Oberhausen, Karlsrühe and Heilbronn. Tito's troops (with Russians) freed Mitrovica (Yugoslavia). 8th Army captured Ravenna. Generalissimo Chiang Kai-shek relinquished Presidency of Executive Yuan.

December 5. U.S. 3rd Army cleared Saarlautern; 7th Army occupied Salestat. R.A.F. heavily attacked Soest, Hamm, Ludwigshaven. Red Army reached shores of Lake Balaton. British and Polish troops crossed Lamone River, S. of Faenza.

December 6. U.S. troops broke into Sarreguemines. R.A.F. heavily attacked Osnabrück and Giessen. 8th Army captured Porto Corsini, port of Ravenna; Poles took Monte San Rinaldo and Brighisella. Japanese bombers attacked Saipan (Marianas).

December 7. Red Army captured Barcs on Hungarian-Yugoslav border. R.A.F. raided Vienna. U.S. landing three miles S. of Ormoc, Leyte (Philippines). Sea and air attack on Iwo Jima (Volcanos).

December 8. U.S. 3rd Army entered Dillingen, near Saarlautern. Fort Driant (Metz) surrendered to Americans. Tushan, Kwangsi (China) recaptured by Chinese.

December 9. Allied armies control whole W. bank of Roer River; U.S. 3rd Army smashed counter-attack at Dillingen. Soviet armies cut off Budapest from three sides, captured Vac and Aszod.

December 10. U.S. 7th Army in Alsace broke into Hagenau. U.S.A.A.F. heavily bombed Coblenz and Bingen railyards. R.A.F. bombed E.L.A.S. column approaching Athens. In Central Burma Indaw and Katha taken by British forces. U.S. troops captured Ormoc, last enemy stronghold on Leyte. Signor Bonomi formed new Government (Italy). Formation announced of British Pacific Fleet. Franco-Soviet treaty signed in Moscow.

December 11. U.S. 7th Army liberated Hagenau (Alsace). Some 1,600 U.S.A. 8th A.F. aircraft bombed Frankfort-on-Main, Hamm and Giessen. Red Army forces captured Veresegyhaz (Hungary). Chinese announced Japanese expelled from Kweichow, Kwangsi re-entered.

December 12. U.S. 3rd Army captured Bliesbrück, crossed Blies River (Saar).

U.S.A. 8th A.F. heavily bombed oil plants in Frankfort area; by night R.A.F. attacked Osnabrück.

December 13. U.S. 7th Army captured Selz, near the Reich frontier; Fort Jeanne d'Arc, last resisting Metz fortress, fell to U.S. 3rd Army. In Italy 8th Army forces cleared Mezzano. Saipan-based Super-Fortresses attacked Nagoya (Japan).

December 12-14. Powerful attacks by U.S. carrier-aircraft on airfields and installations on Luzon (Philippines).

December 14. U.S. 9th Army took Vichoven, S.E. of Kirchberg. French 1st Army launched strong counter-attack in Mulhouse area. Chinese troops reached Tonkwa (Burma). In China, Chinese drove enemy from Cheho, near Hochin.

December 15. U.S. 1st Army split last remaining German bridge-head W. of Roer; 7th Army crossed into Reich in Wissembourg area. R.A.F. bombed R-boat pens at Ijmuiden, chemical works at Ludwigshaven. Chinese 38th Division freed Bhamo on the Irrawaddy (Burma) after a month's siege. U.S. troops landed on S.W. coast of Mindoro (Philippines).

December 16. Germans strongly counter-attacked on 50-mile front between Monschau and Trier. U.S. 7th Army captured Wissembourg. New Zealand troops of 8th Army captured Faenza (Italy); 5th Army evacuated Tossignano.

December 16-17. Luftwaffe, supporting German counter-offensive in the Ardennes, attacked in force. R.A.F. heavily bombed Ulm, Munich, Duisburg, Hanau and Muenster.

December 17. Red Army captured Paszto, rail town near Czech border; Soviet Fleet Air Arm attacked enemy shipping in the Baltic. Saipan-based Super-Fortresses bombed Nagoya (Japan); other Super-Fortresses bombed Hankow.

December 18. U.S. 101st Airborne Division surrounded at Bastoyne (Belgium). R.A.F. Lancasters bombed Gdynia. Red Army crossed Hungarian-Czech frontier on 70-mile front.

December 19. U.S.A.A.F. bombers attacked enemy lines from Trier to Monschau. Tito's forces captured Podgoritza (Montenegro), cutting off German escape route in Albania. Gurkhas took Wuntho (Burma). China-based Super-Fortresses bombed Omura (Japan). U.S. forces captured Valencia (Leyte).

December 19-20 (night). Saipan-based Super-Fortresses bombed Tokyo.

December 20. U.S.A. 15th A.F. bombed Pilsen, Linz, Salzburg. S.E.A.C. announced capture of Kunbaung (N. Burma) and Kandaung (Arakan). British carrier-borne aircraft attacked Belawan-Deli and Sabang (Sumatra).

December 21. Germans by-passed Bastogne and reached St. Hubert. U.S. 3rd Army captured Dillingen (Saar). Red Army liberated Rimaszombat; launched full-scale attack between Lake Balaton and the Danube. Canadians of the 8th Army captured Bagnacavallo (Italy). Super-Fortresses bombed Mukden (Manchuria).

December 22. S.H.A.E.F. announced enemy penetration 40 miles into Belgium; General Eisenhower issued Order

of the Day to A.E.F. "to destroy the enemy on the ground, in the air, everywhere." Saipan-based Super-Fortresses again bombed Nagoya.

December 23. Flying over 7,000 sorties, R.A.F. and U.S.A.A.F. destroyed 84 enemy aircraft in German counter-offensive area; by night R.A.F. bombed Bonn and Coblenz. In Burma British troops took Tigyiang island.

December 24. Major Allied air attacks in St. Vith area; by night R.A.F. attacked Cologne and Bonn. Red Army cut off German and Hungarian retreat route from Budapest to the west; captured Szekesfeharvar and Bicske. Canadians seized Rosetta on Senio River (Italy). Super-Fortresses heavily bombed Iwo Jima.

December 24-25 (night). German spearheads penetrated 59 miles into Belgium.

December 24-26. On Luzon (Philippines) 144 Japanese aircraft destroyed in attacks by U.S. Liberators.

December 25. French 1st Army re-entered Bennweiler, N. of Colmar. Allied air forces again attacked St. Vith and Bastogne areas in strength. U.S.A.A.F. bombed Manila airfield, destroying 72 enemy fighters. Mr. Churchill and Mr. Eden arrived in Athens.

December 26. Luftwaffe raided Paris by night. 3rd Ukrainian Army reached Danube, captured Esztergom and completed encirclement of Budapest. Germans launched counter-attack in Serchio Valley (Italy). British troops occupied Donbaik (Arakan). Iwo Jima bombed and bombarded by U.S. forces. All-Party Conference opened in Athens.

December 27. U.S. 3rd Army relieved Bastogne. Red Army forced E. arm of the Danube, capturing Szentendre. Enemy retook Barga, on the Serchio River (Italy). Saipan-based Super-Fortresses bombed Tokyo by day.

December 27-28 (night). R.A.F. bombed Bonn and München-Gladbach.

December 28. Grandménil (Ardennes) recaptured by Allies. Soviet forces in outskirts of Budapest; Szecseny captured. In Italy U.S. forces evacuated Gallicano. Allied troops reached Foul Point (Arakan). Mr. Churchill and Mr. Eden left Athens.

December 29. Allies strongly counter-attacked towards Rochefort and between St. Hubert and Bastogne. Heavy R.A.F. and U.S.A.A.F. attacks on Frankfort, Bingen and Aschaffenburg. 5th Army troops reoccupied Barga (Italy). Enemy resistance on Mindoro (Philippines) ceased. U.S.A.A.F. bombed Iwo Jima.

December 30. Rochefort (Ardennes) recaptured; fresh Allied attack between St. Hubert and Bastogne. Japanese suffered heavy naval losses in Limgayen Gulf, Luzon (Philippines).

December 31. R.A.F. bombed Gestapo H.Q. in Oslo. Heavy R.A.F. and U.S.A.A.F. attacks on enemy troop concentrations at Houffalize (Ardennes). U.S.A.A.F. attacked Luzon. Archbishop Damaskinos appointed Regent of Greece. Polish Committee of National Liberation in Lublin assumed title of "Provisional Government" of Poland.

Chapter 344

INDIA FREED FROM THE JAPANESE MENACE

The end of the war in the Far East left British authorities and Indian parties alike free once more to take up without reserve consideration of India's future, and this chapter is mainly concerned with efforts made by Lord Wavell, the Viceroy, during the year 1945 to enlist the co-operation of politicians of all opinions in a new attempt to reach a solution of the constitutional problem. India's history in 1944 is described in Chapter 298

THE unexpected swiftness of Japan's collapse after Germany's unconditional surrender — victory over Japan was celebrated on August 15, little more than three months after Germany's surrender—quickened the pace of political and administrative developments in India during the year 1945. The Government of Lord Wavell had a heavy burden. When the year opened it had still to provide for the due contribution of Indian effort in the final stages of the war in the west. It had to expect a far-flung extension of the hostilities against Japan for which India was an important base. The strain of over five years' war on India's economy was matched by that on her administrative machine. The civil services and industrial life of the country were acutely feeling the pressure. The sharp cleavage between the two chief political parties, and between them and the Government, added to this pressure. Lord Wavell had given a clear lead in directing attention to the problems of post-war reconstruction. He was vigilant in encouragement of any attempt to solve the political deadlock so as to harness all the best minds of India in a common advance to economic and political security. Provincial Governments—whether Ministerial or bureaucratic—were stimulated to plan for the future.

Government Post-War Plans

The Government of India's own programme covered a wide field of educational, rural, public health, housing, town planning and labour activities at an estimated cost of £750 millions in the first five-year period after peace had come. An " Economic Brains Trust " was set up by Sir Ardeshir Dalal, Planning and Development Member of the Viceroy's Council, to be composed of a Consultative Committee of Scientists. Panels of experts were formed to advise the Government on the development of industries. Indian industrialists were encouraged to visit the United Kingdom, the United States of America, and Australia.

INDIA AND VICTORY IN EUROPE

To celebrate the Allied victory over Germany in Europe, this impressive memorial to George V, Emperor of India, and also public buildings at New Delhi were floodlit. The Indian Army made an outstanding contribution to the Allied war effort both in Burma and in the west. In Tunisia, the 4th Indian Division—the renowned ' Red Eagles '—helped to pierce the Mareth Line and took part in the final break-through to Bizerta. In Italy, at Cassino, against the Gothic Line and elsewhere, Indian units fought magnificently.   *Photo, Topical Press*

Lord Wavell was profoundly impressed by the need for a further effort to clear the political air. The rapid progress of the Allied campaign in Europe toward what was seen to be the inevitable end and the brilliant advance of General Slim's army in Burma had naturally brought more firmly into the picture discussion of India's post-war status. The Government of India was manfully shouldering a colossal responsibility with a public support that vindicated its leadership but did not really remedy its lack of what might be called truly political sanction. It was a Government of public-spirited men under a soldier-statesman to whom was denied the co-operation of the accepted political leaders of the country.

With some leaders Lord Wavell, during the eighteen months which had elapsed since his assumption of

Viceroy's Visit to London

office, had managed to keep in touch, albeit informally. The declared policy of the British Government still rested on the Cripps proposals, the development of which required Indian political endorsement, still withheld because of the inability of the two chief parties—the Congress Party and the Muslim League—to reconcile their differences. The Viceroy, on March 23, arrived in London by air to confer with Mr. Winston Churchill's Government. The inspiration of this journey was well crystallized by a " Punch " cartoon which depicted Lord Wavell, watch in hand, standing over a game of chess between Mr. M. K. Gandhi and Mr. M. A. Jinnah, whose postures elicited the caption " Time for a Move."

The visit was prolonged by the home Government's pre-occupation with direction of the concluding stages of the war against Germany. Lord Wavell returned to India just at the moment when the Coalition Government was breaking up and giving place to the interim " Caretaker " Government. He had been able, nevertheless, to secure the outgoing Government's support for a new effort to canvass Indian political co-operation. Shortly after his return,

BENGAL'S GOVERNOR

Mr. Frederick Burrows was appointed on November 6, 1945, to succeed Mr. R. G. Casey as Governor-General of Bengal. Knighted on his appointment, the new Governor had been a railway porter at Ross-on-Wye when, in 1942, he was elected President of the National Union of Railwaymen. *Photo, Topical Press*

of the representation in the Council, the remaining 20 per cent being reserved for the minority parties. The Councillors (with the exception of the Viceroy and the Commander-in-Chief) would be all Indians. Readiness to prosecute the war against Japan with all available resources was an essential condition of the proposals.

This offer constituted an important advance in that, although the Viceroy was to retain his personal control of dealings with the Indian States, the portfolio of Foreign (External) Affairs would pass to Indian hands and India would have her own representatives in foreign countries (in extension of the interchange of diplomats with the U.S.A. and China begun in 1940). It was also decided to appoint a United Kingdom High Commissioner for India to represent British interests and thus to relieve the Viceroy of the embarrassment of having to continue to represent those interests while being primarily concerned with Indian interests as head of the Government of India.

The Viceroy announced on June 14 that a conference would open at Simla on the 25th, to which leaders of the groups in the Central Legislature and leaders of the political parties, as well as premiers and ex-premiers of the Provinces, would be invited; and that Congress Party leaders still in detention (who included Pandit Jawaharlal Nehru and Dr. Maulana Azad) were to be released immediately.

Mr. Gandhi accepted the invitation but emphasized that he was not an

official representative of the Congress Party, that function belonging to Dr. Azad, the Congress President, or someone appointed by him. In opening the conference, Lord Wavell asked for help in a spirit of broad co-operation towards the good of India as a whole. He disclaimed any attempt at a final settlement of India's problems. He sought a temporary agreement for the purpose of paving the way towards a settlement. The various parties were invited to submit panels of names from which the Viceroy could make a suitable selection for his expanded Council.

The atmosphere at the outset seemed favourable, but the discussions broke

GOVERNOR OF MADRAS

In succession to Sir Arthur Hope, Lt.-General Sir Archibald Edward Nye, K.B.E., C.B., M.C., Vice-Chief of the Imperial General Staff, was appointed on November 28, 1945, Governor of Madras. Director of Staff Duties in 1940, he had enlisted in the ranks on the outbreak of the First Great War. He was born in 1895. *Photo, Topical*

down owing to the inability of the Muslim League, through Mr. Jinnah, to secure the sole right to recommend Mahomedan names for the panels. Full responsibility for the breakdown was accepted by Lord Wavell. Nevertheless it was hoped that the discussions had improved the political situation and cleared the way for the removal of misunderstandings at a later date.

Certainly Lord Wavell's action in releasing the Congress Party leaders had removed one obstacle to the restoration of the currents of political life. But acerbity did not diminish.

The Viceroy, announcing the end of the war in the Far East in a broadcast from New Delhi, said : " Japan was a close and deadly menace to India, and

an official announcement was made on June 14, outlining the Government's proposals. Generally they followed the lines of the Cripps plan, but, in providing for the reconstruction of the Viceroy's Executive Council in the transitional period, they gave the Muslims and Hindus each 40 per cent

LORD WAVELL'S EFFORTS FOR INDIAN PEACE

In India the year 1945 was remarkable for the efforts of the Viceroy, Lord Wavell, to achieve agreement with and between Congress and Muslim leaders. In late August he came to London for the second time in 1945, for talks with the new Secretary of State, Lord Pethick-Lawrence. He is here seen (left) with the Secretary of State and the High Commissioner for India in London, Sir Samuel Runganadham (centre). *Photo, Topical Press*

PLYMOUTH CELEBRATES VICTORY AMONG HER RUINS

A section of Plymouth's Victory Parade passes the burnt-out Guildhall (right) : it included contingents of the
women's Red Cross and the U.S. Navy. Plymouth was one of the most heavily attacked of British towns. Raids
began towards the end of 1940—that on the night of November 27, when almost the entire centre of the town was
destroyed, being particularly fierce. Thousands of homes were wiped out in the raids, as well as shops, hospitals,
churches, schools and public buildings. Neighbouring Devonport was another frequent target for the Luftwaffe.

3 x ³

NO GREATER DAY THAN THIS

At six p.m. on V.E. day (May 8, 1945) the Prime Minister appeared on the balcony of the Ministry of Health in Whitehall. 'This is your Victory,' he told the crowds, 'Victory in the cause of freedom in every land. In all our long history we have never seen a greater day than this. Everyone has done their bit. Everyone has tried. Neither the long years, nor the dangers, nor the fierce attacks of the enemy, have in any way weakened the resolve of the British nation. God bless you all.'

BRITISH 36th DIVISION DRIVES ALONG THE RAILWAY 'CORRIDOR' IN BURMA

Thrusting southwards along the Mogaung–Mandalay railway 'corridor' towards Katha on the Irrawaddy in October and November 1944, the British 36th Division, under Major-General F. W. Festing, D.S.O., encountered much local resistance; anti-personnel mines were also freely sown. On November 2 the Division captured Mawlu, 16 miles north of Naba junction where the line to Katha branches off; and on December 1, led by the Royal Scots, occupied Pinwe, which the enemy evacuated only after prolonged and stubborn resistance. Here, men and supplies of the 36th Division move into Pinwe station shortly after its capture. (See map in page 3536.)

Photo, S.E.A.C. Official

INDIAN WOMEN
GO TO WAR

Over 10,000 Indian women were in uniform as members of the Women's Auxiliary Corps (India) and the Women's Royal Indian Naval Service. Dressed in flowing saris and regulation tunics, these N.C.O.'s of the W.A.C.(I.) were inspected by the Countess of Carlisle, Chief Commander of the Corps, at a ceremonial parade in Delhi in February 1945. Left, a Second Officer of the W.R.I.N.S.

Photos, Indian Official; Associated Press

her defeat is in a special sense India's victory." Immediately after Japan's defeat it was decided to hold general elections for the Central Legislative Assembly in the autumn and—so as to give time for the preparation of revised registers—for the Provincial Legislatures in the spring of 1946.

Lord Wavell paid another and shorter visit to London at the end of August to confer with the new Secretary of State (Lord Pethick-Lawrence). Back **Viceroy on British Policy** in India again, he broadcast on September 19 reaffirmation of the Government's intentions to convene a constitution-making body as soon as possible. He had been authorized, when the general elections were over, to ascertain from the representatives in the Legislatures whether the Cripps Proposals were acceptable or whether some alternative or modified scheme was preferable. In the meantime, when all the elections were completed he was to bring into being an Executive Council which would have the support of the main Indian parties. He intimated that he intended to act on these lines by holding in due course the appropriate discussions with the elected representatives in the provinces of British India and with the representatives of the Indian States, for the purpose of determining the form, powers and procedure of the proposed constitution-making body. Mr. Attlee in a broadcast to the British people at the same time confirmed this policy.

The election campaign for the new Legislative Assembly at Delhi was viewed by the two chief parties as a dress rehearsal for the later provincial elections. The electorate, based on the pre-1935 Constitution (because the plan for Federation had not materialized) comprised about 1½ million voters, whereas the total of the eleven provincial electorates based on the 1935 Constitution was well over 30 million voters. Yet it was considered that the results of the central elections would give a fairly accurate pointer to probabilities in the provinces.

The Congress Party maintained that it

was national in its appeal. Certainly its first aim when it was founded in 1885 by Mr. Allan O. Hume, a retired Indian Civil Servant, was " the fusion into one national whole of all the different and discordant elements that constitute the population of India." But the Muslim League, founded in 1906, claimed the sole right to represent the 90,000,000 Mahomedans of India. Mr. Jinnah indicated that his success at the

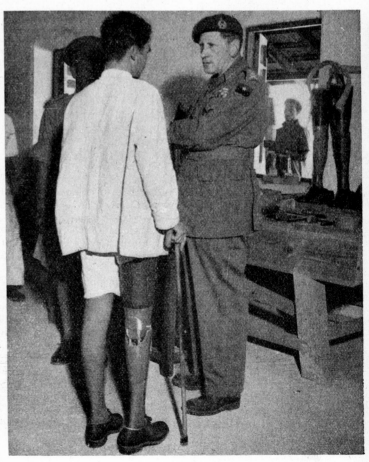

C.-IN-C. WITH THE DISABLED

General Sir Claude John Eyre Auchinleck, G.C.I.E., C.B., C.S.I., D.S.O., after being C.-in-C., Middle East, was appointed C.-in-C., India, on June 18, 1943, when the land, air and sea forces under his command totalled over 2,000,000. He is seen here visiting a depot where disabled Indian ex-servicemen were fitted with artificial limbs.

Photo, Illustrated

KARACHI WAS R.A.F. FLYING-BOAT BASE

The R.A.F. flying-boat base at Korangi Creek, Karachi, was one of the largest in India. An important maintenance base, it was from here that R.A.F. Catalinas and Sunderlands arriving from Britain were 'routed' on to their forward destinations. These flying-boats played a many-sided war rôle—from cruising on anti-submarine patrol and bombing enemy targets to ferrying wounded and exterminating locusts. *Photo, British Official*

polls would confirm him in the determination to demand a separate Mahomedan state (" Pakistan "), and consequently a separate constitution-making body so as to relieve the bulk of Indian Mahomedans from the fear of Hindu domination. The elections gave sweeping victories to the Congress Party in non-Muslim, and to the Muslim League in Muslim constituencies—a result which appeared to prove the contentions that the League represented the majority of Muslims, and the Congress Party was in essence a Hindu organization. Whether this result in the limited field of the Central Assembly electorate would be reflected in the provincial elections of 1946 remained to be seen.

Political passions aroused by the election campaign—Pandit Jawaharlal Nehru and other Congress Party leaders were bitter in their attacks on British policy—were further stirred by controversy over Allied policy in Indonesia and by a furious press and platform agitation in favour of the officers and

men of the Japanese-sponsored " Indian National Army " which had fought against the Allies in Burma. The Government exercised a generous clemency toward the large majority of the 20,000 who out of a total of 65,000 Indian Army officers and men taken prisoner by the Japanese went over to the enemy. (Total Indian casualties from September 3, 1939 to August 14, 1945 were 179,935, of whom 24,338 were killed, 11,754 missing, 64,354 wounded, 79,489 prisoners—the last figure including 20,147 missing but presumed prisoners of war.) Some 2,500 were exonerated altogether as they had joined the Japanese with the object of getting back to the British lines as soon as possible, or of assisting the Allies from behind the enemy front. Of the remainder most were sent back to their villages with only the loss of their military status and rights of pension. Fewer than 50 in all were sent for trial. Three of these—former officers of the Indian Army—were tried by court martial at

Delhi. Round this trial popular excitement raged. Demonstrations were staged in many cities, and in Calcutta serious disturbances occurred. In the event the sentences on the three officers were remitted. This act of exceptional grace did not prevent the exploitation of these men as " national heroes."

Lord Wavell felt impelled at Calcutta on December 10 (*see* Historic Document 295, page 3529) to remind India that of the 45,000 officers and men of the Indian Army who as Japan's prisoners of war " under pressure and punishment, under hardships and want stood firm to their ideals of a soldier's duty," 11,000 of them had died in captivity from diseases and murder, whereas of the 20,000 who went over to the enemy only 1,500 lost their lives. The Viceroy added, " Whatever your political views, if you cannot acclaim a man who prefers his honour to his ease, who remains steadfast in adversity to his pledged faith, then you have a poor notion of the character which is required to build up a nation."

Lord Wavell's rebuke was timely. In electioneering speeches Pandit Jawaharlal Nehru had even gone to the lengths of applauding the Japanese-

Viceroy on ' Indian National Army'

MORE HEROES OF THE INDIAN ARMY WIN THE VICTORIA CROSS

Jem. RAM SARUP SINGH
(1st Punjab Regiment)

In Burma, in October 1944, troops of the 1st Punjab Regiment were ordered to attack a heavily-guarded enemy hill-fortress. The jemadar, though wounded, led the charge, during which he was killed. 'It would be difficult to find a finer example of cool bravery, cheerfulness, leadership and determination,' ran the citation.

BHANBHAGTA GURUNG
(2nd Gurkha Rifles)

Under deadly fire, a company of the 2nd King Edward VII's Own Gurkha Rifles was ordered to attack an enemy hill-position on 'Snowden East' in Burma, in March 1945. This rifleman five times advanced single-handed, clearing enemy foxholes and killing Japanese with his kukri. His action was 'decisive in capturing the objective.'

Havildar UMRAO SINGH
(Indian Artillery)

The havildar was in charge of a gun in an advanced section of his battery in the Kaladan Valley, Burma, in December 1944, when it came under heavy fire. Though badly wounded and with all his detachment except himself and two others either killed or wounded, he beat off four violent counter-attacks.

Naik GIAN SINGH
(15th Punjab Regiment)

On the Kamye-Myingyan Road, Burma, in March 1945, the naik was in command of a leading section ordered to dislodge the enemy from a strong position. Displaying 'magnificent gallantry,' he advanced alone, clearing fox-holes, killing Japanese and capturing an anti-tank gun single-handed. 'His leadership could not have been surpassed.'

Jemadar ABDUL HAFIZ
(9th Jat Regiment)

'The inspiring leadership and great bravery' shown by this soldier near Imphal, Burma, in April 1944, 'would be difficult to equal,' ran the citation. Though twice wounded (once mortally), he so encouraged his men that a vital position was captured and casualties inflicted on an enemy force several times stronger than his own.

Sepoy ALI HAIDAR
(13th Frontier Force Rifles)

During the crossing by the sepoy's section of the River Senio, near Fusignano (Italy) in April 1945, only three men managed to get across. Thanks to his single-handed silencing of two enemy posts—during which he was severely wounded—the rest of the company charged across the river and established a bridge-head preparatory to the building of a bridge.

Rifleman LACHHIMAN GURUNG *(8th Gurkha Rifles)*

Lord Wavell, the Viceroy, decorating Lachhiman Gurung with the V.C. he won in May 1945 while bravely fighting at Taungdaw, Burma. By his 'magnificent example,' he so inspired his comrades that, although surrounded and cut off for three days and nights, they smashed every attack.

Sepoy NAMDEO JADHAO
(5th Mahratta Light Infantry)

In Italy, in April 1945, this sepoy, fighting on the River Senio, not only saved the lives of his comrades, but his 'outstanding and personal bravery' enabled them to hold the river banks firmly and, eventually, the Battalion to secure a deeper bridge-head which led to the collapse of all German resistance in the area.

Co.Hav.-Maj. CHHELU RAM
(6th Rajputana Rifles)

This outstandingly brave N.C.O. was mortally wounded during an attack on the Djebel Garci feature in Tunisia in April 1943. In fierce hand-to-hand fighting he showed 'utter contempt for danger' and inspired his men to hold vital ground until he himself fell unconscious from his wounds.

Lt. KARAMJEET SINGH
(15th Punjab Regiment)

In an attack on the outskirts of Myingyan, Burma, during March 1945, this young officer 'dominated the entire battlefield by his numerous and successive acts of superb gallantry,' eliminating ten enemy bunkers. He was mortally wounded while mopping up a last enemy strongpoint as the battle finished.

Jemadar PARKASH SINGH
(13th Frontier Force Rifles)

In command of a platoon at Kanlan Ywathit, Burma, in February 1945, the jemadar died from his wounds while inspiring his men to withstand fierce counterattacks. Although suffering intense pain and unable to walk, he crawled among his wounded comrades, directing and encouraging them.

Sepoy BHANDARI RAM
(10th Baluch Regiment)

At East Mayu, Arakan, in November 1944, this young sepoy 'by his outstanding gallantry, determination to destroy the enemy at all cost, and entire disregard for his personal safety' in scaling a precipitous slope under fire, enabled his platoon to capture what he knew to be the key to the enemy position.

Rfm. THAMAN GURUNG
(5th Royal Gurkha Rifles)

It was due to this Indian rifleman's 'superb gallantry' and sacrifice of his life that his platoon was able to withdraw from an extremely difficult position at Monte San Bartolo (Italy) in November 1944 without many more casualties than it incurred. Information obtained led to the mountain's capture.

THE SIMLA CONFERENCE

Lord Wavell called a conference of Indian leaders to form a new Executive Council 'more representative of organized public opinion,' which opened at Simla on June 25, 1945, but broke down on July 14. 1. Left to right, Master Tara Singh, representative of the Sikhs; the Hon. Malik Khizar Hayat Khan Tiwana, Premier of the Punjab; Mr. M. A. Jinnah, President of the Muslim League; and the Hon. Imam Hussain, Muslim League Leader in the Council of State. 2. Pandit Jawaharlal Nehru goes to the talks on horseback. 3. Lord Wavell and Dr. Azad, President of the Congress Party. 4. Arrival of Mr Gandhi.

sponsored I.N.A. under Subhas Chandra Bose and had dismayed his own champions in Great Britain by claiming for himself the credit of helping to organize the disturbances of August 1942 which, but for the firmness of the authorities, might have gravely dislocated the lines of communication of the forces defending India against the Japanese advance. (Bose died on August 19 following an air crash on Formosa while he was on his way from Singapore to Tokyo.)

In this atmosphere a special delegation from both Houses of Parliament not charged to make any official enquiry, but designed to establish informal contacts with political personalities, left London on January 2, 1946, for a short visit to India. (*See* also Historic Document 294, page 3529.)

Against this political background the general direction of India's fortunes by the Government in 1945 must be considered. Lord Wavell's **Industrial Policy** anxiety to put his Executive Council on a less restricted basis was justified by the difficulties which it encountered increasingly in making its influence felt. Sir Ardeshir Dalal, whose appointment as Planning and Development Member had given satisfaction, and who had paid a brief visit to Great Britain in the course of the year, found it necessary for personal reasons to tender his resignation on January 10, 1946. Before he left India he had expounded the Government of India's industrial development policy in forthright terms and had gone far to meet the views of at least some members of the Opposition regarding the measures necessary to encourage Indian industrial enterprise. In London he declared that this policy was not framed with any intention of treating British industry unfairly. Rather was it hoped to arrive at a settlement which would lead to enduring permanent relationships based on goodwill and co-operation. This declaration was reaffirmed by the Viceroy toward the end of the year in his expression of the belief that " co-operation between British and Indian enterprise in an atmosphere of goodwill provided the best means for the industrial development of India in the quickest and most fruitful manner."

The transition from war to peace presented problems which the Government tackled alertly. The economic strain of the war was aggravated by anxiety over the food supply. Serious crop failures in early 1946, owing to cyclone and drought damage, led to considerable uneasiness for the future, and the probability that the machinery

which the Bengal Famine of 1943 brought into action would be tested to the utmost.

Sir John Woodhead's Famine Inquiry Commission completed and issued its final report, which was regarded as a classic contribution to the study of the food problem and attracted attention, not only in India, for much of its material was described by experts in U.N.R.R.A. as most valuable for general guidance.

Demobilization of the armed forces of India—totalling some 2,500,000—was expected to come into operation rapidly after the defeat of Japan. In addition to these troops the Army had employed eight million workers in auxiliary jobs, five million had been working in the munitions factories—double the number engaged in factory labour in peace time. Railway staffs had increased from three-quarters of a million to one million men. Expectation was that, before many months of 1946 had passed, something like 10 million of the civil population who had earned high wages during the war might be unemployed unless there was a quick transition to production for peace-time needs.

The magnitude of the problem can be realized when it is explained that, as a result of the war, the total expenditure of British India for all purposes, Central and Provincial, rose from £150 million to £900 million. Although a good deal of the latter figure was borne by the British Exchequer, a huge gap remained to be filled from Indian resources if the level of spending in the country was to

be maintained and prices were not to experience a catastrophic fall.

Indians looked to the sterling balances of something like £1,200 million to help bridge the gap, but a large proportion of these balances could not be made immediately available. The Government had also **Lack of Skilled Staff** to bear in mind the question of the employment of the demobilized soldier on return to his own village. The Provincial Government mainly concerned was that of the Punjab, which drew up a reconstruction programme at an estimated cost of £75 millions sterling. A major difficulty in all these plans for reconstruction was the paucity of skilled staff both in the administration and in industry generally. The wave of economic nationalism sweeping over the East did little to facilitate solution of this aspect of the problem.

The decision to hold a general election in 1946 showed that the Government hoped to see in that year a complete return in the Provinces to parliamentary government. When 1945 ended, ministerial functions were still in the hands of the respective Governors under the emergency section of the Constitution in the following Provinces: Bombay, Bengal, Bihar, Central Provinces, Madras, Orissa, United Provinces. In Assam, North-West Frontier Province, Punjab, Sind, ministerial governments were in charge. The Bengal Ministry fell during the year and Mr. R. G. Casey took over charge of the Administration. Under his governorship

INDIA HAD MILLIONS OF WAR WORKERS

Apart from 2,500,000 in the Forces, there were during the Second Great War 8,000,000 Indians in auxiliary Army jobs and 5,000,000 in munitions. Indian workmen are here inspecting auxiliary petrol tanks at a Bangalore factory. Used by India- and China-based aircraft, these tanks could be dropped from the air when emptied and vastly increased the aircraft's range.

the much-needed overhaul of the administrative machinery (on which a Committee under the chairmanship of Sir Archibald Rowlands had submitted a comprehensive report) was pressed forward. Mr. Casey publicly disclosed that he had been appalled by the " haphazard and unco-ordinated system of administration " that had grown up in Bengal " with consequent wastefulness and inefficiency." The Rowlands Report underlined this opinion in no uncertain terms.

Mr. Casey had accepted the Governorship of Bengal as a wartime obligation. It was recognized when he came to
Mr. Casey Goes Home England during the summer after the defeat of Japan that he would want to be relieved to return home to Australia. His successor (announced on November 6) was Mr. Frederick John Burrows, a former President of the National Union of Railwaymen, made a knight on his appointment.

The Governor of Madras, Sir Arthur Hope, was due to retire in March 1946, and Lieutenant-General Sir Archibald Nye, Vice-Chief of the Imperial General Staff, was appointed to succeed him (announced November 28,

MAHATMA GANDHI 'TALKS' WITH MR. CASEY

In December 1945 Mr. Richard G. Casey, Governor of Bengal, had a series of talks with Mr. Gandhi. The third was held on a Monday, which is Mr. Gandhi's self-imposed weekly day of silence, when he answered Mr Casey's oral questions in writing. He here hands a reply to the Bengal Governor as they sat in the latter's study at Government House, Calcutta.
Photo, Sport & General

1945). Sir Archibald Rowlands became Finance Member (Minister) of the Viceroy's Executive Council in succession to Sir Jeremy Raisman, whose able handling of India's war finances received tributes from all parties at the time of his presentation of the 1945–46 (his last) Budget. The retirement of the Metropolitan of India, Dr. Foss Westcott, marked the end of a long and distinguished charge during which the Church of India had become autonomous. His successor, Dr. George C. Hubback, was enthroned in Calcutta Cathedral in October. Impending changes in Provincial governorships were provided for during the year by the appointment of Sir Francis Wylie, Sir Olaf Caroe, Sir Hugh Dow, Sir Francis Mudie, Sir Evan Jenkins (Lord Wavell's Private Secretary) and Sir Chandulal Trivedi to succeed Sir Maurice Hallett (United Provinces), Sir George Cunningham (North-West Frontier), Sir Thomas Rutherford (Bihar), Sir Hugh Dow (Sind), Sir Bertrand Glancy (Punjab) and Sir Hawthorne Lewis (Orissa) respectively. Sir Chandulal is the first Indian officer of the Indian Civil Service to become a Governor, but not the first Indian to hold that position—a distinction which fell to the late Lord Sinha who became Governor of Bihar and Orissa in 1920. During Lord Wavell's two absences in England, Sir John Colville, Governor of Bombay, acted as Viceroy and Governor-General.

Plans for the complete Indianization of the Indian Army (that is to say,

the eventual elimination of British officers) were announced by General Sir Claude Auchinleck, C.-in-C. India, on October 22, as a result of the deliberations of a committee appointed on November 26, 1944, headed by Lieutenant-General H. B. Willcox (G.O.C., Indian Southern Command). Permanent commissions in the Indian Army were in future to be given only to Indians or other persons domiciled in India who were British subjects or subjects of an Indian Prince—a restriction already applicable to the R.I.A.F.

The total number of British officers in the Indian Army at the outbreak of war was about 3,000, some 1,600 of whom had permanent commissions. The **Indianization** total number of casual- **of the Army** ties by retirement and death, whether in action or on service, was about 1,600. It was recognized that for some time the Indian Army would require the services of British officers, in addition to those whose permanent commissions would eventually be completed by fluxion of time, and the proposal was that officers from the British Services should be seconded to Indian regiments for certain periods.

In recognition of its distinguished services in the war, the Indian Air Force, in March, was permitted to use the prefix Royal ; and in October the Indian Artillery—seven regiments strong in 1939, 61 in 1945—was renamed the Royal Regiment of Indian Artillery.

CALCUTTA OUTBREAK

As a protest against the trial of officers of the Japanese sponsored 'Indian National Army,' riots broke out in Calcutta on November 22, 1945. Eleven Indians were killed and 125 injured. Police casualties totalled 40 injured. Supporting a general transport strike, these Indian boys and men held up the trains by squatting on the track.
Photo, Associated Press

Historic Documents.   CCXCIV—CCXCV

BRITAIN OFFERS INDEPENDENCE TO INDIA

On Sunday, March 24, 1946, three British Cabinet Ministers arrived in Delhi with power to negotiate an agreement for the handing over to Indians of the government of India.   Here are the chief points from the Prime Minister's speech explaining their mission.   Extracts from an important speech by the Viceroy are also given

Speech made by the Prime Minister, Mr. Clement Attlee, in the House of Commons on March 16, 1946 :

THIS is a critical stage in the relationships between the two countries [Great Britain and India], a time of high tension. . . . Every one in the House realizes the difficulty of the task which the Cabinet Ministers have undertaken in conjunction with the Viceroy, and every one will desire to say nothing that will make that task more difficult. . . .

The mission are going out in a positive mood.   It is a time emphatically for very definite and clear action. . . . Nothing increases the pace of the movement of public opinion so much as a great war.   I am certain that at the present time the tide of nationalism is running very fast in India, and indeed all over Asia.   India is affected by what happens elsewhere in Asia.   Today we find that Hindu, Muslim, Sikh, Mahratta, politicians—among all of them the conception of nationality has been growing stronger and stronger. Today that national idea has spread right through, and not least perhaps among some of those soldiers who have done such wonderful service in the war.   Whatever the difficulties may be, there is this underlying demand among the Indian people. . . .

The obvious reason for sending out the Cabinet Ministers is to send out persons of responsibility who are able to take decisions. . . . Twice in 25 years India has played a great part in the defeat of tyranny.   Is it any wonder that today she claims, a nation of 400,000,000 people that has twice sent her sons to die for freedom, that she should herself have freedom to decide her destiny ?   My colleagues are going to India with the intention of using their utmost endeavours to help her to attain that freedom as speedily as possible.

What form of government is to replace the present regime is for India to decide.   Our desire is to help her to set up forthwith the machinery for making that decision.   There you are sometimes met with the initial difficulty of getting that machinery set up.   We are resolved it shall be set up, and we seek the utmost co-operation of all Indian leaders to do so.   India herself must choose what shall be her future Constitution, and what will be her position in the world.

I hope that the Indian people may elect to remain within the British Commonwealth.   I am certain that she will find great advantages in doing so, that in these days demands for complete isolated nationhood apart from the rest of the world are out-dated.   Unity may come through the United Nations or the Commonwealth, but no great nation can stand alone. . . . If she does so elect, it must be by her own free will. The Commonwealth and Empire is not bound together by external compulsion.   It is a free association of free peoples. If she elects for independence, in our view she has a right to do so, and it will be for us to help to make the transition as smooth and easy as possible.

We believe that the British have done a great work in India.   We have united India and given her that sense of nationality she had lacked over the previous centuries.   She has learned from us the principles of democracy and justice. When Indians attack our own rule, they base their attack not on Indian principles but on the basis of standards derived from Britain.

I am well aware that I am speaking of a country containing a congeries of races, religions, and languages, and I know well all the difficulties thereby created.   They can be overcome only by Indians.   We are very mindful of the rights of minorities, and minorities should be able to live free from fear.   But we cannot allow a minority to place a veto on the advance of the majority.   We cannot dictate how these difficulties will be overcome.   Our duty is to get the machinery of decision set up, and that is the main purpose of my right honourable friends and the Viceroy.

Speech by Lord Wavell to the Associated Chambers of Commerce of India at Calcutta, December 10, 1945.

SINCE I spoke here a year ago, our enemies have collapsed ; have collapsed more suddenly and completely than anyone could have expected. . . . The sudden ending of the war found India unprepared for peace.   But that is not to say that there had been lack of foresight.   Preparations to meet the outbreak of peace had been going on for more than a year ; but it is much easier to prepare for war during a peace than to prepare for peace during a war. . . .

Wartime controls do not arise from the actual fighting, but from causes which continue to operate long after the fighting ends, and cannot immediately be eliminated. . . . Controls will have to be relaxed   ·   in an orderly way.

It is alleged against controls that they cause black-marketing and corruption. . . . But it is shortages that cause the corruption not the controls.   Wherever there is shortage, the anti-social greedy man flourishes in his black market or languishes in gaol, in proportion to the lack or existence of public honesty and public spirit. . . .

Short-term planning . . . includes the training of Service men and women for civil life ; the establishment of Employment Bureaux all over the country :   the resettlement of soldiers ;   and the preparation in all Provinces of works projects on which unskilled labour can be absorbed. . . . Our long-term planning is based on the parallel development of agriculture and industry. . . . There is not now a great deal of new land that can easily be made fertile ; but the yield of the land already under cultivation can be greatly increased by improved methods and improved seeds. . . .

For industrial development, we have available abundant raw material, labour and enterprise.   Our chief need is power, of two kinds—hydro-electric power to run the machinery and skilled manpower to direct it.   A number of important hydro-electric schemes have been planned and will soon be taken in hand. . . . We are doing all we can to provide training for technicians of every kind. . . .

I come to the political situation. . . . India has before her great opportunities, the greatest she has ever had. . . . But there are certain elements of the problem which we must recognize.   It is not a simple problem ; it cannot and will not be solved by repeating a password or formula.   " Quit India " will not act as the magic " Sesame " which opened Ali Baba's cave.   It cannot and will not be solved by violence. . . . There are various parties to the settlement. . . . The objective of all is the same—the freedom and welfare of India. . . . I do not believe an agreed solution between the parties is impossible ;   I do not believe it would even be very difficult, given goodwill, commonsense and patience on all sides. . . .

I will now refer to a matter on which as a soldier I hold strong views.   A great deal of political heat and feeling has been engendered by the way in which the I.N.A. trials have been represented to the public.   I will say nothing of the trials themselves or of the men under trial, it would be quite improper for me to do so.   But I do propose to say something for the men who were prisoners of war, but did not join the I.N.A., who under pressure and punishment, under hardships and want, stood firm to their ideals of a soldier's duty, a soldier's faith. . . . Whatever your political views, if you cannot acclaim the man who prefers his honour to his ease, who remains steadfast in adversity to his pledged faith, then you have a poor notion of the character which is required to build up a nation. . . . As a proof of what they endured . . . I will tell you this : the 45,000 Indian prisoners of war who stood firm are estimated to have lost about 11,000 or one quarter of their numbers, from disease, starvation and murder ; the 20,000 who went over to our enemy's side lost only 1,500 or 7½ per cent.

Chapter 345

ALLIES TAKE THE ROAD TO MANDALAY

Chapter 299 describes the 1944 campaign in Burma to the capture of Myitkyina in August. Operations in all areas were then brought to a temporary standstill by monsoon conditions. In this chapter Charles Gardner continues the history of the Burma fighting. He describes the capture of Mandalay, the clearance of the enemy from Arakan, and the reopening of the Burma Road

WHEN South-East Asia Command was established in August 1943 Admiral Mountbatten's plan for the reconquest of Burma was by use of amphibious forces landing at Rangoon. This was, to quote the "Supremo," the "sensible way round." Unfortunately the amphibious equipment on which this plan was based was taken from the Burma theatre for use in the European theatre (*see* page 2997). S.E.A.C. had therefore to plan the reconquest of Burma from the north. Many said it could not be done. Certain it was that, on account of the great difficulties of communication, it would be the toughest task of the whole war. The nearest supply port for any offensive from the Indian borders was Calcutta—over 500 tortuous and ill-linked miles from even the rear defensive positions of Imphal. Rangoon, next useful port, lay nearly 700 miles farther on—with barriers of mountains, rivers and jungles interposed, barriers through which there were only two roads (to Tiddim and to Tamu) and no railways.

There could be no relief from this land supply problem until Rangoon was reached, and the 14th Army would have to depend on Calcutta as its port, on the overloaded Bengal–Assam railway as far as Manipur, and then on jungle roads, all the way to Rangoon. By the time Rangoon was reached the lines of communication would be 1,200 to 1,500 miles long. It was obvious that this supply route could not be expected to sustain a major force in action in central and southern Burma. Unless, therefore, an alternative could be found, the recapture of Burma from the north would not be possible.

An alternative was found—air supply. The Mountbatten-Slim plan for the reconquest of Burma was this:

1. The 14th Army was to chase the defeated Japanese through the jungle to the Chindwin river, reaching the Chindwin just at the end of the monsoon (November). For this stage it would draw supplies from Calcutta and Manipur, and the front line would be kept going by air-lift (the Tiddim Road being "out" during the rains).

2. In Arakan the 15th Indian Corps (Lieutenant-General Sir Philip Christison) would advance on Akyab. This would ensure the safety of the Bengal port

Lieutenant W. B. WESTON
(The Green Howards)
In Burma, on March 3, 1945, Lieutenant William Basil Weston's platoon was ordered to clear a fanatically defended way through Meiktila. With 'magnificent bravery' he inspired his men (nearly all of whom were seeing active service for the first time) to 'superb achievements.' Lying wounded, he withdrew the pin from a grenade, killing himself and most of the enemy inside a bunker. He was posthumously awarded the V.C.

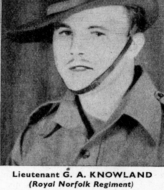

Lieutenant G. A. KNOWLAND
(Royal Norfolk Regiment)
Such was the inspiration of Lieutenant George Arthur Knowland's 'magnificent heroism' in action in Burma on January 31, 1945, that, though 14 of the 25 men in his platoon became casualties at an early stage, and six of his positions were overrun by the enemy, his men held on through twelve hours of continuous and fierce fighting until reinforcements arrived. Mortally wounded in the action, he was awarded the V.C. posthumously.

Photos, Daily Mirror ; News Chronicle

of Chittagong, and when (by January) Akyab had been secured the 14th Army could be supplied through these two ports for their big fight southwards to Rangoon. But as no roads run eastward from them over the mountains to central Burma, the only link between these seaports and General Slim's troops would be by air.

3. As this vital air-lift could not be sustained once the new monsoon started (May or June) General Slim had to be at Rangoon by then—*i.e.* he would have to advance 700 miles in exactly six months from crossing the Chindwin.

In the event of the rains coming early, or of the race against the monsoon becoming a "near thing," 15th Indian Corps was to mount an amphibious force to capture Rangoon from the sea. It was estimated that by April 1945 the theatre would have the equipment to do this, and that, by then, 15th Corps would have completed its main task of securing the Arakan air-supply ports of Akyab and, later, Ramree.

Changes in the command in South-East Asia were announced in November : Lieutenant-General Raymond A. Wheeler, U.S. Army, who had been chief of the U.S. Military Mission to Iraq, Persia and India in 1941–42, and Commanding General, U.S. Services of Supply in India, Burma and China in 1942, was appointed Deputy Supreme Commander, South-East Asia (in succession to General Stilwell) under Admiral Mountbatten ; and a new command, Allied Land Forces, South-East Asia (A.L.F.S.E.A.), comprising the 11th Army Group (including General Slim's 14th Army) and the U.S. Forces in the India-Burma theatre (commanded by Lieutenant-General Daniel I. Sultan) was created under Lieutenant-General Sir Oliver Leese, formerly commanding the 8th Army in Italy.

In October 1944, as the monsoon tailed off, the major operations began. The 14th Army had three great obstacles between it and the first great prize at which it was aiming— **Major Operations Begin Again** Mandalay. First the massif of the Chin Hills ; then the Chindwin River—broad, deep and fast at that time of year ; more hills, then the great Irrawaddy river.

Across the hills the Japanese army, broken but ever ready to stand and fight a do-or-die rearguard action, was streaming down the valleys. Diseased and hungry, the enemy was short of everything, it seemed, except ammunition. Chasing after the Japanese, the East Africans took again the road through the dreaded Kabaw valley, one of the unhealthiest parts of Burma, while the veterans of the 5th Indian Division under Major-General Evans, pursued them across the jungle tracks of the Chin Hills and down the road through Tiddim—the road which had seen the British withdrawal in the previous spring.

Each column had its path to follow. Both paths led to the same spot—Kalewa. Tiddim village, a collection of huts with a few solid buildings, formerly

Allies Capture Tiddim the administrative centre of the Chin Hills territory, was captured on October 19. The Japanese, outwitted by the 5th Division's astute flanking approaches, had quit, to stand and fight farther down the road. With the 5th Division came tanks. They were winched up the steep slopes, and on the level were carried by lorries whose drivers accomplished miracles in negotiating the bends and turns of the precipitous road.

The tanks had their part to play at the feature nicknamed by the British the "Chocolate Staircase," where the Japanese tried hard to make a stand. There, and at Kennedy Peak, 9,000-foot mountain into which the enemy had dug innumerable strongpoints, the tanks were taken up the steep slopes to blast him out of his holes at point-blank range.

FOURTEENTH ARMY TROOPS SEIZE TIDDIM

Capture of Tiddim on October 19, 1944, brought the road from Imphal, nearly a hundred miles to the north, under 14th Army control. Little more than a village, it was in peace-time the administrative centre of the Chin Hills territory. After the defences had collapsed under air attack, troops of the 5th Indian Division went in. Here a 14th Army patrol above Tiddim keeps a look-out for snipers. *Photo, British Official*

From the Peak (where tanks actually attacked from cloud cover), captured on November 7, the going was swifter, though the Japanese were still full of fight.

On November 15, an Askari of the 11th East African Division (Major-General Dimoline) met a Sepoy of the 5th Indian Division on the track that runs along the bank of the Myittha

river from Kalemyo to the Chindwin at Kalewa. Kalemyo fell to the 11th Division on the 16th.

On the track to Kalewa the Japanese were expected to stand firm, for it runs through defiles in which a handful of men could hold up an army. But for some reason the enemy failed to do so. **East Africans Reach Kalewa** The East Africans reached Kalewa, which they found a mass of bomb craters, on December 2, and established a solid bridge-head on the east bank of the Chindwin. The second great

KENNEDY PEAK AND THE 'CHOCOLATE STAIRCASE'

Important objective of the 5th Indian Division advancing from Tiddim was Kennedy Peak, a 9,000-ft. height in the Chin Hills honeycombed with enemy strongpoints, captured on November 7, 1944. Below, left, 5th Division troops move up its slopes to consolidate. Right, the 'Chocolate Staircase' on the Tiddim Road, also scaled by British tanks. It has 40 hairpin bends.
Photos, Indian Official

WORLD'S LARGEST BAILEY PONTOON BRIDGE

An outstanding achievement by the Bengal Sappers and Miners in Burma was a pontoon bridge across the Chindwin at Kalewa some 1,000 feet long, made from Bailey bridge units and here seen in course of construction—the longest in any theatre of war. Troops of the 11th East African Division reached Kalewa on December 2, 1944, and established a bridge-head over the river which (below) they are preparing to cross in 'Ducks.'   *Photos, British Official*

obstacle on the march back into central Burma was overcome.

The country south of Tiddim, cleared of organized enemy units, was now turned over to the Lushai Brigade, a polyglot force expert in ambushes and sudden sorties and including Indian Army regulars, men of the Assam Rifles, Chin Hill levies and a force called the Lushai Scouts. The 5th Division,

already earmarked for a great role in the final campaign, was pulled out for a well-earned rest.

The British 2nd Division (Major-General C. G. G. Nicholson) took over the Chindwin bridge-head from the East Africans. Already the Engineers had thrown across the river a pontoon-bridge some 1,000 feet long, constructed from Bailey bridge units. Great

volumes of traffic poured across it night and day. For the first time in months the Japanese air force responded to the challenge: five aircraft came over in an effort to put out of action this vital link in Allied communications. They did not achieve a single hit on the bridge, and one enemy machine was shot down. The bridge-head was expanded, despite Japanese resistance, and the 2nd Division began to take the long road to Mandalay.

On the right flank of the 2nd Division's advance, the 20th Indian Division, under Major-General Douglas Gracey (its commander since he raised the Division in 1942), crossed the Chindwin lower down (*see* page 3534). On the left flank, Major-General T. W. Rees's 19th Indian Division pushed across the river to link up with the 2nd Division at Shwebo on January 7, 1945. The troops were deployed on the right side of the river, on the right side of the great Chin Hills barrier, in readiness for the next phase of the campaign—the drive to Mandalay.

The capture of Mandalay was entrusted to 33rd Corps, under Lieutenant-General Sir Montagu Stopford. It had three divisions for the task—the British 2nd, the 19th Indian (Daggers), and the 20th Indian. By January all three of these divisions were east of the Chindwin, and, as air supply took over the L. of C., the slogan "Rangoon Before the Monsoon" became the 14th Army's battle cry. **Composition of 33rd Corps**

During November, the 19th Division had crossed the Chindwin in the north (among other places, at Paungbyin on the 30th). It had marched 400 miles and fought 18 battles in seven weeks, capturing "Oil" Indaw (so-called to distinguish it from "Rail" Indaw, taken by the British 36th Division on December 10: *see* page 3543) and Pinlebu, and on December 16 it had joined hands with the 36th Division near Banmauk, to assist in the clearing of the northern sector where General Sultan was driving the Ledo Road through to China (*see* page 3538). Only marching fitness and air supply made possible the speed and success of these operations. The 19th Division was, for this work, under 4th Corps.

From Banmauk it marched down the Mogaung-Mandalay railway and through the Chindit country to Wuntho, secured by December 19, which brought the valuable Japanese airfields in the Wuntho area into Allied hands. Pushing the enemy before it through the central Burma plain in a series of sharp battles, 19th Division also arrived to join 2nd Division in the first week of

DRIVE DOWN THE VALLEY OF THE IRRAWADDY

1. Pushing east to make contact with the 36th Division (on December 16, 1944), British and Indian units of the 19th Division cross the upper Chindwin in the Sittaung area on November 17. 2. After taking Katha on December 10, Scottish and Welsh troops of the 36th Division cross the Irrawaddy in that area.   3. Army telephonists test a circuit across the river, linking the east bank with the rear. 4. At Tigyiang, an island in the Irrawaddy 42 miles south of Katha, U.S. aircraft drop supplies by parachute to the 36th Division, which captured it on December 23.

Photos, British and S.E.A.C. Official

MYSTERY OF JAPANESE WITHDRAWAL AT MONYWA

After a fierce three days' struggle, the Japanese at Monywa—important rail-river communications centre of the Chindwin, sixty miles west of Mandalay—on January 22, 1945, unexpectedly withdrew before troops of the 20th Indian Division under Major-General Douglas Gracey, M.C. Garrisoned by the crack Japanese 33rd Division, the town (here seen after its capture), had previously been bombed by Allied aircraft.   *Photo, British Official*

January, at Shwebo, where it passed under command of 33rd Corps.

The British 2nd Division crossed the Chindwin at Kalewa in mid-December and followed the road to Yeu. On the way it captured intact the important Kabo weir which controls the irrigation of all the fertile Shwebo plain. In twenty days the Division, spearheaded by the Royal Berkshires and the Royal Welch Fusiliers, the Dorsets and the Camerons, marched 130 miles from Kalewa to Shwebo, into which the Worcesters broke on January 7. Both town and airfield were in British hands by the 10th.

The 20th Division crossed the Chindwin at Mawlaik in November, and then

Chindwin Crossed at Mawlaik

moved south to Budalin and Monywa, an important railhead Chindwin town, taken on January 22. The Northamptons, the

Devons and the Border Regiment formed part of this division together with three regiments of British artillery and two British tank regiments.

After crossing the Chindwin, the 14th Army left the jungle behind, and was in open country. The central Burma plain is flat and sandy and, from a tactical point of view, much resembles the desert.

The drive on Mandalay started from Shwebo, 50 miles to the north of it and the last big town on the Myitkyina–Mogaung–Mandalay railway before that city, Burma's second largest, is reached.

On the night of January 14, troops of 19th Division slipped across the Irrawaddy to build up a bridge-head

in the Singu sector, some forty miles north of Mandalay. This bridge-head was held and enlarged, despite the heaviest concentration of Japanese artillery met up to that time in Burma. This was developing the left of three blows aimed at Mandalay.

In the centre, 2nd Division threatened Sagaing, which, lying on the west bank of the Irrawaddy in the right-angle bend which the river makes at this point, is only ten miles west of Mandalay, but on the opposite bank of the river.

The right-hand blow was made by 20th Division.

To deceive the enemy, 2nd Division's Reconnaissance (Armoured) Regiment advanced towards Sagaing. The Japanese, expecting the big attack against Mandalay to be made at this vital point, were **Deception of the Enemy** caught with a large number of troops and guns on the wrong side of the river when the actual attack on the city came.

On the night of February 11-12, 20th Division crossed the Irrawaddy opposite Myinmu to establish a bridge-head thirty miles west of Mandalay. Little opposition was encountered in the initial landings, but within a few days the Japanese began reacting fiercely. They attacked in force, and on the third day even sent over some bombers. But within a week the bridge-head was enlarged to five miles long and two deep.

Then on February 25, a little east of 20th Division's bridge-head, the main body of 2nd Division made its crossing. The boats were met by heavy fire from well-dug-in Japanese, and a good many were sunk.

At both 19th Division's Singu bridge-head, north of Mandalay, and 2nd and 20th Divisions' bridge-head near Myinmu, west of Mandalay, the R.A.F.

AT SHWEBO, LAST BIG TOWN BEFORE MANDALAY

Armour in strength was assembled when a British armoured division, operating in late December 1944 near Pyingyaing, between Kalewa and Shwebo, pushed forward 30 miles in three days against stiff opposition. Shwebo, on the Myitkyina–Mandalay railway, was cleared on January 10, 1945. Left, British infantry cross a bridge (left intact by the enemy) during their three days' 'push.' Right, infantry and bren-carriers enter Shwebo.   *Photo, British Official*

and the U.S.A.A.F. gave invaluable assistance in preparing the crossings and wearing down Japanese resistance to the bridge-heads.

To meet this serious threat to Mandalay from the west, the Japanese began withdrawing troops from their forces containing the 19th Indian Division's Singu bridge-head. This proved their undoing. For 19th Division had been preparing to break out of its bridge-head. The whole of the Division was got across with tanks, which now joined the Division for the first time. The Japanese assumed that the chief thrust would be down the main road to Mandalay. In fact it was made, with the full weight of guns and tanks behind it, down a little used track which hugged the east bank of the Irrawaddy.

On March 6, the 19th Division really got going. Next day it was fighting in the streets of Madaya, from which

Outskirts of Mandalay Reached

a road and a railway run into Mandalay, only 12 miles to the south. By the evening, British troops were within 4½ miles of Mandalay and could see the spires of the pagodas. 19th Division entered the northern outskirts of the city early in the morning of the 8th.

While fighting was still going on in Mandalay, General Rees dispatched a force of Gurkhas to capture Maymyo, in order to cut off the enemy's retreat and also to prevent any reinforcements from reaching him. The attack on this hill station (residence of the Governor of Burma in peace-time), on March 13, involved secret marches for three nights over ancient smugglers' tracks and was a complete surprise to the Japanese.

By March 12, the only serious obstacle remaining in Mandalay was Fort

ROAD TO MANDALAY
On March 20, 1945, Lord Louis Mountbatten issued a special announcement : ' The fall of Fort Dufferin today marks the capture of Mandalay by the 14th Army.' Here Gurkhas and other units of the 19th Indian ('Dagger') Division—commanded by Major-General T. Wynford Rees (right)—cross the Irrawaddy during the drive to Mandalay. The Division later took part in the city's capture *Photos, Indian Official ; Illustrated*

Dufferin, with its massive walls. The Japanese defended this fanatically. But three days later it was encircled. The end came suddenly and dramatically. On March 19, Mitchell bombers using 2,000-lb. bombs breached the walls of Fort Dufferin. Next day at 12.45 the besieging troops were astonished to see an Anglo-Burmese walk out of the north gate carrying a Union Jack and a white flag. The Japanese—nearly 500 of them—had pulled out of the Fort at noon, leaving there 346 refugees,

mostly Anglo-Burmese and Anglo-Indians, and a number of missionaries.

In Arakan, meanwhile, 15th Corps, no longer part of the 14th Army, was securing the vital air-supply ports. The 15th Corps defensive victory in Arakan in early 1944 (*see* page 3001) had left it in a strong position—but exploitation had been delayed when the 5th and 7th Divisions had to be withdrawn and flown to the Imphal battle. Immediately the '44 monsoon ended, and concurrently with the first

BRITISH SECOND DIVISION SEIZES AVA BRIDGE
English and Scottish troops of the British 2nd Division on March 19, 1945, captured the ancient town of Ava, ten miles from Mandalay. East of the town they took the 1,200-yards-long Ava road-rail bridge—the only bridge across the Irrawaddy between Ava and Myitkyina, some 400 miles to the north (right). British troops mop up at Ywathitgyi (left) on the road to Sagaing.
Photos, British Official

Chindwin crossings by 33rd Corps, the 15th Corps started to push south towards Akyab. They raced down the peninsula. Men of the 25th Division (Major-General Chambers) and the 82nd West Africans (Major-General Stockwell) took Buthidaung and Maungdaw (reported on December 19), and on the 28th, the 25th Division reached Foul Point opposite Akyab, four miles across the water.

Meanwhile the 82nd West African Division had advanced down the east bank of the Mayu River. They reached

Advance on Akyab

the river through the old railway tunnels which go under the Mayu hills between Maungdaw and Buthidaung. They, and a force of 25th Division, brought with them an armada of small boats—all manhandled through the famous tunnels. The 82nd West African Division had the job of protecting the 25th Division's left flank as it struck at Akyab, and, later, of delivering a left hook to cut the Jap east-west L. of C. to that port, and effecting a

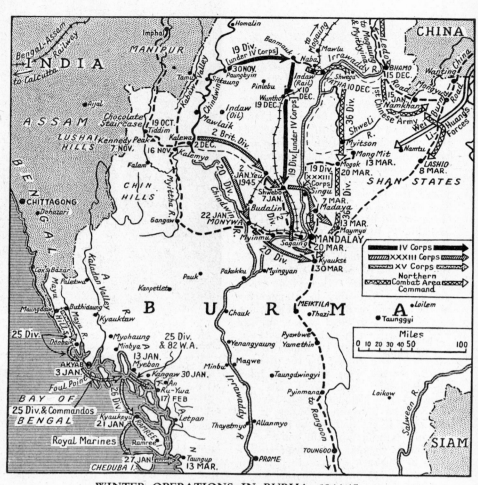

WINTER OPERATIONS IN BURMA, 1944-45

This map indicates (i) the moves by the various divisions of the 14th Army entrusted with the recapture of Mandalay, (ii) the landings which led to the reconquest of the Arakan coast and the freeing of the seaport of Akyab, (iii) the advances in the Northern Combat Area which made possible the completion of the Ledo Road. The operations which preceded the crossings of the Irrawaddy below Mandalay are described in Chapter 371.

ACROSS THE SHWELI

After an intense air and land bombardment, British and Indian troops of the 36th Division forced the Shweli River at Myitson early in February 1945. Crossing of this last river-barrier between northern and central Burma was bitterly opposed, the Japanese using flame-throwers for the first time in this theatre. Here an assault pontoon is unloaded for the crossing. *British, Official*

link with the 81st West African Division (Major-General Loftus Tottenham) which was coming south down the jungly Kaladan Valley farther inland. The two West African Divisions met at Myohaung, and then concentrated on Japanese escape routes as the 25th Division and commandos forced the enemy to pull out of Akyab.

There had been indications that the Japanese were evacuating Akyab, but intelligence reports from this quarter were not reliable. General Christison, Rear-Admiral B. C. Martin and the local Air Commander, the Earl of Bandon, therefore assembled a powerful Combined Operations force which landed and occupied Akyab without opposition on January 3.

Meanwhile, 26th Indian Division (Major-General Chambers) of 15th Corps was assembling at Chittagong for another successful amphibious operation —the largest undertaken to date in the area—this time on Ramree Island (January 21), followed on the 26th by

a landing on Cheduba Island by Royal Marines.

Operations in the Arakan had locked up four Allied divisions ; General Leese saw a way of amending this by staging a series of landings in the enemy's rear along the Arakan coast while at the same time exerting pressure from the north. Landings

Landings in Arakan

were made at Myebon (January 13) ; on the coast 35 miles south-east of Akyab (January 22) to take Kangaw on the 30th ; at Ru-Ywa (February 17) and at Letpan (March 13) in which commandos, infantry, tank-crews, gunners and naval and air forces all played a part. A full-scale Japanese retreat south followed.

Some of the battles resulting from these landings were of the bloodiest. That of Kangaw, where the Commandos and 25th Division distinguished themselves, went on at fever pitch for four weeks. The Japanese trying to hammer through to escape from the West Africans closing down on them from

THE BATTLE FOR MANDALAY'S FORT DUFFERIN

The 19th Indian ('Dagger') Division entered Mandalay on March 8, 1945. By March 12 the only serious enemy strongpoint remaining was Fort Dufferin, a powerful fortification, fanatically defended, with sides 1¼ miles long, walls 30 feet high and 12 feet thick, and surrounded by a moat 70 yards wide. R.A.F. Hurri-bombers unsuccessfully attacked the walls, which withstood all onslaughts until March 19 when they were breached by Mitchells with 2,000-lb. bombs. 1. An observation officer watches the battle for the Fort from Pagoda Hill. 2. Indian troops man machine-guns sited on roof-tops on the hill. 3. R.A.F. drops supplies for troops outside the town ; Pagoda Hill is seen in background.

SEABORNE ATTACKS ON THE ARAKAN COAST

1. 'Z' craft beached on the Myebon Peninsula with 25-pdr. guns used for shelling the Japanese lines six miles from the beach-head established by the 15th Indian Corps on January 13, 1945. 2. Assault craft go forward near Ru-Ywa for the landing of British and Indian troops of the 15th Corps on February 17.   3. These tanks of King George V's Own 19th Lancers drove the Japanese from the Kangaw area. They were the first Indian tanks used in a sea-landing. Kangaw was occupied on January 30.   *Photos, British and S.E.A.C. Official*

the north, put in repeated attacks, and on two successive nights poured 600 and 800 shells into the Allied positions. Fighting their way foot by foot up the hill slopes north-east of Kangaw, Indian troops encountered a prepared line of bunkers and trenches defended by concentrations of artillery and machine guns. Recovering from their initial surprise, the Japanese fought back with all they had got. Tanks of the 19th Lancers, the first Indian tanks to take part in a sea landing, did great work in the Kangaw area, where the division cut the Japanese main escape route from Arakan.

The result of this series of Arakan victories was three-fold :

a. To secure the ports of Akyab and Ramree, from which the 14th Army's dash to Rangoon could be fed by air.

b. To tie down and wipe out large enemy forces, and prevent their being switched to other Burma fronts.

c. To release for further operations the forces which had been employed in the area (the 25th and 26th Indian and 81st and 82nd W.A. Divisions, together with 221 Group R.A.F., Commandos, tanks, artillery and ships of the Royal Navy and Royal Indian Navy. The completion of the Arakan campaign also released a certain number of Dakotas for use by the 14th Army).

The campaign to reopen the Ledo Road was completed in January 1945, just as the 14th Army was over the Chindwin.   General **Ledo Road** Stilwell's forces cap- **Campaign** tured Myitkyina on **Reopens** August 4 (*see* page 3015).   Operations in the Northern Combat Area were renewed from there in October, during which month General Stilwell was replaced by Lieutenant-General Daniel I. Sultan. His forces consisted of the Chinese 1st Army (American and British trained and equipped) ; the British 36th Division (Major-General F. W. Festing), and a new American battle group, the " Mars Task Force." In addition there were American, British and Indian road builders, and oil pipe-line experts—the last laying the pipe-line from Calcutta to China which was to supply the American air forces there (*see* illus. in page 3283).

The Chinese advanced south to Bhamo, captured by the 38th Division under Major-General Li Hung on December 15 after one of the fiercest battles of the northern campaign. Yard by yard, as at Myitkyina, they had to clear the Jap from the streets in a siege that lasted a month.

The Chinese pushed on into the Kodaung Hill Tracts and began to come

SUPREME COMMANDER, S.E.A.C.,
AT MANDALAY

Mandalay, capital of Upper Burma and Burma's second largest town, was captured by the 19th Indian Division on March 20, 1945, after a bitter struggle lasting twelve days. The last enemy stronghold was Fort Dufferin, built on the site of the palace of the Kings of Burma and named after the first Marquis of Dufferin and Ava (1826-1902), who was responsible for the British annexation of Burma in 1885. At noon on March 20 the Japanese pulled out of Fort Dufferin, and refugees who had been inside appeared waving a white flag and a Union Jack. They informed Punjabi troops outside that the Japanese garrison had gone. The Union Jack was at once hoisted over the Fort (right), and Mandalay itself officially taken over by Lieutenant-General Sir William Slim, commanding the 14th Army, at a parade of British, Indian and Gurkha troops. The refugees numbered 346. They were mostly Anglo-Burmese and Anglo-Indians, though they included Irish, French, and Italian Roman Catholic missionaries and sisters brought to Mandalay by the enemy from all parts of Burma.

The capture of Mandalay isolated the three Japanese armies in Burma—the 33rd north of Mandalay, facing the Chinese First Army and the British 36th Division, the 15th between Mandalay and Meiktila, and the 26th in Southern Burma. Neither the 15th nor the 33rd had a single road left by which they could withdraw either south towards Rangoon or east to Siam, or receive supplies. The day after Mandalay fell, Lord Louis Mountbatten, Supreme Allied Commander, S.E.A.C., visited the city and congratulated the men who had taken it. He is seen (above) inspecting damage inflicted on the walls of Fort Dufferin by 2,000-lb. bombs dropped by Mitchell aircraft of the R.A.F. On his right is Major-General T. W. Rees, commander of the 19th Indian Division, and on his left Air Marshal Sir Keith Park.

Photos, British Official ; Topical

HAND-TO-HAND FIGHTING IN A MANDALAY TEMPLE

On the southern slopes of Pagoda Hill, Mandalay, where the Japanese still held strong positions among Buddhist temples and monasteries on March 12, 1945, troops of the Royal Berkshire and Baluch Regiments with Gurkhas engaged in bitter hand-to-hand fighting, capturing several enemy machine-gun nests. Mandalay is a comparatively modern town, having been built in 1856-7 by Mindon, King of Burma. It was first occupied by the British in 1885. Here, British troops run to a vantage point in a Buddhist temple.

Photo, Topical

ROYAL WELCH FUSILIERS FORD THE NANKYE CHAUNG

During the 1944 monsoon in north Burma there was much bitter fighting along the 170-miles 'corridor' on the Myitkyina–Mandalay railway. It was the task of General Festing's 36th Division to clear this vital section of railroad and its approaches, from Myitkyina through Mogaung towards Mandalay. In face of almost insuperable difficulties, the Royal Scots Fusiliers and the East Lancashire Regiment, collaborating with British and Indian engineers and Chinese artillery, swept a 75-miles roadway through the jungle between Hopin and Mawlu. *Photo, British Official*

ALLIED AIR FORCES STRIKE AT GERMANY'S RAILWAYS

Photo, U.S. Official

Important bombing objective as the Allied armies closed in on the Reich early in 1945 was Germany's railway network. Among the most frequently struck targets was the Westphalian railway centre of Münster, which served the German armies facing the 21st Army Group. On March 25 R.A.F. 'heavies' gave Münster its last raid. Nine days later the city was taken by the British 6th Guards Armoured Division and the U.S. 17th Airborne Division. In the marshalling yards U.S. troops found this powerful locomotive nosing skywards—result of a well-placed hit on the cab.

up against more resistance from small parties of Japanese. But on January 15, 1945, after an unopposed crossing of the Shweli river, the 30th Division took Namhkam, a small town on the spur road that runs from Bhamo to join up with the Burma road at Mongyu. A few days later they met Marshal Wei Li-huang's forces advancing from Wanting, on the Burma–China border (*see* page 3277), and the land route to China was at last clear. Much of the "mopping-up" along the road fell to Mars Task Force, which in its role of shock troops, was assigned the job of clearing the most stubborn of the enemy strong points.

BHAMO FALLS TO THE CHINESE

Despite repeated Japanese 'suicide' attacks, Bhamo, garrison town on the India-to-China overland supply route and last important enemy bastion in north Burma, fell to the Chinese 38th Division, under Major-General Li Hung, on December 15, 1944, after a month's siege. At Tonkwa, some 50 miles to the south, a new U.S. battle group known as 'Mars Task Force' and commanded by Brigadier-General John P. Willey, was first reported in action fighting alongside Chinese troops on December 16, having marched nearly 260 miles. Left, 'Mars Force' mule team fords a stream.

Photos, Fox Photos; Associated Press

itself. This was also the main axis of advance, down which "jeep trains" were run by Divisional Engineers: but not before they had repaired a large number of bridges, entirely with captured and local material.

The Japanese resisted very stubbornly down the whole of the 170-mile corridor, in which many stern battles were fought in torrential rain and deep mud. The capture of Katha and "Rail" Indaw on December 10 completed the expulsion of the enemy from the "railway corridor," and brought the Division to the west bank of the Irrawaddy river, which was crossed on captured Japanese rafts and local craft.

During the latter half of December, the Division was joined by an Indian brigade, flown in to Mawlu. The advance continued, mopping up scattered parties of the enemy falling back to the river Shweli at Myitson. The fighting for this crossing in February 1945 was bitter. The Japanese used flame-throwers for the first time in this theatre and more artillery than ever before against this Division. The brunt of the fighting was borne by Indian troops, who engaged the enemy at a few yards' range in dense bamboo.

An outstanding feature of this battle was the supply dropping by the 12th Combat Cargo Squadron. The British troops in the very small perimeter across the river were running short of ammunition and food, and as the river crossing was under artillery and small arms fire, everything depended on a "good drop." Without the accurate dropping and skilful flying of these American pilots throughout the battle, a withdrawal might have been unavoidable.

Americans Drop Supplies

Led by men of the Royal Sussex Regiment, troops of the 36th Division, advancing through dense jungle country, had captured Mong Mit, capital of the Shan State of that name, by March 13; as British forward troops hacked their way forward in this advance, bulldozers manned by American and Indian engineers followed and made a path usable by jeeps and other motor traffic. Continuing their advance, they captured Mogok, centre of the world's largest ruby mines, on March 20.

Having successfully completed its task in northern Burma, the Division now turned south-west down the Burma Road to march to Maymyo, where it came under command of the 14th Army.

The Chinese push south went on, troops of the 1st Army taking Old Lashio, terminus of the Burma Road, on March 7, New Lashio, 2 miles away, next day. This brought the whole Burma Road, from Lashio to Yunnan, once more under Allied control.

The British 36th Division acted as left flank guard to the N.C.A.C. forces; its main job was to clear the railway from Myitkyina through Mogaung and down towards Mandalay. The advance down the "railway corridor" began early in August 1944. The monsoon was in full spate, turning the few tracks into quagmires. The only reliable means of communication was the railway

January 1. Luftwaffe made attacks on Allied airfields in Belgium and Holland, losing at least 364 aircraft. R.A.F. bombed Dortmund–Ems canal for first time by daylight, breached Mittelland canal for third time.

January 2. Announced that Moircy and Remagne (Ardennes) had been recaptured and Remagne lost again. By night R.A.F. heavily attacked Nuremberg and Ludwigshaven. 14th Army troops reached Kabo.

January 2-3. U.S. carrier-fleet struck in force at Formosa and Okinawa (Ryukyus), destroying 111 Japanese aircraft and 27 ships.

January 3. U.S. 1st Army opened new attack in Grandménil area. Heavy raid by U.S.A. 8th A.F. on Cologne. British recaptured Akyab (Burma); other 14th Army troops took Yeu, 70 air miles from Mandalay. Chinese forces captured Wanting (Burma–China border). U.S. force landed on Marinduque, S. of Luzon. Plastiras formed Government in Greece.

January 4. U.S. Army troops captured Malempré (Ardennes). Canadians established bridge-head W. of Granarolo River (Italy). British carrier-borne aircraft bombed Pangkalan-Brandan oil refinery in Sumatra. U.S.A.A.F. bombers attacked Manila airfield.

January 5. Allied forces took Arbrefontaine. By night heavy bombers heavily attacked Hanover. In Italy 8th Army reached Reno River, occupied San Alberto. Soviet Union recognized Lublin Committee as Provisional Government of Poland.

January 6. U.S. 1st Army troops took Odeigne. R.A.F. attacked Houffalize, dropping over 1,000 tons of bombs (day); at night R.A.F. struck at Hanau and Neuss. U.S. Super-Fortresses heavily attacked Kyushu (Japan).

January 7. U.S. tanks cut St. Vith–Laroche Road at three points. By night R.A.F. heavily bombed Munich, Hanau, Hanover and Nuremberg. Indian troops entered Shwebo (Burma).

January 8. In Ardennes U.S.A. 8th A.F. kept up offensive on enemy communications, attacked Frankfort marshalling yards. Other U.S. heavy bombers struck at Linz (Austria).

January 9. Red Army captured Kispest, industrial suburb of Budapest. Bombers of M.A.A.F. knocked out Palazzolo rail bridge over the Oglio (Italy). Guam-based Super-Fortresses bombed Tokyo by day. General MacArthur headed landing in force on Lingayen Gulf, N.W. Luzon.

January 10. On S. flank of Ardennes U.S. troops recaptured Tillet; Hodister, Ambly and Bure recovered. U.S.A. 8th A.F. severely attacked communication centres at Karlsruhe, Bonn, Cologne, and Euskirchen. Red Army reported in control of three-quarters of Budapest. Enemy resistance ceased at Shwebo (Burma).

January 11. U.S. 1st Army troops recaptured Laroche, key road centre in Ardennes; British and U.S. forces stormed "Laroche Gap"; strong enemy pocket S.E. of Bastogne wiped out. In Arakan Indian troops entered Ponnagyun. U.S. carrier-based aircraft sank 41 Japanese ships and destroyed 112 enemy planes off Indo-China.

January 11-12. Home Fleet destroyed German convoy of 7-8 ships off Norwegian coast.

January 12. British forces linked up with U.S. 3rd Army near St. Hubert; R.A.F. Lancasters with 12,000-lb bombs attacked U-boat pens at Bergen. 1st Ukrainian Army opened offensive near Sandomierz. Fourteenth Army troops captured Budalin, 60 miles from Mandalay. U.S.A.A.F. bombed Manila airfields.

January 13. U.S. 1st Army launched heavy attack S. of Malmédy and Stavelot. By night R.A.F. Lancasters bombed Poelitz oil-plant (Stettin) and Saarbrücken marshalling yards. XV Indian Corps landed on Myebon Peninsula (Arakan). U.S. carrier-force bombed Hongkong, Swatow and Amoy.

January 14. U.S. troops cut Houffalize–St. Vith Road E. of Houffalize; British captured Champlon; Luftwaffe lost 236 planes in one of its heaviest defeats of the war. 1st and 2nd White Russian Armies take offensive. Fourteenth Army troops entered Wetlet, 30 miles N.N.W. of Mandalay; XV Indian Corps took Myebon. Super-Fortresses bombed Honshu (Japan) and Formosa. Mangatarem (Luzon) captured by Americans.

January 15. U.S. 3rd Army troops took Nennig, Borg and Wies (Germany). First Ukrainian Army captured Kielce, German strongpoint in Poland. Chinese 30th Division seized Nankham near Burma–Yunnan frontier; completion of Ledo Road announced. Tarlac Province (Luzon) penetrated. First civilian cross-Channel service since May 1940 opened.

January 16. British 2nd Army launched attack on German salient E. of Maas. U.S. 1st Army captured Houffalize. Britain-based R.A.F. Lancasters by night bombed oil plants in Sudetenland, Leipzig and the Ruhr. Red Army stormed Radom (Poland), forced Pilica River. Norwegian High Command announced half Finnmark liberated by Norwegian forces.

January 17. U.S. troops took Vielsalm (Ardennes). First White Russian Army captured Warsaw; 1st Ukrainian Army liberated Czestochowa and Radomsko. British 36th Division crossed Irrawaddy in drive towards Mandalay.

January 18. British captured Echt and Susteren, N. of Sittard. Evacuation begun of civilians from St. Nazaire. Red Army in Poland took Krasnysz, Modlin, Piotrkow, Sochaczew, and Lowiec; Pest completely cleared. Mandalay bombed. Paniqui and Bolinao Peninsula (Luzon) captured. Lublin Polish Provisional Government entered Warsaw.

January 19. U.S. troops captured Diekirch, reaching Reich frontier. R.A.F. bombed V2 launching sites in Holland. Red Army took Gorlice and Jaslo (Polish-Czechoslovak frontier), Lodz, Cracow, Tarnow and Wielun (Poland), and Pillkallen (Germany), penetrating E. Prussia. Monywa (Burma) surrounded. Saipan-based Super-Fortresses bombed Akashi (Japan).

January 20. U.S. troops recaptured Deidenberg (Ardennes). French 1st Army attacked 'Colmar Pocket.' Red Army stormed Tilsit, Kaukehmen and Szillen (E. Prussia), and Nowy-Sacz (Poland).

January 21-22. U.S. carrier-aircraft heavily bombed Formosa and Ryukyus.

January 21. First Ukrainian Army invaded German Silesia, capturing Kreuzburg and Rosenberg; 3rd White Russian Army took Gumbinnen (E. Prussia); 2nd White Russian Army occupied Neidenburg and Tannenberg (E. Prussia). XV Indian Corps landed on Ramree Island (Arakan). Tarlac (Luzon) captured. Mr. Roosevelt began fourth term as President.

January 22. U.S.A. 9th A.F. destroyed 1,594 vehicles and 69 tanks in Ardennes; U.S. 3rd Army took Eschweiler. Russians stormed Insterburg, Allenstein and Deutsch Eylau. Monywa (Burma) captured by British and Indian troops. King Peter of Yugoslavia dismissed London Government.

January 23. British captured St. Joost; U.S. troops took St. Vith and in Luxemburg Vianden. First White Russian Army seized Bydgoszcz (Poland).

January 24. British captured Heinsberg (Germany); announced that virtually all Belgian soil again liberated. Red Army took Lyck (E. Prussia) and Oppeln (Upper Silesia).

January 25. U.S. 1st Army took Aldringen (Ardennes). Enemy counter-attack launched N. of Hagenau (Alsace). Russians captured Gleiwitz (Silesia), Ostrov (Poland), and Oels (Germany). Clark airfield, biggest on Luzon, captured.

January 26. Russians reached Gulf of Danzig; other Soviet forces took Hindenburg (Silesia), reached Oder in Breslau area. Royal Marines landed on Cheduba Island, S.W. of Ramree. San Miguel (Luzon) captured.

January 27. Red Army broke through Masurian Lake defences. West Africans captured Myohaung (Arakan). Marianas-based Super-Fortresses bombed Tokyo. Australian-based R.A.A.F. Liberators attacked Java.

January 28. British took St. Odilienburg, S. of Roermond. R.A.F. by night attacked Stuttgart in strength. Moscow announced capture of Memel and liberation of all Lithuania; 1st Ukrainian Army cleared Dabrowa coal region, capturing Katowice. First supply-convoy for 3 years crossed border into China over Ledo–Burma Road.

January 29. U.S. forces captured Bullange, N.E. of St. Vith. Red Army invaded Pomerania, Brandenburg and W. Prussia. New landing on W. coast of Luzon. Yugoslav Regency Council and new Government formed.

January 30. Red Army took Marienwerder and Wartenburg (E. Prussia) and Zakopane (Poland). Kangaw (Arakan) captured.

January 31. U.S. 1st Army crossen Reich frontier to within 2 miles of maid Siegfried Line defences. Russians captured Landsberg, Meseritz, Schibus and Züllichau, forcing Obra defence line. U.S. forces landed on Subic Bay (Luzon), capturing Olongapu.

Chapter 346

LAST SORTIES IN WESTERN EUROPE

Bombing of German oil plants, communications and production centres increased in intensity in the last months of the war in the west. In this chapter, Captain Norman Macmillan, M.C., A.F.C., gives some indication of the devastating power of these Allied attacks, and of the Luftwaffe's hopeless loss of both offensive and defensive strength. The air war in other theatres during 1945 is described in Chapters 356 and 368

THE air war opened on New Year's Day, 1945, with a Luftwaffe raid against airfields in the Low Countries. R.A.F. 2nd T.A.F. and American aircraft were destroyed and damaged on the ground at several airfields where the runways were unusable because of a coating of black ice following a freeze succeeding a thaw (*see illus.* in page 3418). Messerschmitt 262 jet-fighters roared in low and fast, but, instead of returning to their own areas immediately the attack was over, the Luftwaffe pilots continued exultantly to circle the stricken airfields. This gave the Allies time to call British and American fighters from airfields which were not immobilized, and one Tempest wing was deflected while in flight.

The attack, begun promisingly for the Luftwaffe, ended in a disastrous loss, owing to the stupid tactics of the German pilots. By tarrying too long within the danger area, they lost about 364 aircraft, with another probable 81, from a force of about 800, anti-aircraft

gunners claiming 209 and Allied fighters 155. The Luftwaffe made few subsequent appearances in strength.

Allied development of ground and airborne electronic instruments had now brought blind navigation, blind bombing, and night fighting, and the ground control of aircraft in flight into such a state of perfection that the plans of Air Commanders-in-Chief could be carried out with assurance of success in almost any weather.

Aircraft equipped with Gee instruments could pick up one-way radar impulses emitted from ground stations. From these Loran (Long Range Air Navigation) signals, navigators within the aircraft could plot their position rapidly and accurately. The bomb-aiming of aircraft fitted with Oboe radar equipment was controlled from ground radar stations at ranges up to 250 miles, and, even when flying blind, bombs released to the signals of the ground controller fell with certainty within 50 yards of an intended target area. For precision bombing beyond

the range of Oboe methods, bombers were equipped with H2S radar, in whose cathode scope the navigator saw a map depicting the country flown over in green points of light of varying intensity. Gee-H sets and special charts enabled navigators to work out for themselves the correct moment for blind bomb release. Massed bombers operating by night or in cloud carried radar to enable each to detect the presence of other aircraft, and distinguish between friendly and enemy fighters.

IFF radar transmitters within the aircraft emitted a signal which indicated to ground radar stations that the emitting aircraft was friendly. Failure to emit the signal brought anti-aircraft defences and fighters into action. Fighters for night defence and interdiction, and coastal command aircraft, carried radar to enable them to attack enemy aircraft in the air, as well as ground and shipping targets.

Numerous Uses of Radar

Captain EDWIN SWALES
Only member of the South African Air Force to fly with the R.A.F. Pathfinder Force. He met his death on the night of February 23, 1945, when British and Australian heavy bombers attacked the Upper Rhineland town and rail centre of Pforzheim, between Karlsruhe and Stuttgart, in one of Bomber Command's most destructive raids. For his brilliant direction of the raid he was awarded the V.C. posthumously

Flt.-Sgt. G. THOMPSON, R.A.F.V.R.
Wireless operator in a Lancaster which attacked the Dortmund–Ems Canal by day on January 1, 1945, he was posthumously awarded the V.C. for his bravery in rescuing two comrades when their bomber was hit and set ablaze. With complete disregard for himself, he managed to extinguish the flames with his bare hands. He was so badly burnt and frost-bitten that he died three weeks later.

Sgt. N. C. JACKSON, R.A.F.V.R.
Awarded the V.C. for 'outstanding gallantry' during a raid on Schweinfurt on April 26, 1944. His bomber, attacked at 20,000 feet, burst into flames and had to be abandoned despite his 'almost incredible' attempts to extinguish the blaze in which his hands and face were severely burnt as he climbed the aircraft's wing. He was taken prisoner on landing by parachute in enemy territory.

Sqdn.-Ldr. L. H. TRENT, D.F.C.
Serving with the Royal New Zealand Air Force, he was detailed to lead an attack on the power station at Amsterdam on May 3, 1943. Of 11 Venturas only the squadron-leader's succeeded in bombing the target, the others being brought down in a surprise attack by enemy fighters. His own aircraft was hit and he was captured. For his 'cool, unflinching courage in the face of overwhelming odds' he won the V.C.

Photos, *British Official ; The Evening Standard ; Topical Press ; P.A. ; Reuter*

Mobile radar ground stations were used on the Continent to co-operate with fighters. These stations used Plan Position Indicator radar from which the direction, distance and height of aircraft could be simultaneously observed and the fighters accordingly vectored to engage the enemy, either while in flight or from the ground. Anti-aircraft guns were radar controlled, and many batteries (including mixed batteries) on the Continent played an important part in intercepting flying-bombs (*see* illus. in page 3435). (For fuller details of radar, *see* Chapter 379.)

Close air co-operation with the advanced surface forces was made possible by Mobile Forward Control Posts, consisting of armoured vehicles carrying

Forward Control Posts' Work

radio telephony wherein Air and Army officers worked together. Forward infantry and armour, usually operating in columns rather than in lines, were liable to infiltration by enemy columns. But any such dangerous situation was quickly observed by or made known to the F.C.P.s, whose Air control officer called up the aircraft detailed to maintain continuous patrol over the forward zones and directed them to immediate attack in support of the ground troops. These aircraft were usually fighter bombers, equipped with bombs, cannon and rockets, and their instantaneous assault seriously deterred an enemy whose morale was already lowered by air inferiority.

As 1945 began, the last German western offensive was in progress in the Ardennes (*see* Chapter 336). Fog aided the Germans to push forward without air support (*see* page 3414), but between

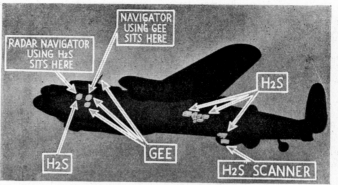

R.A.F. LED WITH RADAR

Secrets of radar ('Radio Detection and Ranging') were not disclosed until August 1945, though it had been used by the R.A.F. for ten years. Left, disposition of radar devices on a bomber. (Compare with radar-equipped Lancaster, below) 'Gee' signals enabled Allied bombers to calculate their exact position.

December 23 and 26, 1944, the weather cleared and the strategic and tactical air forces of the Allies inflicted crushing blows on German armour and supply columns. In January these blows were renewed. On January 22 and 23 the American air forces alone destroyed or damaged some 4,000 vehicles in this area, including over 150 tanks. Air attacks against communications during Von Rundstedt's offensive forced the Germans to withdraw ever farther rearward the most advanced railheads of the Reichsbahn. The offensive failed under the combined air and surface counter-attack.

The advance of the British 2nd Army in the Sittard area (*see* page 3569) called for powerful support from Bomber Command and the Tactical Air Forces. Many German villages were almost completely destroyed by air bombardments intended to drive enemy

infantry from foxholes within and around the houses. Netherlands villages, too, suffered. About this period a new R.A.F. cluster fragmentation bomb came into use. Dropped mostly by the British 2nd T.A.F., it exploded in the air, releasing twenty-six 20-lb. bombs which descended by parachute to explode a few feet above ground. Fragmentation bombs had a devastating effect upon men and transport without unduly wrecking roads which the Allied forces themselves were soon to require.

In February when the 21st Army Group was concentrated for the Battle of the Rhineland (*see* Chapter 349), air reconnaissance became of still greater importance. Without command of the air the roads

Rhineland Battle Preparations

could not have been crowded as they were with long lines of Allied men and material, over which roared flying-bombs aimed at Antwerp.

Everywhere the "taxi-rank" planes were overhead awaiting the call of the F.C.P.s. Army Air Observation Post squadrons operated from landing fields immediately behind the flooded zone. These really were landing "fields" as distinct from airfields, often no more than meadows surrounded by elms or poplars, with a dyked

BOMBING BY AID OF THE 'MAGIC EYE'

Important radar development was 'H2S' (the 'Magic Eye') which gave bomber crews a visual picture of the unseen territory over which they were passing, making possible pin-point 'cloud-bombing' technique, though the ground was completely obscured. The image appeared on the face of a cathode-ray tube. Right, the map-like image with indication of the aircraft's position. Left, conventional map of the same area. (See also diagram above). *Photos, British Official*

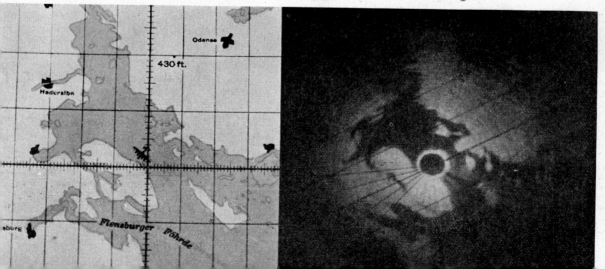

ARMY AIR OBSERVATION AIRCRAFT

The British-built Taylorcraft Auster III was used by the R.A.F. in Tunisia, Sicily, Italy and western Europe. Powered with a 130-h.p. De Havilland Gipsy Major engine, it had a maximum speed of 125 m.p.h. and was highly manoeuvrable. Capable of flying in small circles, it made a difficult target and could climb at 1,000 feet a minute and land on roads and small open areas.

Photo, British Official

canal running past one side. The operating conditions were similar to those of R.F.C. squadrons in France during the First Great War. The aircraft were spread along the front in flights. They flew unarmed, were manned by Gunner officers exclusively, carried wireless and radio telephony, and sometimes an observer. They operated at heights of between 2,000 and 10,000 feet and depended upon the Allied fighter screen to ensure them immunity from enemy fighters. When required they carried cameras, and undertook target photography for the artillery. This was an important task, for in the Second Great War emphasis was on small calibre artillery firing very rapidly.

Army Air Observation Post squadrons collaborated with forward ground observers, thus ensuring to the gunners three points of view—plan, elevation and oblique.

British and Americans used aircraft of similar design for this work — high wing monoplanes with low-powered aircooled engines, and enclosed cabins whose large windows gave exceptionally good downward view. The American aircraft were Piper Cubs and Stinson Sentinels, the British were Taylorcraft Austers. Their chief hazard was enemy flak, through whose shellbursts they flew with impudent assurance. They made excellent communication aircraft, too, for the transport of staff officers.

During these closing months of the war in the west, the Allied air forces were concentrated in a great ring around Germany, with only one opening to the north. Britain's Bomber Command and the U.S.A. 8th Air Force, operating almost exclusively from Great Britain, sealed this opening. The work of the U.S.A. 15th Air Force based in Italy was correlated with that of the 8th in Britain by General Carl A. Spaatz, commanding the U.S. Strategic Air Forces in Europe. The U.S.A. 9th Air Force and 1st Tactical Air Force operated from Belgium, Germany and France. The R.A.F. 2nd Tactical Air Force flew from bases in Britain, France, Belgium and Holland : this was the only Allied force to use jet-planes against the Luftwaffe—Meteors which went into action in 1945. R.A.F. Coastal Command flew from Britain, France, and Belgium ; Fighter Command from the United Kingdom, and Transport Command from wherever its services were required. In the east was the Red Air Force, now much superior in numbers to the Luftwaffe, and composed principally of tactical aircraft to give close support to the Red Army, with a comparatively small strategic heavy bomber force.

Disposition of Allied Air Forces

The Red Air Force was fully engaged on its numerous fronts. But the Allied air forces extended their hitting range to aid the strategic bombing requirements of the Red Army, and as the Allied Army of Liberation pressed ever farther east, the mounting bomber assault fell ever nearer to the German zone behind the Wehrmacht divisions facing the Red Army.

The air forces in 1945 were keyed to the operational plans of the overall commanders. Their priority strategic task was the destruction of the German

R.A.F. COMBATS THE COLD WEATHER

The severe cold spell in Europe during January-February 1945 provided the Allied air forces with additional problems. Below, left, a R.A.F. Typhoon is warmed up on a Continental airfield by a special ' pre-heating ' van. Collapsible tubes conveyed hot air from the van to the air intake and radiator of the aircraft. Right, R.A.F. meteorologist in the Netherlands inflates a ' met.' balloon with hydrogen. *Photos, British Official*

communication system; next came immediate aid to the armies in the field; attack upon the V-weapon launching sites in the Amsterdam–The Hague and the Zutphen–Meppen–Almelo areas; the wrecking of the remaining industrial and oil supplies of the enemy, and the beating down of what remained of the Luftwaffe and the German navy.

How the many operations designed to achieve these aims were interlocked is best illustrated by a few examples.

R.A.F. Hits Germans at Houffalize During the Ardennes offensive Bomber Command gave valuable aid to the American armies by attacking German troop concentrations at the road junction of Houffalize from before dawn on December 31, 1944, and on January 6, 1945, causing serious casualties and confusion.

In the night preceding the beginning of a new attack in the Nijmegen area by the 1st Canadian Army on February 8, Bomber Command bombed Goch and Cleve where German troops and armour were concentrated; and during the same night, to isolate the battle area, attacked transport centres at Magdeburg, Kassel, Mainz, Coblenz, Bonn, Hanover, Düsseldorf and Duisburg. Nijmegen, equally filled with Allied forces, was not bombed by the Luftwaffe. Immediately ahead of the ground attack, medium bombers of 2nd T.A.F. blind-bombed the German defence positions astride the Nijmegen–Cleve road so effectively that the road was cratered in only one place, yet the defences lining the roadway were severely affected, and the attack forces thrust along the road with few casualties.

On February 22, 1945, the Allied strategic and tactical air forces flew more than 7,000 sorties from British, French, Italian and Low Countries bases against transportation targets throughout Germany with the object of paralysing the German railway system and thereby isolating the Western Front for the attack across the Roer river next day by the American 1st and 9th Armies. Bombers of the U.S.A. 8th A.F. attacked the Hanover–Lubeck Bay–Berlin–Nuremberg communications; 15th Air Force bombers from Italy attacked targets in South Germany and Austria, and Bomber Command attacked 14 railway centres in the heart of Germany and viaducts at Bielefeld and Altenbeken. On February 23 U.S. heavy bombers attacked rail targets in the Kassel–Leipzig–Regensburg–Stuttgart area. Day after day the strategic interdiction and tactical pounding from the air backed the advance of the ground forces (described in Chapter 349).

Airborne Descent East of the Rhine Preparations for the 21st Army Group's assault crossing of the Rhine on March 24 were intensified under cover of an artificial smoke screen, and a great air interdiction programme east of the Rhine. Dummy parachutists were sometimes dropped to confuse and alarm the enemy, but, on March 24 the U.S. 17th and the British 6th airborne divisions, descended in parachutes and gliders to the north and north-east of Wesel in a series of carefully planned operations which achieved rapid and decisive success. Some 6,000 Allied bombers, fighters, transport planes, and gliders supported the Rhine crossings. These events succeeded a week of intense air activity, in which U.S. aircraft alone made 14,430 heavy bomber, 7,262 medium bomber, and 29,981 fighter sorties.

In mid-February 1945 Allied strategic air attack had been concentrated upon the isolation of the Ruhr from the rest of Germany. In this assault Bomber Command introduced the new

R.A.F. DESTRUCTION AT CLEVE

The north German frontier town of Cleve seen from the air on the day after its capture on February 12, 1945. It fell to Scottish troops serving with the 1st Canadian Army in a bitter assault led by Crocodile flame-throwing tanks. A strongly defended bastion of the Siegfried Line, Cleve had been heavily bombed by the R.A.F. on October 7, 1944, and on the night of February 7-8, 1945, it was bomb-drenched by over 700 R.A.F. Lancasters and Halifaxes.

GREATEST AIRBORNE OPERATION OF THE WAR

On March 24, 1945, British 6th and U.S. 17th Airborne Divisions supported Allied crossings of the Rhine. Some 6,000 bombers, fighters, and transport aircraft, flying from 26 British and Continental bases, took part; British losses were under three per cent. 1. R.A.F. Dakotas of the vast air armada speed towards the Rhine; above them Stirlings tow gliders. 2. Units of the U.S. 17th Airborne Division, carried in C-46 transports, jump from 600 feet, and 'dig in' (3). 4. British airborne troops take cover after their glider crash-landed.

EFFECTS OF ALLIED AIR POWER AT ESSEN AND HAMBURG

As the Allied armies occupied the industrial areas of N.W. Germany early in 1945 they saw the widespread destruction meted out by the R.A.F.'s sustained bomber offensive. Among the most devastated cities were Essen, seat of the vast Krupps armament works and centre of the Ruhr coal-mining and steel industry ; and Hamburg, second city of Germany and largest port on the Continent. In Essen, cleared on April 10, 1945, no work had gone on in the factories since the R.A.F. attack on March 11. 1. Section of the shattered Krupps works. At Hamburg, surrendered on May 3, less than one-third of the city was habitable. 2. R.A.F. bomb damage in the dock area. 3. Massive flak tower, with four gun-positions, also at Hamburg.

22,000-lb. streamline bomb (*see* illus. in page 3389). These, the heaviest bombs ever used so far in war, scored immediate results. The two parallel

Ruhr Cut off from the East railway viaducts at Bielefeld had been damaged by U.S. heavy bombers with 500-lb. and 1,000-lb. bombs, but the railway track had been repaired by means of steel girders laid across two damaged spans. The first 22,000-lb. bombs used on March 14 against these twin viaducts completely breached them, one bomb bringing down seven spans.

The Arnsberg viaduct, which took the main line over the upper Ruhr a few miles south of the Möhne Dam, also damaged in earlier attacks, was destroyed in one attack on March 19 with 12,000-lb. and 22,000-lb. bombs. The Vlotho bridge, though not destroyed, was rendered impassable in two attacks

R.A.F.'S TELL-TALE PHOTOS

Many secrets of R.A.F. photo-interpretation were not revealed until September 1945. Typical example is illustrated here. From the vertical photograph (above), taken at Kahla, Germany, near the Czechoslovak frontier, and showing an unusual airstrip, was constructed the perspective view (left) of what turned out to be an assembly plant for jet-propelled ME262s, built in the side of the hill, with a runway on top.
Photos, British Official

with 12,000-lb. bombs. The three main railway routes leading east from the Ruhr were thus cut beyond quick repair.

British and American strategic bombers attacked railway targets far and wide behind the German lines. The targets spread eastward into Czechoslovakia and south-eastward into Austria as the ground advance continued with ever-increasing momentum. German industry, dispersed to counteract bombing, was brought almost to a standstill by this transportation assault, for part-finished products could not reach the assembly plants. Meanwhile tactical bombers and fighter-bombers and fighters harried the retreating enemy by day and night.

On March 23 Bomber Command used their 22,000-lb. bombs against railway bridges at Bremen in prosecution of the plan to cut bridges on an arc passing through Bremen, Minden and the Middle Rhine. Four days later 10-ton bombs were employed against the U-boat pens at Vegesack, near Bremen. German naval ports and

shipping were attacked at Hamburg, Bremen, Wilhelmshaven, Kiel and Travemunde, U-boats and other warships being destroyed. Some German losses of heavy warships in harbour through bombing are described in page 3497. In addition, at least 21 merchant and naval vessels were sunk in attacks by U.S. heavy bombers on Bremen and Wilhelmshaven on March 30, and on Hamburg on March 30 and 31, including the cruiser " Köln " sunk at Wilhelmshaven. Red aircraft bombed Swinemünde and Stralsund on April 27, and Swinemünde on May 1. On April 18 and 19 Bomber Command attacked Heligoland and the airfield on the sand island of Düne, three-quarters of a mile away. Fires were left raging, and great destruction was done.

Berlin was heavily raided by U.S.A. 8th Air Force bombers from Britain. R.A.F. Mosquitoes made 37 consecutive night attacks and by the end of the war had dropped over 7,000 tons upon the capital. The U.S.A. 15th Air Force

from Italy bombed it for the first time on March 24. The R.A.F. began to bomb the capital from Continental bases on April 6.

The 8th Air Force now operated in huge fleets. On March 15, 650 bombers, strongly escorted, bombed the German General Staff H.Q. at Zossen, 20 miles south of Berlin. On March 18 no fewer than **Destruction of German Aircraft** 1,000 Flying Fortress and 300 Liberator bombers attacked Berlin in daylight. Sometimes their big air fleets met opposition. On April 7, over 1,300 Fortresses and Liberators with 850 escort fighters attacked airfields, depots and railway targets in north Germany ; they shot down 104 German fighters for the loss of 20 bombers and three fighters. On April 10 American heavy bombers attacking Berlin airfields destroyed 284 enemy aircraft on the ground and 21 in the air for the loss of 25 U.S. bombers and eight fighters. Three days later the U.S. fighter escort destroyed 266 German aircraft on the ground while the bombers attacked rail yards at Neumünster, between Kiel and Hamburg. On April 16, German aircraft totalling 724 were destroyed on the ground and three in the air in attacks on

R.A.F. 'GRAND SLAM' BOMB WRECKS BIELEFELD VIADUCTS

The R.A.F.'s ten-ton bomb was first used on March 14, 1945—against the twin railway viaducts at Bielefeld—severing the chief line connecting the Ruhr with the rest of the Reich. Previously, U.S. 'heavies' had damaged the structure with 500 and 1,000-lb. bombs, but the rail track had been repaired. The R.A.F. daylight attack by Lancasters completely breached it, as shown here, one bomb bringing down seven spans.
Photo, British Official

Regensburg, Landshut, and Plattling. Paralysis following these air attacks dried up the last of the Luftwaffe's oil supplies, and disorganized transport. The Luftwaffe, beaten out of the skies, was in process of being ground into the dust; but to the end enemy flak remained formidable.

From the beginning of the bombing war in 1940, Bomber Command had attacked oil targets on a small scale. But it was not until April 1944 that the British and U.S. strategic air forces began to concentrate against German oil supplies. The result of this assault was everywhere now apparent, and, after the war ended, confirmation of its effect came from high German officials.

On June 30, 1944, Dr. Speer, Reich Minister for Armaments and War Production, wrote to Hitler : "Mein Führer, **German Views** the enemy's [air] **of Attack on** attacks on the hydro-**Oil Production** genation works and refineries were intensified during June. If we do not succeed in protecting the plants better then in September of this year an impossible situation in the fuel supply for the Wehrmacht and the country will arise." When interrogated after the end of the war, Dr. Speer stated : "In the Luftwaffe the shortage of fuel became insupportable from September 1944 onwards. The allocation was cut down to 30,000 tons a month, though the monthly requirement was between 160,000 and 180,000 tons. In the Army the shortage first became catastrophic

at the time of the winter offensive of December 16, 1944. This was substantially responsible for the rapid collapse of the German defensive front against the Russian break-out from the Baranov bridge-head. [*See* opposite page]. There were 1,500 tanks ready for action, but they had only one or two fuel supply units, and were consequently immobilized."

Dr. Speer, Field-Marshal Erhard Milch, Secretary of State for Air, and Dr. Fischer, head of the Oil Department of the Ministry of Armaments, all expressed the view that earlier concentration of attack on oil targets might have ended the war sooner.

Many specialized air attacks were made during the closing months of the war. On January 1 Bomber Command made its fourth attack (the first in daylight) on the Dortmund–Ems Canal, and on February 20-21 (night) attacked the Mittelland Canal ; both canals were kept continuously out of action by bombing from September 1944 to the end of the war. On February 20 U.S. aircraft from Italy bombed Berchtesgaden and railways in the locality; in the succeeding night Red aircraft bombed Stettin, Stargard and Breslau. On March 15 R.A.F. Mosquitos destroyed the Gestapo headquarters in Copenhagen in a daring low-level attack. Two days earlier U.S. bombers from Italy bombed a jet-engined aircraft base at Regensburg. On April 25, using deep penetration bombs, Bomber Command attacked Hitler's chalet and S.S.

barracks, while U.S. bombers attacked rail targets in the same area ; Hitler's famous mountain home was badly damaged in this attack, but his eyrie above, reached by a lift through a vertical shaft cut in the living rock, escaped.

Special air aid was given to ground forces at widely separated points. During the night of April 7-8 parachute troops were dropped east of the Zuider Zee to assist in the rapid liberation of the Netherlands ; on the 9th, Canadian troops made contact with them. On April 14 and 15, U.S.A. 8th Air Force heavy bombers, assisting French ground and naval forces, attacked German forces holding resistance positions at the mouth of the Gironde.

On April 29 R.A.F. heavy bombers dropped 600 tons of food on airfields near The Hague, Rotterdam and Leiden after a truce had been **Relief by Air** arranged with the **For** Germans so that food **Starving Dutch** might reach the starving Dutch (*see* Chapter 358). Next day they dropped another 1,250 tons. On May 1 American bombers joined in this work of mercy, both forces continuing it daily for a fortnight.

It grew increasingly difficult to find targets for heavy bombers as the areas in German hands became more restricted. Berlin itself was now being battered by guns and tactical aircraft. The ring around it drew ever closer to the administrative centre of the city, but despite devastating anti-aircraft fire and the ring of Allied fighters, German communication planes continued to fly in and out of the beleaguered capital until within a day or two of its surrender on May 2. Fräulein Hanna Reisch, test pilot of the flying-bomb (*see* page 3427), was one of the last pilots to leave, with an envoy from Hitler to Himmler, who was in Schleswig-Holstein. R.A.F. Bomber Command's last big attack was made against Kiel in the night of May 2-3.

Germany's surrender was signed on May 8. On May 23 Air Chief Marshal Sir Sholto Douglas was appointed A.O.C.-in-C., British Air Forces in Germany. On May 24 Field-Marshal Ritter von Greim, who had succeeded Goering as C.-in-C. of the Luftwaffe, committed suicide in hospital at Salzburg. And Field-Marshal von Rundstedt said : "Air power was the first decisive factor in Germany's defeat. Lack of petrol and oil (due to bombing) was the second. And the destruction of the railways the third. The other principal factor was the smashing of the home industrial areas by bombing." Field-Marshal Montgomery had summed it up more concisely long before when he said : "The air battle must be won first."

Chapter 347

THE RUSSIANS ADVANCE TO THE ODER

After a short period of relative immobility, the Soviet armies on the frontiers of Germany began another advance in mid-January 1945. The Military Editor, Major-General Sir Charles Gwynn, here describes the rapidity with which it developed : in three months the Russians had captured Königsberg and crossed the river Oder. The Soviet campaigns of the summer and autumn of 1944 are dealt with in Chapters 318, 329 and 340

ALTHOUGH fierce local fighting continued at Budapest, and on the borders of Czechoslovakia and East Prussia, the whole Russian front had become virtually stabilized by the end of 1944. In Hungary the Germans had commenced a series of counter-attacks with the object of restoring the Danube defence line and saving Budapest; and Von Rundstedt's Ardennes counter-offensive also seemed to indicate that they had not lost hope of maintaining a solid defensive front in the east, counting on the exhaustion of the Red Army and its immensely lengthened communications. They had not, it is true, been able to eliminate the bridge-head Marshal Koniev had established across the Vistula and its

bridge-head west of Sandomierz on a wide front in the direction of Kielce. After two days' hard fighting, in which Russian artillery played a major part, penetration up to 25 miles on a 37-mile front had been made in spite of bad weather. Dr. Speer, Reich Minister for Armaments and War Production, interrogated after the surrender of Germany, attributed the rapid collapse of the German defence in this area to the shortage of oil brought about by the (western) Allied bombing offensive : " there were," he said, " about 1,500 tanks ready for action, but they had only one or two fuel supply units, and were consequently immobilized."

Kielce was captured on January 15, but it was not till the following day

that the full implications of Russian strategy were revealed by the announcement that Marshal Zhukov, who had taken over the command of the 1st White Russian Army from Rokossovsky, had broken through the German defences south of Warsaw. After three days' fighting he had linked two bridge-heads on the west bank of the Vistula, and on a front of 75 miles had penetrated to a depth of 37 miles, capturing the important communications and industrial centre of Radom. The German defences were strong and many concrete strongpoints had to be captured by infiltration methods before armour broke through ; but the rapid progress made after the break-through was effected suggests that they may have lacked depth, especially as owing to bad weather the attacking troops were without the air support which contributes so greatly to the swift exploitation of success.

Warsaw Defences Penetrated

KONIEV REACHES THE ODER
First to move in the Soviet offensive renewed on January 12, 1945, was Marshal Koniev's 1st Ukrainian Army whose armoured spearheads drove rapidly westwards from Baranov. Kielce fell to them within three days, and by January 17 their self-propelled guns were rolling through Czestochowa (below). A week later, Koniev's tanks were operating along the banks of the Oder (left).

upper tributaries, but they had had ample time to strengthen the defences on the middle reaches of the river. East Prussia, in spite of its exposed geographical position, was well protected by elaborate fortifications and difficulties of the terrain.

But if the Germans retained hopes that the Eastern front would remain stabilized, these were soon to be shattered. In an offensive which started on January 12 Koniev's 1st Ukrainian Army broke out of its Baranov

The Germans must quickly have realized that their position on the middle Vistula had been hopelessly shattered, and that immediate retreat was inevitable, for Zhukov was able to force another crossing of the river north of Warsaw, and on January 17 captured the city without serious opposition, entering it from north-west and south. They, however, showed no intention of abandoning East Prussia, for Rokossovsky, who had succeeded Zakharov in command of the 2nd White Russian Army, encountered strong opposition when he also, on January 14, launched an offensive from bridge-heads over the Narew. Only after four days' fighting did he succeed in breaking through to a depth of 25 miles on a 60 - mile front. The whole Polish front was now ablaze and Russian progress was amazingly rapid. On January 17 Koniev crossed the Warta, a tributary of the Oder, and captured among other places Czestochowa on its west bank; and his right wing was making towards Lodz, clearly in order to co-operate with Zhukov who, on January 19, captured that city. This rapid progress made it obvious that both generals were using armoured spearheads to thrust boldly in advance, by-passing German centres of resistance when they could not be captured at once.

There were few signs that the German retreat was being carried out in good order or that the expedient of leaving centres of resistance to fight to the last was having the desired effect of interrupting the communications of the Russian spearheads, **Rapid German Retreat** which, apparently by living on the country and on captured supply depots, were able to maintain their momentum. The rate of progress was so great that for some days it was widely assumed that the Germans had intended the Vistula line to be only an outpost and delaying position and that their main defence line would be found somewhere in the neighbourhood of the German frontier. It was difficult, however, to believe that such could have been their deliberate policy because it was not consistent with their evident determination to cling to East Prussia, the danger of whose encirclement would be greatly increased by withdrawal from the Vistula.

Moreover, short of the Oder, there were no natural features which lent themselves to defence, and a withdrawal so far would necessitate the abandonment of much German territory. Only if the Germans had sufficient resources in East Prussia and Pomerania to enable them to stage a major counter-offensive against the flank of the Russian advance could a withdrawal from the Vistula

THE POLISH ARMY COMES BACK TO WARSAW

Advancing in concert with the 1st Ukrainian Army on its left, the 1st White Russian Army under Marshal Zhukov (top) broke through the shallow German defences north-west and south of Warsaw in mid-January, 1945, and liberated the Polish capital on January 17. Units of the 1st Polish Army entered the city with the Soviet forces, and are here seen marching past the Church of the Holy Redeemer.   *Photos, Pictorial Press*

OPENING THE WAY TO KÖNIGSBERG

On the extreme right of the long line of Russian armies moving swiftly west across Central Europe, Army General Chernyakhovsky's 3rd White Russian Army penetrated into East Prussia and took Tilsit on January 20, 1945. Here bridges over the Niemen were blown up by the retreating Germans (left). Two days afterwards the important rail centre of Insterburg (right) was captured, clearing the ground for an advance on Königsberg. *Photos, Pictorial Press*

have been deliberately contemplated. But withdrawal as a purely defensive measure, combined with the retention of East Prussia, Danzig and Eastern Pomerania, entailed an immense lengthening of the front.

It is safe therefore to assume that it was intended to hold both the Vistula and East Prussia, and possibly the results of the autumn fighting may have encouraged the belief that the Russian effort had reached its limit. It is more doubtful whether the Germans, when they lost the Vistula, immediately decided to retire to the Oder. It seems more probable that they may have hoped to rally short of the frontier when the momentum of the Russian drive was lost owing to difficulties of communication—difficulties which would of course be greatly increased if blocks could be maintained on the main avenues of communication.

Whatever the German plans may have been, the speed and vigour of the Russian drives upset them. Koniev's rapid capture of Kielce had broken up a group preparing to counter-attack his flank, and his subsequent rapid advance to Czestochowa tended to isolate the

Problems of German Position

German force in southern Poland round Cracow, and to threaten its communications running through the great railway centre of Katowice. On January 19 Koniev took Cracow and, pressing west from Czestochowa, by January 21 had penetrated 19 miles into German Silesia on a 56-mile front. On his left General Petrov's 4th Ukrainian Army had been operating on both sides of the Carpathians in difficult country; but the latter's northern group now was able to advance westwards, crossing the Wisloka and Dunajec, tributaries of the Vistula, and by January 19 had captured Gorlice and other important towns south-east of Cracow. Maintaining his progress, Koniev on January 24 reached the upper Oder and captured the important town of Oppeln, while farther north he was nearing the Oder both north and south of Breslau.

Meanwhile Zhukov's advance had been at an even more sensational pace. His left, after capturing Lodz (January 19), crossed the Warta the following day, while his right captured Wloclawek on

the south bank of the Vistula. By January 22 his left was approaching Poznan and his right Bydgoszcz (Bromberg). Bydgoszcz, where the Vistula turns north to the Baltic, was taken the following day, but Poznan proved to be strongly defended and was by-passed. It remained, however, such a serious block on the main avenue of communication that separate operations on a considerable scale became necessary for its reduction.

While Koniev's drive into upper Silesia and Zhukov's towards Brandenburg and Pomerania had thus been progressing, Rokossovsky's offensive had developed with startling results. It soon became evident that the isolation of East Prussia was his main object, while at the same time he had the task of clearing the right bank of the Vistula in co-operation with Zhukov's advance along the opposite bank. His left wing on January 18 captured the stronghold of Modlin at the confluence of the West Bug and the Vistula, for which he had prepared the ground during the autumn; and on the following day, exploiting his break-through from the Narew, took Plonsk, Mlawa and Dzialdowo—the

Drive to Isolate East Prussia

RED ARMY DRIVES THROUGH SILESIA

The historic city of Cracow—former capital of Poland, standing on the left bank of the Vistula—was strongly held by the Germans. But, outflanked by Marshal Koniev's fast-moving armour and with its lines of communication menaced, it was entered by the 1st Ukrainian Army on January 19, 1945 (left). Soviet self-propelled guns in Neidenburg (right), captured by Marshal Rokossovsky on January 21. *Photos, Pictorial Press*

ZHUKOV FIFTY-FIVE MILES FROM BERLIN

Although the 1st White Russian Army reached the Oder above Kistrzin (Küstrin) on February 7, 1945, the Germans fought fanatically in defence of this vital bridge-head covering the Danzig–Berlin railway, and it did not fall until March 12 (above). In Pomerania, Schneidemühl, a junction on the same line, had orders to fight to the last, but Zhukov's right wing swept into the town on February 14, killing 7,000 and taking 5,000 prisoners. Right, a Russian command post in Schneidemühl.

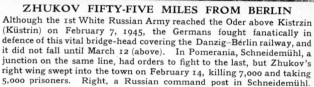

last only three miles from the frontier of East Prussia, indicating that his main advance was in the direction of the lower Vistula and the Gulf of Danzig. This was a bold undertaking, but the risk of serious counter-attacks was diminished and the German situation worsened by a resumption of Army General Chernyakhovsky's offensive, this time with marked success. After five days' fighting, by January 19 it had penetrated 28 miles on a front of 37 miles, capturing Pillkallen and a number of other strongly held places. Chernyakhovsky captured Tilsit on January 20, opening a new line of advance towards Königsberg, and Gumbinnen, a stronghold covering the Insterburg gap, fell on the following day. Insterburg itself was captured on January 22.

Rokossovsky's offensive continued to develop rapidly, and it must have been a bitter blow to all Germans when his forces overran Tannenberg with the memorial to Hindenburg on January 21, although their capture of Allenstein on the next day was a greater strategic disaster, for that town was a nodal centre of railway communication as well as a powerful strongpoint. Farther west on the same day Rokossovsky

took Deutsch Eylau, representing a long stride towards the lower Vistula. The great extent of Rokossovsky's front was further revealed when it was announced that his right wing had captured Lyck (January 24), the fortress town which guards the defile through the great Masurian Lakes region of East Prussia.

That achievement in a notoriously difficult terrain not only brought his offensive into close relation with that of Chernyakhovsky, but suggested that the Germans might have decided to attempt to withdraw from East Prussia, or at the least to concentrate for the defence of Königsberg, which was closely threatened by Chernyakhovsky. If the former were their intention the decision was belated, for on January 26 Rokossovsky's central drive captured Marienburg on the eastern branch of the Lower Vistula and reached the Gulf of Danzig at Tolkemit, thus barring the last avenue for a possible withdrawal.

That the Germans tried to withdraw at least part of their East Prussian force was proved by the violent attempts made by a considerable force, mainly armoured, to break through the ring of encirclement between Allenstein and Elbing during the following week.

The Germans still held Elbing in strength, and not till they lost it on February 10 did they abandon altogether their attempts to escape.

During the latter part of January, Rokossovsky's left continued to clear the right bank of the Vistula, and on January 27 crossed to the left bank at Bydgoszcz. Farther east the old frontier fortress town of Torun still held out, but Zhukov's troops co-operated to surround it, and it was stormed on February 1 by Rokossovsky's forces. Grudziadz (Graudenz), on the east bank of the Vistula below Bydgoszcz, also strongly garrisoned, and with orders to fight to the last, continued to hold out as a "hedgehog" position behind the main front. By the end of January, however, the fate of East Prussia was sealed, and although the complete liquidation of the large force surrounded in the province was to entail hard fighting over a considerable period, it had ceased to be of strategic importance. Whatever hopes the Germans may have had of re-establishing a corridor between East Prussia and the divisions isolated in Courland were

East Prussia's Fate is Sealed

ON THE APPROACHES TO BELEAGUERED BRESLAU

Breslau, junction of the railways and highways leading from the Oder to the interior of Germany, was the German High Command's central stronghold in the Upper and Middle Oder area. Koniev's forces, striking across the river from the north-east, completely encircled Breslau by February 16, 1945 ; but the city did not capitulate until after the general surrender in May. 1. Soviet sappers carry explosives through the suburbs. 2. Red Army mobile rocket battery in action on the city's approaches. 3. Russian artillery take up positions in blazing Neisse, fifty miles south-east of Breslau.

GERMANS CUT OFF IN EAST PRUSSIA

The storming by the 2nd White Russian Army of Elbing, East Prussian stronghold dominating the approaches to Danzig Gulf, completely sealed off enemy forces in this area. Marshal Rokossovsky's men are here seen penetrating the outskirts on February 10, 1945. The German command threw in regulars, cadets, medical units, civil defence squads, policemen, firemen and the Volkssturm in their effort to hold Elbing.

Zhukov's Army, which was rapidly approaching the lower reaches of the Oder near its confluence with the Warta. This entailed forcing the passage of the upper Oder and its tributary the Bober before reaching the Neisse, another tributary farther west. But the upper Oder was in flood and unfrozen, bridges had been blown up and it was strongly held by the Germans. A pause was necessary before a full-scale attempt could be made to force a crossing. On February 6, however, it was announced that after three days' intensive fighting a bridge-head 12 miles in depth and 50 miles in width had been secured south-east of Breslau, and that counter-attacks had failed. This was a magnificent exploit, achieved under most difficult conditions. It started in characteristic Russian fashion with the passage under powerful artillery support of small parties using improvised craft, followed by rapid exploitation as pontoon bridges were constructed.

Another crossing north-west of Breslau quickly followed which, after four days' fighting, resulted in a break-

finally shattered when, on January 28, General Bagramyan stormed Memel, which had been a base of abortive attempts to break out northwards.

After capturing Oppeln (*see* page 3555), and thrusting a wedge between the Germans to the north and those

Clearing Upper Silesia

in the industrial and coalmining district of Upper Silesia, Koniev's immediate object appears to have been to clear that area. On January 25 he captured the large towns of Gleiwitz in Germany and Ostrov in Polish Silesia. On January 28 he took by storm Katowice, the centre of the Dabrowa coalfield, which had been outflanked, and cleared the whole of this important coalfield. During the first week in February mopping up operations east of the Oder continued with Petrov slowly advancing farther south, clearing the country south of Cracow.

The clearing of Upper Silesia, which deprived Germany of fuel and industrial products of vital importance, was a great achievement, but Koniev's chief object was to come up in line with

RUSSIAN GAINS BY THE FIRST WEEK OF APRIL 1945

During the operations in Central Europe from January to April 1945, the grouping from north to south of the Soviet armies was as follows : 1st Baltic (Bagramyan) ; 3rd White Russian (Chernyakhovsky, later Vassilievsky) ; 2nd White Russian (Rokossovsky) ; 1st White Russian (Zhukov) ; 1st Ukrainian (Koniev) ; 4th Ukrainian (Petrov) ; 2nd Ukrainian (Malinovsky) ; and 3rd Ukrainian (Tolbukhin). By early April these forces controlled the ground here shown shaded.

SECOND MEETING OF THE ALLIED BIG THREE

At Yalta, in the Crimea, Mr. Churchill, President Roosevelt and Marshal Stalin had their second meeting, it was announced on February 7, 1945. They had met to consider Germany's fate after defeat, as well as other European problems. Behind the Big Three stand (left to right) : Mr. Anthony Eden, British Foreign Secretary ; Mr. Edward R. Stettinius, Jnr., U.S. Secretary of State ; and Mr. V. M. Molotov, Soviet Foreign Commissar. Between the last two is Sir Alexander Cadogan, Permanent Under-Secretary for Foreign Affairs ; and next to him Mr. Averell Harriman, U.S. Ambassador in Moscow

Direct colour photograph by Pictorial Press

CHIEF OF COMBINED OPERATIONS, 1944

The appointment of Acting Major-General Robert Edward Laycock, D.S.O., as Chief of Combined Operations (in which post he succeeded Admiral Lord Louis Mountbatten—see plate facing page 2570—when Lord Louis was made Supreme Allied Commander, South East Asia) was announced on October 22, 1943. After assisting in the evacuation of Crete, General Laycock was appointed in June 1941 to command a Special Service Battalion in the Middle East, later known as 'Layforce.' He was decorated for bravery in the Sicily landings of July 1943. *Direct colour photograph by Fox Photos*

FIELD-MARSHAL SIR JOHN GREER DILL, G.C.B., C.M.G., D.S.O.

Chief of the British Joint Staff Mission to the U.S.A. from December 25, 1941, till his death in Washington on November 4, 1944, Sir John was an Ulsterman, born in 1881. A veteran of the South African and First Great Wars, he commanded the 1st Army Corps in France in 1939-40. He was appointed Vice-Chief of the Imperial General Staff in May 1940, promoted Chief seven months later, and made Field-Marshal in 1941. He was awarded the Distinguished Service Medal by President Roosevelt—posthumously.   *Direct colour photograph by Karsh, Ottawa*

BRITAIN'S CIVIL DEFENCE AT WORK

The tireless efforts of British Civil Defence workers throughout the war are symbolized in these two photographs. A raid victim in a badly hit residential area (above) reports damage to the Incident Officer, seen wearing a blue cover on his steel helmet for identification (see also illustration in page 1276). Light and Heavy Rescue workers strove night and day, clearing debris, searching for trapped victims. This squad (left) is removing wreckage and girders from Amen Court, London, near St. Paul's, after the big incendiary raid on the City on December 29, 1940. Total civilian air-raid casualties in the United Kingdom during the war were 60,585 killed and 86,175 seriously injured. *Direct colour photographs by Fox Photos*

through reaching a depth of 37 miles and a width of 100 miles by February 11, and Koniev captured Bunzlau on the Bober the following day. There is no doubt that the Germans, expecting a long pause for preparation before attacks on such a formidable position could develop, were taken by surprise and were caught with their main reserves unsuitably placed.

During the remainder of February Koniev's operations were chiefly directed towards clearing Upper Silesia and completing the encirclement of Breslau, which came under close attack. By the end of the month he was pressing into the Sudeten mountains on the borders of Czechoslovakia, with Petrov on his left closing up towards Moravska Ostrava—the gateway of the main route from Silesia, through Moravia, to Vienna.

Meanwhile Zhukov continued his westward advance towards the lower Oder. By January 29 he had crossed
Zhukov Sixty Miles from Berlin
the German frontier into Pomerania, Brandenburg and West Prussia. By February 7 he had closed in on Frankfort-on-Oder and Kistrzin (Küstrin), reaching the Oder on both sides of these towns, which the Germans held as strongly fortified bridge-heads covering the two main railways leading to Berlin from the east. This brought Zhukov to within sixty miles of the capital, but there could be no question of his attempting to cross the river immediately. A pause was inevitable to allow him to close up his army, and it might well be prolonged until the Western Powers, still held up on the Roer, developed their offensive (*see* Chapter 349). The formidable obstacle of the Rhine lay ahead of them, and till it was crossed a premature attempt to reach Berlin from the east might result in failure. Decisions at Yalta (*see* Chapter 348) provided for synchronization.

Zhukov's next moves were to clear the east bank of the lower Oder and to liquidate the block on his main line of communications at Poznan. The by-passing expedient provided for the maintenance of his spearhead, but as his main army closed up, unhampered communications became essential. Moreover, in Pomerania there was a substantial German force which constituted a menace to his flank and also prevented Rokossovsky from coming up in line on the Oder. The liquidation of this group was therefore clearly desirable in order to allow the final offensive to be delivered in full force.

Fierce fighting continued round Poznan throughout February till Zhukov's forces accounted for the last remains of

its garrison on February 23. That the Germans had carried out orders to fight to the last must be admitted. In spite of the facts that the speed of the Russian advance found the outer defences of the city unorganized, and that the inner fortifications soon came under heavy attack from all sides, the siege lasted a full month. After the greater part of the city had been occupied resistance was maintained in the old citadel, which had finally to be stormed with assault ladders and through a breach in its wall—methods reminiscent of sieges two centuries earlier. Large stores of supplies captured at Poznan must, however, have to some extent compensated for the interference with Russian communications the city's stand had caused.

Extension northwards of Zhukov's front on the Oder had also been proceeding, while his right, thrusting northwest through the centre of Pomerania, on February 11 took Deutsch–Krone after by-passing and surrounding Schneidemühl on the Danzig–Berlin railway. Schneidemühl itself he took on February 14, after an abortive attempt by the garrison to break out. Heavy losses of men and material were inflicted on the enemy here, but when the Russians approached Stargard south-east of Stettin they encountered strong resistance in difficult lake country. They repelled

REDUCTION OF THE POZNAN 'HEDGEHOG'
The startling speed of the Red Army's sweep into eastern Germany was largely due to the extensive use by the Soviet Command of armoured spearheads which operated in open country and deliberately by-passed the enemy's powerfully fortified centres of resistance. These were later invested and subdued by supporting troops. Wreckage of battle is here seen in Poznan, one such strongpoint captured only after a month's siege on February 23, 1945

counter-attacks on a considerable scale, but their farther advance was checked on a large and strongly held defence line covering Stettin. Zhukov did not take Stargard till March 5, and Altdamm, the inner defence point at the head of the Oder estuary, not till March 20. To the north-east his forces had reached the Baltic coast and captured, after a stubborn resistance, the small port of Kolberg on March 18. Thus the Germans in Pomerania, like those in East Prussia, were completely isolated.

An important success on the direct line to Berlin was achieved on March 12 when, after four days' intense attack, Zhukov wiped out the German bridgehead at Kistrzin. For the remainder of March and the first half of April, little was heard of Zhukov's armies.

Koniev as early as February 16 had reached the Neisse and had linked up with Zhukov's left, but during March and early April he was mainly occupied with the sieges of Breslau and Glogau (Glogow) on his lines of communication where they crossed the Oder, and with operations towards the Sudeten passes. He captured Glogau on April 1 and Ratibor, in the direction of Moravska Ostrava, the previous day.

Rokossovsky and Chernyakhovsky, on the other hand, continued vigorous action during March and April. Rokossovsky's

DANZIG HELD OUT FOR SIX WEEKS

Eastern Pomerania was cleared by Marshal Rokossovsky's 2nd White Russian Army during February and March 1945, but a German group was left strongly entrenched around Danzig. This enemy garrison did not capitulate until March 30, although the fall of Stolp near the Baltic coast three weeks earlier had isolated it. A Red Army officer is here examining dismounted naval guns in the dockyard at Danzig.
Photo, Planet News

left wing, which at the end of January had crossed the Vistula, operated towards Danzig and into eastern Pomerania, while his right continued, in co-operation with Chernyakhovsky, to effect the liquidation of German forces in East Prussia. This divergence of objectives must have necessitated much regrouping, and Rokossovsky's offensive west of the Vistula did not develop in strength until the end of February, when an advance of 43 miles west of Chojnice, on the Pomeranian frontier, after four days' hard fighting was announced. Farther west he took Neu-Stettin on February 28, this town and Chojnice both lying on the main Danzig–Stettin railway. Stubborn opposition was encountered in this advance, the Volkssturm (*see* page 3173 and illus. in pages 3171 and 3172) being used in considerable numbers to reinforce the defence, and the terrain was difficult. Soviet cavalry was, however, effectively used for outflanking manœuvres. Grudziadz, on the Vistula, by-passed earlier (*see* page 3556), fell to Rokossovsky on March 6 after a fortnight's siege, and on the following day he took Starograd, just outside the Danzig enclave. He captured Stolp, on the coastal railway from Gdynia,

on March 9, thus completing the encirclement of the Danzig group which however, strongly entrenched, did not surrender until the 30th of the month, leaving Rokossovsky free to take part in the final decisive battles.

By the end of January Chernyakhovsky was closing in on Königsberg. On February 6 he captured Arnsdorf, on the 8th Kreuzburg. Thereafter three separate operations were conducted—the siege of Königsberg, attacks on a strong group entrenched in the Samland peninsula to the north-west covering the port of Pillau, and the breaking up of the forces which had attempted to escape through Rokossovsky's encirclement.

The Red Army suffered a great loss when Chernyakhovsky died on February 18 of wounds received while directing operations at Königsberg. Having come to the fore as one of Vatutin's principal subordinates, he had taken a high place among the Soviet commanders. Marshal Vassilievsky, who for long had been Stalin's chief of staff, succeeded him as commander of the 3rd White Russian Army.

Death of Chernyakhovsky

By reaching the shores of the Frisches Haff on March 15 Vassilievsky cut the German central group in two, and on March 20 his capture of Braunsberg eliminated its western half. Towards the end of the month there were signs of a general German collapse, and on April 9 Königsberg surrendered. This left only the Samland group and Pillau to be mopped up.

The loss of the Vistula line had been disastrous to the Germans. It entailed the loss of both East Prussia and Pomerania which, if the line had held, might possibly have become the bases for an effective counter-offensive. The admirable co-ordination and synchronization of the Russian blows, however, were well calculated to upset German plans, and the speed with which they were followed up left the Germans no chance of retrieving the situation. It is well to remember that during January, before the 1945 Allied offensive in the west had opened, the Russians had made these astonishing advances from their original positions in the course of a fortnight: Rokossovsky 160 miles, Zhukov 280 miles, Koniev 220 miles and Petrov 125 miles. Apart from the loss of major groups encircled, it can be imagined what immense losses of men and material were incurred daily by the Germans—losses accentuated by the attempts to check the flood with detachments deliberately sacrificed. There were none of the signs of an orderly retirement shown in the retreat to the Dnieper in 1943.

FALL OF KÖNIGSBERG MARKS THE END IN EAST PRUSSIA

Left, a machine-gun section of the 3rd White Russian Army on the Baltic coast near the East Prussian capital, the collapse of which became inevitable after the Soviet break-through to the Frisches Haff and Braunsberg (see map in page 3558). Right, Red Army men in the Gneisenau Fort, part of the Königsberg defences: the city was entered on April 9, 1945.
Photos, Planet News

Chapter 348

SOVIET UNION REDUCES DEFENCE COSTS

Immense efforts in the field of reconstruction, very great economic advances,
a marked quickening of cultural, political and religious activities, a notable
anxiety to widen ties of every kind with foreign countries—these were the chief
characteristics of Soviet life in 1945, described in this chapter by Mr. Andrew
Rothstein for twenty-one years associated with the Soviet press. For a record
of internal happenings in the Soviet Union in 1944, see Chapter 330

STALIN's declaration: " The period of war in Europe is over. The period of peaceful development has begun " (broadcast on Soviet V.E. Day, May 9), and his congratulations to his compatriots " on the advent of world peace " (broadcast on Soviet V.J. Day, September 2) give the tone of internal affairs in the Soviet Union during 1945.

The gigantic scale of reconstruction work facing the U.S.S.R. can be measured by the figures of the final report (September 13) of the Extraordinary Commission on German Atrocities. In the area ravaged by the Germans and their satellites, there lived a population of 88 million people, with a cultivated area of 170 million acres and 109 million head of livestock. 1,700 towns and 70,000 villages had been destroyed, leaving 25 million people homeless. 32,000 factories, 98,000 collective farms (each comprising fifty to a hundred homesteads) and 84,000 schools and other educational establishments had been burned or blown up. A huge belt of territory in the western part of the U.S.S.R., several times exceeding the United Kingdom in area, was a shattered waste.

Over 1,000 architects were engaged solely on planning or supervising the rebuilding of villages. Scores of small **Rebuilding the Countryside** mobile power stations, with 500 to 4,000 kw. capacity, were manufactured or imported (*see* illus. in page 3357) exclusively to restart industries in the country towns remote from the national power plants. The Agricultural Long-Term Credit Bank gave credit to collective farmers up to 10,000 roubles, repayable over seven years, for rebuilding their cottages and farm buildings. Arrears of agricultural tax were excused for dependents of fallen soldiers, while war invalids and returning soldiers were given substantial rebates ; and 10 per cent of housing space in all new apartment houses was by law reserved for demobilized men, war invalids, orphans or widows of fallen Red Army soldiers. A million houses had been built by November 1—but this was only one-sixth of the number of

buildings destroyed by the Germans, and at the end of 1945 millions of Soviet citizens were still living in dug-outs, barns or basements of ruined buildings.

The State Budget, adopted by the Supreme Soviet (Parliament) at the session which opened on April 24, for the first time since the war allocated less than half the expenditure to defence, and 55 per cent to economic, social and cultural purposes. The Supreme Soviets of the Union Republics adopted Budgets during the following months in which the same tendency was even more strongly marked. For example, 64 per cent of expenditure in Uzbekistan was earmarked for social and cultural purposes ; 42 per cent for economic construction and 45 per cent for social and cultural purposes in Estonia, and so on. The next Supreme Soviet session, on June 22, adopted a law demobilizing thirteen older classes of the Red army. It provided civilian clothing outfit, rations and travel facilities home, gratuity at rates ranging from one year's pay for one year of service, in the case of privates, to five months' pay for four years of service, for officers. Local authorities were ordered within one month to ensure employment (taking account of the man's wartime experience, and in no case at a lesser job than before the war) and living accommodation for demobilized men and their families, with the necessary fuel for the winter, and to provide timber, stock, seeds, cash advances, etc., for rebuilding the farmsteads of demobilized peasants. A further decree in August gave ex-soldiers priority for continued study in technical institutes and universities. On September 26 the demobilization of a further ten age groups was ordered.

A bird's-eye view of basic problems and achievements in reconstruction in Soviet Ukraine, worst damaged of the Republics, was given by its Premier, N. S. Khrushchev, on October 29 ; 123 main pits of the Donetz coalfield restored, out of 306 destroyed, and daily output brought up to 38 per cent of pre-war ; the cultivated area of collective farms brought up to 71 per cent of pre-war, and the area under cereals to 80 per cent ; 20 million square feet of housing space and cultural

buildings restored out of 30 million square feet (two-thirds of the pre-war total of buildings in Ukraine) destroyed by the Germans ; five million children at school (83 per cent of pre-war numbers) ; 99 theatres restored out of 130. Many thousands of collective farmers of the Zaporozhe region provided eight to ten days' voluntary work during the year for the rebuilding of the great Dnieper Dam. One million Ukrainians deported into German servitude returned during the year and many thousands arrived from Poland, exchanged for Polish citizens.

Basic economic construction went on parallel with this work of rebuilding

TREASURES RETURN HOME

Soviet authorities, like others in areas where the enemy threatened destruction, had, on the approaches of the invader, removed their art treasures to places of safety. Many movable treasures of Moscow and Leningrad, for instance, were hidden in Siberia. Here the Soviet artist Churakov prepares for display a portrait by Vasnetsov of the Tsar Ivan the Terrible on its return from the East. *Photo, Pictorial Press*

and reconditioning. On January 10 traffic started on the new Akmolinsk–Kartaly railway, in western Siberia, providing a vital additional channel for heavy industrial freight between the vast Karaganda coalfield and the Magnitogorsk Iron and Steel Works, in the Urals. The year's agricultural plan, announced on February 24 and laying down a further increase of 20 million acres in the sown area over 1944, was over-fulfilled. The fourth War Loan, of 25 milliard roubles, opened on May 5, was over-subscribed within two days. 900,000 youths and girls were being trained in the railway and trade schools by the end of the year, as against 800,000 in 1944. In July, it was announced that work had been resumed on the Manych Waterway—a 200-mile project, linking the Caspian and Azov Seas. On August 19, the Government and Communist Party published a joint resolution giving instructions for the preparation of the fourth Five Year Plan, to provide complete reconstruction and " surpass considerably pre-war levels " by 1950.

With this announcement must be linked a series of far-reaching schemes, such as the Northern Urals (iron ore)-

Long-Term Plans

Pechora (Arctic coal-field) Combine, making available for the metallurgical industry 120 milliard tons of coal (September 29), or the creation of two new People's Commissariats (Ministries)—one for Transport Engineering, based on the wartime People's Commissariat for Tank Building and on all existing large locomotive and automobile works (October 14), and the second for Industrial Crops, set up to direct the production of cotton, sugar beet, flax, tobacco, tea, rubber, etc. (November 11).

By May 23, 11,000 industrial co-operatives (compared with 14,500 before the war) had resumed production of such civilian goods as footwear, clothing, spoons, soap, furniture, toys. Local industries (*i.e.* factories and workshops belonging to town and district Soviets) produced in Russia alone nearly 30 per cent more consumption goods in the first half of 1945 than they had in the whole of 1940 (when the Soviet Union was not yet at war) ; and allotment holders numbered $18\frac{1}{2}$ millions at the end of the year, compared with $16\frac{1}{2}$ millions a year before.

Prices began to fall markedly in September. Thus milk and cereals came down by 50–70 per cent, and potatoes to pre-war prices. An important New Year's present for 1946 was the abolition of all wartime taxes (December 31).

Academies of Sciences were opened in two more Union Republics whose people under Tsarism were illiterate, miserably poor, and disease-ridden—Azerbaijan (February 20) and Kazakhstan (November 11). Among 90 new theatres built since the war, the first Theatre of Opera and Ballet in western Siberia was opened at Novosibirsk, with seating capacity of 2,000 (May 14).

Cultural interest in Britain continued to grow in a country where, among the foreign languages from which all secondary school children must choose at least one for study, English now held first place. The 250th anniversary of the death of Henry Purcell was commemorated in Moscow and elsewhere. The annual Shakespeare Conference opened on April 24. On June 12, the 75th anniversary of the death of Charles Dickens was commemorated in many towns.

The full extent of Britain's material wartime contribution to the Soviet Union, given in the British House of Commons by the Prime Minister (Mr. Attlee) on April 16, 1946, was as follows : 41 outward convoys went to Russia during the war. Between October 1, 1941 and March 31, 1946, military supplies to a total of approximately £308,000,000 in value were dispatched, including 5,218 tanks and 7,411 aircraft. In addition, raw materials, foodstuffs, machinery, industrial plant, medical supplies and hospital equipment to a value of £120,000,000 were sent.

On September 5 the State Committee of Defence—the supreme emergency executive body headed by Stalin, which was set up by the Soviet Government in 1941 to conduct the war—was dissolved, as no longer required. The pendant to this was the announcement on October 7 that a General Election would be held for the Supreme Soviet on February 10, 1946—the first election since 1937. As in other countries, war had prevented dissolution at the normal, constitutional time, which in the Soviet Union would have been 1941.

Delegations from the 27 million Soviet trade unionists attended the World Trade Union Conference in London in February (*see* illus. in page 3511)

Soviet Delegates Abroad

and in Paris in September. Soviet trade union delegations went to Rumania in January, Finland in April, Iran and the U.S.A. in July, Hungary in September, Norway in October, visiting industrial establishments and making contact with labour organizations in all these countries. (Visits were paid to the U.S.S.R. by delegations of the French trade unions in January, Polish in April, British Iron and Steel Trades in the summer, Rumanian and Italian in July, Czechoslovak railwaymen in August and the American C.I.O. in October.) Big Soviet delegations also attended during the year at the World Youth Congress in London, the International Women's Congress at Paris, and the International Conference of Students at Prague. American and British youth delegations (the latter headed by Mr. John Platts Mills, M.P., barrister and " Bevin Boy ") toured

LENINGRAD WELCOMES HOME THE RED GUARDS

A special welcome was given by the people of Leningrad to the Red Guards returning there for demobilization after victory They were pelted with flowers, embraced by the grateful population and loudly cheered as they marched through the streets. Here their commander, Colonel Valentin Yairov, surrounded by enthusiastic citizens, receives the traditional Russian symbol of welcome—a platter with bread and salt.
Photo. Pictorial Press

CRIMEA CONFERENCE

The Big Three—Mr. Churchill, President Roosevelt and Marshal Stalin—held their second and last meeting at Yalta, in the Crimea, from February 4–12, 1945. 1. The conference meets in the Livadia Palace, formerly a summer residence of the Tsars. On Marshal Stalin's left are Mr. Ivan Maisky, Deputy Commissar for Foreign Affairs, and Mr. Andrei Gromyko, Soviet Ambassador to the U.S. 2. President Roosevelt and Mr. Churchill. 3. Mr. Churchill greets Marshal Stalin. Behind the President (seated) stands his Chief of Staff, Admiral William D. Leahy, U.S.N.

Photos, British Official ; Paul Popper

AT THE BRITISH H.Q.
The Foreign Secretaries of the Three Powers held separate meetings at the Vorontsov Palace, the British H.Q., during the Crimea Conference. Above, Mr. Eden and General Sir Hastings Ismay, Chief of Staff to Mr. Churchill, face the camera ; Mr. E. R. Stettinius, U.S. Secretary of State, is on the extreme right, Mr. Molotov, Soviet Foreign Commissar, fourth from left.

the U.S.S.R. ; as did an all-party British Parliamentary Delegation, led by Colonel the Rt. Hon. Walter Elliot, M.P., in January and February.

From February 4 to 12, Mr. Churchill, President Roosevelt and Marshal Stalin with their Foreign Secretaries and Chiefs of Staff met at Yalta in the Crimea. Detailed plans were made for final blows against the enemy. Arrangements were also made for care and repatriation of liberated British and Soviet prisoners of war.

A scheme was worked out for a four-zone occupation and joint control of Germany. Other important announcements on Germany were : " We are determined to disarm and disband all German armed forces . . . eliminate or control all German industry that could be used for military production . . . exact reparation in kind for the destruction wrought by Germans . . . remove all Nazi and militarist influences from public offices and from the cultural and economic life of Germany."

The Big Three declared in favour of " processes which will enable the liberated peoples to destroy the last vestiges of Nazism and Fascism and to create democratic institutions of their own choice." The great Allies would consult, when necessary, on measures to help in

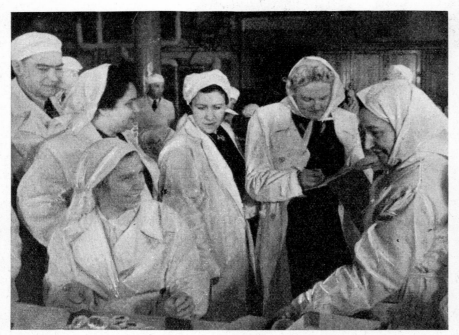

MRS. CHURCHILL VISITS THE SOVIET UNION

Mrs. Winston Churchill, wife of the British Premier, arrived in Moscow on April 2, 1945, tor a five-week tour of Russian institutions at the invitation ot the Soviet Government and the Soviet Red Cross and Red Crescent. It was announced on April 16 that her Aid to Russia Fund had reached a total of over £7,000,000. She is here inspecting a Moscow confectionery factory.
Photo, Pictorial Press

this. Thus, they sanctioned procedure for the establishment of a Polish Provisional Government " on a broader democratic basis," and for unity between Marshal Tito's Government and London Yugoslavs.

A Conference of the United Nations was to be held at San Francisco on April 25, to prepare a Charter on the lines proposed at Dumbarton Oaks (*see* page 3256). Agreement was also reached that, for any security action under a U.N.O. Charter, consent of all five Great Powers would be essential.

Decisions Taken at Yalta

In a secret agreement (not published until February 1946), the U.S.S.R. undertook to enter the war against Japan " two or three months after Germany has surrendered," while Britain and the U.S.A. agreed that the U.S.S.R. would regain certain rights in the Far East lost in the Russo-Japanese war of 1904–5, and would receive the Kurile Islands.

The second meeting, held at Moscow on December 16–27, was of the three Foreign Secretaries of the U.K. (Mr. Bevin), the U.S.A. (Mr. Byrnes), and the U.S.S.R. (Mr. Molotov). They agreed on procedure for drafting the peace treaties, to be submitted by May 1, 1946, to a conference of those United Nations " which actively waged war with substantial military force against European enemy States." They also

established a Far Eastern Commission at Washington to formulate policy, and agreed that an Allied Council for Japan should be established in Tokyo to advise the Supreme Commander for the Allied Powers. A joint Soviet-American Commission would help Korea back to democracy ; and the U.S.S.R. and U.S.A. declared they would withdraw their respective forces from China as soon as practicable.

The Rumanian and Bulgarian Governments were to be advised to accept Opposition members who were " suitable and will work loyally with the Government," as a condition of British and American recognition.

Finally, the three Foreign Secretaries agreed to recommend to the first General Assembly of the United Nations in February 1946 the establishment of a Commission for the Control of Atomic Energy.

Soviet delegations also took part in the Berlin Conference of July (*see* Chapter 380), the Conference of Foreign Ministers in London in September (*see* Chapter 378), the San Francisco **Treaties of Friendship** Conference of the United Nations in April (*see* Chapter 381), and the conference of the jurists of the Big Three, who adopted statutes for the International Tribunal at Nuremberg, in July (*see* Chapter 386). Treaties of friendship and post-war collaboration were signed with Yugoslavia (April 11) and the Provisional (Lublin) Government of Poland (April 21). A treaty of friendship and alliance with China was signed in Moscow on August 14, together with important auxiliary documents, among which were the following : (1) The

REPAIRING WAR DAMAGE AT LENINGRAD

On September 13, 1945, a Soviet State Commission published its report on damage wrought by the invader. It was stated that over 6,000,000 buildings had been destroyed, depriving some 25,000,000 people of shelter. Leningrad (during the siege) was described as one of the worst sufferers. Here Russian women are restoring the Mariinsky Palace in Leningrad. In the background s St. Isaac's Cathedral. *Photo, Pictorial Press*

HOW THEY HAILED VICTORY IN MOSCOW

To celebrate Germany's defeat, Marshal Stalin ordered a Victory Parade in Red Square, Moscow, on June 24, 1945. The salute was taken by the Deputy Supreme Commander-in-Chief, Marshal Georgi Zhukov, Marshal Konstantin Rokossovsky commanding the parade. Units taking part were : combined regiments of the fronts, a combined regiment of the Red Navy, the military academies, military schools and troops of the Moscow Garrison. 1. Red Army men drag standards and banners of the vanquished enemy—including Hitler's personal standard—in the mud of Red Square. 2. Rocket-salute over the Hotel Moskva. 3. Troops at the entrance to Red Square. *Photos, Pictorial Press*

RELEASED BRITISH Ps.O.W.

Plans for the 'protection, maintenance and repatriation' of Allied prisoners of war were made at the Crimea Conference. British prisoners released by the Red Army were to be taken by special train to the Black Sea port of Odessa where, in British ships, they embarked for home via the Middle East. 1. Released British prisoners near Poznan, Poland. 2. Ps.O.W. about to sail. 3. In Russian headgear, others chat with a Soviet officer on the quay.

U.S.S.R. agrees to respect China's sovereignty in Manchuria; (2) China agrees to make the commercial port of Dairen, in Manchuria, a free port for 30 years; although the administration of Dairen will be Chinese, China will lease to Russia, at the latter's request, free of charge, half of the port installations and equipment; (3) Port Arthur will be used jointly by China and the U.S.S.R. as a naval base for 30 years, the U.S.S.R. being responsible for its defence and China for its civil administration; (4) the Chinese Eastern and South Mongolian Railways are to be unified as one railway system, to be owned and operated jointly for 30 years by the U.S.S.R. and China, after which period they will revert to China without compensation; (5) the Russian forces will start to withdraw from Manchuria within three weeks after the Japanese surrender and will complete the withdrawal within three months.

An armistice with Hungary was signed by Marshal Voroshilov on behalf of the United Nations on January 21 (see Chapter 375). Diplomatic relations were established or re-established with Dominica (March 8), Venezuela (March 13), Bolivia (April 18), Guatemala (April 19), Denmark (May 16), Ecuador (June 16), Rumania and Finland (August 6), Hungary (September 25).

Diplomatic Relations

The Soviet-Japanese Neutrality Pact of April 1941 was denounced by the U.S.S.R. on April 5, and war was declared on Japan on August 8 (see Chapter 367). The Soviet-Turkish Treaty of Friendship of December 1925 was denounced on March 19.

On September 7 Colonel-General F. Golikov, Soviet Repatriation Delegate, announced that 5,115,000 Soviet citizens had been brought back so far—2,886,000 having been liberated by the Red Army and 2,229,000 by the western Allies. More than 732,000 nationals of other Allied countries had been repatriated, including 292,000 French and 24,000 British.

FOREIGN SECRETARIES MEET IN MOSCOW

The Foreign Secretaries of Britain, the U.S. and the U.S.S.R. met in Moscow on December 16, 1945. Ending with an all-night sitting on December 27, the talks covered drafting of peace treaties and the proposed establishment of Commissions of Inquiry for the Far East and Atomic Control. Here are Mr. Ernest Bevin (Britain), Mr. V. Molotov (U.S.S.R.), and Mr. James F. Byrnes (United States.).
Photo, Central Press

Chapter 349

THE DECISIVE BATTLE OF THE RHINELAND

In this chapter, Major-General Sir Charles Gwynn, the Military Editor, picks up the threads of the battle of the Western Front, following the defeat of Rundstedt's counter-offensive in the Ardennes (described in Chapter 336), and carries it forward to March 23, 1945, when the Allies stood along the left bank of the Rhine from the Swiss frontier to the sea. The final phases of the war in the West are recorded in Chapters 357 and 369

WITH the opening of the Port of Antwerp and the consolidation of his lines of communication, General Eisenhower in November set in motion preparations for the winter offensive which was to have the object of penetrating the Siegfried line and of placing him in a position to cross the Rhine—his ultimate objective being to isolate the Ruhr and force mobile war on the enemy in the plains of northern Germany. Without the Ruhr the enemy's capacity to continue the struggle must quickly collapse, but it was evident that the enemy had staged a remarkable recovery, and that to reach the Rhine would entail bitter fighting in a winter that gave every promise of bad weather. Nevertheless, it was all important to give the enemy no opportunity for further recovery or to divert forces to meet the Russian offensive due to open.

By the middle of December, General Eisenhower's initial operations had made progress. Field-Marshal Montgomery had been ordered to prepare his 21st Army Group to clear the country between the Maas and the Rhine and to line up on the latter river between Emmerich and Düsseldorf, the most favourable stretch for a major crossing. Acting on these orders, by December 4 he had cleared the whole west bank of the Maas (*see* page 3383) in order to

British Position in December 1944

provide a lightly held defensive flank on the right of the 1st Canadian Army, which was concentrating in the Nijmegen bridge-head preparatory to launching an offensive between the two rivers. Incidentally it should be noted that at least half of this army was composed of British troops, partly in order to bring it up to the required strength, and partly to replace the Canadian corps employed in Italy.* The British 2nd Army was lined up along the Maas as far south as Maeseyck whence its front crossed the river to join the U.S. 9th Army in the Geilenkirchen area. It was given the task of making preparations for the eventual assault across the Rhine.

To the right of the 2nd Army the U.S. 9th and 1st Armies had enlarged the break in the Siegfried line at Aachen, but had come up against strong German resistance on the Roer river and in the Hürtgen forest which covered the approaches to its upper reaches, and to the reservoirs south of Schmidt, the opening of which would flood the river lower down. The 9th Army had reached the Roer between Linnich and Jülich (*see* page 3383), but the 1st Army had not progressed

far along the Cologne and Düren roads or in the forest. The enemy, however, was suffering heavy losses in a battle of attrition. Farther south the U.S. 3rd Army was attacking the strong defences of the Saar front (*see* page 3382) and though it had made some penetrations, had not broken through. Farther south still, the U.S. 7th Army, having captured Strasbourg (*see* page 3382), was attacking northward in the Palatinate, while in Alsace the French 1st Army was driving the Germans out of the Vosges into the pocket they held in the Colmar area (*see* page 3382) as a wedge between forward elements of the French and the U.S. 7th Army at Strasbourg.

American and French Positions

Such was the general situation when Rundstedt's Ardennes offensive (*see* Chapter 336) caused an interruption and disturbed the dispositions of the Allies. The U.S. 1st Army was drawn

---

* During the last months of 1944, the following British Divisions were serving with the 1st Canadian Army : 7th Armoured, 49th Infantry, 50th Infantry, 51st (Highland), & 52nd (Lowland) (which played an outstanding part in the capture of Walcheren), and also the 4th Special Service Brigade (S.S.). The 15th (Scottish), 43rd (Wessex), 53rd (Welch), and Guards Armoured Divisions were among others which served with it.

U.S. ARMIES CROSS THE SWOLLEN ROER

Under pressure of attack by the U.S. 1st Army, the Germans on the night of February 9-10, 1945, blew up the dams containing the Roer reservoirs. The floods made the Roer river impassable for some days, but while they were still high the U.S. 1st and 9th Armies forced a most difficult crossing in the early hours of February 23. U.S. 9th Army engineers here assemble a temporary bridge after the river had considerably subsided. *Photo, U.S. Official*

ALLIED OFFENSIVE AGAINST THE REICH IN THE WEST STARTS AFRESH

After the elimination of the enemy's Ardennes salient, General Eisenhower, in February 1945, resumed his interrupted offensive. Among the most bitterly contested areas was that of the Reichswald, the thickly forested country on the Netherlands-German frontier. 1. British bren-gunners in a shattered attic at Gennep give covering fire for their comrades below. Gennep, heavily fortified Netherlands town and pivotal point in the German defences, was taken on February 12 by Scottish troops serving with the 1st Canadian Army. 2. British tanks await the order to move up the line near Goch, important road junction in the Reichswald area. It was captured by Welsh and Scottish troops serving with the 1st Canadian Army on February 21 after fierce fighting. 3. Generating the smoke screen which covered British troops advancing beyond Goch. 4. Rafts being used to ferry heavy armour across the flooded area behind the lines.

Photos, British Official

L/Cpl. H. E. HARDEN
(Royal Army Medical Corps)

Medical orderly attached to a section of a Royal Marine Commando troop, fighting in N.W. Europe on January 23, 1945, Lance-Corporal Henry Eric Harden sacrificed his life in rescuing, under a hail of machine-gun and rifle-fire directed from four positions, an officer and three other casualties left in the open. For 'superb devotion' he was posthumously awarded the V.C.

Sgt. A. COSENS
(Queen's Own Rifles of Canada)

The V.C. was awarded posthumously to Sergeant Aubrey Cosens for his bravery on the night of February 25-26, 1945, at Mooshof, Holland. He himself killed, single-handed, 20 of the enemy and took an equal number of prisoners, which resulted in the capture of a position vital to the success of the future operations of his brigade. He was shot by a sniper.

Pte. J. STOKES
(King's Shropshire L.I.)

In Holland on March 1, 1945, during the attack on Kervenheim, Private James Stokes displayed 'magnificent courage and devotion to duty' which earned for him the award of a posthumous V.C. Though badly wounded—in all eight times in the upper parts of his body—he single-handed continued to attack enemy positions, firing his rifle until he died.

Fusilier D. DONNINI
(Royal Scots Fusiliers)

Fusilier Dennis Donnini's 'superb gallantry and self-sacrifice' in N.W. Europe on January 18, 1945, won him a posthumous V.C. Though severely wounded in an attack between the Maas and Roer rivers, he drew enemy fire from his platoon on to himself, enabling a strong position to be captured by his comrades before he himself was killed.

Major F. A. TILSTON
(Essex Scottish Regiment)

Though dangerously wounded Major Frederick Albert Tilston silenced an enemy gunpost single-handed in the Hochwald on March 1, 1945, during the advance on the Rhine and took part in vicious hand-to-hand fighting among powerful enemy positions, refusing medical aid till his unit's objectives had been secured. He was awarded the V.C.

Photos, Canadian Official ; G.P.U. ; Topical Press ; Keystone

southwards and the U.S. 3rd Army northwards to repel the breakthrough, while the U.S. 7th Army extended its front as far north as Saarbrücken ; and in the Palatinate, where the enemy launched a subsidiary attack apparently in order to relieve pressure on their forces retreating in the Ardennes, it withdrew to the defences of the Maginot line.

By the end of January, however, the Germans were back on the line from Monschau to Echternach, and the time had come for General Eisenhower to make fresh dispositions for resuming his interrupted offensive.

Already in mid-January the process had begun, and certain preliminary movements and operations had been undertaken. The 1st Canadian Army had completed its concentration in the Nijmegen bridge-head, and the British 2nd Army had on January 16 launched an attack against the enemy's strongly held Sittard salient on the left bank of the lower Roer between Geilenkirchen and Roermond. After some hard fighting, by January 28 the Germans were driven back across the Roer river, and the U.S. 9th Army extended its front to Roermond on the Maas, allowing the 2nd Army to concentrate northwards in order to co-operate with the Canadians.

Down in Alsace on January 20 the French 1st Army had also started an attack in the Colmar pocket in which the XXI American Corps co-operated. By February 9 the pocket was liquidated, and the whole west bank of the Rhine from Strasbourg to the Swiss frontier had been brought under Allied control. As this front could be lightly held, a considerable American force was thereby released for offensive action farther north. As a climax to the Colmar operations, the U.S. 3rd Division achieved a remarkable feat in

Attack in Colmar Pocket

BOTH SIDES USE NEW WEAPONS IN THE WEST

It was disclosed on March 10, 1945, that rocket-firing Sherman tanks were being employed by British and Canadian troops. Sixty 4·5-inch rockets were mounted on the turret (right) and could be fired singly or in salvos. About this time, also, the Germans were using on the U.S. 9th Army front a 15-in. howitzer mounted on a 'Tiger' tank chassis (left).

Photos, Keystone ; Planet News

WIPING OUT THE WESEL POCKET

British troops with the 1st Canadian Army in the Hochwald met strong resistance at Weeze, to reach which on March 2, 1945, they had to cross the River Niers. Left, disembarking from assault craft after the crossing. Capture of Xanten seven days later by the Somerset Light Infantry led to the wiping-out of the Wesel pocket. Right, a prisoner is led through Xanten's ancient gate.
Photos, British Official ; Associated Press

capturing the fortified medieval river port of Neuf Brisach by a night attack on February 6 using assault boats to cross its moats and, in true medieval style, rope ladders to scale the twenty-foot walls—thus emulating a similar feat by the New Zealand Division in 1918.

On February 5, although the U.S. 9th Army remained under Field-Marshal Montgomery's command, the U.S. 1st Army reverted to General Bradley (*see* page 3421) and resumed its attacks towards the heavily fortified village of Schmidt and the Roer reservoirs. It met fierce resistance, but it captured Schmidt on the 8th and by February 11 it had obtained control of the west bank of the Roer from a point two miles west of Gemund to a point two miles

Advance to the Roer River

upstream from Roermond. General Patton's 3rd Army was left to maintain the attack in the Prüm–Trier area.

Redispositions had by now been completed for a general resumption of the offensive, and on February 8 the 1st Canadian Army struck the first blow designed to clear the area between the Maas and the Rhine and to threaten the Ruhr directly. Although this offensive had had to be postponed for six weeks while Rundstedt was being thrown back, it now had improved prospects of achieving success, for the enemy had expended the greater part of his strategic reserve in the Ardennes

and had to transfer his badly mauled 6th Panzer Army eastwards in an attempt to check the Russian offensive on the Vistula and Danube fronts, by now in full blast (*see* Chapters 347 and 354). It was in fact doubtful whether the Germans, having expended their main reserves (*see* page 3422), would accept decisive battle west of the Rhine or would withdraw behind it.

The attack was opened by the XXX Corps under General Crerar's command on a front of five divisions supported by over 1,000 guns and a powerful air bombardment. At first it made rapid progress, but it soon encountered fanatical resistance, appalling weather and flooded country. The movements of troops and supplies through wooded areas lacking solid roads became difficult, and many attacks on the enemy's centres of resistance on the northern

DEVASTATION IN MÜNCHEN-GLADBACH

On their way to the Rhine to join hands with British troops serving with the 1st Canadian Army, forces of the U.S. 9th Army took the German industrial town of München-Gladbach (capture disclosed on March 1, 1945) at the approaches to Düsseldorf. Left, München-Gladbach, previously a target of Allied ' heavies,' after its fall. Right, five miles to the south-west, refugees stream from Rheindahlen.
Photos, British and U.S. Official

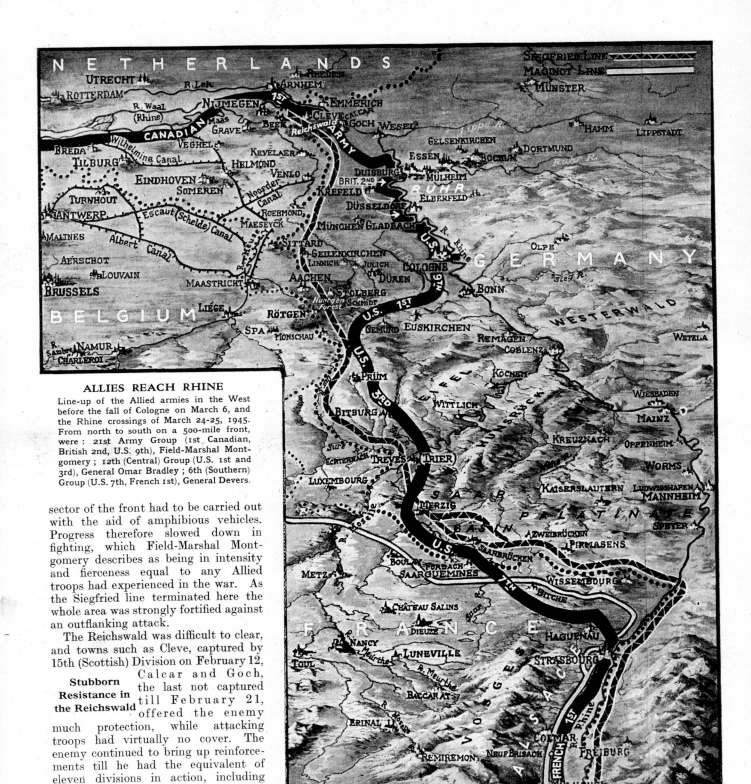

ALLIES REACH RHINE

Line-up of the Allied armies in the West before the fall of Cologne on March 6, and the Rhine crossings of March 24-25, 1945. From north to south on a 500-mile front, were : 21st Army Group (1st Canadian, British 2nd, U.S. 9th), Field-Marshal Montgomery ; 12th (Central) Group (U.S. 1st and 3rd), General Omar Bradley ; 6th (Southern) Group (U.S. 7th, French 1st), General Devers.

sector of the front had to be carried out with the aid of amphibious vehicles. Progress therefore slowed down in fighting, which Field-Marshal Montgomery describes as being in intensity and fierceness equal to any Allied troops had experienced in the war. As the Siegfried line terminated here the whole area was strongly fortified against an outflanking attack.

The Reichswald was difficult to clear, and towns such as Cleve, captured by 15th (Scottish) Division on February 12, **Stubborn Resistance in the Reichswald** Calcar and Goch, the last not captured till February 21, offered the enemy much protection, while attacking troops had virtually no cover. The enemy continued to bring up reinforcements till he had the equivalent of eleven divisions in action, including four parachute and two armoured divisions. The parachutists in particular fought magnificently.

Meanwhile the U.S. 9th Army, which it had been planned should attack on the Roer front between Jülich and Roermond a day or two after the Canadians as the other half of a pincer manoeuvre, had to be held back. It had completed its preparatory movements with remarkable speed and was

all ready, but so long as the enemy controlled the Roer reservoirs its attack could not safely be launched. A flood released by blowing up the dams while a crossing of the river was in progress would have had disastrous effects. On the other hand it was inadvisable to postpone the attack of General Crerar's

army in order to ensure synchronization, after its deployment in assault positions. The deployment had been carried out with great secrecy, and each day's postponement would have risked loss of the element of surprise. Moreover, the condition of troops waiting in forward positions would have deteriorated.

ONE MAN SEIZED THE REMAGEN BRIDGE

Swift initiative of a lieutenant of the U.S. 9th Armoured Division unexpectedly established a bridge-head across the Rhine on March 8, 1945, with the seizure of the Ludendorff railway bridge at Remagen, 12 miles south of Bonn. Dashing across the bridge, troops disconnected the fuses and charges with which the enemy had planned to destroy it a few minutes later. The bridge after capture (above), with U.S. 1st Army units crossing it to the east bank (below).

It was his possession of the flood weapon in reserve that had enabled the enemy to concentrate the bulk of his force against the Canadians, and not until the last minute, when he was in danger of losing control of it under the attacks of the U.S. 1st Army, did his engineers discharge it on the night of February 9–10. The resulting flood made the Roer impassable for some days, but before it completely subsided the U.S. 1st and 9th Armies struck at 3.30 a.m. on February 23, and in bright moonlight, under very difficult conditions, forced a passage across the river, swollen from its normal width of 40–60 feet to 250 feet. As the Americans advanced northwards, it was soon apparent that the postponement of the attack and the consequent concentration of the enemy's forces against the Canadian Army had actually produced a more favourable situation, for once the crust of the enemy's resistance on the Roer was broken there was little behind it.

After some delay in forming bridge-heads over the still flooded river (Jülich was not cleared till February 24), the U.S. 9th Army captured Roermond, München-Gladbach and Krefeld, and armoured columns had reached the Rhine opposite Düsseldorf by March 2. The Germans then began to withdraw across the Rhine, and on March 3 the U.S. 9th Army joined hands with British troops of the 1st Canadian Army striking south from Kevelaer. The enemy, fighting stubbornly as he retired northwards, formed a bridge-head at Wesel, to which he clung tenaciously until March 10, when he withdrew across the Rhine, blowing up the two bridges.

Germans Withdraw Across Rhine

The capture of Wesel brought the Allied line to the Rhine as far south as Düsseldorf, and completed the first objective given to Field-Marshal Montgomery, who was now left free to concentrate on his preparations for the formidable undertaking of crossing the river.

That operation, however, promised to be distinctly less formidable owing to the heavy losses the Germans had sustained—over 100,000 in killed, wounded and prisoners—as a consequence of their hoped for but not altogether expected decision to accept battle west of the river.

While the U.S. 9th Army had attacked north-eastward, the U.S. 1st Army had attacked eastwards towards Düren and Cologne, protecting the 9th's flank. Düren, utterly destroyed, was taken on February 25 and the Erft River was crossed on February 28. By March 5 the outskirts of Cologne were reached. The city, bomb-shattered and torn, fell to the U.S. 3rd Armoured and

8th and 104th Infantry Divisions on March 6. Two days later a more important and totally unexpected success was achieved. While the fight in Cologne was in progress, the right of the Army had been extending towards Bonn, and the U.S. 9th Armoured Division, probing in advance to the south of that city, discovered the Ludendorff railway bridge at Remagen intact. Immediately the officer on the spot, on his own initiative, rushed the bridge, surprising and overrunning the German demolition party before charges already laid could be exploded. The consequences of this fortuitous success are dealt with in Chapter 369; but it meant that something more than a line-up on the river had been achieved in the northern half of the Rhineland.

In the southern half, General Patton's U.S. 3rd Army had from the beginning of February been forcing its way vigorously through the Siegfried defences on the Prüm–Trier front and into the rugged and wooded Eifel region in which the northern tributaries of the Moselle were formidable obstacles. During the first half of February it crossed the Our and Sure rivers, capturing Prüm on February 12. Its advance then continued on both sides of the Moselle and it established bridgeheads across the Kyll on the north and the Saar on the south side, leading up to the capture on March 2 of the ancient city of Trier where the Volkssturm (*see* page 3173) fought, but ineffectively.

By this time the U.S. 7th Army was also closing in on the southern half of the Saar defences, fighting its way into the Saar industrial town of Forbach, five miles south-west of Saarbrücken, by February 22. But it was north of the Moselle that General Patton's unrelenting pressure finally broke down German resistance. On March 6 it was disclosed that his armour had advanced 32 miles in 36 hours, and the following day it reached the Rhine north-west of Coblenz. Two days later it established contact with the 1st Army south of Remagen, and by March 11 the whole of the west bank of the Rhine from Nijmegen to the point at which the Moselle enters it, and on the Alsace front, was controlled by the Allies.

There remained only the Saar pocket to be dealt with, and in it the Germans had few reserves, though they were clinging stubbornly to the Siegfried defences on its western side. It was an opportunity that Eisenhower was not likely to miss, though a few days were needed for reorganization and to complete the mopping up of the Eifel area. General Marshall in his report to the

U.S. 7th and 1st Armies in Contact

Secretary of War quotes the letter received from General Eisenhower at this stage. "Tomorrow morning the XX Corps of Patton's Army begins a local attack in the Trier area as a preliminary to the general attack by 7th Army on the 15th. So far as we can determine, there is not a single reserve division in the whole area. If we can get a quick break-through the advance should go very rapidly. . . . It will probably be a nasty business breaking through the fortified lines. . . . I have given 7th Army 14 Divisions for their part of the job, and XX Corps 3rd Army jumps off with four. Patton will throw in another subsidiary effort north to south across the Moselle with four or five divisions."

That was General Eisenhower's admirable plan, and General Patton was always likely to do even more than was expected of him. Under cover of darkness, and without artillery support, some of Patton's forces crossed the Moselle on a nine-mile front south-west of Coblenz at 2 a.m. on March 15, and drove southward, while his XX Corps struck eastward from Trier. Simultaneously the U.S. 7th Army attacked northwards between Saarbrücken and the Rhine. It made steady progress, through the dense minefields and formidable works of the Siegfried defences, pinning down strong enemy forces. But the 3rd Army thrusts were the more decisive, in particular that from the bridge-head over the Moselle, from which perhaps less was expected because it was faced by very difficult country. Despite that, the spearhead of the 4th Armoured Division broke out on March 16 and, advancing 32 miles, seized two bridges over the Nahe river south of

Kreuznach, cutting the main enemy line of communication to the front.

From that point German resistance crumbled and armoured divisions of the 3rd and 7th Armies encircled the whole pocket, leaving nothing to be done except mop up the troops within it. American columns were able to move in all directions, and as a result well-known places having no particular relation to one another fell rapidly. The 3rd Army entered Coblenz on March 17 (captured on the 18th); while on March 20 troops of the 3rd Army from the north-west and of the 7th Army from the south-west linked up about twelve miles west of Kaiserslautern in the Palatinate after the latter had taken Saarbrücken, Zweibrücken and other towns. The former on the same day passed through Kaiserslautern and, reaching the Rhine, captured Worms and entered Mainz. Next day, 3rd Army tanks took Ludwigshafen, important industrial city opposite Mannheim, and seat of the much bombed chemical works of I. G. Farbenindustrie. On the 23rd, 3rd Army spearheads captured Speyer, like Worms and Mainz prominent in the Middle Ages, and, more important, at Oppenheim south of Mainz, secured a footing across the Rhine by a surprise attack. This again was a purely fortuitous success unplanned by the Higher Command, carried out on the initiative of the infantry commander on the spot, who saw his opportunity and took it. (How the success was achieved and exploited is explained in Chapter 369.)

The elimination of the Saar pocket ended the battle of the Rhineland and

German Towns Fall Rapidly

U.S. FIRST ARMY CAPTURES COLOGNE

Described as 'bomb-shattered and battle-torn,' Cologne, third city of the Reich, fell to units of the U.S. 1st Army, comprising the U.S. 3rd Armoured and 8th and 104th Infantry Divisions, with little opposition on March 6, 1945. This dramatic photograph shows a U.S. tank being hit by a shell. The soldier on the right was blown clean out of it, escaping with the loss of a leg.

Photo, Keystone

completed the line-up along the river which had been General Eisenhower's first major objective. The whole operation from the date the Canadian Army

First Allied Objective Achieved

jump-off had been carried through in the remarkably short period, considering the conditions of weather and terrain, of six weeks. The enemy had suffered crushing losses of men and material and had paid a heavy price for the misuse of his reserves, first, and chiefly, when he expended in Rundstedt's offensive the powerful force he had succeeded in forming ; and, secondly, and more excusably, when he concentrated what reserves he had left against the Canadian Army's attack. It is now known that Hitler not only insisted on Rundstedt's offensive against the advice of his generals, but removed the latter from his command (replacing him by Field-Marshal Albert Kesselring, German C.-in-C. in Italy) when he represented that in spite of initial success the enterprise was bound to fail, and that immediate withdrawal was necessary. Whether the subsequent decision to stand and fight west of the Rhine despite the loss of reserves was Hitler's is not so clear, and it must be admitted that the urgent need to protect the Ruhr confronted the German General Staff with a difficult dilemma. Field-Marshal Montgomery, at any rate, considered that a fatally wrong decision was taken. The decision did not prevent the Allies from recovering the time lost over Rundstedt's offensive, and in doing so they were able to administer crushing defeat on the enemy.

It is interesting to note the difference in method adopted on the two main

EASTWARD THROUGH THE SIEGFRIED LINE
After a heavy preliminary bombardment, troops of General Patton's U.S. 3rd Army on February 12, 1945, entered Prüm, eleven miles inside Germany, strategically important as the converging point of five main roads and situated among the main outer Siegfried defences : infantry of the U.S. 90th Division here pass through the concrete ' Dragon's Teeth ' of the defences near Habscheid, some seven miles east of Prüm. *Photo, U.S. Official*

sectors of the Allied front. In the north the offensive under Field-Marshal Montgomery, with the associated operations of the U.S. 1st Army, was carried through very much according to pre-arranged plans, except in so far as the attacks of the U.S. 9th and 1st Armies were postponed owing to the flooding of the Roer by the Germans, and the capture of the Remagen bridge-head was unexpected.

In the south, although no doubt General Eisenhower had the broad out-

line of the offensive in mind from the start, yet much more was left to be decided as the offensive developed. General Patton's breakthrough to the Rhine north of the Moselle and his subsequent drive south across the Moselle could hardly have been features of the original

Patton's Brilliant Improvisation

plan, but rather brilliant seizures of opportunities that occurred in the course of the fighting. No doubt the character of the country in each case and the condition and strength of the enemy's troops affected the methods employed.

The battle as a whole gave striking proof of the quality of generalship on the Allied side, not least in the smoothness and speed with which dispositions were adjusted and troops moved into position for each phase of the offensive. Whether, if the enemy had husbanded his reserve for the defence of the Siegfried line and the Rhineland instead of expending it in Rundstedt's disastrous offensive, General Eisenhower would have achieved his line-up on the Rhine so speedily and with such decisive results, must always remain an interesting question for speculation. As it was, his success left the enemy in no mood or condition to offer well organized, prolonged resistance, and the German generals realized that the game was up. The decisive battle in the west had been fought.

WEHRMACHT'S BLACK DAY ON THE WESTERN FRONT
March 20, 1945, saw a complete collapse of German resistance west of the Rhine, with fast-moving columns of Allied troops advancing virtually unopposed. Among many places captured by the U.S. 7th Army was Kaiserslautern, most important communications-centre left to the enemy in the Rhine–Moselle–Saar pocket. Below, some of the 11,000 prisoners taken by the U.S. 10th Armoured and 80th Infantry Divisions in that area. *Photo, U.S. Official*

RED ARMY CAVALRY IN GERMAN SILESIA, 1945

Almost alone among the Allied Armies, the Soviet forces employed mounted troops in the Second Great War for active operations in the field from the Crimea westwards. Certain terrain on the vast Eastern front was peculiarly favourable for their use: during the 2nd White Russian Army's stubbornly contested advance along the Danzig–Stettin railway into Eastern Pomerania, Marshal Rokossovsky's cavalry continually outflanked German positions; and horsed units of the 1st Ukrainian Army operated successfully in German Silesia. *Photo, Pictorial Press*

MONTGOMERY'S TROOPS CROSS THE ROER AND TAKE JÜLICH

Photo, British Official

On February 23, 1945, the U.S. 1st and 9th Armies (the latter under Field-Marshal Montgomery) launched a powerful assault across the swollen Roer river, achieving tactical surprise. Next day, thrusting towards the Rhine, the U.S. 9th Army, operating north of Linnich, took by storm the powerfully defended bastion of Jülich, guarding the approaches to Cologne. (See map in page 3571.) Remnants of the enemy garrison unsuccessfully tried to hold out in the ancient moated citadel. Here U.S. troops patrol the ruined town immediately after its capture.